ROUTLEDGE HANDBOOK OF CLIMATE LAW AND GOVERNANCE

Courage, Contributions and Compliance: The Routledge Handbook of Climate Law and Governance recognises calls from the United Nations (UN), the Intergovernmental Panel on Climate Change (IPCC). The elders, and others, for climate justice and urgent action, and convenes insights from leading legal and institutional experts, professors, professionals and early career scholars on emerging climate law and policy challenges, commitments and solutions.

The collection explores the role of law and governance in scaling up global responses to climate change and advancing sustainability. Based on careful study of international advances and the full spectrum of Nationally Determined Contributions (NDCs) to the global response to climate change, as submitted by Paris Agreement Parties to the UN Framework Convention on Climate Change (UNFCCC), the volume compiles a compelling, coherent and systematic topical account from across diverse legal jurisdictions. Analytical chapters by leading experts, practitioners and scholars close to ongoing climate negotiations explore recent legal and institutional innovations related to climate change which can support implementation and compliance with the Paris Agreement and advance the global Sustainable Development Goals (SDGs). They highlight ways to raise ambition through law and policy, to reform national legal and institutional arrangements to implement NDCs and to further develop international law and governance in the face of the existential threat of climate change and the world: sustainable development commitments.

Presenting a pathway for advancing climate ambition in the coming decades, this book will be of interest to government officials, academics, students, professionals and policy makers working in the area of climate law and governance.

Marie-Claire Cordonier Segger, PhD *ad eundem* (Cantab), DPhil (Oxon), MEM (Yale), BCL & LLB (McGill), BA Hons (Carl/UVic) FRSC FRSA WIJA holds the Chair in Sustainable Development Law and Policy at the University of Cambridge, as Law Fellow, Director of Studies and Programme Director in Lucy Cavendish College. She also serves as Senior Director of the Centre for International Sustainable Development Law (CISDL), Executive Secretary of the UN Framework Convention on Climate Change (UNFCCC) Climate Law and Governance Initiative and Vice-President of the International Law Association (ILA) of Canada, among others. As former senior legal advisor to the International Development Law Organization, the UNFCCC Presidency and other intergovernmental organizations, treaty bodies and governments, as well as editor/board of several law journals and book series, she has published over 26 books and 160 papers on law, policy and sustainable development including climate change, and is a co-recipient of the Climate Law and Governance Global Leadership Award, as well as laureate of the *Justicia Fundamentum Regnorum*, the Weeramantry International Justice Award (WIJA) and other distinguished honours.

Christina Voigt, PhD (Oslo), LLM.Env. (Auckland), Rechtswissenschaft (Passau and Munich), is Full Professor of Law in the Department of Public and International Law, University of Oslo, Norway, Chair of the IUCN World Commission of Environmental Law and Member of the IUCN Council. Author of numerous academic articles, a monograph, and several edited volumes including *Non-Compliance Mechanisms versus International Courts*, *Research Handbook on REDD+ and International Law* and *Rule of Law for Nature*, she holds the inaugural Junior Scholarship Prize of the IUCN Academy of Environmental Law, among other distinguished awards and honours. She has served the Norwegian government as lead negotiator on REDD+ and as principal legal advisor in the UN climate negotiations; negotiating, inter alia, the Paris Agreement and its Rulebook. She has served as co-facilitator for the negotiations on the rules for the Paris Agreement's implementation and compliance committee (PAICC). In 2019, she was elected by the first meeting of the Parties to the Paris Agreement as a member of PAICC and currently serves as inaugural Co-Chair of the PAICC.

ROUTLEDGE HANDBOOK OF CLIMATE LAW AND GOVERNANCE

Courage, Contributions and Compliance

Edited by Marie-Claire Cordonier Segger and Christina Voigt

Routledge
Taylor & Francis Group
LONDON AND NEW YORK

earthscan
from Routledge

Designed cover image: Getty images

First published 2025
by Routledge
4 Park Square, Milton Park, Abingdon, Oxon OX14 4RN

and by Routledge
605 Third Avenue, New York, NY 10158

Routledge is an imprint of the Taylor & Francis Group, an informa business

British Library Cataloguing-in-Publication Data
A catalogue record for this book is available from the British Library

ISBN: 978-1-032-23300-0 (hbk)
ISBN: 978-1-032-23303-1 (pbk)
ISBN: 978-1-003-27667-8 (ebk)

DOI: 10.4324/9781003276678

Typeset in Times New Roman
by Apex CoVantage, LLC

CONTENTS

FOREWORD*

Climate change is the justice challenge of our century. As António Guterres, Secretary General of the United Nations, has warned, over half of humanity is in the danger zone from floods, wildfires, droughts and extreme storms. No nation is immune, yet we continue to feed our fossil fuel addiction. We have a choice: collective action or collective suicide. It is in our hands.

The climate crisis is human-induced and implies serious injustice. Climate justice is core in a volume on courage, contributions and compliance in our law and governance responses to the existential threat of climate change. Pursuit of climate justice begins with a recognition of injustices. First, it is an injustice that the climate crisis has hit first and most ferociously the most highly vulnerable countries and communities. The small island states, the Indigenous Peoples, the remote and rural families, the elderly and the children are facing deepening *social injustice.* Secondly, women have different social roles, have less power and sometimes have fewer rights, like access to land and recognition of unpaid labour. Yet, they have to put food on the table, go further in drought for water, make their communities resilient. So, climate change exacerbates *gender injustice.* Thirdly, as the young climate change activists have demonstrated, their generation will be carrying a terrible burden due to our inaction, our irresponsibility, and this is a terrible *intergenerational injustice.* Fourthly, and this is subtle but important, is the rejection of *different pathways to development* in diverse regions of the world – corroded trust in the promises of a different, more sustainable development. Industrialised countries built economies on fossil fuel. Our responsibility is to be grateful to the workers in coal, oil, gas, and in Ireland, peat, who helped us to become modern industrialised countries. Our responsibility is to make sure that we have a just transition away from fossil fuel as quickly as possible, while not leaving behind the communities and the workers who helped us to build our economies. That is the importance of just transition. But what of developing countries, especially the most highly climate vulnerable among them? As the Special Envoy of the Secretary General before the Paris Climate Agreement, I heard from many developing countries in their nationally determined contributions that they wanted to go as green as possible as quickly as possible with clean energy. But the investment, the transfer of technology, with the skills the contributions that had been promised, were not provided at the scale or pace required. This is a *development injustice* and requires a much greater commitment to our obligations to offer opportunities for different, more sustainable development alternatives. The fifth injustice that we face today evokes the terrible loss of biodiversity, the extinction of species, the reports that are coming out that we are not addressing the fact that we are possibly turning nature into an enemy – nature being our greatest friend. The forests and wetlands offer nature-based solutions as carbon sinks, our ocean serves as a significant sink, and yet we are destroying their capacity to help us in our own survival. The climate crisis is an *injustice to nature herself.*

Being aware of these injustices is the first step in a courageous commitment to *climate justice,* and strengthens the moral, ethical and legal case for collective action. Climate scientists worldwide, including Intergovernmental Panel on Climate Change, have warned of our peril. We must reduce carbon emissions by 45% by 2030 and reach zero carbon by 2050. At present, we are on course for 2.7 degrees Celsius warming or more above pre-industrial standards, which would be catastrophic. 2030 is far too soon. The time for gradual, incremental change is gone.

We need to step up, taking up the challenge to build a courageous, committed, climate justice movement for compliance and for transformative action on climate. This volume is an invitation, a call for engagement to everyone with an interest in climate law and governance. To these renowned editors' and authors' invitation, I add a challenge for all readers of this handbook. Many of you are already involved, but this is a call to scale up, tenfold. As though your life, the lives of your family and community, your entire country, depend on it – because they do.

This foreword, therefore, offers a challenge to readers of this handbook: *help us encourage people to talk* to each other more and more about the climate crisis. How can you build on the knowledge in this volume, to create an enabling environment to start this vital conversation? How can you inspire young people to be innovative, to create their own sustainable green internships and jobs, to build a better future? How can you use the insights and wisdom gained by the many perspectives and examples in this volume to motivate people? How can you encourage collective action for change? If you raise awareness of the climate crisis you are joining this global effort, responding to our Secretary General who asks: "Are we going to choose collective suicide?" and invites us all to find the alternative. We can stay negative, or we can choose to be advocates of hope and find the energy, the understanding and the skills to create resilience.

This book, with its contributions from expert jurists, negotiators, professors and practitioners, including early career scholars, from all regions of the world, offers us all the inspiration to work together and to do the impossible. The enormity of the challenge, to secure climate justice may seem impossible, but it will work if every sector, *especially the law and governance sector, our advocates of hope, build on the insights, understandings and experiences in this collection to step up.* For the editors, authors, teachers, current and future law and policy leaders and others reading this important research handbook on climate law and governance, and gathering your strength for the courage, commitment and compliance that is necessary, I commend you and remind you of the words of my friend President Nelson Mandela: "It always seems impossible until it is done".

Hon. President and Elder Mary Robinson
Former President of Ireland and Chair of The Elders

Note

* Foreword shares thoughts with the Hon. President and Elder Mary Robinson's 2022 keynote address for the Opening Ceremony of the World Library and Information Congress.

ACKNOWLEDGEMENTS

We wish to thank our families, colleagues and friends for their encouragement and support during our collaboration on *Courage, Contributions and Compliance: The Routledge Handbook of Climate Law and Governance*. In particular, our warmest gratitude is due to world-class expert jurists and scholars of the Centre for International Sustainable Development Law and the IUCN World Commission on Environmental Law, among others engaged in the global Climate Law and Governance Days over the years, for their insights and expertise. We deeply appreciate the extraordinary depth of analysis and patient collaboration of the chapter authors, especially during the COVID-19 disruptions – this volume would not have been possible without the diversity of experience, insights and ideas of these leading scholars and practitioners from our emerging field. Further, we are very grateful to our assistant editor Advocate Zunaida Moosa Wadiwala, as well as Dr. Antoinette Nestor and Advocates Maeve McDermott, Tejas Rao, Lydia Young, Kaainat Pundir, Susan Ann Samuel and Mrinalini Shinde, also Dr. Freedom-Kai Phillips, Thalsa-Thiziri Mekaouche and Gwyneth Boone, for their substantive contributions and editorial assistance.

We must also sincerely thank the publishers and editorial team at Taylor & Francis for their helpful guidance and engagement, especially Annabelle Harris, Jyotsna Gurung, Rosie Anderson and Pramoth Jaikishan. We gratefully acknowledge the Social Sciences and Humanities Research Council (SSHRC) of Canada, the New Frontiers Research Foundation (NFRF) of Canada and the European Climate Foundation, as well as leading experts and professionals from the UN Framework Convention on Climate Change Secretariat, UN Environment Programme, the UN Development Programme, the International Development Law Organization, the European Bank for Reconstruction and Development (EBRD), the Asian Development Bank (ADB) and the World Bank, among other partners, whose contributions have been essential to the findings shared in this volume. Finally, we greatly appreciate the engagement of current and future law and policy leaders from the International Law Association, the International Bar Association, the Net Zero Lawyers Alliance, the Bennett Institute for Public Policy, the Lauterpatch Centre for International Law, the Kings College London Centre for Climate Law and Governance, the Hughes Hall Centre for Climate Engagement, the Climate Justice Centre of Bangladesh, the Pacific Institute for Climate Solutions, the Sabin Centre for Climate Change Law, the Waterloo Climate Institute, the LSE Grantham Institute on Climate Change and the Environment and the Balsillie School of International Affairs; and of the dedicated professors and graduates from the University of Cambridge, the University of the Witwatersrand, McGill University, Yale University, the University of Paris I: Pantheon-Sorbonne, the University of Victoria, the University of Edinburgh, the University of Glasgow, the University of Dubai, Middlesex University Dubai, Hamad Bin Khalifa University, the University of the South Pacific, the University of Bonn, the Autonomous University of Madrid, the University of Chile and the University of Waterloo, among many renowned universities and other Climate Law and Governance Initiative partners whose world-leading legal and governance research analysis and dialogue has shaped this volume and many significant advances over the years.

Prof. Marie-Claire Cordonier Segger, PhD ad eundem (Cantab) DPhil Intl Law (Oxon) MEM (Yale) BCL & LLB (McGill) BA Hons (UVic/Carl) FRSC FRSA WIJA

Prof. Christina Voigt, PhD (Oslo), LLM.Env. (Auckland), Rechtswissenschaft (Passau and Munich)

ABBREVIATIONS

10YFP	10-Year Framework of Programmes (UN)
ABMTs	area-based management tools
ABNJ	areas beyond national jurisdiction
ABS	access and benefit-sharing
ABs	adaptation benefits
ACP	African Caribbean and Pacific
ACTE	Action Plan for Business Growth and Transformation (France)
ADB	Asian Development Bank
AFA	Advanced Framework Agreement
AfCFTA	African Continental Free Trade Area
AFOLU	Agriculture, Forestry and Other Land Use
AIMS	Atlantic, Indian Ocean, Mediterranean and South China Sea
AMEE	Agency for Energy Efficiency (Morocco)
AOs	Advisory Opinions
AOSIS	Alliance of Small Island States
ASEAN	Association of South East Asian Nations
BBNJ	Biological Diversity of Areas beyond National Jurisdiction
BCCTF	Bangladesh Climate Change Trust Fund
BIT	bilateral investment treaty
CACF	Climate Action Catalyst Fund by ADB
CAFE	Corporate Average Fuel Economy (US)
CAO	Central Arctic Ocean
CAP	Common Agricultural Policy
CBD	Convention on Biological Diversity
CBDR	common but differentiated responsibility
CBDRRC	common but differentiated responsibility and respective capabilities
CBES	Climate Biennial Exploratory Scenario (England)
CBMU	capacity-building management unit
CCAP	Climate Change Action Plan
CCS	carbon capture and storage

CDM	Clean Development Mechanism
CEC	Commission for Environmental Cooperation
CEDAW	Convention on the Elimination of All Forms of Discrimination Against Women
CER	Certified Emission Reduction
CETA	Comprehensive Economic and Trade Agreement
CHM	clearinghouse mechanism
CIL	customary international law
CIS	Commonwealth of Independent States
CITES	Convention on International Trade in Endangered Species of Wild Fauna and Flora
CJEU	Court of Justice of the European Union
CLGD	Climate Law and Governance Day
CLGI	Climate Law and Governance Initiative
CLRTAP	Convention on Long-Range Transboundary Air Pollution
CMA	Conference of the Members of the Paris Agreement
CMS	Convention on the Conservation of Migratory Species of Wild Animals
COMIFAC	Central African Forest Commission
COP	Conference of the Parties
CORSIA	Carbon Offsetting and Reduction Scheme for International Aviation
COSIS	Commission of Small Island States on Climate Change and International Law
COSPAR	Committee on Space Research
CPACC	Caribbean Planning for Adaptation to Climate Change Project
CPRS	Carbon Pollution Reduction Scheme
CRC	Convention on the Rights of the Child
CRPD	Convention on the Rights of Persons with Disabilities
CSDDD	Corporate Sustainable Due Diligence Directive (European Union)
CSR	corporate social responsibility
CSRD	Corporate Sustainability Reporting Directive (European Union)
CVM	Comissão de Valores Mobiliários
D&O	Director and Officers
DOE	Designated Operational Entity
DRC	Democratic Republic of the Congo
DSU	Dispute Settlement Understanding
EA	environmental assessment
EbA	ecosystem-based adaptation
EBRD	European Bank for Reconstruction and Development
EC	European Community
ECA	Environmental Cooperation Agreement
ECACC	Enhancing Capacity for Adaptation to Climate Change
ECC	Environmental Cooperation Commission
ECHR	European Convention on Human Rights
ECJ	European Court of Justice
ECLAC	United Nations Economic Commission for Latin America and the Caribbean
ECOSOC	Economic and Social Council (UN)
ECT	Energy Charter Treaty
ECtHR	European Court of Human Rights
EEC	European Economic Community
EEZ	Exclusive Economic Zone

EIA	environmental impact assessment
ELAC	Economic Commission for Latin America and the Caribbean (UN)
EMG	Environment Management Group
ENACT	Enhancing Nature-based Solutions for an Accelerated Climate Transformation (ENACT) Partnership
ENMOD	Convention on the Prohibition of Military and any other Hostile Use of Environmental Modification Techniques
EPEAT	Electronic Product Environmental Assessment Tool
ER	environmental review
ERPA	Emission Reduction Payment Agreement
ERTs	Expert Review Teams
ESD	ecologically sustainable development
ESG	environment, social and governance
ESM	environmentally sound management
ETM	Energy Transmission Mechanism
ETS	Emissions Trading Schemes
EU	European Union
EU ETS	European Union Emissions Trading Scheme
FAO	Food and Agriculture Organization
FCA	Financial Conduct Authority
FCPF	Forest Carbon Partnership Facility
FDI	foreign direct investment
FEMP	Federal Energy Management (US)
FER	fundamental environmental right
FIDA	Inter-American Forum on Environmental Law
FIPA	Foreign Investment Protection Agreement
FLEGT	Voluntary Partnership Agreement on Forest Law Enforcement, Governance and Trade
FLR	Forest Landscape Restoration
FMAs	free movement agreements
FSB	Financial Stability Board (G20)
FTAs	free trade agreements
GAP	Gender Action Plan
GATS	General Agreement on Trade in Services
GATT	General Agreement on Tariffs and Trade
GBF	Kunming-Montreal Global Biodiversity Framework
GCF	Green Climate Fund
GCM	Global Compacts on Migrants (UN)
GCR	Global Compacts on Refugees (UN)
GDP	gross domestic product
GEA	Green Economy Agreement
GEF	Global Environmental Facility
GFANZ	Glasgow Financial Alliance for Net Zero
GFCM	General Fishery Commission for the Mediterranean
GGGI	Global Green Growth Institute
GHG	greenhouse gas
GHS	Globally Harmonised System

GNI	gross national income
GNP	gross national product
GNSS	global navigation satellite system
GPA	Government Procurement Agreement
GPP	green public procurement
HDI	Human Development Index
HRC	Human Rights Committee (UN)
HRC	Human Rights Council (UN)
IAASB	International Auditing and Assurance Standards Board
IACHR	Inter-American Commission of Human Rights
IACtHR	Inter-American Court of Human Rights
ICAO	International Civil Aviation Organization
ICCPR	International Covenant on Civil and Political Rights
ICESCR	International Covenant on Economic, Social and Cultural Rights
ICJ	International Court of Justice
ICRC	International Committee of the Red Cross
ICRW	International Convention for the Regulation of Whaling
ICSID	International Centre for Settlement of Investment Disputes
ICSU	International Council of Scientific Unions
ICTSD	International Centre for Trade and Sustainable Development
IDB	Inter-American Development Bank
IDP	internally displaced person
IEA	International Energy Agency
IEL	international environmental law
IFRS	International Financial Reporting Standards
IFSD	Institutional Framework for Sustainable Development
IGC	Intergovernmental Council
IGO	intergovernmental organisation
IGY	International Geophysical Year
IIA	international investment agreement
IIL	Institute of International Law
IISD	International Institute for Sustainable Development
IJC	International Joint Commission
IL	International Law
ILA	International Law Association
ILC	International Law Commission
ILO	International Labour Organization
IMF	International Monetary Fund
IMO	International Maritime Organization
iNDCs	Intended Nationally Determined Contributions
IOC	Indian Ocean Commission
IOM	International Organisation for Migration
IOSCO	International Organization of Securities Commissions
IPBES	Intergovernmental Science-Policy Platform on Biodiversity and Ecosystem Services
IPCC	Intergovernmental Panel on Climate Change
IPF	Intergovernmental Panel on Forests

IPLC	Indigenous peoples and local communities
IR	international relations
IRA	Inflation Reduction Act (US)
IRENA	International Renewable Energy Agency
ISDS	Investor–State Dispute Settlement
ISSB	International Sustainability Standards Board
ITA	interim trade agreement
ITLOS	International Tribunal for the Law of the Sea
ITMOs	internally referred mitigation outcomes
ITPGRFA	International Treaty on Plant Genetic Resources for Food and Agriculture
ITTA	International Tropical Timber Agreement
IUCN	International Union for Conservation of Nature
IWL	International Water Law
IWRM	Integrated Water Resource Management
JCM	Joint Crediting Mechanism
JI	Joint Implementation
KP	Kyoto Protocol
KSSB	Korea Sustainability Standards Board
LAC	Latin America and the Caribbean
LBS	land based sources
LCA	long-term cooperative action
LDCs	least developed countries
LEC	Energy and Climate Law
LECCLA	Low Embodied Carbon Climate Leadership Act
LGA	Local Government Act
LME	large marine ecosystem
LMO	living modified organism
LRTAP	long-range transboundary air pollution
LULUCF	Land-use, Land-use Change and Forestry
MASE	Moroccan Agency for Sustainable Energy
MDB	multilateral and regional development banks
MDGs	Millennium Development Goals
MEA	Multilateral environmental agreement
MECC	Migration, Environment and Climate Change Division (IOM)
METs	multilateral environmental treaties
MGR	marine genetic resources
MNC	multinational corporation
MNE	multinational enterprise
MNES	matters of national environmental significance
MoDMR	Ministry of Disaster Management and Relief (Bangladesh)
MOP	Meeting of the Parties
MOPA	mitigation outcome purchase agreement
MPA	marine protected area
MRV	measurement, reporting, and verification
MSP	marine spatial planning
MSY	maximum sustainable yield
MTR	multilateral treaty regimes

NAFTA	North American Free Trade Agreement
NAMAs	Nationally appropriate mitigation actions
NAP	National Adaptation Plan
NATO	North Atlantic Treaty Organisation
NbS	Nature-based solutions
NBSAPs	National Biodiversity Strategies and Action Plans
NCP	National contact point
NDCs	Nationally Determined Contributions
NELD	non-economic loss and damage
NEPAD	New Partnership for Africa's Development
NGO	non-governmental organization
NICFD	Norway's International Climate and Forest Initiative
NIEO	New International Economic Order
NLBI	Non-Legally Binding Instrument on All Types of Forests
NPM	non-precluded measures
NPS	nuclear power source
NTS	non-traditional security
NZIA	Net-Zero Insurance Alliance
OAS	Organization of American States
OAU	Organisation for African Unity
ODS	ozone-depleting substances
OECD	Organisation for Economic Co-operation and Development
OECM	other effective area-based conservation measures
OECPR-6	Open-ended Committee of Permanent Representatives
OECS	Organisation of Eastern Caribbean States
OHCHR	Office of the United Nations High Commissioner for Human Rights
PA	Paris Agreement
PACTE	Action Plan for Business Growth and Transformation (France)
PAICC	Paris Agreement and Compliance Committee
PCA	Permanent Court of Arbitration
PCIJ	Permanent Court of International Justice
PCT	Patent Cooperation Treaty
PDD	Platform on Disaster Displacement
PES	Payment for Ecosystem Services
PIC	prior informed consent
PIFS	Pacific Islands Forum Secretariat
PIL	public interest litigation
PIPA	Phoenix Islands Protected Area
POI	Investment Protocol
POPs	persistent organic pollutants
PPP	public private partnerships
PRA	Prudential Regulation Authority
PRTR	Regional Pollutant Release and Transfer Register
PSNR	permanent sovereignty over natural resources
R&D	research and development
RAP	Regional Action Plan
REAs	sub-regional or bi-lateral environmental agreements

REDD+	Reduced emissions from deforestation and degradation in developing countries
RICO	racketeer influenced and corrupt organisations
RMA	Resource Management Act
RMU	removal unit
ROAM	Restoration Opportunity Assessment Methodology
ROLAC	Regional Office for Latin America and the Caribbean (UNEP)
RONA	Regional Office for North America (UNEP)
RRACC	Reducing risk to human and natural assets resulting from climate change
SAA	Sharm-El-Sheikh Adaptation Agenda
SADC	South African Development Community
SBSTA	Subsidiary Body for Scientific and Technological Advice
SBSTTA	Subsidiary Body for Scientific, Technical and Technological Advice
SDGs	Sustainable Development Goals
SEA	strategic environmental assessment
SEC	Securities and Exchange Commission (United States)
SFAC	Sustainable Finance Action Council (Canada)
SFDR	Sustainable Finance Disclosures Regulation (European Union)
SFDRR	Sendai Framework for Disaster Risk Reduction
SFM	sustainable forest management
SGX	Singapore Stock Exchange
SGX RegCo	Singapore Exchange Regulation
SIA	Sustainability Impact Assessment
SICA	Central American Integration System
SIDS	Small Island Developing States
SIOFA	South Indian Ocean Fisheries Agreement
SIRF Fund	Sustainable Island Resources Framework Fund
SPAR6C	Supporting Preparedness for Article 6 Cooperation program
SPP	sustainable public procurement
STAP	Scientific and Technical Advisory Panel
STEG	Tunisian Electricity and Gas Company
STSC	Scientific and Technical Subcommittee
TAC	total allowable catch
TBT	technical barriers to trade
TCA	The EU-UK Trade and Cooperation Agreement
TCAF	Transformative Carbon Asset Facility
TCFD	Task Force on Climate-Related Financial Disclosures
TEU	Treaty of the European Union
TFD	Task Force on Displacement
TFEU	Treaty on the Functioning of the European Union
TIAS	Treaties and other International Acts Series
TNC	Transnational Corporations
TOMA	tropospheric ozone management area
TRIPS	Trade-Related Aspects of Intellectual Property Rights
TSD	trade and sustainable development
TWAIL	Third World Approaches to International Law
UDRME	Universal Declaration on the Rights of Mother Earth
UK	United Kingdom

UN	United Nations
UNCCD	United Nations Convention to Combat Desertification
UNCED	United Nations Conference on Environment and Development
UNCITRAL	United Nations Commission on International Trade Law
UNCLOS	United Nations Convention on the Law of the Sea
UNCSD	United Nations Commission on Sustainable Development
UNCTC	United Nations Commission on Transnational Corporations
UNDP	United Nations Development Programme
UNDRIP	United Nations Declaration on the Rights of Indigenous Peoples
UNEA-5	United Nations Environmental Assembly 5
UNEA-6	United Nations Environmental Assembly 6
UNECE	United Nations Economic Commission for Europe
UNEP	United Nations Environment Programme
UNESCAP	United Nations Economic and Social Commission for Asia and the Pacific
UNESCO	United Nations Educational, Scientific and Cultural Organization
UNFCCC	United Nations Framework Convention on Climate Change
UNFF	United Nations Forum on Forests
UNGA	United Nations General Assembly
UNGASS	Special Session of the United Nations General Assembly
UNHCR	United Nations High Commissioner for Refugees
UNOPS	United Nations Office for Project Services
UNSC	United Nations Security Council
UNTS	United Nations Treaty System
US	United States
USD	US Dollars
VCLT	Vienna Convention on the Law of Treaties
VOC	volatile organic compound
WCED	World Commission on Environment and Development
WCEL	World Commission on Environmental Law
WCS	World Conservation Strategy
WHC	World Heritage Convention
WHO	World Health Organization
WIM	Warsaw International Mechanism for Loss and Damage Associated with Climate Change
WIPO	World Intellectual Property Organization
WMO	World Meteorological Organization
WRI	World Resources Institute
WSSD	World Summit on Sustainable Development
WTO	World Trade Organization
ZEMA	Zambia Environmental Management Agency

TREATIES

Addis Ababa Action Agenda of the Third International Conference on Financing for Development (17 August 2015) UN Doc A/RES/69/313

Agreement Establishing the African Continental Free Trade Area (adopted 21 March, 2018, entered into force 30 May, 2019)

Agreement on Government Procurement (adopted 15 April 1994, entered into force 1 January 1996)

Agreement on Trade-Related Aspects of Intellectual Property Rights (adopted 15 April 1994, entered into force 1 January 1995) 1869 UNTS 299 (TRIPs)

Agreement under the United Nations Convention on the Law of the Sea on the Conservation and Sustainable Use of Marine Biological Diversity of Areas beyond National Jurisdiction (adopted 19 June 2023, not in force)

American Convention on Human Rights (adopted 21 November 1969, entered into force 18 July 1878) 1144 UNTS 123

Australia-Singapore Green Economy Agreement (signed 8 October 2022)

Australia–United Kingdom Free Trade Agreement (signed 17 December 2021, entered into force 31 May 2023)

Agreement between the Government of the Republic of Belarus and the Government of Hungary for the Promotion and Reciprocal Protection of Investments (signed 14 January 2019, entered into force 28 September 2019) (Belarus-Hungary BIT)

Canada - Ukraine Free Trade Agreement (signed 11 July, 2016, entered into force 1 August 2017)

Cancun Agreements: Outcome of the work of the Ad Hoc Working Group on Long-term Cooperative Action under the FCC Convention. UN Doc FCCC/CP/2010/7/Add.1 (signed 11 December 2010) (The Cancun Agreements 2010)

Charter of the United Nations (adopted 26 June 1945, entered into force 16 October 1945) 1 UNTS 16

Comprehensive Economic and Trade Agreement (signed 30 October 2016, entered into force 21 September 2017)(CETA)

Convention for the Protection of Human Rights and Fundamental Freedoms (ECHR) (adopted 4 November 1950, entered into force 3 September 1953) 213 UNTS 221

Convention on Access to Information, Public Participation in Decision-making and Access to Justice in Environmental Matters (The Aarhus Convention) (adopted 25 June 1998, entered into force 30 October 2001) 216y1 UNTS 459 (No. 37770)

Convention on Biological Diversity (CBD) (adopted 5 June 1992, 30619 UNTS, entered into force 29 December 1993) 1760 UNTS 79; 31 ILM 818 (1992)

Convention on Fishing and Conservation of the Living Resources of the High Seas (adopted 29 April 1958, entered in force 20 March 1966) 559 UNTS 285

Convention on International Trade in Endangered Species of Wild Fauna and Flora (CITES) (adopted 3 March 1973, entered into force 1 July 1975) 993 UNTS 243

Convention on the Conservation of Migratory Species of Wild Animals (CMS) (adopted 23 June 1979, entered into force 1 November 1983) 19 ILM 15

Convention on the Control of Transboundary Movements of Hazardous Wastes and their Disposal (adopted 22 March 1989, entered into force 5 May 1992) 1673 UNTS 57 (Basel Convention)

Convention on the Elimination of All Forms of Discrimination against Women (adopted 18 December 1979, entered into force 3 September 1981) 1249 UNTS 13

Convention on the High Seas (adopted 29 April 1958, entered into force 30 September 1962) 450 UNTS 11

Convention on the Protection and Use of Transboundary Watercourses and International Lakes (UNECE Water Convention) (adopted 9 April 1992, entered into force 6 October 1996) 31 ILM 1312

Convention on the Protection of the Marine Environment of the Baltic Sea Area, 1992 (adopted 9 April 1992, entered into force 17 January 2000) (Helsinki Convention)

Convention on the Rights of the Child (adopted 20 November 1989, entered into force 2 September 1990) 29 ILM 1340

Convention on Wetlands of International Importance Especially as Waterfowl Habitat (adopted 2 January 1971, entered into force 21 December 1975), 996 UNTS 245, 14583 UNTS, as amended by the Paris Protocol, 3 December 1982, Regina Amendments, 28 May 1987 (Ramsar Convention)

Convention Relating to the Status of Refugees, Stateless Persons (adopted 28 July 1951, entered into force 22 April 1954) 189 UNTS 150 (Refugee Convention)

Corporate Sustainability Due Diligence Directive (adopted 24 May 2024, came into force 25 July 2024) (CSDDD)

Corporate Sustainability Reporting Directive (adopted April 21, 2021, entered into force 5 January, 2023) (CSRD)

Energy Charter Treaty (adopted 17 December 1994, entered into force April 1998)

EU-Chile Advanced Framework Agreement (signed 13 December 2023) (AFA)

EU-Chile Association Agreement (signed 2002, entered into force February 2003)

EU-Japan Economic Partnership Agreement (signed 17 July 2018, entered into effect 1 February 2019)

EU-Korea Free Trade Agreement (signed 6 October 2010, came into effect 1 July 2011)

EU-New Zealand Free Trade Agreement (signed 9 July 2023 entered into force 1 May 2024)

EU-Singapore Free Trade Agreement (signed 19 October 2018, entered into effect 21 November 2019)

General Agreement on Tariffs and Trade (GATT, adopted 30 October 1947, entered into force 1 January 1948) 64 UNTS 187

General Agreement on Trade in Services (adopted 15 April 1994, entered into force 1 January 1995) 1869 UNTS 183

Protocol on Cooperation between the Ministry of External Affairs of the Republic of India and the Ministry of Foreign Affairs of the Republic of Kyrghstan (India-Kyrgyzstan BIT) (signed on 4 August 1993)

Geneva Convention for Regulation of Whaling (signed 24 September 1931, entered into force 16 January 1935) 155 LNTS 349

International Covenant on Civil and Political Rights (adopted 16 December 1966, entered into force 23 March 1977) 999 UNTS 171

International Covenant on Economic, Social and Cultural Rights (ICESCR adopted 16 December 1966, entered into force 3 January 1977) 6 ILM 360

International Treaty on Plant Genetic Resources for Food and Agriculture (entered into force 29 June 2004) 2400 UNTS 303

International Tropical Timber Agreement (ITTA) (adopted 27 January 2006, entered into force 7 December 2011) 2797 UNTS 75

Kyoto Protocol to the United Nations Framework Convention on Climate Change (entered into force 16 February 2005) 2303 UNTS 162

Marine Strategy Framework Directive (signed 17 June 2008, entered into force 15 July 2008)

Myanmar–Singapore Bilateral Investment Treaty (signed 24 September 2019, entered into force 9 October 2020)

Plan d'action pour la croissance et la transformation des entreprises (Action plan for business growth and transformation) (adopted 22 May 2019, entered into force on 23 May 2019) (France)

Paris Agreement, parties to the 1992 United Nations Framework Convention on Climate Change (adopted 12 December 2015, entered into force 4 November 2016) 3156 UNTS 79

Protocol on Access to Genetic Resources and the Fair and Equitable Sharing of Benefits Arising from their Utilization (ABS) (adopted 30 October 2010, entered into force 12 October 2014) 3008 UNTS 3

Protocol on Biosafety to the Convention on Biological Diversity (CBD) (adopted 29 January 2000, entered into force 11 September 2003) 39 ILM 1027 (Cartagena Protocol)

Protocol on Substances that Deplete the Ozone Layer (adopted 16 September 1987, entered into force 1 January 1989), 26 ILM 154 (Montreal Protocol)

Regional Agreement on Access to Information, Public Participation, and Justice in Environmental Matters in Latin America and the Caribbean (Escazú Agreement) (adopted 27 September 2018, entered into force 22 April 2021) 56654 UNTS 3398

Rwanda–United Arab Emirates Bilateral Investment Treaty (signed 1 November 2017, entered into force 7 January 2020)

Sustainable Finance Disclosures Regulation (signed on 27 November 2019, entered into force 10 March 2021) (SFDR)

Sustainable Investment Facilitation Agreement between the European Union and the Republic of Angola (signed 17 November 2023, entered into force 4 March, 2024)

UK - Singapore Green Economy Framework (signed 1 March 2023)

UNCITRAL Model Law on Government Procurement (adopted 1 July 2011)

United Nations Convention on the Law of the Sea (adopted 10 December 1982, entered into force 16 November 1994) 1833 UNTS 3

United Nations Convention to Combat Desertification in those Countries Experiencing Serious Drought and/or Desertification, Particularly in Africa (UNCCD) (adopted 14 October 1994, entered into force 26 December 1996) 1954 UNTS 3

United Nations Framework Convention on Climate Change (entered into force 21 March 1994) 1771 UNTS 107

Vienna Convention for the Protection of the Ozone Layer (adopted 22 March 1985, entered into force 22 September 1988) 1513 UNTS 293

Vienna Convention on the Law of Treaties (VCLT) (adopted 22 May 1969, entered into force 27 January 1980), 1155 UNTS 331

Voluntary Partnership Agreement between the European Union and the Republic of Honduras on Forest Law Enforcement, Governance and Trade in Timber Products to the European Union (signed 14 November 2011, entered into force 1 September 2022) (FLEGT)

TABLE OF CASES

African Commission on Human and People's Rights

Centre for Minority Rights Development (Kenya) and Minority Rights Group International on behalf of Endorois Welfare Council v Kenya, African Commission on Human and Peoples' Rights, Comm. No. 276/03 (2009)
Kenneth Good v Republic of Botswana, Communication 313/05 (2009–2010): 219, 223
Malawi African Association v Mauritania, Comm. Nos. 54/91, 61/91, 98/93, 164/97 to 196/97 and 210/98 (1999–2000)
Social and Economic Rights Action Center and Others v Nigeria ('Ogoniland' case), African Commission on Human and Peoples' Rights, Comm. No. 155/96 (2001)

European Court of Human Rights

Association Ekin v France [2001] ECtHR 30882/96
Aydin v Turkey 2000-III ECHR MICT
Carême v France [2024] ECtHR 7189/21
Dayras and Others v France [2005] ECtHR 65390/01
Depalle v France [2010] ECtHR 34044/02
Doğan v Turkey [2005] 41 EHRR
Duarte Agostinho and Others v Portugal and 32 Other States [2024] ECtHR 39371/20
Dubetska v Ukraine [2011] ECtHR 30499/03
Fadeyeva v Russia [2005] ECtHR 55723/00
Fägerskiöld v Sweden [2008] ECtHR 37664/04
Giacomelli v Italy [2006] ECtHR 59909/00
Guerra and Others v Italy [1998] ECHR 7
Hâkasson and Sturesson v Sweden [1990] ECtHR 11855/85
Hamer v Belgium [2007] ECtHR 21861/03
Hatton and Others v The United Kingdom [2003] ECtHR 36022/97
Klass v Germany [1978] 2 EHRR
Ledyayeva and others v Russia [2006] ECtHR 53157/99, 53247/99, 53695/00 and 56850/00

Lopez Ostra v Spain [1994] ECtHR 16798/90
Mamatkulov and Abdurasolovic v Turkey [2005] ECHR 46827/99
Mangouras v Spain [2009] ECtHR 12050/04
McGinley and Egan v UK [1999] 27 EHRR 1
Oneryildiz v Turkey [2002] ECHR 496
Open Door and Dublin Well Woman v Ireland [1992] ECtHR 14234/88
Österreichische Vereeniging zur Erhaltung, Stärkung und Schaffung Eines Wirtschaftlich Gesunden Land und Forstwirtschaftlichen Grundbesitzes v Austria [2013] ECtHR 39534/07
Pine Valley Developments Ltd and Others v Ireland [1991] ECtHR 12742/87
Posti and Rahko v Finland [2002] ECtHR 27824/95
Scordino v Italy (No. 1) [2006] ECtHR 36813/97
Taskin and Others v Turkey [2004] ECtHR 46117/99
Tatar v Romania [2009] ECtHR 67021/01
Turgut and Others v Turkey [2009] ECtHR 1411/03
Verein Klimaseniorinnen Schweiz and Others v. Switzerland [2024] ECtHR 53600/20
Zander v Sweden [1993] ECtHR 14282/88

European Court of Justice

Afton Chemical Limited v Secretary of State for Transport [2010] ECR I-07027
APAS, Case C-435/92, [1994] ECR I-67
ARCO Chemie Nederland, C-418/97 and C-419/97 [2000] ECR I-4475
Bergaderm and Goupil v Commission, Case C-352/98, [2000] ECR I-5291
Bettati v Safety Hi-Tech, C-341/95 [1998] ECR I-4355
Armando Carvalho and others v European Parliament and Council of the European Union, Case C 565/19 P ECLI:EU:C:2021
Commission v Denmark, C-192/01 [2003] ECR I-9693
Commission of the European Communities v Council of the European Union, C-176/03 [2005]
Commission v France, C-333/08 ECR [2010] I-00757
Diego Calì & Figli Srl v Servizi ecologici porto di Genova SpA (SEPG), Case C-343/95 [1996]
Essent Belgium NV v Vlaamse Reguleringsinstantie voor de Elektriciteits-enGasmarkt, C-204/12 & C-208/12 [2014]
Fedesa and Others, Case C-331/88 [1990] ECR I-4023
Fornasar and Others, C-318/98 [2000] ECR I-4785
Govan Commércio Internacional e Serviços Lda v Ministero della Salute, C-77/09, ECR [2010] I-13533
Greenpeace France and Others, Case C-6/99 [2000] ECR I-1651
Hellenic Republic v Council, C-62/88 [1990] ECR I-1527
Kingdom of Spain v Council of the European Union, C-350/92 [1993]
Landelijke Vereniging tot Behoud van de Waddenzee and Nederlandse Vereniging tot Bescherming van Vogels v. Staatssecretaris van Landbouw, Natuurbeheer en Visserij, Coöperatieve Producentenorganisatie van de Nederlandse Kokkelvisserij UA, Case C-127/02, [2004] ECR I-7448
Monsanto Agricoltura Italia, C-236/01 [2003] ECR I-8105
National Farmers' Union and Others, Case C-157/96 [1998] ECR I-2211
Pfizer Animal Health SA v Council [2002] ECR II-03305
PreussenElectra, C-379/98 [2001] ECR I-2099

Queen v Secretary of State for the Environment, Transport and the Regions ex parte First Corporate Shipping Ltd, interveners: World Wide Fund for Nature UK (WWF) and Avon Wildlife Trust Case, C-371/98 ECLI:EU:C:2000:108

Raffinerie Mediterranee (ERG) Spa and Others v Ministero dello Sviluppo economico and Other Authorities, C-379/08 and C-380/08 ECR [2010] I-02007

Santona Marshes, C-355/90 [1993] ECR I-4221

Spain v Council, Case C-179/95, [1999] ECR I-6475

Stichting Greenpeace and Others v Commission, T-585/93 [1995] ECR II-2205

Stichting Greenpeace and Others v Commission, C-321/95P [1998] ECR I-1653

ICJ Cases

Accordance with International Law of the Unilateral Declaration of Independence in Respect of Kosovo, [2010] ICJ Rep 1

Advisory Opinion on the Legal Consequences of the Construction of a Wall in the Occupied Palestinian Territory, [2004] ICJ Rep 178

Advisory Opinion on the Legality of the Threat or Use of Nuclear Weapons, [1996] ICJ Rep. 226

Aerial Herbicide Spraying (Ecuador v Colombia), [2008] ICJ Rep. 174

Anglo-Norwegian Fisheries Case, [1951] ICJ Rep. 131

Armed Activities on the Territory of the Congo (Democratic Republic of the Congo v Uganda), [2005] ICJ Rep. 168

Case Concerning Military and Paramilitary Activities in and against Nicaragua, [1986] ICJ Rep. 98

Case Concerning Sovereignty over Pulau Ligitan and Pulau Sipadan (Indonesia v Malaysia), [2002] ICJ 625

Case Concerning the Continental Shelf (Libyan Arab Jamahiriya v Malta), [1985] ICJ Rep. 13

Certain Activities Carried out by Nicaragua in the Border Area (Costa Rica v Nicaragua)/Construction of a Road in Costa Rica along the San Juan River (Nicaragua v Costa Rica), [2015] ICJ General List Nos. 150 and 152

Certain Phosphate Lands in Nauru, 1992 ICJ Rep. 240

Corfu Channel (United Kingdom v Albania), [1949] ICJ Reports 4

Elettronica Sicula S.p.A. (US v Italy), [1989] ICJ Rep. 15

Gabčíkovo-Nagymaros Project (Hungary v Slovakia), [1997] ICJ Rep. 7

Kasikili/Sedudu Island (Botswana/Namibia), [1999] ICJ 1045

Maritime Delimitation in the Area between Greenland and Jan Mayen (Denmark v Norway), [1993] ICJ Rep. 38

Maritime Delimitation and Territorial Questions between Qatar and Bahrain (Merits), [2001] ICJ Rep. 40: 48, 296

Namibia (SW Africa), [1971] ICJ Rep. 16

North Sea Continental Shelf Cases, [1969] ICJ Rep. 3

Nuclear Tests (Australia v France) (Interim Protection), [1973] ICJ Rep. 99

Nuclear Tests (Australia v France) (Merits), [1974] ICJ Rep. 253

Nuclear Tests (New Zealand v France) (Interim Protection), [1973] ICJ Rep. 135

Nuclear Tests (New Zealand v France) (Merits), [1974] ICJ Rep. 457: 100, 193, 194, 237

Pulp Mills on the River Uruguay (Argentina v Uruguay) (Judgment), [2010] ICJ General List No. 135

Pulp Mills on the River Uruguay (Argentina v Uruguay) (Provisional Measures), [2007] ICJ General List No. 135
Request for Interpretation of the Judgment of 15 June 1962 in the Case Concerning the Temple of Preah Vihear (Cambodia v Thailand), [2013] ICJ Rep. 281
Whaling in the Antarctic (Australia v Japan), [2014] ICJ Rep. 1

Inter-American Court of Human Rights

Case of Claude Reyes et. al. (Chile) (2006), Inter-Am. Ct. H.R. (Ser. C) No. 151
Case of the Sawhoyamaxa Community v Paraguay, Inter-Am. Ct. H.R. (Ser. C) No. 146 (2006)
Case of the Saramaka Peoples v Suriname, Inter-Am. Ct. H.R. (Ser. C) No. 172 (2007)
Case of Velasquez Rodriguez, Judgment of July 29, 1988, Inter-Am. Ct. H.R. (Ser. C) No. 4 (1988)
Case of the Yakye Axa Indigenous Community v Paraguay, Inter-Am. Ct. H.R. (Ser. C) No. 125 (2005)
Gonzales v Mexico, 49 ILM 640 (2009)
Mary and Carrie Dann v USA, 10 IHRR 1143 (2003)
Mayagna (Sumo) Awas Tingni Community v Nicaragua, Inter-Am. Ct. H.R. (Ser. C) No. 79 (2001)

International Arbitration Cases

Trail Smelter (US v Canada), UN RIAA vol. III p. 1905 (1938)
Trail Smelter (US v Canada), UN RIAA vol. III p. 1905 (1941)

International Centre for Settlement of Investment Disputes

Champion Trading Company v Arab Republic of Egypt, Award, ICSID Case No. ARB/02/9 (2006)
Chemtura Corporation v Canada, Award, ICSID Case No. ARB/08/01 (2010)
EDF (Services) Ltd v Romania, Award, ICSID Case No. ARB/05/13 (2009)
Fraport AG Frankfurt Airport Services Worldwide v Republic of the Philippines, Award, ICSID Case No. ARB/03/25 (2007)
F-W Oil Interests v Republic of Trinidad and Tobago, Award, ICSID Case No. ARB/01/14 (2006)
Inceysa Vallisoletana v Republic of El Salvador, Award, ICSID Case No. ARB/03/26 (2006)
Lemire v Ukraine (II), Decision on Jurisdiction and Liability, ICSID Case No. ARB/06/18 (2010)
LESI et al. v People's Democracy Republic of Algeria, Award, ICSID Case No. ARB/05/3 (2008)
Noble Ventures v Romania, Award, ICSID Case No. ARB/01/11 (2005)
Total S.A. v Argentine Republic, Decision on Liability, ICSID Case No. ARB/04/01 (2010)
Waguih Elie George Siag v Arab Republic of Egypt, Award, ICSID Case No. ARB/05/15 (2009)
World Duty Free v The Republic of Kenya, Award, ICSID Case No. ARB/00/7 (2006)

International Tribunal for the Law of the Sea Cases

Arctic Sunrise (Netherlands v Russian Federation), ITLOS Case No. 22 (2013)
Camouco (Panama v France), 125 ILR 151 (2000)
Case Concerning Land Reclamation by Singapore in and around the Straits of Johor (Malaysia v Singapore), ITLOS Case No. 12 (2003)
Chaisiri Reefer 2 (Panama v Yemen), ITLOS Case No. 9 (2001)

Grand Prince (Belize v France), 125 ILR 251 (2000)
Hoshinmaru (Japan v Russian Federation), ITLOS Case No. 14 (2007)
Juno Trader (St Vincent and the Grenadines v Bissau), 44 ILM 4 (2005)
Monte Confurco (Seychelles v France), 125 ILR 203 (2000)
MOX Plant (Ireland v United Kingdom), ITLOS Case No. 10 (2001)
M/V Saiga (Saint Vincent and the Grenadines v Guinea), 110 ILR (1997)
Request for an Advisory Opinion Submitted by the Sub-regional Fisheries Commission (SRFC), ITLOS Case No. 21 (2015)
Responsibilities and Obligations of States Sponsoring Persons and Entities with Respect to Activities in the Area (Advisory Opinion), Case No. 17 (1 February 2011)
Southern Bluefin Tuna (Australia and New Zealand v Japan), ITLOS Case Nos. 3 & 4 (1999)
Southern Bluefin Tuna Case, ITLOS Case No. 17 (2009)
The "Tomimaru" Case (Japan v Russian Federation), ITLOS Case No. 15 (2007)
Volga Case (Russian Federation v Australia), 42 ILM 159 (2003)

North American Agreement on Environmental Cooperation

Council Resolution 00–01 on SEM-97–003 (*Quebec Hog Farms*)
Council Resolution 00–04-Instruction to the Secretariat of the Commission for Environmental Cooperation to make public the Factual Record regarding the assertion that Canada is failing to effectively enforce s. 35(1) of the *Fisheries Act* with respect to certain hydro-electric installations in British Columbia, Canada (SEM-97–001)
Council Resolution 01–10 on SEM-99–002 (*Migratory Birds*)
Council Resolution 02–01 on SEM-98–007 (*Metales y Derivados*)
Council Resolution 03–03 on SEM-99–002 (*Migratory Birds*)
Council Resolution 03–05 on SEM-02–001 (*Ontario Logging*)
Council Resolution 03–06 on SEM-98–006 (*Aquanova*)
Council Resolution 03–12 on SEM-00–004 (*BC Logging*)
Council Resolution 03–13 on SEM-97–006 (*Oldman River II*)
Council Resolution 03–14 on SEM-98–004 (*BC Mining*)
Council Resolution 03–15 on SEM-97–002 (*Río Magdalena*)
Council Resolution 04–05 on SEM-03–005 (*Montreal Technoparc*)
Council Resolution 04–07 on SEM-00–005 (*Molymex II*)
Council Resolution 05–09 on Submission SEM-00–006 (*Tarahumara*)
Council Resolution 06–07 on SEM-04–007 (*Quebec Automobiles*)
Council Resolution 07–02 on Submissions SEM-02–001 (*Ontario Logging*)/SEM-04–006 (*Ontario Logging II*)
Council Resolution 07–03 on Submission SEM-02–003 (*Pulp and Paper*)
Council Resolution 08–01 on SEM-03–003 (*Lake Chapala*)
Council Resolution 08–03 on SEM-04–005 (*Coal-fired Power Plants*)
Council Resolution 12–001 (*BC Salmon Farms*)
Council Resolution 14–04 on SEM-11–03 (*Protection of Polar Bears*)
Council Resolution 14–09 on SEM-12–001 (*BC Salmon Farms*)
Council Resolution 15–01 on SEM-10–002 (*Alberta Tailings Ponds*)
Council Resolution 15–02 on SEM-13–001 (*Tourism Development in the Gulf of California*)
SEM-02–005 (*ALCA Iztapalapa*)

NAFTA Arbitrations

Other International Arbitrations

Parkerings-Compagniet A.S. v Lithuania, ICSID Case No. ARB/05/8 (Norway-Lithuania BIT) (Award, 11 September 2007)

PSEG Global Inc., The North American Coal Corporation, and Konya Ilgin Elektrik Üretim ve Ticaret Limited Sirketi v Republic of Turkey, ICSID Case No. ARB/02/5 (US-Turkey BIT) (Award, 19 January 2007)

Saluka Investment BV v Czech Republic, UNCITRAL (Netherlands-Czechoslovakia BIT) (Partial Award, 17 March 2006)

Técnicas Medioambientales Tecmed, S.A. v United Mexican States, ICSID Case No. ARB (AF)/00/2 (Spain-Mexico BIT) (Award, 29 May 2003)

Seabed Disputes Chamber

Responsibilities and Obligations of States Sponsoring Persons and Entities with Respect to Activities in the Area at the Request of the International Seabed Authority, ITLOS Advisory Opinion (2011)

UNHRC

Ángela Poma Poma v Peru, UN Human Rights Committee, Communication No. 1457/2006, CCPR/C/95/D/1457/2006 (2009)

Anni Äärela and Jouni Näkkäläjärvi v Finland, UN Human Rights Committee, Communication No. 779/1997, CCPR/C/73/D/779/1997 (2001)

Apirana Mahuika et al. v New Zealand, UN Human Rights Committee, Communication No. 547/1993, CCPR/C/70/D/547/1993 (2000)

Ilmari Lansmän v Finland, UN Human Rights Committee, Communication No. 511/1992, CCPR/C/52/D/511/1992 (1994): 457, 463, 467*Jouni E Lansman et al. v Finland*, UN Human Rights Committee, Communication No. 671/1995, CCPR/C/58/D/671/1995 (1996)

Lubicon Lake Band v Canada (1990)

WTO Cases

Australia – Measures Affecting Importation of Salmon, WT/DS18/AB/R (Appellate Body Report) (1998)

Brazil – Measures Affecting Imports of Retreaded Tyres, WT/DS332/16 (2008)

Canada – Continued Suspension of Obligations in the EC-Hormones Dispute, WT/DS321/AB/R (2008)

China – Measures Affecting the Protection and Enforcement of Intellectual Property Rights, WT/DS362/RW (2009)

China – Measures Related to the Exportation of Various Raw Materials, WT/DS394/R and Corr.1/WT/DS395/R and Corr.1/WT/DS398/R and Corr.1 (2011)

China – Measures Related to the Exportation of Various Raw Materials, WT/DS394/AB/R and WT/DS395/AB/R and WT/DS398/AB/R (Appellate Body Reports) (2011–2012)

European Communities – Conditions for the Granting of Tariff Preferences to Developing Countries, WT/DS246/AB/R (Appellate Body Report) (2004)

European Communities – Measures Affecting the Approval and Marketing of Biotech Products, WT/DS291/R (2008)

European Communities – Measures Affecting Asbestos and Asbestos-Containing Products, WT/DS135/AB/R (2001)

National Cases

EDITORS AND CONTRIBUTORS

Editors

Marie-Claire Cordonier Segger, PhD *ad eundem* (Cantab), DPhil (Oxon), MEM (Yale), BCL & LLB (McGill), BA Hons (Carl/UVic) FRSC FRSA WIJA holds the Chair in Sustainable Development Law and Policy at the University of Cambridge as senior Law Fellow, Director of Studies and Programme Director at Lucy Cavendish College. She also serves as Senior Director of the Centre for International Sustainable Development Law (CISDL), Executive Secretary of the UN Framework Convention on Climate Change (UNFCCC), COP29 Climate Law and Governance Initiative and Vice-President of the International Law Association (ILA) of Canada, among others. As former senior legal advisor to the International Development Law Organisation and the UNFCCC Presidency, other intergovernmental organisations, treaty bodies and governments, as well as editor/board of several law journals and book series, she has published over 26 books and 160 papers on law, policy and sustainable development, including climate change, in six languages, and is co-recipient of the Climate Law and Governance Global Leadership Award, as well as laureate of the *Justicia Fundamentum Regnorum*, the Weeramantry International Justice Award (WIJA) and other distinguished honours.

Christina Voigt, PhD (Oslo), LLM.Env. (Auckland), Rechtswissenschaft (Passau and Munich) is Full Professor of Law in the department of public and international law, University of Oslo, Norway, and Chair of the IUCN World Commission of Environmental Law and Member of the IUCN Council. Author of numerous academic articles, a monograph and several edited volumes, including *Non-Compliance Mechanisms versus International Courts* (CUP, 2024), *Research Handbook on REDD+ and International Law* (EEP, 2016), and *Rule of Law for Nature* (CUP, 2013), she holds the inaugural Junior Scholarship Prize of the IUCN Academy of Environmental Law, among other distinguished awards and honours. She has served the Norwegian government as lead negotiator on REDD+ and as principal legal advisor in the UN climate negotiations, negotiating, inter alia, the Paris Agreement and its Rulebook. She has served as co-facilitator for the negotiations on the rules for the Paris Agreement's implementation and compliance committee (PAICC). In 2019, she was elected by the first meeting of the Parties to the Paris Agreement as a member of PAICC and currently serves as inaugural Co-Chair of the PAICC.

Assistant Editor

Zunaida Moosa Wadiwala, LLM (Witwatersrand), CML (U of SA & Pretoria), BLC, LLB (Pretoria) is an attorney, conveyancer and notary of the High Court of South Africa. Her research and publications are focus on Transnational Climate Litigation. Her affiliation is the University of Witwatersrand School of Law, where she works as an assistant and lecturer, and as Fellow of the Claude Leon Chair in Earth Justice and Stewardship. She previously practiced as a property lawyer in Johannesburg. Adv. Moosa Wadiwala also serves as a rapporteur for the Sabin Centre for Climate Change Law at Columbia University, covering South Africa, Saudi Arabia and the Middle East region. She serves as an examiner for the Law Society of South Africa's Legal Practice Council. She is Associate Fellow of the CISDL and an editor with the Voices of Future Generations Initiative. She is also a member of the editorial team at the Global Network for Human Rights and the Environment (GNHRE).

Contributors

Hassan Agouzoul, MBA (ESSEC) is a leading national climate finance and energy transition expert with over 25 years of experience working in the private and public sectors in the field of climate finance, energy and the green economy. He has served as a director of the SDG Action Strategy Center of Morocco since 2019 and is a UNEP Finance Initiative Master in the financial analysis of climate, environmental and social risks for financial institutions. His specializations include sustainable energy systems and climate transition in Morocco and Africa countries, with a special focus on the LT-LEDS, net zero economy, circular economy, SDGs and climate finance, green procurement, green bonds and territorial development.

Sumudu Atapattu, PhD, LLM (Cantab) is a teaching professor and director of the Global Legal Studies Center at the University of Wisconsin Law School. She is also Executive Director of the campus-wide interdisciplinary Human Rights Program. She serves as Lead Counsel for Human Rights at the Center for International Sustainable Development Law. Prof. Atapattu is also on the advisory board of the McGill International Journal of Sustainable Development Law and Policy and is affiliated scholar at the Raoul Wallenberg Institute for Human Rights and Humanitarian Law, Sweden.

Hyfa Azeez, LLM (Cantab), LLB (Groningen) is Legal Counsel at Elements Green, a greenfield developer driving just transition with solar and storage solutions, based in London, United Kingdom. She is an Associate Fellow of the CISDL. She served as rapporteur and legal researcher for the Climate Law and Governance Initiative during the 28th Conference of the Parties to the UNFCCC in Dubai, UAE.

Chhaya Bhardwaj, LLM (Vermont), BA LLB (CCS Meerut) is a United Nations-trained international lawyer and associate professor of law at the Jindal Global Law School and an assistant director of the Center for Environment Law and Climate Change. She is a member of the International Union for Conservation of Nature World Commission on Environmental Law, and a rapporteur for the Sabin Center for Climate Change Law at Columbia University.

Agnieszka Bielska-Brodziak, PhD, DSc (Silesia) is an associate professor of legal theory and philosophy of law at the University of Silesia in Katowice. She is a member of the Climate and

Environmental Crisis Council at the University of Silesia and head of the International Chair in Bioethics Unit. Bielska-Brodziak spoke as a speaker at the Climate Law and Governance Day conference during COP24, COP26 and COP28.

Gwyneth Boone, BCL/JD Cand (McGill) BASc Hons (McGill) is a CISDL legal researcher and passionate about the intersection of environmental law and human rights. In addition to her studies, Gwyneth works with the Canadian Civil Liberties Association and Citizen Lab. She also volunteered as Lead Outreach for Innocence McGill, worked as the Group Assistant for first-year Criminal Justice and served as an Associate Editor for the McGill Journal of Sustainable Development Law.

Megan Bowman, PhD (ANU), LLM (McGill), BA Hons (Monash) is professor of climate law and founding director of the Centre for Climate Law and Governance at King's College London, a visiting professor at Université de Paris-Dauphine in EU Corporate Law, a Centre for International Sustainable Development Law Fellow, and a qualified barrister and solicitor of the High Court of Australia and Supreme Court of Victoria. She consults on Paris Agreement implementation and leads the King's/UN Environment Programme research-impact partnership on *Legal Readiness for Climate Finance*. Prof Bowman's expertise focuses on empirical and transnational analyses of financial regulation and corporate law in the context of climate change and planetary sustainability.

Amelia Burnette, JD (UNC), BA (UNCA) is a doctoral researcher with the Strathclyde Centre for Environmental Law and Governance, pursuing research at the intersection of environmental law, climate change and human rights as a Fulbright Award recipient. She also serves as a director at the Climate Change Legal Initiative and is a visiting scholar with George Washington University Law School. Having practiced law in the US for over a decade, Adv Burnette has developed expertise in complex litigation, specifically in environmental protection, and her bar admissions include the US Supreme Court. Adv Burnette presents regularly on issues relating to climate litigation, biodiversity and human rights.

Jorge Cabrera Medaglia, DCL, MBA, LLM, BCL (UCR) Professor of Environmental Law, University of Costa Rica. Lead Counsel Biodiversity Law, CISDL. International consultant on environmental law, including access and benefit sharing from genetic resources, biotechnology, biotrade and traditional knowledge. Author of more than 140 articles, chapter and papers. He has participated as a negotiator in many different fora, including the Convention on Biological Diversity, the Nagoya Protocol and the International Treaty of FAO and worked in the implementation of MEA in more than 40 countries.

Christopher Campbell-Duruflé, SJD (Toronto), LLM (Notre Dame), BCL/LLB (McGill) is Assistant Professor at the Lincoln Alexander School of Law, Toronto Metropolitan University. His research focuses on international climate law, the Inter-American human rights system, and the reception of international law in Canada. He attended the Conference of the Parties to the UNFCCC from 2016 to 2019, with the CISDL and then with the delegation of Burkina Faso. Before joining Toronto Metropolitan University, he was a Postdoctoral Fellow at the Cambridge Centre for Environment, Energy and Natural Resource Governance (C-EENRG), where he remains associated as fellow and editor of the C-EENRG Research Series. He also serves on the legal committee of the Centre québécois du droit de l'environnement, on behalf of which he appeared before the Senate of Canada during its study of the *Canadian Net-Zero Emissions Accountability Act*. He provided strategic litigation trainings in Colombia, Guatemala, Honduras, and Jamaica, and his profile is part of the Human Rights Defenders exhibit at the Canadian Museum for Human Rights.

Ayman Cherkaoui, MSc (Emlyon), LLB (UdeM), BEng (McGill) is the director of the Hassan International Center for Environmental Training, the academic arm of the Mohammed VI Foundation for Environmental Protection and has previously been Special Advisor to the COP22 Presidency. He serves as Deputy Chair of the IUCN World Commission on Environmental Law, is the Lead Counsel for Climate Change at the CISDL and has been chair of the Climate Law and Governance Initiative for many COPs of the UNFCCC. His interests include international affairs, aeronautics and sustainable development law

Thomas M. Clark, JD (Columbia), AB (Harvard) is general counsel for the Asian Development Bank (ADB), where he is responsible for driving legal strategy and engagement on regulatory and policy reforms to support ADB's mission of achieving a sustainable, prosperous, inclusive and resilient Asia-Pacific region. He has over 30 years of experience in legal and government affairs practice, spanning the financial services, energy and infrastructure sectors, as well as the Americas, Asia-Pacific and European regions, and holds the Climate Law and Governance Global Leadership Award among other international distinctions.

Cosmin Corendea, SJD (Golden Gate), LLM (St. Thomas) is founder Vice Dean for Jindal School of Environment and Sustainability, in Delhi, India and Professor of Climate Law and Policy, Refugee and Migration Law for Jindal Global Law School. He also teaches International Comparative Law as Founder Faculty for the LLM Program in Environmental Law, Energy and Climate Change with WWF and he is a Fellow at the Centre for International Sustainable Development Law. Receiver of multiple awards and grants and author of the book "Legal Protection of the Sinking Islands Refugees", Prof Corendea is credited for initiating and developing the 'international hybrid law' legal concept which synergizes human rights, environmental and refugee/migration law in international climate law.

Pau de Vilchez Moragues, PhD (UIB), Master (Sciences-Po), LLM (Salamanca) is an Associate Professor of International Public Law at the University of the Balearic Islands (UIB), Chair of the Climate Change Committee of the Balearic Islands, Deputy Director of the Interdisciplinary Lab on Climate Change of UIB (LINCC), Legal Advisor at the Climate Change Legal Initiative and member of the Interdisciplinary Human Rights Lab of UIB (LIDIB). He specializes in climate litigation, international environmental law, human rights and the implementation of the energy transition.

Oleksandr Diachuk, PhD (Ukr) is a leading research officer at the Institute for Economics and Forecasting with over 16 years' experience in low-carbon development analysis, modeling, and strategic planning at the national and municipal levels. His focus is on researching strategies to achieve climate neutrality for the Ukrainian economy.

Lara Douvartzidis, Ad. LLM (Leiden), GDLP, LLB & BEnvs (Adelaide) is an Australian qualified lawyer and a senior legal executive of the Net Zero Lawyers Alliance. She has advised and acted for corporate and pro bono clients in the areas of environment and planning, human rights, aboriginal cultural heritage, dispute resolution and class actions, sustainability and modern slavery. She is an Associate Fellow at the CISDL and serves as an Officer of the International Bar Association Business and Human Rights Committee.

Valentina Durán Medina, LLB (Universidad de Chile), Masters (DEA) (University of Paris I Panthéon) is a professor and research coordinator at Centro de Derecho Ambiental at the Universidad de Chile. Professor Duran has participated as a trainer in courses addressed to enterprises and public servants in environmental matters. Her interests include international environmental law, environmental compliance and enforcement, environmental policy, biodiversity and environmental instruments.

Anusheh Fawad, BDEM (York Univ.), MES (Univ. of Waterloo) is a climate communications and marketing specialist. Fawad has dedicated her career to advancing climate sustainability, holding various roles in non-profit organizations and the public sector. Her research focuses on understanding the impact of climate change on marginalized communities, advocating for gender-responsive climate policies, and exploring climate policies through a feminist lens.

Rosa M. Fernández Egea, PhD (UAM), LLM (UAM) is an associate professor of international public law at the Universidad Autónonma de Madrid (UAM), National Rapporteur of the Climate Change Litigation Iniciative (C2LI) for Spain, member of the working group of the Spanish Observatory of Environmental Policies (OPAM) and author of the Environmental International Jurisprudence Chronique of the Revista Catalana de Dret Ambiental (RCDA). She was the leading member of the organizing committee of the Climate Law and Governance Day 2019 Conference as part of the UNFCCC COP 25 in Madrid.

David Gayle, MPhil. (Cantab), BA (UCL) is a Master in Public Policy (MPP) candidate at the Harvard Kennedy School and an Equity Fellow at the Center for Public Leadership. David is currently on sabbatical from the Bank of England, where he is a Policy Adviser on climate change and biodiversity.

Markus W. Gehring, MA (Cantab), LLM (Yale), DrIur (Hamb), JSD (Yale) is Law Fellow and Director of Studies for Hughes Hall at the University of Cambridge, and BIICL former Sir Arthur Watts Fellow. Dr. Gehring is also an associate professor at the Faculty of Law, and serves as Senior Proctor, also Chair of the disciplinary tribunal, in the University of Cambridge. He also serves as the ad personam Jean Monnet Chair in Sustainable Development Law and Lead Counsel for trade, investment and financial law at the CISDL, and holds the Climate Law and Governance Global Leadership Award, among other international distinctions.

Afef Hammami-Marrakchi, PhD (Tunis), is an associate professor of public law at the University of Sfax in Tunisia. She holds a doctoral thesis on "The integration of sustainable development in Tunisian law" (2007) and is a lecturer at the Faculty of Law of Sfax on environmental law and urban planning law and sustainable development law. Dr. Hammami Marrakchi was an expert with the UNDP and a member of the Roster of Experts responsible for providing support to the legislative work of the Assembly of Representatives of the United Nations on the decentralisation bill (2017), the gender bill (2018), the sustainable development body (2019), the sustainable development objectives (2019) and the Water Code (2021).

Vesselina Haralampieva, LLM (Harvard), Masters and BA (Sofia University) is Head of Sustainable Finance Governance and Regulation and Senior Counsel at the European Bank for Reconstruction and Development (EBRD) in London, UK. Ms. Haralampieva leads EBRD's sustainable transition programme for clients (financial institutions and real sector companies) and the climate and sustainability policy and law reform work in the legal department. Prior to EBRD, she has worked at the World Intellectual Property Organisation (WIPO), the Harvard Berkman Klein Centre and in private practice. Ms. Haralampieva is a member of the Climate Change Working Group with the Law Society of England & Wales and holds the CISDL Legal Specialist Awards, among other distinctions. Ms. Haralampieva is admitted to practice as a solicitor in England & Wales and in Bulgaria.

Alexandra Harrington, DCL (McGill), LLM (Albany), BCL&JD (McGill), BA (NYU) is a lecturer in environmental law at the University of Lancaster, Executive Director of the Center for Global Governance and Emerging Law and Chair of the IUCN WCEL Task Force on Plastic Pollution. Dr. Harrington is also the Director of Studies for the International Law Association of Colombia, a member of the ILA Committee on the Role of International Law in Sustainable Natural Resource Management for Development, and is Lead Counsel for Peace, Justice and Governance at the Centre for International Sustainable Development Law.

Barbara Janusz-Pawletta, DCL (Freie), LLM (Moscow), Law (Jagiellonen) is an international law expert with a focus on water and environment. Prof. Janusz-Pawletta was Vice President for International Cooperation and Sustainability at Kazakh-German University and was the UNESCO Chair holder for water management in Central Asia at DKU. She is also the co-editor of the Journal of the Central Asian Journal of Water Research (CAJWR). Her current position is International Water Management Institute Head of Regional Representative Office for Central Asia.

Erick Kassongo, LLM (Salford/UK), Law (Free University of Kinshasa) is Executive Director of the Congolese Center for Sustainable Development Law (CODED) and an attorney at the Environmental Law Alliance Worldwide ELAW-US for French speaking African countries. His research focuses on issues of governance, climate change adaptation and mitigations, NDC, climate litigation, loss and damages, investor states disputes, sustainable landscape investments, sustainable development, REDD+ process, energy projects, public policy and human rights.

M. Hafijul Islam Khan, LL.M (Dhaka University), LLM (CEU) is a climate negotiator with the Least Developing Countries (LDCs) Group from the Bangladesh Delegation for the UNFCCC. He is an advocate affiliated with Supreme Court of Bangladesh and Director for the Centre for Climate Justice-Bangladesh (CCJ-B). Adv. Khan is a Member of the Executive Committee of Warsaw International Mechanism for loss and damage at UNFCCC. He is also advising currently to LDCs Board member to Loss and Damage Fund and was a member of the Transitional Committee for Loss and Damage Fund at UNFCCC. He is involved with New York Law School, USA and the CISDL as Research Fellow.

Avidan Kent, PhD (Cantab), LLM (McGill), LLB (Haifa) is a professor of law and director of research at the University of East Anglia's Law School. He has written and edited books, journal articles and chapters on a varied list of topics, including Environmental Law, Economic Law, international courts, Public Participation and Climate-Induced Migration. His recent publications include a monograph on renewable energy investment in the Global South and a collection on climate migration.

Douglas Leys KC is a former General Counsel of the Green Climate Fund, and previously served as the Government of Jamacia's Solicitor General. Leys holds the rank of Queen's Counsel, a position reserved for persons who have distinguished themselves at the bar in the Commonwealth.

He is also Senior Fellow at the Centre for International Sustainable Development Law and holds the Climate Law and Governance Global Leadership Award, among other international distinctions.

Cassie Lumsden, JD (UVic), BSc (UBC), is an articled student at the Government of British Columbia, with a concentration in environmental law and sustainability. She has contributed to the University of Victoria Climate Change Litigation for Beginners project and was a member of the UVic Environmental Law Centre Board of Directors. Adv. Lumsden completed her JD major thesis project on international marine environmental law and was previously a student researcher with the UBC Climate Justice Research Collaborative.

Kate McKenzie, PhD (Strathclyde), LLM, JD is the CEO and Director of the Climate Change Legal Initiative. She is a licensed attorney in the United States with over 15 years of practical experience across a variety of practice areas, including criminal law, corporate responsibility, mediation and social justice issues. Her research focuses on climate change litigation with an emphasis on ocean-related climate impacts.

Michael A. Mehling, PhD (Helsinki), LLM (Helsinki), Law (Konstanz) is a professor at the University of Strathclyde School of Law, deputy director of the Centre for Energy and Environmental Policy Research at the Massachusetts Institute of Technology, and a non-executive director with the Ecologic Institute in Berlin and Climate Strategies in London. Prof. Mehling is also a founding President of the Ecologic Institute in Washington DC, and a founding board member of the Blockchain & Climate Institute (BCI) in London and the European Roundtable on Climate Change and Sustainable Transition (ERCST) in Brussels. He is also the founding editor of *Carbon & Climate Law Review* (CCLR), the first academic journal focused on climate law.

Wendy Miles KC, LLM (Canterbury), BA (Canterbury) is a specialist in international arbitration and dispute resolution with a focus on private and public international law. Adv. Miles has advised on international law matters and conducted arbitrations under all the major institutions. In the field of climate change and finance, Adv. Miles acts as global coordinating counsel to various major corporations in relation to climate change transition, disclosure, reporting, compliance and investment. She also works closely with the International Chamber of Commerce (ICC), has represented the ICC at the UNFCCC CoP since 2015, and holds the Climate Law and Governance Global Leadership Award among other international distinctions.

Jellie Molino, PhD (Turin), LLM (GWU), EMBA (AIM), JD (Batangas), BA (Philippines-Diliman) is an international legal expert on sustainable public procurement (SPP) with experience working for international organizations, e.g., UNOPS, UNEP, UNDP, the World Bank, IFC, OECD, ITC-ILO and ADB. She is a member of the Philippine Bar with specialization in administrative law, environmental law, and corporate compliance. She is currently a Postdoctoral Fellow at Hughes Hall College, University of Cambridge, with research focusing on private law, procurement, and climate change. She also serves as Procurement Advisor for UNOPS and International SPP Expert for WB in Bangladesh.

Emily Morison, LLM (Cantab), LLM (JD) (Monash) BSc (Melbourne) is a Project Lawyer in the International Bar Association's Legal Policy and Research Unit, leading projects on environment, climate and business and human rights law. Adv Morison is a member of the National

Environmental Law Association (Australia) and was formerly an associate at a leading Australian law firm, specialising in climate change and sustainability.

Margarita Nieves-Zárate, PhD Cand (Groningen), LLM (Universidad Externado de Colombia), JD (Universidad Popular del César) is a PhD Researcher in Energy Law at the University of Groningen and a Senior Advisor to the President to the Agencia Nacional de Hidrocarburos.

Elizabeth Nwarueze, BCL (Oxon), B.L. (Nigeria), LL.B (Ibadan) is a Rhodes Scholar and Doctoral Student in International Law at University of Oxford. She participated in the final negotiations for the BBNJ Agreement and is a member of the UN Pool of Experts for the Development of the Third World Ocean Assessment. Nwarueze's research on ocean governance and maritime security has been published by the Gulf of Guinea Maritime Institute and presented at the US Naval War College and Korea Maritime Institute.

Christina Pak, JD (Rutgers) is a principal counsel of Asian Development Bank and heads the Office of the General Counsel's Law and Policy Reform Program. Adv. Pak specializes in international development finance, law and policy reform, dispute resolution and ESG standards and drives thought leadership on sustainable development issues. She also serves on the Steering Committee of the IUCN World Commission of Environmental Law.

Freedom-Kai Phillips, PhD (Cambridge), LLM (Ottawa), LLB (Dalhousie), MA (Seton Hall), BSc honors (E. Michigan), is Director of the Deloitte Center for Sustainable Progress (DCSP). In addition, Dr. Phillips is a Legal Research Fellow with the CISDL, and a member of the IUCN World Commission on Environmental Law. With over two decades of experience in intergovernmental, multilateral and think-tank environments, Dr. Phillips research focuses on international law, market mechanisms, ocean and nature-climate interfaces, carbon offsetting and renewable energy promotion, and legal measures to support achievement of the Sustainable Development Goals (SDGs).

Tomasz Pietrzykowski, PhD, DSc (Silesia) is a professor of legal theory and philosophy of law at the University of Silesia in Katowice and the head of the Research Center for Public Policy and Regulatory Governance. He is the founder of the "Just Transition Research Group" (2019) to monitor and advise on the processes of just transition in Silesia and other European regions within the EU legal framework.

Maya Prabhu, AB (Harvard), MSc (LSE), MD (Dalhousie), LLB (McGill) is an assistant professor of psychiatry at the Faculty of Law and Psychiatry of Yale University. She is also an Associate Professor (Adjunct) of Law at Yale Law School. Dr. Prabhu is a medical doctor and lawyer. Her research interests include global health, forensic psychiatry, post-trauma stress disorder in post-conflict situations and various issues at the nexus of health and human rights.

Tejas Rao, PhD Cand (Cantab), LLM (Cantab), BA LLB (Hons) (Gujarat) is Senior Manager of the Centre for International Sustainable Development Law and a PhD candidate at the University of Cambridge. His research examines the epistemic communities that participate in international environmental law-making, intersecting his interests in history, politics, economics and law. With a cross-cutting interest across the Sustainable Development Goals, he is a fellow of the Balsillie School of International Affairs, Canada, supporting global governance engagement and research.

Raúl Salas Reyes, PhD Cand (Toronto), MSc (Toronto), Masters (UAG), BEng (UAG) is a researcher in environmental science at the Department of Physical and Environmental Sciences at the University of Toronto Scarborough. His research focuses on the evolution and contestation of the differential treatment norm in the climate regime. He has also worked as a consultant assisting developing countries in the implementation of transparency arrangements as part of their obligations under the UNFCCC and is a member of the UNFCCC's Roster of Experts.

Pamela Towela Sambo, PhD (Manchester), LLM (KwaZulu-Natal), LLB (Zambia) is a Private Law Lecturer at the University of Zambia and Chairperson of the Human Rights Commission of Zambia. Dr. Sambo is specialised in the legal aspects of environmental justice, EIAs and human rights. She has over 24 years of experience in Zambian law practice and research. Her research interests include cross-cutting environmental issues, sustainable development and climate justice. She is past Assistant Dean (Undergraduate) and Head of Private Law Department at the University of Zambia. Her current teaching interests are spread across the law of torts, legal research methodology, human rights and environmental law.

Ignacio Sánchez González, LLB, MA (University of Chile) is an Instructor Professor at the Institute of International Studies of University of Chile, Board Member of the Chile Internet Governance Forum (IGF) and a member of the WTO Chairs Programme Chile. Adv. Sánchez has completed the "Training for International Negotiations on Climate Change", certified by EUROCLIMA+ (European Union) and the Ministry of Environment (Chile). He has experience in internet governance and LAC domain names and their links with sustainability. He has also advised different research and consultancy projects on digital trade integration (ECLAC).

Mrinalini Shinde, LLM Cand (Goethe), MSc (Cologne), BA LLB (Hons) (Nat Law School of India Uni) is a visiting lecturer at the Environmental Law Centre at the University of Cologne. Her previous role was as a Legal Affairs Fellow at the UNFCCC secretariat in intergovernmental matters, treaty implementation and capacity-building. She has acted as litigator and advisor in environmental matters, appearing before the National Green Tribunal in India, and has advised the climate media non-profit 'Climate Tracker Inc.' as Policy Associate. Her research interests include international environmental law, corporate environmental crime, criminal law, climate change law, and carbon taxation.

Francesco Sindico, PhD (UJI), LLM (Madrid), LLB (Turin) is a professor in international environmental law at the University of Strathclyde Law School, and he is Co-Chair of the IUCN World Commission on Environmental Law Climate Change Law Specialist Group. He is an expert in international law and has academic and practical experience in climate change, international water law and sustainable development law. He provides legal advice to international organisations and governments in matters of international law and climate change and enjoys translating his academic work into policy-oriented and practical outputs.

Mariia Stolbova, LLM (NaU-KMA), LLB Hons (NU-OLA) is a member of the Ukrainian Bar, American Chamber of Commerce and European Business Association. She is also a legal consultant to the Ukraine Member of Parliament.

Michael Strauss, JD (Stanford), MALD (Fletcher), BA (Williams College) is General Counsel at the European Bank for Reconstruction and Development. Prior to his appointment, Adv.

Strauss was a partner at Harris, Wiltshire & Grannis LLP, represented the US on the Board of the Asian Development Bank, and served as Senior Advisor to the Assistant Secretary for International Finance at the US Treasury. Adv. Strauss has worked as legal counsel in the World Bank Group and International Monetary Fund, primarily focused on sovereign debt, institutional governance, political risk management and development in Francophone Africa, and holds the Climate Law and Governance Global Leadership Award among other international distinctions.

Magdalena Stryja, Advocate (Polish Bar Council), LLM (Silesia, Katowice) is Director of Sustainable Development at WSB University. Since 2018, she has been chairing and organising expert and leadership panels during the Climate Law and Governance Day conferences within COP24, 25, 26, 27, and 28. She is a legal fellow at the CISDL. She is Chair of the Science and Development Commission at the Silesian Bar Council. She was a spokesperson and director of the legal department at the National Erasmus+ Agency. She was a member of the Just Transition research group, monitoring and advising on the processes of just transition in Silesia and other European regions within the EU legal framework.

Zhen Sun, PhD (Cantab), LLM (Edinburgh), LLM (CUPL), LLB (Hainan) is an associate professor at the World Maritime University's WMU-Sasakawa Global Ocean Institute. Her research focuses on the law of the sea, international regulation of shipping, gender equality in ocean governance, climate action and the protection of the marine environment. Dr. Zhen has also played an active role in launching and executing several high-level research programmes related to the ocean and has previously published a number of book chapters and journal articles on the law of the sea.

Emily Webster, PhD (KCL), LLM (KCL) was an esteemed colleague at Cambridge University as an assistant professor in environmental law in the department of land economy, an Official Fellow of Queens College, and a member of the Hughes Hall Centre for Climate Engagement. Previously, she served as a member of the first PhD cohort of the Centre for Climate Law & Governance at King's College London as an ESRC-funded doctoral candidate and remained a valuable contributor to the Law School as a Senior Research Fellow at the Transnational Law Institute.

Lydia Young, JD (UVic), BSc (UVic) is a member of the Law Society of British Columbia and the Canadian Bar Association (2024). She completed her JD with a concentration in environmental law and sustainability before articling at Tollefson Law Corporation, where she focused on environmental, natural resource and constitutional litigation. Her research interests are biodiversity conservation, natural resource law, green economies and sustainable development.

Abdelnaser Zeyad Hayajneh, PhD (Newcastle), LLM (Jordan), LLB (Yarmouk) is a professor of law at the University of Qatar. As author/co-author of six published books and many articles in civil law, environmental law, Islamic legal literature, human rights, sports law, Jordanian civil law, and environmental liability, he has served as expert/consultant to the Ministry of Justice of Jordan, the Jordan Environment Society and the Law of Jordan Centre, among other distinguished bodies.

Researchers

Samantha Andison, JD (UVic), MPC (Ryerson), BA Hons (Western), is an articling student with a concentration in environmental law and sustainability. Samantha is interested in the intersection of environmental and indigenous law in Canada and around the world, and has volunteered with several legal clinics which work at this intersection. During law school, she was a Senior Editor for the Canadian Law Review and a volunteer editor for UVic's Law Review, Appeal, and was at the top of her class in Water Law and Sustainable Development Law & Governance.

Jay Artley, JD Cand (UVic), BA (Queen's), is a law student at the University of Victoria who is passionate about environmental justice and sustainability. He has volunteered as a student caseworker with UVic's Environmental Law Centre and has worked with the Government of British Columbia, where he brought legislative amendments to support the Province's Clean Transportation Action Plan.

Kendall Damon, MPhil Cand (Cantab), BSc (S. Cal), is a programme coordinator of the Climate Law and Governance Initiative and serves in the Centre for International Sustainable Development Law Secretariat. Her research focuses on equitable climate adaptation policy within urban systems.

Cassandra Hayward, PhD Cand (Cantab), MA (Waterloo), BAHons (Dalhousie/Kings), is a PhD student in Land Economy at the University of Cambridge. She actively supervises at Cambridge, teaching International Organisations and Global Governance, Public Policy, Sustainability in Business and Evidence and Argument. She is a 2023/2024 Canadian Centennial Scholarship Fund Scholar with particular research interests in sustainable development and food systems.

Kaainat Pundir, LLM (Cantab), BA LLB (Jindal), is an arbitration and litigation practitioner, specializing in construction and corporate law. She is an internationally accredited mediator, who coaches and supervises students in mediation and negotiation globally. She led a project for Cambridge Pro Bono consulting for a constitutional court and was a conference associate for the Cambridge Int Law Conference. Her research focuses on alternate dispute settlement, international trade law and sustainability.

1
INTRODUCTION

Marie-Claire Cordonier Segger, Christina Voigt, Lydia Young and Zunaida Moosa Wadiwala[1]

Climate Change Challenges and the Importance of Law to Global Response

Climate change is the justice and sustainability challenge of our century. Anthropogenic greenhouse gas emissions are leading to dangerous global temperature increases and changes in conditions of unprecedented pace. In 2023 alone, the world faced 86 days with temperatures exceeding 1.5 degrees Celsius above pre-industrial levels.[2] Record-breaking temperatures are accompanied by increasing frequency of extreme weather events, melting glaciers and polar ice, devastating floods, rising sea-levels, bleaching corals, changing disease vectors and worsening wildfires, droughts and desertification. As the global climate continues to change, humanity's capacity for mitigation, for instance through adoption of sustainable energy systems, net zero or carbon negative technologies and infrastructure, nature-based solutions and lifestyle transformations, or for adaptation and resilience, including through disaster risk reduction and response measures or for climate finance at sufficient scope and scale remains disturbingly uncertain.

An effective international legal regime, guiding and reflecting insights from myriad domestic legal and institutional reform efforts, is essential to inspire the rules and action necessary to tackle this crisis. The United Nations Framework Convention on Climate Change (UNFCCC) provides a framework for international coordination, increasing ambition, strengthening capacity and improving accountability. The signing of the Paris Agreement inspired a sense of optimism, establishing a common objective to keep the global temperature increase well below 2 degrees Celsius above pre-industrial levels, and to strive towards a 1.5 degrees Celsius limit.[3] Guided by international law, finance and action on climate change is increasing exponentially at all levels, and the 28th Conference of the Parties to the UNFCCC (COP28) in Dubai, United Arab Emirates (UAE), led to an unprecedented call in the Global Stocktake Decision, for "transitioning away from fossil fuels in energy systems, in a just, orderly and equitable manner, accelerating action in this critical decade, so as to achieve net zero by 2050."[4] Prominent national and international litigation efforts are also highlighting the crucial contributions of the law to addressing climate change, and international courts and tribunals, including the International Court of Justice (ICJ), the European Court of Human Rights (ECtHR), the Inter-American Court of Human Rights (IACtHR) and the International Tribunal on the Law of the Sea (ITLOS) among others are increasingly requested by States and others for

DOI: 10.4324/9781003276678-1

advice and dispute settlement.[5] Indeed, as is explored further in this volume, in their 2024 *Advisory Opinion on the Request Submitted by the Commission of Small Island States on Climate Change and International Law*, the International Tribunal on the Law of the Sea found that "climate change represents an existential threat and raises human rights concerns" (para 66) and that "climate change is recognized internationally as a common concern of humankind" (para 122), noting that ITLOS was "conscious of the deleterious effects climate change has on the marine environment and the devastating consequences it has and will continue to have on small island States, considered to be among the most vulnerable to such impacts.[6]" The Tribunal also found that:

> States Parties to the Convention [on the Law of the Sea] have the specific obligations to take all necessary measures to prevent, reduce and control marine pollution from anthropogenic GHG emissions and to endeavour to harmonize their policies in this connection. Such measures should be determined objectively, taking into account, *inter alia,* the best available science and relevant international rules and standards contained in climate change treaties such as the UNFCCC and the Paris Agreement. (ibid, para 243)

It found that "anthropogenic GHG emissions into the atmosphere fall under the definition of pollution of the marine environment," (para 252) and that

> [i]n adopting laws and regulations, States are required to take into account "internationally agreed rules, standards and recommended practices and procedures" . . . Those rules, standards and practices and procedures encompass a broad range of norms, both binding and non-binding in nature. In the context of climate change, they include those contained in climate change treaties such as the UNFCCC and the Paris 97 Agreement. Accordingly, States Parties to the Convention have an obligation to take into account those norms in adopting their laws and regulations to prevent, reduce and control marine pollution from GHG emissions. (ibid, para 270)

Further, ITLOS found: "States have two obligations in this regard: first, the obligation to enforce their laws and regulations; and second, the obligation to adopt laws and regulations and take other measures necessary to implement applicable international rules and standards" (ibid, para 283) and that:

> The obligation of cooperation . . . requires States to make an ongoing effort to formulate and elaborate rules, standards and recommended practices and procedures. The adoption of a particular treaty, such as the UNFCCC or the Paris Agreement, does not discharge a State from its obligation to cooperate, as the obligation requires an ongoing effort on the part of States in the development of new or revised regulatory instruments, in particular in light of the evolution of scientific knowledge. (ibid, para 311)

Despite valiant efforts on many levels, including the landmark Paris Agreement and successive Conference of the Parties serving as the meeting of the Parties to the Paris Agreement (CMA) decisions, however, even if all countries' current 2030 pledges were met, the world would still be on a path toward a terrifying temperature rise of 2.5–2.9 degrees Celsius.[7] For this reason, each round of National Determined Contributions (NDCs) by each Party to the Paris Agreement, including those submitted in 2025 with a time frame to 2035, is critical for global climate action. As Simon

Stiell, Executive Secretary of the UNFCCC, stated in this context: "NDCs may be the most important documents to be produced in a multilateral context so far this century."[8]

The enormity of the challenge for law is clear. While the recent Intergovernmental Panel on Climate Change (IPCC) 2023 AR6 Report finds that a 1.5 degree pathway remains feasible, significant legal and institutional reform is needed. In the first round of NDCs submitted, 169 of the 186 countries explicitly prioritized the need for legal and institutional reforms for countries to meet their pledged NDC targets.[9] Of these, 99 Parties emphasized the need for law and policy capacity building in their NDCs, with many requesting international support and conditioning their targets upon receipt of this assistance. Indeed, the UN Development Programme's Climate Promise, the largest global provider of NDC support, highlights the crucial role for capacity building in enhancing the quality and ambition of NDCs.[10]

Worldwide, the legal community can and must prioritize strengthening the legal and institutional capacity necessary to actualize countries' mitigation and adaptation targets, and to raise the ambition of future NDCs to set the world on a 1.5 degree-aligned pathway. Recent policy, legal and institutional innovations illustrate the role of legal and governance solutions in bridging the growing 'capacity chasm' and addressing the climate crisis. In 2023, studies identified over 3,000 climate-related laws and policies in force across the globe, with new rules being adopted continually.[11] These regulatory changes mainly seek to mitigate greenhouse gas (GHG) emissions through legal reform across energy, forests/land use change and agriculture, industrial processes, waste and water; and to promote strategies, standards and systems for adaptation to the climate impacts already being confronted and enhance resilience toward future climatic impacts. Financial and commercial law is also being deployed, including to raise investment in the more sustainable technologies, infrastructure, goods and services required, enhance requirements for climate-risk disclosures and corporate materiality, and support growing corporate environmental, social and governance (ESG) commitments. Litigation in domestic courts of over fifty countries, including decisions such as the landmark *Urgenda* case in the Netherlands,[12] the Swiss *KlimaSeniorinnen* case in the aforementioned European Court of Human Rights,[13] the *Leghari* case in Pakistan[14] and the *Rocky Hill Mine* case in Australia,[15] suggest that courts are more than able to consider climate change imperatives. Hundreds of ongoing climate lawsuits underline the importance of access to justice and fair, reliable dispute resolution related to climate action. The challenges are great, and innovations in the legal, regulatory and governance spheres are essential to mitigating and adapting to climate change with the requisite urgency.

The Routledge Handbook on Climate Change Law: Courage, Contributions and Compliance

Recognizing the United Nations' calls for urgent action reflected in the Intergovernmental Panel on Climate Change (IPCC) 2023 AR6 Synthesis Report, this handbook convenes insights from leading legal academic experts, specialists and professionals on emerging issues in climate law to present a pathway for advancing climate ambition in the coming decades. The volume explores the role of law and governance in advancing global response to climate change and advancing sustainable development. Based on careful study of international advances and of the full spectrum of NDCs to the global response to climate change, as submitted by Paris Agreement Parties, the Handbook compiles a compelling, coherent and systematic topical account from across diverse legal jurisdictions. Brief analytical chapters by leading international experts, practitioners and early career specialists close to ongoing climate negotiations explore recent legal and institutional innovations related to climate change which can advance the implementation of the Paris Agreement and the global Sustainable Development Goals (SDGs), with a focus on:

- Courage: international efforts to raise climate mitigation, adaptation and resilience and finance ambition through the international law and policy regimes,
- Contributions: reforms of legal and institutional arrangements to implement and achieve NDCs in key countries and regions and
- Compliance: the interactional changes to international law and governance in fostering effective Paris Agreement implementation and compliance.

This generation's ability to adequately mitigate and adapt to climate change – indeed, its very survival – depends on how rapidly and comprehensively country-level commitments and actions can align with the goal to limit global temperature increase under Article 2 of the Paris Agreement, including through cooperative efforts. In this respect, beyond the UNFCCC and the Paris Agreement, new developments in climate legislation and institutional reform, integrated with innovative private law and governance approaches in law and policymaking, will prove crucial to increasing States' climate ambition. With this overarching vision, through thirty-two chapters, the edited volume addresses a series of key themes through five main parts.

Part I: Challenges

In Part I, *Challenges*, the Handbook considers how the challenges of international law and policy might provide a framework to accelerate the transition to a net zero and resilient world, in the context of the global SDGs, providing the contextual foundations for understanding the rest of the volume.

Part I begins with the present Chapter 1, 'Introduction' by the editors, which opens and introduces the volume by highlighting the imperative of global response to climate change, the role of law and policy reform in fostering rapid and effective action on climate change, and the focus and structure of the handbook.

Chapter 2, 'The Urgency of Global Response to Climate Change' written by Adv. Ayman Cherkoui and Adv. Zunaida Moosa Wadiwala, acknowledges that in recent years, climate law and governance structures have evolved in an unprecedented manner, illustrating the depth and importance of the climate change challenge that this book addresses. In calling for climate law and governance to tackle climate change, this chapter frames an urgent global response to climate change to be based on climate science in the context of the eradication of poverty, respect for human rights and sustainable development, taking into account both global and context-specific legal frameworks focused on equity. The chapter concludes with the call for a need to embody transformational positive change with the simultaneous shifting sense of urgency in the perception of climate change.

Chapter 3, 'Climate Courage, Contributions and Compliance in the Context of the Sustainable Development Goals and Principles,' written by Professor Marie-Claire Cordonier-Segger, explains the imperatives of global response to climate change, introducing the UN Sustainable Development Goals (SDGs) and exploring the importance and potential to achieve the objectives of the Paris Agreement in a manner that advances key priorities for sustainability as adopted in the seventeen global SDGs and their 169 targets. The chapter calls for courage through legal and policy innovation and leadership, contributions through full implementation of progressively more ambitious Nationally Determined Contributions, and compliance with commitments in the international regime and at all levels. After a brief discussion of the origins of the SDGs and the Paris Agreement under the UNFCCC, underlining the elements of the Paris Agreement which reflect principles of international law on sustainable development, the chapter examines the contributions of the Paris Agreement to sustainability, especially in highly climate-vulnerable countries. Based on research supported by the New Frontiers Research Fund (NFRF) of Canada, the chapter also highlights how effective, inclusive and rapid implementation of the Paris Agreement can support the SDGs.

Chapter 4, 'The UNFCCC, the Paris Agreement and Legal Obligations on Climate Change,' concludes Part I's discussion of the challenges at hand by providing an overview of the architecture of the UNFCCC and the Paris Agreement. Written by Professor Christina Voigt and Adv. Lydia Young, the chapter explains the legal obligations contained in the agreement and analyzes their legal character. The obligations range from procedural obligations of all Parties, for example to submit and maintain NDCs, to differentiated obligations for developed country Parties only, such as to communicate information on indicative levels of finance, to obligations of conduct, such as the requirement that the NDC will reflect each Party's highest possible ambition and a progression beyond the previous one. The chapter further describes the processes established by the agreement, which in sum are designed to bring parties to the level of ambition needed to address the climate challenge.

Part II: Courage

In Part II on *Courage*, the Handbook investigates the most ambitious new developments in law and governance to implement climate mitigation, climate adaptation and finance through the Paris Agreement under the UNFCCC.

This section opens with Chapter 5, 'Advancing Climate Action in Trade, Investment and Financial Agreements,' written by Professor Markus W. Gehring and Adv. Emily Morison, which reviews the past decade and especially the years following the adoption of the Paris Agreement, noting significant innovation in the way financial instruments and bilateral investment treaties are created to include climate protection in conditionalities. The chapter focuses on exemplary innovations in financial law and regulation that display courage and vision in anticipating climate risks and accounting for climate impacts within international trade and investment transactions.

In Chapter 6, 'Exploring Nature-Based Solutions to Climate Change in International Law,' Professor Jorge Cabrera and Adv. Lydia Young examine the potential for innovation within the development and deployment of nature-based solutions (NbS) to climate change. The role of nature, especially in domestic adaptation efforts, is a significant area of innovation, as these solutions have multiple benefits including restoring ecosystem health and stability, along with providing benefits for human welfare. The chapter defines NbS within the context of international law, provides examples of how it is implemented around the world at a national level and discusses future challenges and opportunities to maximize the benefits of this form of climate action.

Subsequently, Professor Sumudu Atapattu considers climate impacts from sudden events such as extreme weather events and flooding, to slow-onset events such as sea level rise and desertification in Chapter 7, 'Linking International Human Rights Law and Climate Change,' arguing that it is becoming increasingly clear that climate change will affect virtually all rights protected under human rights law. As a global problem, no state or community will be spared adverse consequences, but the impacts will be disproportionately borne by poorer countries and those groups that are already in a vulnerable situation such as women, children, the poor and the elderly. This chapter discusses the impact of climate change on human rights and how a human rights framing is necessary to ensure that vulnerable groups will not be disproportionately affected. It adopts the three-prong application of human rights obligations developed by former UN Special Rapporteur on Human Rights and Environment John Knox in his mapping report: substantive obligations, procedural obligations, and additional obligations applicable to vulnerable groups. These obligations are discussed in relation to mitigation (especially NDCs), adaptation, severe weather events and the loss and damage mechanism, concluding with a case study of the *Teitiota v New Zealand* case decided by the UN Human Rights Committee in 2020 relating to climate refugees.

Chapter 8, 'Promoting Access to Information, Public Participation and Justice on Climate Change' by Professor Valentina Durán Medina and Adv. Ignacio Antonio Sánchez González clarifies the checks and balances between governments and the public through access rights, including those contained within the Paris Agreement. For example, Article 12 of the Paris Agreement includes a requirement for Parties "to cooperate in taking measures, as appropriate, to enhance climate change education, training, public awareness, public participation and public access to information, recognizing the importance of these steps with respect to enhancing actions under this Agreement." Considering the overarching principle and binding requirements toward access to information and public participation, this chapter examines how Parties are deploying innovative tools in law and governance to make good on these obligations, including through public participation in environmental decision-making.

Subsequently, Chapter 9, 'The High Seas Treaty and Interactions with Climate Change,' authored by Adv. Cassie Lumsden, Professor Zhen Sun and Professor Marie-Claire Cordonier Segger, explores how the 2023 Agreement under the United Nations Convention on the Law of the Sea on the Conservation and Sustainable Use of Marine Biological Diversity of Areas Beyond National Jurisdiction interacts with existing climate-related international legal instruments. Based on research supported by the NFRF of Canada, it also addresses the global response to climate change more generally, taking into account findings in the 2024 Advisory Opinion on Climate Change of the International Tribunal on the Law of the Sea (ITLOS).

The text's exploration of *Courage* in Part II concludes with Dr. Maya Prabhu and Dr. Avidan Kent addressing the causes and impact of climate-induced displacement and migration in Chapter 10, 'Expanding the Search on Climate-Induced Migration.' It addresses consideration of climate-induced migration in the UNFCCC process, first in the context of adaptation and increasingly also under the Convention's Loss and Damage Framework. The chapter also addresses the legal foundation and gaps for climate-induced migrants, including human rights implications arising from displacement and extreme weather events. This chapter focuses in particular on the rights associated with health impacts associated with climate-induced migration.

Part III: Contributions

In Part III on *Contributions*, the text examines the most significant legal and institutional reforms being undertaken, in key regions and domestic law, to guide and support state efforts to set and achieve progressively more ambitious NDCs to the global response to climate change.

Chapter 11, 'Private Financing to Implement the Paris Agreement in the United Kingdom' by Professor Megan Bowman and the late Dr. Emily Webster, opens the discussion of contributions through examining the UK's 2021 announcement to become the world's first "net zero aligned financial centre," including its current plans to reach such a goal. The chapter investigates, among other things, relevant mechanisms under the Paris Agreement and the sufficiency of UK regulations for attaining net zero alignment. In doing so, the chapter explores the importance of regulatory creativity to increase finance sector ambition in both private and public sectors to achieve net zero.

Professor Barbara Janusz-Pawletta and Dr. Alexandra Harrington, in Chapter 12 on 'Scaling up Paris Agreement Implementation through Climate Law and International Water Law Regulations with Special Focus on Europe,' provide a good overview of the chapter's contents. This chapter highlights the coherence between the Paris Agreement and areas of international environmental law, and associated national and regional laws which focus on water as one of the main climate-dependent natural resources. It discusses methods for utilizing synergies between these legal regimes, as well as for making additional efforts to strengthen the common customary and conventional provisions relating to climate and water resources, and in this way, further strengthen climate resilience.

In Chapter 13, 'Law and Governance Contributions to Energy Transitions in Latin America,' Dr. Margarita Nieves-Zárate addresses the voluntary adoption of emission reduction commitments by Latin America countries under the Paris Agreement and its impact on the region's energy systems. The chapter also addresses what regulatory mechanisms will be required for transitioning from fossil fuel-dominant energy. Grounded in the theory of regulation, the chapter presents a typology of the mitigation and adaptation measures presented by Latin American countries in their NDCs and the challenges of the region to decarbonize its energy sector.

Chapter 14, 'Legal Aspects of Achieving the Just Transition in Poland,' written by Adv. Magdalena Stryja, Professor Agnieszka Bielska-Brodziak and Professor Tomasz Pietrzykowski, focuses on the "just transition," its origins and the evolution of the concept. The chapter presents arguments examining the concept of a just transition, which, especially in the face of necessary actions aimed at counteracting the climate crisis, appears as one of the most essential instruments of the transition process. The authors discuss the most important acts of international and domestic law, which have built the legal foundation for the application of this concept in practice. The emphasis is placed on Poland, as a country that has received significant financial resources from the European New Green Deal, and is also facing drastic changes in combatting the climate crisis, in which the individual and the concern for their existence cannot disappear from sight. Taking into consideration the Paris Agreement, its "Katowice Rulebook" and the UN Sustainable Development Goals, the authors argue that not only is transition deeply needed, but also – due to legal guarantees – it must be carried out in a manner that is just. In the chapter, the authors also attempt to construct potential future legal consequences of a just transition and how these take on even greater significance when confronted with the effects of the pandemic.

Adv. Erick Kassongo in Chapter 15, 'Legal and Governance Contributions to Climate Ambition through REDD+ in Francophone African Countries,' reviews the REDD+ mechanism referenced under Article 5 of the Paris Agreement. In recent years, the chapter explains, an increasing number of REDD+ activities and initiatives have been implemented in Africa. However, the author argues, these have had little impact on the objectives set and on the communities for which they were designed, particularly rural populations that depend on forest resources. Indeed, the Sub-Saharan African context has faced a range of pressures related to limited financial resources, technical capacity and challenges that have made REDD+ implementation difficult. This chapter identifies the challenges related to the means of implementation and expected results, recalling the institutional actors involved in achieving the objectives agreed upon.

Subsequently, Chapter 16, 'Legal Contributions to Climate Action through Oceans and Marine Resources Stewardship in Small Island States,' written by Adv. Freedom-Kai Phillips, Dr. Alexandra Harrington and Adv. Elizabeth Nwarueze, highlights how marine and ocean resources are vital sources of biodiversity as well as carbon sinks. The chapter explores law and governance approaches that are applied at international, regional and national levels to preserve the marine environment with a focus on Small Island States. The chapter addresses obligations under the United Nations Convention on the Law of the Sea, the Convention on Biological Diversity, the UNFCCC and the Paris Agreement. The chapter then discusses how these obligations are applied under various approaches and highlights pathways for enhancing both climate ambition and cooperation to improve marine governance, taking into account the 2024 Advisory Opinion on Climate Change of the ITLOS.

Chapter 17, 'Legal and Governance Challenges for the Implementation of NDCs in Morocco, Jordan and Tunisia,' authored by Dr. Hassan Agouzoul, Professor Afef Hammami-Marrakchi, Professor Abdelnaser Zeyad Hayajneh, Professor Markus W. Gehring and Gwyneth Boone, reviews current legal structures and explores the possibilities for appropriate and legal innovation to increase Morocco, Jordan and Tunisia's ability to address climate mitigation, adaptation and financial opportunities. The cases of Morocco, Tunisia and Jordan provide lessons learned from efforts to address the legal and governance challenges of climate change at the national level. Based on research and legal assessments supported by the European Bank for Reconstruction and Development (EBRD) and others, this chapter offers insights and potential options for structuring appropriate legal, policy and institutional frameworks at the national level.

In Chapter 18, 'Legal Contributions to Incentivising Investment for Paris Agreement Adaptation and Resilience in Ukraine,' Dr. Oleksandr Diachuk, Adv. Mariia Stolbova, Professor Markus W. Gehring and Gwyneth Boone focus on the importance of investment for countries such as the Ukraine to set and achieve progressively more ambitious NDCs. It considers the legal and governance reforms and measures that can assist Paris Agreement implementation in aspiring EU member states. Based on research and analysis supported by the European Bank for Reconstruction and Development (EBRD) just before the war, the chapter considers good legal practices from across the EU, and analyses appropriate legal, policy and institutional measures to promote investment into climate adaptation and resilience, at the national level, in Ukraine. By examining the case of Ukraine, the chapter offers examples of key challenges implementing the Paris Agreement provisions on mitigation, adaptation and resilience and finance, and identifies potential legal and governance solutions at the national level. By assessing current structures and exploring the possibilities for appropriate and legal innovation, the chapter provides recommendations to enable Ukraine to address climate change and promote more sustainable development.

The exploration of regional and national legal contributions to Paris Agreement implementation concludes with Chapter 19, 'Legal and Governance Response to Loss and Damage in Bangladesh and Zambia,' written by Adv. M. Hafijul Islam Khan and Dr. Pamela Towela Sambo. The chapter assesses the current climate-induced loss and damage structures and explores the possibilities for appropriate legal innovation to enable Bangladesh and Zambia to better address loss and damage. In doing so, the chapter outlines what losses and damages are associated with climate change and notes that such loss and damage are increasing particularly in Least Developed Countries. Bangladesh and Zambia offer helpful case studies as climate-vulnerable countries, providing an opportunity to investigate the reality of loss and damage opportunities at the national level.

Part IV: Compliance

In the penultimate Part IV on *Compliance,* the volume examines the next steps in further developing the compliance regime of the Paris Agreement and how legal scholarship, negotiations and practice can further advance climate action.

Part IV opens with Professor Christina Voigt's Chapter 20, 'Operationalizing the Paris Agreement and Compliance Committee (PAICC),' which addresses the role and function of the PAICC to facilitate implementation of and promote compliance with the provisions of the Paris Agreement, established in Article 15, paragraph 2, of the agreement. The PAICC is an important building-block of the Paris Agreement´s architecture, tasked to enhance mutual trust and confidence, as well as to strengthen parties' accountability for their performance under the agreement. The chapter provides a brief analysis of the historical background behind the establishment of the committee, describes its character and explains its mandate and procedures to facilitate Parties' implementation and promote their compliance.

Chapter 21, 'Submitting Mandatory Reports under the Paris Agreement Transparency Framework,' written by Dr. Christopher Campbell-Duruflé and Dr. Raúl Salas Reyes, explores the requirement under Article 13 of the Paris Agreement to submit National Inventory Reports and Biennial Transparency Reports. The chapter addresses three key challenges associated with these reporting requirements: first, developing countries' challenge to report biennially on emissions and to provide more detailed accounts of mitigation actions when institutional capacity is often lacking; second, all Parties' challenge to report on adaptation progress and challenges in light of the methodological debates surrounding adaptation and of the lack of clarity of the "global goal on adaptation"; and third, developed countries' challenge to explain how their levels of support are "in line with the long-term goals" of the treaty when there is no clear agreement as to how such effort should be divided.

In Chapter 22, 'Operationalizing Article 6 of the Paris Agreement,' Professor Michael A. Mehling briefly traces the negotiating history of Article 6, which enables countries to engage in voluntary cooperation through market and non-market approaches. The chapter dissects the open and contentious issues from a legal perspective and takes stock of emerging state practice under Article 6 with a variety of bilateral pilot activities. Finally, the chapter analyzes the legal options for state implementation in the situations where no agreement on operational rules and guidance for Article 6 can be found.

Chapter 23, 'Incentivising International Finance for Net Zero Paris Agreement Implementation,' authored by Adv. Wendy Miles KC and Adv. Douglas Leys KC, outlines how the Green Climate Fund, among other things, operationalizes Articles 2 of the Paris Agreement of "making finance flows consistent with a pathway towards low greenhouse gas emissions and climate-resilient development." The chapter provides an overview of various instruments available under the Green Climate Fund and their potential uses for implementing Article 2, including grants, concessional loans, equity instruments and results-based payments.

In Chapter 24, 'Advancing Paris Agreement Alignment in International Financial Institutions,' General Counsel Adv. Michael Strauss and General Counsel Adv. Thomas M. Clark, together with co-authors Adv. Christina Pak, Adv. Vesselina Haralampieva and Adv. Hyfa Azeez, consider how leading international financial institutions such as the European Bank for Reconstruction and Development (EBRD) and the Asian Development Bank (ADB) can align investment and finance commitments with the Paris Agreement across all their operations. The chapter underlines the importance of, as noted in the treaty, "making finance flows consistent with a pathway towards low greenhouse gas (GHG) emissions and climate-resilient development."

Chapter 25, 'Exploring Low Carbon and Energy Efficient Procurement as a Tool for Paris Agreement Implementation,' written by Dr. Jellie Molino, highlights how the Paris Agreement recognizes the important role of sustainable patterns of consumption and production in addressing climate change. The chapter discusses the role of environmentally sustainable public procurement, particularly the low-carbon and energy-efficient procurement, as an important tool not only for reducing global greenhouse gas emissions and limiting the global temperature to 2°C, but for raising the ambition to limit the increase further to 1.5°C.

Further, Chapter 26, on 'Regulating the Disclosure of Climate-Related Finance Risks,' authored by Professor Marie-Claire Cordonier-Segger, Adv. Lara Douvartzidis and David Gayle, provides a brief review of the findings of the Task Force on Climate-related Financial Disclosures (TCFD), and the international debates and regulatory trends in relation to climate risk disclosure and sustainability due diligence. The chapter also explores the relationship between litigation claims and insurance products, focusing on the role of board insurance in climate-related financial decision-making, and concludes by considering international frameworks for cooperation on climate risk disclosure in the context of the Paris Agreement and beyond.

The handbook's examination of compliance concludes with Chapter 27, 'Examining Litigation Aspects of Nationally Determined Contributions,' co-authored by Adv. Amelia Burnette, Ms. Kathryn McKenzie and Dr. Francesco Sindico, which addresses how NDCs can be scrutinized at a national level, particularly through the domain of domestic climate change litigation. The chapter explores such litigation, and how a wide variety of legal grounds have been brought around the world, such as human rights, torts and international law, to challenge law and policies in relation to the NDC implementation and Paris Agreement obligations. Overall, the chapter highlights what such NDC-related climate change litigation may imply for future Paris Agreement implementation.

Part V: Conclusions

Part V of the Handbook, *Conclusions*, explores the emerging trends and new directions in the field of climate law and governance, highlighting the essential nature of continued legal and institutional reform in order to meet the Paris Agreement targets.

Professor Rosa M. Fernández Egea and Dr. Pau de Vilchez Moragues open the final section in Chapter 28, 'The Role of International Tribunals in Achieving Increased Ambition,' by highlighting the role of international tribunals and various courts for addressing climate change and advancing the implementation of the Paris Agreement. The chapter provides a general overview of climate litigation before focusing on regional human rights courts in Europe and the Americas. The chapter also addresses progress in the International Court of Justice, the International Tribunal for the Law of the Sea and the World Trade Organization dispute settlement body. The chapter concludes that climate litigation before international courts and tribunals plays a fundamental role in multilevel dialogue needed for an adequate response to the climate emergency.

Chapter 29, 'Prioritising Gender Law and Policy Aspects of Climate Action,' written by Ms. Anushesh Fawad, recognizes that differing gender roles and responsibilities as well as cultural norms cause women and girls to be disproportionately affected by climate change and are often excluded from participating, or fully participating, in climate policy planning. This chapter provides an understanding of the linkages between gender equality, environmental sustainability and the role of gender-responsive climate policies in delivering better environmental and social outcomes.

Then, in Chapter 30, 'Exploring the Potential of the Paris Agreement to Decolonize Law,' Adv. Mrinalini Shinde addresses mechanisms under the UNFCCC and Paris Agreement that can be instrumentalized to decolonize the international legal regime governing climate action. The chapter introduces the legal thought on decolonizing international law with an emphasis on the climate law regime. The chapter discusses how the UNFCCC and Paris Agreement have displayed an ability to construct negotiations and decision-making that recognize historical inequities and responsibilities through the common but differentiated responsibilities principle. The chapter then extends analysis to other 'spaces for decoloniality' in climate law and beyond.

In Chapter 31, 'Addressing Human Mobility in International Law on Climate Change and Beyond,' Dr. Cosmin Corendea and Professor Chhaya Bhardwaj analyze how the component of human mobility is integrated within the Nationally Determined Contributions (NDCs) submitted to the UNFCCC Secretariat. It maps out the types of human mobility and discusses concerning frameworks adopted by members of the Paris Agreement. After mapping out the practices adopted by States in their NDCs, the chapter identifies its impact on global stocktakes and international law.

This *Routledge Handbook on Climate Law and Governance: Courage, Contributions and Compliance* concludes with Chapter 32, 'Advancing the Legal Research and Capacity Agenda for Climate Law and Governance,' by Professor Marie-Claire Cordonier-Segger, Professor Christina Voigt and Adv. Tejas Rao. The chapter delves into the crucial role of advancing legal research and capacity building within the realm of climate law and governance. It highlights the significant capacity gaps present in the current climate law and governance, particularly in developing regions, and underscores the need for enhanced capacity-building and legal frameworks to effectively implement the Paris Agreement and achieve Sustainable Development Goals. It emphasizes the need for interdisciplinary research and training, particularly for climate-vulnerable nations, to foster resilient legal environments. As the concluding chapter in this handbook, it serves as an invitation to intensify research and develop the necessary legal infrastructure to bridge the capacity chasm and to advance and implement climate commitments, calling for global partnerships to play a transformative role in enhancing climate governance worldwide.

Considerations

After a series of international symposia and conferences starting in 2005 at the Montreal CoP11 just after the entry into force of the Kyoto Protocol, the Climate Law and Governance Initiative (CLGI) came together on Climate Law and Governance Day in 2015 at the Paris COP21 as the principal annual forum for informed dialogue between climate law and governance experts, practicing jurists and decision-makers, backed by independent research and analysis. By 2016, the Climate Law and Governance Initiative, as a consortium of law faculties from leading universities of the world, together with the world's leading research institutes, inter-governmental agencies, law associations and judges' networks, experts commissions and others, was leading a series of annual conferences during each Conference of the Parties to the UNFCCC, hosting prestigious Global Leadership Awards and student essay competitions and fostering many growing collaborations. Through annual Climate Law and Governance Days, leading up to over 1,990 registrants to a global Climate Law and Governance Day and related Legal Specialisation Course on Climate Law and Governance in 2023 at the CoP28 in Dubai, United Arab Emirates, and a pledge to join over 6,000 legal specialists in a climate law and governance capacity registry, partners of the CLGI have continued to broaden their reach, engaging more stakeholders and building an active global community of practice. Hosted by the Centre for International Sustainable Development Law (CISDL), the CLGI focus on sustainable development is especially relevant for the leading high-ambition countries, for emerging economies and for the most highly climate-vulnerable countries of the world that can otherwise often be excluded from international law-making.

Over the course of those years, CISDL has partnered on many occasions with IUCN World Commission on Environmental Law (WCEL). The IUCN WCEL provides a forum for capacity-building and networking among environmental law scholars, practitioners and judges to advance legal climate literacy. IUCN WCEL operates on a global scale with individual members engaging in activities aiming at capacity-building as well as developing legal solutions to the climate crisis, both in many national contexts, as well as on the international level. As the core environmental law entity within the International Union for the Conservation of Nature, WCEL also serves to provide support and legal expertise, including on climate law, to both the IUCN Secretariat as well as to the IUCN's many member states and member organizations.

Building on sessions during the Climate Law and Governance Day (CLGD) and many other international collaborations over the years, this volume examines the challenges of climate change, the courageous (ambitious) provisions of the Paris Agreement and how they reflect the priorities and principles of international law on sustainable development, reviews the contributions of domestic legal reform in the context of climate action and sustainable development worldwide, and explores the importance of compliance and implementation, including through inter-actional changes to the climate regime itself, as new legal approaches are developed and tested for their transformative potential as fast as possible.

The volume considers how sustainable development commitments are not only reflected in but are crucial to the success of the Paris Agreement, which inspires and guides parties' global response to climate change. Indeed, based on the available scientific information, there can be no sustainable development if the worst-case scenarios for climate change are not averted. As countries redouble their efforts to implement the Paris Agreement, including through the presentation of new and more ambitious Nationally Determined Contributions and the adoption of domestic laws designing their transition to a low-carbon economy, a profound comprehension of a sustainable development purpose and its operational parameters for climate change will be essential. Moving forward from the first Global Stocktake that concluded in Dubai, United Arab Emirates, in December 2023, this understanding provides a crucial foundation for law and governance. As recognized in the treaty itself, new legal research, education, awareness, capacity building and technical assistance, especially in less-developed countries and small island developing nations, but also in high per-capita emission countries, will be essential to ensure the success of the new Paris Agreement. A great deal is at stake – the avoidance of climate change's most dangerous consequences, and the transformation of the world's economies, societies and ecosystems toward sustainability. The world is watching. Sustainable development of climate action at all levels is more than possible – it is critical for our survival.

Notes

1 The authors would like to thank Ms. Kendall Damon, MPhil (Cantab), Adv. Lydia Young, Adv. Tejas Rao and Adv. Zunaida Wadiwala Moosa for their assistance and insights in drafting and editing this chapter.

2 United Nations Environment Programme (UNEP), 'Emissions Gap Report 2023: Broken Record – Temperatures Hit New Highs, Yet World Fails to Cut Emissions (again)' (2023) <https://wedocs.unep.org/bitstream/handle/20.500.11822/43922/EGR2023.pdf?sequence=3&isAllowed=y>.

3 Paris Agreement to the United Nations Framework Convention on Climate Change (adopted 12 December 2015, entered into force 4 November 2016) FCCC/CP/2015/10/Add.1.

4 UN Framework Convention on Climate Change (UNFCCC), 'COP 28' (UNFCCC 2023) <https://unfccc.int/event/cop-28>.

5 See e.g. *Verein Klimaseniorinnen Schweiz and Others v. Switzerland* (2024) ECtHR 53600/20; *Caso Habitantes de La Oroya vs. Perú (Case of Inhabitants of La Oroya v. Peru)* (2023) Inter-American Court of Human Rights Series C No 511 (27 November 2023); *Obligations of States in Respect of Climate Change* (Request for Advisory Opinion) ICJ General List No. 187 (12 April 2023); *On Climate Change and International Law* (Request for Advisory Opinion) ITLOS (12 December 2022) <www.itlos.org/en/main/cases/list-of-cases/request-for-an-advisory-opinion-submitted-by-the-commission-of-small-island-

states-on-climate-change-and-international-law-request-for-advisory-opinion-submitted-to-the-tribunal/>.

6 *Request for an Advisory Opinion Submitted by the Commission of Small Island States on Climate Change and International Law (No 31)* (Advisory Opinion of 21 May 2024) ITLOS Reports 2024, 66, 122, 243, 252, 270, 283, 311.

7 UNEP (n 2).

8 UNFCCC Secretariat, *Building Support for More Ambitious National Climate Action Plans* (14 March 2024) <https://unfccc.int/news/building-support-for-more-ambitious-national-climate-action-plans>.

9 Marie-Claire Cordonier Segger, Maeve McDermott and others, '169NDCs of 186 Registered to the UNFCCC Explicitly Prioritize Legal and Institutional Reform in Plans to Contribute to the Global Response to Climate Change' (Climate Law and Governance Initiative and Centre for International Sustainable Development Law December 2020). Thanks and recognition are due to CISDL researchers, together with a team of University of Cambridge graduates whose contributions to the study, alongside those of Dr. Alexandra Harrington, Dr. Markus W. Gehring, Adv. Ayman Cherkaoui and Professor Christina Voigt, have proven invaluable <www.cisdl.org> accessed 10 April 2024; <www.climatelawgovernance.org> accessed 10 April 2024. See also Marie-Claire Cordonier Segger, Mirjam Reiner and Alexandra Scott, 'Countries Stress Importance of Legal and Institutional Reforms in their iNDCs' (Climate Law and Governance Initiative, September 2016) <www.climatelawgovernance.org/knowledge-centre.html> accessed 07 September 2016.

10 UN Development Programme, 'UNDP Climate Promise Progress Report' (2022) <https://climatepromise.undp.org/sites/default/files/research_report_document/Climate%20Promise%20Global%20Progress%20Report%202022.pdf>.

11 Ian Higham and Catherine Higham, 'Submission to the Special Rapporteur on the Promotion and Protection of Human Rights in the Context of Climate Change' *Grantham Research Institute on Climate Change and the Environment*, LSE, 2023.

12 *Urgenda Foundation v. State of the Netherlands* (2015) HAZA C/09/00456689.

13 ECHR, 'Judgment Verein KlimaSeniorinnen Schweiz and Others v. Switzerland – Violations of the Convention for Failing to Implement Sufficient Measures to Combat Climate Change' (2024) <https://hudoc.echr.coe.int/eng-press#{%22itemid%22:[%22003–7919428–11026177%22]}>.

14 *Ashgar Leghari v. Federation of Pakistan* (2015) W.P. No. 25501/201.

15 *Gloucester Resources Limited v Minister for Planning* (2019) NSWLEC 7.

PART 1

The Challenge of Global Climate Change and Sustainable Development

2
THE URGENCY OF GLOBAL RESPONSE TO CLIMATE CHANGE

Ayman Cherkaoui and Zunaida Moosa Wadiwala[1]

Introduction

The perception of climate change has largely fluctuated in the last few decades[2] and has included terms such as uncertainty monster,[3] common concern,[4] threat,[5] producing adverse effects,[6] emergency,[7] crisis, existential threat[8] and most recently, its qualification as the defining challenge of our time.[9]

H.M King Mohamed VI, King of the Kingdom of Morocco, provides a compelling example of this evolution and the growing sense of urgency, as shown by this statement from the 2016 High-Level Segment of COP22:

> The time has come to redress the situation. We have no alternative but to work to make up for lost time, through continued, comprehensive mobilization and positive harmonization, so that the coming generations may lead an enjoyable and dignified life together.

In a similar vein, in 2023, H.E Dr. Sultan Al Jaber (UNFCCC COP28 President) stated the following:

> We know, as you know, the gravity of this moment. We feel, as you feel, the urgency of this work. And we see, as you see, that the world has reached a crossroads. And yes, since Paris, we have made some progress. But we also know that the road we have been on will not get us to our destination in time. The science has spoken. It has confirmed that the moment is now to find a new road, a road wide enough for all of us, free of the obstacles and detours of the past.

The Secretary-General of the United Nations' recent remarks to the General Assembly on priorities for 2024 reflect further on the magnanimity of the climate crisis:

> The climate crisis remains the defining challenge of our time. The coming years will largely determine whether we can limit global temperature rise to 1.5 degrees. To stay within that limit, we must cut emissions 45 percent by 2030, compared with 2010 levels. And we need emissions to have peaked by 2025. The good news is, we have never been better equipped to prevent climate breakdown.

DOI: 10.4324/9781003276678-3

This evolution of climate change perception reflects distinct but connected trends: on one hand, the continuous progress of scientific knowledge regarding the physical phenomenon of climate change and its impacts[10] and, on the other hand, the evolution of the political discourse around climate change.[11] While in some geographic areas the consensus achieved around climate change is not only scientific but also of policy makers across the political spectrum, climate change remains a partisan issue in others.[12] Despite elements of continuity in this political stand-off, this should not be viewed solely as a static constant as these elements remain dynamic and connected to other social, economic, environmental and political dimensions.[13]

Climate law and governance stand at the very intersection of these trends, reflecting their ebbs and flows across space and time. At the same time, the past, current and forthcoming negative impacts of climate change across the globe[14] make a particularly compelling case for urgent action across space and in a timely, that is urgent, manner. Whether climate law and governance will grow or shrink in front of the scale of the challenge of climate change is a central question when it pertains to our collective ability to meet the objectives of the United Nations Framework Convention on Climate Change (UNFCCC),[15] the Paris Agreement[16] and the 2030 Agenda.[17] The extent to which climate law and governance will answer that question hinges upon the effectivity and efficiency of its design and implementation, which ought to be measured through transparent, context-specific and science-based indicators, including legal indicators.[18]

While deference is due to ongoing and remaining negotiations connected to climate change across multilateral fora, there is a crucial imperative to accelerate the paradigm shift from negotiations towards implementation, initiated at COP22/CMP12/CMA1 in Marrakech and further cemented most recently at COP28/CMP18/CMA5 in Dubai. Multilateralism must rise above its perception, by some,[19] as a failed hindrance for ambitious action for the climate and fully embrace its potential for concerted, rapid and at-scale action, even in particularly challenging times.[20] An important signal to that effect is contained in the Ministerial Declaration of the 6th session of the United Nations Environmental Assembly[21] and resolutions adopted at that time.[22]

The present introductory chapter will study three key characteristics that the urgent response to climate change need embody for transformational positive change:

- The urgent response to climate change must be based on science.
- The urgent response to climate change must be in the context of the eradication of poverty and sustainable development.
- The urgent response to climate change must hinge upon both global and context-specific legal frameworks focused on equity.

The Urgent Response to Climate Change Must Be Based on Science

In 2023, Professor Ian Fry, the United Nations Special Rapporteur on the promotion and protection of human rights in the context of climate change, called for the judiciary to be trained on the science of climate change.[23] Such a call begs the question – *how does climate law and governance relate to science?* Answered in a nutshell, the understanding of how the people and the planet are affected by climate change, how human influence has unequivocally warmed the atmosphere, ocean and land[24] and how mitigation, adaptation and loss and damage measures address or fail to address climate change, is largely based on the foundations laid by climate science. The ability to act on this scientific knowledge is the challenge facing international law and global climate law and governance structures. In addition, law and governance also plays a role in strengthening the scientific understanding of climate change and its impacts. Studies reveal that advancing scientific knowledge which, *inter alia*, leads to a better understanding of the interdependence of natural systems, results in intensified challenges and opportunities for international law.[25] In recent developments, advancements made in the field of attribution science[26] are expected to alter the climate litigation landscape.[27] It is likely that further findings from attribution science, including when it comes to extreme weather events, will influence ongoing and upcoming climate litigation proceedings.[28]

Climate science can be connected to significant elements of uncertainty, subject to unequal participation and influenced by political considerations, at times challenging its perceived objectivity.[29] However, by and large, science has been cemented as a central component to the advancement of knowledge on climate change, as exemplified in the UNFCCC space.[30] In this regard, the presence of the notion of best available science across the Paris Agreement[31] as both basis and guidance is particularly transformational.

Sources of Climate Science

Of particular note amongst sources of climate science is the Intergovernmental Panel on Climate Change (IPCC), which was established in 1988 by the United Nations Environment Programme (UNEP) and the World Meteorological Organization (WMO). The IPCC serves as an intergovernmental process tasked with assessing the science related to climate change and was created to provide policymakers with regular and updated scientific assessments on climate change impacts.[32] In so doing, the IPCC reports thoroughly cover scientific, technical and socio-economic knowledge regarding climate change, its impacts, future risks and strategies for reducing its pace.[33] The IPCC has 195 parties and regularly holds meetings to adopt its various reports including assessment, special and methodology reports.[34] The assessment reports are prepared by three Working Groups delegated each of the three objectives of the IPCC: (i) to make assessments of available scientific information on climate change, (ii) to make assessments of environmental and socio-economic impacts of climate change and (iii) to formulate response strategies to meet the challenge of climate change.[35] The latest Assessment cycle, the sixth, ran from October 2015 to July 2023 and featured updated methodologies, three Special Reports (Special Report on Global Warming of 1.5°C, Special Report on Climate Change and Land and Special Report on the Ocean and Cryosphere in a Changing Climate), the contributions of Working Group 1 in August 2021, Working Group 2 in February 2023, Working Group 3 in April 2023 and the Synthesis report in March 2023.[36]

Both UNEP and the WMO generate and utilize climate science in their own capacity. The WMO is an authoritative source of climate science that has reaffirmed the crucial significance of the mission of National Meteorological, Hydrometeorological and Hydrological Services in observing and comprehending weather and climate, and in delivering meteorological, hydrological and associated services, including, *inter alia*, through the promotion of long-term observation and collection of meteorological, hydrological, climatological and related environmental data.[37] In this context, with its current 193 member states, the WMO provides frameworks for international cooperation on aspects of cross-border and global weather, climate and water cycle developments.[38] Scientific studies undertaken at WMO periodically contribute significantly to climate science at the global[39] and regional levels.[40] For example, the WMO identified 2023 as the warmest year in the 174-year instrumental record and the past nine years – 2015 to 2023 – as the nine warmest years on record,[41] with the trend set to continue in 2024.[42] In addition, the WMO intends to remain at the 'Frontline of Climate Action'.[43] UNEP, on the other hand, is widely recognised as a leading global authority on the environment,[44] as is set out in its mandate.[45] The establishment of UNEP in 1972 was based, *inter alia*, on the recognition that the international scientific community can make an important contribution to international cooperation in the field of the environment.[46] UNEP's work on the environmental rule of law has recognized the central role of science in informing effective legal frameworks.[47] Furthermore, UNEP's emission gap and adaptation gap reports are important yearly contributions to climate science. The 2023 editions of these two gap reports highlighted a series of findings that further stress the importance of urgent action for the climate, including the following:

- Fully implementing unconditional and conditional Nationally Determined Contributions (NDCs) would put the world on track for limiting temperature rise to 2.5°C,[48] which is significantly higher than not only the 1.5°C but also the 2°C temperature goal of the Paris Agreement.[49]
- Adaptation finance needs of developing countries are 10 to almost 20 times as big as international public finance flows, representing over 50 per cent higher than the previous range estimate.[50]

Other influential sources of climate science include, *inter alia*, the United Nations Development Programme,[51] the World Health Organization,[52] the International Union for the Conservation of Nature (IUCN),[53] the Intergovernmental Science-Policy Platform on Biodiversity and Ecosystem Services (IPBES),[54] the National Aeronautics and Space Administration[55] and the Copernicus Climate Change Service.[56]

The Urgent Response to Climate Change Must Be in the Context of the Eradication of Poverty and Sustainable Development

The interlinked and integrated nature of the Sustainable Development Goals (SDG) is seen as paramount in achieving the purpose of Agenda 2030.[57] While synergies across the 17 SDGs are often highlighted and need be maximized, potential trade-offs and negative spillover effects[58] need also be studied and minimized. Specifically on Climate Change, the United Nations,[59] UNFCCC,[60] Kyoto Protocol,[61] Paris Agreement[62] and Marrakech Partnership for Global Climate Action[63] frame, to different extents, climate action within the broader scope of sustainable development.

Such a framing can be seen as reinforcing the sense of urgency for climate action. Indeed, while the global average temperature is trending higher than a 1.5 degree[64] increase compared to preindustrial levels, the broader 2030 agenda is challenged. The repercussions of the climate crisis, the conflict in Ukraine, a fragile global economy, and the ongoing effects of the COVID-19 pandemic have exposed vulnerabilities and impeded advancements toward the Goals: progress toward over half of the targets of the SDGs is inadequate, and for nearly a third of them, it has either stagnated or regressed.[65]

Climate change exacerbates poverty. Some estimates indicate that climate change may push more than 100 million additional people into poverty by 2030.[66] Climate change exacerbates disparities within nations and among nations, in a manner that bears similarities to the findings of environmental justice.[67] Within nations, the most vulnerable often lack adaptive capacity, which can be defined as a function of: economic resources, technology, information and skills, infrastructure, institutions and equity.[68] At the international level, climate change exacerbates disparities among nations across two main pathways:[69]

- Increasing temperatures resulting from the accumulation of greenhouse gases disproportionately affect developing countries, amplifying their vulnerability, the costs associated with adaptation and loss and damages;[70]
- The expenses associated with mitigating climate change by curbing emissions may impede the economic advancement of developing countries.

Finally, means of implementation are critically important for climate ambition and action and across sustainable development. Specifically on climate change, *full* implementation of all the Nationally Determined Contributions to the Paris Agreement (NDCs) is estimated to lead, by 2030 relative to the 2019 level, to a 5.3 per cent emission reduction, while implementation of all latest NDCs *excluding any conditional elements* is estimated to result in 1.4 per cent higher emissions.[71] As of May 2021, developing countries' NDCs costed needs amount to a nearly $6 trillion by 2030, of which almost 90 per cent provided no information on possible sources of finance.[72] As for sustainable development in general, annual spending needs for developing countries to meet the sustainable development goals have been estimated in the range of the USD trillions across six paths for transformation:[73]

- Social protection and decent jobs: $6.9 trillion, which when compared to a business-as-usual government expenditure trajectory, translates into an annual gap of $370 billion.
- Transforming education: $7.5 trillion, which when compared to a business-as-usual government expenditure trajectory, translates into an annual gap of $400 billion.
- Food systems: $7.6 trillion, which when compared to a business-as-usual government expenditure trajectory, translates into an annual gap of $420 billion.
- Climate change, biodiversity loss and pollution: $7 trillion, which when compared to a business-as-usual government expenditure trajectory, translates into an annual gap of $410 billion.
- Energy transition: $7.3 trillion, which when compared to a business-as-usual government expenditure trajectory, translates into an annual gap of $320 billion.
- Inclusive digitization: $7 trillion, which when compared to a business-as-usual government expenditure trajectory, translates into an annual gap of $540 billion.

Furthermore, capacity building and technology are also strategic means of implementation and need be properly prioritized and resourced to meet the objectives of the Paris Agreement and the 2030 Agenda.

The Urgent Response to Climate Change Must Hinge Upon Both Global and Context-Specific Legal Frameworks Focused on Equity

The global nature of the challenge of climate change necessitates a collective global approach, founded on international solidarity.[74] At the same time, the richness of the diversity of the economic, social and environmental (in particular geographic and climatic) contexts all across the world, combined with core principles such as common but differentiated responsibilities and respective capacities[75] and essentials concepts such as climate justice,[76] indicate that context specific approaches are required.[77]

Climate litigation illustrates eloquently both that the urgent response to climate change must be based on science and that it must hinge upon both global[78] and context-specific legal frameworks[79] focused on equity.[80] This urgency for a global response is further illustrated by the upward trajectory in litigation as has been prevalent in recent years and especially post-2015 and the Paris Agreement.[81]

Climate litigation reconciles the reliance placed by claimants and judges on climate science to the extent that the matter largely hinges on findings from climate science.[82] Furthermore, climate science is the impetus on calls for domestic law and policy regulation, and lastly, the human rights turn in climate litigation is based on climate science. On the other hand, the relevance of global and context-specific legal frameworks focused on equity is evident in climate litigation proceedings.

Climate Litigation's Reliance on Climate Science Regarding Climate Law and Policy Regulation

Building on findings from climate science, the UNEP 2024 Climate Risk Landscape Report highlights on the latest observations in the climate risk landscape.[83]

The following cases, extracted from UNEP Sabin Center Global Climate Litigation Report 2023,[84] which visits forecasts from previous reports for climate litigation based on pre- and post-disaster conditions, climate migration and climate attribution, show the extent of reliance by claimants and judges on climate science.

In *I.L. v. Italian Ministry of the Interior and Attorney General at the Court of Appeal of Ancona* (2021),[85] in consideration of *inter alia* social, environmental and climate degradation against the backdrop of unsustainable exploitation of natural resources in the Niger Delta, ordered the court a quo to re-evaluate the application and to include an analysis of environmental, climate and resource extraction impacts on the claimants' rights to life and dignified existence.[86]

In a similar vein, in the case of *Bushfire Survivors for Climate Action Incorporated v. Environmental Protection Authority* (2021)[87] the Australian court held, in response to the plaintiffs' claim that harm caused by bushfires was intensified by climate change and holding the New South Wales Environmental Protection Authority at fault for failing to develop guidelines and or a regulatory policy with which to align emissions of Green House Gases (GHG) to the Paris Agreement goals, that the duty to prescribe environmental protection measures included climate change protections in its instruments and regulations.[88]

Three cases which addressed extreme weather events[89] highlight that in using existing legislation to seek redress against climate-related extreme events, climate science is once again at the forefront. Various initiatives, such as Hub for Climate Litigation[90] and the Climate Attribution Database,[91] aim to support that linkage.

Climate Litigation's Reliance on Climate Science Regarding the Human Rights Turn

The IPCC released its Sixth Assessment Report on 4 April 2022, noting that climate litigation is shaping climate governance.[92]

Landmark climate litigation across both Global North and Global South jurisdictions have framed decisions from a rights perspective.[93] Judges in such cases have relied extensively on findings from climate science to deduce that there is a threat of 'dangerous climate change'.[94] Using transboundary elements to gauge similarities arising from climate litigation in the Netherlands, Germany and South Africa, studies reveal that a duty of care by states toward their citizens featured prominently in three decisions across all three jurisdictions.[95] Climate change and its associated risks and harms were central to the sphere of transnational considerations included in the three judgments.[96] Domestic legislation was interpreted in accordance with international law, and ultimately human rights provisions were found to underpin the final judgments. These human rights linkages are seen to have led to climate governance; in *Urgenda*[97] by holding the state responsible for increased climate protection, in *Neubauer*[98] by declaring the climate laws as incompatible with human rights and in *Earthlife*[99] by setting precedent for climate considerations to be amongst the necessary factors to consider in the granting of environmental authorizations.[100]

Conclusion

Several quotes were selected to set the scene for this chapter to signify the growing sense of urgency around climate change that has prevailed from the mid-20th century until today, in a manner that aimed to recall the warming stripes data visualization. Indeed, as we will soon celebrate the 10th anniversary of the adoption of the Paris Agreement, the succession of record-breaking warm years in the last decade, as clearly identified by climate science, can rightfully foster a strong sense of discouragement. However, this discouragement must be seen in the light of several genuinely important positive facts.

First, never has a multilateral environmental treaty entered into force as rapidly as the Paris Agreement.[101] Indeed, a year after its adoption in Paris, the world celebrated its entry into force in the Kingdom of Morocco.[102] Second, the Paris Agreement is working. It is not working at the scale and pace that many of us would like, but it is working. Third, solutions that can be seized upon to meet the objectives of the Paris Agreement are a tangible reality. In that regard, the year 2025 will provide perhaps the most critical test yet of the Paris Agreement's Member States' collective ambition to meet the Agreement's objectives.[103] Fourth, a growing array of spaces provide important opportunities for Non-Party Stakeholders to engage meaningfully and coordinate, at various levels, among themselves and with United Nations Member States when it comes to climate action. Specifically on climate change at the global level, the most prominent is the Marrakech Partnership for Global Climate Action.[104] The Paris Committee on Capacity Building[105] has also established a network that connects climate change focused capacity building practitioners.[106] Stakeholders have also networked in parallel to the UNFCCC and Paris Agreement. Such spaces include the major groups and stakeholders system within the United Nations Environment Programme, the International Union for the Conservation of Nature's World Commission on Environmental Law, which has a Specialist Group focused on climate change law[107] and has significantly contributed, *inter alia*, to the IUCN written statements to the International Tribunal Law of the Sea's Advisory Opinion on climate change and international law,[108] the Interamerican Court on Human Right's Advisory Opinion on Human Rights concerning the Climate Emergency and Human Rights[109] and is contributing to the IUCN's written statement to the International Court of Justice's Advisory Opinion on Obligations of States in respect of climate change.[110] The Climate Law and Governance Initiative,[111] through various efforts such as the Climate Law and Governance Day and life-long learning educational endeavors such as the Climate Law and Governance Specialization Course,[112] has also contributed meaningfully to strengthening capacities. Education plays a key role in addressing climate change, and despite several impactful initiatives focused on youth empowerment such as the European Climate Ambassadors and the African Youth Climate Hub,[113] gaps remain. Youth, which must be a core priority when it comes to climate change ambition and action and who have articulated their perspectives and priorities,[114] reinforce further the need for an urgent response to climate change that is based on science, global, in the context of the eradication of poverty and sustainable development, and hinge upon both global and context-specific legal frameworks focused on equity.

Notes

1 With thanks to Adv Lydia Young, CISDL Associate Fellow, and Gwyneth Boone, CISDL Researcher, for their research, drafting assistance and substantive insights.

2 Canadian physicist Gilbert Plass provides an instructive example of the early scientific awareness around the issue of global warming caused by human activities as shown by this 1956 statement: "The extra CO2 released into the atmosphere by industrial processes and other human activities may have caused the temperature rise during the present century". NASA Scientist James E. Hansen famously contributed, in 1988, to the mainstreaming of scientific conclusions based on Climate Science: "My principal conclusions are: (1) the earth is warmer in 1988 than at any time in the history of instrumental measurements, (2) the global warming is now sufficiently large that we can ascribe with a high degree of confidence a cause and effect relationship to the greenhouse effect, and (3) in our computer climate simulations the greenhouse effect now is already large enough to begin to affect the probability of occurrence of extreme events such as summer heat waves." H.R.H Sidi Mohamed, then Crown Prince of the Kingdom of Morocco, indicates an important shift in the political perception of climate change with the following statement from the 1992 UN Conference on Environment and Development (Earth Summit): "Nature is also the product of billions of years of evolution that human recklessness has brought to the brink of destruction. Examples abound of how human beings are currently mistreating nature: depletion of the ozone layer, aggravation of the greenhouse effect, climate warning, desertification and soil degradation, deforestation, impoverishment of fauna and flora, extinction of certain animal species, increased risks of natural disasters, depletion of natural resources, pollution of drinking water sources and oceans, transboundary dumping of toxic or hazardous wastes, and the eternal problem of the inability to recycle industrial or domestic waste on a continuous basis". Still within the landscape of political leadership, H.E Jacques Chirac provides an engaging example of a growing sense of urgency around Climate Change from this statement from the 2002 World Summit on Sustainable Development: "Our house is burning and we are looking the other way".

3 Judith Curry, 'The Climate Change "Uncertainty Monster"' in Judith Curry (ed), *Climate Uncertainty and Risk: Rethinking Our Response* (Anthem Press 2023).

4 IPCC, *Climate Change 2021: The Physical Science Basis. Contribution of Working Group I to the Sixth Assessment Report of the Intergovernmental Panel on Climate Change* (CUP 2021) <https://doi.org/10.1017/9781009157896> (IPCC 2021).

5 Paris Agreement to the United Nations Framework Convention on Climate Change (adopted 12 December 2015, entered into force 4 November 2016) 3156 UNTS 79, Article 2.1.

6 Kyoto Protocol to the United Nations Framework Convention on Climate Change (entered into force 16 February 2005) 2303 UNTS 162.

7 UNEP, 'The Climate Emergency' <www.unep.org/climate-emergency>, accessed 10 April 2024.

8 UN News, 'Climate Change: An "Existential Threat" to Humanity, UN Chief Warns Global Summit' (15 May 2018) <https://news.un.org/en/story/2018/05/1009782> accessed 10 April 2024.

9 Secretary-General of the United Nations, 'Secretary-General's Remarks to the General Assembly on Priorities for 2024' (2024) <www.un.org/sg/en/content/sg/speeches/2024-02-07/secretary-generals-remarks-the-general-assembly-priorities-for-2024> accessed 10 April 2024.

10 IPCC 2021 (n 3).

11 Alexander F Gazmararian and Dustin Tingley, *Uncertain Futures: How to Unlock the Climate Impasse* (CUP 2023); Jale Tosun and B Guy Peters, 'The Politics of Climate Change: Domestic and International Responses to a Global Challenge' (2020) 42(1) IPSR 3.

12 Elizabeth Kolbert, 'How Did Fighting Climate Change become a Partisan Issue?' *New Yorker* (14 August 2022) <www.newyorker.com/magazine/2022/08/22/how-did-fighting-climate-change-become-a-partisan-issue> accessed 10 April 2024; Bo MacInnis and Jon A Krosnick, 'Climate Insights 2020: Surveying American Public Opinion on Climate Change and the Environment' Resources for the Future (2020) <https://media.rff.org/documents/Climate_Insights_2020_Partisan_Divide.pdf> accessed 10 April 2024; Elaine Kamarck, 'The Challenging Politics of Climate Change' (*Brookings,* 23 September 2019) <www.brookings.edu/articles/the-challenging-politics-of-climate-change/> accessed 10 April 2024.

13 Stephen Fisher, 'Expert Comment: European Public Opinion on Climate Change Has Become Politicised' (*University of Oxford News & Events,* 3 November 2022) <www.ox.ac.uk/news/2022-11-03-expert-comment-european-public-opinion-climate-change-has-become-politicised> accessed 10 April 2024.

14 IPCC, *Climate Change 2023: Synthesis Report. Contribution of Working Groups I, II and III to the Sixth Assessment Report of the Intergovernmental Panel on Climate Change* (IPCC 2023) <https://doi.org/10.59327/IPCC/AR6-9789291691647> (IPCC AR6).

15 United Nations Framework Convention on Climate Change (entered into force 21 March 1994) 1771 UNTS 107, Article 2 (UNCCC).

16 Paris Agreement (n 4), Article 2.1.

17 UNGA, 'Transforming Our World: The 2030 Agenda for Sustainable Development' (25 September 2015) UN Doc A/RES/70/1.

18 Jérôme Fromageau, Ayman Cherkaoui and Roberto Coll (eds), *Measuring the Effectiveness of Environmental Law through Legal Indicators and Quality Analyses* (International Union for the Conservation of Nature 2023).

19 Nathalie Tocci, 'Multilateralism Is Broken' (*Politico,* 10 October 2023) <www.politico.eu/article/multilateralism-broken-diplomacy-united-nations-eu-global-governance/> accessed 10 April 2024.

20 Inger Andersen, 'Environmental Multilateralism: Unity in Difficult Times' *UNEP Speech* (20 November 2023) <www.unep.org/news-and-stories/speech/environmental-multilateralism-unity-difficult-times> accessed 10 April 2024.

21 UNEA, 'Draft Ministerial Declaration of the United Nations Environment Assembly at Its Sixth Session: Effective, Inclusive, and Sustainable Multilateral Actions to Tackle Climate Change, Biodiversity Loss and Pollution' (27 February 2024) UNEP/EA.6/HLS/L.1.

22 UNEA, 'Draft Resolution on Fostering National Action to Address Environmental Challenges through Increased Cooperation between the United Nations Environment Assembly, the United Nations Environment Programme and Multilateral Environmental Agreements' (28 February 2024) UNEP/EA.6/L.9; UNEA, 'Draft Resolution on Enhancing the Role and Viability of Regional Forums of Environment Ministers and United Nations Environment Programme Regional Offices in Achieving Multilateral Cooperation in Tackling Environmental Challenges' (28 February 2024) UNEP/EA.6/L.6; UNEA, 'Draft Resolution on Promoting Synergies, Cooperation or Collaboration for National Implementation of Multilateral Environmental Agreements and Other Relevant Environmental Instruments' (28 February 2024) UNEP/EA.6/L.7.

23 UNGA, 'Promotion and Protection of Human Rights in the Context of Climate Change' (28 July 2023) Doc. A/78/255.

24 IPCC, 'Summary for Policymakers' in V Masson-Delmotte and others (eds), *Climate Change 2021: The Physical Science Basis. Contribution of Working Group I to the Sixth Assessment Report of the Intergovernmental Panel on Climate Change* (CUP 2021) 3–32 <https://doi.org/10.1017/9781009157896.001>

25 Marie-Claire Cordonier Segger and Ilaria Espa, 'Exploring the Role of International Law in Sustainable Natural Resources Management for Development' (*LCIL,* 18 March 2021) <www.lcil.cam.ac.uk/blog/exploring-role-international-law-sustainable-natural-resources-management-development-prof> accessed 10 April 2024.

26 L. Delta Merner, 'From Research to Action: The Growing Impact of Attribution Science' (*Union of Concerned Scientists, The Equation,* 7 March 2023) <https://blog.ucsusa.org/delta-merner/from-research-to-action-the-growing-impact-of-attribution-science/> accessed 10 April 2024.

27 Sophie Marjanac and Lindene Patton, 'Extreme Weather Event Attribution Science and Climate Change Litigation: An Essential Step in the Causal Chain?' (2018) 36(3) JENRL 265, 266.

28 ibid.

29 Jasmine Livingston, 'Climate Science for Policy? The Knowledge Politics of the IPCC after Copenhagen' (Doctoral thesis, Lund University 2018); Silke Beck and Martin Mahony, 'The IPCC and the New Map of Science and Politics' (2018) 9(6) WIREs Clim Change e547 <https://doi.org/10.1002/wcc.547>; Zeke Baker, 'Future Times and Spaces – Tracing Objectivity, Scale, and Politics in the Social Life of Climate Science' in Z Baker and others (eds), *Climate, Science and Society: A Primer* (Routledge 2024); Martin Mahony, 'Meteorology, Climate Science, and Empire: Histories and Legacies' in Z Baker and others (eds), *Climate, Science and Society: A Primer (*Routledge 2024).

30 See e.g. Glasgow Climate Pact, Decision 1/CP.26. The UNFCCC Secretariat also provided useful informal compilations of relevant text on systematic observations and research. For example, see UNFCCC,

'Information Paper: Systematic Observations' (December 2023) <https://unfccc.int/sites/default/files/resource/Mandates_systematic_%20observation.pdf> accessed 23 April 2024 and UNFCCC, 'Information Paper: Research' (October 2023) <https://unfccc.int/sites/default/files/resource/Mandates_research.pdf> accessed 23 April 2024.

31 Paris Agreement (n 4) Preamble, Articles 4.1, 7.5, 14.1.

32 IPCC <www.ipcc.ch/> accessed 10 April 2024.

33 ibid.

34 ibid.

35 UNEP and WMO, 'Memorandum of Understanding between the United Nations Environment Programme (UNEP) and the World Meteorological Organization (WMO) on the Intergovernmental Panel on Climate Change' (April 1989) <www.ipcc.ch/site/assets/uploads/2019/06/MOU_between_UNEP_and_WMO_on_IPCC-1989.pdf> accessed 23 April 2024.

36 IPCC AR6 (n 13).

37 Convention of the World Meteorological Organization, adopted by the Washington Conference on 11 October 1947, as amended by Resolutions 1 and 2 adopted by the Third Congress in 1959; Resolutions 1 and 2 adopted by the Fourth Congress in 1963; Resolutions 1, 2 and 3 adopted by the Fifth Congress in 1967; Resolution 48 adopted by the Seventh Congress in 1975; Resolution 50 adopted by the Eighth Congress in 1979; Resolutions 41, 42 and 43 adopted by the Ninth Congress in 1983; Resolutions 39 and 41 adopted by the Fourteenth Congress in 2003; and Resolution 44 adopted by the Fifteenth Congress in 2007: WMO 'Basic Documents No. 1' (*2023 edition,* 2023) WMO-No. 15 <https://library.wmo.int/viewer/48992/download?file=15_2023-edition_en.pdf&type=pdf&navigator=1> accessed 23 April 2024.

38 ibid.

39 WMO, 'State of the Global Climate 2023' (2024) WMO-No. 1347 <https://library.wmo.int/viewer/68835/download?file=1347_Statement_2023_en.pdf&type=pdf&navigator=1> accessed 23 April 2024.

40 WMO, 'State of the Climate in Africa 2022' (2023) WMO-No. 1330 <https://library.wmo.int/viewer/67761/download?file=1330_State-of-the-Climate-in-Africa-2022_en.pdf&type=pdf&navigator=1> accessed 23 April 2024.

41 WMO, 'State of the Global Climate' (n 38).

42 WMO, 'World Had Warmest January on Record' (15 February 2024) <https://wmo.int/media/news/world-had-warmest-january-record> accessed 23 April 2024.

43 WMO, 'World Meteorological Day 2024' <https://wmo.int/site/world-meteorological-day-2024> accessed 10 April 2024; the theme of WMO Day 2024 is 'At the Frontline of Climate Action' which will *inter alia* commit to the progress of SDG 13. This is part of the WMOs programme leveraging global cooperation, innovation and expertise to overcome challenges related to the state of the climate, climate mitigation and adaptation with the ultimate goal of a resilient and safer planet for future generations.

44 Dag Hammarskjöld Library, 'UN Documentation: Environment' <https://research.un.org/en/docs/environment/unep> accessed 23 April 2024.

45 UNEP Governing Council, 'Nairobi Declaration on the Role and Mandate of the United Nations Environment Programme' (1997) UNEP/GC/DEC/19/1 (adopted 7 February 1997).

46 UNGA, 'Institutional and Financial Arrangements for International Environmental Co-operation' Resolution 2997 (XXVII) (15 December 1972).

47 UNEP, 'Environmental Rule of Law: Tracking Progress and Charting Future Directions' (2023) <www.unep.org/resources/publication/environmental-rule-law-tracking-progress-and-charting-future-directions> accessed 23 April 2024.

48 UNEP, 'Emissions Gap Report 2023: Broken Record – Temperatures Hit New Highs, Yet World Fails to Cut Emissions (again)' (2023) <https://doi.org/10.59117/20.500.11822/43922> accessed 22 April 2024.

49 Paris Agreement (n 4) Article 2(1).

50 UNEP, 'Adaptation Gap Report 2023: Underfinanced. Underprepared. Inadequate Investment and Planning on Climate Adaptation Leaves World Exposed' (2023) <https://doi.org/10.59117/20.500.11822/43796> accessed 23 April 2024.

51 UNDP is a particularly active entity in the field of climate change and, as such, generates and utilizes climate science. Recent relevant publications include the following: UNDP and African Group of Negotiators, 'Gender-Responsive Climate Change Actions in Africa: Technical Paper' (*UNDP Research and Reports,* 22 November 2023) <https://climatepromise.undp.org/research-and-reports/gender-responsive-climate-change-actions-africa> accessed 23 April 2024; Kit Nicholson and others, 'Planning Africa's Adaptation Finance: Estimating and Reducing Country Level Adaptation Gaps' (*UNDP*

November2023)<www.undp.org/africa/publications/planning-africas-adaptation-finance-estimating-and-reducing-country-level-adaptation-gaps> accessed 23 April 2024; UNDP, 'UNDP's High-Integrity Carbon Markets Initiative' (December 2023) <https://climatepromise.undp.org/highintegritycarbonmarkets?_gl=1*3hymqk*_ga*MTEzNTkzNjUwOS4xNzA3NjE3MTA0*_ga_3W7LPK0WP1*MTcxMzkw MDY0OS4zLjEuMTcxMzkwMDg5My41Ny4wLjA.> accessed 23 April 2024; Sonia Gautreau and Valeria Correa, 'Blue Economies and Nature-based Solutions: For Enhanced Climate Action in Latin America and the Caribbean Small Island Developing States' (*UNDP*, October 2023) <www.undp.org/latin-america/publications/blue-economies-and-nature-based-solutions> accessed 23 April 2024; Lars Jensen, 'Global Decarbonization in Fossil Fuel Export-Dependent Economies: Fiscal and Economic Transition Costs' (*UNDP*, May 2023) Working Paper <www.undp.org/publications/dfs-global-decarbonization-fossil-fuel-export-dependent-economies#:~:text=May%2015%2C%202023&text=The%20paper%20identifies%2040%20heavily,usual'%20scenario%20reflecting%20stated%20policies> accessed 23 April 2024; and UNDP, 'Re-envisioning Climate Change Adaptation Policy to Sustain Peace – A typology & Analysis of the NAPs' (May2023)<www.undp.org/publications/re-envisioning-climate-change-adaptation-policy-sustain-peace-typology-analysis-naps> accessed 23 April 2024.

52 The World Health Organisation's contribution to climate science focuses mostly on the health impacts of climate change and the health argument for climate action. Recent contributions include: WHO, 'A Framework for the Quantification and Economic Valuation of Health Outcomes Originating from Health and Non-health Climate Change Mitigation and Adaptation Action' (4 May 2023) Technical document <www.who.int/publications/i/item/9789240057906> accessed 23 April 2024; WHO, 'Operational Framework for Building Climate Resilient and Low Carbon Health Systems' (9 November 2023) Report <www.who.int/publications/i/item/9789240081888> accessed 23 April 2024; WHO, 'Measuring the Climate Resilience of Health Systems' (15 November 2022) Technical Document <www.who.int/publications/i/item/9789240048102> accessed 23 April 2024; WHO, 'COP26 Special Report on Climate Change and Health: The Health Argument for Climate Action' (11 October 2021) Special Report <www.who.int/publications/i/item/9789240036727> accessed 23 April 2024.

53 IUCN's contribution to climate science focuses on monitoring the impacts of climate change and guiding the conservation and restoration of ecosystems to help mitigate it. A recent example of the latter is the IUCN, 'Guidance for Using the IUCN Global Standard for Nature-based Solutions: A User-friendly Framework for the verification, design and scaling up of Nature-based Solutions' (1st edn, 2020) <https://acrobat.adobe.com/id/urn:aaid:sc:US:0c93b2bd-3a69-4376-be8e-ff3ce6622b6a> accessed 23 April 2024. It is further worth noting, when it comes to the interface between Climate Science and Law, the work of the IUCN World Commission on Environmental Law.

54 See e.g. ES Brondizio and others (eds), 'Global Assessment Report on Biodiversity and Ecosystem Services of the Intergovernmental Science-Policy Platform on Biodiversity and Ecosystem Services' (*IPBES* 2019) <https://doi.org/10.5281/zenodo.3831673> accessed 23 April 2024. It is also worth noting the collaboration between IPBES and the IPCC as exemplified by the following: Hans-Otto Pörtner and others, 'IPBES-IPCC Co-sponsored Workshop Report on Biodiversity and Climate Change' (*IPCC-IPBES* 2021) <https://doi.org/10.5281/zenodo.4782538>; Hans-Otto Pörtner and others, 'Scientific Outcome of the IPBES-IPCC Co-sponsored Workshop on Biodiversity and Climate Change' (*IPCC-IPBES* 2021) <https://doi.org/10.5281/zenodo.4659158>.

55 NASA, 'Climate Change' <https://science.nasa.gov/climate-change/> accessed 23 April 2024.

56 Copernicus Programme: 'Climate Change Service' <https://climate.copernicus.eu/> accessed 23 April 2024.

57 2030 Agenda (n 16).

58 Christian Kroll, Anne Warchold and Prajal Pradhan, 'Sustainable Development Goals (SDGs): Are We Successful in Turning Trade-offs into Synergies?' (2019) 5(140) Palgrave Comm 1; Huijuan Xiao, Yue Liu and Jingzheng Ren, 'Synergies and Trade-offs across Sustainable Development Goals: A Novel Method Incorporating Indirect Interactions Analysis' (2022) 31(2) Sustainable Develop 1135; Fabrice Renaud and others, 'Synergies and Trade-offs between Sustainable Development Goals and Targets: Innovative Approaches and New Perspectives' (2020) 15 Sustainability Science 1011.

59 UN, 'Synergy Solutions for a World in Crisis: Tackling Climate and SDG Action Together' (1st edn, 2023) Report on Strengthening the Evidence base <https://sdgs.un.org/synergy-solutions-world-crisis-tackling-climate-and-sdg-action-together> accessed 23 April 2024.

60 UNFCCC (n 14) Preamble, Article 4.7.

61 Kyoto Protocol (n 5) Articles 2, 10, 12.

62 Paris Agreement (n 4) Preamble, Articles 2.1, 4.1, 6.8.

63 UNFCCC, 'Marrakech Partnership for Global Climate Action' (2016) <https://unfccc.int/sites/default/files/marrakech_partnership_for_global_climate_action.pdf> accessed 23 April 2024.

64 March 2024 is the tenth month in a row to be the hottest on record and the average global temperature for the period April 2023 – March 2024 is the highest ever recorded, surpassing the 1991–2020 average by 0.70°C and exceeding the pre-industrial average of 1850–1900 by 1.58°C: Copernicus Programme, 'Copernicus: March 2024 is the Tenth Month in a Row to be the Hottest on Record (9 April 2024) <https://climate.copernicus.eu/copernicus-march-2024-tenth-month-row-be-hottest-record#:~:text=The%20global%2Daverage%20temperature%20for,%2D1900%20pre%2Dindustrial%20average> accessed 23 April 2024.

65 UN, 'The Sustainable Development Goals Report: Special Edition' (2023) <https://unstats.un.org/sdgs/report/2023/> accessed 23 April 2024.

66 Stephanie Hallegatte and others, 'Shock Waves: Managing the Impacts of Climate Change on Poverty' (*World Bank Group,* 2016) Climate Change and Development Series <https://openknowledge.worldbank.org/bitstream/handle/10986/22787/9781464806735.pdf> accessed 23 April 2024.

67 Carmen G Gonzalez, 'Environmental Justice and International Environmental Law' in Shawkat Alam and others (eds), *Routledge Handbook of International Environmental Law* (1st edn, Routledge 2014) 77.

68 IPCC, *Climate Change 2001*: *Impacts, Adaptation and Vulnerability, Contribution of Working Group II to the Third Assessment Report of the Intergovernmental Panel on Climate Change* (CUP/IPCC 2001).

69 Nicolas Taconet, Aurélie Méjean and Céline Guivarch, 'Influence of Climate Change Impacts and Mitigation Costs on Inequality between Countries' (2020) 160 Climatic Change 15.

70 R Bharadwaj and others, 'Harnessing Nationally Determined Contributions to Tackle Loss and Damage in Least Developed Countries' (*IIED* 2022) Issue Paper <www.iied.org/21081iied> accessed 23 April 2024.

71 UNFCCC, 'Nationally Determined Contributions under the Paris Agreement: Synthesis Report by the Secretariat' FCC/PA/CMA/2023/12 (14 November 2023).

72 UNFCCC Standing Committee on Finance, 'First Report on the Determination of the Needs of Developing Country Parties Related to Implementing the Convention and the Paris Agreement' (2021) Technical Report <https://unfccc.int/topics/climate-finance/workstreams/determination-of-the-needs-of-developing-country-parties/first-report-on-the-determination-of-the-needs-of-developing-country-parties-related-to-implementing> accessed 23 April 2024.

73 UN Trade & Development, 'UNCTAD Counts the Costs of Achieving Sustainable Development Goals' (18 September 2023) <https://unctad.org/news/unctad-counts-costs-achieving-sustainable-development-goals> accessed 23 April 2024.

74 OHCHR, 'Submission of the Office of the High Commissioner for Human Rights to the 21st Conference of the Parties to the United Nations Framework Convention on Climate Change' (2015) <www.ohchr.org/sites/default/files/Documents/Issues/ClimateChange/COP21.pdf> accessed 23 April 2024.

75 Christina Voigt and Felipe Ferreira, '"Dynamic Differentiation": The Principles of CBDRRC, Progression and Highest Possible Ambition in the Paris Agreement' (2016) 5(2) TEL 285; Phillipe Cullet, 'Common but Differentiated Responsibilities' in Malgosia Fitzmaurice and others (eds), *Research Handbook on International Environmental Law* (2nd edn, Edward Elgar 2021).

76 Shangrila Joshi, 'Climate Justice: Taking Back the Commons' in Zeke Baker and others (eds) *Climate Science and Society: A Primer* (Routledge 2024); Margot Hurlbert, 'Climate Justice: A Call for Leadership' (2015) 8(2) Env Justice 51; Fausto Corvino and Tiziana Andina (eds), *Global Climate Justice: Theory and Practice* (E-International Relations 2023); Sharon Harlan and others, 'Climate Justice and Inequality' in Riley E Dunlap and Robert J Brulle (eds) *Climate Change and Society: Sociological Perspectives* (OUP 2015).

77 Britta Horstmann, 'Context Specific and Yet Transferable? A Reflection on Knowledge-sharing in the Field of Adaptation to Climate Change' in Andrea Prutsch and others (eds) *Climate Change Adaptation Manual: Lessons Learned from European and Other Industrialized Countries* (Routledge 2014); W Neil Adger and others, 'Cultural Dimensions of Climate Change Impacts and Adaptation' (2013) 3(2) Nature Climate Change 112; Dereje Regasa and Nega Akirso, 'Determinants of Climate Change Mitigation and Adaptation Strategies: An Application of Protection Motivation Theory' (2019) 42(337) Rural Sustainability Research 9; Alberto Sanz-Cobena and others, 'Strategies for Greenhouse Gas Emissions Mitigation in Mediterranean Agriculture: A Review' (2017) 238 Agriculture, Ecosystems & Environment 5; Shyamasree Dasgupta, Debrupa Chakrabarty and Joyashree Roy, 'Selected Issues in Economics of Greenhouse Gas Emission Mitigation' (2020) 3 Encyclopedia of Renewable and Sustainable Materials 743; Rico Kongsager, 'Linking Climate Change Adaptation and Mitigation: A Review with Evidence

from the Land-Use Sectors' (2018) 7(4) Land 158; Fang Wang and others, 'Climate Change: Strategies for Mitigation and Adaptation' (2023) 1(1) The Innovation Geoscience 100015; Diana Ivanova and others, 'Quantifying the Potential for Climate Change Mitigation of Consumption Options' (2020) 15 Environmental Research Letters 1.

78 Christina Voigt, 'The Power of the Paris Agreement in International Climate Litigation' (2023) 32(2) RECIEL 237.

79 Francesco Sindico and Makane Mbengue (eds), *Comparative Climate Change Litigation: Beyond the Usual Suspects* (Springer 2021); Anna-Julia Saiger, 'Domestic Courts and the Paris Agreement's Climate Goals: The Need for a Comparative Approach?' (2020) 9(1) Transnational Environmental Law 37.

80 Benito Müller, 'Equity in Climate Change The Great Divide' (*Oxford Institute for Energy Studies,* 2002) <https://acrobat.adobe.com/id/urn:aaid:sc:US:e75f2971-1d69-4eee-9e90-951bd2cd34a9> accessed 23 April 2024; Lavanya Rajamani and others, 'National "Fair Shares" in Reducing Greenhouse Gas Emissions within the Principled Framework of International Environmental Law' (2021) 21(8) Climate Policy 983; Cinnamon Piñon Carlene, 'Balancing Equity and Effectiveness: The Paris Agreement & The Future of International Climate Change Law' (2019). 27 NYU Envtl LJ 107, Ohio State Public Law Working Paper No. 477.

81 See further Michael Burger and Maria Antonia Tigre, 'Global Climate Litigation Report: 2023 Status Review' (Sabin Center for Climate Change Law, Columbia Law School & United Nations Environment Programme, 2023) <https://wedocs.unep.org/bitstream/handle/20.500.11822/43008/global_climate_litigation_report_2023.pdf?sequence=3.> accessed 22 April 2024.

82 Michael Burger, Jessica Wentz and Radley Horton, 'The Law and Science of Climate Change Attribution' (2020) 45(1) Columbia J Environ Law 57.

83 UNEP, 'Climate Risk Landscape Report 2024' (April 2024) <www.unepfi.org/themes/climate-change/2024-climate-risk-landscape/> accessed 10 April 2024.

84 Global Climate Litigation Report (n 81).

85 *I.L. v. Italian Ministry of the Interior and Attorney General at the Court of Appeal of Ancona, Supreme Court of Cassation*, N. 5022/2021, 24 February 2021 (Italy).

86 ibid.

87 Global Climate Litigation Report (n 81) 64. See *Bushfire Survivors for Climate Action Incorporated v. Environmental Protection Authority, Land and Environment Court of Australia*, NSWLEC 92 and NSWLEC 152, 5 March 2021 (Australia).

88 ibid.

89 Global Climate Litigation Report (n 81) 64. See *Conservation Law Foundation v. ExxonMobil Corp.* (2016); *Conservation Law Foundation v. Shell Oil Co.* (2022) and *Conservation Law Foundation v. Gulf Oil LP* (2022).

90 Union of Concerned Scientists, 'The UCS Science Hub for Climate Litigation: Resources and Opportunities for Experts' (3 August 2020) <www.ucsusa.org/resources/science-hub-climate-litigation> accessed 23 April 2024.

91 Sabin Center for Climate Change Law and Lamont-Doherty Earth Observatory, 'Climate Attribution Database' <https://climateattribution.org/> accessed 23 April 2024.

92 IPCC, 'Summary for Policymakers' in *Climate Change 2022: Mitigation of Climate Change. Contribution of Working Group III to the Sixth Assessment Report of the Intergovernmental Panel on Climate Change* (CUP 2022) <https://doi.org/10.1017/9781009157926.001>, '[c]limate-related litigation, for example by governments, private sector, civil society and individuals is growing, with a large number of cases in some developed countries, and with a much smaller number in some developing countries, and in some cases, has influenced the outcome and ambition of climate governance' (E.3.3).

93 Zunaida Moosa Wadiwala, 'Rights-Based Climate Litigation in South Africa and the Netherlands' (2023) 7 CJEL 227–44.

94 Zunaida Moosa Wadiwala, 'The Impact of Climate Change on Human Rights and the Legal Obligations of States to Protect Them – A Comparative Jurisdictional Analysis' (2023) 3 CCLR 123 <https://doi.org/10.21552/cclr/2023/3/5>.

95 ibid.

96 ibid.

97 *The State of the Netherlands v Urgenda Foundation, The Supreme Court of the Netherlands.* (20 December 2019) Case number: 19/00135 Citation for the English Translation ECLI:NL:HR: 2019:2007 (Original Dutch citation from the Supreme Court of the Netherlands: ECLI:NL: 2019:2006)

98 *Neubauer et al v Germany* Bundesverfassungsgericht [BverfG] [Federal Constitutional Court], Mar. 24, 2021. Case No 1 BvR 2656/18. 1 BvR 96/20. 1 BvR 78/20. 1 BvR 288/20.
99 *Earthlife Africa Johannesburg v The Minister of Environmental Affairs and Others* 2017 (5) SA 227 (WCC); (2017) ZAWCHC 50 Case No: 65662/16.
100 Wadiwala (n 100).
101 Yamide Dagnet and others, 'Setting the Paris Agreement in Motion: Key Requirements for the Implementing Guidelines' (2018) PACT Working Paper <https://newclimate.org/sites/default/files/2018/08/PACT-Setting-the-Paris-Agreement-in-Motion-Key-Requirements-for-the-Implementing-Guidelines.pdf> accessed 10 April 2024.
102 UNCC, 'The Paris Agreement: What Is the Paris Agreement' <https://unfccc.int/news/paris-agreement-enters-into-force-celebration-and-reality-check> accessed 10 April 2024.
103 Michael Gerhard, Charlotte Ellis and Selam Abebe, 'On the Road to 2025: Lessons for Effective NDC Update Support' (2022) International Climate Initiative <www.international-climate-initiative.com/fileadmin/iki/Dokumente/Publikationen/Projekte/16_I_298/2022-11-11_IKI_Study_On_the_road_to_2025_-_Lessons_for_effective_NDC_Support.final.pdf> accessed 10 April 2024.
104 Marrakech Partnership for Global Climate Action <https://unfccc.int/files/paris_agreement/application/pdf/marrakech_partnership_for_global_climate_action.pdf> accessed 10 April 2024.
105 UNFCCC, 'Report of the Conference of the Parties on Its Twenty-first Session, Held in Paris from 30 November to 13 December 2015' Decision 1/CP.21 (Adoption of the Paris Agreement) UN Doc. FCCC/CP/2015/10/Add.1, para 71.
106 UNCC, 'PCCB Network: Paris Committee on Capacity-building (PCCB)' <https://unfccc.int/pccb-network
107 IUCN, 'IUCN WCEL Climate Change Law Specialist Group' <www.iucn.org/our-union/commissions/group/iucn-wcel-climate-change-law-specialist-group> accessed 10 April 2024.
108 ITLOS, 'Written Statement of the International Union for Conservation of Nature and Natural Resources – World Commission on Environmental Law, Ocean Law Specialist Group' *Request for an Advisory Opinion Submitted by the Commission of Small Island States on Climate Change and International Law* (13 June 2023) <www.itlos.org/fileadmin/itlos/documents/cases/31/written_statements/2/C31-WS-2–2-IUCN.pdf> accessed 10 April 2024.
109 IUCN, 'Written Opinion by International Union for the Conservation of Nature (IUCN)' *Request by the Republic of Colombia and the Republic of Chile for an Advisory Opinion from the Inter-American Court on Human Rights Concerning the Climate Emergency and Human Rights* (18 December 2023) <www.corteidh.or.cr/sitios/observaciones/OC-32/11_IUCN.pdf> accessed 10 April 2024.
110 *Obligations of States in Respect of Climate Change (Request for Advisory Opinion) – The Court Authorizes the International Union for Conservation of Nature to Participate in the Proceedings* (2023) <https://www.icj-cij.org/index.php/node/202798> accessed 10 April 2024.
111 Climate Law and Governance Initiative, 'Climate Law & Governance Initiative Offers Events, Public Engagement Opportunities to Delegates and Public at COP23' <https://unfccc.int/sites/default/files/resource/CLGI_Events%2BEngagement_Opportunities_at_COP23_0.pdf> accessed 10 April 2024.
112 Marie-Claire Cordonier Segger and Tejas Rao, 'Climate Law and Public Policy Innovation for the Sustainable Development Goals: Accelerating Pre-CoP27 Paris Agreement Compliance' (19 July 2022) University of Cambridge Bennett Institute for Public Policy, Policy Brief <www.bennettinstitute.cam.ac.uk/publications/climate-law-policy-sdgs/> accessed 10 April 2024.
113 African Development Bank Group, 'Leveraging Potentials of the Youth for Inclusive, Green and Sustainable Development in Africa' (2023) Concept Note <https://acrobat.adobe.com/id/urn:aaid:sc:US:3338f847-1910-46eb-8cc5-a5d1f91e9140> accessed 23 April 2024.
114 YOUNGO, 'COP 28 Global Youth Statement: Declaration for Climate Justice' (2023) <www.coy18uae.org/global-youth-statement> accessed 23 April 2024.

3

CLIMATE COURAGE, CONTRIBUTIONS AND COMPLIANCE IN THE CONTEXT OF THE UN SUSTAINABLE DEVELOPMENT GOALS

Marie-Claire Cordonier Segger[1]

Introduction

Climate change is the justice challenge of this century, and it poses critical challenges for global sustainable development. As the Intergovernmental Panel on Climate Change (IPCC) has noted, emissions of carbon dioxide (CO_2) have increased by almost 50 per cent since 1990, and emissions grew more quickly between 2000 and 2020 than ever before in human history. The impacts of climate change threaten to undermine decades of social and economic development, to severely constrain efforts to protect and restore ecosystems and to prevent realization of a wide range of human rights, including the rights to life, health, water, food, shelter and an adequate standard of living.[2] Such changes have already led to serious repercussions and given rise to significant further impacts and risks worldwide.[3] Most effects of climate change will persist for many centuries even if emissions were halted immediately. Perhaps most troubling, current regulatory and financial regimes guiding development continue to privilege carbon-intensive, unsustainable options, rather than promoting sustainable development, and making finance flows consistent with a pathway towards low-GHG and climate-resilient alternatives. However, as argued in this volume, it is still possible, using a wide array of legal and institutional measures among others, to limit the increase in global mean temperature to well below 2°C above pre-industrial levels. Through cooperation governed by international law, major regulatory, institutional, economic and technological transformations, if carried out immediately, offer the world a chance to limit dangerous consequences to below this threshold. Recognizing the groundbreaking work of the many partners in the global Climate Law and Governance Initiative,[4] after a brief discussion of the origins of the Sustainable Development Goals (SDGs) and their links to UN Framework Convention on Climate Change (UNFCCC), underlining the elements of the Paris Agreement which reflect principles of international law on sustainable development, the chapter examines the contributions of the Paris Agreement to sustainability, especially in highly climate-vulnerable countries. The chapter highlights how effective, inclusive and rapid implementation of the Paris Agreement can support the SDGs.

DOI: 10.4324/9781003276678-4

Current global sustainability and justice challenges, particularly the destabilization of the global climate systems upon which our current human societies and States depend, are outcomes of myriad current political, social, economic and environmental development decisions on all levels and across several centuries. In many cases, the choices made and the patterns that they set in place were likely not intended to cause the terrible impacts being seen. Indeed, through international policy and cooperation agendas, States and stakeholders are seeking to redirect global development pathways, especially through the United Nations, towards more sustainable development. One important instance from this century involved the adoption of the Millennium Development Goals, established at the UN Millennium Summit in 2000 in a United Nations Millennium Declaration, whereby all 191 UN Member States committed to eight international policy goals to be achieved by 2015; these included commitments to eradicate extreme poverty and hunger, achieve universal primary education, promote gender equality and empower women, reduce child mortality, improve maternal health and combat HIV/AIDS, malaria and other diseases; as well as a single goal to ensure environmental sustainability and to develop a global partnership for development, with 21 specific time-bound targets.[5] The MDGs offered a landmark global commitment to eliminating poverty and advancing the pillars of sustainable development.[6] In 2015, the UN reported that the MDGs had resulted in many achievements, including *inter alia* between 2000 and 2015, the number of out-of-school children of primary school age worldwide fell by almost half and by 2015, ozone-depleting substances were virtually eliminated; however, they also found that in many areas, more effort was needed.[7] Further critical challenges such as climate change had gained greater prominence in international affairs, expanding the urgency and scale of the global collaboration agenda. Building on these MDGs, in September 2015 the UN set out a further, more comprehensive and integrated sustainable development agenda toward 2030 and beyond,[8] adopting 17 global Sustainable Development Goals (SDGs) with 169 time-bound targets from ending poverty and hunger (SDGs 1 and 2); to securing health, education and gender equality (SDGs 3, 4 and 5); to advancing access to clean water and sanitation, affordable and clean energy, decent work and economic growth, industry, innovation and infrastructure (SDGs 6, 7, 8 and 9); to reducing inequality (SDG 10), to promoting sustainable cities and communities, and responsible consumption and production (SDGs 11 and 12); to advancing climate action, life below water, life on land, and peace justice and strong institutions (SDGs 13, 14, 15 and 16), as well as forming partnerships to advance the goals (SDG 17).[9] Global cooperation to tackle climate change figures heavily in these SDGs, not just as a discrete goal but also as myriad other commitments in relation to further priorities. As the UN recognizes, climate change is a real and undeniable threat to our entire civilization: the effects are already visible and will be catastrophic unless we act now. In committing to "take urgent action to combat climate change and its impacts" (SDG 13), at 13.1 countries prioritized the need to "strengthen resilience and adaptive capacity to climate-related hazards and natural disasters in all countries", at 13.2 to "integrate climate change measures into national policies, strategies and planning", and at 13.3 to "improve education, awareness-raising and human and institutional capacity on climate change mitigation, adaptation, impact reduction and early warning". Further, they underlined their commitment, at 13.a, to

> implement the commitment undertaken by developed-country parties to the [UNFCCC] to a goal of mobilizing jointly $100 billion annually by 2020 from all sources to address the needs of developing countries in the context of meaningful mitigation actions and transparency on implementation and fully operationalize the Green Climate Fund through its capitalization as soon as possible.

Indeed, further annual funds are likely required, and a new quantified collective finance goal remains under review in the UNFCCC. In 13.b they underlined the need to "promote mechanisms for raising capacity for effective climate change-related planning and management in least developed countries and small island developing States, including focusing on women, youth and local and marginalized communities", a commitment that many, including through the Climate Law and Governance Initiative, continue to advance.

In addition to the SDG on Climate Action, there are over 30 other targets under the other SDGs which address the global response to climate change through mitigation, adaptation and resilience, as well as financial, technological and other cooperation. When adopted in 2015, governments sought to achieve most of these targets by 2030, including:

- Under SDG 1 to end poverty in all its forms everywhere, target 1.5 to build the resilience of the poor and those in vulnerable situations and reduce their exposure and vulnerability to climate-related extreme events and other economic, social and environmental shocks and disasters;
- Under SDG 2 to end hunger, achieve food security and improved nutrition and promote sustainable agriculture, target 2.4 to implement resilient agricultural practices that strengthen capacity for adaptation to climate change, extreme weather, drought, flooding and other disasters;
- Under SDG 3 to ensure healthy lives and promote well-being for all at all ages, target 3.9 to substantially reduce the number of deaths and illnesses from hazardous chemicals and air, water and soil pollution and target 3.d to strengthen the capacity for early warning, risk reduction and management of national and global health risks;
- Under SDG 4 to ensure inclusive and equitable quality education and promote lifelong learning opportunities for all, target 4.7 to ensure that all learners acquire the knowledge and skills needed to promote sustainable development;
- Under SDG 6 to ensure availability and sustainable management of water and sanitation for all, target 6.4, to substantially increase water-use efficiency and substantially reduce the number of people suffering from water scarcity;
- Under SDG 7 to ensure access to affordable, reliable, sustainable and modern energy for all, target 7.2 to increase substantially the share of renewable energy in the global energy mix, and target 7.3 to double the global rate of improvement in energy efficiency, as well as target 7.a to enhance international cooperation to facilitate access to clean energy research and technology;
- Under SDG 9 to build resilient infrastructure, promote inclusive and sustainable industrialization and foster innovation, target 9.1 to develop quality, reliable, sustainable and resilient infrastructure, and target 9.4 to upgrade infrastructure and retrofit industries to make them sustainable, with increased resource-use efficiency and greater adoption of clean and environmentally sound technologies, as well as target 9.a to facilitate sustainable and resilient infrastructure development in developing countries through enhanced financial, technological and technical support to African countries, least developed countries, landlocked developing countries and small island developing States;
- Under SDG 10 to reduce inequality within and among countries, target 10.b to encourage official development assistance and financial flows, including foreign direct investment, to States where the need is greatest, in particular the least developed countries, African countries, small island developing States and landlocked developing countries;
- Under SDG 11 to make cities and human settlements inclusive, safe, resilient and sustainable, target 11.5 to significantly reduce the number of deaths and the number of people affected and substantially decrease the direct economic losses caused by disasters with a focus on protecting

the poor and people in vulnerable situations; also target 11.6 to reduce the adverse per capita environmental impact of cities and target 11.b to substantially increase the number of cities and human settlements adopting and implementing integrated policies and plans towards inclusion, resource efficiency, mitigation and adaptation to climate change, resilience to disasters, and develop and implement, in line with the Sendai Framework for Disaster Risk Reduction 2015–2030, holistic disaster risk management at all levels, in addition to target 11.c to support least developed countries, including through financial and technical assistance, in building sustainable and resilient buildings utilizing local materials;

- Under SDG 12 to ensure sustainable consumption and production patterns, target 12.2 to achieve the sustainable management and efficient use of natural resources, target 12.4 to achieve the environmentally sound management of chemicals and all wastes throughout their life cycle, in accordance with agreed international frameworks, and significantly reduce their release to air, water and soil in order to minimize their adverse impacts on human health and the environment, and target 12.5 to substantially reduce waste generation through prevention, reduction, recycling and reuse, as well as target 12.c to rationalize inefficient fossil-fuel subsidies that encourage wasteful consumption by removing market distortions, including by restructuring taxation and phasing out those harmful subsidies, where they exist, to reflect their environmental impacts;
- Under SDG 14 to conserve and sustainably use the oceans, seas and marine resources for sustainable development, target 14.1 to prevent and significantly reduce marine pollution of all kinds, in particular from land-based activities, including marine debris and nutrient pollution;
- Under SDG 15 to protect, restore and promote sustainable use of terrestrial ecosystems, sustainably manage forests, combat desertification and halt and reverse land degradation and halt biodiversity loss, target 15.2 to promote the implementation of sustainable management of all types of forests, halt deforestation, restore degraded forests and substantially increase afforestation and reforestation globally; also target 15.3 to combat desertification, restore degraded land and soil, including land affected by desertification, drought and floods, and strive to achieve a land degradation-neutral world; and target 15.b mobilize significant resources from all sources and at all levels to finance sustainable forest management and provide adequate incentives to developing countries to advance such management, including for conservation and reforestation;
- Under SDG 16 to promote peaceful and inclusive societies for sustainable development, provide access to justice for all and build effective, accountable and inclusive institutions at all levels, target 16.b to promote and enforce non-discriminatory laws and policies for sustainable development; and
- Under SDG 17 to strengthen the means of implementation and revitalize the Global Partnership for Sustainable Development, target 17.7 to promote the development, transfer, dissemination and diffusion of environmentally sound technologies to developing countries on favourable terms, including on concessional and preferential terms, as mutually agreed, and target 17.14 to enhance policy coherence for sustainable development.

While the SDGs are aspirational 'soft law', formulated as collective global policy goals for States and societies rather than legally binding treaties, each commitment is far from irrelevant in international law. Indeed, in 'Transforming Our World: The 2030 Agenda for Sustainable Development' at 18, countries adopting the SDGs reaffirm a "commitment to international law" and emphasize that the Agenda is to be "implemented in a manner that is consistent with the rights and obligations of States under international law". The obligations of States under many international treaties, as well as emerging customary legal principles on sustainable development are directly relevant to advancing all SDGs. With regard to SDG 13 committing to urgent action on climate change, under a rare footnote, the UN acknowledges "that the United Nations Framework Convention on Climate Change is the primary international, intergovernmental forum for negotiating the global response to climate change". Of course, 'primary' by no means suggests 'only', a point recently underscored by the International Tribunal on the Law of the Sea in its comprehensive and unanimous 2024 *Request for an Advisory Opinion Submitted by the Commission of Small Island States on Climate Change and International Law*, which also recognized at 66 that "climate change represents an existential threat and raises human rights concerns" and at 122 that "climate change is recognized internationally as a common concern of humankind".[10]

Only a few months after SDG 13 and the others were announced by the UN, the international Paris Agreement on climate change was concluded during the 21st Conference of the Parties to the UNFCCC (COP21) at Paris in December 2015, and as discussed in the following, this treaty aims to both prevent further greenhouse gas (GHG) emissions through mitigation, and also to promote adaptation and resilience, as well as finance for more sustainable alternative development pathways.[11] If the SDGs offer a common global policy agenda which prioritizes action on climate change, the Paris Agreement provides a structured set of legally binding international obligations which reflects that policy direction by seeking to reduce emissions while also promoting more sustainable development of special relevance for economic and social decisions in leading high-ambition countries, and also development decisions in emerging economies, and especially in the most climate-vulnerable countries that are otherwise often excluded from international law making.

Global response to climate change is still guided by the 1992 UNFCCC, which underpins the 2015 Paris Agreement and provides the framework for deliberations, decision-making and cooperation on many levels, as well as for the negotiation of further instruments, establishing the international climate change regime.[12] Under the UNFCCC, the 1997 Kyoto Protocol[13] included binding emissions reduction targets for Parties, reflecting the international legal principle of common but differentiated responsibilities and respective capabilities (CBDRRC).[14] The first commitment period under the Protocol ended in 2012, and a second commitment period, known as the Doha Amendment, ran to 2020.[15] However, these efforts fell short of what was needed to mitigate and adapt to dangerous climate change.

The Paris Agreement, with binding international commitments that can contribute to SDG 13 on climate action alongside many other SDGs, seeks to address the gap and strengthen the global response to the threat of climate change in the context of sustainable development and efforts to eradicate poverty. In essence, the Paris Agreement presents a core triangle of obligations:

- countries must take nationally determined, quantifiable and progressive action for climate mitigation and adaptation;
- these actions are incentivized by changes in financial flows and related technology transfer, capacity-building, education and other cooperative measures; and
- enforcement is achieved through transparency and reporting, peer review, periodic stocktaking, public participation and compliance mechanisms.

The modalities to operationalize the accord are set out in a 'rulebook' to operationalize the Paris Agreement, guided by the Conference of the Parties serving as the Meeting of the Parties to the Paris Agreement (known as the CMA). Implementation decisions are adopted through a series of further Conferences of the Parties (COPs) to the UNFCCC and the Paris Agreement, including COP 22 in Marrakesh (presided by Morocco) in 2016, COP23 in Bonn in 2017 (presided by Fiji), COP24 in the coal-producing city of Katowice in 2018 (presided by Poland), COP25 in Santiago which was moved to Madrid in 2019 (presided by Chile), COP26 in Glasgow after COVID in 2021 (presided by the UK), COP27 in Sharm-el-Sheikh in 2022 (presided by Egypt), COP28 in Dubai in 2023 (presided by the United Arab Emirates), COP29 in Baku in 2024 (presided by Azerbaijan) and COP30 in the Belem in 2025 (presided by Brazil).

Under Article 2, the Paris Agreement aims to strengthen the global response to the threat of climate change, in the context of sustainable development and efforts to eradicate poverty, by holding the increase in the global average temperature to "well below 2°C above pre-industrial levels" and pursuing efforts to limit the temperature increase to 1.5°C; by increasing the ability to adapt to the adverse impacts of climate change as well as foster climate resilience and low GHG emissions development; and by making finance flows consistent with a pathway toward low GHG emissions and climate resilient development.[16] The Agreement seeks to enhance implementation of the UNFCCC, which in Article 4 includes the commitment to "*enable economic development to proceed in a sustainable manner*."[17]

Specifically, the Paris Agreement aims to implement the commitments in Article 4 UNFCCC in accordance with the principles reflected in Article 3 UNFCCC.[18]

Article 2 of the Paris Agreement further specifies that the Agreement will be implemented to "reflect equity and the principle of CBDRRC, in the light of different national circumstances".[19] The legal obligations of developing countries under the Paris Agreement are thus variable in order to equitably reflect their historical, economic, and social circumstances in comparison with that of other States. Article 3 of the Paris Agreement underscores that all Parties will undertake and communicate ambitious efforts (as defined in articles 4, 7, 9, 10, 11 and 13) to achieve the aim of the agreement through nationally determined contributions (NDCs) to the global response to climate change. In doing so, it recognizes that the efforts of all Parties will progress over time, and that there is a need to support developing country Parties for effective implementation.

Courage and Contributions

Under Article 3 of the Paris Agreement, Parties commit that they "shall prepare, communicate and maintain" successive NDCs to the global response to climate change and pursue domestic mitigation measures to achieve their commitments. Rather than setting out specific mitigation or adaptation targets for each country, the Paris Agreement commits Parties to nationally determine and transparently communicate their own objectives, to inform the international community of the progress in implementing and achieving them and to participate in periodic global stocktaking to inform progressively higher ambition. Adopting a 'bottom up' approach, the Paris Agreement therefore builds on submissions of climate action plans as NDCs by nearly 190 countries and other bodies. The NDCs are communicated every five years (ie 2020, 2025, 2030, etc.). These NDCs, once submitted by a government, are recorded in a public registry maintained by the UNFCCC.A Party may at any time adjust its existing NDC for greater *courage*, i.e., to progressively enhance its level of ambition (Article 4.3, Article 4.11).

Efforts to achieve NDCs are conditioned by climate law and governance. Indeed, research led by the Centre for International Sustainable Development Law (CISDL) for the Climate Law and Governance Initiative has revealed that out of 186 countries with NDCs published online by the UNFCCC registry, 169 countries explicitly prioritize legal and institutional reforms to achieve their contributions.[20] Further, over 120 countries are calling for support from the international community in their NDCs, with more than 60 specifically stressing the need for legal and institutional capacity-building.[21] Across many fields, and at all levels from local to national to international law, the relevant reforms hold the potential to either foster or frustrate the SDGs.

As noted in the 2002 ILA New Delhi Declaration, "sustainable development is now widely accepted as a global objective . . . recognised in various international and national legal instruments, including treaty law and jurisprudence at international and national levels".[22]

Indeed, the SDGs and their targets are reflected in object, purpose and operational provisions of many important international treaties, including the Paris Agreement.[23] The Paris Agreement Adoption Decision explicitly welcomed the global SDGs, particularly SDG 13 on climate action,[24] also recognizing that when taking action on climate change, States must respect, promote and consider human rights obligations and inter-generational equity.[25] The international regime developed in an interactional manner over decades,[26] as countries sought to address climate challenges domestically while also struggling to find an appropriate international cooperative framework. While all Parties, including those with the least historical contributions to global emissions, play a role in emissions reduction, they also benefit from new investment and collaboration for low-GHG pathways for sustainable development and poverty eradication. As an important instrument in the climate regime, therefore, the Paris Agreement holds all the hallmarks of a sustainable development accord.[27] Indeed, the Paris Agreement is predicated upon an expectation that, if NDCs can be shaped and supported by peer review and public awareness, new scientific data on risks, actual impacts and greater political attention will lead to ever-higher ambition from all levels of governments, along with non-State actors in the private sector and civil society. Some hope that countries, perhaps in clubs with higher ambition, can move towards setting and achieving absolute emissions reduction targets, diversified enhanced mitigation actions, or arrangements among donors and beneficiaries to address key sectors. The former would seek to bind Parties to attain net zero emissions levels over the long-term through a quantifiable standard. The latter would set higher ambition, whether or not remaining recalcitrant countries also accept such actions as obligatory.

Several principles of international law, as reflected in decisions of international courts and tribunals,[28] are often found in treaties related to sustainable development, and these include 1) the duty to advance sustainable use of natural resources whereby States have sovereign rights over their natural resources, and a corresponding duty not to cause, or allow, undue damage to the environment of other States in the use of these resources; 2) to promote inter- and intra-generational equity and the eradication of poverty; 3) to respect common but differentiated responsibilities and respective capabilities; 4) to take a precautionary approach to human health, natural resources and ecosystems, transferring the burden of proving lack of significant harm from an undertaking to the proponent in cases of scientific uncertainty; 5) to provide for public participation, backed by access to information and justice; 6) to ensure good governance, with measures to support rule of law, coherence and anti-corruption; and 7) to advance integration and interrelationship of human rights and social, economic and environmental objectives.[29] As has been noted elsewhere, this last principle may sometimes be called – in legal shorthand – a 'principle of sustainable development', holding that States must take into account the environmental and social (including human rights) aspects of economic plans or projects (and vice versa), integrating related measures and costs in order to promote development that is more *sustainable* over the long term.[30]

These principles permeate the Paris Agreement, alongside substantive obligations which advance many targets of the SDGs, as can be elucidated through a few illustrative examples.

GHG Emission Mitigation, Low-Carbon GHG Emission Development Strategies and GHG Sinks and Reservoirs

In Article 4 of the Paris Agreement, the Parties aim to reach global peaking of GHG emissions as soon as possible, recognizing that this will take longer for developing country Parties, and to undertake rapid reductions thereafter in accordance with the best available science, to balance emissions by sources and removals by sinks in the second half of this century (Article 4.1). The notion of balancing emissions and removals can be understood as an objective of 'net zero' emissions, whereby any residual anthropogenic GHG emissions would be annulled by activities removing GHGs from the atmosphere. Such a sequestration of GHGs could occur through expansion of the activities of nature-based solutions such as climate-smart agriculture, ocean, wetlands or forest carbon sinks and reservoirs, such as forests or oceans, or through the deployment of carbon capture technologies,[31] areas that touch on climate-related targets mentioned earlier under SDG 2 zero hunger, SDG 6 access to water, SDG 14 life below water and SDG 15 life on land, among others. Indeed, in the Paris Agreement, parties also agree that they should take action to conserve and enhance GHG sinks and reservoirs as described in UNFCCC article 4.1(d), including forests.[32] They are encouraged to take action to implement and support the existing framework as set out in related guidance and decisions already agreed under the UNFCCC, in order to reduce emissions from deforestation and forest degradation (REDD+ framework), including through results-based payments.[33]

The sustainable development principle of common but differentiated responsibilities is reflected in these provisions. For instance, Article 4 recognizes that developed countries should take the lead by undertaking economy-wide absolute emission reduction targets, while developing countries should continue enhancing mitigation efforts, moving over time toward economy-wide targets (Article 4.4; see also Preamble paragraph 16). Support shall also be provided to developing country Parties for the implementation of mitigation efforts, recognizing that enhanced support for developing country Parties will allow for higher ambition in their actions (Article 4.5; see also Articles 9, 10 and 11). The least developed countries (LDCs) and small island developing States (SIDS) may prepare strategies that reflect their special circumstances (Article 4.6). The duty of States to ensure sustainable use of natural resources is also recognized in the provisions that frame atmospheric and carbon resources as key resources to be managed in a sustainable manner, one which avoids dangerous climate change, as noted in the Treaty preamble and in the substantive provisions on mitigation, such as in Article 5 under which Parties are encouraged to take action on sustainable management of forests as a key natural resource and carbon sink, including through REDD+ and alternative policy frameworks such as joint mitigation and adaptation approaches for the integral and sustainable management of forests. The role of conservation, sustainable management of forests and enhancement of forest carbon stocks in developing countries, but also alternative policy approaches such as joint mitigation and adaptation approaches for integral and sustainable management of forests, is emphasized, while the importance of incentivizing non-carbon co-benefits is also reaffirmed (Article 5.2). The need to build the resilience of socio-economic and ecological systems, including through sustainable management of natural resources, is also prioritized at Article 7.9(e) on adaptation. These provisions reflect the principle of sustainable use of natural resources, particularly in a transboundary context, and can help to achieve the targets of SDG 15 life on land.

Adaptation Goal and Communications, and Efforts to Address Loss and Damage

By virtue of Article 7, a global goal on adaptation is established, to enhance adaptive capacity, strengthen resilience and reduce vulnerability to climate change, with a view to contributing to sustainable development and ensuring an adequate adaptation response (Article 7.1). Each Party should submit and periodically update an Adaptation Communication, which may include a national adaptation plan, priorities, implementation and support needs, plans and actions, without creating additional burdens for developing country parties (Article 7.10, Article 7.11). The Adaptation Communications are recorded in a public registry maintained by the UNFCCC (Article 7.12).

Among sustainable development aspects of Article 7, the Paris Agreement provides that adaptation is recognized as a global challenge faced by all with multiple dimensions, taking into account the urgent and immediate needs of those developing country parties that are particularly vulnerable to the adverse effects of climate change (Article 7.1). Parties strengthen their cooperation on enhancing action on adaptation, taking into account the Cancun Adaptation Framework (Article 7.7); the Global Stocktake (GST) recognizes and enhances these efforts, reviewing the adequacy and effectiveness of adaptation and support for it and overall progress (Article 7.14; also Article 14).[34] Continuous and enhanced international support shall be provided to developing country parties for the implementation of commitments to enhance action on adaptation, to engage in adaptation planning, and to prepare, submit and periodically update their Adaptation Communications (Article 7.13; also Articles 7.7, 7.9, 7.10 and 7.11). The Paris Agreement also recognizes the importance of averting, minimizing and addressing loss and damage associated with the adverse effects of climate change, including extreme weather events as well as slow-onset events, and it specifically highlights the importance of sustainable development in reducing the risk of loss and damage (Article 8.1).[35]

Further, the Paris Agreement also addresses the Warsaw International Mechanism for Loss and Damage associated with Climate Change Impacts, noting that Parties should enhance understanding, action and support on a cooperative and facilitative basis with respect to loss and damage associated with the adverse effects of climate change (Article 8.3; also Article 8.2). Certain key priorities for cooperation and facilitation are identified in the Paris Agreement, such as early warning systems, emergency preparedness, slow-onset events, inter alia, including the resilience of communities, livelihoods and ecosystems (Article 8.4). While the treaty does not go further to define, deny or designate liability or compensation, the adoption decision also does not limit liability, simply stating that Article 8 of the treaty does not involve or provide a basis for any liability or compensation (Adoption Decision, paragraph 52). During the UNFCCC CoP28 in Dubai UAE in 2023, a Response Fund for Loss and Damage was adopted by the CMA, and ensuring that it is rapidly provided with sufficient resources offer a crucial test for the commitment to sustainable development.[36]

Mobilization and Direction of Climate Finance

Under Article 9 of the Paris Agreement, developed country Parties shall provide financial resources to assist developing country Parties with respect to both mitigation and adaptation, in continuation of their existing UNFCCC obligations (Article 9.1), while other Parties are encouraged to provide financial support voluntarily (Article 9.2). At the same time, it holds, all Parties should increase their efforts in mobilizing climate finance from a wide variety of sources, instruments and channels, noting the significant role of public funds, and taking into account the priorities and needs of developing country parties, with the greater onus being on developed country Parties, which shall take the lead (Article 9.3). Prior to 2025, the COP sets a new collective quantified goal on finance from a floor of USD 100 billion per year.[37] Developed country Parties are strongly urged to scale up their level of financial support, and shall biennially communicate indicative quantitative and qualitative information related to scaling up of the provision and as regards mobilizing financial resources, including the balance between adaptation and mitigation (as per Articles 9.1 and 9.3). The provision of scaled-up financial resources should attempt to balance the provision of mitigation and adaptation resources and take into account country-driven strategies and the priorities and needs of developing country Parties, especially those that are particularly vulnerable to the adverse effects of climate change and have significant capacity constraints, such as LDCs and SIDS.

The principle of equity and the eradication of poverty and the principle of common but differentiated responsibilities and respective capacities (CBDRRC) are reflected in these arrangements, as noted by leading legal scholars.[38] In the Preamble of the Agreement, there are two references to equity and intergenerational equity, and it is noted at Articles 2 and 4 that parties should protect the climate on the basis of equity and the principle of CBDRRC. The importance of efforts to eradicate poverty are also highlighted including in relation to cooperation to implement NDCs at Article 6. The Paris Agreement, to reflect CBDRRC, also commits to the provision and the mobilization of financial assistance (Articles 9.1–3), assistance in adaptation efforts (Article 7.7(d)), facilitation of technology transfer (Article 10.6), and capacity-building (Article 11.1–3).

Sustainable Development Aspects of Further Implementation Measures

Transparency, Global Stock-Taking and Peer Review: By virtue of Article 13, in addition to reporting on mitigation and adaptation, Parties should also regularly provide Communications on a national inventory report of GHG emissions by sources and removals by sinks, prepared using good practice methodologies accepted by the IPCC (Article 13.7(a)), and the information necessary to track progress made in implementing and achieving NDCs (Article 13.7(b)). They should also provide information regarding climate change impacts and adaptation (Article 13.8). Of particular interest to developing countries, there are further transparency accommodations. For developing country Parties, information may be presented on financial, technological and capacity-building support needed and received under Article 9 on climate finance, Article 10 on technology transfer and Article 11 on capacity-building (Article 13.10), as well as on progress made on implementing capacity-building plans, policies, actions or measures to implement the Paris Agreement (Article 11.4). The level of support by developed countries to developing countries are the object of a technical expert review and also of a multilateral consideration of progress (Article 13.11, Article 13.12, Article 13.13). As a further ambition/transparency measure, the Paris Agreement stipulates that its Meetings of the Parties shall periodically take stock of the treaty's implementation, to assess collective progress toward achieving the Treaty's purpose and long-term goals – referred to as the 'GST'. The first GST took place in 2023, culminating in Dubai, in order to inform parties in updating and enhancing, in a nationally determined manner, their actions and support, as well as in enhancing international cooperation for climate action (Article 14.3).[39]

Sustainable Development Market Mechanism and Non-Market Approaches: Under Article 6, Parties may engage in "international transfers of mitigation outcomes" toward their NDCs, through voluntary cooperation, to allow "higher ambition in their mitigation and adaptation actions and to promote sustainable development and environmental integrity" (Article 6.1). When using internationally transferred mitigation outcomes, Parties shall promote sustainable development and ensure environmental integrity and transparency, applying robust accounting and governance to avoid double-counting, consistent with guidance to be adopted by the COP meeting of the Parties to the Paris Agreement (Article 6.2).[40] Further, a "sustainable development mechanism" is established to promote mitigation of GHG emissions while fostering sustainable development; to incentivize and facilitate GHG mitigation by public and private entities authorized by a Party; to contribute to the reduction of emission levels in the host Party, which will benefit from mitigation activities resulting in emission reductions that can also be used by another Party to fulfill its NDC;

and to deliver an overall mitigation in global emissions (Article 6.4). There is also recognition of the importance of non-market approaches, and the definition of a framework to promote them, including public and private sector participation and coordination across instruments and relevant institutional arrangements (Articles 6.8 and 6.9). It is not enough, many would perhaps argue, but it provides a platform to build on.[41]

Cooperation for Capacity-Building: Capacity-building under the Paris Agreement, according to Article 11, should enhance the capacity and ability of developing country Parties to take effective climate action, particularly "countries with the least capacity, such as the least developed countries, and those that are particularly vulnerable to the adverse effects of climate change" (Article 11.1). All countries cooperate to achieve this, and there is a specific provision that developed country Parties should enhance support for capacity-building actions in developing country Parties (Article 11.3). Capacity-building should be country-driven, responsive to national needs, and foster country ownership of Parties, including at the national, subnational and local levels, in particular for developing country Parties (Article 11.2). In essence, an effective, iterative process is called for – one that is participatory, cross-cutting and gender-responsive (Article 11.2), not just assisting with technical capacity for implementing adaptation and mitigation actions, the facilitation of technology development, dissemination and deployment and access to climate finance, but also supporting education, training and public awareness, and the transparent, timely and accurate communication of information (Article 11.1, Article 11.4; see also Article 13.15). The Paris Committee on Capacity-Building (PCCB) was also created, with the aim of addressing gaps and needs in implementing capacity-building in developing country Parties and further enhancing capacity-building efforts.[42]

Education and Public Awareness: The Paris Agreement affirms that Parties shall cooperate in taking measures, as appropriate, to enhance climate change education, training, public awareness, public participation and public access to information, recognizing the importance of these steps with respect to enhancing actions under the Agreement (Article 12). Indeed, these provisions appear to reflect the principle of public participation and access to information and justice, as emphasized in the Paris Agreement (Preamble, para 14). The importance of public participation is underlined throughout the Paris Agreement, including in provisions on mitigation (Article 4), adaptation (Article 7) and on the Sustainable Development Mechanism and non-market approaches (Article 6), which aim to enhance public and private sector participation in the implementation of NDCs. Further, Parties shall enhance education, training, public awareness, public participation and public access to information, recognizing their importance in enhancing actions under the Agreement (Article 12). In essence, the treaty depends on public engagement, informed by the data that is made available through the national communications submitted to international registries, the GST, the peer review and other measures, to assist Parties to progressively intensify their contributions to mitigation, adaptation, finance and other aspects of the global response to climate change. Recognizing 'climate justice' is underscored in the Preamble at paragraph 13,[43] which has been explained as ensuring that:

> communities, individuals and governments have substantive legal and procedural rights relating to the enjoyment of a safe, clean, healthy and sustainable environment and the means to take or cause measures to be taken within their national legislative and judicial systems and, where necessary, at regional and international levels, to mitigate sources of climate change and provide for adaptation to its effects in a manner that respects human rights.[44]

Implementation and Compliance: A mechanism to facilitate implementation of the agreement and promote compliance is also established by the Paris Agreement (Article 15.1) as an expert-based and facilitative committee that operates on a transparent, non-adversarial and non-punitive way, as is discussed in later chapters of this volume.

Conclusion

In conclusion, it is clear that the Paris Agreement has great potential to contribute to sustainable development, in principle and in practice. Given available scientific findings, there can be no sustainable development if the worst-case scenarios for climate change are not averted. Compliance with the Paris Agreement, with due consideration of the applicable principles of international law, is crucial to achieve all global SDGs.[45] Indeed, the New Delhi principle of integration and interrelationship, in relation to human rights and social, economic and environmental objectives is found in the reference to 'climate-resilient development' (Article 2.1(c)), and in the linking of economic growth and sustainable development in the context of technology transfers (Article 10.5). Integration of environmental considerations into economic and social development, while ensuring that climate change actions are economically viable and respect human rights, is also highlighted in the Paris Agreement Preamble (paragraph 11), alongside the need to safeguard food security (paragraph 9) and to respect human rights, gender equality, indigenous rights and the integrity of Mother Earth (Preamble, paragraph 13). Integration is also apparent in the references to economic diversification and sustainable resource management in the context of adaptation (Article 7.9(e)), which also highlight the resilience of socio-economic and ecological systems, underlining the need for adaptation measures to integrate all three objectives.

New international legal developments have transformed and informed the roles and engagement of all the actors involved in the UNFCCC, including State delegations, non-State observers from civil society, academia and the private sector among others and intergovernmental organizations.[46] Jurists, legal institutes and associations, law schools, judges networks, decision-makers, advocates and other members of the law and governance community worldwide have long sought legal and institutional reforms on multiple levels, including international, regional, national and sub-national level, to facilitate, incentivize and mandate effective action on climate change.[47] After a series of international symposia and conferences, backed by independent research and analysis that began at a Climate Law and Governance Symposium in 2005 at the Montreal COP11, a consortium of law faculties from leading universities, together with key research institutes, inter-governmental agencies, law associations, judges' networks, experts commissions and others, launched the Climate Law and Governance Day on 4 December 2015 at the Paris COP21, opening a special forum that has grown to promote informed dialogue between over 6,000 registered experts, practicing jurists, negotiators and decision-makers.[48] Indeed, as the International Bar Association has highlighted, "[t]he need for climate change justice is . . . apparent in the unequal geographic distribution of its environmental effects".[49]

Further, as ILA Climate Change Principles affirm, States have an obligation "to employ due diligence efforts to mitigate climate change impacts" in the design of any social and economic development plan which may result in significant emissions of GHGs (paragraph 5).[50] The International Law Association's Committee on International Law on Sustainable Development, through its follow-up Committee on the Role of International Law into Sustainable Resources Management for Development, have further illuminated the principles and good practices of international law which guide efforts in this field.[51] As mentioned previously and in earlier chapters of this volume, in its 2024 Advisory Opinion on Climate Change, the International Tribunal on the Law of the Sea conclusively found that at 311 that:

> The obligation of cooperation . . . requires States to make an ongoing effort to formulate and elaborate rules, standards and recommended practices and procedures. The adoption of a particular treaty, such as the UNFCCC or the Paris Agreement, does not discharge a State from its obligation to cooperate, as the obligation requires an ongoing effort on the part of States in the development of new or revised regulatory instruments, in particular in light of the evolution of scientific knowledge.[52]

For effective responses to climate change under international law, interactional forms of international law-making under framework treaties are proving to be essential.[53] Many countries plan to reform their laws and institutions across diverse economic, environmental and social sectors in order to respond to the challenges of climate mitigation, resilience, technology, finance and accountability.[54] Indeed, as noted earlier, 169 countries explicitly state their intention to undertake legal and institutional reforms, out of 186 countries with 'NDC' published online by the UNFCCC registry, and over 60 stress specifically the need for legal and institutional capacity-building in order to achieve their NDCs. There is a pressing need for innovative legal knowledge, expertise and capacity-building to address the climate law and governance issues discussed in this chapter, in order to ensure a strengthened agenda for the implementation of the Paris Agreement and the broader global SDGs.

As countries seek to further implement the Paris Agreement, including through the presentation of new and more ambitious NDCs in response to the 2023 Global Stocktake (GST) and the adoption of domestic laws designing their transition to a low-carbon economy, a profound comprehension of the principle of sustainable development and its different parameters will be essential. As recognized in the Agreement itself, new legal research, education, awareness, capacity-building and technical assistance, especially in climate-vulnerable but also in high per-capita emission countries, will be essential to ensure the success of the commitments undertaken in Paris, the avoidance of climate change's most dangerous consequences and the transformation of the world's economies, societies and ecosystems toward sustainability.

Notes

1 With thanks to Prof Cristina Voigt, Dr. Zunaida Moosa Wadiwala and Adv Lydia Young for their substantive insights, drafting assistance and guidance. Thanks are also due to colleagues, collaborators and partners from the global Climate Law and Governance Initiative from 2005 to 2025, especially chairs and other Centre for International Sustainable Development Law (CISDL) experts. This chapter shares thoughts with the author's previous works, including Marie-Claire Cordonier Segger, 'Advancing the Paris Agreement on Climate Change for Sustainable Development' (2017) 5(2) CJICL 202 and Marie-Claire Cordonier Segger, 'Sustainable Development through the 2015 Paris Agreement' (2017) 11(2) Canadian International Lawyer 124. It also draws on Caroline Haywood and others, 'Legal Frameworks for Implementing REDD+ in Zambia, Mozambique and Tanzania: Opportunities for a Sustainable Landscapes Approach' (2015) 9(2) Carbon Climate Law Review 130 and Marie-Claire Cordonier Segger and Yolanda Saito, 'Innovative Legal Measures for Climate Change Response in the Green Economy: Integrating Opportunity, Equity and Inclusion' (2013) World Bank Legal Review 5, among other works.

2 UNCHR Res 7/23 (2008) UN Doc A/HRC/RES/7/23; UNGA Res 63/32 (26 November 2008) UN Doc A/RES/63/32; UNCHR Res 10/4 (2009) UN Doc A/HRC/RES/10/4; UNGA Res 63/281 (3 June 2009) UN Doc A/RES/63/281; Report of the Secretary-General 'Climate Change and its Possible Security

Implications' (2009) UN Doc A/64/350; UNSC Presidential Statement (2011) UN Doc S/PRST/2011/15; UNCHR Res 18/22 (2011); UN Doc A/HRC/RES/18/22.

3 IPCC, *Climate Change 2023: Synthesis Report. Contribution of Working Groups I, II and III to the Sixth Assessment Report of the Intergovernmental Panel on Climate Change* Core Writing Team, Hoesung Lee and José Romero, eds, Geneva: IPCC 35-115, <doi:10.59327/IPCC/AR6-9789291691647>; Mizan Khan, David Mfitumukiza and Saleemul Huq. 'Capacity Building for Implementation of Nationally Determined Contributions under the Paris Agreement' *Climate Policy* 20:4 2020 499–510; Xira Ruiz-Campillo, 'Post-Paris Agreement Negotiations: A Commitment to Multilateralism despite the Lack of Funding' (2024) 156 Environmental Science & Policy 103754 <https://doi.org/10.1016/j.envsci.2024.103754>.

4 Climate Law and Governance Initiative partners include CISDL, which hosts the secretariat together with a circle of leading university and independent institutes, governments, the International Law Association and the International Bar Association, in collaboration with experts from the International Development Law Organization, UNDP, UNEP, the IUCN World Commission for Environmental Law, the Asian Development Bank, the European Bank for Reconstruction and Development, the World Bank and other international organizations. <www.climatelawgovernance.org> accessed 10 April 2024.

5 See 'Background' (United Nations Millennium Development Goals, 2000) <https://www.un.org/millenniumgoals/bkgd.shtml> accessed 18 June 2024.

6 See also Malcolm Langford, Andy Sumner and Alicia Ely Yamin (eds), *The Millennium Development Goals and Human Rights* (CUP 2013).

7 See United Nations, *Millennium Development Goals Report 2015* (United Nations 2015) 4–7.

8 Transforming our World: The 2030 Agenda for Sustainable Development UNGA Res 70/1 (25 September 2015) UN Doc A/RES/70/1.

9 Marie-Claire Cordonier Segger and Damilola Sunday Olawuyi, *Sustainable Development Law: Principles, Practices and Prospects* (2nd edn, OUP 2025 forthcoming); Winfried Huck, *Sustainable Development Goals: Article-by-Article Commentary* (Beck C.H. 2022).

10 *Request for an Advisory Opinion Submitted by the Commission of Small Island States on Climate Change and International Law (No 31)* (Advisory Opinion of 21 May 2024) ITLOS Reports 2024, 66, 122, 243, 252, 270, 283, 311.

11 Paris Agreement (adopted 12 December 2015) UN Doc FCCC/CP/2015/L.9/Rev.1.

12 United Nations Framework Convention on Climate Change (adopted 9 May 1992, entered into force 21 March 1994) 1771 UNTS 107 (UNFCCC).

13 Kyoto Protocol to the United Nations Framework Convention on Climate Change (adopted 11 December 1997, entered into force 16 February 2005) 2303 UNTS 148 (Kyoto Protocol).

14 Sandrine Maljean-Dubois and Pilar Moraga Sariego, 'Le principe des responsabilités communes mais differenciées dans le régime international du climat' (2014) 55 Cahiers de Droit 83.

15 In accordance with articles 20 and 21 of the Kyoto Protocol, ratification by 75% of the Parties present and voting at the meeting is necessary for the Doha Amendment to come into force (144 Parties).

16 Paris Agreement (n 7).

17 UNFCCC Article 4 (n 9).

18 The principles in Article 3 UNFCCC (n 9) include intergenerational and intra-generational equity, common but differentiated responsibility, precaution, *right to sustainable development* and nondiscrimination.

19 Note the shift from differentiation as adopted by the UNFCCC (n 9).

20 Marie-Claire Cordonier Segger and others, '169 NDCs of 186 Registered to the UNFCCC Explicitly Prioritize Legal and Institutional Reform in Plans to Contribute to the Global Response to Climate Change' (Climate Law and Governance Initiative and Centre for International Sustainable Development Law December 2021). Thanks and recognition are due to CISDL senior fellows, lead counsel and researchers including Dr. Markus W. Gehring, Adv Ayman Cherkaoui and Prof Christina Voigt, together with a team of University of Cambridge graduates whose contributions to the study have proven invaluable <www.cisdl.org> accessed 10 April 2024; <www.climatelawgovernance.org> accessed 10 April 2024. See also Marie-Claire Cordonier Segger, Mirjam Reiner and Alexandra Scott, 'Countries Stress Importance of Legal and Institutional Reforms in their iNDCs' (Climate Law and Governance Initiative September 2016) <www.climatelawgovernance.org/knowledge-centre.html> accessed 7 September 2016.

21 ibid 5.

22 International Law Association, 'New Delhi Declaration on the Principles of International Law Related to Sustainable Development', Resolution 3/2002; Nico Schrijver and Friedl Weiss (eds), *International Law and Sustainable Development: Principles and Practice* (Martinus Nijhoff 2004) 1–152, 699–706;

Cordonier Segger and Khalfan, Cordonier Segger and Olawuyi (n 6) 95–191; Duncan French, *International Law and Policy of Sustainable Development* (MUP 2005); Marie-Claire Cordonier Segger, 'Significant Developments in Sustainable Development Law and Governance: A Proposal' (2004) 28 Natural Resources Forum 61; Marie-Claire Cordonier Segger and others, 'Prospects for Principles of International Sustainable Development Law after the WSSD: Common but Differentiated Responsibilities, Precaution and Participation' (2003) 12 RECIEL 54. See also seven CISDL Legal Working Papers detailing the meaning, scope and existing status in international law of each ILA New Delhi Declaration Principle, online: <http://cisdl.org/public/docs/new_delhi_declaration.pdf> accessed 12 June 2016.

23 See Marie-Claire Cordonier Segger and Elizabeth Mrema (eds), 'The Contribution of International Law, Policy and Governance to the Sustainable Development Goals' (Issue Briefs, CISDL/UNEP 2016).

24 SDG 13 requires 'urgent action to combat climate change and its impacts, acknowledging that the UNFCCC is the primary international, intergovernmental forum for negotiating the global response to climate change'. See UNGA Res 70/1 (n 3) 14.

25 See John H Knox, 'Linking Human Rights and Climate Change at the United Nations' (2009) 33 Harv Envtl L Rev 477; John H Knox, 'Climate Change and Human Rights Law' (2009) 50 Va J Int'l L 163.

26 See Jutta Brunee and Stephen J Toope, *Legitimacy and Legality in International Law: An Interactional Account* (CUP 2010).

27 Marie-Claire Cordonier Segger and Damilola Sunday Olawuyi, *Sustainable Development Law: Principles, Practices, and Prospects* (2nd edn, OUP 2025 forthcoming). See also Christina Voigt, *Sustainable Development as a Principle of International Law: Resolving Conflicts between Climate Measures and WTO Law* (BRILL 2009).

28 Marie-Claire Cordonier Segger with C J Weeramantry (ed), *Sustainable Development in International Courts and Tribunals* (Routledge 2017).

29 Marie-Claire Cordonier Segger and C J Weeramantry (eds), *Sustainable Justice* (Martinus Nijhoff 2004) 561–92.

30 Marie-Claire Cordonier Segger, 'Sustainable Development in International Law' in David Armstrong (ed), *Routledge Handbook on International Law* (Routledge 2009) 355.

31 Christina Voigt, ed, *Research Handbook on REDD-Plus and International Law* (Cheltenham: Edward Elgar 2016); Christina Voigt et al, 'The Paris Agreement and the Relevance of the Warsaw Framework for REDD+ (WFR)' Review of European, Comparative and International Environmental Law 2024.

32 Nathalie Seddon, Alison Smith, Pete Smith, Isabel Key, Alexandre Chausson, Cécile Girardin, Jo House, Shilpi Srivastava, Beth Turner, 'Getting the Message Right on Nature-Based Solutions to Climate Change' 27 (2021) 1518 Global Change Biology <doi:10.1111/gcb.15513>; Cécile AJ Girardin, Stuart Jenkins, Nathalie Seddon, Myles Allen, Simon L Lewis, Charlotte E Wheeler, Bronson W Griscom and Yadvinder Malhi, 'Nature-Based Solutions Can Help Cool the Planet —If We Act Now' (2021) 191 Nature <www.nature.com/articles/d41586-021-01241-2>; Meinhard Doelle and Tony George Puthucherril, 'Nature-Based Solutions to Sea Level Rise and Other Climate Change Impacts on Oceanic and Coastal Environments: A Law and Policy Perspective' (2023) e03051 Nordic Journal of Botany <doi:10.1111/njb.03051>; Stella Manes et al, 'Nature-Based Solutions Promote Climate Change Adaptation Safeguarding Ecosystem Services' 55 (2022) Ecosystem Services 101439 <doi:10.1016/j.ecoser.2022.101439>; Salvatore Martire et al, *Understanding the Scaling Potential of Nature-based Solutions* (Copenhagen: EEA Europe 2022).

33 María Eugenia Recio, 'Shaping REDD+: Interactions between Bilateral and Multilateral Rulemaking' 34 (1) (2022) Journal of Environmental Law 83 <doi:10.1093/jel/eqab025>; Julia Dehm, *Reconsidering REDD+: Authority, Power and Law in the Green Economy* (Cambridge: Cambridge University Press 2021); Frank Akowuge Dugasseh and Mikael Skou Andersen, 'Non-Carbon Benefits of REDD+ Implementation and Sustainable Emission Reductions: A Review' (2024) 1 Forests, Trees and Livelihoods <doi:10.1080/14728028.2024.2383737>.

34 Chandini Singh, Soundarya Iyer, Mark G New, Roger Few, Bhavana Kuchimanchi, Alcade C. Segnon, and Daniel Morchain, 'Interrogating 'Effectiveness' in Climate Change Adaptation: 11 Guiding Principles for Adaptation Research and Practice' 14:7 (2021) Climate and Development 650–664; Lena I Fuldauer, Scott Thacker, Robyn A Haggis, Francesco Fuso-Nerini, Robert J Nicholls and Jim W Hall, 'Targeting Climate Adaptation to Safeguard and Advance the Sustainable Development Goals' 13 (2022) Nature Communications 3579; Anna McGinn and Cindy Isenhour, 'Negotiating the Future of the Adaptation Fund: On the Politics of Defining and Defending Justice in the Post-Paris Agreement Period' 21:3 (2021) Climate Policy 383–395; Karolina Mordasewicz and Marcin Kowalczyk, 'Legal Aspects of Adaptation

Finance under the UNFCCC Regime with Special Reference to the Adaptation Fund' 23:2–3 (2021) International Community Law Review 168–183; Pranay Arora, 'COP28: Ambitions, Realities, and Future' 7:1 (2024) Environmental Sustainability 107–113.

35 Morten Broberg, 'Interpreting the UNFCCC's Provisions on 'Mitigation' and 'Adaptation' in Light of the Paris Agreement's Provision on 'Loss and Damage'' 20:5 (2020) Climate Policy 527–533; Linda Siegele, "Loss and Damage under the Paris Agreement" in Meinhard Doelle and Sara L Seck, eds, *Research Handbook on Climate Change Law and Loss and Damage* (Cheltenham: Edward Elgar 2021); Harjeet Singh and Sindra Sharma, 'A People-Centred Approach to Assess and Address Impacts of Climate Change-Induced Loss and Damage' in Vositha Wijenayake, Linda Anne Stevenson, Akio Takemoto, Amit Ranjan, Dennis Mombauer, Nafesa Ismail, eds, *Linking Climate Change Adaptation, Disaster Risk Reduction, and Loss & Damage* (London: Palgrave Macmillan 2024) 29–45; Ike Uri, Stacy-ann Robinson, J Timmons Roberts, David Ciplet, Romain Weikmans and Mizan Khan, 'Equity and Justice in Loss and Damage Finance: A Narrative Review of Catalysts and Obstacles' 10:3 (2024) Current Climate Change Reports 33–45.

36 Mario Mendillo, 'COP27 and the Path to Implementing the Paris Agreement Targets: Opportunities and Critical Issues in the Light of the Establishment of the Loss and Damage Fund.' *Biolaw Journal-Rivista di Biodiritto* 2 (2023) 197–215; Moleen Monita Nand, Douglas K Bardsley and Jungho Suh. 'Climate Change Loss and Damage Governance. Where Are We Now? A Case Study from Fiji's Sugar Industry' 28:6 (2023) Local Environment 768–783; Diane Kraal, *A Just Transition to Decarbonisation: Themes of Loss and Damage, Transport, Nature and Youth* (London: Palgrave Macmillan 2023).

37 Sherri Ombuya, Igor Shishlov and Axel Michaelowa, 'International Climate Finance from a Global Perspective' Austrian Foundation for Development Research OFSE Working Paper 76, 2023; Igor Shishlov and Philipp Censkowsky, 'Same but Different? Understanding Divergent Definitions of and Views on Climate Finance' *Handbook of International Climate Finance* (Cheltenham: Edward Elgar 2022) 16–39; W Pieter Pauw, Michael König, Khayala Sadikhova, Tim Stutzmann 'Financing Low-carbon and Climate Resilient Development: Do Countries Integrate Article 2.1(c) of the Paris Agreement in their Long-Term Strategies?' Frankfurt am Main: Frankfurt School - UNEP Collaborating Centre for Climate and Sustainable Energy Finance, 2021.

38 Christina Voigt, 'Equity in the 2015 Climate Agreement' (2014) 4 Climate Law 50.

39 UNFCCC, *2023 Synthesis Report on Global Stocktake Elements* (4 October 2023); UNFCCC, *Technical Dialogue of the First Global Stocktake: Synthesis Report by the Co-facilitators of the Technical Dialogue* FCCC/SB/2023/9 (8 September 2023); Lukas Hermwille, Adis Dzebo, Gabriela Ileana Iacobuţă and Wolfgang Obergassel. 'Global Stocktake and the SDG Midterm Review as Opportunities for Integration' 13:10 (2023) Nature Climate Change 1002–4; Harro van Asselt, Wolfgang Obergassel, Catherine Hall, Lukas Hermwille, Sebastian Oberthür, Simon Otto, María José Sanz, Chun Xia-Bauer, 'Leveraging the Global Stocktake for Effective Sectoral Climate Governance' 2:6 (2023) e0000229 PLOS Clim; Manjana Milkoreit and Kate Haapala, 'The Global Stocktake: Design Lessons for a New Review and Ambition Mechanism in the International Climate Regime' *International Environmental Agreements: Politics, Law and Economics* 19 (2019) 89; Brian Preston, 'Can Litigation Assist in Implementing the Outcome of the Global Stocktake?' *Journal of Energy & Natural Resources Law* 41 (2023) 457; Daniel Puig, 'Loss and Damage in the Global Stocktake' *Climate Policy* 22 (2022) 175; Christopher Campbell-Duruflé, 'A Legal Standard for State Mitigation Efforts: Is National Discretion Bound to Shrink over Time?' in Alexander Zahar, ed, *Research Handbook on the Law of the Paris Agreement* (Cheltenham: Edward Elgar Publishing 2024) 82.

40 See Kishan Khoday, 'Mobilizing Market Forces to Combat Global Environmental Change: Lessons from UN-Private Sector Partnerships in China' (2007) 16 Rev Euro Comm & Int'l Envt 173; Christina Voigt 'WTO Law and International Emissions Trading: Is there Potential for Conflict?' (2008) 2 CCLR 54.

41 Harro van Asselt, Michael Mehling and Kati Kulovesi, `The Evolving Architecture of Global Climate Law; in Leonie Reins and Jonathan Verschuuren, eds, *Research Handbook on Climate Change Mitigation Law* (Cheltenham: Edward Elgar, 2022) <doi:10.4337/9781839101595.00007>; Joanna Depledge, Miguel Saldivia and Cristina Peñasco, `Glass Half Full or Glass Half Empty?: The 2021 Glasgow Climate Conference' 22 (2022) Climate Policy 147.

42 UNFCCC, 'Enhancing the Ownership of Developing Countries of Building and Maintaining Capacity for Climate Action' PCCB Technical Paper UNFCCC 21 January 2022; Mizan Khan, Mizan, David Mfitumukiza and Saleemul Huq 'Capacity Building for Implementation of Nationally Determined Contributions under the Paris Agreement.' 20:4 (2020) Climate Policy 499–510.

43 Cordonier Segger and Weeramantry (n 29).

44 International Bar Association, Climate Change Justice and Human Rights Task Force, *Achieving Justice and Human Rights in an Era of Climate Disruption* (IBA 2014).

45 Marie-Claire Cordonier Segger and Elizabeth Mrema (eds), 'Contributions of International Law to Implementing the Sustainable Development Goals' (CISDL/UNEP 2016). See also Usha Natarajan and Kishan Khoday, 'Locating Nature: Making and Unmaking International Law' (2014) 27 LJIL 573.

46 See for instance Kenneth W Abbott and Duncan Snidal, 'Strengthening International Regulation Through Transnational New Governance: Overcoming the Orchestration Deficit' (2009) Vand J Transnat'l L 501; Matthew Hoffmann, *Climate Governance at the Crossroads: Experimenting with a Global Response after Kyoto* (OUP 2011); Harriet Bulkeley and others, *Transnational Climate Change Governance* (CUP 2014). Christopher Campbell-Durufle is recognized and thanked for excellent insights on these points.

47 Kelly Levin and others, 'Overcoming the Tragedy of Super Wicked Problems: Constraining Our Future Selves to Ameliorate Global Climate Change' (2012) 45 Policy Sciences 123.

48 Report from Climate Law and Governance Day, Middlesex University Dubai/University of Dubai/University of Cambridge, Dubai 5 December 2023 (Climate Law and Governance Initiative Dubai 2023); Report from Climate Law and Governance Day, La Sorbonne Faculty of Law, Pantheon-Sorbonne University, Paris, 4 December 2015 (Climate Law and Governance Initiative Paris 2015); Report from Climate Law and Governance Official Side Event to the UNFCCC COP21 in Paris, 11 December 2014 (Climate Law and Governance Initiative Paris 2015) <www.climatelawgovernance.org>.

49 IBA, Climate Change Justice and Human Rights Task Force (n 33) 45.

50 International Law Association Committee on the Legal Principles Relating to Climate Change, *Legal Principles Relating to Climate Change*' (ILA 2014) 35. See also Expert Group on Global Climate Obligations 'Oslo Principles on Global Obligations to Reduce Climate Change' (adopted 1 March 2015).

51 Nico Schrijver and Friedl Weiss (eds), *International Law and Sustainable Development: Principles and Practice* (Martinus Nijhoff 2004) 1–152, 699–706; Duncan French, *International Law and Policy of Sustainable Development* (MUP 2005); Marie-Claire Cordonier Segger and CJ Weeramantry (eds), *Sustainable Justice* (Martinus Nijhoff 2004) 561–92.

52 *Request for an Advisory Opinion Submitted by the Commission of Small Island States on Climate Change and International Law (No 31)* (Advisory Opinion of 21 May 2024) ITLOS Reports 2024, 66, 311.

53 Toope and Brunnee, *Legitimacy and Legality in International Law* (n 22).

54 See for instance Robert Kibugi, 'Mainstreaming Climate Change into Public Policy Functions: Legal Options to Reinforce Sustainable Development of Kenya' (2012) 8 Fla A & M UL Rev 205; Robert Kibugi, 'Legal Options for Mainstreaming Climate Change Disaster Risk Reduction in Governance for Kenya', in KOH Kheng-Lian (ed), *Adaptation to Climate Change, ASEAN and Comparative Experiences* (WSPC 2015) 409.

4

THE UNFCCC, THE PARIS AGREEMENT AND LEGAL OBLIGATIONS FOR CLIMATE ACTION

Christina Voigt and Lydia Young

The Purpose of the UN Framework Convention on Climate Change (UNFCCC) and Paris Agreement Architecture

The UNFCCC and the Paris Agreement were designed to enable Parties to effectively collaborate on mitigation of and adaptation to climate change.

The UNFCCC and Paris Agreement are legally binding treaties under international law; however, they contain both binding and non-binding components. These agreements are also composed of both substantive and procedural obligations for Parties that are complementary to one another. The UNFCCC sets out a broad objective and foundational principles for mitigating climate change. The Paris Agreement, conversely, sets out a global temperature threshold of holding temperature increases to well below 2°C above pre-industrial levels and pursuing efforts to limit them to 1.5°C, and provides extensive procedural obligations in the form of communication of Nationally Determined Contributions (NDCs) and reporting requirements.

The legal obligations under the UNFCCC and the Paris Agreement were intentionally designed to 'strike a careful balance between broad participation and a level of commitment that matter[s] in the fight against climate change'.[1] Stringent obligations with high climate ambition 'can be detrimental to broad participation' of international agreements.[2] This can be seen, for example, by the Kyoto Protocol, which has been viewed as 'pushing the provisions beyond negotiators' comfort zones'.[3] As such, the Paris Agreement does not incorporate binding targets for individual countries, but instead is based on individual pledges combined with international guidance, reporting and review.

The UNFCCC Legal Architecture

The UNFCCC sets out its objective in Article 2 and guiding principles in Article 3.

Article 2 states that the ultimate objective of the Convention, and any related instruments (such as the Paris Agreement) are as follows:

> The ultimate objective of this Convention and any related legal instrument that the Conference of Parties may adopt is to achieve, in accordance with the relevant provisions of the Convention, stabilization of greenhouse gas concentrations in the atmosphere at a level that

DOI: 10.4324/9781003276678-5

would prevent dangerous anthropogenic interference with the climate system. Such a level should be achieved within a time frame sufficient to allow ecosystems to adapt naturally to climate change, to ensure that food production is not threatened and to enable economic development to proceed in a sustainable manner.[4]

There are several principles under Article 3 that Parties 'shall be guided' by during implementation of the UNFCCC, including:

1) Intergenerational equity and the principle of common but differentiated responsibilities and respective capabilities;[5]
2) 'The specific needs and special circumstances of developing country Parties, especially those that are particularly vulnerable to the adverse effects of climate change, and those Parties, especially developing country Parties, that would have to bear a disproportionate or abnormal burden under the Convention, should be given full consideration';[6]
3) The precautionary principle;[7]
4) The right to sustainable development;[8] and
5) Sustainable international economic growth and development and the avoidance of 'unjustifiable discrimination or a disguised restriction on international trade'.[9]

Article 4 sets out Parties' commitments under the UNFCCC. There are three levels of obligations contained under Article 4. First are obligations of all Parties, which are set out in Article 4(1). Second, Article 4(2) sets out differentiated obligations for *developed* country Parties and other Parties under Annex I, which include adopting national policies and measures on the mitigation of climate change which are supposed that those Parties demonstrate taking the lead. This provisions also contains flexibilities for these Parties in implementing their commitments (which eventually led to the creation of global carbon markets) under Article 4(6) and communicating 'supplementary information' under Article 12(2). Third are obligations of financial and technological assistance to be undertaken only by those developed country Parties listed in Annex II.

The Paris Agreement Legal Architecture

The Paris Agreement was adopted in 2015 at the 21st UNFCCC Conference of Parties and is considered to be a successful reflection of years of negotiation that 'instill[s] a sense of fairness and trust among parties by striking the necessary balance between the efforts of developed and developing countries'.[10] The adoption shortly followed the IPCC's 2014 Fifth Assessment Report, which clearly stipulated that anthropogenic climate change was 'unequivocal'.[11] As mentioned earlier, the Paris Agreement sets a global threshold of limiting temperature increases to well below 2°C above pre-industrial levels and pursuing efforts to limit them to 1.5°C,[12] and provides a combination of substantive and procedural legal obligations that are intended to ensure effective and ambitious climate mitigation and adaptation.

The Paris Agreement is composed of a Preamble and 29 operative articles, which set out the Agreement's scope and definitions, main objectives, obligations and institutional provisions.[13]

Article 4 contains some of the binding components under the Paris Agreement (although there are also non-binding components). One of the most notable legally binding requirements under Article 4 is the requirement for Parties to develop progressively more ambitious NDCs:

> Each Party shall prepare, communicate and maintain successive nationally determined contributions that it intends to achieve. Parties shall pursue domestic mitigation measures, with the aim of achieving the objectives of such contributions. (Article 4.2)

> Each Party's successive Nationally Determined Contribution <u>will</u> represent a progression beyond the Party's then current Nationally determined Contribution and reflect its highest possible ambition, reflecting its common but differentiated responsibilities and respective capabilities in light of different national circumstances. (Article 4.3)
>
> In addition, the Paris Agreement contains legal guidance on the scope of NDCs in Article 4.4:
>
> Developed country Parties should continue taking the lead by undertaking economy-wide absolute emission reduction targets. Developing country Parties should continue enhancing their mitigation efforts, and are encouraged to move over time towards economy-wide emission reduction or limitation targets in the light of different national circumstances. (Article 4.4)

Article 4.9 established the frequency of NDC communication and the requirement that NDCs are informed by the outcome of the global stocktake:

> Each Party shall communicate a nationally determined contribution every five years in accordance with decision 1/CP21 and any relevant decisions of the Conference of the Parties serving as the meeting of the Parties to this Agreement and be informed by the outcomes of the global stocktake referred to in Article 14. (Article 4.9)

Paris Agreement Objectives

The Paris Agreement's primary objective is the overarching temperature threshold under Article 2.1, which can be described as an 'collective goal':[14]

This Agreement, in enhancing the implementation of the Convention, including its objective, <u>aims</u> to strengthen the global response to the threat of climate change, in the context of sustainable development and efforts to eradicate poverty, by:

(a) Holding the increase in the global average temperature to well below 2°C above pre-industrial levels and pursuing efforts to limit the temperature increase to 1.5°C above pre-industrial levels, recognizing that this would significantly reduce the risks and impacts of climate change;
(b) Increasing the ability to adapt to the adverse impacts of climate change and foster climate resilience and low greenhouse gas emissions development, in a manner that does not threaten food production; and
(c) Making finance flows consistent with a pathway toward low greenhouse gas emissions and climate-resilient development.[15]

Further, in order to achieve this long-term temperature goal, Article 4(1) stipulates the following:

> In order to achieve the long-term temperature goal set out in Article 2, Parties aim to reach global peaking of greenhouse gas emissions as soon as possible, recognizing that peaking will take longer for developing country Parties, and to undertake rapid reductions thereafter in accordance with best available science, so as to achieve a balance between anthropogenic emissions by sources and removals by sinks of greenhouse gases in the second half of this century, on the basis of equity, and in the context of sustainable development and efforts to eradicate poverty.[16]

Other substantive objectives include Article 5(1), for preserving ecosystems through climate mitigation efforts, including conserving greenhouse gas reservoirs and sinks, 'including biomass, forests and oceans as well as other terrestrial, coastal and marine ecosystems'.[17] Article 5(2) incorporates the entire framework of existing decisions on REDD+ (reducing emissions from deforestation and forest degradation in developing countries) and encourages Parties to take action to implement and support REDD+.[18] Article 7 establishes a 'global goal on adaptation of enhancing adaptative capacity, strengthening resilience and reducing vulnerability to climate change'.[19] Article 7 acknowledges that adaptation efforts should

> follow a country-driven, gender-responsive, participator and fully transparent approach, taking into consideration vulnerable groups, communities and ecosystems, and should be based on and guided by the best available science as, as appropriate, traditional knowledge, knowledge of indigenous peoples an local knowledge systems.[20]

Obligations under the Paris Agreement

Most of the Paris Agreement obligations are 'procedural in nature and require Parties to submit certain types of information at certain points in time or in regular periods or to report or account in accordance with agreed rules'.[21] These procedural obligations are set out in Articles 4, 7, 9, 10, 11 and 13. Such obligations 'require certain action (or omission) and can, therefore, be considered to establish obligations of result that are also judicially or quasi-judicially reviewable'.[22]

One of the Paris Agreement's primary procedural obligations pertains to 'preparing, communicating and maintaining' NDCs (see *supra* for relevant text). Under Article 4(2), each party 'shall communicate and maintain successive nationally determined contributions'. Moreover, when communicating their NDCs, Parties must provide sufficient information for 'clarity, transparency and understanding' (Article 4(8)).[23] NDCs must be communicated every five years and 'be informed by the outcomes of the "global stocktake" referred to in Article 14 (Article 4(9))'.[24] The first global stocktake occurred in 2023 at CMA5 in Dubai.[25]

The Agreement further provides guidance and expectations on the substantive content of these plans which Parties need to take into account when preparing and communicating their NDC. These parameters establish as an obligation of conduct or due diligence obligation in relation to the primary obligation of communicating an NDC. Examples of such due diligence obligations are that each NDC must 'represent a progression beyond the Party's then current [NDC] and reflect its highest possible ambition' (Article 4.3).[26]

A second set of obligations lies in Article 13, which establishes the enhanced transparency framework. Article 13 requires each Party to provide certain information, including a national inventory report and information required to effectively track progress in implementing and achieving its NDC under Article 4.[27] Relatedly, the governing body of the Paris Agreement, the Conference of the Parties serving as the Meeting of the Parties to the Paris Agreement (CMA), will utilize, *inter alia*, such information to periodically undertake the global stocktake, which is to assess collective progress of implementing the goals of the Paris Agreement under Article 14.

The Paris Agreement also sets out differentiated collective legal obligations depending on whether a Party is considered 'developed' or 'developing'. Under Article 9(1), developed country parties 'shall provide financial resources to assist developed country parties with respect to both mitigation and adaptation', while other parties are encouraged to provide or continue to provide such support voluntarily (Article 9(2)).[28] Article 9(3) establishes collective obligations on the mobilization of finance where

> As part of a global effort, developed country Parties should continue to take the lead in mobilizing climate finance from a wide variety of sources, instruments and channels, noting the significant role of public funds, through a variety of actions, including supporting country-driven strategies, and taking into account the needs and priorities of developing country Parties.

It is in this context that the collective finance goal of 100bn USD annually applies, which is currently under negotiation to adopt a new quantified collective goal by 2024.

The Paris Agreement intentionally uses the term 'developed country Parties', rather than the reference to Annex I and Annex II employed by the UNFCCC. However, developed and developing countries are not defined, nor are there criteria for establishing these categories, under the Paris Agreement (see more discussion on this *infra*).

Note that there are further procedural and capacity building objectives under the Agreement not addressed in detail within this Chapter. Moreover, Article 8 addresses loss and damages associated with climate change challenges and impacts. Under Article 8, parties 'recognize' the need to avert, minimize and address loss and damage, and to utilize the Warsaw International Mechanism for Loss and Damage associated with Climate Change Impacts to achieve this end.[29] Further, Article 11 states that the Paris Agreement should enhance the capacity of development countries and least developed countries such that these countries can, *inter alia,* 'take effective climate change action'.[30]

Design Features for Increasing Ambition

The Paris Agreement has been intentionally designed to constantly increase state ambition in implementing climate action at a domestic level. These design features include the iterative, 5-yearly processes for communication of successive NDCs and the Global Stocktakes to inform the next round of NDCs. Moreover, a dynamic application of the common but differentiated responsibilities and respective capabilities principle, in the light of different national circumstances (CBDRRC) and the principles of highest possible ambition and progression contained in the NDC requirement also aim at increasing ambition.

CBDRRC is reflected, albeit differently, under both the Paris Agreement and the UNFCCC.[31] CBDRRC can increase state ambition because it can create perceptions of fairness and equity, which in turn can increase state participation.[32] A key feature of the Paris Agreement design that distinguished it from the Kyoto Protocol and UNFCCC was the notion that the Paris Agreement would be 'applicable to all' to reflect the 'need to increase the collective level of ambition and ensure the highest possible mitigation efforts by *all* parties'.[33] As such, the Paris Agreement's CBDRRC approach is 'more diversified' than the UNFCCC by adding the qualifier 'in the light of different national circumstances'. Moreover, while the categories 'developing' and 'developed' country parties are still relevant, they are not defined or categorized in an Annex, which represented a 'big shift' in design.[34] The aim of this dynamic and diversified CBDRRC approach was to 'reflect the responsibilities, capacities, and circumstances of all parties'.[35] This general principled character of CBDRRC allows parties to adjust their Paris Agreement obligations to 'changing political, social and economic circumstances'.[36]

A second design feature are the principles of highest possible ambition and progression built into Article 4's NDC requirement. These principles 'inform the level of ambition of the Parties' efforts'.[37] Article 4 requires each successive NDC to 'reflect its highest possible ambition, reflecting its common but differentiated responsibilities and respective capabilities, in the light of different national circumstances'.[38] Such expressive language is 'a potent and powerful tool' for raising ambition; it 'reflects an expectation that all Parties will deploy their best efforts in setting their national mitigation targets and in pursuing domestic measures to achieve them'.[39]

The principle of the highest possible ambition aligns with the duty of due diligence in international law, and essentially requires that Parties deploy their best efforts in setting their national mitigation targets and in pursuing domestic measures to achieve them. In the context of the Paris Agreement, this standard requires Parties to act in proportion to the risk at stake and to their individual capacity, considering that those efforts should progress over time.[40]

Accordingly, Parties must make every effort within their means to progressively protect the rights and interests at stake, which includes limiting the rise in global temperature to below 2°C and striving to limit it to 1.5°C. Additionally, in line with the due diligence principle, Article 4(3) mandates the identification of the highest achievable mitigation ambition that is not overly burdensome or impossible to achieve economically. This mitigation goal should be comprehensive and based on a thorough assessment of mitigation options in all relevant sectors. The Parties must utilize all political, legal, socio-economic, financial and institutional capacities and possibilities in defining such a target. 'Highest possible ambition' as a standard of conduct and due diligence needs to be adopted by the Parties while formulating and communicating their NDCs every five years. States must act with care and use appropriate measures in matters of international importance. The level of care required is proportional to the degree of risk they may face or are exposed to. As the level of potential harm increases, so does the duty of care required to prevent it.

Furthermore, they must plan their climate policies holistically and with a long-term outlook, as stipulated in Article 4(19), which requires Parties to aim to formulate and communicate long-term strategies for low GHG emissions.

Moreover, Article 4 also establishes in paragraphs 4 and 5 that developed country Parties should continue taking the lead by undertaking economy-wide absolute emission reduction targets. Developing country Parties should continue enhancing their mitigation efforts and are encouraged to move over time towards economy-wide emission reduction or limitation targets in the light of different national circumstances.

It further states that '[s]upport shall be provided to developing country Parties for the implementation of this Article, in accordance with Articles 9, 10, and 11, recognizing that enhanced support for developing country Parties will allow for higher ambition in their actions'.

Conclusion

This chapter provides a brief overview of the legal framework and obligations contained under the UNFCCC and Paris Agreement. It discusses the overarching objectives and principles of these agreements, in addition to binding legal requirements. The chapter offers some analysis of the Paris Agreement's design for increasing States' ambition for domestic climate action. Overall, the chapter provides context that will assist the reader in their understanding of other chapters contained within this *Routledge Handbook*.

Notes

1 Christina Voigt, 'The Compliance and Implementation Mechanism of the Paris Agreement' (2016) 25(2) RECIEL 161 <https://doi.org/10.1111/reel.12155>, 161 (Voigt).
2 ibid.
3 Trudy Fraser, 'A Comparative Architectural Analysis of the 1997 Kyoto Protocol and the 2015 Paris Agreement and Other to Counter Environmental "Ratification Fatigue"' in Vesselin Popovski (ed), *The Implementation of the Paris Agreement on Climate Change* (Routledge 2019) 47.
4 United Nations Framework Convention on Climate Change (entered into force 21 March 1994) 1771 UNTS 107, Article 2 (UNFCCC).
5 ibid Article 3(1).
6 ibid Article 3(2).
7 ibid Article 3(3).
8 ibid Article 3(4).
9 ibid Article 3(5).
10 Fraser (n 3) 45–46; quoting Huang, 'The 2015 Climate Agreement: Key Lessons Learned and Legal Issues on the Road to Paris' (2015), SSRN <https://dx.doi.org/10.2139/ssrn.2724109>.
11 IPCC, 'Climate Change 2014: Synthesis Report. Contribution of Working Groups I, II and III to the Fifth Assessment Report of the Intergovernmental Panel on Climate Change' (2014) 2.
12 Paris Agreement, Parties to the 1992 United Nations Framework Convention on Climate Change (adopted 12 December 2015, entered into force 4 November 2016) 3156 UNTS 79, Article 2(1)(a).
13 Leonie Reins and Geert van Calster, 'Introduction' in Geert van Calster and Leonie Reins (eds), *The Paris Agreement on Climate Change: A Commentary* (Edward Elgar 2021) 1.
14 ibid.
15 Paris Agreement (n 12) Article 2(1).
16 ibid Article 4(2).
17 ibid Article 5(1) referring to UNFCCC (n 4) Article 4(1)(d).
18 Paris Agreement (n 12) Article 5(2).
19 ibid Article 7(1).
20 ibid Article 7(5).
21 Christina Voigt, 'The Paris Agreement: What Is the Standard of Conduct for Parties?' (2016) 18 QIL 17 at 17. Christina Voigt, 'The Power of the Paris Agreement in International Climate Litigation' (2023) 32 RECIEL 2, 237–249 (open access).
22 ibid 18. An indication of which provisions contain legally binding obligations for Parties can be found in the modalities and procedures for the Paris Agreement Implementation and Compliance Committee, Decisions 20/CMA.1, Annex, para 22(a).
23 ibid Article 4(8).
24 ibid Article 4(9).
25 Decision 1/CMA.5, 'Outcome of the first global stocktake' FCCC/PA/CMA/2023/16/Add.1.
26 Paris Agreement (n 12) Article 4(3).
27 Paris Agreement (n 12) Article 13(7).
28 ibid Article 9(1), emphasis added.
29 ibid Article 8.
30 ibid Article 11(1).
31 Christina Voigt and Felipe Ferreira, '"Dynamic Differentiation": The Principles of CBDRRC, Progression and Highest Possible Ambition in the Paris Agreement' (2016) 5(2) Trans EL/CUP <https://doi.org/10.1017/S2047102516000212 285>.
32 ibid 288 ('[w]hat can be concluded from all this is that, while effectiveness depends on participation, participation in turn depends on States' *own* perception of fairness and equity').
33 ibid 291, emphasis original. Conversely, the UNFCCC and Kyoto Protocol focused obligated action on 'developed countries'.
34 ibid 294.
35 ibid.
36 ibid 294–95.
37 ibid 295.
38 Paris Agreement (n 12) Article 4(3).
39 Voigt and Ferreira (n 31) 295.
40 Christina Voigt, 'The Paris Agreement: What Is the Standard of Conduct for Parties?' (2016) QIL 17, 20.

PART 2

Courage in Advancing International Law on Climate Change for Sustainable Development

5

ADVANCING CLIMATE ACTION IN TRADE, INVESTMENT AND FINANCIAL AGREEMENTS

Markus W. Gehring and Emily Morison

Introduction

Aligning finance flows with a pathway towards low greenhouse gas emissions and climate-resilient development is an aim of the Paris Agreement,[1] and this has important implications for international trade and investment law.

The vast influence of trade over the global economy highlights its importance as a tool for responding to climate change.[2] A recent report by the World Trade Organization (WTO) found that while trade itself generates significant carbon emissions, stronger international trade cooperation is an essential component of effective climate mitigation and adaptation.[3] Among other things, the report found that trade has the potential to reduce the cost of climate change mitigation and speed up the low-carbon transition while also supporting green job creation.[4] It also found that trade can help countries – particularly least developed countries, small island developing states, and land-locked developing states – adapt to climate change through facilitating access to technologies and critical goods and services, such as food and healthcare.[5]

Free trade agreements (FTAs) cover the majority of today's global trade flows and play a dominating role over the trade policies and relations between countries.[6] Significantly, leading scholars have observed a general drive towards 'more sustainable' trade agreements over the past decade.[7] Today, FTAs are increasingly incorporating provisions that support and reaffirm existing legal commitments to reduce carbon emissions under the international climate regime, and recently negotiated FTAs involving the EU go further to include cooperative measures aimed at facilitating climate action legislation and regulation.[8] Distinct chapters on trade and the environment (or trade and sustainable development [TSD]) now feature in many FTAs,[9] with some modern agreements containing innovative commitments specifically linked to climate change mitigation, and chapters dedicated to 'climate action'.[10] Examples are also emerging of trade instruments which are specifically directed toward facilitating the transition to a net zero economy, such as the Australia-Singapore Green Economy Agreement and UK-Singapore Green Economy Framework.[11]

Meanwhile, the role of international investment in environmental protection has long been the subject of debate. In one view, foreign investment offers environmental benefits through a variety

DOI: 10.4324/9781003276678-7

of channels (for example, through supporting energy efficiency and carbon emissions reductions), while in another, foreign investment can adversely impact the environment of a host state (for example, through biodiversity destruction).[12] As the climate crisis deepens, however, foreign investment has been identified as a crucial tool for supporting private capital flows for climate change mitigation.[13] This was acknowledged recently in the decision on the outcomes of the First Global Stocktake under the Paris Agreement, which noted challenges with respect to mobilising private finance as part of the mitigation finance gap.[14]

In parallel, traditionally simplistic bilateral investment treaties are being slowly replaced by more textually complex agreements with specific provisions or chapters devoted to sustainable development and climate change.[15]

This chapter considers the roles of FTAs and International Investment Agreements (IIAs) in advancing climate action, as well as future steps that may enhance the roles of these instruments in achieving the goals of the Paris Agreement.

Advancing Climate Action Through Free Trade Agreements

Safeguarding the Right to Regulate and Committing to High Levels of Environmental Protection

Price-based measures, such as taxes and tariffs, market-based mechanisms, and subsidies, are all potential climate mitigation tools which may intersect with trade rules and procedures. For example, WTO rules impose general non-discrimination principles and a general prohibition against border quotas, as well as specific rules on subsidies.[16] This illuminates a tension between the need for States to retain freedom to introduce domestic laws and policies to combat climate change, and compliance with WTO rules. This tension was recently acknowledged in the decision on the outcomes of the First Global Stocktake, which explicitly noted that measures to combat climate change should not constitute arbitrary or unjustifiable discrimination on international trade.[17]

Acknowledging this tension, according to the WTO, its general approach is to recognise that a degree of trade restriction may be necessary to achieve certain policy objectives provided that certain conditions are respected.[18]

FTAs have dealt with this tension by developing mechanisms for safeguarding States' right to regulate for the purposes of environmental protection, and more specifically, climate action. These may be combined with commitments by parties to establish high levels of environmental protection. Examples include the 'Trade and Environment' chapter of the Comprehensive Economic and Trade Agreement (CETA).[19] Meanwhile, more recent agreements (for example, the NZ-EU FTA) may explicitly protect the right to regulate for climate change purposes.[20]

Non-Regression Commitments and Essential Element Clauses

In a similar vein, modern FTAs may also include non-regression clauses, which constitute a commitment by the Parties not to regress on internationally recognised environmental standards and obligations in order to secure trade advantages or economic gains.[21] An early example of this is the EU-Korea FTA,[22] which includes a commitment by each Party not to weaken or reduce the environmental or labour protections afforded in its laws to encourage trade or investment by derogating from its laws or regulations in a way that affects trade between the Parties.[23]

The EU-UK Trade and Cooperation Agreement (TCA) contains arguably the strongest formulation of a non-regression norm.[24] Article 391(2) adopted mandatory language prohibiting the weakening or reduction or lack of enforcement of levels of environmental or climate protection as defined in Article 390(1) below levels applicable at the end of the transition period. This level of climate protection mandates, for the Union, the 40% economy-wide 2030 target, including the Union's system of carbon pricing and for the United Kingdom, the UK's economy-wide share of this 2030 target, including the United Kingdom's system of carbon pricing.

In law, that means a 37% reduction of greenhouse gas emissions by 2030 based on 2005 levels for the UK.[25] While such a strong definition of the level of climate protection should be welcomed, it should be noted that neither of these commitments is as ambitious as the UK's or the EU's Nationally Determined Contribution (NDC). There is a condition in Article 391(2) that only regressions which are 'affecting trade or investment' are covered. However, if interpreted as in the WTO panels, 'affecting trade' means having an economic impact without any qualitative level beyond *de minimis*.[26]

Perhaps more significantly, the TCA lists climate change as an 'essential element' in its preamble and body.[27] An 'essential elements' clause provides a legal basis to act when a Party derogates from a certain principle or set of rules. If an essential element of an agreement is frustrated, a Party can inter alia justify countermeasures, suspension, or even termination of the agreement.[28] This type of clause constitutes a powerful tool that stands in contrast to most environmental protection provisions, which often lack an effective enforcement mechanism.[29] The inclusion of climate change action as an essential element in the TCA is, therefore, a significant development in international trade's capacity to help drive the net zero transition.[30]

Article 764 of the TCA sets out the Parties' commitment to fighting climate change by requiring that parties 'respect the Paris Agreement' and 'refrain from acts or omissions that would materially defeat [the Agreement's] object and purpose'. Significantly, the TCA not only notes that fighting climate change is an essential element, but it specifically describes compliance with the Paris Agreement as part of this element.[31] It remains to be seen how compliance with such a commitment will be enforced by the Parties.

Recently, more trade agreements have declared or agreed to declare in the future that climate change constitutes an essential element of the trade relationship. The TCA was the first of what will likely be many EU agreements to include climate change as part of the 'essential element' clause and to consider derogation from the Paris Agreement as a material breach of trade obligations. Combined with the full implementation of the parties' respective NDCs, this marks an important and new shift. Indeed, climate change may well become part of the standard 'essential element' clause in all EU trade agreements. In June 2022, the European Commission asserted a general aim to include 'the possibility of trade sanctions as a matter of last resort, in instances of serious violations of core TSD commitments, namely the ILO fundamental principles and rights at work, and of the Paris Agreement on Climate Change'.[32]

This new policy found expression in the EU's trade agreement with New Zealand signed in July 2023. Although climate change is not mentioned in the 'essential element' clause in the EU NZ Partnership Agreement, Article 27.4 (3) of the FTA states that Parties can take the same measures that they would in the event of the breach of an essential element 'in the event of an act or omission which materially defeats the object and purpose of the Paris Agreement'. In doing so, it effectively elevates Paris Agreement compliance to the status of an essential element. The inclusion of 'materially defeats the object and purpose' means that this provision itself (similar to Article 50 of the Treaty on European Union) is not designed to ever be used. This does not mean that it could not be used if politicians in either Party suddenly decided to abandon the Paris Agreement or envisioned action on climate change. In that sense it also binds the EU to not deviating significantly from its climate commitments.

A recent example is the EU's new Advanced Framework Agreement (AFA) with Chile, which takes an innovative approach to including climate change in an 'essential element' clause of the treaty. In the interests of swiftly concluding the legal texts, the Parties decided that the new AFA will not *ab initio* contain a treaty provision declaring climate change an essential element – even though the new Chilean government and the EU share a strong commitment to climate action – instead committing to a review within 12 months of the TSD obligations in the treaty text, upon entry into force of the interim trade agreement (ITA).[33] They agreed that '[w]ithout prejudice to the outcome of the review, the Parties will also consider the possibility of including the Paris Agreement on Climate Change as an essential element of the Agreements'.[34] While the caveat of not pre-empting the negotiations might seem a lesser commitment, it should be highlighted that, by including an 'essential element' clause discussion, the Parties have committed themselves to a reform of the treaties, which would have to include a discussion of the current treaty practice of the EU which, after the TCA and the EU-New Zealand Trade Agreement, has solidified, at least on the EU side.

The EU-Chile Joint Declaration on TSD also committed the trading partners to not only declare their 'joint objective of addressing the urgent threat of climate change' but also to 'underline their commitment to effectively implement the United Nations Framework Convention on Climate Change and the Paris Agreement adopted thereunder, including their commitments with regard to their respective Nationally Determined Contribution'.[35] While the verb 'underline' might be seen as less of a substantive obligation, the provision calls the NDC a commitment that should be effectively implemented. Accordingly, the text of the ITA contains a dedicated Article 26.10 on 'trade and climate change' pursuant to which Parties commit to implementing the Paris Agreement, including commitments with regard to their NDCs.

Although the mere requirement to negotiate regarding essential elements might appear disappointing compared to previous agreements like the EU-NZ FTA, which included the 'essential element' clause, we shouldn't overlook the legal and political significance of joint statements, such as the one between the EU and Chile. As exemplified by the Windsor Political Declaration by the European Commission and the Government of the United Kingdom, which set the stage for several draft changes to the Windsor Framework in the context of Brexit, joint statements can serve as crucial platforms for subsequent negotiations.

The EU had proposed a similar though less ambitious approach[36] for the EU-Mercosur Agreement,[37] in the form of a new side letter (or 'joint instrument'). The instrument included seemingly mandatory interpretations of existing TSD chapter provisions, such as Article 2, which mandated implementation of a number of obligations under the Paris Agreement including (among other things) timely communication and implementation of NDCs reflecting the highest possible ambition; pursuit of domestic mitigation measures with the aim of achieving the objectives of such NDCs; and engagement in adaptation planning processes. This joint instrument has not to date removed the deadlock on the EU-Mercosur FTA. Indeed, multiple studies have shown that the current draft is significantly less ambitious in sustainable development terms than the TCA or EU-New Zealand FTA.[38] It is expected that climate change and biodiversity will remain high on the EU's agenda.

Eliminating Barriers to Trade of Environmental Products

One of the key challenges facing the environmental goods market is the significant barriers to trade experienced by this industry,[39] with carbon-intensive industries tending to face lower tariff and non-tariff barriers than clean industries.[40] In that light, removing barriers to trade in environmental goods is one way to facilitate climate action:[41] modelling by the WTO indicates that eliminating tariffs and reducing non-tariff measures on certain energy-related environmental goods and environmentally preferable products could increase global exports in these products by 5% and 14% respectively by 2030, while resulting energy efficiency and renewable energy uptake would reduce global emissions by 0.6%.[42]

Accordingly, several FTAs include specific commitments by Parties to work to reduce barriers to trade in environmental products. A recent example may be found in the EU-NZ FTA 'trade and climate change' provision,[43] which includes commitments to:

- promote the mutual supportiveness of trade and climate policies and measures;
- facilitate the removal of obstacles to trade and investment in goods and services of particular relevance for climate change mitigation and adaptation, such as renewable energy and energy-efficient products and services, for instance through addressing tariff and non-tariff barriers or through the adoption of policy frameworks conducive to the deployment of best available technologies; and
- promote emissions trading and environmental integrity in the development of international carbon markets.

The efficacy of this type of clause remains to be seen, including whether it will be incorporated into future FTAs negotiated by the EU, NZ, and others.

Cooperation

International trade cooperation can facilitate climate action by minimising trade frictions and investor uncertainty.[44] For example, international cooperation on trade-related aspects of climate policy (such as carbon pricing and decarbonisation standards) can mitigate risks associated with a country taking unilateral measures to prevent carbon leakage and loss of competitiveness of domestic industry, which could lead to trade tensions as countries implement their NDCs.[45]

In the FTA context, 'cooperation' refers broadly to mutual commitments by relevant parties to 'engage in new joint collaborative ongoing ventures, projects or other actions in ongoing processes with the aim of realising specific benefits and transformative outcomes'.[46] A study of FTAs found that cooperation (in a wide variety of forms) has been the main operational framework in which climate action measures are incorporated into FTAs. It argued that sustained and substantive climate action cooperation fostered through FTAs has the potential to help shape what kind of trade develops in the longer term, and this can lead to positive climate action outcomes: for example, trade partners could work collaboratively to strengthen trade capacity in their clean energy sectors or on designing carbon trading instruments.[47] The study also argued, however, that the impact of cooperative measures in FTAs could be difficult to assess in light of their open-ended nature and that, instead, legally binding commitments in FTAs to undertake specified climate actions within certain timeframes may be more likely to result in defined, quantifiable impacts and lead to more substantial positive results than diffuse cooperation commitments.[48]

Examples of EU FTAs that provide for broad cooperation on climate and environmental issues include the 2019 EU-Singapore FTA (which contains a chapter on renewable energy), and the 2019 EU-Japan Economic Partnership Agreement (the first trade deal to contain a comprehensive commitment to implementing the Paris Agreement), which explicitly commits Parties to work together to realise UNFCCC aims, to take steps to meet Paris objectives, and to promote trade as a means of reducing greenhouse gas emissions and of achieving climate-resilient development, including full implementation of the Paris Agreement.[49] It is likely that such provisions will continue to be incorporated into FTAs in the future.[50]

A recent example of a cooperation clause is found in the EU-NZ FTA, which contains (at Article 13.12(1)) a commitment by Parties to 'promote cooperation between the regulators or standardisation bodies located within their respective territories in the area of energy efficiency and sustainable renewable energy, with a view to contributing to sustainable energy and climate policy'. To facilitate this process, Parties 'shall endeavour to identify relevant initiatives of mutual interest concerning standards, technical regulations, and conformity assessment procedures related to energy efficiency and sustainable renewable energy'.[51]

In late 2022, Australia and Singapore signed the Green Economy Agreement (GEA), which builds on the FTA between the two countries[52] and blends trade, economic, and environmental objectives to facilitate trade in environmental goods and services, as well as promote investment to propel the transition to a green economy. The GEA has a particular focus on cooperation, including with respect to identifying and improving each country's access to environmental goods and services; supporting both countries' net zero commitments through investment in green and transition activities; and cooperating towards establishing green shipping channels.[53]

Advancing Climate Action Through Investment Agreements

Safeguarding the Right to Regulate and Enabling Environmental Protection

While pre-2010 ('old-generation') IIAs paid little or no attention to host countries' regulatory flexibility for environmental protection or climate action, post-2010 IIAs have begun to incorporate specific provisions protecting states' right to regulate and are also incorporating provisions on environmental protection and climate mitigation.[54]

While post-2010 IIAs do not generally contain explicit references to climate action, a number do contain general environmental provisions and provisions dealing with sustainable development. Despite not explicitly referring to climate action, these types of clauses facilitate climate action because climate action forms part of sustainable development.[55]

One example is the preamble to the Myanmar–Singapore Bilateral Investment Treaty (BIT) (2019), which recognises 'the important contribution investments can make to sustainable economic growth and development, and seeking to promote, protect, and facilitate such investments within the territories of the parties' and reaffirms 'Parties' right to regulate and to introduce new measures, such as health, safety, and environmental measures relating to investments in their territories in order to meet legitimate public policy objectives'.[56] The right to regulate for environmental protection is also embedded in the body of recent BITs, including CETA and the Rwanda–United Arab Emirates BIT (2017).[57]

Several IIAs now include substantive environmental protection provisions in various forms, including reaffirming commitments to effectively implement multilateral environmental agreements in their laws and practices;[58] commitments to facilitate and promote investment and dissemination of goods, services, and technologies beneficial to the environment;[59] and non-regression clauses. An example of a non-regression clause in the IIA context is found in the Belarus–Hungary BIT (2019),[60] which provides as follows:[61]

> The Contracting Party shall not encourage investment by lowering domestic environmental, labour or occupational health and safety legislation or by relaxing core labour standards. Where a Contracting Party considers that the other Contracting Party has offered such an encouragement, it may request consultations with the other Contracting Party and the two Contracting Parties shall consult with a view to avoid any such encouragement.

Significantly, environmental protection has also emerged as a carve-out in clauses on indirect expropriation, national treatment, and the prohibition of performance requirements. A recent example is the India–Kyrgyzstan BIT (2019), which specifies that non-discriminatory regulatory measures that are designed and applied to protect legitimate public interest or public purpose objectives, such as public health, safety, and the environment, shall not constitute expropriation.[62]

At the multilateral level, investment is governed by a number of legal instruments. The Energy Charter Treaty (ECT), which entered into force in 1998, is a multilateral framework for energy cooperation, designed to promote energy security through open and competitive energy markets while respecting sustainable development principles and sovereignty over natural resources. Several key parties including the EU have announced their withdrawal from the ECT; its future is thus uncertain. It focuses on protection of foreign investments, based on the extension of national treatment or most-favoured nation treatment (whichever is more favourable) and protection against key non-commercial risks. Additionally, the ECT provides for non-discriminatory conditions for trade in energy materials, products, and energy-related equipment based on WTO rules, and it seeks to ensure reliable cross-border energy transit flows through pipelines, grids, and other means of transportation. The resolution of disputes between participating States, and – in the case of investments – between investors and host states, forms a core aspect of the ECT's requirements, as do the promotion of energy efficiency and attempts to minimise the environmental impact of energy production and use.[63] ECT Article 19 deals specifically with environmental aspects of energy as an industry and regulatory field. It is an extensive provision, requiring each Contracting Party to 'strive to minimise in an economically efficient manner harmful Environmental Impacts occurring either within or outside its Area from all operations within the Energy Cycle in its Area'.

The outcomes of investment disputes arising under the ECT with respect to renewable energy regulation have produced important signals for states looking to implement laws that facilitate the aims of the Paris Agreement. In one view, recent cases suggest that states have the ability to alter the regulatory frameworks that form the basis for renewable energy investments as long as this is done within reasonable limits. In another view, however, the variability of dispute outcomes, exemplified by the different decisions resulting from the disputes over Spain's solar feed-in tariff regulations, may operate as an obstacle to low-carbon investment.[64]

There remains a dearth of evidence as to whether the ECT has had a positive impact on investment flows in the renewable energy sector or other sectors[65] and whether its commitment to neutral investment protection may risk encouraging fossil fuel investment rather than facilitate the renewable energy transition. The ECT's potential to be reformed so as to more actively promote sustainable development and to be more aligned with Paris Agreement objectives has been the subject of much recent discussion, particularly since all ECT Member States have committed to the Paris Agreement and the Sustainable Development Goals. It has been suggested that the ECT should expressly discriminate between carbon-intensive energy industries, which would receive less favourable treatment, and low-carbon energy investments, which should be encouraged.[66] In May 2019, the European Commission recommended that the ECT be altered to incorporate stronger sustainable development provisions, including on clean energy and climate change, and to clarify rules with respect to foreign investment protection, for example, by including a specific right to regulate provision.[67] While many of these proposals were accepted, not all found agreement among current parties. The Commission has thus since recommended a coordinated withdrawal but has yet to suggest rules that could be put in its place.

Responsible Business Conduct

One feature of trade and investment agreements that has begun to gain momentum over the past decade is the incorporation of corporate social responsibility (CSR) provisions,[68] and recent IIAs are increasingly recognising investors' responsibility in contributing to the transition to a low-carbon economy.[69]

Canada is a leading example: the CETA preamble encourages responsible business conduct,[70] and Canada's model Foreign Investment Promotion and Protection Agreement (FIPA) (which was recently revised in 2021 and will serve as the basis for Canada's future negotiations) article on responsible business conduct,[71] states that each Party:

> 'reaffirms the importance of internationally recognized standards, guidelines and principles of responsible business conduct that have been endorsed or are supported by that Party, including the OECD Guidelines for Multinational Enterprises and the United Nations Guiding Principles on Business and Human Rights, and shall encourage investors and enterprises operating within its territory or subject to its jurisdiction to voluntarily incorporate these instruments into their business practices and internal policies',

and agrees to cooperate on joint initiatives to promote responsible business conduct.

The impact of this integration of 'soft law' instruments into FTAs and investment instruments should not be underestimated. As we concluded elsewhere:

> a widespread and systematic reliance on CSR guidelines could be useful for signaling to investors exactly what kind of standards or behavior are expected of them. Such pre-investment signaling could facilitate the long-term investor-state relationship and prevent future disputes. This type of explicit 'expectation' could also play a role in the manner in which 'hard' investment provisions are being interpreted by tribunals, for example through CSR-oriented interpretations of legal terms such as 'FET', the definition of 'investment', or the determination of the appropriate compensation. It could also be that the increasing frequency of CSR language in IIAs implies a process of normative evolution, in which CSR norms are increasingly regarded as expected and appropriate behavior, a process that may end in the future with the 'hardening' of CSR obligations.[72]

Especially in the light of proliferation of supply chain legislation such as the new EU Corporate Sustainability Due Diligence Directive, these investment CSR commitments should be regarded as important in the transition to a net zero future.

Specific Climate Action Provisions

Importantly, examples are also emerging of climate-specific provisions in international investment instruments (albeit usually in the investment chapters of FTAs rather than standalone IIAs).[73] One example is the Australia–United Kingdom FTA (2021), which contains a specific clause on promoting climate-friendly investment, under which parties recall various provisions in the agreement geared toward promoting mutually supportive investment and environmental outcomes and that are consistent with the sovereign right of each Party to set its levels of environmental protection.[74]

Some instruments go further than cooperation: the new Investment Protocol (POI) of the African Continental Free Trade Area (AfCFTA) is considered one of the most progressive and sustainable development-friendly investment treaties.[75] As Danish et al.[76] concluded:

> The preamble is a key part of the POI, as it introduces the objectives and intentions of the negotiators of the agreement and serves as guidance for its application and interpretation by various stakeholders, including communities, governments, and investors today and in the future. Importantly, the preamble has a sustainability criterion incorporated in it, which is also reflected in the POI's objectives (Article 2) and scope (Article 3), immediately underscoring the centrality of this theme.

POI Chapter 4 ('Sustainable development-related issues') includes investment promotion and facilitation provisions relating to specific thematic areas including climate action. In particular, Article 26 ('Investment and Climate Change') sets out Parties' agreement to (in accordance with their domestic climate change policies, the Principle of Common but Differentiated Responsibilities, and relevant international climate change instruments) promote and facilitate investments that: support actions to mitigate greenhouse gas emissions and measures to adapt to the negative impacts of climate change; create initiatives conducive to financing regional climate mitigation and adaptation programmes; and support just transition. Parties also agree to encourage new investment regimes (e.g. low or zero carbon Special Economic Zones) and investments that mitigate climate change impacts on exhaustible natural resources. These commitments constitute a new dimension of climate commitments in IIAs.

Two further examples echo this move towards inclusion of climate change provisions in investment instruments. Article 32 of the 2023 EU-Angola Sustainable Investment Facilitation Agreement includes commitments from each Party to 'effectively implement' the UNFCCC and the Paris Agreement, including their NDCs; and promote the mutual supportiveness of investment and climate policies and measures. Article 32 also commits the Parties to work together to strengthen their cooperation on investment-related aspects of climate change policies and measures bilaterally, regionally, and in international fora.

While this might just sound like a more detailed cooperation provision, we should not underestimate the effect of the commitment to'effectively implement' NDCs, which must be read as a binding commitment and thus shape the implementation of the entire agreement.

Similarly, the 2023 Canada-Ukraine Updated FTA highlights the Environment Chapter as applicable to the Investment Chapter. In Article 13.8, it mandates, like Article 34 of the AfCFTA POI, the conduct of an Environmental Impact Assessment, and Article 13.10 contains several commitments with respect to climate change, stating that 'the Parties are resolved to demonstrate international leadership and work together to pursue domestic and global efforts to limit the global temperature increase to 1.5 degrees Celsius above pre-industrial levels and transition to net-zero greenhouse gas emissions by 2050'. It sets out a range of commitments to cooperate, including to enhance Parties' efforts to implement the Paris Agreement; increase energy efficiency; promote the rapid transition from unabated coal power to clean energy sources; and encourage development and deployment of cost-effective, low-emissions technologies and alternatives. Interestingly, the parties also affirm their commitment to the Global Methane Pledge and agree to cooperate to reduce methane emissions. All these provisions must be seen also in the context of Article 17.3 on the relation to other Chapters, which highlights that chapters other than the investment chapter shall prevail.

In this field, materials outside of the treaty text can also prove impactful. A 2017 joint statement by the EU and Canada on CETA (made at the time of signing CETA) provided their agreed interpretation of provisions which had been subject to public debate. The statement recognised (among other things)[77] that CETA commits the Parties to provide for and encourage high levels of environmental protection; recognises their right to establish their own levels of environmental protection (mindful of their international obligations); contains an agreement not to lower levels of environmental protection; and also 'includes commitments to cooperate on trade-related environmental issues of common interest such as climate change': in other words, while the right to regulate gives each Party discretion, such discretion ends when the implementation of international obligations under other treaties is concerned.

Climate Change and Investor–State Dispute Settlement (ISDS)

Despite the emergence of innovative climate action provisions in recent IIAs, one ongoing hurdle that IIAs face to facilitating climate action is the risk of ISDS being used to challenge climate policies, and investors in the fossil fuel sector are frequent ISDS claimants.[78] Equally, however, the past decade has seen a growth in ISDS cases from renewable energy sector investors (perhaps most famously, the 'Spanish Solar' disputes).[79]

UN Trade and Development (UNCTAD) has recently observed that the IIA regime is still dominated by 'old-generation' IIAs,[80] and that reform is 'essential' to ensure that IIAs and associated ISDS claims do not hinder countries' efforts to respond to challenges such as addressing climate change.[81] It has also noted that while new-generation IIAs feature more refined provisions aimed at safeguarding states' right to regulate and reforming ISDS, questions remain as to whether the refinements are sufficiently robust to achieve the desired effects.[82]

Future Directions

The past decade has seen an emergence of innovative clauses in both FTAs and IIAs directed at facilitating climate action.

With respect to trade, the EU has been leading on incorporating climate and sustainable development provisions into its FTAs; however, the efficacy of these largely cooperation-focused clauses remains to be tested. As Dent contends that, on balance, legalisation will be important for enhancing the climate action impact of future FTAs, but as he acknowledges, this approach may be more feasible for some subject matters (for example, environmental and technical standards, and promotion and liberalisation of trade) than others (for example, carbon tariffs or border carbon adjustments are often viewed as forms of trade protectionism, which creates challenges to including such provisions in FTAs).[83]

From a broader perspective, incorporation of provisions in FTAs directed toward combatting climate change and facilitating compliance with the Paris Agreement fundamentally changes trade relationships in several ways. Even provisions that are designed to never be used could fulfil an important backstop to Parties implementing damaging policy changes which risk undermining global efforts to implement the Paris Agreement. In the case of the EU in particular, the inclusion of climate change in FTAs has had the effect that the EU's constitutional aim of combating climate change has become an objective of all EU foreign policy.[84]

It remains to be seen whether such an approach will be adopted more broadly outside the EU in the future; however, recent developments such as the AfCFTA, Canada-Ukraine FTA, and

Singapore's green economy agreements with Australia and the UK may indicate an increasingly global recognition of the importance of trade to driving the net zero transition.

With respect to investment law, both investment protection and investment liberalisation chapters in IIAs have the potential to contribute to climate change mitigation to the extent they are accompanied by proper investment regulation standards and environmental-climate change provisions.[85] Investment protection standards may provide adequate protection for carbon-low and renewable energy investors in host states, while investment liberalisation increases positive spillover effects by the movement of goods and services and the establishment of high-technology actors in the market.[86] However, growing evidence indicates that the most valuable piece of investment law is investment facilitation, including regulatory cooperation, technical assistance, exchange of best practices, and positive motivation between states on more ambitious plans for climate change mitigation.[87] In this light, future IIAs should take a holistic approach to facilitating climate action through combining positive commitments and should be supplemented with investment facilitation and regulation clauses.[88]

The interaction of trade and investment law with climate change is undoubtedly complex. Certain rules are important, if not essential, for a rapid transition to net zero, while others might seem to stand in the way of such a transition. Embedding clear and carefully crafted provisions in FTAs and IIAs that promote – and safeguard – states' capacity to implement ambitious climate mitigation and adaptation measures is one important element of achieving financial flows aligned with the goals of the Paris Agreement.

Notes

1 Article 2(1)(c).

2 Christopher Dent, 'Trade, Climate and Energy: A New Study on Climate Action through Free Trade Agreements' (2021) 14(14) *Energies* 4363, 25 <https://doi.org/10.3390/en14144363>.

3 World Trade Organisation Secretariat, 'World Trade Report 2022: Climate Change and International Trade' 11 <https://www.wto.org/english/res_e/publications_e/wtr22_e.htm>.

4 ibid 8.

5 ibid.

6 Dent (n 2) 25.

7 Marin Duran, 'Sustainable Development Chapters in EU Free Trade Agreements: Emerging Compliance Issues' (2020) 57(4) Common Market Law Review 1031; Marie-Claire Cordonier Segger, 'Integration as a Principle of European Law, and its Relevance to the Negotiation of Trade and Investment Agreements' in *Crafting Trade and Investment Accords for Sustainable Development: Athena's Treaties* (OUP 2021) 89; Markus W. Gehring, 'EU Constitutional Aims and External Relations – Legal Consequences of Climate Provisions in EU Trade Accords' (2023) University of Cambridge Faculty of Law Research Paper No. 2/2023, 7.

8 Dent (n 2) 26.

9 See E Lydgate, 'Beyond Non-regression: Mainstreaming Climate Action into FTAs' Centre for Inclusive Trade Policy, Working Paper 001 (2023) <https://citp.ac.uk/publications/beyond-non-regression-mainstreaming-climate-action-into-ftas>; European Commission, 'Sustainable Development in EU Trade Agreements' <https://policy.trade.ec.europa.eu/development-and-sustainability/sustainable-development/sustainable-development-eu-trade-agreements_en> accessed 22 August 2024. See also Dent (n 2).

10 See, for example, Association Agreement between the European Union and the Republic of Moldova (signed 27 June 2014) Chapter 17 Climate action.

11 Australia-Singapore Green Economy Agreement (signed 18 October 2022); Memorandum of understanding on the Green Economy Framework between the Government of the United Kingdom and the Government of the Republic of Singapore (signed 1 March 2023).

12 Pierre-Marie Dupuy and Jorge E Viñuales, *International Environmental Law* (2nd edn, Cambridge University Press 2018) 453; Markus Gehring, Marie-Claire Cordonier Segger and Andrew Newcombe, eds, *Sustainable Development in World Investment Law* (Wolters Kluwer, 2010).

13 Nikolaus Lang, Rami Rafih and Cristian Rodriguez-Chiffelle, 'Why Foreign Direct Investment Is Needed to Fulfil the Climate Justice Agenda' (*World Economic Forum Centre for Nature and Climate*, 8 February 2023) <https://www.weforum.org/agenda/2023/02/why-foreign-direct-investment-is-needed-to-fulfil-the-climate-justice-agenda/> accessed 22 August 2024.

14 Report of the Conference of the Parties serving as the meeting of the Parties to the Paris Agreement on its fifth session, held in the United Arab Emirates from 30 November to 13 December 2023 (FCCC/PA/CMA/2023/16/Add.1) para 80 of Decision 1/CMA.5 Outcome of the First Global Stocktake.

15 Markus Gehring and Marios Tokas, 'Synergies and Approaches to Climate Change in International Investment Agreements: Comparative Analysis of Investment Liberalization and Investment Protection Provisions in European Union Agreements' (2022) 23(5–6) The Journal of World Investment & Trade 778–812, 778 <https://doi.org/10.1163/22119000-12340270>.

16 World Trade Organisation Secretariat, 'Climate Change and the Potential Relevance of WTO Rules' <https://www.wto.org/english/tratop_e/envir_e/climate_measures_e.htm> accessed 22 August 2024.

17 Para 154 of Decision 1/CMA.5.

18 World Trade Organisation Secretariat (n 16).

19 See in particular Article 24.3 of the CETA between Canada and the EU (signed 30 October 2016) 'Right to regulate and levels of protection'.

20 NZ EU FTA (signed 9 July 2023) Preamble; Chapter 10 'trade in services and investment'; Article 10.1 objectives; Chapter 12 'digital trade'; Article 12.3 'right to regulate'.

21 Markus W. Gehring and Freedom-Kai Phillips, 'Legal Options for Post-Brexit Climate Change and Energy Provisions in a Future UK-EU Trade Agreement' Legal Working Paper (ECF 2019) 10 <https://www.cisdl.org/wp-content/uploads/2019/07/Post-Brexit_Provisions_report_final.pdf>.

22 Signed 6 October 2010.

23 Article 13.7.

24 MW Gehring, 'Analysis 5 of the Brexit Deal: Environment and Climate Provisions' (22 January 2021) <http://eulawanalysis.blogspot.com/2021/01/analysis-5-of-brexit-deal-environment.html> accessed 22 August 2024.

25 Gehring, 'EU Constitutional Aims and External Relations – Legal Consequences of Climate Provisions in EU Trade Accords' (n 7).

26 See Panel Report, *China – Publications and Audiovisual Products*, para 7.1450 and Appellate Body report, *EC – Bananas III*, para 220, cited in Gehring, 'EU Constitutional Aims and External Relations – Legal Consequences of Climate Provisions in EU Trade Accords' (n 7).

27 Article 771 TCA affirms that Article 764(1) (fight against climate change) TCA is an essential element of the agreement; and paragraph 1 of the Preamble states that the fight against climate change (among other things) constitutes an essential element of the TCA and supplementing agreements. It should be noted that such preambular language can be relevant to interpreting other provisions of instruments, as seen in the *US – Shrimp* dispute: Appellate Body Report, *US – Shrimp*, paras 152–53 and 155.

28 TCA Article 772; Aust, *Modern Treaty Law and Practice* (3rd edn, CUP 2013) 260.

29 Gehring, 'EU Constitutional Aims and External Relations – Legal Consequences of Climate Provisions in EU Trade Accords' (n 7) 13.

30 ibid; Cordonier Segger, Athena's Treaties (n 7).

31 ibid 14.

32 EU Commission, *Communication from the Commission to the European Parliament, the Council, the European Economic and Social Committee and the Committee of the Regions – The Power of Trade Partnerships: Together for Green and Just Economic Growth*, 22 June 2022. COM(2022) 409 final, para 3.6.

33 EU-Chile Advanced Framework Agreement – Joint Statement on Trade and Sustainable Development (2 December 2022) <https://circabc.europa.eu/rest/download/96cafa19-80fe-4455-b63b-ea36adf2635a?>. The modernisation of the 2002 EU-Chile Association Agreement entails two parallel legal instruments, being the AFA and an ITA. These instruments were signed in parallel on 13 December 2023. The ITA will remain in force only until the AFA is fully ratified and enters into force.

34 ibid.

35 ibid.

36 See Fabiano De Andrade Correa and Alessandra Lehmen, 'Trade, Sustainable Development and Climate Change: How Can Free Trade Agreements Be Leveraged for Increased Climate Action? Perspectives on the EU-MERCOSUR Agreement' (2023) 50(3) Legal Issues of Economic Integration 287–306.

37 See European Commission, 'EU proposal for a Joint Instrument tabled to Mercosur in the context of discussions to finalise the EU Mercosur agreement' (March 2023) <https://policy.trade.ec.europa.eu/eu-trade-relationships-country-and-region/countries-and-regions/mercosur/eu-mercosur-agreement/documents_en> accessed 22 August 2024.
38 See Javiera Cáceres and others, 'Environment and Climate Change in the Draft EU-Mercosur Trade Agreement' (2021) Centre for International Sustainable Development Law Working Paper (CISDL 2021) <https://www.cisdl.org/environment-and-climate-change-in-the-draft-eu-mercosur-trade-agreement-2021>.
39 World Trade Organisation Secretariat (n 3) 12.
40 ibid, citing Joseph S Shapiro, 'The Environmental Bias of Trade Policy' (2021) 136(2) The Quarterly Journal of Economics 831–86.
41 ibid 12.
42 ibid 8, 13.
43 Article 19.6.
44 World Trade Organisation Secretariat (n 3) 8.
45 ibid.
46 Dent (n 2) 11.
47 ibid.
48 ibid.
49 Gehring and Phillips (n 21) 10; Article 16.4 of the EU-Japan Economic Partnership Agreement (entered into force 1 February 2019); Chapter 7 of the EU-Singapore FTA (signed 19 October 2018).
50 Gehring and Phillips (n 21) 10.
51 Article 13.12(2) 'Cooperation on standards, technical regulations and conformity assessment procedures'.
52 Singapore-Australia Free Trade Agreement (SAFTA). SAFTA entered into force on 28 July 2003 and has been subsequently amended.
53 Para 9. More detail is set out in the annexes to the GEA.
54 UNCTAD, 'The International Investment Treaty Regime and Climate Action' (IIA Issues Note, Issue 3, September 2022) 9 <https://unctad.org/system/files/official-document/diaepcbinf2022d6_en.pdf>.
55 ibid 4.
56 ibid.
57 Rwanda–United Arab Emirates BIT (2017), Article 9; Canada–EU CETA (2016), Chapter 8 Investment, Article 8.9 cited in UNCTAD (n 54).
58 UNCTAD (n 54).
59 ibid.
60 Article 2(7).
61 UNCTAD (n 54) 5.
62 Article 5(5), cited in UNCTAD (n 54).
63 See Energy Charter Treaty (signed 17 December 1994, entered into force 16 April 1998); International Energy Charter, 'The Energy Charter Treaty' <https://www.energycharter.org/process/energy-charter-treaty-1994/energy-charter-treaty/> accessed 22 August 2024.
64 Yulia S Selivanova, 'Changes in Renewables Support Policy and Investment Protection under the Energy Charter Treaty: Analysis of Jurisprudence and Outlook for the Current Arbitration Cases' (2018) 33(2) ICSID Review – Foreign Investment Law Journal 433 <https://academic.oup.com/icsidreview/article/33/2/433/5087801>.
65 Kyla Tienhaara and Christian Downie, 'Risky Business? The Energy Charter Treaty, Renewable Energy, and Investor-State Disputes' (2018) 24 Global Governance 451.
66 Nathalie Bernasconi-Osterwalder and Martin Dietrich Brauch, 'Redesigning the Energy Charter Treaty to Advance the Low-Carbon Transition' (2019) Transnational Dispute Management 1, 11 <https://iisd.org/sites/default/files/publications/tv16-1-article08.pdf>.
67 European Commission, 'Recommendation for a Council Decision Authorising the Entering into Negotiations on the Modernisation of the Energy Charter Treaty' COM(2019) 231 final (14 May 2019).
68 R Peels and others, 'Corporate Social Responsibility (CSR) in International Trade and Investment Agreements: Implications for States, Business And Workers' (2016) ILO Research Paper Series No. 13.
69 UNCTAD (n 54).
70 The preamble provides that Parties 'encourage' 'enterprises operating within their territory or subject to their jurisdiction to respect internationally recognised guidelines and principles of corporate social

responsibility, including the OECD Guidelines for Multinational Enterprises, and to pursue best practices of responsible business conduct'. See Cordonier Segger, Athena's Treaties (n 7).

71 Article 16.

72 Avidan Kent and Markus W Gehring, 'Investment Law and the Environment' in E Techera and others (eds), *Routledge Handbook of International Environmental Law* (2nd edn, Routledge 2020) <https://doi.org/10.4324/9781003137825>.

73 UNCTAD (n 54) 8.

74 Article 13.8, cited in ibid.

75 See Protocol to The Agreement Establishing the African Continental Free Trade Area on Investment – January 2023 <https://edit.wti.org/document/show/e5d51824-c467-4e24-922b-3fb376d89550>.

76 Danish and others, 'The Protocol on Investment to the Agreement Establishing the African Continental Free Trade Area: What's in it and what's next for the Continent?' (*IISD Investment Treaty News*, 1 July 2023) <https://www.iisd.org/itn/en/2023/07/01/the-protocol-on-investment-to-the-agreement-establishing-the-african-continental-free-trade-area-whats-in-it-and-whats-next-for-the-continent/> accessed 22 August 2024.

77 Joint Interpretative Instrument on the Comprehensive Economic and Trade Agreement (CETA) between Canada and the European Union and its Member States [2017] OJ L11/3, para 9 <https://eur-lex.europa.eu/legal-content/EN/TXT/?uri=CELEX%3A22017X0114%2801%29>.

78 See Annex 2 of UNCTAD, 'Treaty-based Investor-State Dispute Settlement Cases and Climate Action' (IIA Issues Note, Issue 4, September 2022) <https://investmentpolicy.unctad.org/publications/1270/treaty-based-investor-state-dispute-settlement-cases-and-climate-action>.

79 See ibid 5.

80 UNCTAD, 'Trends in the Investment Treaty Regime and a Reform Toolbox for the Energy Transition' (IIA Issues Note, Issue 2, August 2023) <https://unctad.org/system/files/official-document/diaepcbinf2023d4_en.pdf>.

81 UNCTAD, 'Review of 2021 Investor-state Arbitration Decisions: Insights for IIA Reform' (IIA Issues Note, Issue 1, July 2023) 11 <https://unctad.org/system/files/official-document/diaepcbinf2023d3_en.pdf>. See also UNCTAD, 'Investment Treaty Regime Needs Reforms to Support Climate Action' (6 September 2022) <https://unctad.org/news/investment-treaty-regime-needs-reforms-support-climate-action> accessed 22 August 2024.

82 UNCTAD, 'Trends in the Investment Treaty Regime and a Reform Toolbox for the Energy Transition' (n 80).

83 Dent (n 2) 26.

84 Article 191 Treaty on the Functioning of the European Union; Gehring, 'EU Constitutional Aims and External Relations – Legal Consequences of Climate Provisions in EU Trade Accords' (n 7) 22.

85 Gehring and Tokas (n 15) 778–812, 811 citing Markus W. Gehring and Marie-Claire Cordonier Segger, 'Overcoming Obstacles with Opportunities: Trade and Investment Agreements for Sustainable Development' in Stephan W Schill, Christian J Tams and Rainer Hoffmann (eds), *International Investment Law and Development* (Edward Elgar 2015) 93.

86 ibid; Marie-Claire Cordonier Segger, Ted Gleason and Sean Stephenson, *Research Handbook on Investment Law and Sustainable Development* (Edward Elgar, 2025 Fc).

87 ibid.

88 ibid; Cordonier Segger, Athena's Treaties (n 7).

6

EXPLORING NATURE-BASED SOLUTIONS TO CLIMATE CHANGE IN INTERNATIONAL LAW

Jorge Cabrera Medaglia and Lydia Young

Introduction

The role of nature-based solutions (NbS) to address the climate crisis has been increasingly recognized by the international community. It is now incredibly important that such utility is realized as the scientific community warns of humanity's continued failure to effectively address climate change.[1] While some may argue nature should be preserved in its own right, NbS to climate change is a critical component for global climate mitigation and adaptation efforts.

Nature can assist with climate mitigation by decreasing emissions related to deforestation and land use and sequestering emissions from the atmosphere. Nature can assist with climate adaptation by enhancing ecosystem[2] resilience to climate impacts, such as flooding, heatwaves and wildfires. Many of these solutions are synergistic, which makes NbS an attractive solution to achieving climate action and sustainable development goals.[3] For example, conserving and restoring ecosystems for carbon sequestration can create positive co-benefits for climate adaptation through enhanced ecosystem services and sustainable development through related economic benefits and improved livelihoods.[4] It is important to note, however, that NbS is not a single answer to climate change; it must be employed alongside 'rapid, deep and sustained reductions in greenhouse gas emissions'.[5] Further, poorly implemented NbS can cause its own problems. For example, large-scale afforestation and bioenergy plantations for climate mitigation can create maladaptation, negatively impact ecosystem services, biodiversity,[6] food systems, livelihoods[7] and intensify social conflict.[8] However, assuming effective and nuanced governance that minimizes such trade-offs, NbS provides a crucial tool for increasing states' courage and contributions to climate action.

This chapter begins by defining NbS and situating it alongside similar terminology. It then addresses where NbS arises in international law, specifically within the climate, biodiversity, desertification and ocean regimes. One example is provided of how NbS is implemented nationally throughout these regimes. The chapter ends with a discussion of current challenges and opportunities in implementing NbS for effective climate mitigation and adaptation.

DOI: 10.4324/9781003276678-8

Defining Nature-Based Solutions

The international law community has used a variety of terminology to address how nature can be utilized for tackling complex problems. These terms, such as 'ecosystem-based approaches', may be distinct from NbS depending on the context of their use. Note that 'nature-derived solutions' are entirely distinct from NbS, and encompasses renewable energy, such as solar energy, or 'nature-inspired solutions,' which address material designs 'modelled on biological processes.'[9]

The concept of NbS initially arose in 2009 when the World Bank and the International Union for Conservation of Nature (IUCN) each released reports outlining the benefits of 'ecosystem-based adaptation' and 'ecosystem-based approaches' to climate change.[10] Ecosystem-based approaches has remained a commonly used term, particularly with the International Panel on Climate Change (IPCC) and within the Convention on Biological Diversity (CBD) regime.[11] Ecosystem-based approaches refers to both ecosystem-based mitigation and ecosystem-based adaptation to climate change and does not expressly require social or economic benefits outside of what is immediately derived from the climate mitigation, adaptation and biodiversity conservation.

In 2022, the UN Environment Assembly (UNEA-5) provided the first multilateral definition of NbS, clarifying that it means actions to protect the environment while also providing human benefit:

> [N]ature-based solutions are actions to protect, conserve, restore, sustainably use and manage natural or modified terrestrial freshwater, coastal and marine ecosystems which address social, economic and environmental challenges effectively and adaptively, while simultaneously providing human well-being, ecosystem services, resilience and biodiversity benefits.
> (the 'UNEA-5 definition')[12]

The UNEA-5 definition clearly links the importance of NbS as a tool for achieving the UN Sustainable Development Goals,[13] indicating the NbS are 'among the actions' necessary for addressing major sustainable development challenges, such as climate change, in addition to other related issues facing humanity, such as biodiversity loss, land degradation, desertification, food security, disaster risks, urban development, water availability and poverty eradication, among others.[14] This sustainable development connection distinguishes NbS from 'traditional' biodiversity and climate change approaches.[15] Notably, the UNEA-5 definition connects NbS to the phrase 'ecosystem-based approaches', stating that NbS, while not equivalent, is 'cognizant of and in harmony with the concept of ecosystem-based approaches identified under the Convention on Biological Diversity and other management and conservation approaches carried out under existing national policy and legislative frameworks'.[16] The takeaway from this semantical analysis is that NbS does not necessarily equate to climate action, whereas ecosystem-based approach is used solely in the context of climate change.[17] For the purposes of this chapter, NbS refers specifically to nature-based solutions to climate change problems.

Of note, while the UNEA has agreed on a definition of NbS, its implementation remains controversial. Cameroon proposed on behalf of the African Group a draft resolution for the 2023 UN Environmental Assembly (UNEA-6) that would set out developing NbS norms, standards and guidelines 'to support sustainable development'.[18] A draft NbS resolution was then subject of debate and further revisions at the Open-ended Committee of Permanent Representatives (OECPR-6), which discussed resolutions that were to be forwarded to the UNEA-6 for final negotiations.[19] A draft resolution was not agreed on at OECPR-6, nor were Parties able to reach consensus at UNEA-6.[20] As such, while there is an internationally agreed definition, there remains to date no global consensus on what constitutes appropriate standards of NbS implementation. The IUCN Global Standard for NbS remains the most authoritative instrument available in this regard.[21]

How Nature Provides Solutions to Climate Change Problems

Nature provides solutions to climate change through the availability of natural carbon sequestration, and to climate adaptation, such as the ability to provide natural flood control. This next section provides a non-exhaustive overview of the benefits of nature for climate action, in addition to a discussion of its effectiveness and possible shortcomings.

Climate Mitigation Benefits

Land use can provide both climate mitigation benefits and exacerbate climate change:[22]

> Land can be simultaneously a source and a sink of CO_2 due to both anthropogenic and natural drivers, making it difficult to separate anthropogenic from natural fluxes. The IPCC reports that activities related to Agriculture, Forestry and Other Land Use (AFOLU) accounted for around 13% of CO_2, 44% of methane (CH4), and 81% of nitrous oxide (N2O) emissions from human activities globally during 2007–2016, representing 23% of total net anthropogenic GHG emissions. This is a significant share, and is, in fact, superior to total emissions from other key sectors such as transportation. Further, agricultural emissions have increased since the turn of the century and, under a business-as-usual scenario, and in the face of an expected increase in demand for agricultural products, are expected to rise sharply over the coming years and decades, largely due to the projected increase in the world population . . . and in changes in diets due to a wealthier middle class particularly in emerging economies.[23]

On the other hand, agriculture and forests can provide significant mitigation benefits. Agriculture has a climate mitigation potential equivalent to approximately 6 billion tons of CO_2 per year, the majority of which is from soil carbon sequestration, reducing emission from soil inputs such as fertilizers and livestock management.[24] An NbS to climate mitigation involves promoting soil as a carbon sink including through the use of 'agroforestry, improved grazing land management, crop rotations and fallows, residue management, reduced tillage and restoration of degraded lands'.[25] Forests also 'play a crucial role' in climate mitigation as they remain the only large-scale means of removing CO_2 from the atmosphere.[26] Notably, 'healthy soil' provides a number of NbS to climate mitigation and adaptation: it stores more carbon, absorbs more water, which makes the soil resilient in a dry year, it improves water quality 'by retaining more water, which reduces runoff from cropland' and it 'goes further in meeting the needs of a growing population and food production'.[27]

For the forest sector, '[a]voiding deforestation is the biggest single opportunity' for climate mitigation while other actions 'include growing new forests, restoring old forests and better forest management'.[28] Forest management such as the REDD+ strategy under the Paris Agreement 'has its own set of benefits and challenges', which requires 'careful land planning, safeguards for biodiversity and indigenous people and local communities, comprehensive and integrated polices for agriculture and forests, as well as addressing deforestation along the supply-chain of products'.[29]

Non-forested ecosystems, such as freshwater wetlands, salt marshes, created wetlands, tropical and subtropical grasslands and coastal ecosystems have significant climate mitigation potential, yet have not received as much scholarly attention compared to forests.[30] According to Chausson and others, this bias towards utilizing forests 'is reflected in existing NbS policies and pledges, which focus on the use of nature for contributing to GHG reduction objectives primarily through afforestation and reforestation'.[31] Wetlands and grasslands are important carbon stores.[32] Further, the ocean is a major emissions sink, having sequestered 'more than 25% of excess carbon dioxide emitted into the atmosphere since the mid 1990s'.[33] 'Blue carbon' is a term to describe the carbon sequestration ability of marine ecosystems. This can include carbon storage within vegetated coastal ecosystems, such as mangroves, salt marshes and sea grass[34] in addition to the deep sea, which is the world's largest carbon sink.[35] Blue carbon initiatives typically focus on coastal ecosystems; however, recent developments in deep sea mining may raise questions as to the impacts of anthropogenic disturbance to a carbon sink once considered inaccessible.[36]

Climate Adaptation Benefits

Nature provides myriad benefits for adapting to climate change, specifically in three dimensions: reducing physical exposure, reducing ecosystem sensitivity and supporting adaptative capacity.[37] These types of NbS are often referred to as 'ecosystem-based adaptation' or EbA.

NbS to reduce exposure include using nature to protect from erosion, inland flooding, coastal hazards and sea-level rise, moderating urban heat waves and heat island effects, managing stormwater and flooding in urban areas and 'sustaining natural resources in drier and more variable climates'.[38] For example, effective use of forests can protect communities from soil erosion and inland flooding.[39] Natural coastal habitats, including coral reefs, saltmarshes, sea grass, kelp beds and mangroves can significantly reduce wave heights that threaten communities and infrastructure.[40] Further, 'urban greening', including increasing canopy cover within urban spaces, can significantly reduce daytime air temperature to create cooling effects, thereby reducing exposure to heatwaves and extreme heat.[41] In this regard, NbS can replace 'hard infrastructure' while providing the co-benefits of healthy ecosystems, such as carbon sequestration, biodiversity and habitats for 'commercially important fisheries, and tourism and recreation'.[42]

Nature can also increase ecosystem resiliency to climate change, particularly through biodiversity. NbS that support biodiversity are more resilient to climate change because biodiversity increases an ecosystem's 'capacity to resist and recover from perturbation and maintain the flow of ecosystem services'.[43] Ecosystem resiliency is a necessary feature that ecosystems must possess to be effective solutions to climate change mitigation and adaptation.[44] As such, policy makers must take care to ensure that NbS implementation supports resilient and long-lasting benefits.[45] For example, grasslands do not receive as much attention as forests.[46] However, grasslands 'may be more reliable as carbon sinks than forests in regions facing increased drought and wildlife risk . . . and forest dieback because of increasing climate stress'.[47] Grasslands also 'store over 10% of terrestrial biomass carbon . . . and could sequester one billion tons of carbon annually if sustainably managed'.[48] Ecosystem sensitivity can be managed by protecting the ecosystem integrity, which may include controlling pollution, invasive species and over-exploitation, in addition to conserving and improving biodiversity.[49] Biodiversity is important for reducing ecosystem sensitivity to climate change because it 'safeguarded the evolutionary potential of ecosystems, allowing for ecological adaptation . . . and reduces the likelihood of trade-offs among different ecosystem services'.[50]

Nature-Based Solutions in International Law

If states want to formulate and implement NbS in national legislation, 'the starting point is an appraisal of relevant international legal instruments and principles that will provide the overall normative framework for proposals at the national level'.[51] As such, this next section highlights where in international law one can find support for the implementation of NbS.

NbS are recognized implicitly and expressly throughout the Rio Conventions treaties, which are the United Nations Framework Convention on Climate Change (UNFCCC),[52] the CBD and the United Nations Convention to Combat Desertification (UNCCD).[53] References to NbS can also be found in the multilateral agreements flowing from the Rio Conventions, including the Paris Agreement, the Sharm El Sheikh Adaptation Agenda and the Kunming-Montreal Global Biodiversity Framework (GBF).[54] Recently, NbS can now be located in the United Nations Convention on the Law of the Sea (UNCLOS) regime with the adoption of the Agreement under the United Nations Convention on the Law of the Sea on the Conservation and Sustainable Use of Marine Biological Diversity beyond National Jurisdiction (High Seas Treaty, not in force).[55]

NbS within the Climate Law Regime

The 1992 UNFCCC does not contain express language on NbS. However, the Preamble and Article 4 recognizes the importance of ecosystems for mitigating climate change. The Preamble illustrates that parties are '[a]ware of the role and importance in terrestrial and marine ecosystems of sinks and reservoirs of greenhouse gases'.[56] Under Article 4, Parties to the Convention have committed 'as appropriate' to '[p]romote sustainable management and promote and cooperate in the conservation and enhancement' of ecosystems that act as greenhouse gas sinks and reservoirs'.[57] Further, Article 3 requires parties to be 'guided' by the precautionary principle '[i]n their actions to achieve the objectives of the Convention'.[58] The precautionary principle requires that '[w]here there are threats of serious or irreversible damage, lack of full scientific certainty should not be used as a reason for postponing such measures'.[59] This principle could support the implementation of NbS, particularly conservation efforts where an ecosystem that offers a high degree of climate mitigation or adaptation potential is at risk of irreversible damage.

The Kyoto Protocol was adopted in 1997, coming into force in 2005.[60] The Protocol 'operationalizes the UNFCCC by committing industrialized countries and economies in transition to limit and reduce greenhouse gases emissions in accordance with agreed individual targets'.[61]

In 2015, Parties to the UNFCCC adopted the Paris Agreement,[62] which responds to the threat of global warming by, *inter alia,* seeking to halt 'global temperatures to well below 2°C, pursuing efforts toward a 1.5°C limit' above pre-industrial temperatures.[63] The Paris Agreement does not specifically refer to NbS or ecosystem-based approaches to climate change mitigation. However, the Preamble recognizes the importance of conserving greenhouse gas reservoirs and sinks within the context of the UNFCCC,[64] which necessarily include ecosystems that act as a greenhouse gas reservoirs and sinks. Further, Article 4 requires that parties 'achieve a balance between anthropogenic emissions by sources and removals by sinks of greenhouse gases . . . on the basis of equity, and in the context of sustainable development and efforts to eradicate poverty'.[65] As with the Preamble, the use of nature-based carbon sinks is implied under Article 4 through Article 5(1), which situates the greenhouse gas sinks within the context of the Convention.[66] Additionally, the Preamble, Article 4 and Article 5 support that Parties' Nationally Determined Contributions (NDCs)[67] should support the conservation of natural greenhouse gas reservoirs and sinks. Indeed, as of 2020, over half of Paris Agreement signatories included NbS in their NDCs.[68] The Paris Agreement also encourages parties to take action to implement and support the reduction of emissions from deforestation and forest degradation,[69] which has led to REDD+ initiatives.

NbS within Non-Binding Climate Instruments

NbS are also located in non-binding instruments flowing from the UNFCCC, such as REDD+, the Enhancing Nature-based Solutions for an Accelerated Climate Transformation (ENACT) Partnership and the Sharm-El-Sheikh Adaptation Agenda (SAA).

REDD+ stands for Reducing Emissions from Deforestation and Forest Degradation, 'plus conservation sustainable management of forests and enhancement of forests carbon stocks'.[70] REDD+ was established within the UNFCCC regime in 2007 at CoP 13[71] as a results-based climate finance mechanism offering 'developing countries financial incentives for reducing GHG emissions'.[72] In 2013 at CoP 19, the Warsaw Framework for REDD+ was adopted, which 'presents rules and guidelines for REDD+ design and implementation', including methods of measuring, reporting and verifying emissions.[73] There are various global initiatives outside of REDD+ that also focus on tree-planting and avoiding forest loss and degradation, including the Bonn Challenge,[74] the New York Declaration on Forests[75] and the Glasgow Leaders' Declaration on Forest and Land Use.[76]

The ENACT Partnership was launched by Germany, Egypt and the IUCN in 2022 at CoP 27.[77] This Partnership aims to 'accelerate collective global efforts to address climate change, land and ecosystem degradation, and biodiversity loss through [NbS]' specifically by providing a 'hub for Parties and non-state actors working on NbS to collaborate and build support across the Rio Conventions'.[78] Germany, Egypt, Canada, the European Union, Spain, Malawi, Norway, South Korea, Japan, Slovenia and the IUCN were the founding partners.[79] However, in 2023 at CoP 28, France, the United States, Belgium, the Netherlands, Switzerland, Pakistan and the UN Environment Programme joined the ENACT Partnership.[80] The IUCN released the inaugural ENACT NbS Goals in 2024.[81] This report addresses remaining gaps in effective NbS implementation, which it states arise from confusion on what constitutes as NbS, the need for contextualised overviews and case studies 'on system-focused implementation' and 'limited clarity on the status of achieving the full potential of NbS address climate change, biodiversity loss and land degradation'.[82]

The Sharm-El-Sheikh Adaptation Agenda (SAA) is another example of a non-legal instrument that provides a mechanism for NbS implementation that was launched at CoP 27.[83] SAA is an aspirational agenda that sets out 30 global climate adaptation targets for 2030. The 2022 Launch Report provides the following NbS-specific outcomes for increasing water and nature resilience: (1) protect 45 million hectares of land and inland water, sustainably manage 2 billion hectares and restore 350 million hectares of land;[84] (2) utilize NbS investment opportunities to eliminate commodity-driven deforestation; and (3) utilize natural wetland filtration systems for wastewater.[85] In its 2023 Implementation Report, the SAA Task Force highlights opportunities for implementing NbS to achieve its 2030 outcomes for increasing resilience in water and natural systems, such as protecting shallow-water tropical coral reefs and seagrass ecosystems.[86] The SAA provides a shared understanding of what states must do to fulfill their adaptation obligations under the UNFCCC (see Article 4) and the Paris Agreement (see Article 7), which can assist states with implementation under the interactional theory of international law.[87] The GBF provides an analogous shared understanding of how states can implement their legal obligations under the biodiversity regime.

NbS within the Biodiversity Law Regime

The CBD does not expressly refer to NbS, although it does seek to conserve and sustainably use biodiversity.[88] Biodiversity 'is understood as comprising all forms of life on Earth, including ecosystems, animals, plants, fungi, micro-organisms and genetic diversity'.[89] Biodiversity conservation, if implemented through ecosystem-based approaches, can increase an ecosystem's resilience to climate impacts and constitute a form of climate adaptation (see discussions on climate adaptation *supra*).

There are various bodies under the Convention that are working on projects related to NbS. For example, in 2004 the CBD CoP established the Ad Hoc Open-ended Working Group on Protected Areas.[90] This Protected Areas Working Group has a mandate to, *inter alia,* explore options for establishing marine protected areas (see Ocean Regime section), options for mobilizing financial resources for protected areas, develop 'tool kits' for designing *infra* and implementing protected areas, ecological networks and buffer zones, among other national and regional systems. Protected areas can evidently function as effective NbS to climate mitigation and adaptation.

The CBD regime also creates national obligations. Similar to the NDCs under the climate regime, Article 6 of the CBD requires parties to develop national strategies, plans or programs for the conservation and sustainable use of biological diversity (NBSAPs).[91] These NBSAPs can be used as a vehicle for utilizing international law for domestic climate adaptation through NbS.

The GBF, which was adopted at the CBD CoP 15 in 2022,[92] is meant to facilitate the implementation of the CBD through the CBD's 'ecosystem approach'. As with the SAA, the GBF is a non-legal tool that assists states in implementing their obligations under the CBD and UNFCCC by increasing a shared understanding of what is needed to meet these collective goals, including climate mitigation and adaptation. The GBF recognizes the alarming continued loss of biodiversity, the threat this loss poses 'to nature and human well-being',[93] and seeks to 'galvanize' strategic implementation of the CBD and its Protocols.[94] The GBF is composed of four overarching goals and 23 targets. The GBF targets are split into three general categories: conserving biodiversity; meeting people's needs through sustainable use and benefit sharing; and tools and solutions for implementation and mainstreaming. NbS is expressly referenced in Target 8 and 11. Target 8 sits under the conserving biodiversity section and seeks to minimize the impacts of climate change on biodiversity 'through nature-based solutions and/or ecosystem-based approaches'.[95] Target 11 sits under the '[m]eeting people's needs' section and seeks to utilize 'nature-based solutions and/or ecosystem-based approaches' to restore, maintain and enhance, among other things, nature's ecosystem services to people.[96]

According to the IPCC, 30–50% of land, freshwater and ocean must be effectively (and equitably) conserved in order to ensure the world's ecosystems remain resilient to climate change impacts.[97] The GBF helps to achieve this through its '30x30' targets. Target 2 encourages parties to restore 'at least 30 per cent' of degraded terrestrial, inland water and marine and coastal ecosystems by 2030.[98] Similarly, Target 3 encourages parties to ensure that 'at least 30 per cent' of terrestrial and inland water areas, and marine and coastal areas ('especially areas of particular importance for biodiversity and ecosystem functions and services') are effectively conserved and managed through protected areas and 'other effective area-based conservation measures' (OECM).[99]

The Global Environment Facility ratified and launched the Global Biodiversity Framework Fund in 2023.[100] This Fund, which addresses financing requirements under Target 19 of the GBF, will be crucial for implementing NbS to climate adaptation under Targets 8 and 11.

Beyond the CBD, it is also important to highlight the International Treaty on Plant Genetic Resources for Food and Agriculture (ITPGRFA), which was adopted in 2001 at the 31st FAO

Conference.[101] The ITPGRFA 'recognizes the vast contribution of farmers to the diversity of crops' sustaining humanity and 'establishes a global system to provide farmers, plant breeders and scientists with access to plant genetic materials, and ensures that recipients share benefits they derive from the use of these genetic materials with the countries where they originated'.[102] The ITPGRFA is therefore an important tool for implementing NbS for climate adaptation through agricultural diversity, while also achieving the CBD's third objective of fair and equitable benefit sharing of genetic resources.[103]

NbS within the Combatting Desertification Regime

The 1992 United Nations Convention to Combat Desertification (UNCCD) 'is the only legally-binding international agreement linking environment and development to sustainable land management'.[104] The UNCCD targets drylands, particularly in Africa, where there are ecosystems and communities particularly vulnerable to climate change.[105] The Food and Agriculture Organization of the United Nations (FAO) summarizes the UNCCD's Framework for reducing and restoring land degradation:

> The UNCCD 2018–2030 Strategic Framework is a comprehensive global commitment designed to achieve Land Degradation Neutrality in order to restore the productivity of vast expanses of degraded land, improve the livelihoods of people, and reduce the impacts of drought. The Strategy will be implemented primary through actions at national or sub-regional levels, with the support of UNCCD institutions, partners and other relevant stakeholders. National Action Programmes (NAPs) to combat desertification and/or alleviate the impacts of drought are the key legal instruments for implementing the Convention. Given the importance of sustainable land management for climate change mitigation and adaptation, coordination of implementation between national actions on the NAPs and the NDCs, among other instruments [such as the CBD NBSAPs], is strongly recommended.[106]

NbS within the Ocean Regime

In 2023, the UN adopted the 'Agreement under the United Nations Convention on the Law of the Sea on the Conservation and Sustainable Use of Marine Biological Diversity beyond National Jurisdiction' (High Seas Treaty), which is not yet in force under international law.[107] The High Seas Treaty does not contain express language for NbS but does require parties to be guided by 'an ecosystem-approach'.[108] Marine biodiversity 'contributes substantially to carbon sequestration and storage'[109] and is therefore an important aspect of climate mitigation. Marine biodiversity is also important for climate adaptation.[110] Therefore, there is an argument that this Agreement's objective 'to ensure the conservation and sustainable use of marine biological diversity of areas beyond national jurisdiction',[111] in addition to provisions on marine protected areas, sustainable use and area-based management, may be utilized for implementing NbS in marine contexts.

Examples of Implementing NbS: REDD+ in Indonesia

There are three categories of NbS implementation: actions that 'protect natural ecosystems from loss and degradation'; actions that 'restore ecosystems that have been degraded'; and actions that 'more sustainably manage working lands such as fields and managed forests'.[112] Efficient and effective conservation, restoration or sustainable management must be 'designed on a context-specific basis' and adhere to the best available science.[113] Conversely, poorly implemented NbS can create unwanted trade-offs. The UNFCCC's REDD+ instrument can be used for any of the aforementioned NbS actions (protecting, restoring or sustainably managing).

Enhancing forests as carbon stocks is critical for climate mitigation and achieving the goals of the Paris Agreement, as it represents the most viable approach of sequestering CO_2 at a large scale. As such, avoiding loss of forests (or deforestation) is 'the biggest single opportunity at climate mitigation'.[114] REDD+ is one tool that can help states increase NbS for climate mitigation through reducing deforestation. Indonesia provides an example of REDD+ policies successfully reducing deforestation-related emissions, but some failure to ensure that the state receives reliable payment highliting shortcomings on REED + implementation.

The Government of the Republic of Indonesia created a REDD+ national strategy in 2007 for the period 2012–2020, implemented this strategy and has achieved emissions reductions from reduced deforestation from 2013–2020.[115] For 2018–2020, Indonesia's emission reductions were equivalent to 577,449,160 tCO_2eq.[116] Indonesia, however, did not receive any payments for these successes until 2020, when the Green Climate Fund approved US$103.8 million in results-based payments for Indonesia's REDD+ emission reductions that occurred from 2014 to 2016.[117] Part of this delay in payments may be due in part to difficulties between Indonesia and Norway, which partnered in 2010 to implement REDD+ in Indonesia but had undergone termination and renegotiation after Norway failed to pay for Indonesia's emission reductions.[118]

As REDD+ payment is based on climate mitigation, it does not necessarily protect climate adaptation benefits such as biodiversity. Indeed, carbon mitigation through REDD+ may in practice create adaptation trade-offs, including biodiversity loss.[119] This can be seen with Indonesia's success at reducing deforestation emissions. While the emissions have reduced, this is in part because Indonesia's Environment and Forestry Ministry defines plantations as forests in the context of REDD+ implementation.[120] This definition is somewhat contentious and raises concerns that ecologically valuable forests may be logged under REDD+ implementation.[121] However, Indonesia does state that 'natural forest' and biodiversity conservation are part of its National Strategy.[122]

Overall, it will be important to ensure that REDD+ solutions are implemented carefully so that climate mitigation, adaptation and sustainable development trade-offs are minimized. While REDD+ appears to be producing climate mitigation benefits in Indonesia, it remains unclear whether the same mechanism will protect the state's rainforests and biodiversity.

The Forest Carbon Partnership Facility and the East Kalimantan ER Program

The Forest Carbon Partnership Facility (FCPF) is a separate, non-UN REDD+ instrument that can assist in REDD+ implementation. It is a 'global partnership of governments, businesses, civil society, and Indigenous People's organizations' managed by the World Bank that focuses on reducing emissions through 'activities commonly referred to as REDD+'.[123]

In 2020, Indonesia's Ministry of Environment and Forestry and the World Bank FCPF signed a landmark Emission Reduction Payment Agreement (ERPA) that would provide up to US$110 million for the Government of Indonesia to lower emissions from deforestation and forest degradation between 2020 and 2025, specifically in the East Kalimantan province.[124] This agreement provides that Indonesia will receive results-based payments under the FCPF Carbon Fund. In 2022, Indonesia was provided an advance payment of US$20.9 million under the ERPA to 'facilitate the start of the East Kalimantan program's Benefit Sharing Plan', with the full payment being released after independent verification of the reported emission reductions.[125] Indonesia is the first country in the East Asia Pacific region to receive payments through the FCPF.[126]

The ERPA is a legally binding contract that provides payment for ecosystem services (PES), specifically payment 'for Indonesia's efforts to preserve tropical forests and in so doing reduce the emissions of greenhouse gases into the atmosphere'.[127] The East Kalimantan ERPA is publicly available.[128]

Challenges and Future Opportunities for Implementing NbS

NbS is evidently an important means of tackling climate mitigation and adaptation, and the prior sections highlight where it can be utilized though international law and legal instruments. However, there are challenges for implementing NbS at a national and regional level. This chapter identifies three such challenges.

First is the lack of global consensus on what standards and procedures are necessary to implement effective NbS at a regional, state or local level. This issue was raised earlier in the chapter and presents one of the more immediate and pressing opportunities to increase the application of NbS for climate action, particularly in national legislation. For example, the REDD+ case study contained in this chapter highlights the need for clarification over whether and how plantations (or working forests and crops), either in the context of agroforestry or monocultures, fit into NbS approaches to climate mitigation and adaptation. The IUCN did release its own 'Global Standard for NbS' in 2020, which sets out eight criteria.[129] However, much more detail is necessary, and state consensus is needed imminently to establish the method of determining NbS standards and implementation procedures under the UNFCCC and/or CBD regimes. Without a global consensus, it will be difficult for states to ensure effective NbS at a national level within their NDC and NBSAP requirements. Standardization is also necessary to avoid state and corporate greenwashing and unnecessary trade-offs between carbon sequestration, biodiversity and ecosystem conservation and sustainable development.

A second challenge arises where there are jurisdictional overlaps to nature. A prominent example are Indigenous sovereignty claims to nature that may overlap and conflict with a state's claim. Such overlap creates an interesting legal environment. The principle of sovereignty over natural resources still applies solely to the state pursuant to customary international law. However, the United Nations Declaration on the Rights of Indigenous People, while non-binding, makes it clear that states need to respect Indigenous people's rights to their traditional lands and natural resources, including development strategies.[130] There are examples of nation-to-nation agreements arising between states and Indigenous nations and governments to create benefit-sharing agreements. There will certainly be future opportunities and continued development in this area to determine how NbS can be implemented on Indigenous territory through benefit-sharing and nation-to-nation partnerships. Future research may also be needed to determine whether there are relevant linkages between access and benefit-sharing, protecting Traditional Knowledge and implementing NbS.

A somewhat related legal challenge is jurisdictional barriers to nature in federalist states, such as Canada, the United States, Brazil, and India, to name a few. In these instances, depending on constitutional divisions of power, the federal government may wish to implement NbS to fulfill its international legal obligations under the UNFCCC and CBD, but not have the domestic jurisdiction to legislate such action without the cooperation of the states/provinces within the country. For example, in Canada, the Federal government can establish protected areas over federal lands and has jurisdiction over some wildlife; however, the Provinces have wide jurisdiction over the country's provincial Crown lands, including forest resources.[131] As such, future research is needed to determine how federalist states can effectively implement NbS in areas that may be outside their constitutional jurisdiction.

Conclusion

NbS offer myriad positive opportunities and co-benefits for urgent, near-term and long-term climate action. This chapter has outlined how NbS is defined, how it can address climate mitigation and adaptation, discussed examples of how NbS has been incorporated in different instruments of international law and provided one example of its implementation on the ground using international and domestic mechanisms. This chapter has highlighted how complicated effective application can be, and it stresses the need for strategic, locally contextualized application of NbS that avoids unnecessary trade-offs between carbon sequestration, biodiversity and ecosystem conservation and local livelihoods and development. This chapter has detailed how international law offers many tools, particularly through NDCs and NBSAPs, for states to implement NbS domestically. However, there remain various challenges and opportunities that need to be addressed, including clear norms, standards and guidelines of NbS for sustainable development and climate action. Relatedly, more examples are needed of national implementation of NbS and international law principles to provide guidance to other parties and stakeholders, including national legislation of NbS.

Notes

1 See IPCC, 'Climate Change 2023: Synthesis Report. Contribution of Working Groups I, II and III to the Sixth Assessment Report of the Intergovernmental Panel on Climate Change' (IPCC, Switzerland 2023) <https://doi.org/10.59327/IPCC/AR6-9789291691647> accessed 1 April 2024.

2 Ecosystem 'means a dynamic complex of plant, animal and micro-organism communities and their non-living environment interacting as a functional unit'; Convention on Biological Diversity (adopted May 1992, entered into force 29 December 1993) 1760 UNTS 79 (CBD) Article 2.

3 Transforming our world: the 2030 Agenda for Sustainable Development, UNGA Res 70/1 (21 October 2015) UN Doc A/RES/70/1 (2030 Agenda).

4 IPCC 2023 (n 1) 108; 2030 Agenda (n 3).

5 UNEP/EA.5/Resolution 5, Article 1 (NbS Resolution).

6 Biodiversity (or biological diversity) 'means the variability among living organisms from all sources, including, *inter alia,* terrestrial, marine and other aquatic ecosystems and the ecological complexes of which they are a part; this includes diversity within species, between species and of ecosystems'; CBD (n 2) Article 2.

7 IPCC 2023 (n 1) 108; Nathalie Seddon and others, 'Understanding the Value and Limits of Nature-based Solutions to Climate Change and Other Global Challenges' (2020) 374(20190120) Phil Trans R Soc B.

8 Fabiano de Andrade Correa and Christina Voigt, 'The Paris Agreement and Net-Zero Emissions: What Role for the Land-Sector' (2021) 15(1) CCLR 1, 7.

9 Lera Miles and other, 'Nature-based Solutions for climate Change Mitigation' (2021) UNEP and IUCN <www.unep.org/resources/report/nature-based-solutions-climate-change-mitigation> accessed 1 April 2024 (UNEP-IUCN).

10 World Bank, 'Convenient Solutions to an Inconvenient Truth: Ecosystem-based Approaches to Climate Change' (2009) <http://hdl.handle.net/10986/3062> accessed 17 March 2024; A Colls, N Ash and N Ikkala, 'Ecosystem-based Adaptation: A Natural Response to Climate' (2009) IUCN <https://portals.iucn.org/library/node/9439> accessed 1 April 2024.

11 CBD (n 2). The Convention on Biological Diversity does not contain the word 'ecosystem-based approach'; however, it is used frequently in CBD-related documents such as C. Epple and others, 'Managing Ecosystems in the Context of Climate Change Mitigation: A Review of Current Knowledge and Recommendations to Support Ecosystem-based Mitigation Actions That Look beyond Terrestrial Forests' (2016) Technical Series No. 86, Secretariat of the Convention on Biological Diversity.

12 NbS Resolution (n 5).
13 2030 Agenda (n 3).
14 NbS Resolution (n 5); Seddon and others (n 7).
15 Seddon and others (n 7).
16 NbS Resolution (n 5); see also the CBD, Kunming-Montreal Global Biodiversity Framework (19 December 2022) COP/DEC/15/4 (GBF) with regard to examples of NbS and ecosystem-based approaches being used as distinct concepts.
17 Holly Jones and others, 'Global Hotspots for Coastal Ecosystem-based Adaptation' (2020) 15(5) PLoS ONE, 2 with regard to ecosystem-based adaptation referring specifically to climate change solutions.
18 TWN Info Service on Biodiversity and Traditional Knowledge, 'UNEA-6: No Agreement on an Intergovernmental Process for Guidelines on Nature-based Solutions' (9 April 2024) <https://wp.twnnews.net/sendpress/email/?sid=NjIyODk&eid=NzE0MA&utm_medium=email&utm_source=sendpress&utm_campaign> (TWN).
19 ibid.
20 ibid.
21 IUCN, 'IUCN Global Standard for Nature-based Solutions: A User-friendly Framework for the Verification, Design and Scaling Up of NbS' (1st edn, 2020) <https://acrobat.adobe.com/id/urn:aaid:sc:US:dd16bc24–3867–449a-9183–4b8a01ac1b85> accessed 22 April 2024.
22 Fabiano de Andrade Correa and Voigt (n 8) 1, 5.
23 ibid.
24 **24** Fabiano de Andrade Correa, Margret Vidar and Tejas Rao, 'UNFCCC CoP 26: Key Outcomes for Soil Management' in Harald Ginzky and others (eds), *International Yearbook of Soil Law and Policy 2022* (Springer 2024) 146.
25 de Andrade Correa and Voigt (n 8) 6; Fabiano de Andrade Corrêa, Vidar and Rao (n 24) 146.
26 de Andrade Correa and Voigt (n 8) 6.
27 de Andrade Corrêa, Vidar and Rao (n 24) 146–47.
28 de Andrade Correa and Voigt (n 8) 6.
29 ibid 6–7.
30 Alexandre Chausson and others, 'Mapping the Effectiveness of Nature-based Solutions for Climate Change Adaptation' (2020) 26 Global Change Biol 6134, 6148–49.
31 ibid 6148.
32 ibid 6149.
33 Nathalie Hilmi and others, 'Deep Sea Nature-based Solutions to Climate Change' (2023) 5(1169665) Front Clim <https://doi.org/10.3389/fclim.2023.1169665> 2.
34 IPCC 2023 (n 1) 106; Cuicui Feng and others, 'Sustainability Developing Global Blue Carbon for Climate Mitigation and Economic Benefits Through International Cooperation' (2023) 14(6144) Nature Comm 1.
35 Hilmi (n 33).
36 ibid.
37 Seddon and others (n 7).
38 ibid.
39 ibid.
40 ibid. Note that salt marshes may be vulnerable to sea level rise, which could impact NbS effectiveness; ibid.
41 Seddon and others (n 7); IPCC 2023 (n 1) 8.
42 Jones (n 16) 2.
43 Seddon and others (n 7) 3.
44 ibid 6.
45 Seddon and others also stress that more research is needed to 'model how the performance of NbS varies under climate change'; Seddon and others (n 7) 6–7.
46 Chausson and others (n 30).
47 ibid 6149 (citations omitted).
48 ibid.
49 Seddon and others (n 7) 6.
50 ibid.
51 Food and Agriculture Organization of the United Nations, 'Agriculture and Climate Change – Law and Governance in Support of Climate Smart Agriculture and International Climate Change Goals' (2020) FAO Legislative Studies No. 115 <https://doi.org/10.4060/cb1593en> 86 (FAO 2020).

52 United Nations Framework Convention on Climate Change (adopted May 1992, entered into force 21 March 1994) 1771 UNTS 107.
53 United Nations Convention to Combat Desertification in those Countries Experiencing Serious Drought and/or Desertification, Particularly in Africa (adopted 17 June 1994, entered into force 26 December 1996) 1954 UNTS 3 (UNCCD); IUCN, 'State of ENACT NbS Goals Report: Year One Roadmap' (2024) <https://iucn.org/resources/grey-literature/state-enact-nbs-goals-report-year-one-roadmap> accessed 1 April 2024 (ENACT Report).
54 ENACT Report (n 53).
55 Agreement under the United Nations Convention on the Law of the Sea on the Conservation and Sustainable Use of Marine Biological Diversity of Areas beyond National Jurisdiction (adopted 19 June 2023) (High Seas Treaty).
56 UNFCCC, article 4).
57 ibid Article 4.
58 ibid Article 3.
59 ibid.
60 Kyoto Protocol to the United Nations Framework Convention on Climate Change (Signed 11 December 1997, entered into force 16 February 2005) 2303 UNTS 162.
61 Fabiano de Andrade Corrêa, Vidar and Rao (n 24) 150–51.
62 Adoption of the Paris Agreement (12 December 2015) CP/2015/L.9/Rev/1.
63 Paris Agreement (adopted 12 December 2015, entered into force 4 November 2016) 3156 UNTS 79.
64 Paris Agreement (n 62).
65 ibid Article 4(1).
66 Paris Agreement (n 62) arts 4, 5; Fabiano de Andrade Corrêa, Vidar and Rao (n 24) 153.
67 Paris Agreement (n 62) Article 4.
68 Chausson and others (n 30) 6135.
69 Paris Agreement (n 62) Article 5.
70 Frances Seymour and Jonah Busch, *Why Forests? Why Now? The Science, Economics and Politics of Tropical Forests and Climate Change* (Center for Global Development 2016) 10.
71 Reducing emissions from deforestation in developing countries: approaches to stimulate action 3/CP.13 (14 March 2008) FCCC/CP/2007/6/Add.1.
72 Michael Köhl, Prem Raj Neupane and Philip Mundhenk, 'REDD+ Measurement, Reporting and Verification – A Cost Trap? Implications for Financing REDD+ MRV Costs by Results-based Payments' (2020) 168(106513) Ecol Econ 1. Carbon pricing is currently not high enough, which results in states needing financial support to implement REDD+; Köhl (n 63).
73 Köhl (n 63); Christina Voigt and Felipe Ferreira, 'The Warsaw Framework for REDD+: Implications for National Implementation and Access to Results-based Finance' (2015) 9 CCLR Special Issue 113.
74 The Bonn Challenge <www.bonnchallenge.org/> accessed 22 April 2024.
75 Nathalie Seddon and others, 'Getting the Message Right on Nature-based Solutions to Climate Change' (2020) 27 Global Change Biol 1519.
76 Glasgow Leaders' Declaration Dashboard, 'Tracking Progress toward 2030 Goals to Protect and Restore Forsts and Land' <https://dashboard.forestdeclaration.org/> accessed 22 April 2024.
77 IUCN, 'Six Countries and UN Agency Joint Vital Global Partnership to Advance Nature-based Solutions' (9December2023)<www.iucn.org/news/202312/six-countries-and-un-agency-join-vital-global-partnership-advance-nature-based> accessed 22 April 2024.
78 ibid.
79 ibid.
80 ibid.
81 IUCN, 'State of ENACT NbS Goals Report: Year One Roadmap: A Report by the ENACT Partnership – Enhancing Nature-based Solutions for Accelerated Climate Transformation' (n 53).
82 ibid iii.
83 Sharm-El-Sheikh Adaptation Agenda, 'Implementation Report 2023' <https://acrobat.adobe.com/id/urn:aaid:sc:US:a40c0399-e7de-4fec-882c-4a8c13026479> accessed 1 April 2024.
84 Note that this target interacts with the Bonn Challenge and New York Declaration of Forests and the GBF's 30 x 30 Targets 2 and 3.
85 Sharm-El-Sheikh Adaptation Agenda (2022) <https://acrobat.adobe.com/id/urn:aaid:sc:US:5ba99698-00ca-4fa6-92a6-5e990d155509> accessed 1 April 2024.
86 SAA 2023 (n 83) 17.

87 Jutta Brunée and Stephen Troope, 'Interactional Legal Theory, the International Rule of Law and Global Constitutionalism' in Lang and Wiener (eds), *Handbook of Global Constitutionalism* (Edward Elgar 2017) with regard to interactional theory.
88 CBD (n 2) Article 1 with regard to the CBD's objectives, which are 'the conservation of biological diversity, the sustainable use of its components and the fair and equitable sharing of the benefits arising out of the utilization of genetic resources, including by appropriate access to genetic resources and by appropriate transfer of relevant technologies'.
89 FAO 2020 (n 51) 89.
90 <https://www.cbd.int/convention/wgpa.shtml>.
91 CBD (n 2) Article 6.
92 GBF (n 16).
93 ibid.
94 ibid.
95 GBF (n 16) Target 8.
96 ibid Target 11.
97 IPCC 2023 (n 1) 106.
98 GBF (n 16) Target 2.
99 ibid Target 3.
100 CBD, 'Launch of the Global Biodiversity Framework Fund' (2023) <www.cbd.int/article/launch-global-biodiversity-framework-fund> accessed 31 August 2023.
101 FAO 2020 (n 51) 93.
102 ibid.
103 See also International Law Association, Kyoto Conference, 'The Role of International Law in Sustainable Natural Resources Management for Development' (2020) Resolution No. 4/2020.
104 FAO 2020 (n 51) 91.
105 ibid, with regard to 'ecosystems and peoples' in Africa being vulnerable.
106 FAO 2020 (n 51) 92.
107 Agreement under the United Nations Convention on the Law of the Sea on the Conservation and Sustainable Use of Marine Biological Diversity of Areas beyond National Jurisdiction (adopted 19 June 2023, not in force).
108 ibid Article 7(f).
109 Md Saiful Karim and William WL Cheung, 'The New UN High Seas Marine Biodiversity Agreement May Also Facilitate Climate Action: A Cautiously Optimistic View' (2024) 3(8) npj Climate Action <https://doi.org/10.1038/s44168-023-00088-9> 1.
110 ibid.
111 ibid Article 2.
112 UNEP-IUCN (n 9) 5.
113 NbS Resolution (n 5).
114 Fabiano de Andrade Correa and Voigt (n 8) 6.
115 REDD+ Web Platform <https://redd.unfccc.int/submissions.html?country=ID> accessed 2 April 2024; REDD+ Story Indonesia (5 September 2023) <https://redd.unfccc.int/submissions.html?country=ID> accessed 1 April 2024 (REDD+ Story).
116 ibid.
117 UN-REDD Programme, 'Indonesia Receives Results-based Payments from the Green Climate Fund' (1 December 2020) <www.un-redd.org/news/indonesia-receives-results-based-payments-green-climate-fund> accessed 2 April 2024.
118 Hans Nicholas Jong, 'Indonesia and Norway Give REDD+ Deal Another Go after Earlier Breakup' (*Mongabay,* 12 September 2022) <https://news.mongabay.com/2022/09/indonesia-and-norway-give-redd-deal-another-go-after-earlier-breakup/> accessed 2 April 2024. Note that in 2022, Indonesia did receive
119 Micah L Ingalls and Michael B Dwyer, 'Missing the Forest for the Trees? Navigating the Trade-offs between Mitigation and Adaptation under REDD' (2016) 136 Clim Change 353, 354 (citations omitted).
120 Hans Nicholas Jong, 'Is a Plantation a Forest? Indonesia Says Yes, As It Touts a Drop in Deforestation' (*Mongabay,* 31 January 2018) <https://news.mongabay.com/2018/01/counting-plantations-as-forests-indonesia-claims-decline-in-deforestation/> accessed 2 April 2024.
121 ibid.

122 Ministry of Environment and Forestry of the Republic of Indonesia, 'Indonesia REDD+ National Strategy, 2021–2023' (November 2022) <https://redd.unfccc.int/files/indonesia_redd__national_strategy_2021-2030.pdf> accessed 2 April 2024.

123 Forest Carbon Partnership Facility, 'About the FCPF' <www.forestcarbonpartnership.org/about> accessed 22 April 2024.

124 The World Bank, 'Indonesia and the World Bank Sign Milestone Agreement on Emission Reductions' (8 December2020)<www.worldbank.org/en/news/press-release/2020/12/08/indonesia-and-the-world-bank-sign-milestone-agreement-on-emission-reductions> accessed 22 April 2020; The World Bank, 'Indonesia Receives First Payment for Reducing Emissions in Easy Kalimantan' (8 November 2022 <www.worldbank.org/en/news/press-release/2022/11/08/indonesia-receives-first-payment-for-reducing-emissions-in-east-kalimantan> accessed 2 April 2024 (World Bank First Payment).

125 World Bank First Payment (n 124).

126 ibid.

127 ibid. See

128 Forest Carbon Partnership Facility (FCPF) Carbon Fund Emissions Reductions Program Document (ER-PD), East Kalimantan Jurisdictional Emissions Reductions Program, Indonesia (2019) <https://acrobat.adobe.com/id/urn:aaid:sc:US:e9da6e5d-2a8a-49dc-b5a1-3ff50164d10e> accessed 22 April 2024.

129 <https://www.iucn.org/news/europe/202007/iucn-global-standard-nbs>.

130 UNGA, 6/295 'United Nations Declaration on the Rights of Indigenous Peoples' (13 September 2007) A/RES/61/295, Articles 26, 32.

131 The Constitution Act, 1867 (UK), 30 & 31 Victoria, c. 3, s. 92(5).

7

LINKING INTERNATIONAL HUMAN RIGHTS LAW AND CLIMATE CHANGE

Sumudu Atapattu

Introduction

The link between climate change and human rights has strengthened since the Inuit Petition to the Inter-American Commission of Human Rights (IACHR) in 2005.[1] From Human Rights Council (HRC) Resolutions[2] to the request for an advisory opinion from the ICJ in 2023,[3] the impact of climate change on the enjoyment of rights has received considerable attention in recent years,[4] culminating in the creation of a special mandate on climate change and human rights in 2021.[5] The Paris Agreement includes a reference to human rights in its Preamble: 'Parties should, when taking action to address climate change, *respect, promote and consider* their respective obligations on human rights'.[6] The link between human rights and the environment (including climate change) received a considerable boost with the adoption of the HRC resolution recognizing access to a clean, healthy and sustainable environment as a human right,[7] which was closely followed by a UN General Assembly (UNGA) resolution endorsing this right in almost identical language.[8] The most recent and welcome addition to the burgeoning body of environmental rights is General Comment No 26, adopted by the Committee on the Rights of the Child.[9]

This chapter discusses the link between climate change and human rights and why a rights-based approach to climate change is necessary.[10] It first discusses the impact of climate change on the enjoyment of rights and rights that are being infringed due to adverse consequences of climate change. A discussion of the resolutions of the HRC and the analytical reports prepared by the Office of the High Commissioner for Human Rights (OHCHR) on climate change follows in Section 3. Section 4 summarizes climate litigation as well as pending requests for Advisory Opinions (AOs); Section 5 surveys vulnerable groups and countries that are disproportionately affected by climate change and briefly considers the justice framework and the principle of intersectionality. Section 6 discusses pros and cons of applying a human rights framework to climate change, and Section 7 concludes with final reflections. The chapter argues that despite the challenges of applying a human rights framework to climate change, the obligations of States to adopt both mitigation and adaptation measures under the human rights framework are now well-established, and States have obligations to protect the rights of their citizens from the adverse consequences of climate change.

DOI: 10.4324/9781003276678-9

Impact of Climate Change on the Enjoyment of Rights

From sudden events such as severe weather and floods to slow-onset events such as sea level rise and desertification, it is becoming clear that climate change will have a range of impacts on many of the rights protected under human rights law. As a global problem, no State or community will be spared these adverse consequences, but the impacts will be disproportionately borne by poorer countries and those who are already in a vulnerable position, such as women, children, the poor and the elderly. Moreover, vulnerable communities who have historically contributed least to climate change are disproportionately affected.[11]

Furthermore, extreme heat events, climate-related food and water-borne diseases, increased incidence of vector-borne diseases and mental health challenges have contributed to adverse health impacts seen in many economic sectors, especially climate-exposed sectors like agriculture, forestry, fisheries and tourism. Infrastructure, livelihoods and transportation sectors have also been affected. Certain parts of the world have become too dangerous to live in, or severe weather events have intensified so people are either forced to move or are being relocated to safer areas.[12] Forcible displacement associated with climate change is increasing, and many small island states are facing the prospect of losing their territory to rising seas and severe weather events.

In his thematic report on climate change, UN Special Rapporteur on Human Rights and Environment David Boyd discussed the causes of the climate crisis and its consequences.[13] Noting that 'our society is addicted to fossil fuels', the Special Rapporteur observed that despite three decades of commitments under the UNFCCC, 'the world is neither headed in the right direction, nor addressing the crisis at an adequate pace'.[14] Since 1990, global energy consumption has increased by 57 per cent, while GHG emissions have *increased* by 60 per cent. Instead of phasing out fossil fuels, States provided subsidies amounting to $5.2 trillion in 2017.[15] The SR stressed that States have obligations to protect human rights from environmental harm, and the potentially catastrophic effects of climate change require States to take immediate action to prevent those harms.[16]

Stressing that climate change is already infringing the human rights of billions and exacerbating inequality and injustice, the SR called upon States to submit ambitious NDCs to reduce GHG emission by 45 per cent by 2030, as recommended by the IPCC.[17] He stressed that the 'failure to fulfil international climate change commitments is a prima facie violation of the State's obligations to protect the human rights of its citizens'.[18]

The tripartite typology of obligations proposed by former Special Rapporteur John Knox is also useful.[19] Substantive obligations include the obligation to adopt and implement a legal and institutional framework that protect against environmental harm; the obligation to protect against environmental harm from private actors; and obligations relating to transboundary environmental harm. The procedural obligations include the duty to assess environmental impacts; provide access to information; the duty to facilitate public participation in environmental decision-making; and the duty to provide access to legal remedies.[20]

Resolutions of HRC and OHCHR Reports

The HRC's first resolution on climate change was adopted in 2008, soon after the Inuit petition was dismissed by the IACHR.[21] Concerned that 'climate change poses an immediate and far-reaching threat to people and communities around the world and has implications for the full enjoyment of human rights',[22] HRC requested the OHCHR to conduct an analytical study on the relationship between climate change and human rights,[23] and encouraged States to contribute.

In Resolution 10/4, the HRC noted that climate change has a range of implications for the enjoyment of human rights, including the rights to life and safe drinking water and sanitation, and recognized that the effects of climate change will be felt by those who are already in vulnerable situations due to poverty, gender, age, Indigenous or minority status and disability.[24] The HRC encouraged special mandate holders to consider climate change within their mandates.[25] The HRC, stressing the importance of holding the temperature increase to below 2 degrees Celsius above pre-industrial levels and trying to limit it to 1.5 degrees, called upon States to consider human rights within the UNFCCC and to 'adopt a comprehensive, integrated and gender-responsive approach' to adaptation and mitigation policies.[26] The HRC has thus far requested the OHCHR to prepare studies on a gender-responsive approach to climate action,[27] rights of persons with disabilities, rights of migrants and the rights of older persons in the context of climate change.[28]

Resolution 41/21 referred to the importance of facilitating interaction between human rights and climate change communities at national and international levels to build capacity, considering the Geneva Pledge for Human Rights in Climate Action[29] and similar efforts, and expressed concern that climate change is contributing to the increased frequency and intensity of both sudden-onset and slow-onset events. It urged states to implement policies to increase the participation of persons with disabilities in climate responses.[30]

Reaffirming the commitment to implement the UNFCCC and Paris Agreement, Resolution 47/24 stressed that responses to climate change should be integrated with social and economic development.[31] Recognizing that climate change posed an existential threat to some countries, the HRC expressed concern that adverse effects are felt more acutely by those who are already in a vulnerable situation due to geography and other factors and called upon states to *consider* human rights within the UNFCCC.[32] Additionally, the HRC requested the Secretary-General to submit a report on the adverse impact of climate change on human rights of people in vulnerable situations.[33] It encouraged States to discuss the possible creation of a new special procedure addressing the impact of climate change on human rights.[34]

The OHCHR's first major report on climate change was the analytical report prepared pursuant to HRC's 2008 resolution on climate change.[35] Noting that while human rights treaties do not embody a right to a healthy environment, treaty bodies have recognized the link between human rights and the environment,[36] and the report discussed the impact of global warming on specific rights. It also discussed the impact on specific groups, especially women, Indigenous peoples and children,[37] and that States must address these vulnerabilities under principles of equality and non-discrimination. The report noted that 'climate refugees' do not have a legal basis in international law. Likewise, while the eventual submergence of small island states is a possibility, human rights law does not provide answers to the status of these populations.[38]

Moreover, the report noted that there are human rights implications of measures that States adopt to address climate change, such as agro-fuel production and the REDD program.[39] While there is consensus that climate change has negative implications for the enjoyment of human rights, the report cautiously concluded that 'it is less obvious whether, and to what extent, such effects can be qualified as human rights violations in a strict legal sense'.[40] Nonetheless, human rights obligations provide protections to people whose rights are affected by climate change and require international cooperation among States.[41]

Climate Litigation

One of the fastest-growing areas of action on climate change relates to litigation,[42] which has become a tool to enforce or enhance commitments made by governments. While most common grounds are based in constitutional or administrative law, the use of human rights arguments continues to rise – over 100 human rights cases have been identified globally, with 29 of them filed in 2020.[43]

The IACHR was the first human rights body to receive a petition on climate change.[44] The petitioners alleged that the impacts of climate change violate their rights protected by the American Declaration of Rights and Duties of Man,[45] including the rights to culture, property, health, life, physical integrity, security, means of subsistence and residence, the freedom of movement and the inviolability of the home.[46] The Commission dismissed the petition *without prejudice*, stating that the information provided was insufficient to make a determination,[47] but did hold a hearing on Global Warming and Human Rights.[48] Although the petition did not reach the merits phase, it had a cascading effect, giving rise to a flurry of activity in human rights circles.[49]

The Inter-American system was again the forum for a groundbreaking AO that had implications for climate law.[50] This was the first opportunity for the Court to elaborate on States' obligations relating to environmental protection under the ACHR.[51] It affirmed the right to a healthy environment as a right in itself, and that multiple human rights are vulnerable to environmental degradation.[52] It emphasized

> that the right to a healthy environment is an autonomous right which protects elements of the environment, such as forests, rivers, seas . . . as legal interests in themselves, even in the absence of the certainty or evidence of a risk to individuals. . .

thus, recognizing both the right to a healthy environment and the rights of nature.[53]

The effective control test established by the Court with regard to extraterritorial obligations has been followed by other human rights bodies.[54]

In their 2023 request for an AO, Chile and Colombia referred several questions on climate change to the Court.[55]

The latest development is the UN GA's request for an advisory opinion from the ICJ on the obligations of states in respect to climate change pursuant to the campaign spearheaded by Vanuatu.[56] An AO from the world court, while not binding, will go a long way in clarifying states' obligations in relation to climate change.

The European Court of Human Rights (ECtHR) has become the site of most climate-related cases.[57] *Duarte Agostinho and Others v Portugal and 32 Other States*,[58] although dismissed by the ECtHR, is unprecedented as it was filed against *all* signatories to the ECHR. A group of youth from Portugal petitioned about climate-related violations linked to, *inter alia*, rights to life and a healthy environment, as harmed by 33 States under the jurisdiction of the ECtHR.[59] The petitioners referred to catastrophic climate events, including forest fires in Portugal, heatwaves that force them to spend time indoors and that young people stand to experience the worst effects of climate change. They linked such harms to years of contributions to climate change by the respondent States.[60] The Court declined to pronounce on extraterritorial obligations of States relating to climate change, despite emerging jurisprudence on this issue.

In *Greenpeace Nordic and Others v. Norway*,[61] currently pending, the petitioners alleged that in issuing new licenses for oil and gas exploration in the Arctic, the Norwegian government violated the petitioners' rights under Articles 2 and 8 of the ECHR. They also alleged that the government failed to assess their claims and to provide them with access to an effective remedy under Article 13 of the ECHR. According to the petition, the applicants experience 'climate anxiety, emotional distress and worry greatly about the current and imminent risks of serious climate effects in Norway, and how this will impact their lives, life-choices, and the lives of future generations'.[62] Norway requested that the Court pronounce the complaint inadmissible and inexplicably claimed that

Russia's invasion of Ukraine justified more oil and gas exploration, 'thus increasing greenhouse gas emissions for another 30 years or more'.[63]

KlimaSeniorinnen v. Switzerland[64] involved allegations by the group *Senior Women for Climate Protection Switzerland* about the failure by the Swiss government to protect their health from heat waves which are worsened by the climate crisis, and they requested the case to be expedited pursuant to the Rules of the Court. Complaints included that the Swiss government's inadequate climate policies violate women's right to life and health under Articles 2 and 8; the Federal Supreme Court's rejection of their case on arbitrary grounds violated the right to a fair trial under Article 6; and the Swiss authorities' and courts' failure to deal with the content of their complaints violated the right to an effective remedy under Article 13 of the ECHR. In a decision hailed as a major victory for climate change, the ECtHR held in favor of the NGO "KlimaSeniorinen" and that Swiss government's failure to act on climate change violated Articles 2, 6 and 8 of the ECHR.

UN Treaty Bodies have also received complaints on climate change. While not successful, *Sacchi and others v. Argentina*[65] was a major communication submitted to the Committee on the Rights of the Child (CRC Committee).[66] In October 2021, the Committee on the Rights of the Child Committee issued its decision in all five cases.[67] The Committee pointed out that the harm suffered by the victims needs to have been reasonably foreseeable to the State party *at the time of its acts or omissions*, even for the purpose of establishing jurisdiction. With regard to climate as a global problem, the Committee's observations are noteworthy:

> The Committee notes the authors' claims that, while climate change and the subsequent environmental damage and impact on human rights it causes is a global collective issue that requires a global response, *States parties still carry individual responsibility for their own acts or omissions* in relation to climate change and their contribution to it.[68] (emphasis added)

Turning to the issue of domestic remedies, the Committee noted that authors must make use of all judicial or administrative avenues available unless they objectively have no prospect of success, but 'mere doubts or assumptions about the success or effectiveness of remedies do not absolve the authors from exhausting them'.[69]

The decision of the Committee is significant in that it recognized that climate change posed a significant risk to the enjoyment of rights protected under the Convention, and it accepted that States may be held responsible for any significant damage caused to persons *outside* their borders by activities originating in their territory or under their effective control or authority. In deciding whether activities are under the effective control of states, the Committee held that children are under the jurisdiction of the State in whose territory the emissions originated if there is a *causal link* between the acts or omissions of the State in question and the negative impact on the rights of children located outside its territory, *when the State of origin exercises effective control over the sources of the emissions in question.* Further, the collective nature of the causation of climate change does not absolve the State party of its individual responsibility to limit its emissions; scientific evidence showed that the potential harm of the state party's acts or omissions regarding carbon emissions was reasonably foreseeable to the state party; harm must lead to a real detrimental effect; and states have a heightened responsibility to protect children from foreseeable harm.[70]

In *Teitiota v. New Zealand*,[71] the UN Human Rights Committee was confronted with the issue of 'climate refugees' for the first time.[72] The communication by Mr. Teitiota, a citizen of the Republic of Kiribati, was the culmination of a series of failed applications for refugee status in New Zealand.[73] The Committee believed that the question is whether the author had substantiated his claim that deportation would cause a real risk of irreparable harm to his right to life[74] and is thus a 'victim' under the Optional Protocol to the ICCPR. The Committee noted that the author's claims are not hypothetical future harm, but 'a real predicament caused by lack of potable water and employment possibilities, and a threat of serious violence caused by land disputes'.[75] Relying on GC No 31,[76] the Committee noted that States are under an obligation not to remove a person from their territory when there is *a real risk of irreparable harm* under Articles 6 and 7 of the ICCPR.[77]

This decision breaks new ground for several reasons: *first*, the Committee recognized that both sudden events and slow-onset events associated with climate change can trigger the movement of people, essentially accepting the notion of 'climate refugees'; *second*, it accepted that climate change could, in extreme situations, affect the right to life, triggering the application of the *non-refoulement* principle;[78] *third*, sea-level rise could render the Republic of Kiribati (and, by implication, other small island states) uninhabitable; and *finally*, it indirectly referred to the obligation of the international community to assist these countries to take affirmative action, including relocating the populations.

In *Daniel Billy et al v. Australia*,[79] the UN Human Rights Committee decided in favor of a group of eight Torres Strait Islanders,[80] who alleged that Australia's contribution to GHG emissions and its failure to adopt adaptation measures violated their human rights under the ICCPR. The authors claimed that the state party had failed to adopt both adaptation measures and mitigation measures to reduce GHG emissions and to stop the promotion of fossil fuel extraction and use. They relied on GC No 36 to show that climate change is a human rights issue.[81] Australia requested that the petition be dismissed on the grounds, *inter alia*, that it cannot be held responsible for a global problem.[82]

Australia maintained that the communication is inadmissible because the alleged violations of treaties such as the Paris Agreement and the ICESCR are outside the scope of the Covenant, and 'interpreting the Covenant through the Paris Agreement would be contrary to the fundamental principles of international law'.[8384]

On merits, the Committee noted that Article 6 cannot be interpreted in a restrictive manner and it requires States to adopt positive measures to protect life; this obligation extends to reasonably foreseeable threats and life-threatening situations, even if such threats do not result in the loss of life.[85]

With regard to mitigation measures, the Committee noted that as one of the largest producers of GHG emissions, the alleged actions or omissions fall under the state party's jurisdiction. With regard to adaptation measures, the Committee noted that the state party has positive obligations to protect the rights of individuals under their jurisdiction. Additionally, by not addressing the delay in seawall construction, the reduction of marine resources used for food and the loss of crops, the state violated the authors' private life, family and home. The Committee thus held the State liable for full reparation to individuals whose Covenant rights had been violated.[86]

Vulnerable Groups, Vulnerable Countries and Climate Refugees

It is well recognized that those who contributed least to climate change are the most affected by it. This inverse relationship between cause and effect has led many scholars to argue that a justice approach to climate change is necessary to protect these vulnerable communities.[87] There are many reasons why these communities are more affected than others – while some reasons are geographic and social, others are historic and structural.[88] Vulnerable and marginalized groups and communities for whom states have heightened obligations include women, children, minorities, Indigenous peoples, older persons, people in poverty, people with disabilities, LGBTQI+ people and rural people. Many of these vulnerabilities and injustices intersect with one another to create greater vulnerabilities and injustices.[89] OHCHR recognized in its analytical report that:

> The effects of climate change will be felt most acutely by those segments of the population who are already in vulnerable situations due to factors such as poverty, gender, age, minority status, and disability. Under international human rights law, States are legally bound to address such vulnerabilities in accordance with the principle of equality and non-discrimination.[90]

The 2017 OHCHR report[91] noted that both slow-onset and sudden events have a devastating impact on people and the planet. Since 2008, about 221.5 million people per year have been displaced, internally and across borders, by weather- or climate-related disasters. Unjustly, climate change disproportionately harmed people who had contributed the least to it.[92] The report pointed out that migrants fled the effects of climate change not out of choice but because of the need to escape conditions that could not provide basic fundamental rights. Throughout their migration they faced violations of other rights, including xenophobia. While human rights law did provide for the protection of those who are on the move, there are gaps with regard to those fleeing the adverse consequences of climate change, especially slow-onset impacts.[93]

The report highlighted the need to address the underlying causes of migration.[94] While most displaced persons remained within their own country, some crossed international borders, but international law did not provide a right of admission and stay. The Nansen Initiative showed that human rights played a role here:[95] first, reducing displacement risks in countries of origin by addressing poverty, population density, bad governance and discrimination. Second, ensuring access to food, water, shelter and health for those who are migrating. Finally, a rights-based approach could help in relation to admission to other countries in disaster-affected situations. States should protect the rights of migrants regardless of their status, and millions of people are on the move due to climate change; some regions and countries are particularly affected, exacerbated by the protection gap in international law.[96]

Pursuant to HRC resolution 38/4, the OHCHR prepared an analytical study on gender-responsive climate action.[97] It noted that diverse factors, including social status, gender and poverty affects one's capacity to adapt to climate change. While human rights law prohibits gender-based discrimination, women often face systemic discrimination, including limited access to financial assets and services, education, land resources and decision-making.[98]

The report examined the relevant provisions of the ICESCR and CEDAW, both of which prohibit gender-based discrimination. In 2017, the parties adopted the Gender Action Plan under the Lima Work Program to guide gender-responsive approaches to climate change.[99] Climate finance is another area that requires a gender-responsive approach.[100]

Pursuant to HRC resolution 41/21, the OHCHR prepared a study on the promotion and protection of rights of persons with disabilities in the context of climate change.[101] An estimated 1 billion people who have a disability may experience the adverse impacts more severely than others, especially during emergencies, sustaining higher rates of morbidity and mortality.[102] The IPCC notes that the poorest people will continue to experience the worst impacts of climate change due to lost income, displacement, hunger and health problems. Multiple intersecting factors of discrimination related to gender, poverty, displacement, disability, age and indigeneity increase the risks of climate change experienced by persons with disabilities. Thus, their participation will allow for tailored action that addresses their specific needs.[103]

The report discusses health care inequities, food insecurity, access to accessible homes, access to water and sanitation, livelihoods and decent work and mobility faced by persons with disabilities. Persons with disabilities are at risk of being left behind in a degraded environment without support networks, and they face related challenges when members of their family or community migrate due to climate change impacts.[104] The report recommended fully integrating human rights and disability into climate action.[105]

Pursuant to Human Rights Council resolution 44/7, in 2021, OHCHR prepared an analytical study on the protection of rights of older person in relation to climate change.[106] Older persons do not constitute a homogenous group and there is enormous variance among them; neither is there an agreed-upon definition. However, they are often overlooked in research and data collection, and individuals may not self-identify within the 'older persons' category.[107] Moreover, their mental health is affected due to loneliness and isolation.

Rights affected include rights to food, water and sanitation, social protection, care and support, decent work and livelihoods, human mobility and cultural rights. The report also discussed multiple and intersecting forms of discrimination in relation to gender, disabilities, minorities and Indigeneity.[108] Discussing the key human rights instruments, the report pointed out that treaties such as the ICCPR, ICESCR, CEDAW and the CRPD protect older persons' human rights, even though age is not specifically identified as a prohibited ground of discrimination. Moreover, States have legal obligations to implement climate policies that empower all people by ensuring their full participation in climate action,[109] and several general comments refer to older persons.[110]

Another group that is especially vulnerable to climate change is Indigenous peoples. UN Special Rapporteur on Cultural Rights Karima Bennoune recognized the impact of climate change on Indigenous peoples for whom connections to place, land and relationships with culturally important animals, plants and ecosystems play an important role. Lack of respect for land rights exacerbate their vulnerabilities, especially for Indigenous women who care for the land and face resource scarcity of traditional foods and medicines.[111] Adaptation and mitigation measures taken in response to climate consequences without free, prior and informed consent of Indigenous peoples or without their participation could further undermine cultural rights.[112] Special Rapporteurs on Indigenous Peoples also discussed the disproportionate impact of climate change (and environmental pollution) on Indigenous peoples,[113] as well as the ever-expanding conservation measures, including World Heritage sites.[114] In addition, a complaint was submitted to 10 special mandate holders by the Alaska Institute for Justice on behalf of five tribes located in Louisiana and Alaska facing climate displacement.[115]

It is well recognized that children are more susceptible to climate change than other groups, both because their immune systems are not yet well-developed and because climate consequences will worsen in the future. The adoption of General Comment No 26 by the Committee on the Rights of the Child in August 2023 recognized that the triple planetary crisis – climate change, loss of biodiversity and pollution – poses an urgent and systemic threat to children's rights globally.[116] It calls upon States to apply a child rights-based approach to the environment that requires the full consideration of children's rights under the Convention on the Rights of the Child. The GC stressed the need to phase out the use of coal, oil and natural gas, create just transition of energy sources and invest in renewable energy.[117]

Part V of the GC is devoted to climate change, organized under mitigation, adaptation, loss and damage, finance and the business sector. It calls for the urgent collective mitigation action by all States, especially by major emitters, to reduce greenhouse gas emissions in line with their human rights obligations and best available science and with a view to achieving net zero carbon emissions by 2050.

Regarding adaptation, the GC calls upon states to identify climate change-related vulnerabilities among children concerning essential services such as water, sanitation, nutrition, healthcare and education. Adaptation measures, including disaster risk reduction and preparedness, should be targeted to reduce both short-term and long-term impacts, including protecting schools and developing sustainable water management systems.

In terms of loss and damage, States are encouraged to consider that, from a human rights perspective, it is closely related to the right to remedy and reparations, and they are required to take all necessary and reasonable measures to protect against harms to children's rights related to climate change perpetrated by business enterprises, including reductions in emissions and due diligence procedures.

While the prior discussion referred to groups of people who are especially susceptible to climate change, no other group of countries is as vulnerable to climate change as small island states which could lose territory – and with it, perhaps statehood.[118] Both scientists and human rights groups have recognized this possibility – in the *Teitiota case*, the UN Human Rights Committee recognized that Kiribati (and by implication other small island states) could become uninhabitable in 10 to 15 years' time.[119] While several proposals have been advanced, it is not clear what the legal status of these states is going to be if some of them lose territory (or population, or both) altogether. Despite loss and damage being included in the Paris Agreement, it remained contentious and was recognized as a separate fund at COP27 and operationalized at COP28, 10 years after the Warsaw International Mechanism for Loss and Damage was established.[120]

Advantages and Challenges of Using a Human Rights Framework for Climate Change

Victims of climate change have turned to international human rights regimes and compliance mechanisms to seek redress and to deter future rights violations. As the Paris Agreement acknowledges, States are required to ensure that they do not violate the rights of their citizens when acting on climate change.[121] Although there are challenges to using the human rights framework discussed here, victims have an avenue to seek relief for the violations of their rights caused by climate change by resorting to the sophisticated network of treaties and institutions. This gives a human face to climate change, illustrating the dimension of actual victims and pressing the need for more climate action.

Despite the burgeoning jurisprudence on climate change using human rights law and the increasing willingness of human rights bodies to address them, cases shed light on the legal hurdles that hinder human rights litigation, viz exhaustion of local remedies, imminent threat, enforceability, the global nature of climate change involving multiple emitters and multiple victims, causality and extraterritoriality.[122]

Regarding attribution issues, there is no reason why responsibility of States cannot be based on the common but differentiated responsibility principle (CBDR).[123] After all, the international community was willing to base their obligations on this principle – a significant breakthrough in international law.[124] If obligations are based on the CBDR principle, the legal regime that comes into play when a violation of that obligation occurs[125] should also be based on that principle. In *Daniel Billy*'s case, the Human Rights Committee dismissed Australia's argument that it cannot be held responsible for a global problem. In *Sacchi v Argentina*, the CRC Committee specifically referred to the CBDR principle in endorsing states' individual responsibilities to address climate change.[126]

Climate change involves multiple actors in every State, but the current responsibility principles, mostly bilateral in nature, are ill-suited to apply to the global climate problem. However, this traditional approach to climate litigation, relying on archaic principles, seems to be giving way to a much more robust and innovative approach – both *Sacchi v Argentina* and *Daniel Billy v Australia* recognized that the global nature of climate change did not absolve states of their individual responsibility to address climate change, which was later endorsed by the CRC Committee in its GC 26.

Despite the innovative approach taken by these bodies, some challenges remain – for example, what constitutes 'an imminent threat' in the context of climate change is closely linked to the *non-refoulement* principle under human rights law (called 'complementary protection'). In the *Teitiota case*, the Human Rights Committee asserted that the threat to the life of the author and his family was not imminent, despite its recognition that Kiribati could become uninhabitable in 10–15 years' time. Does this decision imply that victims should wait until it becomes *impossible to live* in their country, or wait until there is actual loss of life?[127] In the face of climate change, how imminent is imminent?

Thus, returning individuals to countries where there are *substantial grounds for believing that they face a real risk to their lives* violates Articles 6 and 7 of the ICCPR,[128] and since these threats can come from environmental degradation and climate change,[129] climate change consequences can trigger the application of the *non-refoulement* principle. The main obstacle to this is the requirement that the risk of harm must be personal in nature, *except in the most extreme cases*. Non-establishment of personal injury was one of the reasons why Teitiota's claim failed.[130] Given the widespread and pervasive nature of the adverse consequences of climate change, it may be difficult to establish personal injury (or risk of harm) above and beyond the risk of harm to others. Additionally, what constitutes 'extreme cases'? Does rendering these islands uninhabitable constitute 'an extreme case'? If so, can we be more flexible with the rigid requirement of personal injury? Does this provide a potential window for future claims?[131]

Furthermore, in the *Teitiota case*, the Human Rights Committee considered the adaptation measures taken by the national country, Kiribati, as one of the reasons for rejecting the author's request. Would the communication have been successful had the national country *not* taken any adaptation measures to help the citizens, even though that would be a violation of its obligations under international law?[132] Indeed, in *Daniel Billy*, Australia was held accountable for not taking adequate adaptation measures. This raises a dilemma and a disincentive for developing States, especially small island States, to engage in adaptation measures if that could mean their nationals may not succeed in their asylum claims.

Conclusion

This chapter surveyed the legal landscape governing climate change and human rights, and why a rights-based approach to climate change is necessary. There is no doubt that climate change is human-induced. In fact, the 6th IPCC report refers to 'human-caused climate change' in several instances.[133]

Similarly, the impact of climate change on the enjoyment of rights is no longer doubted. From the rather lukewarm reception to the Inuit petition in 2007 to the unanimous UNGA resolution for an ICJ advisory opinion in 2023, a rights-based approach to climate change is now firmly entrenched. There is also a recognition that some communities and States are disproportionately affected and States need to take additional measures to protect them. Climate litigation using the human rights framework has seen a remarkable global increase with some success.

Notes

1 Martin Wagner and Donald M Goldberg, An Inuit Petition to the Inter-American Commission on Human Rights for Dangerous Impacts of Climate Change (2004) CIEL/Earthjustice (Inuit Petition).

2 The first resolution was adopted in 2008. See HRC Res 7/23, Human Rights and Climate Change (28 March 2008) A/HRC/RES/7/23.

3 UNGA, 'Request for an Advisory Opinion of the International Court of Justice on the obligations of States in Respect of Climate Change' (1 March 2023) A/77/L.58 (Climate Change Obligations Advisory Opinion Request); Human Rights Watch, 'UN General Assembly Seeks World Court Ruling on Climate Change' (New York, 29 March 2023) <https://www.hrw.org/news/2023/03/29/un-general-assembly-seeks-world-court-ruling-climate-change>; A similar request was before the International Tribunal for the Law of the Sea (ITLOS) and ITLOS rendered its opinion in May 2024 holding that anthropogenic GHG emissions constitute a form of marine pollution and states parties have specific obligations to take all necessary measures to prevent marine pollution from these emissions (para. 243): *Request for an Advisory Opinion Submitted by the Commission of Small Island States on Climate Change and International Law (No 31)* (Advisory Opinion of 21 May 2024) ITLOS Reports 2024. <https://verfassungsblog.de/the-itlos-advisory-opinion-on-climate-change/>.

4 See e.g. Donald K Anton and Dinah L Shelton, *Environmental Protection and Human Rights* (CUP 2011); Ben Boer, *Environmental Law Dimensions of Human Rights* (OUP 2015); Sumudu Atapattu, *Human Rights Approaches to Climate Change, Challenges and Opportunities* (Routledge 2016); Svitlana Kravchenko and John E Bonine, *Human Rights and the Environment: Cases, Law & Policy* (Carolina Academic Press 2008); Sumudu Atapattu and Andrea Schapper, *Human Rights and the Environment: Key Issues* (Routledge 2019).

5 HRC Res 48/14, Mandate of the Special Rapporteur on the Promotion and Protection of Human Rights in the Context of Climate Change (13 October 2021) A/HRC/RES/48/14 (adopted by 42 votes to 1; 4 abstentions).

6 UNFCCC Decision 1/CP.21, Report of the Conference of the Parties on its twenty-first session, held in Paris from 30 November to 13 December 2015 'Adoption of the Paris Agreement' (2015) FCCC/CP/2015/10/Add.1 (2016) (Paris Agreement), Preamble of the Paris Agreement contained in the Annex. It is unfortunate that the established typology of human rights – respect, protect and fulfill – was diluted by this wording. See Sam Adelman, 'Human Rights in the Paris Agreement: Too Little, Too Late?' (2018) 7 TEL 17.

7 HRC Res 48/13 (8 October 2021) UN Doc A/HRC/RES/48/13 (adopted by 43 votes to none; 4 abstentions).

8 UNGA Res 76/L75 (26 July 2022) UN Doc A/76/L./75, which endorsed a stand-alone right to a healthy environment (The HRC resolution connects the right to a healthy environment to the enjoyment of other rights) and also calls upon States, international organizations and the business community to give effect to the right.

9 Committee on the Rights of the Child 'General Comment No. 26 (2023) on children's rights and the environment, with a special focus on climate change' (22 August 2023) CRC/C/GC/26 (Children's Climate Change Rights).

10 This chapter draws from the author's prior work on this topic.

11 ibid A.2. Pointing out that approximately 3.5 billion people are highly vulnerable to climate change (half the entire population of the world), the report highlights that acute food and water insecurity has increased.

12 In the US, several communities are being relocated or are awaiting relocation. These communities include Isle de Jean Charles in Louisiana, and Kivalina, Shishmarof and Newtok in Alaska; see Abrahm Lustgarten, 'How Climate Migration will Reshape America' *New York Times Magazine* (15 September 2020) <https://www.nytimes.com/interactive/2020/09/15/magazine/climate-crisis-migration-america.html>.

13 UNGA, 'Report of the Special Rapporteur on the issue of human rights obligations relating to the enjoyment of a safe, clean, healthy and sustainable environment' UNGA 74th Session (15 July 2019) UN Doc A/74/161.

14 ibid para 16.

15 ibid para 32.

16 ibid para 62. To comply with their international human rights obligations, States should apply a rights-based approach to all aspects of climate change and climate action clarifying the obligations of States and businesses.

17 ibid para 75. They should prepare 'rights-based deep decarbonization plans' to achieve net zero emissions by 2050.

18 ibid para 74. He called upon States to immediately terminate all fossil fuel subsidies and to ramp up climate finance to fulfill the commitment made by developed countries to mobilize at least $100 billion per year to finance mitigation and adaptation needs of developing countries.

19 HRC, 'Report of the Independent Expert on the Issue of Human Rights Obligations relating to the Enjoyment of a Safe, Clean, Healthy and Sustainable Environment' (30 December 2013) A/HRC/25/53 (Mapping Report). He pointed out that states have *substantive* and *procedural* human rights obligations in relation to environmental issues as well as *heightened obligations* to protect the rights of vulnerable populations.

20 ibid. Many of these are already well-established obligations under international law, and States are required to fulfill them in relation to climate change as well.

21 This section draws from Sumudu Atapattu, *UN Human Rights Institutions and the Environment: Synergies, Challenges, Trajectories* (Routledge 2023).

22 HRC Res 7/23 (n 2), Preamble.

23 See discussion at text to n 35.

24 HRC Res 10/4 (25 March 2009) UN Doc A/HRC/RES/10/4.

25 ibid.

26 HRC Res 38/4 (16 July 2018) UN Doc A/HRC/RES/38/4.

27 ibid. It again encouraged special mandate holders to consider climate change within their respective mandates.

28 These are discussed later in the chapter.

29 See Mary Robinson Foundation – Climate Justice, 'Geneva Pledge on Human Rights and Climate Action Announced' (13 February 2015).

30 HRC Res 41/21 (12 July 2019) UN Doc A/HRC/RES/41/21.

31 HRC Res 47/24 (26 July 2021) UN Doc A/HRC/RES/47/24 (adopted by 46 votes to none; 1 abstention).

32 ibid arts 3–4.

33 See HRC, 'Report of the Secretary General, The Impact of Climate Change on the Human Rights of People in Vulnerable Situations' (6 May 2022) UN Doc A/HRC/50/57.

34 A special rapporteur position was created by Res 48/13 (n 7) on climate change and human rights.

35 HRC, 'Report of the Office of the UN High Commissioner for Human Rights on the Relationship Between Climate Change and Human Rights' (15 January 2009) UN Doc A/HRC/10/61 (OHCHR report).

36 ibid para 8.

37 ibid para 42 (footnotes omitted).

38 ibid para 60.

39 REDD program refers to Reducing Emissions from Deforestation and Forest Degradation, a solution put in place to address deforestation as well as climate change. See <https://redd.unfccc.int>.

40 OHCHR report (n 35) 70 (footnotes omitted). This view seems to have changed since then. See text to n 71 and n 79.

41 ibid para 84–85.

42 This section draws from author's book chapter 'Climate Litigation, International Human Rights, and Right to a Healthy Environment: Connecting the Dots' in Francesco Sindico and others (eds), *Research Handbook on Climate Change Litigation* (Edward Elgar 2024) 304–327.

43 See Joana Setzer and Catherine Higham, 'Global Trends in Climate Change Litigation: 2021 Snapshot' (Grantham Research Institute on Climate Change and the Environment and the Centre for Climate Change Economics and Policy, July 2021) 5, who note that most cases involve action to address climate change, some have the goal of opposing climate action while some cases challenge the way climate action is carried out or its impact on the enjoyment of rights which is seen in the new wave of 'just transition' litigation.

44 Inuit Petition (n 1) 9. The Inuit petition brought by the Inuit Circumpolar Conference on behalf of the Inuit of US and Canada against the US was the first case to utilize the human rights framework to litigate climate change. The petitioners alleged that the US, as the highest emitter of greenhouse gases (GHGs) at that time, bore the greatest responsibility for the damage to the Arctic, adversely affecting their traditional way of life and their human rights.

45 Organization of American States, 'American Declaration of the Rights and Duties of Man' adopted at the 9th International Conference of American States (New York 10 June 1948); Petitioners invoked the American Declaration as the US has not ratified the ACHR.
46 ibid 5.
47 Emphasis added. See Jessica Gordon, 'Inter-American Commission to Hold Hearing after Rejecting Inuit Climate Change Petition' (2007) 7 Sustainable Development L & Policy 55.
48 Earthjustice, 'Inter-American Commission on Human Rights to Hold Hearing on Global Warming' (Washington, DC 6 February 2007) <https://earthjustice.org/press/2007/inter-american-commission-on-human-rights-to-hold-hearing-on-global-warming>.
49 See Hari M Osofsky, 'The Inuit Petition as a Bridge? Beyond Dialectics of Climate Change and Indigenous Peoples' Rights' in William CG Burns and Hari M Osofsky (eds), *Adjudicating Climate Change: State, National, and International Approaches* (CUP 2009) 273.
50 *The Environment and Human Rights*, Advisory Opinion OC-23/17, Inter-American Court of Human Rights (15 Nov 2017); See also Maria L Banda, 'Inter-American Court of Human Rights' Advisory Opinion on the Environment and Human Right' (10 May 2018) 22(6) ASIL Insights 3. In 2016 Colombia requested an AO from the IACtHR on whether: (i) and when a person outside a state's territory falls under its jurisdiction for environmental damage; (ii) serious harm to the marine environment would be incompatible with the American Convention of Human Rights (ACHR); and (iii) the ACHR implies an obligation to respect principles of international environmental law, including those on environmental impact assessment.
51 ibid para 46.
52 ibid para 55.
53 ibid para 62.
54 See *Sacchi v Argentina*, discussed at text to n 65.
55 Ministry of Foreign Affairs, 'Request for an Advisory Opinion on the Scope of the State of Obligations for Responding to the Climate Emergency' (9 January 2023). Unofficial translation of petition available at <https://climatecasechart.com/wp-content/uploads/non-us-case-documents/2023/20230109_18528_petition-3.pdf>. Questions posed to the court include: (a) what are the obligations of states to prevent and guarantee human rights with regard to the climate emergency; (b) what is the scope of substantive and procedural obligations on human rights and the environment; (c) clarify the differentiated obligations of states to protect the rights of children and future generations from climate change; (d) clarify obligations to protect environmental defenders, especially Indigenous people and women; (e) clarify the shared and the differentiated obligations amongst the states in the region; and (f) what actions should be taken regarding climate migration. For further reading see: Maria Antonia Tigre and others, 'Advisory Opinion on Climate Change: Summary of Written Observations Submitted to the Inter-American Court of Human Rights (Part 1)' (Sabin Center for Climate Change Law, Columbia Law School 2024) <https://scholarship.law.columbia.edu/cgi/viewcontent.cgi?article=1222&context=sabin_climate_change>.
56 Climate Change Obligations Advisory Opinion Request (n 3) UNGA, 'recognizing that climate change is an unprecedented challenge of civilizational proportions' referred the following questions to the Court: (a) what are the obligations of states under international law to ensure protection of the climate system from anthropogenic GHG emissions and (b) what are the legal consequences under these obligations for states where they have caused, by their acts and omissions, significant harm to the climate system, to states, especially small island states, and peoples and individuals of the present and future generations affected by adverse consequences of climate change?; see also Maria Antonia Tigre and Jorge Alejandro Carrillo Banuelos, 'The ICJ Advisory Opinion on Climate Change: What Happens Now? *Climate Law – A Sabin Center Blog* (29 March 2023) <https://blogs.law.columbia.edu/climatechange/2023/03/29/the-icjs-advisory-opinion-on-climate-change-what-happens-now/>
57 See Ministry of Foreign Affairs (n 55).
58 *Duarte Agostinho and Others v Portugal and 32 Other States* App no 39371/20 (2020). For similar cases see, *De Conto v Italy and 32 other states*, App no 14620/21(2021); and *Uricchio v Italy and 32 other States*, Appl no 14615/21 (2021).
59 The complaint relied on Articles 2, 8 and 14 of the ECHR.
60 ESCR-Net, 'Members Intervene in Pair of Groundbreaking Climate Change-related Human Rights Cases Pending at the Grand Chamber of European Court of Human Rights' (9 September 2022) <https://www.escr-net.org/news/2022/members-intervene-pair-groundbreaking-climate-change-related-human-rights-cases-pending>

61 *Greenpeace Nordic and Others v. Norway* App no 34068/21 (2021).
62 ibid.
63 ibid.
64 *KlimaSeniorinnen v. Switzerland* App no 53600/20 (2020). Several other cases have been dismissed or are pending. For a complete list of cases see http://climatecasechart.com/non-us-jurisdiction/european-court-of-human-rights/.
65 Committee on the Rights of the Child, Decision adopted by the Committee under the Optional Protocol to the Convention on the Rights of the Child on a communications procedure, concerning communication No. 104/2019 (11 November 2021) UN Doc CRC/C/88/D/104/2019 (*Sacchi*).
66 ibid Article 3.3. The authors argued that the climate crisis is not an abstract future threat and children around the world already carry the burden of climate change. They believe that the climate crisis is a children's rights crisis, mitigating climate change is a human rights imperative and human rights obligations are informed by principles of international environment law. They claimed that the acts and omissions of states have exposed them to 'foreseeable, life threatening risks' of climate change, including jeopardizing subsistence practices of Indigenous authors from Alaska to the Marshall Islands, affecting their cultural identity. They invoked Article 6 (right to life), Article 24 (right to health), Article 30 (minority rights and the right to enjoy culture, language and religion) as well as Article 3, which embodies the best interests of the child principle.
67 ibid.
68 ibid Article 10.8. The Committee further noted that there is scientific evidence that carbon emissions from the State party contribute to worsening climate change, having an adverse effect on the enjoyment of rights by individuals both within and beyond the territory of the State party. Relying on scientific evidence, the Committee considered that the potential harm of the State party's acts or omissions regarding carbon emissions was reasonably foreseeable.
69 ibid Article 10.17.
70 See Tigre and Maria Antonia Tigre and Victoria Lichet, "The CRC Decision in Sacchi v. Argentina," *Insights, American Society of International Law*, Vol 25: 26, 13 December 2021, https://www.asil.org/sites/default/files/ASIL_Insights_2021_V25_I26.pdf, who believe that the decision 'contributes to a broader toolbox of responses at local, national, regional, and international levels to the climate emergency. Overall, the CRC highlighted that climate change is indeed a child rights crisis and that states are responsible for their emissions. Children willing to sue states for failing to address climate change now have a direct legal framework to bring a case before the CRC if they exhaust local remedies'. They referred to the CRC Committee's decision to draft a General Comment on children's rights and the environment with a special focus on climate change 'thus signaling the potential of human rights litigation to contribute to normative development beyond a specific case'.
71 HRC, Views adopted by the Committee under article 5(4) of the Optional Protocol, concerning communication No. 2728/2016 (23 September 2020) UN Doc CCPR/C/127/D/2728/2016 (*Teitiota*). This section draws from Sumudu Atapattu, 'Human Rights and the Environment' in Michael Goodhart (ed) *Human Rights in Theory and Practice* (4th edn, OUP 2022) 297 and 'Migrating with Dignity: Protecting the Rights of "Climate Refugees" with the *Non-refoulement* Principle' in Simon Behrman and Avidan Kent (eds), *Climate Refugees: Global, Local and Critical Approaches* (CUP 2022) 127; See also, Simon Behrman and Avidan Kent, 'Prospects for Protection in Light of the Human Rights Committee's Decision in Teitiota v New Zealand' (2021) Polish Migration Review, 24–35.
72 The term 'climate refugees' is not a legally accepted term. It simply describes those who are compelled to move due to adverse consequences of climate change, whether internally or across borders.
73 Simon Behrman and Avidan Kent, 'Climate-Induced Migration: Will Tribunals Save the Day?' (2020) 2(2) HKJLPA 26. The 1951 Geneva Convention on Refugees protects only political refugees.
74 *Teitiota* (n 71) para 8.5.
75 ibid.
76 HRC General Comment No. 31 [80], The Nature of the General Legal Obligation Imposed on states Parties to the Covenant (26 May 2004) UN Doc CCPR/C/21/Rev.1/Add.13.
77 *Teitiota* (n 71).
78 The non-refoulement principle under human rights law requires states not to return a person to their home country if their rights are likely to be violated. Its application under human rights law is wider than under the refugee law.
79 HRC, Views adopted by the Committee under article 5(4) of the Optional Protocol, concerning communication no. 3624/2019 (22 September 2022) UN Doc CCPR/C/135/D/3624/2019 [Advance unedited version] (*Daniel Billy*).

80 This is the first climate change legal action against Australia alleging a violation of human rights and the first legal action filed by the inhabitants of a low-lying island against a national government for inaction on climate change; See Miriam Cullen, 'Climate Change and Human Rights: The Torres Strait Islanders' Claim to the UN Human Rights Committee' (*Groningen JIntlL*, 27 June 2019) <https://www.grojil.org/blog2/2019/06/27/climate-change-and-human-rights-the-torres-strait-islanders-claim-to-the-un-human-rights-committee.; and Miriam Cullen, 'Eaten by the Sea: Human Rights Claims for the Impacts of Climate Change upon Remote Subnational Communities' (2018) 9(2) JHRE 171.

81 In this case, too, the Special Rapporteurs on Human Rights and Environment filed an amicus brief. See M Faa, 'Torres Strait Islander Complaint against Climate Change Inaction Wins Backing of UN Legal Experts' (*ABC News*, 11 December 2020) <https://www.abc.net.au/news/2020-12-11/torres-strait-islander-complaint-against-climate-change-inaction/12972926>.

82 In *Sacchi* (n 65), the CRC Committee stressed that the global nature of climate change does not absolve states of their *individual responsibility* to address climate change (emphasis added).

83 *Daniel Billy* (n 79) para 4.1.

84 ibid para 4.3. It claimed that none of the alleged failures to take mitigation measures fell within the scope of the Covenant and it is not possible under international human rights law to attribute climate change to the State party, and legally 'it is not possible to trace causal links between the State party's contribution to climate change, its efforts to address climate change, and the alleged effects of climate change on the enjoyment of the authors' rights'.

85 ibid para 8.7. Identical language was used in the *Teitiota case (n 71)*. It observed that regional human rights tribunals have also established that environmental degradation can compromise the enjoyment of the right to life and that severe environmental degradation can affect individuals' well-being, thereby threatening the right to life. The authors' claims under Article 6 mainly relate to their culture which falls within Article 27 of the Covenant. Without robust national and international efforts, climate impact may expose individuals to a violation of Article 6 in the future. Relying on the *Teitiota case*, the Committee said: 'given that the risk of an entire country becoming submerged under water is such an extreme risk, the conditions of life in such a country may become incompatible with the right to life with dignity before the risk is realized'.

86 ibid para 11.

87 While there are many definitions of environmental justice, the four-part definition encompassing distributive justice, procedural justice, corrective justice and social justice is useful. See Robert R Kuehn, 'A Taxonomy of Environmental Justice' (2000) 30 Env't L.Rep. 10681; Carmen G Gonzalez, 'Global Justice in the Anthropocene' in Louis Kotze (ed), *Environmental Law and Governance for the Anthropocene* (Hart Publishing 2017).

88 See Carmen G Gonzalez, 'Racial Capitalism and the Ecological Crises of the Anthropocene' (2022) 21 Perspectives on Global Development and Technology 323; OHCHR report (n 35); HRC, Report of the Special Rapporteur on the issue of human rights obligations relating to the enjoyment of a safe, clean, healthy and sustainable environment (24 January 2018) A/HCR/37/59 (Special Rapporteur's Report); HRC, Women, girls and the right to a clean, healthy and sustainable environment (5 January 2023) UN Doc A/HRC/52/33.

89 Intersectionality and compound injustice are two lenses to study these vulnerabilities and injustices. See Kimberly Crenshaw 'Demarginalizing the Intersections of Race and Sex: A Black Feminist Critique of Antidiscrimination Doctrine, Feminist Theory, and Antiracist Politics' (1989) (1) U Chi Legal F 139.

90 OHCHR report (n 35) para 42 (footnotes omitted).

91 HRC, 'Report of the Office of the United Nations High Commissioner for Human Rights, Summary of the panel discussion on human rights, climate change, migrants and persons displaced across international borders' (14 November 2017) UN Doc A/HRC/37/35 (Panel Report).

92 ibid para 6.

93 ibid para 8.

94 ibid para 12. A key issue is to address the protection needs of all those compelled to move by complex factors and to design long-term solutions, particularly when returning home is not an option, paying greater attention to gender aspects, as 48% of migrants are women.

95 The Nansen Initiative, *Agenda for the Protection of Cross-Border Displaced Persons in the Context of Disasters and Climate Change* (December 2015), vol 1.

96 Under the 1951 Convention Relating to the Status of Refugees, only political refugees are protected as persecution based on certain grounds must be established. A protection gap thus exists with regard to 'climate refugees', which is not a legally accepted term.

97 HRC, Report of the Office of the United Nations High Commissioner for Human Rights, Analytical study on gender-responsive climate action for the full and effective enjoyment of the rights of women (1 May 2019) UN Doc A/HRC/41/26 (Gender Study); see also UN Special Rapporteur's Report (n 91).

98 ibid para 4 (footnotes omitted). The report noted that many smallholder farmers are women whose livelihoods and food sources are at risk due to climate change which contribute to increasing food insecurity among women. Likewise, male-dominated structures that govern land ownership, unequitable distribution of domestic and care work as well as discriminatory laws that restrict women's ownership of land negatively impact their adaptation to climate change. Moreover, climate change can disproportionately affect the physical and mental health of women especially during severe weather events due to scarcity of water, poor air quality and spread of vector-borne diseases. Noting that human mobility poses unique risks to women, the report points out that they are exposed to gender-based violence, as are LGBTQ+ persons. The report also addressed the situation of women human rights defenders.

99 See UNFCCC, 'The Enhanced Lima Work Programme on Gender' <https://unfccc.int/topics/gender/workstreams/the-enhanced-lima-work-programme-on-gender>. Other relevant instruments discussed include the 2030 Agenda, Sendai Framework for Disaster Risk Reduction, Beijing Declaration and the Addis Ababa Declaration.

100 Gender Study (n 97) para 47. In addition, a panel discussion was held on women's rights and climate change: HRC, Report of the Office of the United Nations High Commissioner for Human Rights, Summary of the panel discussion on women's rights and climate change: climate action, good practices and lessons learned (24 July 2019) UN Doc A/HRC/42/26.

101 HRC, Report of the Office of the United Nations High Commissioner for Human Rights, Analytical study on the promotion and protection of the rights of persons with disabilities in the context of climate change (22 April 2020) UN Doc A/HRC/44/30 (Disability Study). It noted that impairment due to disability results from the interaction with attitudinal and environmental barriers which hinder their full participation in society on par with others. Thus, persons with disabilities are at risk of harm due to climate change, which has both direct and indirect impacts on the enjoyment of rights.

102 ibid para 5.

103 ibid para 7.

104 ibid para 21.

105 Disability Study (n 101) at 39.

106 HRC, Report of the Office of the United Nations High Commissioner for Human Rights, Analytical study on the promotion and protection of the rights of older persons in the context of climate change (30 April 2021) A/HRC/47/46. Noting that by 2050 there will be approximately 1.5 billion people aged 65 years and older, the report pointed out that while age itself does not make individuals more vulnerable to climate change, in combination with physical, political, economic and social factors, older persons may be at more risk, as we saw during the COVID-19 pandemic.

107 ibid para 9. Human rights-impacts of climate change are aggravated by ageism and older persons are often considered as passive and incapable. They do not have a specific treaty dedicated to them and environmental instruments often do not mention them. At the same time, climate impacts could affect older persons disproportionately. They are especially affected by heatwaves, extreme cold and during severe weather events. During the 2003 heatwave in Europe, 80% of additional deaths occurred in persons over 75, while during Hurricane Katrina in the U.S., 75% of those who died were over the age of 60.

108 Ibid para 64. In emergencies, they may have difficulty reaching safety while they may not be aware of warnings and evacuation orders, especially if new technologies are used to disseminate such information. If they are displaced, they face additional hurdles in accessing humanitarian aid if they are unfamiliar with new technology to access networks and information.

109 ibid para 41.

110 ibid para 67–68. The recommendations include strengthening the international legal system by conducting empirical research on the impact of climate change on older persons and their rights; including the rights of older persons in future climate COP decisions; adopting an international legal instrument on human rights of older person; and taking urgent action to mitigate and adapt to climate change that protects the human rights of all.

111 UNGA, Note by the Secretary General, Field of cultural rights, UNGA 75th Session (19 August 2020) UN Doc A/75/298 (10 August 2020 para 53.)
112 ibid para 54.
113 HRC, Report of the Special Rapporteur on the Rights of Indigenous Peoples, James Anaya, Addendum: The Situation of Indigenous Peoples in the United States of America (30 August 2012) UN Doc A/HRC/21/47/Add.1.
114 UNGA, Report of the Special Rapporteur of the Human Rights Council on the rights of Indigenous Peoples, Victoria Tauli-Corpuz, UNGA 71st Session (29 July 2016) UN Doc A/71/229.
115 Summary available at <https://climatecasechart.com/non-us-case/rights-of-indigenous-people-in-addressing-climate-forced-displacement/>.
116 Children's Climate Change Rights (n 9), and *Sacchi* (n 65) recognized this vulnerability.
117 ibid para 64. Moreover, it notes that the right to a clean, healthy and sustainable environment is a human right in itself and necessary to enjoy other rights. Thus, environmental degradation and climate change adversely affect the enjoyment of a range of rights, especially by children in disadvantaged situations. In addition to discussing the rights that could be affected by environmental degradation and climate change, GC 26 lays down obligations of states in this context. Elaborating on the right to a clean, healthy and sustainable environment which is implicit in the rights embodied in the CRC, GC 26 noted that the substantive elements of the right are important for children as they include clean air, a safe climate, healthy ecosystems and biodiversity, safe water, healthy food and non-toxic environments. The GC calls upon states to prepare children's rights impact assessment of all proposed legislation, policies, projects, regulations and budgets relating to the environment. They should require the assessment of possible direct and indirect impacts on the environment and climate, including transboundary, cumulative and production and consumption effects on the enjoyment of children's rights, both before and after implementation.
118 See Jenny Grote Soutenburg, 'When Do States Disappear? Thresholds of Effective Statehood and the Continued Recognition of "Deterritorialized" Island States' in Michael B Gerrard and Gregory E Wannier (eds), *Threatened Island Nations: Legal Implications of Rising Seas and a Changing Climate* (CUP 2013) 57.
119 *Teitiota* (n 71).
120 UNFCCC, 'Warsaw International Mechanism for Loss and Damage Associated with Climate Change Impacts (WIM)' <https://unfccc.int/topics/adaptation-and-resilience/workstreams/loss-and-damage/warsaw-international-mechanism#:~:text=The%20COP%20established%20the%20Warsaw,that%20are%20particularly%20vulnerable%20to>
121 Paris Agreement (n 6) Preamble. The Special Rapporteur on Human Rights and the Environment, David Boyd, identified three distinct advantages of bringing human rights into a discussion on climate change: 'First, advocacy grounded in human rights can spur stronger action. . . . Second, human rights norms clarify how States should respond to climate change . . . . Third, human rights bodies can inform and improve climate policy by providing forums for issues concerning climate change and human rights that might otherwise be overlooked'. HRC, 'Report of the Special Rapporteur on the Issue of Human Rights Obligations Relating to the Enjoyment of a Safe, Clean, Healthy and Sustainable Environment' (1 February 2016) UN Doc A/HRC/31/52. HRC, 'Report of the Special Rapporteur on the Issue of Human Rights Obligations Relating to the Enjoyment of a Safe, Clean, Healthy and Sustainable Environment' (1 February 2016) UN Doc A/HRC/31/52.
122 Stephen Humphreys (ed), *Human Rights and Climate Change* (CUP 2010) 32.
123 Lavanya Rajamani, *Differential Treatment in International Law* (OUP 2006); Sumudu Atapattu, *Emerging Principles of international Environmental Law* (Transnational Publishers 2006) ch. 5.
124 See United Nations Framework Convention on Climate Change (adopted 9 May 1992, entered into force 21 March 1994) 1771 UNTS 107 Article 3; Kyoto Protocol to the United Nations Framework Convention on Climate Change (adopted 11 December 1997, entered into force 16 February 2005) 2303 UNTS 162.
125 See International Law Commission, Draft Articles on Responsibility of States for Internationally Wrongful Acts ILC 53rd Session (2001).
126 *Sacchi* (n 65) para 10.10.
127 Behrman and Kent (n 73) argue this can be interpreted as meaning that there has to be actual and widespread loss of life, not simply a threat to life.
128 *Teitiota* (n 71) para 55 (emphasis added).
129 Ibid para 62.

130 Cf. dissenting opinion of Committee member Muhumuza (text to n 71).

131 See Matthew Scott, 'Natural Disasters, Climate Change and *Non-Refoulement*: What Scope for Resisting Expulsion under Articles 3 and 8 of the European Convention of Human Rights?' (2014) 26(3) IJRL 404, who contends that in the context of disasters and the non-refoulement principle, the question of causation of movement is immaterial. The relevant perspective is forward-looking, to the conditions the individual can expect to find on return. Thus, the issue here is not whether it is possible to establish the causal link between climate change and the movement of people, but whether the prevailing conditions in the home country could pose a threat to the right to life and dignity in the event citizens are deported there.

132 See Paris Agreement (n 6) Article 7, and *Daniel Billy* (n 79).

133 IPCC, Summary for Policymakers (2023), https://report.ipcc.ch/ar6syr/pdf/IPCC_AR6_SYR_SPM.pdf, A.1.

8

PROMOTING ACCESS TO INFORMATION, PUBLIC PARTICIPATION AND JUSTICE ON CLIMATE CHANGE

Valentina Durán Medina and Ignacio Sánchez González

Introduction

Climate change is probably the most pressing challenge of all time; therefore, it demands creative and comprehensive strategies and solutions through global cooperation. However, stakeholders must not only be States or public authorities; rather, we must also seek to include individuals, non-governmental organizations and different groups like Indigenous People, diverse ethnicities, migrants, women and children.

This chapter deals with the dynamic that the international legal framework provides between States and the public, especially shedding light on the meaning of green access rights as human rights and their importance on climate action. Key legal instruments will be examined to achieve the latter purpose. The Paris Agreements, the Aarhus Convention and the Escazú Agreement all encompass the actual three pillars of climate change action, meaning the access to environmental information, the right to public participation in decision-making processes and the right of access to justice on environmental matters.

In democratic societies nowadays, it is necessary to ensure these rights as they serve to hold public authorities accountable for their actions while also mandating a high level of transparency to promote robust citizen engagement mechanisms.

Finally, this chapter seeks to clarify how pivotal it is to engage people in climate action or climate governance, proving that States alone cannot the reach the 2030 Agenda common goal of reducing greenhouse gas emissions in order to decrease global warming.

The Importance of Access to Information and Public Participation

The management of contemporary governments and international organisations should be based on a model governed by principles of transparency and probity, allowing citizens and all stakeholders in general to have access to the information they require, whatever it may be, and as a corollary, the possibility in principle of exercising citizen control over the actions of the State.

DOI: 10.4324/9781003276678-10

Indeed, this is what is expected of a state governed by the rule of law conceived as the correlative fruit of the overcoming of monarchies and absolutist states.

Democratic theories indicate that the political authorities fulfil a function in the service of the *demos*, of the common good, in an impersonal way, subject to the laws and within a framework of powers granted only by them. Among the indirect responsibilities is that of being accountable to their constituents, the citizens, by giving an account of their performance. Citizens can exercise a function of participation, supervision or oversight and control of state management, not only through periodic elections, but at all times through the exercise of their rights of expression, association, demonstration and petition.

It follows that it is not enough for rulers, or those who exercise roles of institutional representation or are in decision-making spaces of important global governance schemes, to be democratically elected, but that their functions must also be exercised democratically, and for this there must be mechanisms of control and effective mechanisms of public participation.

This can only be possible when transparency of public management and information is the general rule. The confidentiality of public information is a self-evident contradiction; therefore, to omit this obligation of transparency there must be a real reason proven with facts and sustained in law that justifies placing contingent conditions on this important right that the public possesses.[1]

The right of access to information has been recognised as a human right; however, without the existence of suitable mechanisms to make it effective, it increases the likelihood that both authorities and people in positions of power and decision-making exercise cronyism and opens the possibility that through the weight of undue influence, control or capture of the political establishment by interest groups can be achieved through improper means.[2]

Citizenship, civil society and participation are semantically distinct but closely intertwined concepts. Various initiatives carried out by NGOs, social movements, civic associations or independent media, guided by a common concern to improve the transparency and accountability of government action, monitor the behaviour of public officials, denounce violations of the law or call for investigations and corresponding sanctions.[3]

In essence, the greater the transparency and access to information, the higher the standard and quality of the democratic system, including on environmental and climate justice issues. Any activity related to public affairs must be duly and timely known by all, and above all, accountability must be ensured with the utmost transparency in everything related to public funds, and it must be possible for citizens to access this information for auditing purposes. In this regard, the Organisation of American States has called on the countries of the region to update their transparency systems, indicating that neither the actions of the state, which are owed to its citizens, cannot remain indefinitely outside the public domain, nor can the reasons decisions were taken, since it is part of the *acquis communautaire* to know the facts and the acts carried out by the state.[4]

In the Ibero-American context, the Ibero-American Charter of Citizen Participation defines public participation as

> the process of social construction of public policies that, in accordance with the general interest of democratic society, channels, responds to or expands the economic, social, cultural, political and civil rights of individuals, and the rights of the organisations or groups of which they are a part, as well as those of communities and indigenous peoples.[5]

Green Access Rights: Environment and Climate Action

Defining Green Access Rights

In environmental and climate law, access rights have been understood as one of the specific manifestations of environmental justice, and therefore part of the human right to live in a healthy environment. There is an intersection with the three rights of access: access to information, access to public participation and access to justice in environmental matters.

Access rights have been shaped by various international instruments dealing with environment and development. Indeed, Principle 10 of the Rio Declaration on Environment and Development, adopted in 1992 at the United Nations Conference on Environment and Development, known as the "Earth Summit", states that "[e]nvironmental issues are best handled with the participation of all concerned citizens, at the relevant level". In Rio +20 Conference, Principle 10 was also confirmed in the declaration called "The future we want", recognizing the indispensable role of access rights in the framework of sustainable development. Sustainable development

> requires the meaningful involvement and active participation of regional, national and subnational legislatures and judiciaries, and all major groups: women, children and youth, indigenous peoples, non-governmental organizations, local authorities, workers and trade unions, business and industry, the scientific and technological community, and farmers, as well as other stakeholders, including local communities, volunteer groups and foundations, migrants and families as well as older persons and persons with disabilities.

Thus, it is understood that access rights in environmental matters have been configured as fundamental pillars in various areas and have become the basis of "environmental democracy".[6]

Green access rights have three components: access to information on the environment and its provision by the authorities, effective and informed public participation in decision-making that affects the environment and access to justice, where people have the right to access the mechanisms of justice administration to institutionally demand environmental rights. Various instruments have consolidated this approach; for example, SDG 16 ("Peace, Justice and Strong Institutions") has encompassed these elements since a healthy environment is crucial for peace and security, while environmental justice protects communities that are vulnerable and/or seek to enforce their rights. It also strengthens this link by promoting public participation and the rule of law.[7] Furthermore, both the Escazú Agreement, which expressly encompasses these three areas under the concept of "access rights", and the Aarhus Agreement, which refers to them jointly and in a correlated manner, have been reaffirming these insights and extending them to other areas, such as climate action.

Green Access Rights are Human Rights

It is important to highlight that the rights of access to information, participation and justice in environmental matters and decisions follow the same principles and logic detailed supra, i.e., conceptually, even though they are *environmental*, they are indeed human rights and contribute directly to the access and guarantee of access to justice.[8]

These rights do not operate in isolation but are inextricably linked. If one is diminished, the effectiveness of the others is compromised, while the guarantee of one is indispensable for the realisation of the others. This complex interdependence is the basis of environmental democracy, which in turn is a fundamental component of environmental justice[9] and has been so understood, even in the Inter-American Human Rights System.

In relation to this last point, it is relevant to consider that the Inter-American Court of Human Rights has developed this interpretation in its advisory and jurisdictional powers.

On the one hand, Advisory Opinion OC-23/17 of the Inter-American Court of Human Rights, issued in 2017 and requested by the Republic of Colombia, represents a fundamental milestone in analysing the relationship between human rights and the environment. The Court establishes a clear interdependence and indivisibility between environmental protection, sustainable development, and the enjoyment of human rights. This analysis recognises that the adverse effects of climate change, such as environmental degradation and pollution, directly impact the effective enjoyment of various basic human rights. The Court emphasises that the vulnerability of certain social groups, such as Indigenous Peoples or impoverished communities, makes them more susceptible to these violations. The Advisory Opinion also underlines the importance of procedural rights, such as access to information, public participation and access to environmental justice, pointing to them as essential tools to guarantee substantive rights and support States in the fulfilment of their environmental obligations.[10]

The well-known case of *Claude Reyes et al. v. Chile*, which has been decisive in defining the rights of access to information and participation, is noteworthy. The Court established that information is essential for public participation in the development of communities, as it allows people to know the risks and benefits of projects or activities and to make informed decisions about their future. The Court established that the refusal to provide environmental information must be exceptional, justified by law and guided by the principle of maximum disclosure. In addition, the denial is only valid if it is made within a reasonable period of time, is presented in writing, is based on a pre-established legal reason, responds to an imperative public interest and restricts access to information to the least extent possible.[11]

Green Access Rights and Climate Action

As mentioned at the beginning of this chapter, access rights arising from strictly environmental matters are now intrinsically related to climate change and its normative and conceptual developments.

The severe climate crisis demands a strong response. SDG 13 calls for ambitious climate action that prioritises the most vulnerable. This action must be fair and consider human rights and the rule of law.

In terms of legal instruments, historic milestones have been achieved in the fight against climate change at the level of binding international treaties. The Paris and Aarhus Agreements, for instance, and the Escazú Agreement in particular (which will be discussed in detail in the following section), mark a "before and after" in community participation to meet the 2030 Agenda. These agreements are a fundamental tool for achieving climate justice and realising the theoretical and conceptual considerations summarised at the beginning of this chapter.

It should also be noted that regional and international cooperation can be strengthened by ensuring access to information, public participation and climate justice. For example, the Regional Agreement on Access to Information, Public Participation, and Justice in Environmental Matters in Latin America and the Caribbean promotes these principles as fundamental elements of effective climate policy.[12]

When it comes to promoting good governance in climate change, public awareness, participation and access to information are crucial. The United Nations Framework Convention on Climate Change (UNFCCC) stresses the importance of public awareness, participation and access to information in the context of climate change.

In this regard, it is clear that access to information, climate and environmental justice and public participation are essential to address climate change at both local and global levels. These elements enable climate policies to be effective, transparent and accountable, ultimately leading to better outcomes for communities and the environment. By promoting these principles, governments, organisations and individuals (i.e. the multi-stakeholder community) can combine efforts to develop and implement sound solutions to climate change.

Paris Agreement Provisions on Access to Information and Justice, and Public Participation

The Paris Agreement Preamble

For more than a decade, it has been increasingly confirmed that the climate crisis reinforces situations of risk and vulnerability, directly affecting human development and certain disadvantaged groups: the poor, women, children, the elderly and Indigenous Peoples.[13] Therefore, it has been of particular importance to have binding legal instruments at the international level to address this issue through access to information, justice and public participation.

In this regard, the Paris Agreement recognises the fundamental role of public participation, access to information and justice in effectively addressing climate change. Already at the preambular level, these important safeguards are recognised.

The preamble of the Paris Agreement recognizes the importance of the right to development and meeting the specific needs and concerns of developing countries that are particularly vulnerable to the adverse effects of climate change. This involves ensuring access to justice for those affected by the impacts of climate change.

In other preambular provisions, the parties reaffirm the importance of education, training, public awareness, public participation, public access to information and cooperation at all levels on the issues addressed in the Agreement. It also introduces for the first time and recognises the importance of climate justice regarding the actions that can be taken to address climate change.

Substantive Provisions for Access to Information, Justice and Public Participation

There are also substantive provisions of the Agreement that address the aforementioned acknowledgements. For example, Article 7 refers to communications on adaptation, where parties must periodically communicate their adaptation plans and needs, promoting transparency and public access to this information.

Article 12 addresses improving education, training, public awareness, public participation and public access to information: This article encourages all countries to work together to improve public understanding of climate change and ensure that people can participate in decision-making processes related to climate action. These elements are particularly important, because although Article 12 does not detail aspects related to, for example, the actions involved in such guarantees, it is possible to provide content through the expertise of international legal doctrine.

Thus, public awareness necessarily involves increasing public understanding of climate change and its impacts.[14] This provides the basis for effective and meaningful public participation, which can be understood as enabling people to participate in the decision-making and implementation processes related to climate action.[15]

The Paris Agreement Transparency Framework

Finally, in relation to public access to information, the aim is to ensure transparency and accessibility of information on climate change, including national contributions (NDCs), adaptation plans and financial support provided.[16]

Article 13 refers to transparency frameworks. This article establishes a robust transparency framework for monitoring and reporting on progress toward the Agreement's objectives. It includes provisions for public access to information submitted by countries, promoting transparency and accountability.

The Paris Agreement Transparency Framework ('Transparency Framework'), established by virtue of Article 13, constitutes one of the most important aspects of the Paris Agreement, as it involves monitoring and tracking progress towards the objectives of the Agreement, increasing trust between parties and ensuring clear information on climate action.

Transparency Framework introduces a number of elements of crucial importance for the international institutional framework for climate action.

First, it establishes the biennial transparency reports, which are submitted by all parties and describe greenhouse gas emissions, mitigation efforts, adaptation actions, support received and provided and other relevant information. Next, it refers to the Technical Expert Review, which involves a rigorous and independent assessment of the data by international experts to ensure the quality and consistency of the data. Third, the Facilitative Multilateral Review promotes a dialogue between party representatives and experts to share experiences, clarify issues and provide feedback on business monitoring reports.[17]

It should be noted that support and transparency from developed countries to less-developed countries is encouraged.

Given these important developments at the international level, it is important to keep in mind that while the Agreement encourages these elements, concrete implementation measures are left to each country; and civil society organisations and activists play a crucial role in pushing for stronger enforcement of these provisions and ensuring meaningful public participation and access to information and justice.[18]

Other Important Instruments for Access to Information and Justice and Public Participation

The Aarhus Convention

Formally known as the United Nations Economic Commission for Europe Convention on Access to Information, Public Participation in decision-making and Access to Justice in Environmental Matters, this agreement was adopted back in 1998 and was considered a "new kind" of international tool as it aimed to link environmental rights with human rights, focusing on the interaction between governments and the public, then pursuing the involvement of all stakeholders with check and balances in order to achieve – in principle – a regional sustainable development. Specifically, its regulation within three pillars is key to hold governments accountable by giving people and NGOs a series of rights.

Firstly, Articles 4 and 5 regulate access to information covering two bases; on one hand, public authorities must be transparent when dealing with public requests of information while also actively providing it through periodical environmental updates and information dissemination.

The instrument aims for securing the receipt of data applying the *presumption in favour of access* principle, meaning that any public information is subject to disclosure unless it falls under certain exceptions, such as national security. Also, this right extends broadly to any person proving to have a reason for requesting information, and it must be delivered in a fixed period.[19]

Secondly, Articles 6 to 8 deal with public participation in environmental decision-making. When permitting certain activities *inter alia* chemicals installations and waste-water treatment plants, State Parties are obliged to comply with certain requirements of public participation, such as notifying them in time while giving them the right to inspect the relevant information and providing reasonable timeframes for participation.[20]

Thirdly, access to justice is treated within Article 9 regarding appeals to access information and public participation. Thus, if a person requests information and the authority responds in an unsatisfactory manner, a review procedure before a court of law or an independent body is possible, whereas seeking a review of either substantive or procedural matters in decision-making processes is also doable when proven to have a "sufficient interest". Additionally, if established by national law, persons can also challenge the general violations of environmental law done by authorities or private corps.[21]

Through its Compliance Committee, Aarhus has proven to be a key tool for the public and NGOs to hold governments accountable. In fact, over 200 communications from the public have been received since 2001, 60% of which have come from NGOs and almost 30% from individuals, demonstrating a very high level of public engagement is vital to achieve compliance.[22] Out of this, the Committee has adopted 96 findings, assisting parties to remedy their noncompliance; for example, Denmark reduced their court fees for NGOs appealing, and Slovakia amended nuclear-related environmental information so it could no longer be deemed unconditionally confidential with no possibility of disclosure.[23]

Now, as a regional-born instrument, Aarhus challenges with a rather low number of ratifications (47), but it is open to accession by any United Nations member; while it is mostly a European-centred body, other continents might enhance their environmental policies if entering the treaty. Further, some national implementation reports show that the provisions dealing with access to justice have had some difficulties, and effective practice operation of access to information and public participation has been challenging.[24]

At any rate, the Convention has been regarded as a highly valuable contribution and nowadays has a Strategic Plan for 2022–2030 aiming to minimise the depletion of environmental resources, ensuring its remanence to future generations while addressing climate change.[25]

The Escazu Agreement

More recently, a new regional instrument appeared in the international sphere: the Regional Agreement on Access to Information, Public Participation and Justice in Environmental Matters in Latin America and the Caribbean, known as Escazú Agreement. Adopted on 4 March 2018, it entered into force on 22 April 2021. It is the first treaty in the region to deal with environmental matters and the first one in history to include regulations on environmental human rights defenders.[26] It had its foundation in Principle 10 of the Rio Declaration and was also initiated within the context of Rio+20, mainly characterised for offering a wide protection of human rights while safeguarding the environment.

As established in Article 1, the objective of the Agreement is to fully guarantee and effectively implement the rights of access to environmental information, public participation in the environmental decision-making process and access to justice in environmental matters.

Articles 5 and 6 deal with the right to access environmental information, its denial, the conditions to deliver information, its generation and dissemination. Escazú enshrines and systematises environmental regulations from other international treaties, giving a bigger-picture approach when, for example, facilitating and guaranteeing access to information for vulnerable people and groups, such as Indigenous People.[27] Further, any person can ask for information without the need to prove they have a special interest, while the authorities must disclosure the information within 30 business days unless its disclosure falls under the exceptions regulated, such as when it would create adversities for national security. Additionally, transparency plays an essential role. Each State party must ensure the generation, collection, publicisation and dissemination of relevant information in an effective, proactive, timely, regular, accessible and comprehensive manner.

Escazú utilises the IACtHR reasoning, expanding the framing of the boundaries of access to information through the test of necessity and proportionality, thus proving once again the importance of human rights elements within the analyzsing method.[28]

Article 7 regulates rights of public participation, seeking to enhance the empowerment of the public in the decision-making process. In the international arena, it has been understood that public consultation derives from cultural construction; taking the people's opinion on the matter helps build a more legitimate project through effective participation.[29] Inclusiveness of all stakeholders, not leaving anyone behind, participation and equity are the goals.

For its part, Article 8 provides the right of access to justice in environmental matters. Although at first sight very similar to the provisions set in the Aarhus Agreement, Escazú acknowledges that mere access to justice is not sufficient, thus going beyond due process, stipulating the facilitation of justice access through reducing economic barriers, amplifying the *locus standi,* adopting precautionary measures, facilitating evidence production and adequate mechanisms of enforcement, reparation and settlement of disputes.[30]

Access to information, participation and justice are key to achieve the goal of sustainable development and provide a healthy environment, especially for future generations. Even though there have been some difficulties in the ratification process and the implementation of the Agreement's provisions, it is fundamental that the rest of signatory parties ratify it. For example, in the *Quintero and Puchuncaví case* regarding sacrifice zones, the judiciary was not able to condemn private companies because of the lack of information, thus convicting State organs for omitting the delivery of preventive and exposure information to the public.[31] Escazú aims to avoid these types of situations, believing that becoming an enforcing party is a major public necessity.

Future Directions

All three instruments encompass similar aims, but if we take a closer look, the Paris Agreement has the specific and time-fixed goal of reducing global warming below 2°C, preferably 1.5°C, by reducing global greenhouse emissions: a worldwide concern that conjugated the greatest quantity of countries working towards a common environmental objective. Nevertheless, an issue arose in its implementation since change of policies and application of international provisions in internal law are left to each State Party, therefore leaving a – not small – window for lack or delay of compliance.

The latter is why Aarhus and Escazú are vital to strengthening the implementation of the Paris Agreement: they are regional instruments that monitor each of their parties closely, as their compliance mechanisms have more rapid effectiveness while the cumulation of their diverse aims helps – at the end – in reaching the ultimate goal.

In addition, these treaties provide a settlement of disputes clause, establishing that parties must go first through negotiations or any other peaceful means before giving compulsory jurisdiction to the international court of justice and/or an arbitral tribunal. This means that, as usual, diplomatic methods are always the first priority, but it does not close the door on litigation when they fail to be successful. In fact, if a controversy arises, then parties must resolve it through the jurisdictional means mentioned.

Concluding Remarks: Is This Useful at All?

It is clear that access to information, justice and public participation are crucial to addressing climate change at both the global and national levels. These aspects are interconnected and contribute to the effectiveness of climate policies and the overall well-being of communities. The current complex climate change situation requires concrete action on these issues.

For example, regarding informed decision-making, access to information allows individuals and communities to make informed decisions about climate change, enabling them to take appropriate actions and adapt to changing environmental conditions.[32] On the other hand, direct engagement in climate change policies and decision-making processes helps build trust, bring expertise and strengthen legitimacy. It ensures that the voices of diverse stakeholders are heard and considered in the development and implementation of climate policies[33] on the stakeholder networking mechanisms that are possible in this area, in order to improve and adapt policies and actions.[34]

In addition, accountability and public oversight allow individuals and communities to evaluate policies and hold decision-makers accountable for their actions. This helps to ensure transparency and accountability in climate governance, as well as helping close gaps in accountability by involving affected communities in the decision-making process, ensuring that their concerns and needs are addressed.[35]

Notes

1 JA Morales, 'Transparencia: Derecho Fundamental y Antídoto Contra La Corrupción' (2016) 55 Revista De Derecho Puertorriqueño.

2 Centro de Derechos Humanos, *Anti-corrupción: actualizando los desafíos. Informe sobre la segunda reunión regional de especialistas en transparencia, rendición de cuentas y lucha contra la corrupción en América Latina* (Universidad de Chile 2009).

3 E Peruzzotti, 'La Política de Accountability Social En América Latina' *Democratización, rendición de cuentas y sociedad civil: participación ciudadana y control social* (Honorable Cámara de Diputados, LIX Legislatura; CIESAS; Universidad Veracruzana; Miguel Ángel Porrúa 2006).

4 L García-Corrochano, 'Presentation of the Proposal of the Inter-American Juridical Committee. Paper presented at the Virtual Forum: "Presentation of the Proposal for a Model Law 2.0 on Access to Public Information, Organised by the Secretariat for Legal Affairs of the OAS' (2020) <https://www.oas.org/es/sla/foro_virtual_CJI_Ley_Modelo_Acceso_Informacion_Publica.asp> accessed 20 March 2024

5 Ibero-American Charter for Citizen Participation in Public Management 2009, Adopted by the XIX Ibero-American Summit of Heads of State and Government, artículo 2.

6 V Durán and C Nalegach, 'Justicia climática, construcción de sociedades' *El Acuerdo de Escazú sobre democracia ambiental y su relación con la Agenda 2030 para el Desarrollo Sostenible* (CEPAL; Universidad del Rosario 2021).

7 CEPAL, *Cambio climático y derechos humanos: Contribuciones desde y para América Latina y el Caribe (LC/TS.2019/94/Corr.1)* (Naciones Unidas 2019).

8 Ibid.; V Durán and B González, 'Artículo 2. Definiciones' *Comentario al Acuerdo de Escazú sobre derechos ambientales en América Latina y el Caribe* (Konrad Adenauer Stiftung 2023).

9 ibid.

10 *Advisory Opinion OC-23/17, Requested by the Republic of Colombia* (2017) IACtHR.

11 *Case of Claude-Reyes et al. v. Chile (Merits, Reparations and Costs)* (2006) IACtHR.

12 J Diamond and C Bruch, 'The International Architecture for Climate Change Adaptation Assistance' in *Climate Change Adaptation and International Development: Making Development Cooperation More Effective* (Routledge 2012).

13 UNDP, *Human Development Report 2007/8: Fighting Climate Change: Human Solidarity in a Divided World* (United Nations 2008).

14 F Khatibi and others, 'Can Public Awareness, Knowledge and Engagement Improve Climate Change Adaptation Policies?' (2021) 2(1) Discover Sustainability.

15 S Hügel and AR Davies, 'Public Participation, Engagement, and Climate Change Adaptation: A Review of the Research Literature' (2020) 11(4) Wiley Interdisciplinary Reviews: Climate Change.

16 CEPAL, *Acceso a la información, la participación y la justicia en asuntos ambientales en América Latina y el Caribe: hacia el logro de la Agenda 2030 para el Desarrollo Sostenible* (Naciones Unidas 2018).

17 H Winkler, B Mantlana and T Letete, 'Transparency of Action and Support in the Paris Agreement' (2017) 17(7) Climate Policy.

18 BB Derman, 'Climate Governance, Justice, and Transnational Civil Society' (2014) 14(1) Climate Policy.

19 UNECE, 'Access to information', Aarhus Convention. Content of the Convention <https://unece.org/environment-policy/public-participation/access-to-information>

20 UNECE, 'Public Participation', Aarhus Convention. Content of the Convention <https://unece.org/environment-policy/public-participation/public-participation>

21 UNECE, 'Access to Justice', Aarhus Convention. Content of the Convention <https://unece.org/environment-policy/public-participation/access-to-justice>

22 UNECE, 'After 25 years of the Aarhus Convention, Stats's compliance with Environmental Rights Obligations Matters More Than Ever' (2023) <https://unece.org/environment/press/after-25-years-aarhus-convention-states-compliance-environmental-rights>

23 ibid

24 UNECE, 'Decision VII/11 on the Strategic Plan for 2022–2030'. Excerpt from the addendum to the report of the seventh session of the Meeting of the Parties (ECE/MP.PP/2021/2/Add.1) (2021) 2.

25 ibid; Submission by the UNECE Aarhus Convention Secretariat, 'The Role of the Aarhus Convention in Promoting Good Governance and Human Rights' (2012) 5.

26 Secretary General of the United Nations, 'Foreword', Regional Agreement on Access to Information, Public Participation and Justice in Environmental Matters in Latin America and the Caribbean (2018) 5.

27 D Soberón and C Trinidad, 'Artículo 5. Acceso a la información ambiental' *Comentario al acuerdo de Escazú sobre derechos ambientales en América Latina y el Caribe* (Konrad Adenauer Stiftung 2023) 166.

28 D Soberón and C Trinidad, 'Artículo 5. Acceso a la información ambiental'. *Comentario al acuerdo de Escazú sobre derechos ambientales en América Latina y el Caribe* (Konrad Adenauer Stiftung 2023) 166.

29 G Aguilar, 'The Content and Contemporary Scope of the Right to Access to Environmental Participation' (2020) 26(2) Ius et Praxis 85–86.

30 H Jiménez and G Parola, 'Artículo 8. Acceso a la justicia en asuntos ambientales' *Comentario al acuerdo de Escazú sobre derechos ambientales en América Latina y el Caribe* (Konrad Adenauer Stiftung 2023) 272.

31 V Duran and C Nalegach, '¿Por qué Chile debe adherir al Acuerdo de Escazú? Análisis jurídico de los argumentos esgrimidos por el Gobierno de Chile para la no suscripción del Acuerdo Regional sobre el Acceso a la Información, la Participación Pública y el Acceso a la Justicia en Asuntos Ambientales en América Latina y El Caribe' (2020) 2 Perspectivas CDA 18.

32 S Hügel and AR Davies, 'Public Participation, Engagement, and Climate Change Adaptation: A Review of the Research Literature' (2020) 11(4) Wiley Interdisciplinary Reviews: Climate Change. UNDP, *Scaling Up Climate Action to Achieve the Sustainable Development Goals* (United Nations 2016).

33 Climate Change Committee, *The Role of Deliberative Public Engagement in Climate Policy Development* (Lancaster University 2022); I Suboticki, S Heidenreich, M Ryghaug and T M Skjølsvold, 'Fostering Justice Through Engagement: A Literature Review of Public Engagement in Energy Transitions' (2023) 100 Energy Research & Social Science 102233, 5–8.

34 J Razzaque, 'Information, Public Participation and Access to Justice in Environmental Matters' in *Routledge Handbook of International Environmental Law* (Routledge 2021).

35 S Brunelli and others, 'Accountability for Climate Change: A Research Synthesis through the Lenses of the Integrated Thinking Approach' (2021) 29(4) Meditari Accountancy Research.

9

NAVIGATING HIGH SEAS BIODIVERSITY AND CLIMATE CHANGE

Cassie Lumsden, Zhen Sun, and Marie-Claire Cordonier Segger

Introduction

The ocean is the largest biome on Earth, making up over 70% of the surface of the planet, with areas beyond national jurisdiction ("ABNJ") – or the high seas – encompassing over two-thirds of Earth's surface and 95% of the total volume of the world's oceans.[1] As such, it is logical that the oceans provide widespread benefits for the planet and human populations alike. For example, the oceans are responsible for driving the overall climate on Earth, and they provide humans with important food sources and economic support.[2] However, while the connections between humans and the ocean widely benefit communities, the same connections are also the reason that sustainable development and protection of the marine environment is dire. Cumulative anthropogenic impacts, including anthropogenic climate change, have placed marine environments under stress, which will continue to impact marine biodiversity, as well as humans, as climate change continues.[3]

The oceans and climate change are directly linked.[4] As greenhouse gases (GHGs) continue to be emitted into the atmosphere and the planet continues to warm, the ocean continues to absorb this extra heat and carbon dioxide. This results in the warming of the entire ocean, a decrease in dissolved oxygen, ocean acidification, changes to ocean currents, and declines in nutrient supplies, which stresses marine biodiversity.[5] As climate change continues to increase, the risk of marine biodiversity loss is also expected to increase, further impacting global food supplies and economies.[6] Furthermore, these same changes also will result in more severe weather events on land and at sea, as well as rising sea levels, putting human communities at even further risk.[7] Therefore, these negative impacts on the oceans and marine biodiversity from climate change mean that limiting warming of the planet is important for oceans and society going forward, but also sets ocean conservation as an important piece of the global response to climate change.[8] The connection between the ocean and climate change has been acknowledged in the recent 21 May 2024 Climate Change Advisory Opinion issued by the International Tribunal for the Law on the Sea ("ITLOS").[9] ITLOS determined that anthropogenic GHG emissions are a form of pollution under the United Nations Convention on the Law of the Sea ("UNCLOS"), which expands the environmental obligations under UNCLOS to now place climate change obligations on States.[10] Now States have obligations to prevent, reduce, and control GHG emissions and to protect and preserve the marine

DOI: 10.4324/9781003276678-11

environment from climate change impacts through the international law of the sea, in addition to international climate change measures.

Because the high seas make up such a large portion of the total ocean environment that not only concerns the over 150 coastal States but also the 44 landlocked States, and because "the problems of ocean space are closely interrelated and need to be considered as a whole," global ocean conservation and the mitigation of climate change on marine biodiversity needs to be focused on the high seas, and it requires a "multilateral solution" involving coordination with other relevant agreements and bodies.[11] Indeed, the ITLOS Climate Change Advisory Opinion emphasized that "coordination and harmonization" between the law of the sea and other relevant legal frameworks is necessary to inform the meaning of the provisions of UNCLOS and ensure that UNCLOS "serves as a living instrument" such that it is able to respond to growing concerns, such as climate change.[12]

The recently adopted BBNJ Agreement has the potential to provide the avenues for States to fulfill their climate change obligations in the framework across the law of the sea and climate law.[13] The provisions of the BBNJ Agreement create processes that require cooperation between relevant international law instruments and bodies to ensure that the goals to protect the marine environment and to conserve marine biodiversity as included in the Agreement and UNCLOS, as well as highlighted in the ITLOS 2024 Climate Change Advisory Opinion, are achieved. However, because the BBNJ Agreement is relatively new and not in force, yet contains broadly worded provisions, there is general uncertainty about how the Agreement will apply in relation to existing regulatory regimes. Therefore, this chapter will explore possibilities for intersection and cooperation between the BBNJ Agreement and existing climate change instruments such that the cooperation sought by the ITLOS Climate Change Advisory Opinion may be achieved.

The BBNJ Agreement and Its International Context

The BBNJ Agreement was created under the UNCLOS as the third implementation agreement to fill the legal gaps on the conservation and sustainable use of marine biodiversity of the high seas and the Area.[14] The general obligations of States to protect and preserve the marine environment and to prevent, reduce, and control marine pollution as laid down in Part XII of UNCLOS apply to the high seas and the Area.[15] Despite expressing the importance of cooperation for the protection and preservation of the marine environment, some have argued that the UNCLOS alone provides "limited institutional opportunities for collective action to address transboundary problems," such as the impacts that climate change are having on ABNJ, and that the UNCLOS "does not provide guidance or rules concerning the impacts of climate change."[16] However, the ITLOS Climate Change Advisory Opinion has clarified that this is not the case. It dictated that climate change and GHG emissions have just as much of a place within existing international law of the sea frameworks as the law of the sea has within international climate change frameworks.

In 2022, the Commission of Small Island States on Climate Change and International Law ("COSIS") requested an opinion from the ITLOS on the obligations of States under international law in relation to climate change and the oceans.[17] The ITLOS concluded that climate change fit well within the environmental obligations imposed by the UNCLOS.[18] First, as a prerequisite, the ITLOS determined that anthropogenic GHG emissions are captured as a form of marine pollution under the UNCLOS, resulting in a number of existing obligations under the UNCLOS now placed on States in relation to GHG emissions.[19] In relation to the impacts of climate change, the general obligation to protect and preserve the marine environment entails two distinct elements: that States have "the duty to prevent, or at lease mitigate, environmental harm," and to maintain "ecosystem health and the natural balance of the marine environment."[20] Under Article 194.1 UNCLOS, States are obligated "to take all necessary measures to prevent reduce and control" anthropogenic GHG emissions.[21] In a similar vein, States also have obligations under Article 194.2 UNCLOS to: prevent the pollution of GHGs in transboundary settings, "adopt laws and regulations and take other measures necessary to implement applicable international rules and standards" in relation to GHG pollution, and cooperate in an ongoing manner to "formulate and elaborate rules, standards and recommended practices and procedures," beyond just adopting a particular climate change instrument.[22] Thus, it has been made clear by the ITLOS Climate Change Advisory Opinion that States have a "substantive legal obligation to protect the ocean from climate change impacts" by reducing GHG emissions in accordance with the UNCLOS and other international legal frameworks.[23]

While it has been determined by the ITLOS that the UNCLOS applies in the context of anthropogenic climate change, the provisions of the UNCLOS still do not provide specifically how these obligations may be met by States and the Climate Change Advisory Opinion demands that States need to take more action, both individually on a national level and jointly on an international level.[24] Nevertheless, ITLOS also reaffirmed that "treaties do not operate in isolation but are 'interpreted and applied within the framework of the entire legal system prevailing at the time of the interpretation'".[25] Therefore, the interpretation and implementation of States' general environmental obligations in relation to GHG emissions must consider relevant climate-related treaties and other instruments.[26] The BBNJ Agreement has the ability to address the need for international collective action for the conservation and sustainable use of marine biodiversity in ABNJ in the face of climate change.[27] In pursuance of collective action and the need for coordination with existing regulatory structures, the BBNJ Agreement was thus developed to interact with other instruments and bodies to effectively apply its provisions, as reflected by the objectives of the Agreement.[28] However, given the broad language of the Agreement, it is difficult to currently predict what such interaction will resemble. Therefore, the potential for the BBNJ Agreement to interact within the ocean-climate change connection will be examined, with a focus on the potential for interaction and cooperation with the Paris Agreement.

Interactions with the Paris Agreement

What Is the Paris Agreement?

The Paris Agreement is a multilateral agreement developed in pursuance of the United Nations Framework Convention on Climate Change ("UNFCCC") as a global response to climate change in 2015.[29] The central aim of the Paris Agreement is to "strengthen the global response to the threat of climate change" by keeping the rise in the average global temperature to below 2°C above pre-industrial levels, and preferably limiting the increase in temperature to 1.5°C above pre-industrial levels.[30] The Paris Agreement seeks to achieve this goal by reducing global emissions of GHGs by requiring State parties to pursue reductions through national climate action plans – called nationally determined contributions by the Agreement – and by providing a framework to provide support for developing States in order to help those States deal with climate change and the requirements of the Paris Agreement, reflecting a global need for "common but differentiated responsibilities" in addressing transboundary environmental issues.[31]

Possible Interactions between the BBNJ Agreement and the Paris Agreement

The BBNJ Agreement comprises four elements that are designed to address conservation and sustainable use of marine biodiversity in ABNJ. Three of these elements have the potential to interact with the Paris Agreement: area-based management tools ("ABMTs"), environmental impact assessments

("EIAs"), and capacity building and technology transfer measures. However, ABMTs and EIAs are most likely to address the threat of climate change in general on marine biodiversity.[32] The BBNJ Agreement requires States to "[strengthen] and enhanc[e] cooperation with and promot[e] cooperation" among relevant legal instruments and bodies in the achievement of its objectives.[33] In so doing, the interpretation and implementation of the BBNJ Agreement shall not undermine relevant legal instruments and bodies, but shall promote coherence and coordination with them.[34] These requirements apply to the interactions between the BBNJ Agreement and the Paris Agreement.

In order to achieve the objectives of the BBNJ Agreement, parties shall be guided by the following principles and approaches (Article 7):

(a) the polluter-pays principle;
(b) the principle of the common heritage of humankind which is set out in the [UNCLOS];
(c) the freedom of marine scientific research, together with other freedoms of the high seas;
(d) the principle of equity and the fair and equitable sharing of benefits;
(e) the precautionary principle or precautionary approach, as appropriate;
(f) an ecosystem approach;
(g) an integrated approach to ocean management;
(h) an approach that builds ecosystem resilience, including to adverse effects of climate change and ocean acidification, and also maintains and restores ecosystem integrity, including the carbon cycling services that underpin the role of the ocean in climate.
(i) the use of the best available science and scientific information;
(j) the use of relevant traditional knowledge of Indigenous Peoples and local communities, where available;
(k) the respect, promotion and consideration of their respective obligations, as applicable, relating to the rights of Indigenous Peoples or of, as appropriate, local communities when taking action to address the conservation and sustainable use of marine biological diversity of areas beyond national jurisdiction;
(l) the non-transfer, directly or indirectly, of damage or hazards from one area to another and the non-transformation of one type of pollution into another in taking measures to prevent, reduce and control pollution of the marine environment;
(m) full recognition of the special circumstances of small island developing States and of least developed countries;
(n) acknowledgment of the special interests and needs of landlocked developing countries.

Interactions Regarding ABMTs

ABMTs have been found to be beneficial in protecting marine environments and marine biodiversity by improving marine ecosystem function, reversing declines in fish stocks, protecting ecosystems from direct damage by humans, and improving the overall resilience of ecosystems to other external stressors.[35] Furthermore, the ITLOS Climate Change Advisory Opinion has noted that under the UNCLOS, States are required to take conservation, adaptation, and resilience-building measures to "protect and preserve the marine environment in response to climate change impacts," which they acknowledge can include measures such as ABMTs.[36] Historically, though, there has been a lack of implementation of ABMTs outside the jurisdiction of States.[37] The BBNJ Agreement seeks to remedy this issue by providing an ABMT framework for ABNJ. The framework provided by the BBNJ Agreement involves regulating the implementation of ABMTs in ABNJ, including providing for other instruments and bodies to participate in the coordination of implementation with the Agreement, and providing that other instruments and bodies, such as OSPAR, the International Maritime Organization or the International Seabed Authority should coordinate and cooperate with the Agreement to ensure implemented ABMTs are respected.[38] The Conference of the Parties of the BBNJ Agreement, taking into account the inputs of these relevant instruments and bodies, as well as of "the scientific advice and recommendations of the Scientific and Technical Body," shall take decisions on the establishment of ABMTs or recommend States to adopt measures that fall within the competences of other bodies.[39] However, the interaction with an instrument such as the Paris Agreement remains to be developed.

In the preamble of the Paris Agreement it is stated that the Parties to the Agreement recognize "the importance of the conservation and enhancement, as appropriate, of sinks and reservoirs of the GHGs referred to in the [UNFCCC]", which includes oceans, as the oceans play a vital role in absorbing and storing carbon.[40] Furthermore, the Paris Agreement also notes "the importance of ensuring the integrity of all ecosystems, including oceans, and the protection of biodiversity," thus overlapping with the main themes of the implementation of ABMTs through the BBNJ Agreement.[41] It is expected that the BBNJ Agreement will enter into force rapidly once it has been ratified by more than sixty State Parties. For States that are parties to both the BBNJ Agreement and the Pairs Agreement, they must consider how their obligations under one Agreement must be fulfilled while implementing the other. It is within this overlap that the Paris Agreement and BBNJ Agreement indirectly interact, although the Paris Agreement itself does not provide for the creation of ABMTs specifically.

Through the development of ABMTs on the high seas through the BBNJ Agreement framework, the harmful effects of climate change can be addressed by "reducing other sources of damage in areas designated for [ABMTs]. . . that will enhance ocean health and build ecological resilience to stressors."[42] For example, Annex I of the Agreement provides a list of criteria for identifying areas appropriate for ABMT designation, including factors such as vulnerability (including to climate change) and cumulative and transboundary impacts. (footnote: BBNJ Agreement, Annex I (f) and (q)) The consideration of criteria such as these may lead to the use of ABMTs to protect areas of the high sea that will help oceans respond to the pressures of climate change. Therefore, the creation of ABMTs in ABNJ through the BBNJ Agreement would support the overall goals of the Paris Agreement by seeking to conserve, enhance, and increase the integrity of marine ecosystems. Vice versa, the emission reduction goals in the Paris Agreement would likewise support the goal of protecting marine biodiversity and increasing ecosystem resilience through ABMTs in the BBNJ Agreement by potentially reducing GHG emissions. However, this interaction between the two documents is indirect. In order to develop more direct coordination and cooperation between the two instruments in relation to ABMTs so they may be "implemented in a complimentary and mutually reinforcing manner" beyond the indirect connections mentioned, direct linkages may have to be developed.[43] This may be possible to create due to the BBNJ Agreement's mandate to enhance cooperation and coordination, as well as the Paris Agreement's openness to coordination with relevant instruments as found in Article 6 of the Agreement.[44]

Interactions Regarding EIAs

EIAs are tools that are used to assess the potential impacts from proposed projects or activities, determine whether any mitigation measures are necessary, and decide whether the project or activity should proceed.[45] Due to increasing pressures on the marine environment, EIAs are necessary to ensure the conservation and sustainable use of the marine environment and biodiversity. In recognition of this fact, the ITLOS Climate Change Advisory Opinion has stated that "the obligation to conduct environmental impact assessments is crucial to ensure that activities do not harm the marine environment" and that, as such, planned activities that "may cause substantial pollution to the marine environment or significant and harmful changes thereto through anthropogenic GHG emissions, including cumulative effects" need to be subject to an EIA process.[46] However, implementing EIAs in ABNJ has historically been a difficult exercise due to gaps in the overarching legal regime.[47] By providing a comprehensive process for completing EIAs for projects and activities in ABNJ, particularly with the requirement to consider potential cumulative impacts and the possibility to undertake strategic environmental assessments, the BBNJ Agreement seeks to fill this gap and the requirement stated by the ITLOS.[48]

Similar to ABMTs, cooperation and coordination related to EIAs in the BBNJ Agreement is related to providing a baseline standard for conducting EIAs in ABNJ, as well as interacting with other instruments and bodies to develop guidelines for conducting EIAs.[49] There is scope for more direct interaction between the BBNJ Agreement and the Paris Agreement in regard to EIAs in comparison to ABMTs. For example, the BBNJ Agreement seeks to establish certain guidelines related to determining whether an activity has passed the threshold for triggering an EIA, as well as for assessing cumulative impacts, which includes impacts related to climate change, in ABNJ.[50] This interaction could contribute to the considerations and debates associated with climate engineering options that are developed to limiting climate change.[51] The BBNJ Agreement requires that the development of such requirements involve collaborating with relevant legal instruments and bodies.[52] Given that climate change is a consideration in the EIA process under the BBNJ Agreement, and that EIAs will be required for proposed activities that could have "significant adverse impacts on the environment, including those that contribute to climate change," the Paris Agreement very well could be a relevant instrument that could collaborate with the BBNJ Agreement to generate these guidelines for EIAs, which will further its own emissions goals, as well as the objectives of the BBNJ Agreement.[53]

Interactions Regarding Capacity-Building

Furthermore, in addition to calling for the use of ABMTs and EIAs, the ITLOS Climate Change Advisory Opinion also called for the provision of "scientific, technical, educational and other assistance to developing States that are particularly vulnerable to the adverse effects of climate change" as a means to address the "inequitable situation" placed on States which are suffering more severely from the effects of GHG emissions on the marine environment.[54] Under the BBNJ Agreement, this is referred to as capacity-building and the transfer of marine technology that also demands international cooperation.[55] The Paris Agreement may open potential for cooperation with the BBNJ Agreement in relation to capacity-building and technology transfer to provide for addressing the inequitable position spoken of by the ITLOS. Within the BBNJ Agreement, the element of capacity-building and technology transfer is intended to assist developing States in participating in the substantial provisions of the Agreement and in attaining its goals.[56] In particular, the BBNJ Agreement states that

> Parties shall cooperate, directly or through relevant legal instruments . . . to assist Parties, in particular developing State Parties, in achieving the objectives of the [BBNJ Agreement] through capacity-building and the development and transfer of marine science and marine technology.

This includes sharing knowledge and technology in relation to ABMTs and EIAs in ABNJ.[57]

Similar provision for capacity-building of, and technology transfers to, developing States and those that are more vulnerable to the effects of climate change, such as small island developing

States, are included in the Paris Agreement.[58] Given this overlap, both instruments may be able to bolster the goals of the other by providing for the sharing of knowledge and technology related to GHG emissions and climate change mitigation in regards to the marine environment between their associated State Parties in order to best address the impacts of climate change in ABNJ. However, like the issue with ABMTs, it is likely that this coordination would require a more formal process to be developed in order to better align conservation goals between the two instruments as those goals relate to capacity-building and technology transfer.

Interactions with Climate Change More Generally

In addition to interacting with a specific climate change text, such as the Paris Agreement, there may be potential for the BBNJ Agreement to interact with climate change more generally as well. The ITLOS Climate Change Advisory Opinion notes that, as the largest carbon dioxide sink in the world, the ocean plays an important role in mitigating climate change by "storing heat trapped in the atmosphere caused by increasing concentrations of GHGs and storage of excess carbon dioxide."[59] As such, the obligation of protecting and preserving the marine environment in the UNCLOS and reflected in the BBNJ Agreement not only promotes "the conservation and resilience of living marine resources," but also involves the mitigation of "anthropogenic GHG emissions by enhancing carbon sequestration through measures to restore the marine environment."[60] One of these measures to improve carbon sequestration could involve the interaction between the BBNJ Agreement and the idea of "blue carbon."

Blue carbon is the concept that living marine organisms act as a sink for atmospheric carbon.[61] While the idea of blue carbon is generally associated with coastal ecosystems where the BBNJ Agreement would have limited effect, blue carbon can also exist in deep-sea areas where the BBNJ Agreement would apply.[62] While the use of ABMTs in ABNJ may be able to provide some protection to areas of the high seas that may provide for deep-sea blue carbon, there is not enough knowledge on how the different deep-sea blue carbon processes interact to say for certain that ABMTs created through the BBNJ Agreement would have any certain effect.[63]

Conclusion

"[T]he duty to cooperate is a fundamental principle in the prevention of pollution of the marine environment under . . . the [UNCLOS] and general international law."[64] As such, the ITLOS has found that "the global nature of climate change calls for the widest possible cooperation by all countries and their participation in an effective and appropriate international response."[65] The BBNJ Agreement has the potential to provide for this cooperation with other legal instruments and bodies. One such instrument is the Paris Agreement. While there is potential for interaction, coordination, and cooperation between the BBNJ Agreement and the Paris Agreement in relation to ABMTs, EIAs, and capacity-building, the interactions between the two instruments are not necessarily direct enough to fully facilitate cooperation as the instruments currently stand. Similarly, in order for the BBNJ Agreement to interact with climate change on a wider level, more must be known about the processes of the high seas to have full faith that any actions taken through the BBNJ Agreement would actually protect blue carbon. Therefore, the development of knowledge on ABNJ and the creation of processes to facilitate interaction between the BBNJ Agreement and the Paris Agreement are necessary before it can be said with certainty what the interaction between the BBNJ Agreement and climate change may resemble.

Notes

1 Cymie Payne, 'Responsibility to the International Community for Marine Biodiversity beyond National Jurisdiction' (2022) 11(1) Cambridge International Law Journal 24, 28; Cymie Payne, 'New Law for the High Seas' (2019) 46(1) Berkeley Journal of International Law 191, 192.
2 United Nations, *The Second World Ocean Assessment: Volume 1* (UN 2021) 5; Alistair Hobday and Richard Matear, 'The Impact of Climate Change on Oceans: Physical, Chemical and Biological Responses' in J McDonald, J McGee and R Barnes (eds), *Research Handbook on Climate Change, Oceans and Coasts* (Edward Elgar Publishing Ltd. 2020) 32; United Nations Educational, Scientific, and Cultural Organization (UNESCO) (Intergovernmental Oceanographic Commission), 'The Contribution of the UN Decade of Ocean Science for Sustainable Development to the Achievement of the 2030 Agenda' (2022) IOC/2022/ODS/34 Rev. 5.
3 UNESCO, 'The Contribution of the UN Decade of Ocean Science' (n 2) 5.
4 Stephen Minas, 'The Ocean-climate Nexus in the Unfolding Anthropocene: Addressing Environmental Challenges through International Law and Cooperation' in M Lim (ed), *Charting Environmental Law Futures in the Anthropocene* (Springer 2019) 84.
5 Hobday and Matear (n 2) 32–41; Nilüfer Oral, 'UNCLOS and Sea Level Rise' (2023) 149(1) Marine Policy 1, 2.
6 Minas (n 4) 84; Payne, 'Responsibility' (n 1) 28.
7 Hobday and Matear (n 2) 36; OECD, 'The Transition to a Sustainable Ocean Economy Is a Global Imperative' in *Sustainable Ocean for All: Harnessing the Benefits of Sustainable Ocean Economies for Developing Countries* (OECD 2020); Oral, 'UNCLOS and Sea Level Rise' (n 5) 2.
8 Alexandre Magnan and others, 'Implications of the Paris Agreement for the Ocean' (2016) 6(1) Nature Climate Change 732, 733; Minas (n 4) 91.
9 *Request for an Advisory Opinion Submitted by the Commission of Small Island States on Climate Change and International Law (No 31)* (Advisory Opinion of 21 May 2024) (ITLOS Climate Change Advisory Opinion), ITLOS Reports 2024.
10 ITLOS Climate Change Advisory Opinion (n 9), paras 179, 243, and 258.
11 Minas (n 4) 91; Payne, 'New Law for the High Seas' (n 1) 192 and 206; United Nations Convention on the Law of the Sea (adopted 10 December 1982, entered into force 16 November 1994) 1833 UNTS 3 (UNCLOS), Preamble.
12 ITLOS Climate Change Advisory Opinion (n 9), paras 122 and 130.
13 Agreement under the United Nations Convention on the Law of the Sea on the Conversation and Sustainable Use of Marine Biological Diversity of Areas beyond National Jurisdiction (adopted 19 June 2023) UNTS C.N.203.2023.TREATIES-XXI.10 (BBNJ Agreement).
14 BBNJ Agreement, Preamble, Articles 1(2) and 2.
15 UNCLOS, Articles 192 and 194. BBNJ Agreement, Preamble, Article 5(1).
16 Payne, 'Responsibility' (n 1) 25; Nilüfer Oral, 'Implementing the Duty to Cooperate under the 1982 UNCLOS for the Conservation and Sustainable Use of Biodiversity in Areas beyond National Jurisdiction under a New BBNJ Agreement' (2021) 9(1) Korean Journal of International and Comparative Law 174, 175 and 181; Oral, 'UNCLOS and Sea Level Rise (n 5) 4. UNCLOS, Articles 197–201.
17 ITLOS Climate Change Advisory Opinion (n 9), para 1.
18 Constantinos Yiallourides and Surya Deva, 'A Commentary on ITLOS' Advisory Opinion on Climate Change' (*BIICL*, 24 May 2024) <https://www.biicl.org/blog/77/a-commentary-on-itlos-advisory-opinion-on-climate-change> accessed 8 June 2024.
19 ITLOS Climate Change Advisory Opinion (n 9), paras 179 and 180.
20 Ibid, para 385.
21 Ibid, para 243.
22 Ibid, paras 258, 283, and 311.
23 IUCN, 'IUCN WCEL Welcomes the Advisory Opinion on Climate Change by the International Tribunal on the Law of the Sea' (*IUCN*, 21 May 2024) <https://www.iucn.org/news/202405/iucn-wcel-welcomes-advisory-opinion-climate-change-international-tribunal-law-sea> accessed 8 June 2024; Yiallourides and Deva (n 18).
24 ITLOS Climate Change Advisory Opinion (n 9), para 202.
25 Ibid, para 135.
26 Ibid, paras 137, 214, 243 and 441(3)(b) and (f)–(i).

27 Payne, 'Responsibility' (n 1) 25–26; Oral, 'Implementing' (n 16) 182 and 187.
28 BBNJ Agreement. Article 2 states that the objective of the Agreement "is to ensure the conservation and sustainable use of marine biological diversity of areas beyond national jurisdiction, for the present and in the long term, through effective implementation of the relevant provisions of the [UNCLOS] and further international cooperation and coordination."
29 Hobday and Matear (n 2) 30; Paris Agreement to the United Nations Framework Convention on Climate Change (adopted 12 December 2015, entered into force 4 November 2016) FCCC/CP/2015/10/Add.1 ("Paris Agreement").
30 Paris Agreement Article 2(1).
31 Paris Agreement Articles 3, 4(2), and 4(3); UNFCCC, 'Key Aspects of the Paris Agreement' (UNFCC) <https://unfccc.int/most-requested/key-aspects-of-the-paris-agreement> accessed 20 March 2024.
32 Payne, 'Responsibility' (n 1) 30.
33 BBNJ Agreement, Article 8(1).
34 BBNJ Agreement, Article 5(2).
35 Dan Laffoley and others, 'Marine Protected Areas' in Charles Sheppard (ed), *World Seas: An Environmental Evaluation* (Elsevier 2019) 552.
36 ITLOS Climate Change Advisory Opinion (n 9), paras 407, 438, and 440.
37 Giovanni Ardito, Gemma Andreone, and Marzia Rovere, 'Overlapping and Fragmentation in the Protection and Conservation of the Marine Environment in Areas beyond National Jurisdiction' (2022) 9(1) Frontiers in Marine Science 1, 8.
38 BBNJ Agreement Part III, Articles 17(b), 20–22 and Articles 25–26.
39 BBNJ Agreement, Article 22(1).
40 Paris Agreement Preamble; United Nations Framework Convention on Climate Change (adopted 9 May 1992, entered into force 21 March 1994) 1771 UNTS 107, Article 1; Hobday and Matear (n 2) 36.
41 Paris Agreement Preamble; BBNJ Agreement Article 17(c).
42 Payne, 'Responsibility' (n 1) 30.
43 Minas (n 4) 92.
44 BBNJ Agreement Article 2; Paris Agreement Article 6(8)(c).
45 Kevin Hanna and Lauren Arnold, 'An Introduction to Environmental Impact Assessment' in K Hanna (ed), *Routledge Handbook of Environmental Impact Assessment* (Routledge 2022) 3.
46 ITLOS Climate Change Advisory Opinion (n 9), paras, 354 and 367.
47 Deqiang Ma, Qinhua Fang, and Song Guan, 'Current Legal Regime for Environmental Impact Assessment in Areas beyond National Jurisdiction and Its Future Approaches' (2016) 56(1) Environmental Impact Assessment Review 23, 26.
48 BBNJ Agreement Part IV.
49 BBNJ Agreement Articles 29 and 38.
50 BBNJ Agreement Articles 38(1)(a) and (b).
51 A Neil Craik and William C G Burns, *Climate Engineering under the Paris Agreement: A Legal and Policy Primer* (Centre for International Governance Innovation 2016); Mark G Lawrence and others, 'Evaluating Climate Geoengineering Proposals in the Context of the Paris Agreement Temperature Goals' (2018) 9 Nature Communications 3734.
52 BBNJ Agreement Article 29(3).
53 Payne, 'Responsibility' (n 1) 30.
54 ITLOS Climate Change Advisory Opinion (n 9), para 327.
55 BBNJ Agreement, Articles 40–41.
56 Cymie Payne, 'Negotiation and Dispute Prevention in Global Cooperative Institutions: International Community Interests, IUU Fishing, and the Biodiversity Beyond National Jurisdiction Negotiation' (2020) 22(1) International Community Law Review 428, 430–31.
57 BBNJ Agreement Articles 40(e) and 41(1).
58 Paris Agreement Articles 10 and 11; Nilüfer Oral, 'International Law as an Adaptation Measure to Sea-level Rise and Its Impacts on Islands and Offshore Features' (2019) 34(1) The International Journal of Marine and Coastal Law 415, 424.
59 ITLOS Climate Change Advisory Opinion (n 9), para 390.
60 Ibid.
61 Minas (n 4) 84.

62 Nathalie Hilmi and others, 'Deep Sea Nature-based Solutions to Climate Change' (2023) 5(1) Frontiers in Climate 1, 2.
63 Ibid 10 and 14.
64 ITLOS Climate Change Advisory Opinion (n 9), para 296.
65 Ibid, para 298.

10

CLIMATE-INDUCED MIGRATION: LEGAL AND HEALTH IMPLICATIONS

Avidan Kent and Maya Prabhu

Introduction

One of the most significant consequences of climate change will be mass human displacement. While the ubiquitous image of climate-induced migration is that of an Atlantis-like sinking island nation, the reality will be far more varied. Rising sea levels may indeed cause small island states to slowly submerge. Equally likely are slow-onset events, such as increased heat levels and droughts[1] which will propel individuals to migrate.[2] Extreme weather events, such as typhoons, wildfires and floods, will affect the habitability of certain regions, leading to land erosion and increased salinization of agricultural land.[3] Some of these impacts will lead directly to rapid displacement, whereas others will more indirectly influence economic, social or political conditions.[4] Some of these push factors are permanent in nature; in other cases, the damage may be temporary and could be remedied.

Just as the reasons for migration are varied, so does the act of migration itself take many different forms. Some affected communities will react to eroding coastlines by moving their homes several hundred meters inland.[5] Others will engage first in internal migration to different regions or large cities, or seek to cross borders in order to avoid the long-term impacts of climate change.[6] Some affected persons who reside in the richest communities in the world[7] will benefit from financial and governmental institutions and the availability of adaptation options. Others will be entirely unprotected. Some migrants will have easy routes to other well-resourced countries,[8] while others will not. Some will consider their displacement a temporary condition, hoping that future adaptation efforts will allow their return. Others will settle down in their new locations and build new lives eking out whatever livelihoods and communities they can.

In short, there is no single lens through which to view the process of climate-induced migration. Not surprisingly, efforts to address this phenomenon at the international level are abstract and fragmented. The purpose of this chapter is to provide a historical overview of legal interventions and to consider important gaps in the social and health needs of migrants.

Climate-Induced Migration and International Law: A Timely Opportunity

International climate change laws and policies have traditionally focused on the environmental and economic impacts of climate change. It was not until 2008 that social development and human

DOI: 10.4324/9781003276678-12

rights received more attention. Several Human Rights Council Resolutions became the bellwether, addressing the link between climate change and human rights.[9] These Resolutions 'trickled down' into the UNFCCC process, leading to explicit references to human rights in a number of UNFCCC COP decisions.[10] The process of linking climate change with social development peaked with the 2015 Paris Agreement, characterized by John Knox as a 'human rights treaty' due to its clear emphasis on the human and social dimension.[11]

Within this broader context came the 2010 Cancun Agreements,[12] which called on the UNFCCC's member states to

> enhance action on adaptation . . . by undertaking, inter alia. . . Measures to enhance understanding, coordination and cooperation with regard to climate change induced displacement, migration and planned relocation, where appropriate, at the national, regional and international levels.[13]

This statement was the first international recognition of human displacement as linked to, and resulting from, climate change. This placed the topic of climate-induced migration on the UNFCCC negotiations table, sparking international recognition within the climate regime and beyond.[14]

Steps beyond declaratory statements were undertaken in 2015, as part of COP Decision 1/CP.21 ('Adoption of the Paris Agreement'). The UNFCCC Member States established the Task Force on Displacement, mandated to "develop recommendations for integrated approaches to avert, minimize and address displacement related to the adverse impacts of climate change".[15] In line with the expansion of climate negotiations into the 'social sphere', the Task Force assembly included organizations such as Red Cross, International Organisation on Migration (IOM), UN High Commisioner for Refugees (UNHCR), International Labour Organisation (ILO), UN Development Programme (UNDP), Platform on Disaster Displacement (PDD), and civil society representation.[16]

Additional measures occurred in 2018 with the adoption of the UN Global Compacts on Migration (GCM) and Refugees (GCR). These initiated further actions such as the GCM review process and the identification of specific issues for negotiations like the Task Force Report.[17] However, none of these developments defined new rights and obligations in the context of climate-induced migration. More recently, the decisions establishing and operationalising the UNFCCC Loss and Damage Fund have made important references to climate migration, which may represent a promising step forward. The size of this fund and its future usefulness remain to be seen.

It is important to note the institutional framing for climate-migration. For many years, the topic was 'institutionally homeless', outside of international institutions' mandate and off-limits from any meaningful negotiation table. The COP 1/CP.21 Decision and the Task Force on Displacement established the UNFCCC as an institutional home for climate-induced migration negotiations. Other notable institutional developments that have taken place in the last decade include the creation of the highly active Migration, Environment and Climate Change (MECC) Division at the UN Migration Agency (IOM); the establishment of the Nansen Initiative (later on transformed into the Platform on Disaster Displacement); and increased attention from IGOs, such as the Red Cross and the UNHCR.

The processes described here are still in early stages. Global, regional and domestic policy responses are all being framed,[18] and different legal approaches are being considered. As such, there is 'a window of opportunity for international action on climate-induced migration'[19] in which new norms could be developed.

The Legal Foundations and the Missing Pieces

Though the existing legal framework regulating climate-induced migration is insufficient,[20] it does include several important legal elements.[21] First, a wide body of human rights laws secure climate migrants' most basic rights.[22] Second, other instruments, such as the Sendai Framework, the Nansen Protection Agenda, the UN Guiding Principles on Internal Displacement, the Convention Related to the Status of Stateless Persons, together with certain regional instruments (e.g., the Kampala Convention, the Cartagena Declaration) address specific situations, regions or elements related to climate-induced migration.

At the same time, there are notable gaps in the legal framework[23] which adversely affect the protection of climate migrants' rights. The following section provides a preliminary review of some of those gaps with a specific focus on migrants' rights to physical and mental health.

No Right to Cross a Border and Legally Stay in the Host State

The most discussed legal gap concerns climate migrants' lack of a recognized legal right to seek refuge in other states. The 1951 Refugee Convention provides a 'refugee' status only to those who cannot return to their home countries due to a well-founded fear of persecution "for reasons of race, religion, nationality, membership of a particular social group or political opinion".[24] While UNHCR[25] and certain domestic courts[26] confirm that climate-related events *may impact* asylum decisions, this can only happen where climate-related considerations affect Convention grounds and depend on claimants demonstrating a 'well founded persecution'.

Other regional instruments, notably the Kampala Convention (African Union) and the Cartagena Declaration (Latin America), provide wider definitions which may allow climate-induced migrants to seek a refugee status in these specific regions. These instruments address more general events that disturb the public order as grounds for protection. To date, however, there are only few indications that states accept a wide interpretation of this wider language to also include climate-related events.

The Financial/Funding Gap

Another identified protection gap concerns the lack of an appropriate financial mechanism to support *inter alia* host states' costs of hosting migrants (whether internal or international).[27] These costs could be substantial, especially where states ambitiously try to secure 'costly' rights for migrants, such as the right to education, shelter and healthcare. These costs are substantial in the context of high-income countries, and are beyond the reach of low- and middle-income countries, where the vast majority of climate-induced migration is taking place.

Statehood and Statelessness

Many questions remain regarding notions of statehood and statelessness. In legal terms, it is not clear what the future status of 'sinking' states will be, and whether their citizens will become stateless.[28] This scenario also suggests severe financial implications,[29] ranging from the loss of property, housing and land[30] to the loss of the much wider states' rights vis-à-vis their resources (including their Exclusive Economic Zones).[31] The UN International Law Commission is currently researching statehood issues together with issues that are related to the protection of individuals affected by sea level rise.[32]

The Enforcement Gap

As stated earlier, a wide body of human rights laws provides protection for climate migrants' most basic needs.[33] Similarly, the need to protect climate migrants' human rights has indeed been recognized by the international community.[34] In reality, there is a recurring "gap between law and practice. [. . .] in practice these rights are rarely fully realized, especially for IDPs."[35]

Human rights laws often require victims to establish that the threat to their rights is imminent.[36] Due to the slow nature of many climate-related effects, the threat in these cases may not be regarded as imminent until it becomes nothing short of extreme. This point was demonstrated in the Human Rights Committee's (HRC) iconic *Teitiota* ruling. Even whilst accepting the claim that "sea level rise is likely to render the Republic of Kiribati uninhabitable",[37] the Committee did not regard the threat as sufficiently imminent. The Committee commented that the next decade "could allow for intervening acts by the Republic of Kiribati, with the assistance of the international community" in order to protect the petitioner's right to life. Two dissenting members observed that the current living conditions were already dire due to the lack of access to clean water and habitable space, the destruction of food crops, flooding and severe health issues relating to poor water quality.[38] This suggested that the right to life could be invoked only "where all hopes are gone, when it is clear that the nation island's future is doomed".[39] Opined Committee member Duncan Laki Muhumuza: "[i]t would indeed be counterintuitive to the protection of life, to wait for deaths to be very frequent and considerable; in order to consider the threshold of risk as met".[40]

The 'individualised' nature of human rights protection presents yet another challenge for climate migrants' rights. The HRC has noted that States must refrain from returning individuals to countries in which there are substantial grounds for a real risk: "Such a risk must be personal in nature and cannot derive merely from the general conditions".[41] However, the impact of climate change is never 'personal in nature', leaving one to wonder whether this body of law is indeed appropriate in these circumstances.[42] The UNHCR Secretariat has explicitly commented on this issue,

> The fact that many or all members of a community are impacted does not undermine the validity of any individual member's claim . . . . In some cases, the adverse effects of climate change and disasters on an entire community may strengthen rather than weaken the evidence that justifies the fear of an individual being persecuted.[43]

The Right to Physical and Mental Health for Climate-Induced Migrants

Part II reviewed the legal framework addressing climate-induced migration. The following section will amplify the discussion on the context of the right to physical and mental health.

The Human Right to Physical and Mental Health

The 1946 World Health Organization's Constitution defines 'health' as "a state of complete physical, mental and social well-being and not merely the absence of disease or infirmity".[44] It adds that "[t]he enjoyment of the highest attainable standard of health is one of the fundamental rights of every human being without distinction of race, religion, political belief, economic or social condition".[45] The 1948 Universal Declaration of Human Rights further consolidated the notion,

> [e]veryone has the right to a standard of living adequate for the health and well-being of himself and of his family, including food, clothing, housing and medical care and necessary social services, and the right to security in the event of unemployment, sickness, disability, widowhood, old age or other lack of livelihood in circumstances beyond his control.[46]

Article 12(1) of the 1966 International Covenant on Economic, Social and Cultural Rights similarly states that "[t]he States Parties to the present Covenant recognize the right of everyone to the enjoyment of the highest attainable standard of physical and mental health".[47] The right to health is enshrined in a multitude of international documents,[48] and, as noted in a OHCHR Fact Sheet, "every State has ratified at least one international human rights treaty recognizing the right to health".[49]

The right to health has also been recognized in several UNFCCC decisions. Most prominently, the preamble to the Paris Agreement calls on the member states to take action 'to address climate change, respect, promote and consider their respective obligations on human rights, the right to health'.[50] Decision 3/CP.25 further acknowledges that as "climate change is a common concern of humankind, Parties should, when taking action to address climate change, respect, promote and consider their respective obligations on human rights, the right to health".[51]

There is ample research that demonstrates the link between health considerations and climate-induced migration in both the pre and post migration stages.[52]

Pre-Migration Phase: Health Considerations as Push Factors or Migration

The impact that climatic changes have on humans' health has been thoroughly addressed in a number of authoritative sources, including in the 2014 Intergovernmental Panel on Climate Change (IPCC) report[53] and the 2020 Lancet Countdown on Health and Climate Change report.[54] Climate change is affecting human health in a number of ways due to extreme weather events, heat waves, flooding, infectious diseases, air quality, undernutrition, reduced food availability, availability of water, poverty and more.[55]

With respect to the impact on mental health, the Lancet Countdown report noted that "[c]orrelating climate change and mental health is challenging for several reasons, including local and global stigma and under-reporting, differences in health systems, and variations in cultural understandings of wellbeing".[56] The IPCC report nevertheless noted that

> [f]looding and storms may have profound effects on peoples' mental health [FN omitted]. The prevalence of mental health symptoms (psychological distress, anxiety, and depression) was two to five times higher among individuals who reported flood water in the home compared to non-flooded individuals.[57]

The IPCC report further describes how "floods, droughts and heat waves tend to increase the stress on all those who are already mentally ill [. . .]". Post-traumatic stress responses, "generalized anxiety, depression, aggression and complex psychopathology [. . .]" are all known stress reports. Prolonged slow-onset events increase the risk of suicide. Extreme weather conditions threaten agricultural productivity, fishing, forestry and other economic activities. The impact on cities with high concentrations of mentally ill persons will be destructive. In addition, as stated by the IPCC, "there may be a distressing sense of loss, known as 'solastalgia', that people experience when their land is damaged (Albrecht et al., 2007) and they lose amenity and opportunity".[58]

The health dangers do not arise only from heat and water. In the colder regions of the world, climatic changes have been described as "an emerging mental health challenge for Circumpolar Indigenous populations".[59] Climate-related impacts will affect the ability to hunt, travel and maintain a traditional way of life. Such impacts, it is explained, may cause a variety of mental health problems, including anxiety, stress and grief.[60] Another notable concern relates to the deteriorating state of existing infrastructure and living conditions: "these added stressors may contribute to mental health impacts associated with anxiety and distress from current or anticipatory loss and displacement".[61] Other climate-related impacts, such as prolonged droughts, economic impacts, the effect of certain adaptation and mitigation efforts and more, are also identified in the literature as potentially leading to a variety of mental health-related problems.[62]

All of these impacts adversely affect living conditions and could potentially contribute to one's decision to migrate. These factors, if severe enough, could be enough to directly push individuals to migrate, or alternatively, contribute – alongside other social and economic factors – to the overall deteriorating human experience, eventually leading to migration.

Post-Migration: The Impact of Climate-Induced Migration on Individuals' Physical and Mental health

Access to Health Services and Support Abroad (No Right to Cross a Border)

As stated earlier, one of the main gaps in the legal framework addresses climate migrants' lack of a legal right to cross a border and to (legally) stay in their host state. The lack of a clear legal right to cross a border and reside in the host state could affect migrants' access to health services in two meaningful ways. The first is in the case of internal displacement, where health services are unavailable, and the only way to access health services is via cross-border migration. The lack of a right to cross borders in these cases naturally implies limitations on the ability to enjoy a right to physical and mental health.

The second scenario addresses the situation where the individual has already crossed a border, but their access to health services is impaired due to the lack of a legal right to stay in the host country. The need to secure migrants' access to health services was explicitly addressed by the Global Compact for Migration (GCM) in many different contexts. For example, in the context of unaccompanied and separated children, it asks states to "provide access to health care services, including mental health".[63]

Lack of Access to Health Services in the Home Country as a Reason to Delay Return (No Right to Cross a Border and Legally Reside in Host States)

Another related issue addresses the situation of those who have already crossed a border, but due to the lack of legal right to stay (e.g., no refugee status) might be sent back to their home countries, which may not be able to protect their right to health. An interesting case study relates to the situation of the 2010 Haiti earthquake, following which many Haitians sought refuge in neighboring states. The UNHCR and the OHCHR co-evaluated the possibility of returning them to Haiti. The two organizations concluded that the home state's inability to provide *inter alia* health services should stop host countries from conducting returns.[64]

Another important clarification on this topic (and more related to the specific context of climate change) was made by the UNHCR's Secretariat, in a document titled 'Legal considerations regarding claims for international protection made in the context of the adverse effects of climate change and disasters'.[65] The Secretariat explained in this document that where conditions are bad enough to affect the protection of human rights, "affected populations may be exposed to a risk of human rights violations that amount to persecution within the meaning of the 1951 Convention".[66] In other words, where the human right to health is unprotected, it could be that a claim to deny return to the country of origin could be sustained.

The Financial Gap: Resources for Supporting the Provision of Health/Mental Health Services (The Finance/Funding Gap)

As stated earlier, the effective protection of rights often requires resources. This point has been stressed in policy documents, *inter alia* the UNFCCC Task Force Report and the Nansen Protection Agenda.[67] This financial gap has also been emphasized by many of the authors who have proposed regulatory frameworks for the protection of climate migrants, most of which address the need to link such proposed frameworks with a dedicated fund.[68]

Another point concerning resources links the protection of the right to mental health to the ability to exercise other rights, notably to apply for refugee status. The UNHCR's 'In Harm's Way' study reports on Haitians seeking refuge in Latin American countries following the 2010 earthquake. The report mentions – in several places – the difficulties of those suffering from trauma due to the environmental disaster that they have just faced, when applying for visas/refugee status in their host countries: "assessing claims within the criteria of the Refugee Convention was difficult because Haitians were suffering from serious psychosocial harms and struggling to articulate coherent claims".[69] Allocating resources for supporting these individuals seems necessary in order to allow them to exercise their rights.

Loss of Homeland, Culture, Communities, Identity (Statehood, Loss and Damage)

The legal analysis presented here discusses terms such as 'statehood' and 'loss and damage'. In the more extreme examples (e.g., sinking nation islands) the loss of a state's statehood may lead to certain legal questions and consequences, such as, *inter alia*, the possible statelessness of its citizens and the loss of sovereignty over territory and natural resources. In most cases, however, the existence of the state will not be in question, as the state will not disappear. Rather, parts of its territory will be degraded and the environment will gradually change. All these changes – from the complete loss of state to the more common degraded environment – could affect an individual's mental health.

The experience of climate-induced migration inherently embeds a sense of loss; the migrant's homeland has often been changed – degraded enough to induce displacement. Authors are increasingly discussing terms such as 'solastalgia'[70] or 'ecological grief',[71] essentially reflecting the impact of environmental change, degradation and loss on local communities.

Certain case-studies report the mental health impacts that are associated with climate-induced migration. With respect to the Alaskan Iñupiat community, it was noted that "[m]ental health impacts related to safety and security concerns as well as a sense of loss due to changing sociocultural and environmental conditions have also been reported".[72]

Moreover, the loss of homeland could mean a variety of incidental losses that may exacerbate the aforementioned sense of grief and its impact on an individual's mental health. For example,

Adger et el. link displacement with loss of culture: "[w]hen people are displaced from places that they value, there is strong evidence that their cultures are diminished, and in many cases endangered".[73] A different study examining the impacts of climate change on mental health commented on the impacts of acculturation in the case of migration.[74]

Other authors have focused on the mental health impacts associated with the disruption of social ties resulting from climate-induced migration.[75] In short, the loss of homeland, even if not complete and extreme, may lead to a line of adverse effects on one's community, culture, way of life, landscapes, sense of security and certainty and more. These situations are all common to climate migrants and can all affect their mental health.

Notes

1 Jesse Bell and others, 'Changes in Extreme Events and the Potential Impacts on Human Health' (2018) 68(4) Journal of the Air & Waste Management Association 265.

2 E.g., Amir Reza Khavarian-Garmsir and others, 'Climate Change and Environmental Degradation and the Drivers of Migration in the Context of Shrinking Cities: A Case Study of Khuzestan Province, Iran' (2019) 47 Sustainable Cities and Society; Stephen Sherwood and Matthew Huber, 'An Adaptability Limit to Climate Change Due to Hear Stress' (2010) 107(21) Proceedings of the National Academy of Sciences of the United States of America 9552.

3 E.g., Virginie Duvet and others, 'Risks to Future Atoll Habitability from Climate-driven Environmental Changes' (2021) 12(3) WIREs Climate Change 1–28.

4 UK Government Office for Science, *Foresight: Migration and Global Environmental Change* (2011) <https://assets.publishing.service.gov.uk/government/uploads/system/uploads/attachment_data/file/287717/11-1116-migration-and-global-environmental-change.pdf>.

5 See for example Arne Harms, 'Under the Climate Radar: Disaster and Displacement in the Bengal Delta' in Ali Nobil Ahmad (ed), *Climate Justice and Displacement in the Global South* (Heinrich Boll Foundation 2020) 150.

6 See for example the case of Ioane Teitiota and his family – residents of Kiribati – who asked to seek refuge in New Zealand, claiming that the impacts of climate change on their home county will pose a risk to their lives. Mr Teitiota's case was litigated before New Zealand Courts, and eventually before the UN Human Rights Committee, UN Human Rights Committee (HRC), Ioane Teitiota v New Zealand (advance unedited version now available: 23 September 2020) UN Doc CCPR/C/127/D/2728/2016 (7 January 2020).

7 Alan Taylor, 'Alaska's Climate Refugees' *The Atlantic* (7 July 2015) <https://www.theatlantic.com/photo/2015/07/alaskas-climate-refugees/397862/>.

8 See for example the USA-Marshall Islands Compact of Free Association, which allows citizens of the Marshall Islands to immigrate to the USA.

9 See for example UN Human Rights Council Resolutions 7/23 (2008), 10/4 (2009), 18/22 (2011), 26/27 (2014), and, importantly, the Paris Agreement (2015).

10 Notably, Decision 1/CP.16 (2010) (the Cancun Agreements) states: 'Noting resolution 10/4 of the United Nations Human Rights Council on human rights and climate change, which recognizes that the adverse effects of climate change have a range of direct and indirect implications for the effective enjoyment of human rights and that the effects of climate change will be felt most acutely by those segments of the population that are already vulnerable owing to geography, gender, age, indigenous or minority status, or disability'.

11 John Knox, 'The Paris Agreement as a Human Rights Treaty' in Dapo Akande and others (eds), *Human Rights and 21st Century Challenges: Poverty, Conflict, and the Environment* (OUP 2020).

12 Attempts to address the human elements were made in different forms/areas; see for example the negotiations over the establishment of the Sustainable Development Mechanism – the successor of the Kyoto Protocol – and the calls to incorporate human rights mechanisms in this market-based legal instrument. See for example John Knox, 'Human Rights and Safeguards in the New Climate Mechanism Established in Article 6, Paragraph 4 of the Paris Agreement' 3 May 2016 <https://www.ohchr.org/Documents/Issues/Environment/Letter_to_SBSTA_UNFCCC_May2016.pdf>.

13 UNFCCC Decision 1/CP.16, para 14(f).
14 See developments within the UN General Assembly (notably the Global Compacts), and other institutions such as the IOM, the PDD, Red Cross, and more.
15 UNFCCC Decision 1/CP.21, para 49.
16 UNFCCC, 'Task Force on Displacement – Membership' <https://unfccc.int/process/bodies/constituted-bodies/WIMExCom/TFD/membership>.
17 Task Force on Displacement, 'Report of the Task Force on Displacement' (17 September 2018) <https://unfccc.int/sites/default/files/resource/2018_TFD_report_17_Sep.pdf>.
18 Simon Behrman and Avidan Kent (eds), *Climate Refugees: Global, Local and Critical Approaches* (CUP 2022).
19 Elin Jakobsson, 'Lessons from the Past: Momentum Going forward. Norm Dynamics and the Process of Protection for Climate-induced Migration and Displacement' in Behrman and Kent (eds) (n 18) 85.
20 The reader should be aware that many of these legal instruments are limited in one way or another. For example, some are 'soft laws', while others are limited in terms of memberships/geographic coverage. These issues were all discussed elsewhere and are beyond the scope of this chapter's discussion.
21 A number of authors have mapped the variety of legal instruments that are addressing climate-induced migration; see for example Kälin and Schrepfer (n 23); Sumudu Atapattu, 'A New Category of Refugees?' in Simon Behrman and Avidan Kent (eds), *Climate Refugees: Beyond the Legal Impasse?* (Routledge 2018) 34; Avidan Kent and Simon Behrman, *Facilitating the Resettlement and Rights of Climate Refugees* (Routledge 2018) 9.
22 Sumudu Atapattu, 'Climate Change, Human Rights, and Forced Migration: Implications for International Law' (2009–2010) 27 Wisconsin International Law Journal 607.
23 Walter Kälin and Nina Schrepfer, 'Protecting People Crossing Borders in the Context of Climate Change: Normative Gaps and Possible Approaches' (2012) UNHCR Legal and Protection Policy Research Series <https://www.unhcr.org/uk/media/no-24-protecting-people-crossing-borders-context-climate-change-normative-gaps-and-possible>; Behrman and Kent (n 18).
24 Article 1(A)2, Convention Relating to the Status of Refugees, 28 July 1951, United Nations, Treaty Series, vol. 189, p. 137.
25 UNHCR, 'Legal Considerations Regarding Claims for international protection made in the context of the adverse effects of climate change and disasters' (2020) <https://www.refworld.org/docid/5f75f2734.html>.
26 Camilla Schloss, 'The Role of Environmental Disasters in Asylum Cases: Do German Courts Take Disasters into Account?' in Behrman and Kent (eds) (n 18) 243.
27 Nansen Protection Agenda (Vol 1, 2015), 18–19; Task Force Report (n 17) 30–32; Katrina Miriam Wyman, 'Response to Climate Migration' (2013) 37 Harvard Environmental Law Review 167, 181.
28 See full analysis of the relevant legal situation in Kent and Behrman (n 21).
29 Ori Sharon, 'Tides of Climate Change: Protecting the Natural Wealth Rights of Disappearing States' (2019) 60(1) Harvard International Law Journal 95.
30 Scott Leckie, *Finding Land Solutions to Climate Displacement: A Challenge Like Few Others* (Displacement Solutions 2013).
31 Sharon (n 29).
32 ILC, 'Sea-level Rise in Relation to International Law' (2018) A/73/10 <https://legal.un.org/ilc/reports/2018/english/annex_B.pdf>.
33 This protection is provided whether via the key human rights conventions, *inter alia* International Covenant on Civil and Political Rights (ICCPR) and the International Covenant on Economic, Social and Cultural Rights (ICESCR), The International Convention on the Elimination of All Forms of Racial Discrimination, Convention on the Rights of the Child, Convention on the Rights of Persons with Disabilities, Convention on the Elimination of All Forms of Discrimination against Women, Convention against Torture and Other Cruel, Inhuman or Degrading Treatment or Punishment. Importantly, certain human rights are universally protected under customary international law; see Olivier De Schutter, *International Human Rights Law* (CUP 2019) 59.
34 For example, The Global Compact for Safe, Orderly and Regular Migration (GCM) states that it is 'based on international human rights law and upholds the principles of non-regression and non-discrimination. By implementing the Global Compact, we ensure effective respect for and protection and fulfilment of the human rights of all migrants, regardless of their migration status, across all stages of the migration cycle. We also reaffirm the commitment to eliminate all forms of discrimination, including racism, xenophobia

and intolerance, against migrants and their families'. Global Compact for Safe, Orderly and Regular Migration, para 15(f).

35 Walter Kälin and Rhodri Williams, 'Introduction' in Walter Kälin and others (eds), *Incorporating the Guiding Principles on Internal Displacement into Domestic Law: Issues and Challenges* (ASIL/Brookings 2010) <https://www.refworld.org/pdfid/4b6c164e2.pdf> at 6.

36 Jane McAdam, 'Climate Change Displacement and International Law: Complementary Protection Standards', UNHCR background paper (May 2011) <http://www.unhcr.org/4dff16e99.pdf> 50–52.

37 Human Rights Committee, 'Views adopted by the Committee under Article 5(4) of the Optional Protocol, concerning communication No. 2728/2016'), 7 January 2020, para 9.12.

38 See dissenting views by Duncan Laki Muhumuza and Vasilka Sancin, Human Rights Committee (n 6).

39 Simon Behrman and Avidan Kent, 'Prospects for Protection in Light of the Human Rights Committee's Decision in Teitiota v New Zealand' (2021) Polish Migration Review 6, 24–35.

40 Dissenting views by Duncan Laki Muhumuza, Human Rights Committee (n 6).

41 Human Rights Committee, 'General comment No. 36 (2018) on article 6 of the International Covenant on Civil and Political Rights, on the right to life' (30 October 2018) CCPR/C/GC/36, para 30.

42 It should be noted on the other hand that the HRC did leave an opening, allowing an 'except in the most extreme cases' exception to the personalization requirement.

43 UNHCR Legal Considerations (n 25) Para 8.

44 Constitution of the World Health Organization (1946), Preamble.

45 ibid.

46 Universal Declaration of Human Rights (1948), Article 25.

47 International Covenant on Economic, Social and Cultural Rights (1966), Article 12(1).

48 For a thorough review, see Margaretha Wewerinke-Singh and Melina Antoniadis, 'Climate Displacement and the Right to Mental Health' in Simon Behrman and Avidan Kent (eds), *Climate Refugees: Global, Local and Critical Approaches* (CUP 2022) 146.

49 OHCHR and WHO, 'The Right to Health' (2008) Fact Sheet No 31 <https://www.ohchr.org/documents/publications/factsheet31.pdf> 1.

50 Paris Agreement (2015), Preamble.

51 UNFCCC, Decision 3/CP.25 'Enhanced Lima work programme on gender and its gender action plan' (2019) FCCC/CP/2019/13/Add.1.

52 Wewerinke-Singh and Antoniadis (n 48).

53 See for example IPCC Fifth Assessment Report (2014), Chapter 11 (Human Health: Impacts, Adaptation, and Co-Benefits' <https://www.ipcc.ch/site/assets/uploads/2018/02/WGIIAR5-Chap11_FINAL.pdf>; IPCC, 'Global Warming of 1.5°C' (2018), chapter 3 (Impacts of 1.5°C global warming on natural and human systems) <https://www.ipcc.ch/sr15/>.

54 Nick Watts and others, '*The 2020 Report of the Lancet Countdown on Health and Climate Change: Responding to Converging Crises*' (Lancet 2020).

55 See review in Kirstie Ebi and others, *The 1.5 Health Report: Synthesis on Health & Climate Science in the IPCC SR1.5* <https://www.who.int/globalchange/181008_the_1_5_healthreport.pdf>.

56 Watts and others (n 54) 142.

57 IPCC 2014 (n 53) 722.

58 ibid 732.

59 Ashlee Cunsolo Willox and others, 'Examining Relationships between Climate Change and Mental Health in the Circumpolar North' (2015) 15 Reg Environ Change 169, 171.

60 ibid.

61 ibid 176.

62 Susanta Kumar Padhy and others, 'Mental Health Effects of Climate Change' (2015) 19(1) Indian Journal of Occupational & Environmental Medicine 3, cited in UNHCHR, *Report of the Office of the United Nations High Commissioner for Human Rights: Analytical Study on the Relationship between Climate Change and the Human Right of Everyone to the Enjoyment of the Highest Attainable Standard of Physical and Mental Health* (2016) A/HRC/32/23.

63 Global Compact for Safe, Orderly and Regular Migration (2018) <https://refugeesmigrants.un.org/sites/default/files/180711_final_draft_0.pdf>, para 23(f).

64 A letter from High Commissioner for Human Rights and High Commissioner for Refugees, 'Joint UNHCR-OHCHR Return Advisory Update on Haiti' (9 June 2011) <https://www.unhcr.org/protection/operations/4e0305666/joint-unhcr-ohchr-return-advisory-update-haiti.html>.

65 UNHCR Legal Considerations (n 25) para 7.
66 ibid.
67 Nansen Protection Agenda (Vol 1, 2015), 18–19; Task Force Report (n 17) 30–32.
68 See for example Frank Biermann and Ingrid Boas, 'Protecting Climate Refugees: The Case for a Global Protocol' (2008) 50(6) Environmental Science and Policy for Sustainable Development 8; CRIDEAU, *Draft Convention on the International Status of Environmentally-Displaced Persons* (3rd version, 2013); Bonnie Docherty and Tyler Giannini, 'Confronting a Rising Tide: A Proposal for a Convention on Climate Change Refugees' (2009) 33 Harvard Environmental Law Review 349; David Hodgkinson and others, 'The Hour When the Ship Comes in: A Convention for Persons Displaced by Climate Change' (2010) 36 Monash University Law Review 69.
69 In Harm's Way, 82, 97, 200.
70 Glenn Albrecht, 'Solastalgia: The Distress Caused by Environmental Change' (2007) 15 Australasian Psychiatry S95.
71 Ashlee Cunsolo and Nevile Ellis, 'Ecological Grief as a Mental Health Response to Climate Change-related Loss' (2018) 8 Nature Climate Change 275.
72 Patricia Schwerdtle and others, 'The Health Impact of Climate-Related Migration' (2018) 16(1) BMC Medicine.
73 W Neil Adger and others, 'Cultural Dimensions of Climate Change Impacts and Adaptation' (2012) 3 Nature Climate Change 112.
74 Kumar Padhy and others (n 62).
75 Jacqueline Torres and Joan Casey, 'The Centrality of Social Ties to Climate Migration and Mental Health' (2017) 17 BMC Public Health.

PART 3

Contributions to Increasing Ambition on Climate Change through Law

11

LEGAL CREATIVITY AND PRIVATE FINANCING TO IMPLEMENT THE PARIS AGREEMENT IN THE UNITED KINGDOM

Megan Bowman and Emily Webster[*]

Introduction

It is now clear that green investment is critical to meet the global net zero target and manage climate-related risks at national levels.[1] Equally as important, but less discussed in policy circles, is the fact that finance flows for polluting activities and unsustainable development must be exponentially reduced and phased out. To this end, the 2021 *Marrakech Partnership Climate Action Pathway on Finance* provides that 'In a net-zero, resilient economy by 2050, every financial decision will take climate change into account and financial flows will drive low-emission and climate-resilient development'.[2]

These realisations, while relatively recent, are anchored in the objectives of the 2015 Paris Agreement. Specifically, Article 2.1c provides that the Paris Agreement

> aims to strengthen the global response to the threat of climate change, in the context of sustainable development and efforts to eradicate poverty, including by *making finance flows consistent with a pathway towards low GHG emissions and climate resilient development*' (emphasis added).

Indeed, it is becoming very clear that the global temperature objective in Article 2.1a cannot be met without making *all finance* (not just public funding or niche environment, social and governance projects) consistent with Paris Agreement goals on mitigation and adaptation under Articles 2.1b and 2.1c.

Close attention to the meaning and implementation of Article 2.1c only began in earnest at the 2021 climate negotiations in Glasgow, also known as COP26, co-hosted by the United Kingdom (UK) and Italy. Indeed, the sentiment that 'every financial decision will take climate change into account' was echoed in the UK-driven Private Finance Agenda in the lead up to COP26.[3] This can be understood as a natural progression from the 2019 UK *Greening Finance Strategy*, which coined the terms 'financing green' (increasing finance for clean energy projects) and 'greening finance' (mainstreaming climate and environmental factors in financial decision making and

DOI: 10.4324/9781003276678-14

market products globally).[4] Indeed, Mark Carney, UN Special Envoy on Climate Action and Finance and former Governor of the Bank of England, has stated that 'Net zero is now an organizing principle that is cascading from the global to the country and the company'.[5]

Consistent with these ambitions, the UK announced its goal at COP26 to become the world's first 'net zero aligned financial centre' by focusing on expanded reporting requirements as the predominant means to decarbonise financial institutions and listed companies.[6] Such a pronouncement has gravitas: in addition to the UK's role as COP26 Co-President, the city of London is an internationally important financial centre and the UK has early-mover status regarding climate-related financial regulation, even despite political vicissitude.[7] Thus, the UK is an apt case study for contemplating the levers and limits of turning net zero aspirations into action through reliance on enhanced climate-related corporate disclosure.

Climate-related reporting and disclosure by corporate actors and financial institutions has seen exponential proliferation around the globe since the publication of the 2017 final recommendations of the Financial Stability Board's *Task Force on Climate-related Financial Disclosures* (TCFD).[8] Those recommendations encourage firms to voluntarily provide information to stakeholders (notably investors, lenders, and insurers) on risks and opportunities posed to their business by climate change using forward-looking scenario analyses regarding governance, strategy, risk management, and metrics and targets.

Currently, TCFD-based disclosure is the predominant climate-related financial regulatory tool in the UK and, in a relatively short time, it has evolved into a mandatory legislative regime. Specifically, there has been a laudable coordinated effort between the UK government and financial regulators to introduce economy-wide climate disclosure requirements to support the resilience of the financial system.[9] The hope is that mandatory TCFD-aligned reporting can, indirectly and eventually, help finance to flow at scale toward 'Net Zero and a green recovery'.[10]

This chapter critically assesses the steps that have been taken by the UK to reach its goal of becoming the first net zero financial centre by examining the sufficiency of climate risk disclosure regulation and extant accountability and enforceability modalities. It makes recommendations for ways forward through comparative analyses of other jurisdictions and by exploring the importance of legal and regulatory creativity for increasing public and private sector ambition to achieve a net zero transition. The key message of this chapter is that compliance with Article 2.1c of the Paris Agreement will require not only courage but also creativity.

Climate-related Disclosure: *Compliance and Courage*

Since 2017, the UK has moved swiftly from voluntary to mandatory climate risk disclosure. Although voluntary uptake of climate-risk disclosure increased after publication of the TCFD recommendations, upon review by the TCFD it was found that few disclosures properly identified the potential financial impacts and resilience of a company's strategy.[11] The UK government specifically noted that, within the UK, 'levels of disclosure overall are low and many companies are often not disclosing in line with all the TCFD recommendations'.[12] Consequently, mandatory disclosure requirements were introduced from 2021 to ensure higher levels of reliability, comparability, credibility, and mass uptake across all four core TCFD pillars (governance, strategy, risk management, and metrics and targets).

The logic of disclosure can be imagined as three prongs of a trident. One prong is pointing to the macro-economic level indicating early identification of systemic risks to financial stability by regulators; the second prong is pointing to the meso-market level whereby market players require accurate data to inform responsible capital allocation decisions; and the third prong is pointing to the micro-firm level, whereby the very process of doing disclosure can enable intra-firm identification of vulnerabilities and inflection points for change.[13] In these ways, disclosure can prompt markets to price-in climate risks to assets or potential investments and to identify greener companies and investment opportunities.[14] The disclosure of more and better information may also help to scale up investment in adaptation measures to ensure that the UK is better able to cope with the impacts of climate change.[15] Moreover, transparency has been identified as an important element of the transition to net zero with climate risk disclosure positioned as a mechanism by which to increase the transparency of financial markets.[16]

The following regulatory initiatives have ensured that TCFD-aligned reporting is being implemented across the whole UK economy:[17]

- Since 1 January 2021, premium-listed companies have been required to disclose their climate-risks in alignment with the 11 detailed TCFD recommendations on a comply or explain basis via changes to the Financial Conduct Authority's *FCA Listing Rules*.[18] Companies must include a statement in their annual report confirming disclosures have been made (or explain why they have not) and where in the annual report or supplemental document they can be found.[19] The first disclosures against this Listing Rule were published in early 2022 and a thematic review was co-published by the FCA and Financial Reporting Council in July 2022.[20]
- Since April 2022, changes to the *Companies Act 2006* (UK) require TCFD-aligned disclosures on a comply or explain basis by all large companies (including financial institutions)[21] which are required to produce a non-financial and sustainability statement within the strategic report.[22] This obligation to disclose covers a range of different company types, although small and medium-sized companies (which make up the majority of companies in the UK) are excluded.[23]
- Since October 2021, trustees of certain occupational pension schemes are required to 'establish and maintain oversight of the climate-related risks and opportunities which are relevant to the scheme' over the short-, medium-, and long-term.[24] These schemes are required to, amongst other things, produce and publish a TCFD-aligned report annually, conduct scenario analysis every three years, obtain emissions data of the scheme's assets and use them to assess the risks and opportunities of the scheme on an 'as far as they are able' basis (to allow for the company data deficiencies with which Trustees had to initially wrangle). Schemes must also set a target (absolute, intensity, or other metric) against which they can measure the Scheme's performance. The Pensions Regulator can issue compliance notices and penalties for failure to produce a report.[25]
- Since 1 January 2022, updated Financial Conduct Authority (FCA) Rules also require TCFD-aligned disclosures at entity- and product-levels by asset managers and FCA-regulated asset owners (life insurers and pension providers) on an absolute mandatory basis (not comply or explain).[26]

Consistent with the 'trident logic' of disclosure outlined earlier, the stated goal of these statutory obligations was to ensure that companies and financial institutions 'take actions against climate-related risks and opportunities'.[27] Nevertheless, the current insufficiency and low quality of data, combined with the tick-box mentality of many reporting organisations,[28] pose very serious threats to attaining this goal. Indeed, without quality data and comparability between disclosures, the usefulness of reporting is limited in terms of offering investors the requisite information to accurately price their current or potential investments.[29]

Acknowledging this limitation, in 2021 the UK government proposed a *Sustainability Disclosure Requirement (SDR) Framework* to build on the TCFD-aligned disclosure regulations. It is an ambition touted as Phase 1 of 'greening the financial system' and 'an integral part' of 'kick-start[ing] a green industrial revolution'.[30] The full-scale roll-out of that Framework was initially delayed; however, in November 2023, the FCA finally published the new SDR and associated fund-labelling regime, which took effect from 2024 and applies only to UK firms and their UK-domiciled products marketed in the UK.[31] Importantly for data comparability, the SDR seeks to align UK disclosure rules with reference to newly developed reporting standards by the International Sustainability Standards Board (ISSB). The ISSB was established at COP26 to develop a comprehensive global baseline of sustainability disclosures for capital markets and will work together with the International Accounting Standards Board (IASB) to ensure compatibility with financial reporting standards. The hope is that this will put financial and sustainability reporting on equal footing to ensure commensurate outputs of quality, relevance, and audit rigor.[32] It is unclear yet how it will interact with other standards, notably the EU Corporate Sustainability Reporting Directive (CSRD) or United States' Securities and Exchange Commission (SEC) requirements in development. To this end, the International Financial Reporting Standards (IFRS) Foundation has created the Sustainability Standards Advisory Forum as 'a mechanism for formal engagement on standard-setting between the ISSB and jurisdictional representatives', to promote interoperability and a 'building blocks' approach for an effective global baseline.[33]

These disclosure-related legislative and regulatory initiatives are very encouraging, especially when taken together as a whole-of-economy approach. Nonetheless, mandatory climate-related financial reporting is procedural in nature, which has limited implications for far-reaching change. In the early stages of legislative roll out, regulators focused primarily on compliance with regulatory requirements rather than accuracy or ambition as aligned to Paris Agreement goals.[34] Although there are enforcement mechanisms associated with disclosure rules, the penalties can be small for non-compliance; for example, in 2022 the penalty for trustees was £5,000 and for corporate bodies £50,000.[35] In addition, regulators face challenges (capacity or funding) to monitor and enforce every errant disclosure especially given the wide scope of their everyday regulatory functions beyond climate issues. In short, there is a very real concern that TCFD reports become tick-box in nature rather than embedding risk identification, management, and reduction throughout the organisation,[36] which would undermine the purpose of reports and thus their utility in practice.

In addition to these uncertainties that are specific to the UK, the utility of disclosure to facilitate green finance may be limited for several general reasons. The implementation of the obligation to identify, assess, and disclose such information is a slow process. Identifying such information throughout the organisation and also its supply and value chains requires not only the collection of significant amounts of information but also the expertise to understand and complete the necessary analysis, including the use of scenario analysis, to the extent that it may take several years for the information to truly reflect the climate risks and opportunities of the company in question. The response to climate change must be rapid, given that global greenhouse gases must be halved by 2030 if we are to have a chance at staying within temperature guardrails, so significant progress towards net zero must be made very quickly and by developed states in particular.[37]

In this respect, it is important to note that the role of auditors and assurance providers as enforcers of standards are crucial to the reliability and therefore integrity of climate-related disclosures. Yet the concern is that most external auditors do not yet fully account for climate-related risks in financial statements, despite the significance of those risks in the context of net-zero pledges by audited firms.[38] Moreover, assurance in Environmental, Social and Governance (ESG) non-financial reporting is uneven due to a lack of uniform standards, unlike in financial auditing,[39] and such assurance tends to favour managerial interests, 'thereby eroding transparency'.[40]

Given that transparency is so key to market integrity, and that new regulations like the EU CSRD require enhanced assurance of sustainability risks, the prudence of auditors and assurers requires more scrutiny in forthcoming reporting cycles. In this regard, the International Organization of Securities Commissions (IOSCO) and international audit and assurance standard setters such as the International Auditing and Assurance Standards Board (IAASB) need to step up work on implementation of international audit and assurance standards for sustainability.

Nonetheless, disclosures may be useful if they can be used as evidence in litigation, as happened in the Dutch case of *Milieudefensie v Royal Dutch Shell*.[41] But in the UK, this approach is not so clear. For example, Lord Briggs JSC in *Vedanta Resources Plc,* a case concerned with environmental damage by the defendant's subsidiary, noted that liability of the parent company for the negligent activities of the subsidiary 'would depend heavily upon the contents of the documents internal to each of the defendant companies'.[42] However, such 'internal' documents would only become available to claimants at the point in the litigation process where parties reveal relevant documents to each other (known as *discovery* in litigation parlance). The result is that, for summary judgements and those requiring the court's permission to proceed (namely shareholder derivative actions under UK Company Law as clearly demonstrated in *ClientEarth v Shell plc & Individual Directors [2023] EWHC 1897 (Ch)*), claimants may face challenges in demonstrating to the court that they have an arguable case.[43] Climate-related reporting or other company disclosures, due to their public nature, may make it easier for claimants to provide evidence to the courts at a preliminary stage without having to proceed to full trial to obtain the requisite information. However, this in turn could motivate companies and financial institutions to be circumspect about identifying their climate-related risks. In short, if there is a lack of enforcement or scrutiny of the content of the disclosures by financial regulators, and an over-reliance on internal corporate monitoring and identification of risks, then the threat of litigation may have the perverse effect of undermining accurate disclosures, thus limiting their efficacy.

A ray of hope is in the dynamic nature of the disclosure regulation space, which is moving at quite a fast pace. Internationally. For example, in Europe pursuant to the EU *Sustainable Finance Action Plan,* double materiality (the sustainability impacts of business on the planet, not just the financial impacts of climate on business), due diligence obligations regarding supply chains and inclusion of biodiversity and nature-related risks and impacts in reporting requirements are required by new legislation such as the CSRD and Article 29 of the 2019 French *Energy and Climate Law* (LEC). In the UK, double materiality is not favoured to date.[44] However, there is some early attention to due diligence and biodiversity considerations, currently limited to a specific list of forest risk commodities and illegal deforestation as a result of agricultural activity, but which may be extended subject to successful implementation.[45] Such a development would be consistent with transnational due diligence obligations via the UN Guiding Principles on Business and Human Rights and the OECD Guidelines for Multinationals, as well as EU legislative developments such as the 2023 *Corporate Sustainability Due Diligence Directive*.[46]

Nonetheless, an overarching concern about the efficacy of reporting to address planetary crises is that production of more information – no matter how ambitious in scope – cannot guarantee that meaningful action will be subsequently taken by market players. In other words, disclosure by itself does not guarantee that more finance will be channelled towards sustainable investments or ensure that companies adapt to climate change or protect the planet from risks created by their activities. Although the identification and disclosure of climate risks and opportunities is in the long-term interests of a firm, many directors and investors operate on short-term time horizons and principles of wealth maximisation. In addition, company directors and managers often have deficiencies in knowledge and understanding of climate change and its impacts, and many require support to ensure that the organisation will be resilient. These issues are explored in the next Part.

Ultimately, the obligation to identify, assess, and disclose climate and sustainability information cannot, by itself, ensure a significant net benefit to the planet in terms of directing all finance towards projects and investments that are consistent with net zero.

Supplementing Disclosure Regulation: *Creativity and Comparison*

As evidenced in Part 2, mandatory climate-related disclosure can best be described as a logical first step in the transition process. It is a regulatory tool that, when implemented and utilised efficaciously, can provide data (via reporting) and assessments (via scenario analysis and stress testing) to regulators and market participants to assist with accurately pricing risk, identifying micro- and macro-prudential vulnerabilities, realigning investment portfolios, and gauging net zero progress. Nonetheless, it cannot single-handedly deliver the systemic change to mainstream sustainable finance as exhorted by Article 2.1c of the Paris Agreement.

Thus, disclosure regulation needs to be supplemented with other regulatory tools. The types, form, and intent of such tools, and who can or should wield them, have been discussed in depth elsewhere,[47] and new tools will likely need to be created and deployed as the climate emergency escalates. So this Part will focus in on two categories of emerging tools: anti-greenwashing endeavours through taxonomies and mandatory transition plans; and cultural change through director responsibility and firm-wide training.

Anti-Greenwashing: Taxonomies and Transition Planning

Mandatory TCFD-aligned reporting does not change the fact that the green *assessment* of a company, asset or product is left up to interpretation by readers of the disclosures. Unsurprisingly, a proliferation of spurious green messaging within markets is starting to confuse readers,[48] which has ramifications for market integrity along with the timely move to net zero. Moreover, firms and financial institutions that make net zero promises are coming under increased scrutiny. For example, an international consortium of private finance actors under the banner of the Glasgow Finance Alliance for Net Zero (GFANZ), which together supervise US$130 trillion of assets under management, promised at COP26 to help deliver the multi-trillion-dollar funding required for a net zero transition.[49] Yet the faithfulness of that promise will be judged against how many of those trillions are mobilised to address global warming, and whether GFANZ-supported fossil fuel funding is exponentially reduced.

In short, concrete steps for achieving targets in the few years left to 2030 must become the imperative for firms as well as governments. As the IPCC report revealed so starkly, net zero by 2050 is not possible without hitting at least 50% reduction of emissions by 2030. This necessarily requires regulatory oversight of firm-level transition planning to counter greenwashing and increase ambition in line with national and international targets.

In response, Taxonomy regulation is being developed with the objective of addressing greenwashing and providing a common understanding of key terms such as ‘green’, ‘sustainable/unsustainable’, and ‘transition’. In 2021, the UK Treasury announced the creation of a national Green Taxonomy and, subsequently, a government consultation on Technical Screening Criteria; however, as at 2024 we have not yet seen further developments. By contrast, the EU is much further along this path and a forerunner amongst developed countries for its 10-point *Action Plan on Financing Sustainable Growth* which commenced in 2018 in response to the Paris Agreement[50] and comprises the EU Green Taxonomy Regulation (in force July 2020). This taxonomy is a classificatory tool for assessing economic activities as ‘sustainable’. It defines six environmental objectives against which an economic activity can be assessed as sustainable if that activity contributes to at least two objectives whilst Doing No Significant Harm to any others. Reporting against the first two objectives of Mitigation and Adaptation came into force in January 2022; the other four objectives followed in 2023. Specifically, Article 8 of the EU Taxonomy imposes disclosure obligations on in-scope financial and non-financial companies to report on how and to what extent their activities are associated with 'environmentally sustainable' economic activities as defined under the Taxonomy Regulation. That obligation is also integrated into the Sustainable Finance Disclosure Regulation (SFDR) (in force from March 2021) pursuant to which financial market participants and advisers must disclose how and to what extent financial products that '*promote* environmental or social characteristics' (Article 8) or have 'sustainable investment as their *objective*' (Article 9) are aligned with the EU Taxonomy; that is, the extent to which they are environmentally sustainable and address any adverse impacts of their business on sustainability.

In addition, the European Commission is considering the introduction of a Red Taxonomy of outright unsustainable activities, and has already proposed the creation of an Amber taxonomy to cover intermediate activities that are not yet green but are not environmentally harmful under the Do No Significant Harm principle. Yet some critics have warned that an Amber category could encourage greenwashing and should therefore only be a short-term bridging step.[51] Indeed, EU taxonomy development has attracted criticism at various stages (e.g., for classifying natural gas and nuclear as green transition activities), which reflects the complex and inherently political nature of classification, and which is providing salutary lessons for the UK.

Alongside anti-greenwashing regulation, mandatory transition planning – for firms as well as national governments – is emerging. The concept of transition plans involves concrete actions, metrics, targets, and methodologies of how entities and institutions will decarbonise over specific horizons to 2030. Indeed, this will be crucial for translating net zero commitments into action and helping to track economy-wide progress whilst also holding firms accountable by investors and society. As such, transition planning goes well beyond mere disclosure.

There is no internationally accepted template for high-quality and effective transition plans as yet, and regulatory approaches are embryonic and experimental.[52] In the EU and indeed the world, French Article 29 of the LEC 2019 represents one of the first forays into transition planning. In 2021, Article 29 LEC replaced the pioneering Article 173 of the *Energy Transition for Green Growth Law 2015* and amended the *French Monetary and Financial Code* to enhance and expand the previous climate-related disclosure regime, which was the first to require institutional investors and financial institutions (not just listed companies) to report on a comply-or-explain basis about their risk exposure and strategy towards a low-carbon economy. Article 29 LEC goes much further. It also incorporates biodiversity and double materiality objectives. Firms must disclose their strategies for reducing negative impacts and their alignment with the *UN Convention on Biological Diversity* goals; additionally, they must disclose how their businesses *depend on* climate and biodiversity, as well as their impacts. As such, Article 29 LEC aligns with EU-level SFDR (for financial institutions) and the CSRD (for companies). Indeed, under the CSRD, double material sustainability information is included on the balance sheet thus eradicating financial/ESG distinctions; and mandatory digital tagging will enable machine readability with intent for vertical comparability (same company across different years) and horizontal comparability (different companies).

Importantly, although the French Article 29 LEC does not explicitly require a company transition plan, the inclusion of double materiality and disclosures *over specific horizons to 2030* on matters such as financial services provision, new products such as green bonds, and engagement policy/voting rights all trigger the requirement of net zero targets. In other words, complying with Article 29 LEC requires transition planning; it goes well beyond disclosure of climate risk.

In the UK, the Transition Plan Taskforce was launched in April 2022 comprising industry, academia, and regulators to develop a 'gold standard' for transition plan disclosures. The Taskforce published a Sector-Neutral Framework for public comment in May 2022 and launched the final version of its 'TPT Disclosure Framework' with implementation guidance and draft sector guidance in October 2023, all of which have been described by the FCA as providing 'a set of good practice recommendations to help companies across the economy make high quality, consistent and comparable transition plan disclosures'.[53] HM Treasury extended the TPT's mandate well into 2024 to support the proposed Transition Finance Market Review, which will aim to

> consider what the UK financial and professional services ecosystem needs to do to become a leading hub for and provider of transition financial services – by facilitating UK and international companies and investors to invest to align with credible net zero pathways.[54]

Moreover, the FCA had referenced the TCFD's guidance on transition plans in its rules on climate-related disclosures for listed companies, asset managers, and asset owners, and will continue to draw on TPT Disclosure Framework outputs to strengthen its disclosure expectations.[55]

Certainly, we will need courageous leadership from the FCA and the Transition Plan Taskforce to help make real the promise of net zero in the UK. Historically there has been uncertainty in government rhetoric and ambitions about the extent to which transition plans will indirectly impose net zero targets on companies in this space. In 2021, the UK government stated that it would introduce the requirement for transition plans by certain large companies that lay out how the company will contribute to the government achieving its statutory net zero target.[56] Yet at that time the government also stated that it would not impose net zero targets directly upon companies.[57] Clarity and coherence is required to move forward in an impactful way.

Cultural Change via Accountability and Education

It is clear from Part 2 that regulatory success for a net zero transition will be evidenced by cultural and behavioural change whereas tick-box compliance would signify regulatory failure.[58] As such, disclosure requirements cannot stand alone; rather, they need to be nested within a suite of complementary legal and regulatory measures aimed at transforming business-as-usual.

Since the 2008 global financial crisis, the concept of 'regulating culture' by financial regulators via governance considerations has become acceptable on the basis that director responsibility and good board decision-making is integral to risk management and mitigation. Accordingly, extant regulatory tools, especially those of central banks that are directed at the Board culture of supervised firms, have been extended to include climate-related accountability in some jurisdictions.

The UK is a leader on this issue. The UK *Senior Managers and Certification Regime* establishes the link between seniority and accountability in banks and insurers that are supervised by the Bank of England's Prudential Regulation Authority (PRA) by ensuring that individual officers assume a 'duty of responsibility' to take reasonable steps to prevent or stop regulatory breaches in their area of responsibility. In 2019, this Regime was updated to include the identification and management of climate-related financial risks by virtue of the Bank of England's Prudential Regulation Authority (PRA) *Supervisory Statement Enhancing Banks' and Insurers' Approaches to Managing the Financial Risks from Climate Change* (SS3/19). SS3/19 builds climate risk into the UK Senior Managers and Certification Regime by adding it to the list of controlled functions allocated to individual officers who assume responsibility for them – known as Senior Management Functions. Those Functions are subject to a number of statutory and regulatory requirements as monitored by the PRA and FCA (as relevant). In so doing, the PRA was the first central bank to set out supervisory expectations for banks and insurers to manage the financial risks from climate change on threat of personal liability.

SS3/19 also required supervised firms to establish strategic plans that, amongst other things, enhance transparency through a robust disclosure approach, delineate clear roles and responsibilities for Boards regarding management of climate risk, use scenario analysis, and incorporate financial risks from climate change into risk management practice. In addition, senior management committees share collective responsibility; and international banks active in the UK are also expected to consider climate risks. Relevant firms were expected to embed those expectations as far as possible by the end of 2021.

Similarly, the Dutch Central Bank (DNB) and Dutch Markets Authority (AFM) employ qualitative measures to help assess the safety and soundness of supervised firms. They have a legal duty to conduct *Fit and Proper Assessments* of incoming Board members to supervised firms, and those assessments were updated after 2020 to include climate risk. In so doing, these regulators evaluate whether someone can meet the responsibility of directing a firm's strategy and corporate culture by assessing that person's technical knowledge, experience, skills, and competencies. Prospective directors must now demonstrate knowledge of climate risks by identifying, for example, relevant law and regulations, responsible company officers, and ways of managing those risks. This mechanism for climate risks dovetails with *Professional Conduct and Culture Supervision* which the DNB pioneered in 2011, comprising qualitative assessment of the integrity, suitability, behaviour, and culture of firms' board members. If problems emerge at a bank during the supervisory process, then DNB can scrutinise board meetings and other participatory processes to identify root causes of potential risks in the governance culture of a firm.

Yet, whilst these qualitative supervisory approaches are laudable, they also have limitations. The time-consuming, resource-intensive, and highly abstract nature of qualitative supervision makes the practice of it challenging. Moreover, one can certainly query whether fit and proper assessments are too superficial to actually ensure better decision-making by boards, or whether assessment of climate risk even by a named individual is sufficient to change broader firm behaviour. Nonetheless, personal accountability is a powerful motivator for directors to do the right thing. Indeed, UK supervisors have reported that, due to the *Senior Managers and Certification Regime,* positive changes have been discernible in firm governance such that director attitudes about climate change are no longer tokenistic; rather, they treat it as a serious risk and opportunity to be addressed.[59]

Thus, individual accountability is a very powerful lever; and the UK and Dutch measures reveal a positive beginning. The challenge for moving forward is to ensure that behaviour and culture awareness (and consequential change) spreads beyond the board level throughout whole organisations. To this end, 'institutional irrigation' of climate and sustainability-related knowledge and responsibility needs to occur within firms. This can happen in different ways. Certainly, proper training and education is key,[60] and this is starting to happen around the world. For example, the French Markets Authority (AMF) established a voluntary certification dedicated to sustainable finance for supervised firms (aimed particularly at sales professionals) pursuant to which exams began in 2022. This certification is offered alongside the mandatory AMF certificate (that must be studied by people with certain roles in firms) which has been strengthened by new modules since 2021 that test professional knowledge about green and responsible finance.

Similarly, in March 2022, the regulatory functions arm of Singapore's Stock Exchange (SGX), known as Singapore Exchange Regulation (SGX RegCo), commenced mandatory sustainability training courses for all directors of companies listed on the SGX. Directors must attend one of the eight courses to meet enhanced SGX sustainability reporting rules, and confirmation of their attendance must be included in the first sustainability report (issued from 2023) for financial years commencing 1 January 2022.[61]

These educational initiatives are very encouraging. Yet the fact remains that any sustainability-related certification and training must be mandatory for *all employees* (not just titled roles) to reach the critical mass required. It must also be undertaken annually (not just as a one-off) until we actually achieve net zero due to the dynamic nature of planetary crises, the fast pace of climate-related financial regulation, and the potential for knowledge loss if the lone climate expert in a firm departs. Finally, the subject matter of such training must be broader than simply 'Reporting 101': it needs to cover basic climate science, doughnut economics, planetary boundaries, and emerging laws and regulation that can give trainees the requisite 'full picture' of what is at stake, why meaningful action needs to occur promptly, and what actions they can take within their professional role.

Conclusion: Creativity and Corporate Purpose

This chapter has identified encouraging initiatives as well as legitimate concerns with the UK government's approach to reach net zero by focusing predominantly on climate-related corporate disclosure. It is clear that relying on disclosure as the preferred modality to motivate companies and investors to self-direct private finance towards sustainable investments will never meet required ambitions, especially when it is done in a piecemeal and reactive way.[62] Indeed, such an approach is exemplified by the history of the *Companies Act 2006* (UK), which featured several revisions in light of changing norms whereby the initial refusal to introduce notions of corporate social responsibility into the statute was superseded by the later recognition that environmental and social factors do need to be incorporated. This in turn led to the introduction of new requirements for, respectively, a strategic report, a s172(1) statement, and climate-related disclosure in less than a decade. The result is that chapter 4A of the *Companies Act 2006* (UK) has now become unwieldly for regulatees to understand and thus discharge their obligations.

Yet the unique hallmark of climate change is that it triggers several regulatory paradoxes.[63] For example, its inherent scale and complexity is unprecedented, which necessitates iterative and experimental regulatory responses (which by their nature can be slow) but also creates a planetary emergency (which requires urgent action). In short, the legal and business preference for certainty is at odds with planetary and regulatory realities.

We can make a compelling argument here that the underlying problem – and potential solution – is the thorny corporate governance issue of corporate purpose. As defined by Eccles et al, corporate purpose is 'the key to their [company] strategies and capital allocation decisions' and ought to 'reflect the problems they aim to solve profitably'.[64] Pointedly, Sjåfjell et al. argue that dominant legal-economic theories and the social norm of shareholder primacy have 'disembedded' the corporation from its rightful place within society and the environment.[65]

With this in mind, measures such as enhanced disclosure requirements or even anti-greenwashing regulations sit at the periphery but do not get to the heart of the matter. Attention to directors' personal liability is getting closer; but how efficacious is it to compel a director to care about planetary crises on pain of penalty, while concomitantly compelling that same director to ensure profits at any cost? When normative messaging is mixed, businesses will not make radical change.

Indeed, it is not surprising that an extensive 2022 study of institutional investors in the USA and Europe revealed that, despite 'widespread appreciation amongst investors of the significance and potential of corporate purpose', they were cynical about any serious correlation between stated company purposes and enlightened director/board behaviour.[66] The findings showed that corporate purpose is not regarded by companies as integral to the relationship between ESG issues and financial performance; yet that relationship is of key concern to asset managers and their asset owner clients. So there is a disconnect between different links in the investment chain, namely companies and investors.[67] The authors posit that part of the solution requires investors to get clear about their own purpose in order to prioritise the purposes of companies, thereby holding each other to account.[68]

Yet, there is also an important role for law and regulation in this endeavour. Animating Article 2.1c requires not just compliance and courage but also *creativity*, especially from legal and regulatory experts. We are seeing initial steps in this direction. For example, the 2019 French *PACTE Law (Action Plan for Business Growth and Transformation)* requires French companies to take into consideration social and environmental issues; and it encourages companies to incorporate social objectives into their corporate purpose (their 'raison d'être').[69] Moreover, the American outdoor clothing company Patagonia Inc., a privately-held B-Corp, changed its corporate form in 2022 to guarantee continuation of the owners' values and vision for a sustainable earth. Rather than selling the company or publicly listing it, they created a new corporate form through a trust mechanism.[70] Further, in corporate law research, a 2022 study proposed an 'integrated corporate capital solvency standard' which implies that all three forms of capital (financial, natural, human) are to be included on the corporate balance sheet, in recognition that 'the triple threats of climate change, depleting ecosystems, and the global health pandemic' require a new approach to integrated reporting to fulfil the promise of sustainable corporate purpose.[71]

These are just a few exciting examples of creative legal forms and thought experiments seeking to bring a truly sustainable corporate purpose to life. The key question now is how can this sort of creativity be mainstreamed for the betterment of planet and people? Implementing Article 2.1c of the Paris Agreement requires that all messaging (legal, political, financial, corporate) is aligned and heading in the same direction: towards a low-carbon, sustainable and resilient global economy. Tweaks at the edge of business-as-usual do not – and cannot – get to the heart of systems change, in the UK or anywhere else.

Notes

* Dr. Emily Webster was an Assistant Professor in Environmental and Climate Law at the Department of Land Economy, University of Cambridge, an Official Fellow at Queens' College, and a truly wonderful person. *To dear Emily from Megan: I dedicate this chapter to you. I am particularly grateful for your critical analysis of the legal barriers to transforming business-as-usual, delivered with your trademark smile and twinkly eyes. In so doing, your self-declared cynicism balanced out my unbounded optimism, and this chapter is only the better for it. We miss you.*

1 'Consultation on Requiring Mandatory Climate-Related Financial Disclosures by Publicly Quoted Companies, Large Private Companies and Limited Liability Partnerships (LLPs)' (2021) <https://www.gov.uk/government/consultations/mandatory-climate-related-financial-disclosures-by-publicly-quoted-companies-large-private-companies-and-llps 12>; Climate Change Act 2008 s 2.

2 UNFCCC Climate Champions, 'Today's Top of the COP: Finance Goes Green and Resilient' (3 November 2021) <racetozero.unfccc.int/finance-goes-green-and-resilient/>.

3 Bank of England, 'Media: COP26 Private Finance Strategy to Drive Whole Economy Transition' (February 2020) <www.bankofengland.co.uk/-/media/boe/files/events/2020/february/cop26-private-finance-strategy.pdf?la=en&hash=4D961E25E8E80EAB2108EEA09628DBA461D60750>.

4 HM Government, 'Green Finance Strategy: Transforming Finance for a Greener Future' (July 2019) <assets.publishing.service.gov.uk/government/uploads/system/uploads/attachment_data/file/820284/190716_BEIS_Green_Finance_Strategy_Accessible_Final.pdf>.

5 Mark Carney, *Clean and Green Finance: A New Sustainable Financial System Can Secure a Net Zero Future for the World* (IMF, 21 September 2021).

6 HM Treasury, 'Chancellor: UK Will the World's First Net Zero Financial Centre' (3 November 2021) <www.gov.uk/government/news/chancellor-uk-will-be-the-worlds-first-net-zero-financial-centre>.
7 Megan Bowman, *Regulatory Leadership for a Net Zero Transition: Central Banks and Financial Regulators: Levers and Limits* (King's College London, September 2022) <www.kcl.ac.uk/climate-law/assets/regulatory-leadership-for-a-net-zero-transition-dr-megan-bowman.pdf≥; Rob Macquarie and Brendan Curran, 'Shifting the Trillions: Financial Regulation Reforms in the UK and Their Relevance for Climate Action' LSE Grantham Institute (24 March 2022) <www.lse.ac.uk/granthaminstitute/news/shifting-the-trillions-financial-regulation-reforms-in-the-uk-and-their-relevance-for-climate-action/?mc_cid=c87ec9661d&mc_eid=c44a763982>.
8 TCFD, 'Recommendations of the Task Force on Climate-Related Financial Disclosures. Final Report' (Task Force on Climate-related Financial Disclosures 2017) ii.
9 'Independent Assessment of UK Climate Risk' (Committee on Climate Change 2021) 26.
10 ibid.
11 TCFD, '2020 Status Report' (Task Force on Climate-related Financial Disclosures 2020) 4.
12 'Explanatory Memorandum to the Companies (Strategic Report) (Climate-Related Financial Disclosure) Regulations 2022' 2022 No. 31 para 7.4
13 Megan Bowman and Daniel Wiseman, 'Finance Actors and Climate-Related Disclosure Regulation: Logic, Limits, and Emerging Accountability' in Cameron Holley, Liam Phelan and Clifford Shearing (eds), *Criminology and Climate* (Routledge 2020)
14 'Are Climate Risk Disclosures the Key to Green Recovery?' (*Grant Thornton UK LLP*) <www.grantthornton.co.uk/en/insights/are-climate-risk-disclosures-the-key-to-green-recovery/> accessed 1 July 2021
15 'Independent Assessment of UK Climate Risk' (n 9) 113–14.
16 TCFD (n 8) ii.
17 'A Roadmap towards Mandatory Climate-Related Disclosures' (HM Treasury 2020) 2 <assets.publishing.service.gov.uk/government/uploads/system/uploads/attachment_data/file/933783/FINAL_TCFD_ROADMAP.pdf>.
18 *FCA Listing Rules* per FCA Policy Statement PS20/17 'Proposals to enhance climate-related disclosures by listed issuers and clarification of existing disclosure obligations' (December 2020)
19 FCA Handbook LR 8.8.6B-LR 9.8.6E.
20 FCA, 'Review of TCFD-aligned Disclosures by Premium Listed Commercial Companies' (29 July 2022) <fca.org.uk>; FRC, 'CRR Thematic Review of TCFD Disclosures and Climate in the Financial Statements' (July 2022) <frc.org.uk>.
21 Defined as: within the financial year, are not small or medium-sized, and are a traded, banking, insurance, or undertaking insurance market activity, is a company trading securities on the Alternative Investment Market, or a high turnover company (more than £500 million) in the financial year: Companies Act 2006 s 414CA(A2)(1)(a)-(e) and (1A)
22 ibid 414CB(1); ibid 414CA(A1)-(2); (2A); 'Explanatory Memorandum to the Companies (Strategic Report) (Climate-Related Financial Disclosure) Regulations 2022' (n 12) para 2.1
23 'Business Population Estimates for the UK and Regions 2021: Statistical Release (HTML)' (*GOV.UK*) <www.gov.uk/government/statistics/business-population-estimates-2021/business-population-estimates-for-the-uk-and-regions-2021-statistical-release-html> accessed 7 July 2022.
24 *Occupational Pension Schemes (Climate Change Governance and Reporting) Regulations 2021 (2021/839)* in force 1 October 2021.
25 The Occupational Pensions Schemes (Climate Change Governance and Reporting) Regulations 2021.
26 Per FCA Policy Statement (PS 21/24) 'Enhancing climate-related disclosures by asset managers, life insurers and FCA-regulated pension providers' (December 2021)
27 'Explanatory Memorandum to the Companies (Strategic Report) (Climate-Related Financial Disclosure) Regulations 2022' (n 12) para 7.3
28 See e.g. FRC, *Improving the Quality of 'Comply or Explain' Reporting*, Financial Reporting Council (February 2021).
29 TCFD (n 8) ii.
30 HM Government, *Greening Finance: A Roadmap to Sustainable Investing* (HM Government October 2021) 2, 7.
31 The aim of this regime is stated by the FCA as follows: 'financial products that are marketed as sustainable should do as they claim and have the evidence to back it up', 'Policy Statement PS23/16 Sustainability

Disclosure Requirement (SDR) and investment labels' at page 3, www.fca.org.uk/publication/policy/ps23-16.pdf.

32 Robert Eccles, 'A Personal Message to the Cantankerous Critics of the International Sustainability Standards Board' *Forbes.com* (19 February 2022)

33 IFRS Foundation, 'About the Sustainability Standards Advisory Forum (SSAF)' (2023) <https://www.ifrs.org/groups/international-sustainability-standards-board/issb-frequently-asked-questions/>.

34 Bowman (n 7).

35 The Occupational Pensions Schemes (Climate Change Governance and Reporting) Regulations 2021 s 9(4)(a)(i)-(ii).

36 Justina Lipskyte and Harold Koster, 'Evaluation of Sustainability Reporting under EU Directive 2014/95' (2018) 29(8) International Company and Commercial Law Review 522, 522; Constance Z Wagner, 'Evolving Norms of Corporate Social Responsibility: Lessons Learned from the European Union Directive on Non-Financial Reporting' (2018) 19 Transactions: The Tennessee Journal of Business Law 619, 633–34.

37 IPCC, 'Summary for Policymakers' in Valérie Masson-Delmotte and others (eds), *Global Warming of 1.5°C. An IPCC Special Report on the Impacts of Global Warming of 1.5°C above Pre-industrial Levels and Related Global Greenhouse Gas Emission Pathways, in the Context of Strengthening the Global Response to the Threat of Climate Change, Sustainable Development, and Efforts to Eradicate Poverty* (World Meteorological Organization 2018).

38 Carbon Tracker, 'Flying Blind: The Glaring Absence of Climate Risks in Financial Reporting' *carbontracker.org* (September 2021).

39 V Harper Ho, '"Comply or Explain" and the Future of Nonfinancial Reporting' (2017) 21(2) Lewis & Clark Law Review 318–55.

40 Lipskyte and Koster (n 36) 522–34, 533.

41 *Milieudefensie et al v Royal Dutch Shell plc* (2021) The Hague District Court C/09/571932/HA ZA 19–379.

42 *Vedanta Resources PLC and another (Appellants) v Lungowe and others (Respondents)* (2019) UKSC 20 [44].

43 ibid 45.

44 Eccles (n 32).

45 Environment Act 2021 s 116. Although at the time of writing the provisions were not in force and further regulations are required to add detail.

46 United Nations Human Rights, 'Guiding Principles on Business and Human Rights' (United Nations 2011); OECD, 'OECD Guidelines for Multinational Enterprises' (OECD Publishing 2011); Proposal for a Directive on Corporate Sustainability Due Diligence 2022 (COM/2022/71 final).

47 See e.g. Bowman (n 7); P Bolton and others, *The Green Swan: Central Banking and Financial Stability in the Age of Climate Change* (Bank for International Settlements 2020); N Gunningham, 'A Quiet Revolution: Central Banks, Financial Regulators, and Climate Finance' (2020) 12(22) Sustainability 1–22.

48 Eccles (n 32).

49 'COP26 and the Glasgow Financial Alliance for Net Zero (GFANZ)' <https://climatechampions.unfccc.int/wp-content/uploads/2021/04/GFANZ.pdf>.

50 EC 'Commission Legislative Proposals on Sustainable Finance' (May 2018) <ec.europa.eu>.

51 G Redgrave, 'EU Taxonomy Amber Category "Could Lead to Greenwashing"' (2022) Environmental Finance <www.environmental-finance.com/content/news/eu-taxonomy-amber-category-could-lead-to-greenwashing.html>.

52 Bowman (n 7).

53 <https://www.fca.org.uk/news/news-stories/fca-welcomes-launch-transition-plan-taskforce-disclosure-framework>.

54 <https://www.gov.uk/government/publications/transition-finance-market-review/transition-finance-market-review-terms-of-reference#:~:text=The%20Transition%20Finance%20Market%20Review,with%20credible%20net%20zero%20pathways>.

55 ibid.

56 HM Government (n 30) 16.

57 'Fact Sheet: Net Zero-Aligned Financial Centre' <https://www.gov.uk/government/publications/fact-sheet-net-zero-aligned-financial-centre/fact-sheet-net-zero-aligned-financial-centre> accessed 16 December 2021.

58 Bowman (n 7).
59 Ibid.
60 Ben Caldecott, 'Achieving Alignment in Finance' (September 2020) *EIT Climate-KIC*.
61 SGX, 'Sustainable Finance: Capacity Building and Training' *SGX website* (undated) <https://www.sgx.com/sustainable-finance/capacity-building-training>.
62 See also Emily Webster, 'Information Disclosure and the Transition to a Low-Carbon Economy: Climate-Related Risk in the UK and France' (2020) 32 Journal of Environmental Law 279; Bowman and Wiseman (n 13).
63 Bowman (n 7).
64 Robert Eccles, Colin Mayer and Judith Stroehle, 'Companies say they're serious about corporate purpose, but investors aren't convinced' *Fortune Magazine* (10 January 2022) <https://fortune.com/2022/01/20/corporate-purpose-institutional-investors-skepticism-research-esg-investing/>.
65 Beate Sjåfjell, Re-embedding the Corporation in Society and on Our Planet: Company Law as a Vehicle for Change' in Beate Sjåfjell, Carol Liao and Aikaterini Argyrou (eds), *Innovating Business for Sustainability: Regulatory Approaches in the Anthropocene* (Edward Elgar Publishing 2022) Chapter 12.
66 Eccles, Mayer and Stroehle (n 64).
67 *Supra* note 61.
68 ibid.
69 Article 169, LOI n° 2019–486 du 22 Mai 2019 relative à la croissance et la transformation des entreprises.
70 Lora Kolodny, 'Patagonia Founder Just Donated the Entire Company, Worth $3 Billion, to Fight Climate Change' *CNBC* (14 September 2022) <https://www.cnbc.com/2022/09/14/patagonia-founder-donates-entire-company-to-fight-climate-change.html>.
71 Yue S Ang and Tineke Lambooy, '(Re)defining Corporate Solvency for Sustainability' (2022) 15(2) International and Comparative Corporate Law Journal 56–92.

12

SCALING UP PARIS AGREEMENT IMPLEMENTATION THROUGH CLIMATE LAW IN INTERNATIONAL WATER LAW REGULATIONS WITH SPECIAL FOCUS ON EUROPE

Alexandra Harrington and Barbara Janusz-Pawletta

Introduction

The climate crisis requires flexible global frameworks for resilience to restore links between biophysical and social aspects of life. International environmental law offers an important framework for integration of climate concerns into interstate cooperation, providing a complimentary normative framework that scales up existing climate relevant norms reinforced in the Paris Agreement. Climate-focused provisions of international environmental law continue to evolve to meet climate-induced challenges.

This chapter highlights the normative coherence between the Paris Agreement and selected areas of international environmental law; specifically, International Water Law (IWL) and associated national and regional laws which focus on water as one of the main climate-dependent natural resources. It discusses methods for recognising and making increased use of existing synergies between these legal regimes, as well as for making additional efforts to strengthen the common customary and conventional provisions relating to climate and water resources to strengthen climate resilience.

Ecosystems of water and associated biodiversity resources selected for this analysis are of critical importance for climate mitigation and adaptation efforts. Climate pressure is growing upon water ecosystems, while sustainable management of these systems can contribute strongly to climate resilience. Countries managing water resources properly are on track to implement the 2030 Sustainable Development Goals Agenda, where water plays a clearly cross-sectoral role.[1] Additionally, biodiversity and climate change are interwoven. On one hand, climate change negatively impacts the biological diversity of plants and animals and, on the other hand, protected biodiversity can make sufficient contributions to both climate mitigation and adaptation through the ecosystem services it supports.

The international legal framework regulating water resources and biodiversity includes clear links to existing global climate governance established in the 1992 United Nations Framework

DOI: 10.4324/9781003276678-15

Convention on Climate Change (UNFCCC) and the 2015 Paris Agreement on Climate Change adopted through the UNFCCC system. The Paris Agreement aims first at reduction of greenhouse gas emissions and second to increase the ability to adapt to the adverse impacts of climate change.[2] The overlap between the provisions relevant for climate change mitigation and adaptation are present in the other sources of the international environmental law, as discussed here, in two complementary instruments governing transboundary waters, the 1997 Convention on the Law of the Non-Navigational Uses of International Watercourses (UN Watercourses Convention) and the 1992 Convention on the Protection and Use of Transboundary Watercourses and International Lakes (UNECE Water Convention), as well as in the water-related Ramsar Convention on wetlands. The interlinkage of water and climate change is indispensable in the proper implementation of conventions which support the Paris Agreement. In its decision related to the San Juan River dispute between Costa Rica and Nicaragua, the International Court of Justice demonstrated how the legal regimes of the Convention on Biological Diversity, Ramsar, and water and environmental law in transboundary cases interact to achieve a regulatory continuum.[3] Still, the body of legal norms across the international environmental legal regimes is disjointed and fragmented[4] and requires more efforts in their coherent implementation to strengthen the resilience of legal action on climate change.

The active engagement of all stakeholders is needed to guarantee the long-term success of building up the normative continuum between international climate, water, and biodiversity. Climate change impacts all resources essential to sustain life, guarantee development, and uphold the environment. Providing for active engagement of affected citizens and other stakeholders within society contributes to climate resilience and sustainable development through greater transparency when implemented in three dimensions: (1) participation in decision-making processes, (2) public access to adequate and relevant information, and (3) access to justice for those affected.[5] The right to participation is a part of international civil and political rights, such as human rights to assembly, freedom of speech, and expression,[6] as well as a means to realise economic, social, and cultural rights.[7]

The following subsections examine existing normative frameworks on management of water resources, including wetlands, with special focus on their climate-related regulations. They analyse how these international regulations support scaling up the implementation of the Paris Agreement. First, focus is given to the overview of IWL, especially its climate-relevant regulations. The interrelation of wetlands and climate change within international law is then discussed. These sections provide an introductory background to an analysis of supporting the Paris Agreement commitments through water law, with the example of the European Union. It is followed by the EU law regarding water resources and management and concludes with the transboundary water laws in EU context.

Climate Change and Water Law

According to the World Economic Forum Risk Reports, four out of five of the worst global risks between 2015–2020 were linked to two issues: climate action failure and water.[8] Existing provisions of IWL integrate climate concerns into transboundary water cooperation, offering a complimentary climate-relevant normative framework for the existing climate governance reflected in the Paris Agreement. Laws related to climate mitigation and adaptation remain directly linked to management of water resources. Climate mitigation in the water sector requires, for instance, cutting greenhouse gas (GHG) emissions, mainly on a national level through, among other methods, low-carbon urban water supply and wastewater management.[9] The increase in use of hydropower and rising interest in the use of hydrogen contributes to lowering the use of traditional emission-heavy energy sources, and to climate mitigation goals.[10] The Paris Agreement introduces enhancing the climate adaptive capacity of states, which, in the context of the transboundary basins, means adopting a basin-wide approach to water allocation issues, ongoing evaluations of the use of water resources, and effective enforcement measures. Still, flexible adaptation to climate change remains an important obstacle for management of transboundary water resources and therefore continues to be one of the main challenges for IWL.

Water might be seen as simultaneously part of the problem and part of the solution.[11] Proper management of water resources strengthens states' climate resilience, especially in light of a significant number of water-related climate risks.[12] For example, climate change is negatively affecting freshwater ecosystems, changing the steam flow and water quality. It causes a net loss of stream run-off as glaciers melt and annual winter snow cover diminishes. Disasters, including those excessively impacted by climate change, are overwhelmingly water-based and will become more frequent and intense.[13] The expected number of droughts as well as flooding due to increased rainfall events will have a significant impact on the social and economic development of many areas worldwide.[14]

The only option for countries and areas of underwater stress due to climate impact is to adapt to the inevitable changes. Since most of the transboundary basins lack any regulatory framework, they are already problematic responses to climate change. Originally, one of the goals of the water law was to create secure rights to encourage infrastructure investment. At present, the climate impact water law seeks to secure flexible real-time allocation to adjust to changing conditions. Water law should help to create basin-wide benefits, and they are shared in an equitable and reasonable way as a basis for new patterns of allocation, pollution protection, and conservation. Certainly, this will require more data sharing from the transboundary states as well as strengthening of flexible institutions, allowing better preparation and management of disasters and tailored modification of allocation of water resources.

To overcome these challenges, there is an urgent need for comprehensive interstate cooperation: the search for resilient water management must be based on basin-wide planning coordinated among all stakeholders on the international, national, and sub-national levels. The 1997 UN Watercourses Convention and 1992 UNECE Water Convention contain substantive and procedural rules that might contribute to developing climate adaptation approaches. First, they include the duty to cooperate, the principles of equitable, reasonable use, ecosystem protection, and institutional mechanisms, all of which allow for the adaptation of a regulatory framework to remain the core of adaptation provisions of both conventions. The joint management arrangements (JMAs) serve as an effective platform for facilitating the needed interstate cooperation. They take a form of joint bodies/joint cooperation mechanisms or commissions with divergent scope of activities,[15] and a differing scope of functions which contribute to the climate change adaptation.

The protection of watercourses can become a part of climate litigation, as demonstrated by the Colombian Supreme Court's 2018 finding that the Amazon shall be regarded as a legal subject with the right to protection in large part for climate change mitigation.[16]

Cooperation among transboundary states sharing common transboundary watercourses, as well as cooperation on the multilateral global level, may contribute to establishing and adaptation of regulatory mechanisms capable of climate-proofing transboundary water basins.

The Sustainable Development Goals (SDGs), adopted in 2015, do not offer a source of international law, but represent a commitment of states, which can help to achieve international legal obligations and to ensure the right to water.[17] The SDG6 seeks to '[e]nsure availability and sustainable management of water and sanitation for all', including encouraging transboundary cooperation in water management (SDG 6.5). The Helsinki Convention and the New York Convention contribute to achieving Integrated Water Resource Management (IWRM), including on a transboundary level. The Ramsar Convention's inclusive definition of wetlands strengthens the legal protection of transboundary water and contributes to achieving SDG6. Similarly, a number of regional water treaties (on the Senegal, Niger, Rhein, Danube rivers as well as Lake Chad and Guarani Aquifer) provide for legal coordination in achieving sustainable development. However, the limited states' participation in the global water legal framework, as well as the nonexistence or gaps in regulating many transboundary watercourses and the lack of common institutional management, creates a legal obstacle to achieving sustainable management of freshwater resources and decelerates the achievement of SDG6.

Climate Relevant Regulations in the International Water Law's Sources

Out of 263 transboundary river and lake basins and approximately 300 transboundary aquifers worldwide, only some are regulated by relevant agreements.[18] Out of 153 states sharing transboundary basins, 58 percent of transboundary basin areas are in a state that has an existing operational arrangement. Moreover, 32 countries now report having 90 percent or more of their transboundary basin area covered by operational arrangements, in comparison to only 22 countries in 2017.[19]

This speaks to the limitations in the transboundary water regulatory framework in providing for interstate cooperative actions, including on climate resilience measures. The international law reflected in existing agreements and within customary rules plays an important role in governing transboundary waters,[20] facilitating transboundary cooperation and offering substantive norms or principles and procedural mechanisms guiding states towards sustainable, mutual interactions. There are two global instruments regulating international legal status and regime of international watercourses: the UN Watercourses Convention,[21] and the UNECE Water Convention,[22] as well as the special framework for regulating groundwater resources, the 2008 Law of Transboundary Aquifers.[23] There are also related soft law documents helping states with water management and climate change adaptation.[24]

Although neither Conventions explicitly mentions climate change, they offer important legal frameworks for cooperation on transboundary aspects of climate change and on the development of adaptation strategies. Firstly, both Conventions adopted an ecosystem approach, which is crucial to adapt to the changing climate, increasing resilience within all related systems, and accommodate stress, such as floods and droughts, as they impact the availability, quantity, and quality of water. Aquatic ecosystems exchange materials and energy with surrounding ecosystems and legal frameworks for valuing of ecosystem services and ecosystem integrity, as well as for the application of mitigation measures within an overarching ecosystem-based management, is crucial for climate resilience.[25] Secondly, including substantive and procedural rules relevant to climate change adaptation allows both Conventions to provide for water quality obligations, precautionary principles, data and information exchange, consultations, monitoring and assessment, emergency systems, and technology exchange and joint research. They provide for institutional arrangements for interstate cooperation, including on transboundary adaptation, implying effective water management and ensuring climate resilience and the conclusion of basin-specific agreements. All these provisions are based on three main IWL principles, which offer a customary law framework for management of water resources that is able to accommodate the climate change-prone global impact on water resources.

The three basic principles of the IWL sources may contribute to developing adaptation approaches.[26] They all allow for adopting reasonably flexible allocation mechanisms, which makes

IWL instrumental for providing an enabling environment for sustainable and peaceful management of transboundary resources. This is especially true for the first principle of equitable and reasonable utilisation, binding the cornerstone of customary IWL, which guarantees flexibility for climate change adaptation. The principle of reasonable and equitable use plays a primary role in the use and protection of shared water resources.[27] The factors used in this context include geography, hydrography, climate, ecology, as well as other factors of natural, social, and economic character.[28] The weight for the aforementioned factors is not legally determined; rather, 'all relevant factors are to be considered together and a conclusion reached on the basis of the whole'.[29] Climate is mentioned as one of the main factors to be considered in the determination of equitable and reasonable use of transboundary waters. Such an adaptive management approach allows states to cope with future hydrological and development changes and other constant changes.[30] Respectively, it contributes to less predictability and legal certainty in transboundary water management.[31]

The second principle of IWL reflects states' sovereignty and their right to freely develop their economy and use their natural resources, which is limited by states' obligation not to cause harm to the environment of other states.[32] States are obligated to take actions to prevent harm and to pay compensation to allow an environment to recover.[33]

Third, the principle of cooperation foresees common activities of states aimed at preventing, reducing, and eliminating negative environmental impact, and at restoring natural resources.[34] All three principles of IWL render this legal framework appropriately equipped to adapt to the changing climate, and set a framework for flexible water allocation where needed.

IWL principles are being applied rather rarely in adjudication. Some examples include the *Gabčíkovo-Nagymaros*[35] and *Pulp Mills*[36] ICJ cases, and the 2013 *Kishenganga* case of the Permanent Court of Arbitration.[37]

Wetlands and the Climate Change Impact in the International Law

Resilience to water-related hazards can be increased thanks to coastal and inland wetlands, which regulate the availability, quantity, and quality of water by absorbing water during floods and releasing it in dry times, as well as protecting against coastal storms.

Management should consider the protection of wetlands to lower vulnerability to impacts of climate change, including scarcity of water resources. Resilience in water management contributes to the mitigation of GHG and other emissions due to sequestration of carbon through surface water ecosystems, including wetlands, peatlands, and mangroves. Wetlands, whether natural or artificial, permanent or temporary, serve as carbon sinks, working alongside the goals of the Paris Agreement to limit carbon in the atmosphere. The Convention on Wetlands of International Importance of 1971 (Ramsar Convention)[38] unites 168 states in the regulation of wetlands and may scale up the implementation of Paris Agreement, especially regarding climate adaptation and building resilience.

Coastal wetlands, including salt marshes, mangroves, and seagrass beds, are carbon-dense ecosystems;[39] coral reefs and mangroves absorb the shock of storms, surges, and tsunamis. On land, wetlands absorb rainfall, reduce droughts, and help to accumulate flooding.[40] Wetlands also reduce $CO2$ emissions. Peatlands, being organic carbon stocks, prevent $CO2$ emission into the atmosphere, and their drainage, conversion, and burning has a significant impact on the global carbon budget.[41]

Wetland ecosystems decline rapidly worldwide through mismanagement of water and land resources, contributing to global warming when these natural carbon sinks turn into sources of emissions.

Some priorities on wetlands have been identified in the framework of the Talanoa Dialog Platform to enhance climate action.[42] There is a need for safeguarding and restoring production systems linked with wetlands. Improving the condition and extent of high mountain lakes, peatlands, and floodplains to reduce the incidence and impacts of human-induced water scarcity downstream is necessary. Another priority is to invest in multifunctional green infrastructure solutions to minimise encroachment on wetlands. Also, accelerating global action to safeguard and re-wet peatlands to avoid drainage is required. Safeguarding and restoring floodplains, mudflats, salt marshes, and mangroves for resilient coasts and deltas is of high importance, as is conserving and restoring coastal wetlands. Finally, there is a need to identify wetland hotspots and restore peace.

These goals are possible only with proper implementation of international agreements on conservation, restoration, and sustainable use of inland freshwater ecosystems including wetlands, like IWL, the Ramsar Convention, and the climate governance framework. Such implementation will lead to the scaling up of the climate resilience goals included in the Paris Agreement.

The goal of the Ramsar Convention is to halt the worldwide loss of wetlands and to conserve wetlands through wise use and management. Article 2 of the Ramsar Convention foresees national activities and international cooperation in the conservation and wise use of areas of marsh, fen, peatland, or water, whether natural or artificial, permanent or temporary, with water that is static or flowing, fresh, brackish, or salt, including areas of marine water, the depth of which at low tide does not exceed six metres. It regulates transboundary wetlands, shared wetland systems, and shared species, offering a framework for managing the interrelations between water and soil covered by the wetlands. Endorsements of the Ramsar Convention's provisions over transboundary Ramsar sites offer a mechanism of water and soil protection and conservation. States are required to designate wetlands of international significance within their territories to be included in the List of Wetlands of International Importance.[43]

Links between wetlands and climate are defined by referring to the framework of the international climate relevant regulations. Global States have recognised the impact of climate change on wetland ecosystems, including changes in water availability. To adapt to climate change, countries should increase the capacity of wetlands to better provide ecosystem services.[44] There is a need for increased recognition of the importance of different wetland types in the global carbon cycle. The degradation of wetlands, especially peatlands, which are an even more important carbon store than the forest biomass, will lead to the increase of annual $CO2$ emissions.[45] Conversion of wetlands, due to the associated increase of biofuel-driven land use, might additionally add to the growth of greenhouse gases.[46]

Scaling up the Paris Agreement Through Water Law in the European Union

Throughout the history of the European Union (EU), environmental and natural resource issues have played a significant role in the law and policy generated. Efforts to regulate water use and water resources in EU Member States were among the earliest measures taken after the formal creation of the EU. The following section grounds critical aspects of water law in the EU's early measures and expands outward to demonstrate how the EU has used this structure to scale up the Paris Agreement through the water sector. While an exhaustive study of all water-related laws and policies adopted at the EU level is beyond the scope of this chapter, the measures discussed here emphasise responsiveness to climate issues, as well as efforts to protect the EU's water resources for the advancement of human and environmental health. In this way, the measures discussed address the nexus of these issues upon which the EU's efforts to implement the Paris Agreement are based and through which they can be understood.

EU Commitments under the Paris Agreement and Associated Laws and Policies

The EU is bound by the terms of the Paris Agreement, as are its constituent Member States. The EU's Nationally Determined Contributions (NDC) submissions thus far have been arguably rudimentary in content; however, it can be assumed that this will need to change as the NDC system is entrenched and filings are subject to oversight, including that of the Paris Agreement Committee on Compliance.

To fulfil its commitments under the Paris Agreement, the EU adopted the European Green Deal (Green Deal) in December 2019. The underlying aim of the Green Deal is to ensure that the EU can meet its commitments to achieve net zero carbon emissions by 2050, while using this as an opportunity to advance society, technology, and the economies of the EU and its Member States.[47]

There is a critical nexus between water resources and agriculture, including the soil necessary for agricultural production and the need to protect groundwater resources from potential pollution stemming from agriculture. This is recognised in the Green Deal, which calls for the production of a "Farm to Fork" strategy that will advance the Green Deal's goals in a way that is tailored to the agricultural and food production sectors.[48] Included in the intended scope of the EU's policies relating to food and agriculture is the fishing and aquaculture sector.[49]

The Green Deal provides the basis upon which the EU is to construct a 'zero pollution ambition for a toxic-free environment', including water pollution and land-based sources of water pollution, such as runoff into lakes and rivers.[50] In conjunction with this, the Green Deal provides:

> The natural functions of ground and surface water must be restored. This is essential to preserve and restore biodiversity in lakes, rivers, wetlands and estuaries, and to prevent and limit damage from floods. Implementing the 'Farm to Fork' strategy will reduce pollution from excess nutrients. In addition, the Commission will propose measures to address pollution from urban runoff and from new or particularly harmful sources of pollution such as micro plastics and chemicals, including pharmaceuticals. There is also a need to address the combined effects of different pollutants.[51]

In the Green Deal, the EU commits to being at the forefront of international climate leadership and climate responsiveness, including working with neighbouring States and those sharing natural resources to promote the implementation of commitments under the Paris Agreement.[52]

The implementation strategy and focus of the Green Deal was, perhaps obviously, impacted by the emergence of the COVID-19 pandemic in early 2020, at a time when much of the groundwork for laws and policies were to be laid. Despite this, the EU continued to work towards adopting a number of policies and, ultimately, the EU Climate Law in 2021.[53] While these policies and laws do bear the indelible imprint of being created in the shadow of the pandemic and the attendant need to include pandemic responsiveness, they nevertheless maintain the focus of raising climate ambition and addressing issues including water use and water resources.[54]

The 2021 EU Climate Law (Climate Law) represents the culmination of efforts to ensure legal parity in climate responses across all EU Member States and within the EU as a whole.[55] One of the core principles underlying the Climate Law is the understanding that 'it is necessary to address the growing climate-related risks to health, including more frequent and intense heatwaves, wildfires and floods, food and water safety and security threats, and the emergence and spread of infectious diseases'.[56] A core component of the Climate Law is the requirement that EU Member States use national adaptation plans that include water security measures, and that they submit these plans for EU-based review.[57]

Relatedly, in 2020, the EU issued the EU Biosecurity Strategy for 2030: Bringing nature back into our lives (Biosecurity Strategy).[58] The Biosecurity Strategy creates an express link between the EU's efforts to address climate change and climate change at a global level, stressing the impacts of both on water and marine resources.[59] A critical component of the Biosecurity Strategy is the recognition that many areas containing vital natural resources and ecosystems should be designated as protected areas, including marine resources that would directly relate to water health and protection.[60]

The EU Action Plan: Towards Zero Pollution for Air, Water and Soil (Action Plan) was issued in 2021 and stresses the inherent links between environmental degradation, climate change impacts, and negative health outcomes.[61] The Action Plan highlights that the EU's Drinking Water Directive was set to be updated in 2023 and that these revisions should include increased standards for drinking water, stronger regulation of water pollution sources, and efforts to reduce plastics in the water sector.[62] The Action Plan similarly stresses the potential for planned reviews of the EU Bathing Water Directive and EU Urban Waste Water Treatment Directive to play an important role in promoting safer water sources across the EU.[63] Further, the Action Plan seeks to ensure that standards for groundwater protection and prevention of pollution for groundwater resources are updated to ensure they take into account the full state of scientific knowledge.[64] At the same time, the Action Plan is critical of existing Member State legislation regarding protection of freshwater resources and calls for more robust EU oversight and monitoring in order to ensure that these resources are being used in a way that furthers climate ambition under the Paris Agreement.[65]

The EU Circular Economy Action Plan (Circular Economy AP) is founded on the understanding that the majority of emissions, as well as water stress, at the global level is attributable to the extraction and subsequent processing and use of natural resources.[66] Thus, the Circular Economy AP seeks to ensure that the EU decouples from these forms of extraction and resource use in a way that is sustainable and fosters industrial innovation.[67]

EU Law Regarding Water Resources and Management

Prior to the formal creation of the EU in 1991, the European Economic Communities adopted the Directive concerning the protection of waters against pollution caused by nitrates and agricultural sources.[68] The Directive noted the potential for transboundary harms associated with these forms of water pollution, as well as the need to ensure that terrestrial activities did not have a negative impact on water resources throughout the EEC.[69]

In 2000, the EU adopted what has come to be known as the Water Directive, in recognition that '[w]ater is not a commercial product like any other but, rather, a heritage which must be protected, defended and treated as such'.[70] The scope of the Water Directive extends to methods which

(a) prevent[s] further deterioration and protects and enhances the status of aquatic

> ecosystems and, with regard to their water needs, terrestrial ecosystems and wetlands directly depending on the aquatic ecosystems; (b) promote[s] sustainable water use based on a long-term protection of available water resources; (c) aim[s] at enhanced protection and improvement of the aquatic environment, inter alia, through specific measures for the progressive reduction of discharges, emissions and losses of priority substances and the cessation or phasing-out of discharges, emissions and losses of the priority hazardous substances; (d) ensure[s] the progressive reduction of pollution of groundwater and prevents its further pollution, and (e) contribute[s] to mitigating the effects of floods and droughts.[71]

The EU Directive concerning the management of bathing water quality was adopted in 2006 and is based on the necessity to intertwine sustainable development and the protection of water as a natural resource, along with concerns about public health.[72] The Directive is underpinned by two fundamental understandings:

> Water is a scarce natural resource, the quality of which should be protected, defended, managed and treated as such. Surface waters in particular are renewable resources with a limited capacity to recover from adverse impacts from human activities . . . [And] Community policy on the environment should aim at a high level of protection, and contribute to pursuing the objectives of preserving, protecting and improving the quality of the environment and of protecting human health.[73]

The terms of the Directive require continued monitoring of bathing water resources by Member States, as well as frequent bathing water quality reviews, especially for areas known to be frequented by bathers.[74] Importantly, the Directive requires transboundary cooperation and information-sharing when there are threats to the quality of bathing waters shared by Member States.[75] Further, Member States are required to provide the public with information on bathing water quality and potential harms from bathing water, thus promoting the awareness of the public to environmental and public health issues.[76]

Also in 2006, the EU adopted the Directive on the protection of groundwater against pollution and deterioration in recognition of the status of groundwater as a major and essential natural resource throughout the EU territory that is fundamental to the health of all.[77] The Directive establishes requirements and parameters for Member State assessments of the chemicals found in groundwater, efforts to combat groundwater pollution and identify benchmarks in these efforts, and further identify chemicals and pollutants for the purposes of groundwater regulation throughout the EU.[78]

Existing EU water laws were largely supplemented by the 2008 Directive on environmental quality standards in the fields of water policy, which incorporated the precautionary principle and related environmental and sustainable development law principles within its terms.[79] This Directive establishes the concept of environmental quality standards for a variety of pollutants and substances identified in earlier Directives and policies in order to counter the pervasive presence of such pollutants in waters across the EU's territory.[80] There are significant transboundary elements in this Directive, including reporting requirements for pollution with transboundary impacts and the recognition that States which suffer from transboundary water pollution should not be considered to have violated their obligations under EU law.[81] The Directive adopted a stringent reporting, monitoring, and oversight system for Member States in terms of environmental quality standard implementation.[82]

The EU adopted the Directive on the quality of water intended for human consumption in 2020, with the goal of advancing several earlier directives relating to water quality.[83] This Directive was issued with the understanding that

> Member States should take the necessary measures to ensure that water intended for human consumption is free from any micro-organisms and parasites and from any substances which, in numbers or concentrations, in certain cases, constitute a potential danger to human health, and that it meets those minimum requirements.[84]

Rather than solely focusing on the exclusion of pollution from drinking water, the Directive also stresses the need for drinking water to retain minerals that are important for human health and creates space for localities to adopt minimum mineral content requirements for drinking water.[85] Again, the precautionary principle is stressed as a core element of the Directive and the regulatory systems which Member States adopt to comply with it.[86] To protect the health and safety of humans and ecosystems, the Directive requires that Member States ensure all aspects of the water supply chain – from source to storage to delivery – comply with pollution restrictions.[87] Reflecting many aspects of the Paris Agreement, the Directive contains significant terms relating to risk assessment and reduction.[88] Monitoring, reporting, and oversight requirements play an important role in the Directive's efforts to ensure Member State compliance and to address issues which arise.[89]

Conclusion

Climate change poses a threat to water security worldwide. IWL integrates these concerns into its regulation of interstate cooperation over transboundary waters. In this way, it scales up existing climate change law recently reinforced in the Paris Agreement. Climate-focused interpretation of the substantive and procedural norm of the IWL lays the basis for climate action in the transboundary basins worldwide.

This chapter has focused on the normative coherence between climate law and IWL, with an example of the associated water law regulation developed for the European Union region. The chapter emphasised how existing water laws and regulations within the European Union context have been used as building blocks for the implementation of the Paris Agreement in the post-2015 period. The chapter highlights how the European Union has used its legal and regulatory systems to scale up water law commitments under the Paris Agreement, as well as using the same methods to assist in the entrenching of climate law throughout the EU as a whole.

Notes

1 UN Water, 'UN-Water Policy Brief: Climate Change and Water (Final Draft)' (2019).

2 Paris Agreement to the United Nations Framework Convention on Climate Change (adopted 12 December 2015, entered into force 4 November 2016) 3156 UNTS 79.

3 *Certain Activities Carried Out by Nicaragua in the Border Area (Costa Rica v Nicaragua)* and *Construction of a Road in Costa Rica along the San Juan River (Nicaragua v Costa Rica)* (2015) ICJ Rep 665 (San Juan River Judgement).

4 Daniel Barstow Magraw and Patsorn Udomritthiruj, 'Water and Multilateral Environmental Agreements: An Incomplete Jigsaw Puzzle' in Stephen C McCaffrey, Christina Leb and Riley T Denoon (eds), *Research Handbook on International Water Law* (Edward Elgar Publishing 2019); Margaret A Young, 'Fragmentation and International Environmental Law' in Lavvanya Rajamani and Jaqueline Peel (eds), *Oxford Handbook of International Environmental Law* (2nd edn, OUP 2021); Owen McIntyre, *Environmental Protection of International Watercourses under International Law* (Routledge 2016); Jing Lee, *Preservation of Ecosystems of International Watercourses and the Integration of Relevant Rules: An Interpretative Mechanism to Address the Fragmentation of International Law* (Brill Nijhoff 2014).

5 Marie-Claire Cordonier Segger and Ashfaq Khalfan, *Sustainable Development Law: Principles, Practices, and Prospects* (OUP 2004); see also Marie-Claire Cordonier Segger and Damilola Olawwyi, *Sustainable Development Law: Principles, Practices and Prospects*, 2nd ed (OUP, 2025 Fc).

6 International Covenant on Civil and Political Rights (adopted 16 December 1966, entered into force 23 March 1976) 99 UNTS 171 Article 25; Universal Declaration of Human Rights (adopted 10 December 1948 UNGA Res 217 A(II) (UDHR) Article 21; Economic and Social Council, Human Rights and the Environment: Final Report' (6 July 1994) Commission on Human Rights Sub-Commission on Prevention of Discrimination and Protection of Minorities 46th session UN Doc E/CN.4/Sub.2/1994/9, Annex I containing Draft Principles on Human Rights and the Environment para. 18.

7 Declaration on the Right to Development, UNGA Res 41/128 (4 December 1986) Article 1.

8 World Economic Forum, 'Reports' <https://www.weforum.org/reports#filter> accessed 6 September 2022.

9 Simon Parkinson, 'Guiding Urban Water Management Towards 1.5 °C '(2021) 4 NPJ Clean Water.

10 Fuel Cells and Hydrogen 2 Joint Undertaking, 'Hydrogen Roadmap Europe: A Sustainable Pathway for the European Energy Transition' (2019).

11 Patricia Wouters and Sergei Vinogradov, 'Reframing the Transboundary Water Discourse: Contextualized International Law in Practice' (2020) 29(3) RECIEL 385.

12 Alistair Rieu-Clarke, Ruby Moynihan and Bjørn-Oliver Magsig, 'Transboundary Water Governance and Climate Change Adaptation: International Law, Policy Guidelines and Best Practice Application' (UNESCO World Water Assessment Program 2015).

13 World Meteorological Organization (WMO-No. 1333), *State of Global Water Resources 2022* (2023) https://wmo.int/publication-series/state-of-global-water-resources-2022.

14 IPCC, AR6 Synthesis Report: Climate Change 2023 https://www.ipcc.ch/report/sixth-assessment-report-cycle/.

15 Convention on the Law of Non-Navigable Uses of International Watercourses (adopted 21 May 1997, entered into force 17 August 2014) 2999 UNTS 77 (UN Watercourses Convention) arts 8, 24; Convention on the Protection and Use of Transboundary Watercourses and International Lakes (adopted 17 March 1992, entered into force 9 October 1996) 1936 UNTS 269 (UNECE Water Convention) Article 9.

16 Nicholas Bryner, 'Colombian Supreme Court Recognizes Rights of the Amazon River Ecosystem' (*IUCN*, 20 April 2018) <https://www.iucn.org/news/world-commission-environmental-law/201804/colombian-supreme-court-recognizes-rights-amazon-river-ecosystem> accessed 2 September 2022.

17 Otto Spijkers, 'The Cross-Fertilization between the Sustainable Development Goals and International Water Law' (2016) 25(1) RECIEL 39.

18 'Shared Waters Partnership' (Stockholm International Water Institute) <http://www.siwi.org/priority-area/transboundary-water-management/> accessed 2 September 2022.

19 UN Water, 'Progress on Transboundary Water Cooperation: Global status of SDG Indicator 6.5.2 and Acceleration Needs 2021' (United Nations and UNESCO 2021).

20 Patricia Wouters, 'Dynamic Cooperation' in International Law and the Shadow of State Sovereignty in the Context of Transboundary Waters (Part 2) (2013) 4 Env. Liability 131.

21 UN Watercourses Convention (n 13).

22 UNECE Water Convention 1992 (n 13).

23 The Law of Transboundary Aquifers, UNGA Res 63/124 (15 January 2009) UN Doc A/RES/63/124.

24 UNECE, 'Guidance on Water and Adaptation to Climate Change' (2009); UNECE and INBO, 'Water and Climate Change Adaptation in Transboundary Basins: Lessons Learned and Good Practices' (United Nations 2015).

25 UNECE, 'Protection of Water Resources and Aquatic Ecosystems' (1993); Allistair Rieu-Clarke and Chris James Spray, 'Ecosystem Services and International Water Law: Towards a More Effective Determination and Implementation of Equity?' (2013) 16(2) Potchefstroom Electronic LJ <https://www.ajol.info/index.php/pelj/article/view/91215>.

26 Dante A Caponera, 'Patterns of Cooperation in International Water Law: Principles and Institutions' (1985) 25 Natural Resources Journal 563; Narong Jaiharn and Naporn Popattanachai, 'An Analysis of Thai Water Management Legislation from an International Law Perspective,' (2013) Yonsei LJ 4, 2.

27 Richard Paisley, 'Adversaries into Partners: International Water Law and the Equitable Sharing of Downstream Benefits' 2002 3(2) MJIL 280.

28 UN Watercourses Convention (n 13).

29 ibid Article 6.

30 Stephen C McCaffrey, 'The Need for Flexibility in Freshwater Treaty Regimes' (2003) 27(2) Natural Resources Forum 156; J C Neuman, 'Adaptive Management: How Water Law Needs to Change' (2001) 31(12) Environmental Law Reporter 11432.

31 J Rainne, 'The Work of the International Law Commission on Shared Natural Resources: The Pursuit of Competence and Relevance. Natural Resources: The Pursuit of Competence and Relevance' (2006) 75(2) Nordic Journal of International Law 321.

32 Charter of Economic Rights and Duties of States, UNGA Res 3281(XXIX) (12 December 1974) UN Doc A/RES/29/3281 Article 1; Annex I: Rio Declaration on Environment and Development (3–14 June 1992) UN Conference on Environment and Development UN Doc A/CONF.151/26 (Vol. I) Principle 2.; Gretta Goldenman, 'Adapting to Climate Change: A Study of International Rivers and their Legal Arrangements' (1990) 14(4) Ecology Law Quarterly 741.

33 Owen McIntyre, 'State Responsibility in International Law for Transboundary Water-Related Harm: The Emergence of a New Ecosystems-Based Paradigm?' (2020) 29(3) RECIEL add first page or pinpoint reference; Andrea M Keessen, Jasper JH van Kempen, Helena FMW van Rijswick, 'Transboundary River Basin Management in Europe: Legal Instruments to Comply with European Water Management Obligations in Case of Transboundary Water Pollution and Floods (2008) 4(3) Utrecht Law Review 35.
34 James Pittock and others, 'Changing Character: The Ramsar Convention on Wetlands and Climate Change in the Murray-Darling Basin, Australia' (2010) 127 EPLJ 401.
35 *Gabčíkovo-Nagymaros Project (Hungary/Slovakia)* (Judgment) (1997) ICJ Rep 7.
36 *Pulp Mills on the River Uruguay (Argentina v. Uruguay)* (Judgment) (2010) ICJ Rep 14.
37 *Indus Waters Kishenganga Arbitration (Pakistan v India)* (Final Award) ICGJ 478 (PCA 2013).
38 Convention on Wetlands of International Importance Especially as Waterfowl Habitat (adopted 2 February 1971, entered into force 21 December 1975) 996 UNTS 245 (Ramsar Convention).
39 Elizabeth Mcleod and others, 'A Blueprint for Blue Carbon: Toward an Improved Understanding of the Role of Vegetated Coastal Habitats in Sequestering CO2 (2011) 9(10) Frontiers in Ecology and the Environment 552.
40 Eric Wolanski, Thematic Paper: 'Synthesis of Protective Functions of Coastal Forests and Trees against Natural Hazards' in *Coastal Protection in the Aftermath of the Indian Ocean Tsunami: What Role for Forests and Trees?* (Regional Office for Asia and the Pacific 2006).
41 Pierre Taillardat and others, 'Climate Change Mitigation Potential of Wetlands and the Cost-Effectiveness of their Restoration (2020) 10(5) Interface Focus.
42 Talanoa Dialogue Platform (*Wetlands International*, 2018) <https://www.wetlands.org/news/countries-can-strengthen-climate-plans-2020-peatland-mangrove-targets/talanoa-dialogue-platform/> accessed 5 September 2022.
43 Ramsar Convention (n 36) preamble, Article 2; Strategic Framework and Guidelines for the Future Development of the List of Wetlands of International Importance – 2012 Revision, Resolution XI.8 Annex 2 (2012) 11th Meeting of the Conference of the Parties to the Convention on Wetlands (Ramsar, Iran, 1971).
44 Wetlands and Human Health and Well-Being, Resolution X. 23 (2008) 10th Meeting of the Conference of the Parties to the Convention on Wetlands.
45 Climate Change and Wetlands, Resolution X.24 (2008) 10th Meeting of the Conference of the Parties to the Convention on Wetlands.
46 Wetlands and "Biofuelsm" Resolution X.25 (2008) 10th Meeting of the Conference of the Parties to the Convention on Wetlands.
47 European Commission, 'The European Green Deal' (11 December 2019) 640 s. 1.
48 ibid s. 2.1.6.
49 ibid
50 ibid s. 2.1.8.
51 ibid.
52 ibid. sect 3.
53 See Official Journal of the European Union, 'Regulation (EU) 2021/1119 of the European Parliament and of the Council' (30 June 2021).
54 ibid.
55 ibid.
56 ibid preamble (5).
57 Ibid Article 5(4).
58 European Commission, 'EU Biodiversity Strategy for 2030: Bringing nature back into our lives,' (20 May 2020) COM 380.
59 ibid s. 1.
60 ibid. ss. 2.1, 2.2.6, 2.2.7.
61 European Commission, 'Pathway to a Healthy Planet for All: EU Action Plan: Towards Zero Pollution for Air, Water and Soil' (12 May 2021) COM400.
62 ibid s. 2.2.
63 ibid.
64 ibid.
65 ibid s. 2.3.
66 European Commission, 'Circular Economy Action Plan: For a Cleaner and More Competitive Europe (3 March 2020) s. 1.

67 ibid.
68 European Council, 'Directive Concerning the Protection of Waters Against Pollution Caused by Nitrates and Agricultural Sources' (31 December 1991) OJ L 375/1.
69 ibid preamble.
70 European Parliament and Council, 'Directive 2000/60/EC, Establishing a Framework for Community Action in the Field of Water Policy,' (22 December 2000) OJ L 327/1 preamble (1).
71 ibid Article 1.
72 ibid preamble.
73 ibid
74 ibid arts 3, 4.
75 ibid Article 10.
76 ibid at Article 12.
77 European Parliament and Council 'Directive 2006/118/EC on the Protection of Groundwater against Pollution and Deterioration' (27 December 2006) OJ L 372/19.
78 ibid Article 1.
79 European Parliament and Council, 'Directive 2008/15/EC, on Environmental Quality Standards in the Fields of Water Policy' (24 December 2008) OJ L 348/54 at preamble.
80 ibid Article 1.
81 ibid Article 6.
82 See generally ibid arts 8–12.
83 European Parliament and the Council, 'Directive (EU) 2020/2184 on the quality of water intended for human consumption' OJ L 435/1 (23 Dec 2020).
84 ibid preamble.
85 ibid preamble.
86 ibid Article 4(2).
87 ibid Article 7.
88 ibid.
89 ibid arts 13, 18, 19, 20.

13

LAW AND GOVERNANCE CONTRIBUTIONS TO ENERGY TRANSITIONS IN LATIN AMERICA

Margarita Nieves-Zárate[1]

Introduction

Traditionally, the development of water resources for electricity generation and energy access have been the drivers for advancing renewable energy in Latin America. Since the 1990s, the region's vulnerability to climate change has emerged as a new driver for the incorporation of renewable energy into energy systems. While the scientific community gets more certainty on the dangers posed by climate change to humanity and the contribution of fossil fuels to this threat, the transition to a new low-carbon energy system comes forth as a new model for sustainable development.

Until the adoption of the Paris Agreement, the international legal regime of climate change did not provide for specific Greenhouse Gas (GHG) reduction commitments for Latin American countries. With the voluntary adoption of GHG reduction commitments by Latin American countries under the Paris Agreement, questions arise whether such commitments mark the end of the participation of fossil fuels in the region's energy system and what regulatory mechanisms will contribute to such a transition.

The first part of this chapter addresses the relationship between climate change and energy transition. Secondly and thirdly, it explores the vulnerabilities of Latin America to climate change, as well as the opportunities and challenges of the energy transition for the region. Fourthly, it provides an overview of the international climate change regime, particularly the Paris Agreement as a new driver of the energy transition. Grounded on the theory of regulation, the fifth and final part of this chapter identifies the regulatory mechanisms used in Latin America to advance the energy transition and whether they have changed with the adoption of the Paris Agreement.

Energy Transition: Towards a New Low-Carbon Paradigm

The modern debate on climate change shows evidence that the use of fossil fuels brings GHG emissions as a negative externality, including CO_2, methane[2] and nitrogen dioxide (NO_2). Of these gases, CO_2 most affects the equilibrium of the Earth's atmosphere,[3] contributing around two-thirds of GHG.[4] According to the Intergovernmental Panel on Climate Change (IPCC), atmospheric CO_2 concentrations have increased by 40% since the pre-industrial era. The main cause of this increase are emissions from the use of fossil fuels.[5]

DOI: 10.4324/9781003276678-16

While the Earth has its own mechanisms for removing excess CO_2 emissions from the atmosphere through natural sinks such as forests and oceans,[6] these mechanisms are not sufficient and also have negative externalities. An example of these externalities are the oceans. The oceans are natural sinks of CO_2, absorbing about 30% of anthropogenic CO_2 emissions. However, in the process of absorbing CO_2, oceans have also become acidified.[7] The CO_2 that is not absorbed by natural sinks remains in the atmosphere, exacerbating global warming. In addition, the climate system shows a delayed response to the emission of GHGs, which means that the warming produced by the GHGs emitted today will only be evident in thirty or forty years.[8]

The IPCC reports include measurements of the increase of CO_2 in the atmosphere relative to the pre-industrial era, a period in which fossil fuels were not used to any significant amount. The rise of fossil fuels as the basis of the world energy system began from the end of the eighteenth to the nineteenth centuries with the first Industrial Revolution. During this period, the development of the coal-powered steam engine replaced animal force as the main means of transportation and biomass (wood) as the main fuel,[9] turning coal into the foundation of the energy paradigm.

In the first half of the twentieth century, the second Industrial Revolution introduced another massive fossil fuel: petroleum. Petroleum facilitated the use of the internal combustion engine. From the Industrial Revolution until today, the basis of the global energy system has been the use of fossil fuels. In 2018, fossil fuels supplied more than 84% of primary energy consumption,[10] meeting basic human needs such as electricity and transport. Of this percentage, 33% corresponds to oil, 27% to coal and 24% to natural gas.

With burning fossil fuels as the most CO_2-emitting anthropogenic activity, much of the modern climate change debate places decarbonisation at the heart of the solution to this problem. This change in energy use is known as the energy transition, which refers to the decarbonisation of the energy system, reducing its carbon intensity; that is, reducing GHG emissions per unit of energy produced.

In its Fifth Report, the IPCC identified energy mitigation and adaptation strategies that may contribute to reducing and managing climate change risks.[11] These strategies consist of energy-efficiency measures and the introduction of zero- or low-carbon energy sources,[12] including renewable energy,[13] nuclear energy, fossil energy with Carbon Capture and Storage (CCS) or bioenergy with CCS.[14] As climate change is a global phenomenon, all regions of the world are affected in different ways. In this context, the contribution and vulnerability of Latin America to climate change, and how such vulnerability is one of the drivers of the energy transition in the countries of the region, are analysed.

The Vulnerability of Latin America to Climate Change

Latin America contributes about 8% of global GHG emissions.[15] While the region has a lower share of GHG emissions[16] than Asia, Europe and North America,[17] its climatic, geographic, economic and social conditions make it one of the region's most vulnerable to climate change.[18] Climate phenomena affecting the region have been extensively documented by, among others, the Fourth Assessment Report (AR4) of the IPCC in 2007 and the United Nations Economic Commission for Latin America and the Caribbean (ECLAC).

Climatic phenomena include the El Niño and La Niña phenomena, heavy rainfall, floods, droughts, storms and hurricanes. Geographical factors include the location of Central America within the hurricane belt,[19] the existence of numerous island states and low-lying coastal areas, dependence on the melt of the Andes Mountain Range for water supply and its exposure to floods[20] and forest fires.[21]

Social and economic factors include population growth, unplanned urban growth, poverty, rural migration and low investment in infrastructure and services.[22] These aspects make the poorest communities the most vulnerable to the effects of climate change.[23]

The impacts of climate change in Latin America range from the decrease of electricity production due to its high dependence on hydropower to the forced displacement of millions of people. Regarding the latter impact, the World Bank has warned that if GHG emissions are not significantly reduced, climate change could cause the permanent displacement of approximately 17 million people in Latin America by 2050.[24]

Likewise, the IPCC's special report on Climate Change 1.5°C underlines the high vulnerability of the Amazon, Central America and the Caribbean Islands in the scenario where global temperatures increase to 1.5°C relative to the pre-industrial era.[25] Given their vulnerability to climate change, Latin American countries have actively participated in the international conventions on climate change and introduced measures to decarbonise their energy systems. The following section briefly analyses the energy transition in Latin America, as well as the challenges and opportunities of the region in such a transition.

Energy Transition in Latin America

While coal and oil are the main source of electricity globally,[26] the main source in Latin America is renewable energy, particularly hydroelectricity. In 2018, approximately 70% of electricity in Latin America came from renewable energy.[27] In the same year, half of total electricity generation came from hydroelectricity.[28] Hydroelectricity is categorised as a conventional renewable energy, to distinguish it from other renewable energy sources such as wind, solar and biomass, known as non-conventional renewable energy.

For their part, non-conventional renewable energies are the third-largest source of electricity generation in the region after natural gas.[29] Among unconventional renewable energy sources, biomass stands out. Although there is vast potential for the development of solar and wind power in Latin America, their share in electricity generation is still modest.[30] Notable cases are Uruguay, Honduras, Nicaragua, Costa Rica and Chile, which in 2018 were among the 25 countries globally with the largest share of wind and solar energy in the electricity generation matrix.[31]

Opportunities for the Energy Transition for Latin America

Decarbonisation of the electricity system in Latin America through the increased participation of non-conventional renewable energies is an opportunity to address three major challenges in the region: the first is to strengthen energy security; the second is to achieve universal electricity access; and the third is to contribute to the provision of modern energy sources in the region.

Energy security in Latin America is particularly vulnerable to climate change.[32] The variability of the climate means that during dry periods the level of precipitation decreases, affecting the water level of the rivers and the production of hydroelectricity. In the summers of 2017 and 2018, the La Niña phenomenon caused severe droughts affecting countries such as Argentina, Uruguay, Venezuela and Brazil.[33] The effects varied by country, as did the measures to deal with them, from the increase in electricity imports into Brazil from Argentina and Uruguay to electricity rationing in Venezuela.[34]

Another measure to address periods of low hydropower production in the region is to increase the generation of fossil fuel-based power plants such as coal and natural gas. However, as the thermal plants enter into operation, the GHG emissions from the electrical system inevitably increase.

Increasing the share of non-conventional renewable energies such as wind and solar can help to counteract the effect of climate change on the decrease of hydroelectricity production in Latin America,[35] which also serves to strengthen the energy security of the countries of the region.

Ensuring universal access to electricity is another driver for the development of non-conventional renewable energies in Latin America. While 98% of the population has access to electricity, 12 million people do not have access to this valuable resource,[36] mostly in remote rural areas with low population densities.[37] Providing these populations with access to electricity by connecting them to electricity transmission networks is costly and inefficient. For this reason, non-conventional renewable energies, through the provision of decentralised electricity generation located close to the places of consumption, are a great opportunity to achieve universal electricity access in Latin America.[38]

Finally, a major challenge for the region is to provide access to modern energy sources for the 83 million people who depend on traditional uses of biomass for cooking[39] and heat supply, such as wood. Because of this deficit in the provision of modern energy sources, the World Health Organization (WHO) has identified that 13% of the population in Latin America does not consume safe food, putting their lives at risk and increasing the risk of diseases.[40]

Challenges of the Energy Transition for Latin America

The slow or accelerated pace of the energy transition in Latin America is influenced by, among other factors, (a) increases in energy demand, (b) the economic dependence of countries in the region on the production of fossil resources, (c) the decarbonisation of the transport sector, (d) the attraction of investments to boost the energy transition and (e) regional energy integration.

The first challenge of the energy transition relates to the growth of energy demand in the region. Demand for primary energy in Latin America is projected to increase by more than 60% between 2012 and 2040.[41] This means that the countries of the region will be in constant need in terms of meeting the growing demand for energy. Over the long term, projections indicate that between 2005 and 2100, primary energy demand in the region will not only grow exponentially but will be in parallel with the use of fossil fuels, particularly oil and natural gas.[42] This can be explained by observing the fossil resources available in Latin America.

It is precisely when observing the natural resources to supply energy demand that we find the second challenge of the energy transition in Latin America; several countries have substantial proven reserves of fossil resources on which their economies depend. Indeed, Latin America has the world's largest proven oil reserves, while its proven reserves of gas and coal account for 4% and 1%, respectively.[43] The exploitation and export of fossil resources have been the basis of the economies of countries such as Venezuela, Brazil, Mexico, Bolivia, Ecuador and Colombia. This availability represents a tension between different interests of countries that possess fossil resources. On the one hand is the interest of meeting energy demand and increasing revenues from the export of fossil resources, and on the other, the need for combating climate change.

The eventual reduction in global demand for fossil fuels, the decline in international prices of hydrocarbons and coal and the possibility of abandoning the exploitation of these resources pose a threat to the economies of fossil fuel exporter countries.[44] Similarly, the abundance of fossil resources is a challenge for the decarbonisation of the energy system in Latin America, since countries can meet the demand for energy through the use of fossil fuels. At the same time, there are incentives for the use of hydrocarbons in the form of subsidies, for example, subsidies for petrol in the transport sector.[45] These subsidies facilitate access to energy in the transport sector, and at the same time, they constitute a barrier to decarbonisation.

Fuel subsidies, together with the use of renewable energy such as biomass to decarbonise the transport sector, are the third challenge of the energy transition. Indeed, one of the main measures adopted by some Latin American countries, such as Brazil, Argentina and Colombia, to reduce petrol imports, strengthen agro-industry and decarbonise the transport sector, has been to promote the production and use of biofuels.[46] However, land use for biofuel production also represents a tension for food security.[47]

The fourth challenge of the energy transition relates to its financial dimension. The development of non-conventional renewable energy depends on the policies of each country to attract investment in the energy sector. Each country in Latin America has implemented measures to promote these investments.[48] The most successful cases are Chile, Brazil, Mexico and Peru, which globally rank among the ten most attractive emerging markets for investment in clean energy.[49] Investments have also not only come from the private sector. In Brazil, direct state investment has been predominant in the development of non-conventional renewable energies.[50]

The fifth challenge of the energy transition is to advance regional energy integration. More energy integration through joint policies and the development of infrastructure at the regional level, such as electricity interconnections, may contribute to incorporating renewable energy into the energy system more efficiently, taking advantage of resources and economies of scale.[51] Although Latin America does not have a regional or international agreement to promote investment and integration in the energy sector,[52] agreements such as the Central American Electricity Market framework treaty and binational electrical interconnections stand out at the sub-regional level.[53]

Until 2015, the energy transition in Latin America had been driven by the individual efforts of each country to ensure its energy security, without specific commitments in the international climate change regime to reduce their GHG emissions. However, with the entry into force of the Paris Agreement, Latin American countries have committed to reduce their GHG emissions. Hence, the Paris Agreement has emerged as a new driver for the decarbonisation of energy systems in the region.

A Look at the Legal International Climate Change Regime and the Paris Agreement as a New Driver of the Energy Transition

The UNFCCC established a division between Annex 1 (developed) and Non-Annex 1 (developing) countries, with the responsibility of developed countries to take the lead in combating climate change and its adverse effects.[54] One of the specific obligations of Annex 1 countries was to return in 2000 to the level of anthropogenic GHG emissions they had in 1990.[55] In 1997, the Kyoto Protocol sought to implement the GHG reduction obligations of developed countries by requiring Annex I countries to the UNFCCC to reduce their total GHG emissions by at least 5% below 1990 emission levels for the first period of the protocol, from 2008 to 2012.[56]

Despite its entry into force in 2005, not all developed countries committed themselves to the Kyoto Protocol. The United States did not ratify the protocol, and Canada announced its withdrawal in 2011.[57] In 2012, the Doha amendment to the Kyoto Protocol established a new GHG emission reduction period and commitments. However, the amendment has not yet entered into force due to the lack of ratifications of the UNFCCC Parties.[58]

In parallel, emerging economies with no GHG emission reduction commitments under the Kyoto Protocol, including China, India, South Africa and Brazil, increased their GHG emissions.[59] Such growth increased pressure from developed countries to commit emerging economies to specific emission reduction agreements.

In this context, the Paris Agreement emerged as a solution to engage all developed and developing countries in reducing GHG emissions. On 12 December 2015, during the 21st Climate Change Conference (COP 21), the 195 countries that took part in the Conference adopted the Paris Agreement. To date, 195 of the 198 Parties to the UNFCCC have ratified the Paris Agreement,[60] which entered into force on 4 November 2016. The Paris Agreement seeks to strengthen the global response to the threat of climate change in the context of sustainable development and poverty eradication efforts.[61] To this end, the Paris Agreement has three key objectives that may be categorised as objectives for mitigation, adaptation and the orientation of financial flows towards low-GHG-emissions development.[62]

The mitigation objective is to maintain the global average temperature increase well below 2°C above pre-industrial levels, and to continue efforts to limit this temperature increase to 1.5°C above pre-industrial levels, recognising that these measures would significantly reduce the risks and impacts of climate change.[63] The adaptation objective seeks to increase capacity to cope with the adverse effects of climate change and promote climate resilience and low-GHG emission development, without compromising food production.[64] In turn, the objective of orientating financial flows is to make financial flows conform with a pathway towards low GHG emissions and climate-resilient development.[65]

One of the specific obligations acquired by the parties that ratified the Paris Agreement is to define how they will contribute to meeting the objectives established in the Agreement. Unlike the Kyoto Protocol, the definition of this contribution is an autonomous exercise of each party under the principle of national sovereignty.

The mechanism established in the Paris Agreement to define the individual contribution of each party to the overall objective is called Nationally Determined Contributions (NDCs).[66] When ratifying the Paris Agreement, each party was required to report its contributions to the UNFCCC Secretariat,[67] which in turn maintains a public register of the NDCs.[68] On the assumption that all Parties will represent a progression of their efforts over time,[69] the parties may at any time adjust their NDCs with a view to increasing their level of ambition in reducing emissions[70] and must update their contribution every five years.[71]

While the Paris Agreement commits all Parties to GHG reduction, it also preserves the guiding principles of equity, and common but differentiated responsibilities and respective capabilities, in light of different national circumstances.[72] Applying these principles means that while all parties must contribute to the global temperature mitigation objective, the obligations of developed and developing countries are different. To this end, the Paris Agreement maintains the UNFCCC division between Annex 1 and Non-Annex 1 countries.

In the case of Latin America, all countries of the region have individually ratified the Paris Agreement[73] and are considered Non-Annex 1 countries.[74] The Paris Agreement states that developed countries should continue to lead efforts, adopting absolute emission reduction targets for their economies as a whole,[75] while developing country parties should continue to scale up their mitigation efforts, and are urged, over time, to adopt economy-wide emission reduction or limitation targets, in light of different national circumstances.[76]

Developed countries, in turn, assume the obligation to provide financial resources to developing countries for both mitigation and adaptation assistance, thus continuing to meet their obligations under the UNFCCC.[77]

Unlike the UNFCCC,[78] the Paris Agreement does not mention GHG reductions in the energy sector in any of its paragraphs but refers to GHG reduction in the economy as a whole.[79] However, in 2018, the Paris Agreement Rulebook, adopted at COP 24, provided further details on how the parties to the Agreement should report on the implementation of their commitments. The Paris

Agreement Rulebook establishes energy as one of the key sectors when reporting the actions implemented to comply with NDCs.[80]

Furthermore, the Paris Agreement cannot be understood in isolation, but as part of the international climate change regime, of which not only international conventions but also other guiding instruments such as IPCC reports are a part.

From the IPCC reports, particularly the Fifth Report, it is the identification of mitigation and adaptation strategies in the energy sector that can contribute to reducing and managing climate change risks.[81] Strategies include energy efficiency measures and the introduction of zero or low-carbon energy sources,[82] such as renewable energy,[83] nuclear energy, fossil energy with CCS or bioenergy with CCS.[84]

The Paris Agreement and Regulatory Mechanisms for the Energy Transition in Latin America

Reducing GHG emissions from the energy system requires the commitment of the different actors that are part of the energy sector. The international climate change regime has taken an important step by committing states, which are with few exceptions the owners of the fossil resources that lie underground, and who have the sovereignty and authority to make rules within their jurisdictions.

However, the energy sector is made up of a chain of actors that includes, among others, the private sector and final energy consumers. The private sector is key to orientate investments to decarbonise the energy sector. For their part, consumers constitute the demand for energy and their actions can influence the decarbonisation of the energy system, either by reducing consumption, by choosing energy products and services low in GHG emissions or even by generating their own energy.

Under the Paris Agreement, Latin American countries have committed to reducing GHG emissions through their NDCs. In addition, the Paris Agreement Rulebook states that each party must report on the type of instruments used to comply with its NDCs, indicating, for example, whether they are regulatory or economic instruments.[85]

With regard to this commitment, it is worth pondering what mechanisms states have to intervene in the energy sector, reduce their GHG emissions and involve other actors of the energy system.

The theory of regulation identifies two main mechanisms that states traditionally use to intervene in the economy and implement their policies.[86] These instruments consist of command-and-control mechanisms and economic incentives. While command-and-control mechanisms regulate with the imposition of rules and sanctions,[87] regimes based on economic incentives promote that regulatees contribute to the achievement of the state's objectives with positive or negative economic incentives.[88] Among the positive mechanisms are subsidies and tax reductions, as well as the granting of contracts, concessions or loans.[89] Among the negative mechanisms are the payment of fees and taxes.[90]

Regarding the types of regulatory mechanisms used to foster the energy transition, with few exceptions, the preferred mechanism has been economic incentives. This choice is also supported by empirical research which shows that at least in the promotion of renewable energy, the increased participation of these energy sources in the electricity system is mainly influenced by tax incentives and guarantees of access to the grid.[91]

Transferring the regulatory mechanisms of the theory of regulation to the regulation of the energy sector in Latin America, we observe that each country in the region has adopted its own combination of regulatory instruments to increase the participation of renewable energy sources according to their energy resources.[92] Some mechanisms are more used than others and are also implemented differently in each country.

In turn, the International Renewable Energy Agency (IRENA) classifies the mechanisms adopted by Latin American countries for the promotion of renewable energy in national policies, fiscal incentives, access to the network, regulatory and financial instruments.[93] National policies include renewable energy laws and targets to increase their share in the energy matrix. In 2015, 11 countries in Latin America had adopted national laws or strategies for the promotion of renewable energy, and 14 countries had laws promoting specific technologies for the generation of renewable energy.[94]

The setting of renewable energy targets reflects the commitment of countries in the short-, medium- or long-term.[95] In most cases, renewable energy generation targets are not accompanied by sanctions for non-compliance (command-and-control).[96] Chile is the only country in the region that has set its targets as mandatory, defining fines in the event of non-compliance, accompanied by a monitoring and compliance mechanism.[97]

In most Latin American countries, the enactment of non-conventional renewable energy laws is followed by the adoption of specific regulatory frameworks.[98] Regulatory mechanisms adopted by the countries in the region include auctions to contract renewable energy, feed-in tariffs, premiums, mandatory quotas for the generation of renewable energy in the electrical matrix, certificate systems, net metering, ethanol and biodiesel blending obligations and obligations to incorporate solar energy into the electric matrix, among others.[99]

Fiscal incentives include tax exemptions, carbon taxes and accelerated depreciation. Access to the electricity grid includes priority in the dispatch of plants with electricity generation from renewable energies in the case of grid congestion, exemptions or discounts of transmission tariffs, guaranteed or regulated access to the electricity grid and preferential dispatch of electricity from renewable energy sources.[100]

While many of these mechanisms can be considered within the general category of economic incentives identified in the theory of regulation, the IRENA classification gives an idea of the multiple regulatory mechanisms implemented in the region.

Similarly, the main nonconventional renewable energies promoted by the regulatory frameworks include wind, solar, geothermal, small hydropower[101] and biomass. In Latin America, less attention has been paid to the development of other technologies identified by the IPCC's Fifth Report, such as nuclear power and fossil energy with CCS or bioenergy with CCS.

When reviewing the NDCs submitted to the UNFCCC Secretariat pursuant to the Paris Agreement, we observe that 31 Latin American countries have proposed mitigation and/or adaptation measures in the energy sector to reduce GHG emissions.[102] Most of the measures are mitigation measures, focusing mainly on the promotion of renewable energy and energy efficiency.[103] The proposed adaptation measures, although smaller in quantity, also relate primarily to the promotion of renewable energy.[104]

Of the measures presented in the NDCs, most of them continue with the policies and regulatory mechanisms that Latin American countries had been implementing before the adoption of the Paris Agreement. What the Paris Agreement may eventually bring is the commitment to more ambitious measures, since the NDCs have to be updated at least every five years.

Beyond the measures proposed in the NDCs, it is necessary to consider the role of governance in advancing the energy transition in Latin America. The term governance refers to the multiple non-state actors involved in regulation at the subnational, national, supranational and global levels, a task traditionally considered as exclusive to the state.[105] In this context, governance implies recognising that not only state but also non-state actors such as the private sector are involved in the regulatory process and their role in the energy transition.

This chapter has explained how climate change and the Paris Agreement are the new drivers of the energy transition in Latin America. However, projections for Latin America indicate that in the short-, medium- and long-term, primary energy demand, mainly from the transport and industrial sector, will exponentially grow. The growth in energy demand will be in parallel with the use of fossil fuels, particularly oil and natural gas. These projections call into question a real paradigm shift in the energy sector in Latin America that includes decarbonisation of both the electricity and transport sectors. The region's vulnerability to climate change and the commitments made in the Paris Agreement should serve as reasons to counterbalance these projections and to decouple Latin American development from GHG emissions. Only in this way can the region take advantage of the energy transition and overcome the challenges and tensions identified in this chapter.

Conclusion

This chapter explored whether the voluntary adoption of GHG reduction commitments by Latin American countries under the Paris Agreement will mark the end of fossil fuels in the region's energy system, and what regulatory mechanisms will contribute to such a transition.

Three of the opportunities identified are to promote energy security in Latin America, reach universal electricity access and provide modern energy sources to 83 million people who lack it in the region. These opportunities, along with the high availability of water resources in the region, have been the traditional drivers of the energy transition in Latin America. With the certainty that the scientific community has acquired over the years about the dangers of climate change to humanity, and the contribution of fossil fuels to this threat, climate change has emerged as a new driver of the energy transition in Latin America.

Projections indicate that primary energy demand in the Latin American region will grow exponentially and in parallel with the use of hydrocarbons.

There is also a close link between energy sector GHG emissions and economic growth.[106]

Reducing GHG emissions and moving towards energy transition and sustainable development are in the interests of Latin America because of its high vulnerability to climate change.

Notes

1 This chapter shares thoughts with the author's perspectives from Margarita Nieves-Zárate, 'The Paris Agreement as a New Driver of the Energy Transition in Latin America: The End of the Fossil Fuels Paradigm?' in Geoffrey Wood and others (eds), *The Palgrave Handbook of Zero Carbon Energy Systems and Energy Transitions* (Palgrave Macmillan 2023) <https://doi.org/10.1007/978-3-030-74380-2_34-1>; a Spanish version of this chapter was published in *Retos del Sector Energético para el Desarrollo Sostenible en Iberoamérica* <www.marcialpons.es/libros/retos-del-sector-energetico-para-el-desarrollo-sostenible-en-iberoamerica/9789563929485/>.

2 Intergovernmental Panel on Climate Change, *Climate Change 2013 – The Physical Science Basis: Working Group I Contribution to the Fifth Assessment Report of the IPCC* (CUP 2013) 52.

3 On CO_2 as the main anthropogenic GHG, see IPCC (n 2) glossary carbon dioxide.

4 United Nations, 'Climate Change' (United Nations) <www.un.org/en/global-issues/climate-change> accessed 28 March 2024.

5 IPCC (n 2). The second cause is emissions originated in land use changes, mainly deforestation.

6 ibid 96.

7 ibid 11.

8 *The State of the Netherlands v Urgenda Foundation*, NL:GHDHA:2018:2591 (The Hague Court of Appeal, 9 October 2018) *'global warming is expected to accelerate further, mainly because emitted*

greenhouse gases reach their full warming effect only after 30 or 40 years'; on the accumulation of CO_2 in the atmosphere over decades, see IPCC (n 2) 19, 27.

9 Kostas Bithas and Panos Kalimeris, *Revisiting the Energy-Development Link. Evidence from the 20th Century for Knowledge-Based and Developing Economies* (Springer 2015) 7.

10 British Petroleum, 'BP Statistical Review of World Energy 2019: 68th edition', 9 <www.bp.com/content/dam/bp/business-sites/en/global/corporate/pdfs/energy-economics/statistical-review/bp-stats-review-2019-full-report.pdf> accessed 28 March 2024.

11 IPCC, *Climate Change 2014: Synthesis Report. Contribution of Working Groups I, II and III to the Fifth Assessment Report of the Intergovernmental Panel on Climate Change* (Core Writing Team, RK Pachauri and LA Meyer eds) (IPCC 2014) 17.

12 ibid 20, 21, 23.

13 IPCC, *IPCC Special Report on Renewable Energy Sources and Climate Change Mitigation* (CUP 2011).

14 IPCC, *Climate Change 2014: Synthesis Report* (n 11) 23.

15 Figures from: ECLAC, 'Economics of Climate Change in Latin America and the Caribbean' (United Nations 2018) 22.

16 ibid (n 40) 22.

17 In 2018, China, the United States of America, India, the European Union, Russia and Japan emitted 67.5% of CO_2 global fossil fuel emissions. See total CO_2 emissions at Monica Crippa and others, *Fossil CO2 and GHG Emissions of All World Countries – 2019 Report* (Publications Office of the European Union 2019) 6.

18 ECLAC, *Cambio Climático y Desarrollo en América Latina y el Caribe: Una Reseña* (Naciones Unidas 2009) 10.

19 IPCC, *Climate Change 2007: Impacts, Adaptation and Vulnerability. Contribution of Working Group II to the Fourth Assessment Report of the Intergovernmental Panel on Climate Change* (CUP 2007) 585.

20 ibid.

21 These factors are cited by ECLAC, *Cambio Climático y Desarrollo* (n 18) 10.

22 ibid; IPCC, *Climate Change 2007* (n 19) 585.

23 ibid; See IPCC, 'Global Warming of 1.5°C. An IPCC Special Report on the Impacts of Global Warming of 1.5°C above Pre-Industrial Levels and Related Global Greenhouse Gas Emission Pathways, in the Context of Strengthening the Global Response to the Threat of Climate Change, Sustainable Development, and Efforts to Eradicate Poverty' (Valérie Masson-Delmotte and others eds, 2018, In Press) c 9.

24 Kanta Kumari Rigaud and others, *Groundswell: Preparing for Internal Climate Migration* (The World Bank 2018).

25 Valérie Masson-Delmotte and others (n 48), c 4–5.

26 British Petroleum (n 10) 55.

27 ibid.

28 ibid.

29 ibid 3, 55.

30 See figures at ibid 52.

31 IEA, *Annual Shares of Wind and Solar pv in Electricity Top 25 Countries in 2018* (IEA 2018).

32 World Energy Council, *World Energy Trilemma Index 2019* (WEC 2019) 8, 56.

33 International Hydropower Association, *2019 Hydropower Status Report* (IHA 2019) 65.

34 ibid.

35 See World Energy Council (n 32) 8; International Hydropower Association (n 33) 65.

36 United Nations, *Accelerating SDG7 Achievement SDG 7 Policy Briefs* (United Nations 2019) 120; IEA, IRENA, UNSD, WB, WHO, *Tracking SDG 7: The Energy Progress Report 2019* (IEA, IRENA, UNSD, WB, WHO 2019) 4, 20.

37 World Energy Council (n 32) 8, 57.

38 ibid.

39 United Nations, *Accelerating SDG7 Achievement SDG 7 Policy Briefs* (n 36) 120.

40 ibid 124.

41 Sybille Röhrkasten, 'Regional Energy Integration: The Global Energy Governance and the Latin American Scenario' in Konrad-Adenauer-Stifgtung (ed), *Regional Energy Integration* (Konrad-Adenauer-Stifgtung 2015) 29, figures based on IEA (2014) 678. On the projections of energy demand in Latin America see also ECLAC, 'Economics of Climate Change in Latin America and the Caribbean' (n 15) 43.

42 ECLAC, 'Economics of Climate Change in Latin America and the Caribbean' (n 15) 43.

43 British Petroleum (n 10) 9, 14.
44 On the role and challenges of hydrocarbon exporting countries in the energy transition, see: The Oxford Institute for Energy Studies, *The Rise of Renewables and Energy Transition: What Adaptation Strategy for Oil Companies and Oil-exporting Countries?* (University of Oxford 2018).
45 IRENA, *Renewable Energy Market Analysis Latin America* (IRENA 2016) 38.
46 ibid 38, 73.
47 On the tensions between biofuels and food security see: David L McCollum and others, 'Connecting the Sustainable Development Goals by their Energy Inter-Linkages' (2018) 13 Environmental Research Letters 3, 7; IRENA (n 45) 74.
48 IRENA (n 45) 62.
49 BloombergNEF, *Climatescope 2018* (BloombergNEF 2018).
50 ibid 48–49.
51 IRENA (n 45) 146.
52 Margarita Nieves-Zárate, 'The Relevance of the Energy Charter to Develop Renewable Energies in Latin America' in Vicente López-Ibor Mayor (ed) *Clean Energy Law and Regulation: Climate Change, Energy Union and International Governance* (Wildy, Simmonds and Hill Publishing 2017); On the need for a South American treaty in the energy sector see: Jason Pierce, 'A South American Energy Treaty: How the Region Might Attract Foreign Investment in a Wake of Resource Nationalism' (2011) Cornell Int'l LJ 417.
53 On the need to promote more energy integration in Latin America see World Energy Council (n 32) 8, 56.
54 ibid Article 3(1).
55 ibid Article 4(2).
56 Kyoto Protocol to the UNFCCC, 2303 UNTS 162 (entered into force 16 February 2005) Article 3.
57 Meinhard Doelle, 'The Paris Agreement: Historic Breakthrough or High Stakes Experiment?' (2016) 6 Climate L 1–2.
58 According to num 4 Article 20 of the Kyoto Protocol, to enter into force the amendment requires 144 parties. To date, the Doha amendment only has 136 ratifications. The status of ratifications of the Doha Amendment was consulted on 2 February 2020 at <https://treaties.un.org/Pages/ViewDetails.aspx?src=TREATY&mtdsg_no=XXVII-7-c&chapter=27&clang=_en>
59 Doelle (n 57) 1–2.
60 UNFCCC, 'Paris Agreement – Status of Ratification' <https://unfccc.int/process/the-paris-agreement/status-of-ratification> accessed 28 March 2024.
61 Paris Agreement (n 2) Article 2(1)(a-c).
62 ibid.
63 ibid Article 2(1)(a).
64 ibid Article 2(1)(b).
65 ibid Article 2 (1)(c).
66 ibid, Article 3.
67 COP, 'Adoption of the Paris Agreement', FCCC/CP/2015/10/Add.1, dec 1/CP 21, para 22.
68 Paris Agreement (n 2) arts 4(12) and 17.
69 ibid Article 3.
70 ibid Article 4(11).
71 ibid Article 4(9).
72 Paris Agreement (n 2) preamble, Article 2(2).
73 See ratification status of the Paris Agreement (15 February 2020) <https://treaties.un.org/Pages/ViewDetails.aspx?src=TREATY&mtdsg_no=XXVII-7-d&chapter=27&clang=_en>.
74 United Nations Climate Change, *Parties to the United Nations Framework Convention on Climate Change* <https://unfccc.int/process/parties-non-party-stakeholders/parties-convention-and-observer-states?field_national_communications_target_id%5B514%5D=514>.
75 Paris Agreement, Article 4(4).
76 ibid.
77 ibid Article 9(1).
78 UNFCCC, Article 4(1)(c).
79 Paris Agreement, Article 4(4).
80 Paris Agreement Rulebook, for more references to the energy sector see Annex I, 4, d, ii; II E, 2, 50.
81 IPCC, *Climate Change 2014: Synthesis Report* (n 11) 17.

82 ibid, 20, 21, 23.
83 IPCC, *IPCC Special Report on Renewable Energy Sources and Climate Change Mitigation* (n 38).
84 IPCC, *Climate Change 2014: Synthesis Report* (n 11) 23.
85 Paris Agreement Rulebook (n 116) X, Annex Modalities, procedures and guidelines for the transparency framework for action and support referred to in Article 13 of the Paris Agreement, III, D, 82, C.
86 Robert Baldwin, Martin Cave and Martin Lodge (eds), *Understanding Regulation* (2nd edn, OUP 2011).
87 Julia Black, 'Decentric Regulation Understanding the Role of Regulation and Self-Regulation in a "Post-Regulatory" World' (2001) 54 Current Legal Problems 1, 105.
88 Anthony Ogus, *Regulation: Legal Form and Economic Theory* (Clarendon Press 1994) quoted by Bronwen Morgan and Karen Yeungan, *Introduction to Law and Regulation* (CUP 2007) 86; Baldwin and others, *Understanding Regulation* (n 122) 112; Barry Barton and others, *Regulating Energy and Natural Resources* (OUP 2006) 21.
89 Ogus (n 88) 86.
90 ibid.
91 See Inter-American Development Bank, *The Role of Renewable Energy Laws in Expanding Energy from Non-Traditional Renewables* (IDB Working Paper Series, 2014) 24; see also UNEP, *Emissions Gap Report 2018* (27 November 2018).
92 See Inter-American Development Bank (n 91) 24.
93 IRENA (n 45) 68–69.
94 ibid 67.
95 ibid 70.
96 ibid 67–69.
97 ibid 70.
98 Inter-American Development Bank (n 91) 6.
99 IRENA (n 59) 11.
100 ibid 25, 73.
101 Inter-American Development Bank (n 91) 5.
102 Climate Watch NDC Content (World Resources Institute: Washington, DC) <www.climatewatchdata.org>
103 ibid.
104 ibid.
105 Julia Black, 'Constructing and Contesting Legitimacy and Accountability in Polycentric Regulatory Regimes' (2008) Regulation & Governance 2, 141.
106 ECLAC (n 40) 43.

14

LEGAL ASPECTS OF ACHIEVING THE JUST TRANSITION IN POLAND

Magdalena Stryja, Agnieszka Bielska-Brodziak and Tomasz Pietrzykowski

Introduction

The concept of just transition has evolved over the last half-century from a political slogan to a legal concept. Born out of the American trade union movement in the 1980s, it became the subject of the 'Silesian Declaration on Solidarity and Just Transition' signed by more than 50 countries at the 2018 UN Climate Summit in Katowice, Poland,[1] and in 2021 the central concept of the Regulation establishing the Just Transition Fund adopted by the EU.[2] In this way, a political slogan has become a legal concept, co-shaping the key objectives and policies of the European Union and assigning rights and obligations related to the spending of tens of billions of euros allocated to the instruments of the so-called 'Just Transition Mechanism'.

In Poland, economic transformation processes associated with coal mining and high-emission industries began as early as 1989. However, they were related to the building of a market economy after the collapse of the communist system, whose economy was artificially focused on heavy industry and the development of large industrial plants (the working class was supposed to be the dominant force in this system).

In 1990, ten laws from the so-called Balcerowicz Plan came into force, setting out new rules for the functioning of enterprises and the state's financial system and regulating trade in goods with foreign countries and new labour relations. The changes were introduced through 'shock therapy', i.e., radically and comprehensively, which on the one hand allowed the economy to return to a path of growth more quickly, but on the other hand burdened society with high costs. Balcerowicz's 'shock therapy' is to this day in Poland synonymous with an economic transformation geared towards an immediate economic effect and without regard for social costs, almost entirely based on trust in the balancing act of the invisible hand of the free market.

It is worth mentioning that between 1990 and 2012, GDP per capita (PPP) increased in Poland at an average annual rate of 3.7% – the highest rate among all transition countries in Central and Eastern Europe. Moreover, over the past decades, GDP per capita has increased from 37.6% of the OECD average recorded in 1990 to 65.4% in 2016. At the same time, many regions and occupational groups have been doomed to years of stagnation, spikes in unemployment, loss of prospects and the collapse of the economic basis of the cultural and social order.[3] Overcoming these difficulties took many years in most cases, and in some instances has not succeeded to this day.

DOI: 10.4324/9781003276678-17

The climate policy implemented by the European Union marks the next phase of transformation processes, perhaps even more profound and more far-reaching than the economic transformations taking place in the post-communist countries over the past 30 years. Irrespective of the fact that the shift is now being driven primarily by ecological rather than economic reasons, the challenges it poses to regions and communities with more difficult initial conditions for its implementation are partly similar to those of the economic transformations of previous decades.

In the European Union's ambitious climate policy, which aims to make Europe the first fully climate-neutral economic area in the world by 2050, Poland has a special position. It is not only the European leader in coal mining but also in the generation of energy from coal. From the point of view of climate policy, it is therefore the most problematic and crucial area of the European Union. In 1990, Poland extracted 40% of Europe's coal, and in recent years this percentage has exceeded 90%.[4] Despite 30 years of transformation, over 70% of electricity in Poland is generated by burning coal, while in the European Union the share of coal in the energy mix has fallen to below 20%.[5] Of the 50 most polluted cities in Europe, 36 are Polish.[6] Without successful transformation in Poland, European climate policy has no chance of success. This makes Poland a particularly important participant in the transformation processes and the discussion on their conditions and course.

These factors resulted in the COP24 Climate Summit being held in Katowice – the region's capital city, where the Polish hard coal mining and high-emission industry is concentrated. The choice of this place should be perceived as a symbolic declaration of the need and willingness of Poland to fully engage in the implementation of the objectives of the Paris Agreement and the European Green Deal. This, however, requires an enormous effort, determination, financial mobilisation and, last but not least, the know-how necessary for this purpose. That is why the greatest achievement of COP24 is the 'Katowice Package', also known as the Katowice Rulebook, which is to constitute a road map for the implementation of the Paris Agreement.

In the national dimension, COP24 contributed to a surprising development of social activity. A large part of Polish society reacted with civic action (school strikes, climate protests, activation of many new educational organisations, civic movements and social campaigns) to the reluctant policy of successive governments towards climate challenges, as well as intensive propaganda in defence of the Polish mining industry as a national treasure ('black gold') and a centuries-old tradition.

Since 2018, we have seen an avalanche of economic activity in Poland, especially in the energy and new technology sectors, where pro-climate innovations are sought. We can also see the evolution and synergy of the argumentation for climate protection in Poland – for example, an unambiguous joint articulation of animal protection arguments and ideas about the need for climate protection. There have been and are also entirely new, creative interpretations of the law in Poland that extend the status quo. One example is the precedent-setting court decisions recognising the state's liability to compensate a citizen for negligence resulting in exceeding smog standards.[7]

A positive evolution can also be seen in governmental activities. After COP24, the promotion of attitudes that contradict the challenges of the EU climate policy weakened, and the pro-climate legislative activity increased. Although somewhat chaotic and inconsistent, it aims to introduce legal mechanisms that favour emission reductions and build an environmentally sustainable economy.

There are many indications that, in retrospect, COP24 in Katowice may be regarded as a symbolic turning point significantly influencing the level of social awareness and the readiness of the political and economic establishment to come to terms with the inevitability of a profound economic transformation. It is a transformation that must be carried out, even at the cost of incurring political losses and making unpopular decisions in still very strong circles downplaying climate threats or determined to protect their particular interests.

Just Transitions in Historical and Legal Perspective

Just Transition – From a Political to Legal Concept

The concept of just transition originated in the trade union movement. Therefore, it was initially understood rather narrowly – primarily as a need to care for workers in factories and industries closed down due to economic and political change. In this sense, it is concerned with ensuring that 'nobody is left alone' among workers. In particular, a fair social dialogue and the participation of those working circles most exposed to the negative consequences of the transformation in the planning and implementation of measures intended to respond to the risks and needs arising in this connection were considered an indispensable condition for a just transition. In this view, the notion of just transition has also been disseminated in documents of the International Labour Organization (2013–2015). According to them, just transition is to combine the pursuit of environmentally sustainable development with values such as 'social dialogue, social protection, rights at work and employment', as well as opportunities to promote 'social inclusion and eradication of poverty'.[8]

Over time, however, the concept broke away from its trade union origins and took on a much broader meaning. First and foremost, it came to encompass the provision of an adequate scale of assistance to regional communities exposed to the negative consequences of the rapid closure of industries on which they were economically, culturally and socially dependent. Just transition is sometimes understood even more broadly as the redress of damage and injustice produced by past global economic development. The most economically developed parts of the world are primarily responsible for the exploitation of the environment that threatens climate catastrophe. They, too, have reaped the main profits from this exploitation. However, the negative consequences will also be borne by those countries and continents that have contributed incomparably less to greenhouse gas emissions and the climate threat. At the same time, they do not have the capacity to effectively prevent this damage, which is accumulated in developed countries.

In legal terms, however, just transition has first and foremost the dimension of an obligation to support occupational groups, regions and local communities that are in a particularly difficult situation due to their most significant dependence on carbon-intensive industries and their own insufficient capacity to make a rapid and effective transition to a climate-neutral economy. These communities are particularly exposed to the risk of severe developmental regression, impoverishment, including energy poverty, and anomie associated with the breakdown of existing cultural and social patterns often strongly linked to the dominant industrial activity.

In terms of a legal concept, just transition is intended to respond primarily to such needs. This is reflected in the most critical legal acts in which the idea of just transition plays a central role.

The Silesian Declaration on Solidarity and Just Transition, adopted at COP24, emphasises 'imperatives of a just transition of the workforce and the creation of decent work and quality jobs' as well as 'the intrinsic relationship to the climate change actions, responses and impacts have with equitable access to sustainable development and eradication of poverty'.

Despite noticing 'specific needs and special circumstances of developing countries, especially those that are particularly vulnerable to the adverse effects of climate change and that natural disasters and other exogenous shocks, exacerbated by climate change,' the greatest emphasis was placed on 'challenges faced by sectors, cities and regions in transition from fossil fuels and high emitting industries, and the importance to ensure a decent future for workers impacted by the transition, while working to ensure sustainable development and community renewal'.

However, the declaration recognises

> the importance of a participatory and representative process of social dialogue involving all social partners to promote high employment rates, adequate social protection, labour standards and wellbeing of workers and their communities, when developing nationally determined contributions, long-term low greenhouse gas emission development strategies and adaptation planning processes.

The Silesian Declaration on Solidarity and Just Transition combines an emphasis on worker protection and social dialogue with a broader dimension of global energy and climate justice. The Regulation on the Just Transition Fund adopted by the European Union takes another step towards the legal concretisation of the concept of just transition. Unlike the Silesian Declaration, which is international soft law, the Regulation is a legal act of the European Union directly applicable to its Member States, which have a population of almost 450 million people.

The regulation aims at providing assistance to the most vulnerable and fossil fuel-dependent EU regions in financing projects diversifying and converting its industries and labour force into one better fitting the targeted renewable energy and low-emission economy model. It is then an attempt to translate the ideal of just transition into a set of legal rules, rights and duties aiming to make the transition toward the European Green Deal fair and just.

The solutions adopted in the Regulation indicate that just transition is understood in three dimensions, corresponding to the distributive, compensatory and procedural understanding of justice. Measures aimed at supporting the transformation processes are to reach the regions most exposed to the negative effects of decarbonisation and rapid phasing out of high-emission industries. In addition, financial rewards are to be given to those regions that do most to make rapid progress towards the objectives of the European Green Deal. This reflects the distributive dimension of a just transition in the European Union, based on the principle of distribution in proportion to need and the effort and commitment of the individual regions concerned.

As a rule, these funds may be used to create a new economic basis for the development of the regions affected by the transition and to repair the damage caused by the previous exploitation of fossil fuels and environmental pollution. This constitutes the restorative dimension of a just transition in the meaning of European Union law. Justice here means compensating for particularly severe losses – both those caused by the transition itself and by previous industrial activities. In particular, it concerns the creation of new jobs to replace those that must be lost due to the phasing out of carbon-intensive industries and decarbonisation. However, it also concerns repairing damage necessary to improve the quality of life in regions affected by environmental exploitation. This is to reduce the risk of the attractiveness of life in such regions rapidly declining, thereby reducing their opportunities for development.

Finally, just transition is also understood as a process involving all relevant stakeholders and giving them the right to be heard at the stage of planning, implementation and evaluation of the course of the transformation. Thus, it is also to be a just transformation procedurally, in which the circles most interested in its shape and success are not merely objects but play a subjective and creative role. All these aspects constitute integral and inalienable dimensions of the justice of the transformation process, as expressed in the current legal regulations of the European Union.

Decarbonisation in Poland before the COP24

The sector of coal, lignite, peat and bituminous shale mining, as well as its related energy production and energy-intensive sectors such as the manufacture of cement, steel, aluminium, fertilisers or paper, are located and often highly concentrated in specific regions. These areas require radical economic diversification, repairing environmental damage, ensuring that social cohesion is maintained and, above all, creating new life prospects for large groups of their inhabitants.

The transformation process, especially one that is to take place over the next three to four decades, is an almost existential challenge and certainly critically important for their identity and further development opportunities. It is estimated that in the regions most affected by the adverse effects of transformation, the problem of job losses may concern up to 32% of currently existing positions.[9] They are often relatively highly paid, deeply rooted in multi-generational traditions and culture and highly capable of articulating their interests through strong and representative trade union organisations. In Poland, 20 mines remain in operation (some were created by merging several previously independent mines), employing over 80,000 people.[10] This state of affairs has been achieved after almost 30 years of Polish industry and economic changes. After the fall of communism in 1989, more than 70 mines in Poland employed around 415,000 workers.[11] Their gradual phasing out had primarily economic and, to a much lesser extent, ecological reasons.

The most important and radical phase of this transformation was the reforms carried out in 1998–2002. In just four years, employment in the mining sector was reduced by more than 104,000 people, and more than 20 mines were closed or partially closed.[12] It is worth noting that despite the very high level of unionisation of employees in this sector, these changes were carried out in a way that hardly caused significant social unrest.

As the authors of this reform emphasise, the reductions in mining output and employment carried out at that time were much faster and more radical than those carried out a decade earlier in Great Britain by Margaret Thatcher's government. At the same time, they were achieved without riots, strikes or bloody police pacifications, while during the fights between police and protesting miners in Great Britain in the 1980s, several thousand people were injured, 14 died, and several hundred were sentenced to prison.[13]

However, from the point of view of just transition standards, the reforms of 1998–2002 should not be assessed unequivocally. The government's active cooperation with trade union circles (which at the time were the political backbone of those in power) deserves some credit. However, this cooperation was missing in relation to local communities, local government authorities and the scientific community. As a result, many cities and territories were left without assistance to compensate for the economic losses caused by rapid deindustrialisation.

Social peace was ensured by relatively high severance payments for those leaving the mining industry. However, they did not become the basis for other professional activities and mainly were spent on simple consumption purposes. A massive group of skilled and experienced workers was prematurely withdrawn from the labour market. Therefore, the Polish reforms can be a source of both positive and negative experiences, which should be taken into account in planning and conducting the transition process towards the objectives of the European Green Deal.

The pace and scale of phasing out of the Polish coal mining industry contrast sharply with the current plans to end coal mining in Poland. Although the number of existing mines and the number of miners they employ is similar to, or even less than, the number by which the coal sector was reduced during the four years of the 1998–2002 reforms, the process of its phasing out has been spread over almost 30 years. According to the government's current plans and the agreement reached with the mining unions, the last Polish mine will cease production in 2049. Employees currently working in the mines are to have the opportunity to work in mining until they reach retirement age.

However, it should be remembered that the pace of these changes is limited not only by social resistance and the desire of trade unions to protect jobs for as long as possible. Its basic limitations are the dependence of the energy sector on coal and the time needed to ensure a sufficient amount of energy from other sources (particularly renewable sources). At present, this does not seem possible in less than 20 years. Greenhouse gas emissions do not come from coal mining itself but from coal combustion. Achieving reduction targets is therefore primarily dependent on the transformation of the energy industry, not mining. A premature reduction in coal mining will only mean that more coal will have to be imported.

Impacts of the Paris Agreement and COP24 on Just Transition

Just Transition in the Paris Agreement and its Executive Instruments

The 2015 Paris Agreement is the primary legal reference for global climate policy.[14] The agreement, signed by 190 countries, contains rules to implement the United Nations Framework Convention on Climate Change goals to limit the average temperature increase to as low as 2 degrees Celsius above pre-industrial levels.[15]

The agreement also recognizes that adaptation is a global challenge faced by all with local, subnational, national, regional and international dimensions and that it is a key component of and makes a contribution to the long-term global response to climate change to protect people, livelihoods and ecosystems, taking into account the urgent and immediate needs of those developing country parties that are particularly vulnerable to the adverse effects of climate change (Article 7.2).

The concept of just transition in the Paris Agreement is explicitly expressed only once – in its preamble. The understanding of just transformation adopted therein clearly refers to ILO documents, linking it primarily with appropriate care for the workforce affected by the transformation processes, particularly the creation of decent work and quality jobs. This understanding can be complemented by the following stipulation that when taking action to address climate change, respect, promote and consider their respective obligations of human rights, the right to health, the rights of Indigenous Peoples, local communities, migrants, children, persons with disabilities and people in vulnerable situations and the right to development, as well as gender equality, empowerment of women and intergenerational equity.

The Agreement additionally notes 'the importance for some of the concept of "climate justice", when taking action to address climate change'. Linked to this mention, it seems, is Article 2.2 of the Agreement, mandating that implementation of the UNFCCC's objectives should 'reflect equity and the principle of common but differentiated responsibilities and respective capabilities, in the light of different national circumstances' (Article 2.2).[16]

Despite the limited role that the notion of just transition plays in the Paris Agreement, its presence indicates that tackling the effects of climate change and the necessary reductions in greenhouse gas emissions cannot be divorced from the notion of equity – both in its global dimension and in the dimension of protecting vulnerable groups and regions within individual countries. Secondly, the Agreement represents a further step towards legitimising just transition. It links the concept both to its original meaning as developed by the trade union movement and to its broader reference to human rights and the need to take into account the diverse capacities and needs associated with climate change and the effects of the actions needed to mitigate it.

The very need for a transition to avert climate catastrophe is primarily linked to the concept of intergenerational justice and the interests of people who are yet to be born. On the other hand, the equitable manner of implementing the transition should respect the interests and values of people who are already faced with carrying a particularly heavy burden and exposed to the unpreventable adverse effects of climate change and mitigation efforts. This makes just transition one of the 'key challenges for local transitions and the restructuring of real economy sectors'.[17]

The most important document concretising the way of implementing the Paris Agreement is the so-called Katowice Rulebook, adopted during COP24.[18] It is an extensive, complicated and largely technical set of rules which enables the reporting and monitoring of individual countries' progress towards achieving their reduction goals. A significant achievement of the Katowice Package is the provisions that indicate ways of transferring aid funds to the poorest countries to combat climate change.

The text of the Katowice Package contains detailed requirements for the communication and accounting of *nationally determined contributions* (NDCs).[19] Commitments made by countries in this regard are determined by the type of NDC and not by the country's level of development. It also includes specific arrangements for ICTUs.[20] This will enable the collection and evaluation of data on ongoing adaptation activities. The result should be a knowledge and experience platform, which will allow one to learn from each other and a tool to stimulate more effective and efficient cooperation at the international and regional level. As stated in the Katowice Rulebook, data and guidance will be updated in 2025.

The Katowice Package also contains principles, procedures and guidelines to serve the primary purpose of implementing the Paris Agreement. It covers all key areas, including finance, mitigation and adaptation. It also ensures transparency and comparability of reporting through the adoption of common reporting methods and measures of emissions reductions.

An essential element of the Katowice Package is the planning of the Global Stocktake, which according to the original assumptions was to take place in 2021. The Global Stocktake is to be the basis for the preparation of reduction plans by 2030. The package also establishes a Committee of Experts to analyse and evaluate countries' implementation of their emission reduction targets. The Committee will also report on countries' failure to meet their emission reduction or reporting commitments and other activities to achieve the Agreement objectives.

The Katowice Rulebook is a viable implementation tool for the first-ever global climate agreement.[21] Although it does not refer explicitly to the concretisation of the concept of just transition, it contains two references to this concept. One is the reference to the drafting and adoption of the Silesia Declaration on Solidarity and Just Transition.[22] The second is the inclusion of Just Transition as an element of the Work Plan of the Forum on the Impact of the Implementation of Response Measures and its Katowice Committee of Experts on the Impacts of the Implementation of Response Measures. This plan was finally adopted at COP25 in Madrid in 2019.[23]

One of the direct consequences of COP24 for the situation in Poland was the development of the Just Transition Toolbox. It was an outcome of the People and Climate – Solidarity and Just Transition Conference held in Warsaw on 3 July 2019.[24] The toolbox links the three themes of transition of the labour market, sustainable consumption and production and inclusive transition, emphasising the need for multi-actor dialogue.[25] It also recommends product standardisation and transparent labelling with campaigns to promote informed consumer choice, material efficiency and other zero-waste economy measures, as well as government purchasing policies to stimulate the production of climate-friendly goods and services and promote green jobs.

A just transition is understood in this document as also including a non-exclusive, participatory decision-making process – the procedural dimension of a just transition signalled previously is therefore visible here. In particular, this should apply to groups most at risk of marginalisation. It is also important to ensure equal access to newly created green jobs and special training, upskilling and reskilling programmes for these groups.

COP24 has also influenced fundamental legal initiatives of the European Union, which in turn are directly reflected in the laws of member states, including Poland. In 2019, the European Commission presented the European Green Deal to implement the UN climate neutrality policy and sustainable development goals. An essential part of the European Green Deal became the Just Transition Mechanism, which included the Regulation establishing the Just Transition Fund.[26] The European Climate Pact followed this in the subsequent year as an EU-wide initiative inviting people, communities and organisations to participate in climate action, build a greener Europe and draft a new European climate law (which was finally adopted in June 2021).[27] These were reinforced by the presentation of the 'Fit for 55' package in 2021. It includes changes to several existing instruments of EU law aimed at achieving a 55% reduction in the European Union's emissions (relative to 1990) by 2030.[28]

Implementing the Just Transition in Poland after COP24

The political and legislative activities of the European Union also have a direct legal significance for Poland as a Member State obliged to fulfil the resulting objectives and obligations. This is particularly important since, due to the inconsistent national climate policy, the decrease in emissions in the Polish energy sector slowed down between 2014 and 2018. During this period, emissions remained virtually unchanged and even recorded slight increases. However, in 2019 there was a rather significant change, and the amount of gases emitted by burning fossil fuels fell by 5.7% in Poland (while the EU average for 2019 was -4.3%). This was the result of an increase in the amount of energy produced using renewable sources and natural gas and an increase in energy imports. At the same time, very high prices of CO_2 emission allowances make electricity generated in Poland the most expensive in the European Union in 2020.

Although the Energy Policy of Poland, developed and adopted in early 2021, still does not fully reflect all the targets and indicators provided for in the rapidly changing European regulations, it is much more focused on the fastest possible reduction of emissions than previous documents of this kind.[29] According to its assumptions, the share of coal in energy production is to fall to 50–60% by 2030, while the share of energy from renewable sources will rise to 21–23%. There is also a significant improvement in energy efficiency and supplementation of energy sources with a nuclear power plant. However, the emission reduction by 2030 is still set at 30%, which is well below the 55% level resulting from the European solutions in force in Poland.

The Energy Policy of Poland was based on three pillars: just transition (Pillar I); zero-emission energy system (Pillar II) and good air quality (Pillar III). Under the just transition pillar, a specific objective was set for the transformation of coal regions. This process is to be supported by the financial instruments of the EU Just Transition Mechanism, including in particular the Just Transition Fund.

As indicated in the Energy Policy of Poland, a just transition means providing new development opportunities for the regions and communities most adversely affected by the low-carbon energy transition. At the same time, it is supposed to provide them with new jobs and build new industries contributing to the transformation of the energy sector. The activities related to the change of the coal regions are to be supported with funds of a total value of ca. PLN 60 billion (ca. EUR 15 billion).

In addition to the regional approach, the transformation will involve individual energy consumers encouraged to actively participate in the energy market. The transformation model ensures the use of national competitive advantages, creates new development opportunities, and initiates extensive modernisation changes. According to government estimates, the transformation supported by allocated funds may create up to 300,000 new jobs in high-potential industries, particularly related to RES, nuclear energy, electromobility, network infrastructure, digitisation, thermal upgrading of buildings, etc.[30]

At the same time, it is necessary to take measures to support the development of social awareness of the need for transformation and the benefits that can be achieved. It is also essential to prevent the processes of social stratification and mitigate the socially harmful effects of changes in the economic structures of mining regions. This requires close cooperation with local and regional governments and social partners, scientific institutions, and the business environment. Only in this way will it be possible to effectively give post-mining and post-industrial areas and infrastructure new social, economic, cultural, tourism, recreational and educational functions.

The central part of programme solutions aiming at distributing resources from the Just Transition Fund is still in the preparation phase. This concerns the National Plan for Just Transition and territorial plans for a just transition for individual regions covered by EU support.

In Poland, territorial plans for a just transition are being prepared for several regions particularly strongly linked to coal-based energy. These are regions where hard coal is mined or associated with the production of electricity from lignite. There is an interesting case of the Wałbrzych sub-region, where the last mines were closed 20 years ago, but since then, these areas have experienced serious economic and social difficulties, which can be solved by including the sub-region in the just transition plan.[31]

Support from the Just Transition Fund will only be available for those regions where mines are closed or mining is significantly reduced by 2030 – with the notable exception of Upper Silesia, which will be supported even though mine closures have been spread over almost 30 years. In turn, because of plans to extract lignite from the Turów mine until 2044, the European Commission refuses to support the Zgorzelec district from the Just Transition Fund.[32]

Among the regions where territorial plans are prepared, the most ambitious emission reduction targets are set in the Wałbrzych sub-region and in Eastern Wielkopolska – where CO_2 emissions are to be reduced by 55% by 2030 and the goal of carbon neutrality is to be achieved by 2040 (10 years earlier than at EU level).[33] Other projected territorial plans can be criticised for some significant shortcomings in this respect. For example, the plan for Upper Silesia assumes a 62% reduction in emissions by 2030. Still, this is only in the energy sector – it is not clear what the target is for the whole economy.[34] The plan for the Bełchatów region, on the other hand, envisages emission reductions of as much as 80% by that date, but it is not clear how this goal is to be achieved, given that the decommissioning of coal-fired units at Poland's largest power plant in Bełchatów will not begin until 2030.[35]

However, despite this, several solutions have appeared in Polish law in recent years to support the achievement of climate objectives and improve air quality and other environmental elements.

An example of such solutions is the provisions supporting the thermal modernisation of single-family dwellings inhabited by people suffering from energy poverty and replacing or liquidating solid fuel boilers with low-emission heating devices.[36] Financial support, in this case, is a condition for the effective reduction of emissions associated with the massive use of coal for heating homes and the relatively low cost of such fuel. This is the only way to significantly improve air quality in Poland (to combat smog), prevent energy poverty and improve residential buildings' energy efficiency.[37] In turn, the "My Electricity" programme promotes and financially supports the construction of photovoltaic micro-installations on buildings such as residential houses.[38] The owners of such installations can satisfy their demand for electricity with this renewable energy source, thus reducing demand from other sources and increasing the share of renewable energy sources in the Polish energy mix. It should be noted, moreover, that the total capacity of photovoltaic installations in Poland has been growing rapidly in recent years.[39]

Summary

In recent years, just transition has become one of the key concepts of European and Polish climate policy. After the Silesia Declaration on Solidarity and Just Transition was adopted within COP 24, the concept gained its direct legal dimension – primarily in normative acts of the European Union. The most important of them is the EU Regulation 2021/1056, establishing the Just Transition Fund. It focuses on understanding just transition from the perspective of specific support provided to groups and territories most vulnerable to the adverse effects of transition and least able to cope with their neutralisation on their own.

Justice is understood here both in its distributive dimension, which makes the amount of support dependent on needs and the effort put into effectively overcoming barriers to transformation and in its corrective dimension – directing support measures primarily towards repairing economic and social damage caused by transformation and environmental damage resulting from intensive exploitation of natural resources. At the same time, fairness of the change has an essential procedural dimension – it requires the participation of the main stakeholders in the process and ensuring its sufficiently inclusive character.

Following the legalisation of this notion at the level of the European Union, it is also more and more broadly reflected in Polish legal regulations. This applies primarily to programme documents – the National Plan for Just Transition and territorial plans of equitable transformation for individual regions. They have a formal status determined by the provisions of the EU Regulation 2021/1056, which is directly applicable in Polish law. At the same time, a just transition has been made the first pillar of the Energy Policy of Poland of 2021 – a formally adopted government programme document setting out the main directions and methods of action until 2040.

The reduction targets set out in it represent significant progress compared to Poland's previous Energy Policy of 2009. However, they are not ambitious enough compared to the European Union's targets, particularly those set out in the Fit for 55 package, under which emission reductions at the EU level are to reach 55% by 2030. At the same time, many territorial plans for a just transition set even more ambitious targets for the regions covered than those in the package and provide for faster or deeper reductions than those expected at the EU level.

COP24 and the Katowice Rulebook agreed upon in its outcome also have real consequences in domestic solutions. Legislative changes occurring after 2018 and investment and financial priorities indicate that Poland is no longer a country reluctant to join actual actions aimed at limiting the effects of climate warming. For the first time in many years, there has been a noticeable reduction in CO_2 emissions by the energy sector, faster than the EU average. After a period of long-term stagnation, actions were accelerated to stimulate faster development of renewable energy sources and search for possibilities for replacing coal in the Polish energy mix (also through the development of nuclear energy, which has not been present in Poland so far).

There are many indications that in retrospect, 2018, the year in which Katowice was made the climate policy capital of the world, will prove to be a breakthrough not only in terms of the pace of resolving the most serious barriers to achieving the ambitious reduction targets set by the European Union but also in terms of making just transition a central concept in the process leading up to it.

Notes

1 Solidarity and Just Transition. Silesia Declaration (2018) <https://cop24.gov.pl/fileadmin/user_upload/Solidarity_and_Just_Transition_Silesia_Declaration_2_.pdf> accessed 7 October 2021.
2 Regulation (EU) 2021/1056 of the European Parliament and of the Council of 24 June 2021 establishing the Just Transition Fund (2021) OJ L 231/1
3 Urszula Zagóra-Jonszta, 'Polscy ekonomiści o przebiegu i skutkach transformacji' ['Polish Economists on the Course and Effects of the Transformation'] (2017) 316 Studia Ekonomiczne (Zeszyty Naukowe Uniwersytetu Ekonomicznego w Katowicach) 208 208ff
4 'Coal Production and Consumption Statistics' <https://ec.europa.eu/eurostat/statistics-explained/index.php?title=Coal_production_and_consumption_statistics> accessed 13 October 2021
5 'Electricity Mix in the European Union, January-September 2020' <https://www.iea.org/data-and-statistics/charts/electricity-mix-in-the-european-union-january-september-2020> accessed 13 October 2021
6 'European City Air Quality Viewer' <https://www.eea.europa.eu/themes/air/urban-air-quality/european-city-air-quality-viewer> accessed 13 October 2021.
7 See judgements of District Court in Warsaw from 24 January 2019, VI C 1043/18 and District Court in Warsaw from 1 October 2019, II C 661/19.
8 International Labour Organization, 'Guidelines for a Just Transition towards Environmentally Sustainable Economies and Societies for All' <https://www.ilo.org/wcmsp5/groups/public/---ed_emp/---emp_ent/documents/publication/wcms_432859.pdf> accessed 7 October 2021.
9 Patricia Alves Dias and others, *EU Coal Regions: Opportunities and Challenges Ahead* (Publications Office of the European Union 2018) 59.
10 Marek Antosiewicz and others, 'Dekarbonizacja i zatrudnienie w górnictwie węgla kamiennego w Polsce' ['Decarbonisation and employment in bituminous coal mining in Poland'] (2021) 1 IBS Research Paper 1, 8
11 See on that topic Henryk Paszcza, 'Procesy restrukturyzacyjne w polskim górnictwie węgla kamiennego w aspekcie zrealizowanych przemian i zmiany bazy zasobowej' ['Restructuring processes of hard coal sector in Poland in the aspect of realized transformation and changes in reserve base'] (2010) 34(3) Górnictwo i Geoinżynieria 63, 64
12 ibid 72.
13 Piotr Jachowicz, 'Strajk górników brytyjskich 1984–1985' ['The British Miners' Strike in 1984–1985'] (1999) 31(2) Dzieje Najnowsze 137, 139ff.
14 Paris Agreement to the United Nations Framework Convention on Climate Change from 12 December 2015, Journal of Laws 2017, item 36 (Agreement)
15 United Nations Framework Convention on Climate Change from 9 May 1992, Journal of Laws 1996, no. 53, item 238, hereinafter referred to as 'Convention'.
16 On that principle see Janina Ciechanowicz-McLean, 'Implementacja Porozumienia Paryskiego w sprawie ochrony klimatu' ['Implementation of the Paris Agreement on climate protection'] (2017) XXXVIII Gdańskie Studia Prawnicze 491, 495ff and sources cited therein.
17 Rebekka Popp and Lisa Fischer, 'The EU Long-Term Strategy as an Opportunity for Just Transition: Five Elements for Success' (2019) E3G <http://www.jstor.com/stable/resrep21749> accessed 7 October 2021 1, 3
18 Katowice Rulebook, 'Getting Ready for the Implementation Era' <https://cop24.gov.pl/fileadmin/DEKLARACJE/Katowice_Ruleboo_E-BOOK_mini.pdf≥ accessed 7 October 2021.
19 NDC – Nationally Determined Contributions
20 ICTU – Features and information to facilitate clarity, transparency and understanding (funkcje i informacje ułatwiające jasność, przejrzystość i zrozumienie)
21 Krzysztof Bolesta, 'Klimatyczne mikołajki' ['Climatic Saint Nicholas' Day'] <https://www.polityka insight.pl/_resource/multimedium/20269105> accessed 7 October 2021
22 Katowice Rulebook (n 18) decision 1/CP.24 48: 'Notes the Solidarity and Just Transition Silesia Declaration, which recognizes the need to take into account the imperatives of a just transition of the workforce and the creation of decent work and quality jobs'
23 Report of the Conference of the Parties on its twenty-fifth session, held in Madrid from 2 to 15 December 2019 <https://unfccc.int/sites/default/files/resource/cp2019_13a01_adv.pdf> accessed 7 October 2021 decision 4/CP.25
24 *Solidarity and Just Transition. Summary Report of the Actions* <https://cop24.gov.pl/fileadmin/KONFERENCJA_JT/Just_transition_E-BOOK.pdf> accessed 7 October 2021, 1, 45ff

25 Peter J Glynn, Andrzej Błachowicz, and Mark Nicholls, 'Incorporating Just Transition Strategies in Developing Country Nationally Determined Contributions' (2020) Climate Strategies i, 27.

26 Communication from the Commission. The European Green Deal. COM(2019) 640 <https://eur-lex.europa.eu/legal-content/EN/TXT/HTML/?uri=CELEX:52019DC0640&from=PL> accessed 7 October 2021

27 'European Climate Pact' <https://europa.eu/climate-pact/index_en> accessed 7 October 2021; Regulation (EU) 2021/1119 of the European Parliament and of the Council of 30 June 2021 establishing the framework for achieving climate neutrality and amending Regulations (EC) No 401/2009 and (EU) 2018/1999 ('European Climate Law') OJ L 243/1

28 'Fit for 55. The EU's plan for a green transition' <https://www.consilium.europa.eu/en/policies/eu-plan-for-a-green-transition/> accessed 7 October 2021

29 EPP2040 – Energy Policy of Poland Until 2040. Announcement of the Minister of Climate and Environment of 2 March 2021 on Energy Policy of Poland Until 2040, MP 2021, item 264. That document has replaced previous Energy Policy of Poland Until 2030, announced in 2009. English version available at <https://www.gov.pl/web/klimat/polityka-energetyczna-polski> accessed 7 October 2021

30 EPP2040, 6.

31 Hanna Schudy, 'Wałbrzych ma przyszłość dzięki, a nie pomimo transformacji energetycznej' ['Wałbrzych Has Future Thanks to, Not Despite the Energy Transformation'] <https://biznesalert.pl/walbrzych-transformacja-energetyczna-europejski-zielony-lad-gornictwo/> accessed 7 October 2021

32 Emilia Ślimko, Magdalena Bartecka, Alina Pogoda, 'Terytorialne plany sprawiedliwej transformacji polskich regionów węglowych. Raport Związku Stowarzyszeń Polska Zielona Sieć 2021' ['Territorial Just Transition Plans of Polish Coal Regions. Report of the Union of Associations Polish Green Network 2021'] <http://sprawiedliwa-transformacja.pl/wp-content/uploads/2021/09/POLSKIE-TPST_sierpien.pdf> accessed 7 October 2021, 1, 6–7.

33 ibid 14, 16.

34 ibid 15.

35 ibid 16.

36 These measures materialised in the Act of 6 December 2018 on amending the Act on supporting thermomodernisation and renovations and some other acts (Journal of Laws 2019, item 51) and the Act of 28 October 2020 on amending the Act on supporting thermomodernisation and renovations (Journal of Laws 2020, item 2127).

37 Cf. justification of the bills from n 30: <https://www.sejm.gov.pl/Sejm8.nsf/druk.xsp?nr=2906> accessed 7 October 2021 1, 26 and <https://www.sejm.gov.pl/Sejm9.nsf/druk.xsp?nr=574> accessed 7 October 2021 1, 49

38 See description of Polish priority program 'My Electricity' <https://mojprad.gov.pl/images/program_priorytetowy_moj_prad_mp3.pdf> accessed 7 October 2021

39 'Moc zainstalowana fotowoltaiki wynosi 5,6 GW' ['The Installed Capacity of Photovoltaics Is 5.6 GW'] <https://www.rynekelektryczny.pl/moc-zainstalowana-fotowoltaiki-w-polsce/> accessed 7 October 2021.

15

LEGAL AND GOVERNANCE CONTRIBUTIONS TO CLIMATE AMBITION THROUGH REDD+ IN FRANCOPHONE AFRICAN COUNTRIES

Erick Kassongo

Introduction: Controversy over the REDD+ Solution

Reducing emissions from deforestation and forest degradation (REDD+), a mechanism designed to reward actors who conserve or restore forests in order to reduce carbon emissions, has been a central dimension of the contemporary international forest regime for more than a decade. In fact, the REDD+ political strategy consists of innovating existing sustainable forest management and conservation systems to achieve REDD+ results.[1] In doing this, the United Nations Framework Convention on Climate Change (UNFCCC) aims to address the problem of mitigating climate change due to forest loss.

Under Article 5 of the Paris Agreement, parties are "encouraged to take action to implement and support, including through results-based payments, the existing framework" relating to REDD+. Such action may target emissions reduction from deforestation and forest degradation in developing countries, and focus on the role of conservation, sustainable management of forests, and enhancement of forest carbon stocks in developing countries.

In recent years, an increasing number of REDD+ activities and initiatives have been implemented in Africa. However, these have had little impact on the objectives set and on the communities for which they were designed, particularly rural populations that depend on forest resources. Indeed, the Sub-Saharan African context has faced a range of pressures related to limited financial resources, technical capacity, and challenges that have made REDD+ implementation difficult.

Many of the specialists consider carbon rights, understood as titles to carbon credits, to have a sui generis connotation in the REDD+ debate. Since the beginning of this process, the holding of these titles has been closely associated with the conviction, or even certainty, that REDD+ will generate economic rents.[2] In other words, revenues will exceed the total cost of the corresponding effort.[3] This implies framing the discussion in terms of a right to income that goes beyond more financial compensation.

This chapter identifies the challenges related to the means of implementation and expected results, and discusses the institutional actors involved in achieving the objectives agreed upon. The chapter

DOI: 10.4324/9781003276678-18

draws on documentation of REDD+ policy events, policy texts, and relevant analysis from members of government, civil society organizations, research organizations, development partners, and the private sector, from various scientific reports, articles, and books across the African continent.

It is important now to review a few key points on the REDD+ challenges in order to frame a bit of context on this forest management regime in francophone African countries.

Key Points on Challenges that Have Made REDD+ Implementation Difficult in Francophone African Countries from Expected Results

The Congo Basin in Central Africa is home to the world's second largest contiguous rainforest, which is a source of income for millions of people. Men and women have a different relationship with the forest and rely on it for differing uses, and consequently, they have different experiences of climate change.[4] This recognition is crucial for climate change adaptation, as well as for mitigation policies such as Reducing Emissions from Deforestation and Forest Degradation (REDD+). The REDD+ aim is to offset carbon emissions in developed countries by encouraging actions to reduce deforestation and degradation in developing countries.[5]

The notion of carbon rights leads to rent-seeking: remuneration may be disconnected from the active contribution to the production of emission reductions, which is a public good by nature. Another interpretation of carbon rights is the right to benefit from the sale of carbon credits, a framework in which the issue is the sharing of benefits derives from human production and the sale of these benefits, which is a traditional social issue. However, the majority of developing countries engaged in the REDD+ program depend on financial and technical assistance from developed countries.[6]

The francophone African countries' REDD+ process evolved through a particular context, which is important to better understand the main constraints of its implementation. The following points illustrate REDD+ specialists' opinion on the disappointments, or missed opportunities, of this forest management system. The following sections note several such problems.

Lack of Interaction between Constellations of Actors (State and Non-State) and Institutions (Formal and Informal) to Produce Policy Outcomes and Dysfunctional Rules for Effective Engagement of Existing Coordination Mechanisms

A major weakness in many African countries is the dysfunctional rules for effective engagement of existing coordination mechanisms,[7] and lack of interaction between the actors (state and non-state) and institutions (formal and informal) involved in producing policy outcomes. A case in point is the Democratic Republic of Congo (DRC), where the REDD+ process was making progress on the technical front, but at the same time faced numerous challenges in terms of dialogue between institutions.

UNDP, FAO, UNEP (UN-REDD), and the World Bank's Forest Carbon Partnership Facility (FCPF) worked in close collaboration and jointly supported the national REDD+ process.[8] Other partners including ONFI, WWF, GTZ, etc. were integrated during the following years. REDD+ stakeholder networks in the DRC are characterized by a multiplicity of actors and categories, a multiplicity of interventions, and a highly unstable context with regular conflicts between different parties with divergent political interests. These actors got involved in the key events of the REDD+ process in the DRC: the 2009 decree on REDD+ architecture in the DRC, the validation of the R-PP, the validation of the national REDD+ framework strategy, and the validation of the Mai-Ndombe Emission Reduction Development Program (ER-PD).

For the purposes of this study, we only mention the example of the DRC to illustrate this problem of the lack of collaboration between institutions. In fact, during the preparation and subsequent phases, REDD in the DRC operated with the Scientific Council and National Coordination, advisory and coordinating bodies, as well as with the National Committee and Interministerial Committee, guidance, decision-making, and planning bodies.

These bodies' responsibilities included national coordination, overall steering, IEC, consultations and mobilization, community anchoring, construction of the National Strategy, technical, institutional and regulatory preparation, elaboration and implementation of an experimental program, and elaboration and implementation of the anticipated deployment of the REDD strategy:

a) **National Committee's** mission is to define the orientations and guidelines of the REDD process and to decide on the actions to be taken; to approve the respective work plans of the Interministerial Committee and the National Coordination; to monitor, control, and evaluate the implementation of the REDD process; to set up a national fund and to establish the terms and conditions for the management and redistribution of subsidies and resources from the REDD process. (Chaired by the SG of the MECNT, the Presidency and the Primature, 7 seats for the State and the government, and 7 seats for other stakeholders.
b) **Interministerial Committee** is in charge of planning the implementation of the National Committee's decisions and assigning responsibility for their execution to the relevant State structures, as well as identifying and mobilizing national and international technicians to deal with the problems encountered in the field in implementing the REDD process.
c) **National Coordination**: was in charge of coordination, day-to-day management, secretariat, advisory support, steering of process implementation.[9]

Main structures in charge of the REDD+ process at national level in the DRC

National REDD+ Committee	National REDD+ Coordination (CN-REDD)	National REDD+ Fund (FONAREDD)
Chaired by the Secretary General for the Environment, the National Committee is made up of 14 members (including a delegate from the Presidency of the Republic, the Prime Minister's Office, the Ministry of Decentralisation, the Ministry of Agriculture, a representative of the environmental NGOs and a representative of the Federation of Enterprises of the Congo).	As a coordination and day-to-day management body, the CN-REDD's mission is in particular to : -Ensure coordination of the REDD+ process in the DRC with government initiatives and donors in the forestry sector; -Ensure the day-to-day management of the National REDD+ Coordination and monitor the activities set out in the annual work plan; -Act as Technical Secretariat to the National Committee and the Interministerial Committee; Formulate proposals for the Minister for the Environment and ensure the mobilisation of national and international experts, etc.	Provided for in the National REDD Framework Strategy, FONAREDD is an instrument for mobilising funding, cross-sectoral coordination and monitoring of funding linked to reducing emissions from deforestation and forest degradation (REDD+), as well as mitigating the effects of climate change [https://fonaredd-rdc.org/qui-sommes-nous/].

Figure 15.1 This table illustrates the main structures in charge of the REDD+ process at national level in the DRC (UNFCCC REDD+ 2010).

The construction of the REDD+ strategy required numerous studies and a process of open dialogue to build a national consensus between the various parties, as this table of the main structures in charge of the REDD+ process at the national level in the DRC rightly illustrates. The reality is that only the National Coordination was a functional institution. Other structures, such as the Interministerial Committee and the National Committee, were not operational.

This lack of interaction between constellations of actors (state and non-state) and institutions (formal and informal) to produce political results is one of the causes of the failure of this process, as well as the delay on the part of various actors in following the National Coordination in its various advances.

Finally, it is important to note that the role of state actors in REDD+ is crucial to its success. Countries such as Papua New Guinea, Costa Rica, and Norway, which adopted and then promoted REDD+, motivated by the potential for cheap forestry credits or access to resources to finance their forestry sector, are a strong illustration of this.

Weak Institutional Coordination, Lack of Integration and Limited Use of the Scientific Knowledge Produced, Despite the Creation of Coordinating Institutions (Challenges Involved in Designing a Governance Structure for a REDD+ Strategy)

The enormous governance challenges associated with REDD+ implementation in tropical forest countries have received considerable attention.[10] In particular, multi-level governance, institutional coordination, and limited use of scientific knowledge have been identified as major challenges, as REDD+ aims to tackle local deforestation activities through a results-oriented global financial system. The design of a solid governance structure is necessary to successfully achieve a REDD+ program.

The type of multi-level coordination issues that emerge with regard to horizontal and cross-sectoral coordination reveal institutional complexity at the level of responsibilities.[11] Authors such as Korhonen and others argue that coordination problems have emerged due to a failure to recognize key multi-level issues. Indeed, they believe that REDD+ is not sufficiently integrated into existing policies, and there is "a gap . . . between REDD+ and sectoral and national development policies."[12] This leads to overlapping regulations and unequal allocation of resources between sectors.

The authors' analysis suggests that effective coordination mechanisms for REDD+ should build on existing mechanisms and experience, include all stakeholders, ensure the flow of information at all levels, and exploit the potential of REDD+ itself to overcome multi-sectoral problems.[13] It is important that, at national level, there is a high level of awareness of the problems hindering effective coordination and REDD+ implementation,[14] but this awareness is still rather low.

Many researchers have argued that the success of REDD+ will depend to some extent on the availability of sufficient funds for REDD+ countries; this contention remains true today.[15] Kanninen and others argue that overall success will depend on the quality of policy reforms undertaken in REDD+ countries, the identification and design of effective country-specific REDD+ policies, and the availability of institutions in REDD+ countries that have the capacity to oversee the management of the REDD+ program.[16]

This is all the more relevant today, as institutional problems and shortcomings in the various reforms undertaken after the REDD+ processes were launched are one of the causes of the failure.

The Inconsistency of National Safeguard Standards and the Proliferation of Existing Forest Governance Initiatives

Approaches to avoiding deforestation have been the subject of discussion for many years under the United Nations Framework Convention on Climate Change (UNFCCC). The non-carbon social and environmental dimensions of REDD+, such as benefit sharing, the rights and livelihood development of Indigenous Peoples and local communities, and biodiversity conservation, feature prominently in the various international and national frameworks on REDD+.

UN-REDD and a number of international multi-stakeholder platforms have formulated REDD+ social standards, such as REDD+ Social and Environmental Standards (REDD+ SES), which are considered to be the clearest, most comprehensive, and most rigorous. Most REDD+ countries in Africa apply an approach based on principles, criteria, and indicators.[17]

In terms of process, the REDD+ SES initiative is very strong because its principles, criteria, and indicators have been generated by multi-stakeholder processes at the international level, and the criteria and indicators are then adapted to individual national contexts by national multi-stakeholder processes. This approach significantly improves understanding of the issues at the local level while building consensus and promoting responsibility for REDD+ and its social norms. It also provides a framework for monitoring and reporting.

Generally speaking, safeguards and standards are integral to investor confidence and the viability of REDD+ in the future. Studies have shown that 'safeguard' policies and processes that only aim to minimize the negative impacts of REDD+ are not sufficient.

Clearly structured and interlocking standards at the project, national, and international levels are also needed, particularly to deliver the benefits and opportunities presented by REDD+, as well as robust but adaptable compliance mechanisms to ensure they are respected. None of the existing systems of safeguards or standards reviewed covers the full range of social issues under REDD+.[18]

Yet the same findings attest that the simplicity of safeguards and standards should be the key to achieving results, and social (and environmental) standards employing 'principles and criteria' offer the clearest logic for REDD+ designers and implementers to be involved at all levels.[19] It is therefore questionable whether the guarantees offered by safeguards and standards to date will really have reduced the risks for all investors by demonstrating efforts to document and mitigate the risk of social or environmental concerns compromising the delivery of emission reduction benefits, or leading to declining social support for project activities.

Collaboration between development partners is crucial to develop a common approach to social and environmental safeguards (policies) and standards, and then disseminate and publicly uphold them in order to establish socially responsible REDD+ as the international norm.[20]

Heavy Reliance on External Funding and Foreign Experts to Produce Technical Reports and Provide Technical Assistance

The scale of REDD+ requires a high level of funding.[21] However, funding issues are at the heart of persistent disagreements between countries over who should pay and how.[22] This is why contributions to the REDD+ programme come mainly from public funds in wealthier countries, such as Norway's agreements with Brazil, Indonesia, and Guyana.[23] Investors in REDD+ come not only from the public sector but also from the private sector.

Reality shows that methods, skills, and funding required for the carbon measurements under REDD+ are exclusively provided by Western donors,[24] and all targeted forests and beneficiary actors were located in 'weak' or 'fragile' tropical countries.[25] Examining the weakness of national ownership of REDD+ and the threat it poses to undermine Cameroon's climate mitigation and sustainable development objectives, Ngwome analyzes the reasons for this lack of national ownership, identifying in particular the lack of national budget allocation and reliance on conditional external funding that appears to hinder true national ownership in REDD+ implementation.[26]

Ngwome concludes that strong and meaningful national ownership is an essential prerequisite for REDD+ to contribute effectively to climate change mitigation and socio-economic development in Cameroon. He encourages the government to implement and enforce international guidelines on REDD+ national ownership, through legislative reforms that can guarantee national ownership and its proper implementation on the ground.

This conclusion could be extended to all African countries with REDD+ potential.[27] While today the major impacts of REDD+ in terms of reducing forest loss are difficult to document, many practitioners including Fletcher and others believe that REDD+ has been hyped in some circles, creating unrealistic expectations among policy makers and forest dwellers alike.[28] The reason for this is the lack of progress on the principles of payment for environmental services, as well as, in part, the misunderstanding of the payments for environmental services (PES) concept.

The Paris Agreement failed to create the binding national caps needed to stimulate demand for global carbon trading. Around US$10 billion in cumulative international pledges come mainly from multilateral and bilateral aid agencies.[29] This is a far cry from the US$10–15 billion a year needed to halve deforestation worldwide.[30]

For Angelsen, international REDD+ funding has evolved into a light form of results-based aid, exemplified by Norway's International Climate and Forest Initiative (NICFD) and Germany's REDD Early Movers (REM) program. The Green Climate Fund, which is expected to increasingly finance REDD+, will also follow a non-market-funded, non-compensatory model with elements of performance-based payments. Tapping into global economic markets may remain only a minor source of funding.[31]

The experts are convinced that REDD+ has been blocked by powerful actors interested in maintaining the status quo, and that it is conceptually flawed in its conception as a PES and forest management program. The same is true of the financing of REDD+ credits sold on a carbon market, and REDD credits used as offsets to comply with national emissions caps. This historic vision of REDD+ now represents no more than a reality that is unlikely to emerge.

Lack of Formal Platforms Set up to Share Scientific Knowledge at the Local Level

Kankeu and others note that "[a]part from discussions within ad hoc UNFCCC scientific working groups led by Western scientists, such as SBSTA1, there are few formal platforms set up to communicate scientific knowledge at the local level."[32] However, there remains a significant technical capacity gap that needs to be addressed before REDD+ can be fully implemented. For CGIAR, in its analysis report entitled REDD+ in Africa: Context and Challenges,[33] the prevalence of a capacity deficit for forest carbon monitoring in Africa could potentially limit the possible benefits of REDD+ in Africa.[34]

Since its inception, REDD+ has led to significant changes in discourses, practices, policies, and legal frameworks in forest territories in developing countries.[35] While REDD+ has helped to increase the engagement of non-state actors in the international governance of climate change,[36] it has been slower to recognize the ecological knowledge and practices of forest dwellers that have historically maintained the balance and well-being of these ecosystems.[37]

By making the success of the whole process dependent on scientific knowledge that, while important, has been developed at the international level, it is highly inappropriate to the local context. That is what Bidone calls the predominance of ecological modernism, which claims to reduce the scope of perspectives, knowledge and values integrated into sustainability policies.[38] While the opposite should be the case, multi-stakeholder environmental governance mechanisms propose to integrate a plurality of perspectives and legitimate knowledge bases. In other words, innovative approaches that envisage 'win-win' solutions for environmental policy may ultimately rest on the endorsement of alternative frameworks about nature and society that move away from the constrained paradigms of efficiency within the theories and discourse of ecological modernization.

Weak Definition of Carbon Rights, Benefits Sharing and Land or Tree Tenure Rights are the Critical Issues to Address

REDD+ governance covers issues such as land tenure, resource rights, benefit sharing, and forest management policies and forms.[39] This governance in Africa's forest sector is characterized by poor institutional capacity and performance, weak forest conservation programs, and uncertain land and forest rights for indigenous and local communities.[40] In addition, the aforementioned lack of cross-sectoral coordination on REDD+ and compatibility between REDD+ and national land and agriculture policy are considered obstacles to REDD+ implementation.[41]

Weak political and governance systems have been one of the main obstacles to pre-REDD+ forest management policies, such as the Tropical Forest Action Plan (TFAP) and National Forest Programmes (NFPs).[42] As a result, REDD+ implementation requires governance reforms, such as land tenure, and institutions that consider the rights and interests of a wide range of stakeholders, particularly local and indigenous communities.[43]

Carbon rights are poorly defined and linked to a project- and market-based approach. Carbon rights rhetoric obscures a critical distinction between economic rent and benefits: linking carbon rights to land tenure confuses social justice and rent-seeking. Carbon rights can be interpreted as deriving from conservation easements.[44]

Different contractual arrangements have affected the behavior of private investors in REDD+. For some authors, such as Sheng, examining the dynamic effects of benefit-sharing, cost-sharing, and incentive-coordination contracts on actors' behavior during the project period is important.[45] This is because it can demonstrate that incentive coordination contracts under REDD+ are a fair and effective mechanism for motivating actors to reduce emissions, guaranteeing the equal decision-making status of all actors. But the main shortcomings of current REDD+ contracts lie in their command-and-control instruments.

In Africa, land tenure is the most serious governance concern, as rural land remains the most important resource for development across the continent. Hence, land tenure reforms are at the top of the REDD+ development agenda. Although the states claim legal title to land, particularly forest land, they appear to have little control over the forests themselves. The same is true of the rural population (individuals and communities), which depends on forests they do not legally own. Over 90% of Africa's rural land is not legally documented,[46] and less than 2% of Africa's tropical forests are legally owned or designated for use by forest communities or indigenous groups, compared with nearly a third of all forests in Latin America, Asia, and the Pacific.[47]

Weak Integration of Monitoring, Reporting and Verification (MRV) Knowledge

Monitoring, reporting and verification (MRV) is a set of methods for tracking REDD+ activities and results. MRV activities include measuring carbon stocks and emissions of carbon dioxide and other greenhouse gasses, reporting these measurements at different levels (global/national/local), and verifying the effectiveness of planned reductions.[48] It is also a priority to ensure that REDD+ is implemented with environmental and social safeguards, co-benefits, and strengthened governance.

Other challenges identified by the national REDD+ implementation structure in the case of the DRC include going beyond the technical dimension of REDD+ to meet the human challenge; bringing technical instruments, such as MRV, reference scenarios, etc., under control; building an effective and operational sustainable development strategy; combining the political and the technical; and reconciling the short- and the long-term. These challenges must be overcome in order to build a solid foundation while avoiding tunnel effects, and to improve the credibility of the State and the confidence of stakeholders to engage them in the envisaged transformation. This will bring all sectors together and mobilize the country's forces in a more coherent direction, integrating the international and the local, through impact monitoring, complaints and safeguards, financial mechanisms, etc.[49]

As REDD+ payments require a demonstrated reduction in emissions from REDD+ activities, the UNFCCC decided that countries wishing to get involved in REDD+ will need to establish an MRV system to quantify emission reductions and removals. Countries were then required to develop reference (emission) levels for forests,[50] which provide a benchmark for estimating emission reductions from REDD+ activities.[51]

For example, the Warsaw Framework for REDD+ sets minimum reporting requirements before countries can benefit from results-based financing.[52] However, there remains a significant technical capacity gap that needs to be addressed before REDD+ can be fully implemented.

Institutional Actors Involved in Achieving REDD+ Objectives

In the DRC, the institutional players involved in REDD+ were largely limited to the Ministry of the Environment and Sustainable Development. Indeed, the institutions that were brought together within frameworks, such as the National Committee or the Interministerial framework, struggled to function due to a lack of financial resources. This was probably due to a lack of interest in REDD+ on the part of institutional players at the highest level.

REDD+ had been attracting strong political and scientific attention as a climate change mitigation approach due to Africa's large and still well-preserved forest cover. African countries' governments with high REDD+ potential such as Cameroon, the DRC, and Gabon have expressed interest in getting involved in REDD+. Moreover, national deliberations on a policy strategy have attracted the interest of various actors regarding the adoption of REDD+ framework strategies, but with weak results.

Specialists have noticed that Africa is characterized by poor institutional capacity and performance of institutional players, weak forest conservation programs, and uncertain land and forest rights for indigenous and local communities.[53] In addition, the lack of cross-sectoral coordination on REDD+ and compatibility between REDD+ and national land and agriculture policy are barriers to REDD+ implementation.[54] As Caroline Haywood, David Wardell, Marie-Claire Cordonier Segger argued, Institutional mandates need to be reviewed and streamlined and mechanisms for institutional coordination strengthened. Furthermore, the government institutions that oversee the forestry, agriculture, mining and energy sectors in African countries are subject to distinct mandates, which include distinct development strategies that can lead to inconsistent or confused government actions with regard to the different uses of the same areas.[55]

Current REDD+ Policies Delaying Implementation in Africa

Since the year 2000, a set of methods and tools designed at the international level has been transferred to the national level in many developing countries, in order to generate information on how these countries contribute to the reduction of global emissions through local forest landscapes.[56] The aim of these knowledge transfers was to improve the MRV system at the national level, as well as the level of knowledge transfer and the role of the players involved at various levels – global, regional, national, and local.

The results show that the transfer of MRV knowledge from the global to the local level is weak, and vice versa. MRV knowledge comes from research, integration of MRV knowledge is weak, and direct use is limited. MRV, which refers to forest monitoring or measurement, is a challenge for forest-rich countries. For some researchers, measurement is part of monitoring:[57] it's the first step. Measurement provides data on deforestation, enabling stakeholders to track its evolution.[58] The Congo Basin has been highlighted as a region with insufficient monitoring capacity for REDD+ purposes.[59]

In the meantime, the potential for slowing deforestation in high-forest cover African countries depends on the effectiveness of the REDD+ policy strategy, its effectiveness in achieving its objectives at the lowest cost,[60] and its ability to equitably distribute the costs and benefits associated with the program.

Along with the DRC and other countries in the region, Cameroon is an active member of the Central African Forest Commission (COMIFAC) and has been a member of the FCPF since 2008.[61] These countries are committed to other elements of international forest legislation, such as the Forest Principle and Chapter 11 of Agenda 21, the Non-Legally Binding Instrument on All Types of Forests (NLBI), the International Tropical Timber Agreement (ITTA), and the Voluntary Partnership Agreement on Forest Law Enforcement, Governance and Trade (FLEGT).[62]

These elements of international forest and non-forest legislation, together with a range of national policies, legislation, and climate change strategies, constitute important policy elements guiding the design and implementation of a national REDD+ policy strategy in Africa. Researchers who have argued that the success of REDD+ will depend, to some extent, on the availability of sufficient funds for REDD+ countries[63] could be proven right today. But others have argued that overall success will depend on the quality of policy reforms undertaken in REDD+ countries, the identification and design of effective country-specific REDD+ policies, and the availability of institutions in REDD+ countries that have the capacity to oversee the management of the REDD+ program.[64]

Conclusions and Recommendations

African countries' interest in the REDD+ mechanism has demonstrated the continent's willingness to contribute to the global mitigation effort. But as the governance system is largely determined by interactions between political actors (states and non-state actors) and institution-building systems, these actors and systems are the key to success.

The multiple benefits promised by REDD+, such as poverty reduction, biodiversity conservation, and economic development, were essential to the legitimacy of the mechanism, but there have been very few notable results. Some authors argue that the concept of carbon rights is misleading. Compensation for easements would be a more appropriate framework for designing incentive schemes, such as payments for environmental services (PES).[65]

Reforming land tenure codes to enable individuals, families, and communities to claim property rights or collective tenure rights over land and trees is an important issue to address, which will facilitate equity in REDD+ and PES initiatives. African countries have significant differences in terms of their political dynamics and forest governance, this predisposes them to a management system for the transfer.

Like Karsenty, Vogel, and Castell, we believe that in a desirable REDD+ scheme, the possibility of rents being granted under REDD+ would be very limited. In the real world, rent could be created through strategic behavior by setting a reference emission level, which would happen under a business-as-usual scenario, and through the eventual acceptance, for political reasons, of inappropriate rules such as payment for the entire carbon stock.

Strategies to encourage effective participation by all stakeholders are essential to ensure that gender is taken into account in issues of climate change, forest access, forest management, and the distribution of carbon benefits. For instance, building a data system for the national context involves gathering real information using different local examples in the field. This can help provide an accurate picture of the actual carbon stock situation, as well as past emissions, and guide future trends in local deforestation and carbon stock dynamics.

To meet the requirements, recipient African countries engaged in the REDD+ process must have in-depth knowledge of their forest carbon stocks and the capacity to monitor these carbon stocks in space and time at a national level.[66] The methods, skills, and funding required for these carbon measurements were provided by Western donors if the targeted forests and beneficiary actors were in 'weak' or 'fragile' tropical countries.[67]

Consequently, these tropical countries had a recurring need for technical knowledge and financial resources to carry out the process, particularly in the areas of forest monitoring, biomass and carbon stock assessment, and the forest mapping and reporting systems required to claim payment,[68] but they also require that the local communities be given the opportunity to share their knowledge.

To complement the national/local expertise that exists in Central African countries, external knowledge has been brought in through projects and programs in the form of external scientists and experts from universities and other private, bilateral, and multinational actors. New REDD+ features to be integrated into policy are important to adapt national interpretation processes so that they become more effective spaces for influencing the localization of international standards, in order to promote more equitable pathways toward reducing deforestation and forest degradation.

Notes

1 Olufunso A Somorin and others, 'REDD+ Policy Strategy in Cameroon: Actors, Institutions and Governance' (2014) 35 Environmental Science & Policy 87.
2 Alain Karsenty, Aurélie Vogel and Frédéric Castell, '"Carbon Rights", REDD+ and Payments for Environmental Services' (2014) 35 Environmental Science & Policy 20.
3 ibid.
4 H Carolyn Peach Brown, 'Gender, Climate Change and REDD+ in the Congo Basin Forests of Central Africa' (2011) 13(2) International Forestry Review 163.
5 Morganne Blais-McPherson and Peter Rudiak-Gould, 'Strengthening Inter-Disciplinary and Inter-Ideological Collaboration on REDD: A Cultural Theory Approach' (2017) 42 Global Environmental Change 13.
6 Gillian A Cerbu, Brent M Swallow, and Dara Y Thompson, 'Locating REDD: A Global Survey and Analysis of REDD Readiness and Demonstration Activities' (2011) 14(2) Environmental Science & Policy 168.
7 Kaisa Korhonen-Kurki and others, 'Coordination and Cross-Sectoral Integration in REDD+: Experiences from Seven Countries' (2016) 8(5) Climate and Development 458.
8 UNFCCC REDD+ 'Le Processus REDD+ en RDC' [The REDD+ Process in the DRC] (2010).
9 ibid 4.

10 Neil M Dawson and others, 'Barriers to Equity REDD+: Deficiencies in National Interpretation Processes and Constrain Adaptation to Context' (2018) 88 Environmental Science & Policy 1.
11 Esteve Corbera and Heike Schroeder, 'REDD+ Crossroads Post Paris: Politics, Lessons and Interplays' (2017) 8(12) Forests 508.
12 Korhonen-Kurki and others (n 7) 469.
13 ibid.
14 Arild Vatn and others, 'Governance Structures for REDD+ Experiences from Tanzania' in *Climate Change Impacts and Adaptation and Mitigation Project (CCIAM)* (Sokoine University of Agriculture 2016).
15 Markku Kanninen and others, 'Do Trees Grow on Money? The Implications of Deforestation Research for Policies to Promote REDD' (CIFOR 2007).
16 ibid.
17 Catherine Mackenzie, 'REDD+ Social Safeguards and Standards Review: Forest Carbon, Markets and Communities (FCMC) Program' (FCMC 2012).
18 ibid.
19 ibid.
20 Daniela Ray, Wahida Patwa Shah and Steve Swan, 'Country Approaches to REDD+ Safeguards: A Global Review of Initial Experiences and Emerging Lessons' (UN-REDD Programme Secretariat 2015).
21 Arild Angelsen and others, 'Learning from REDD+: A Response to Fletcher et al.' (2017) 31(3) Conservation Biology 718.
22 Timothy Laing, Luca Taschini and Charles Palmer, 'Understanding the Demand for REDD+ Credits' (2016) 43(4) Environmental Conservation 389.
23 ibid.
24 Gideon Fosoh Ngwome, 'The Legal Guarantee of National Ownership of REDD+' (2020) 14(3) CCLR 150.
25 Alain Karsenty and Symphorien Ongolo, 'Can "Fragile States" Decide to Reduce their Deforestation? The Inappropriate Use of the Theory of Incentives with Respect To the REDD Mechanism' (2012) 18 Forest Policy and Economics 38.
26 Ngwome (n 24).
27 Charles E Ngoma, 'Carbon Trading Mechanism in Semi-Arid Areas of North–Western Tanzania: A Case Study of Kahama District' (MSC thesis, University of Dodoma 2012).
28 Angelsen and others (n 21), citing Fletcher and others, 'Questioning REDD+ and the Future of Market-Based Conservation' (2016) 30(3) Conservation Biology 673.
29 Marigold Norman and Smita Nakhooda, 'The State of REDD+ Finance-Working Paper' (2014) Center for Global Development Working Papers 378.
30 Angelsen and others (n 21), citing Nicholas Stern, *Stern Review: The Economics of Climate Change* (CUP 2006).
31 Angelsen and others (n 21) 718.
32 Richard Sufo Kankeu and others, 'Governing Knowledge Transfer for Deforestation Monitoring: Insights from REDD+ Projects in the Congo Basin Region' (2020) 111 Forest Policy and Economics 2, citing Bérenger Tchatchou and others, 'Déforestation et Dégradation des Forêts dans le Bassin du Congo: État des Lieux, Causes Actuelles et Perspectives' [Deforestation and Forest Degradation in the Congo Basin: Current Situation, Current Causes and Prospects' (2015) CIFOR Occasional Paper 120, and citing HC Peach Brown and Denis Sonwa, 'Rural Local Institutions and Climate Change Adaptation in Forest Communities in Cameroon' (2015) 20(2) *Ecology and Society;* see also Heike Schroeder and Nidia C Gonzalez, 'Bridging Knowledge Divides: The Case of Indigenous Ontologies of Territoriality and REDD+' (2019) 100 Forest Policy and Economic*s* 198.
33 Belachew Gizachew and others, 'REDD+ in Africa: Contexts and Challenges' (2017) 41(2) Nat.Res.F 92.
34 See e.g. Martin Herold, 'An Assessment of National Forest Monitoring Capabilities in Tropical Non-Annex I Countries: Recommendations for Capacity Building' (Global Observation of Forest and Land Cover Dynamics Land Cover Project Office 2009); Erika Romijn and others, 'Assessing Capacities of Non-Annex I Countries for National Forest Monitoring in the Context of REDD+' (2012) 19(33) Environmental Science & Policy.
35 Adelaide Glover and Heike Schroeder 'Legitimacy in REDD+ Governance in Indonesia' (2017) 17 Intl Environmental Agreements: Politics, L and Economics 695.
36 Maria Brockhaus, Monica Di Gregorio and Rachel Carmenta, 'REDD+ Policy Networks: Exploring Actors and Power Structures in an Emerging Policy Domain' (2014) 19(4) Ecology and Society; Aarti Gupta,

Till Pistorius and Marjanneke J Vijge, 'Managing Fragmentation in Global Environmental Governance: The REDD+ Partnership as Bridge Organization' (2016) 16(3) Intl Environmental Agreements 355; Hannah Betts and Heike Schroeder, 'Multi-Stakeholder Governance' in Karin Bäckstrand and Eva Lövbrand (eds), *Research Handbook on Climate Governance* (Edward Elgar Publishing 2015); Peter Newell, Phillip Pattberg and Heike Schoeder 'Multiactor Governance and the Environment' (2012) 37 Annual Revision of Environment and Resources 365; Naghmeh Nasiritousi, Mattias Hjerpe and Björn-Ola Linnér, 'The Roles of Non-State Actors in Climate Change Governance: Understanding Agency through Governance Profiles' (2016) 16 Intl Environmental Agreements: Politics, Law and Economics 109.

37 Romijn and others Assessing Capacities of Non-Annex I Countries for National Forest Monitoring in the Context of REDD+' (n 34); Darrell Addison Posey, 'Indigenous Management of Tropical Forest Ecosystems: The Case of the Kayapó Indians of the Brazilian Amazon' (1985) 3 Agroforestry Systems 139; Darrell Addison Posey, *Kayapó Ethnoecology and Culture* (Kristina Plenderleith ed, 1st edn, Routledge 2002); Angayuqaq Oscar Kawagley and Ray Barnhardt, 'Education Indigenous to Place: Western Science Meets Native Reality (Alaska Native Knowledge Network 1998).

38 Francisco Bidone, 'Driving Governance Beyond Ecological Modernization: REDD+ and the Amazon Fund.' (2022) 32(2) Environmental Policy and Governance 110.

39 Jacob Phelps, Edward L Webb and Arun Agrawal, 'Does REDD+ Threaten to Recentralize Forest Governance?' (2010) 328 Science 312.

40 Romijn and others Assessing Capacities of Non-Annex I Countries for National Forest Monitoring in the Context of REDD+' (n 34); Arun Agrawal, Daniel Curtis Nepstad and Ashwini Chhatre, 'Reducing Emissions from Deforestation and Forest Degradation' (2011) 36(1) Annual Review of Environment and Resources 373.

41 Joanes O Atela and others, 'Implementing REDD+ at the National Level: Stakeholder Engagement and Policy Coherences between REDD+ Rules and Kenya's Sectoral Policies' (2016) 65 Forest Policy and Economics 37.

42 Romijn and others Assessing Capacities of Non-Annex I Countries for National Forest Monitoring in the Context of REDD+' (n 34); Olufunso A Somorin and others, 'The Congo Basin Forests in a Changing Climate: Policy Discourses on Adaptation and Mitigation (REDD+) 2012 (22)1 Global Environmental Change 288.

43 Gizachew and others (n 33).

44 Karsenty, Vogel and Castell (n 2).

45 Jichuan Sheng, 'Private Sector Participation and Incentive Coordination of Actors in REDD+' (2020) 118 Forest Policy and Economics.

46 Frank F K Byamugisha, *Securing Africa's Land for Shared Prosperity: A Program to Scale Up Reforms and Investments* (World Bank 2013).

47 Gizachew (n 33); (Allen 2011).

48 Ben Palmer Fry, 'Community Forest Monitoring in REDD+: The 'M' in MRV?' (2011) 14(2) Environmental Science & Policy 181; Pamela A Jagger and others, 'Multi-Level Policy Dialogues, Processes, and Actions: Challenges and Opportunities for National REDD+ Safeguards Measurement, Reporting, and Verification (MRV)' (2014) 5 Forests 2136.

49 UNFCCC REDD+ (n 8).

50 ibid.

51 Angelsen and others, 'Modalities for REDD+ Reference Levels: Technical and Procedural Issues' (Meridian Institute 2011).

52 UNFCCC, 'Warsaw Framework for REDD+' <https://unfccc.int/topics/land-use/workstreams/redd/redd-resources#Warsaw-Framework-for-REDD>.

53 Agrawal, Nepstad and Chhatre (n 40).

54 Atela and others (n 41)

55 Dalupan, Caroline Haywood, David Anderson Wardell, Marie-Claire Cordonier-Segger, & Robert Kibugi. (2015). *Building enabling legal frameworks for sustainable land-use investments in Zambia, Tanzania and Mozambique: A synthesis* (Vol. 140). CIFOR.

56 Kankeu and others (n 32)

57 Palmer Fry (n 48); Alejandra Larrazábal, 'The Role of Community Carbon Monitoring for REDD+: A Review of Experiences' (2012) 4(6) Current Opinion in Environmental Sustainability 707.

58 ibid.

59 Kankeu and others (n 32).

60 Richard S Mbatu, 'Domestic and International Forest Regime Nexus in Cameroon: An Assessment of the Effectiveness of REDD+ Policy Design Strategy in the Context of the Climate Change Regime' (2015) 52(C) Forest Policy and Economics 46; Romijn and others Assessing Capacities of Non-Annex I Countries for National Forest Monitoring in the Context of REDD+' (n 34); Erica Romijn and others, 'Assessing Change in National Forest Monitoring Capacities of 99 Tropical Countries' (2015) 352 Forest Ecology and Management 109.
61 (World Bank 2008).
62 Atyi R Eba'a and others, 'Etude de l'Importance Économique du Secteur Forêt-Faune au Cameroun' [Study of the Economic Importance of the Forest-Wildlife Sector in Cameroon] (MINFOF/CIFOR 2013).
63 See e.g. Kanninen and others (n 15).
64 Jeremy Rayner, Alexander Buc and Pia Katila (eds), *Embracing Complexity: Meeting the Challenges of International Forest Governance'* (IUFRO 2010).
65 Lisa Westholm and Seema Arora-Jonsson, 'Defining Solution, Finding Problems: Deforestation, Gender, and REDD+ in Burkina Faso' (2015) 12(2) Conservation and Society 189.
66 Gupta, Pistorius and Vijge (n 36).
67 Karsenty and Ongolo (n 25).
68 Romijn and others, Assessing Capacities of Non-Annex I Countries for National Forest Monitoring in the Context of REDD+' (n 34), Romijn and others, 'Assessing Change in National Forest Monitoring Capacities of 99 Tropical Countries' (n 59).

16

LEGAL CONTRIBUTIONS TO CLIMATE ACTION THROUGH OCEANS AND MARINE RESOURCES STEWARDSHIP IN SMALL ISLAND STATES

Freedom-Kai Phillips, Alexandra Harrington and Elizabeth Nwarueze

Introduction

Global oceans are the largest CO_2 sink in the world, absorbing around 25% of all CO_2 emissions.[1] Additionally, they are home to an estimated 94% of the wildlife of the entire planet, making them an invaluable source of existence.[2] Increasingly, the marine environment has been threatened by climate shocks – including ocean warming, thermal expansion, deoxygenation, stratification, coral bleaching and acidification due to increasing CO_2 concentrations – accounting for growing negative climatic effects on the planet and calling attention to the imperative for global preservation as an extension of preserving human existence.[3] Having deep intersection with several sustainable development goals (SDGs) related to ocean governance (SDG 14), poverty eradication (SDG 1), food (SDG 2), health (SDG 3), water (SDG 6) and biodiversity (SDG 15), oceans and the marine environment hold particular significance to coastal and island States which depend on the ecosystem for their livelihoods, provide cultural and spiritual significance and are especially vulnerable to the negative impacts of climate change on the socio-cultural and economic foundations of the jurisdictions.[4]

This chapter explores law and governance approaches applied at the international, national and regional level to preserve and protect the marine environment, with a special focus on Small Island Developing States (SIDS). First, international treaty obligations at the ocean and climate nexus are surveyed, including the United Nations Convention on the Law of the Sea (UNCLOS),[5] the *Convention on Biological Diversity* (CBD),[6] the United Nations Framework Convention on Climate Change (UNFCCC)[7] and the Paris Agreement on Climate Change.[8] Second, modalities' and legal approaches at the national and regional level are outlined, illustrating policy implementation, institution approaches, capacity building and reliance, indigenous knowledge and finance pathways to meet climate objectives. Finally, intersections are identified and discussed, highlighting avenues for enhanced climate ambition and continued cooperation to implement sustainable strategies for marine governance.

DOI: 10.4324/9781003276678-19

International Obligations at the Ocean and Climate Nexus

The international legal architecture governing intersections of ocean governance and climate change comprise a body of interconnected and mutually supportive regimes which form the bulwark for protection and preservation of the marine environment. This section summarizes obligations under the international ocean, biodiversity and climate regimes. Analysis highlights principles, strategic, institutional and governance approaches, and illustrates the rich mosaic of measures for preservation of the marine environment, conservation of biodiversity and action on climate change.[9]

United Nations Convention on the Law of the Sea (UNCLOS)

UNCLOS (1982) provides a comprehensive governance regime for oceans and supports a strong foundation for climate resilience.[10] The general obligation found in Article 192 to 'preserve and protect the marine environment',[11] as noted in the Advisory Opinion by the International Tribunal on the Law of the Sea (ITLOS) on the *Request for an Advisory Opinion Submitted by the Commission of Small Island States on Climate Change and International Law*, contains the duty to prevent, or at least mitigate, environmental harm, noting explicitly that GHG emissions constitute pollution under Article 1(1)(4) of UNCLOS, and clarifying the obligation to preserve the marine environment, which entails maintaining ecosystem health and the natural balance of the marine environment from the impacts of climate change.[12]

The all-encompassing nature of the provisions of Part XII was emphasized in the *South China Sea* Arbitration, where the Tribunal stressed Article 192 of the UNCLOS imposes a general obligation on States to protect the marine environment from future damage and preserve the marine environment by maintaining or improving its present condition.[13] Additionally, the Tribunal noted that obligations within UNCLOS, other related instruments and the general corpus of international law inform the interpretation and applications of the obligations under Article 192 and Part XII which are applicable to all States and in all maritime zones.[14] The Tribunal noted a stringent due diligence obligation on States to prevent and mitigate significant harm to the environment,[15] and responsibilities for developed State Parties to assist developing State Parties with issues of pollution and pollution prevention, including technology transfer and capacity building.[16]

Article 194 of the UNCLOS provides several core elements as noted by the Tribunal. Article 194(1) requires State Parties to take all necessary measures to 'prevent, reduce and control' all sources of pollution to the marine environment, including by GHG emissions, based on the best available science and within available means and capabilities; Article 194(2) obliges States to take all necessary measures to ensure activities under their jurisdiction and incidents arising from activities do not cause transboundary harm; and Article 194(5) concerns protection of 'rare or fragile ecosystems' using the best available means in accordance with their capabilities.[17] Importantly, linkages have also been drawn with the Convention on Biological Diversity (CBD), which defines 'ecosystem' to mean 'a dynamic complex of plant, animal and micro-organism communities and their non-living environment interacting as a functional unit'.[18] In a similar regard, the *Chagos Marine Protected Area Arbitration* Tribunal emphasized that Article 194(5) serves as the basis of measures for the conservation of ecosystems such as marine protected areas and enactment and enforcement of laws or the undertaking of monitoring and assessment,[19] reflective of the ecosystem approach as a fundamental of marine protection.[20]

As an important milestone, the Agreement under the United Nations Convention on the Law of the Sea on the Conservation and Sustainable Use of Marine Biological Diversity of Areas beyond

National Jurisdiction (BBNJ Treaty) (2023) addresses critical governance gaps on the high seas. Agreed upon in June 2023, the BBNJ Treaty advances ecosystem governance through the integration of, among other aspects, strategic environmental assessment, area-based management practices, such as protected areas, use of environmental impact assessment, support for capacity building and technology transfer.[21] Establishment of marine protected areas may be used to 'protect, preserve and restore' marine ecosystems to strengthen resilenance to climate change with the importance, fragility and sensitivity of the habitat, as well as vulnerability to climate change impacts provided as indicative factors informing selection.[22] Passage of an international legally binding instrument governing areas beyond national jurisdiction (ABNJ) lays the groundwork for cooperative approaches to climate action on the high seas.

Obligations under UNCLOS have deep intersections with the climate framework. Foremost, the recognition that anthropogenic GHG emissions are pollution to the marine environment, coupled with application of a stringent due diligence standard for marine protection obligations, provides important clarity to obligations underpinning national climate ambition. As a uniform legal mechanism for ocean governance, grounding resilience in the 'precautionary principle' and reinforcing the integrity and mutual supportiveness of the broader international legal architecture, UNCLOS provides an important complementarity to obligations under the international climate framework.[23]

Convention on Biological Diversity (CBD)

The Convention on Biological Diversity (CBD) (1992) is the preeminent instrument addressing conservation and sustainable use of biodiversity. Having a threefold goal of the conservation of biological diversity, sustainable use of its components and fair and equitable sharing of benefits from the use of genetic resources,[24] the CBD provides a framework for Parties to develop National Biodiversity Strategies and Action Plans (NBSAPs), establish a system of protected areas and management guidelines, utilize environmental impact assessments and further cooperation domestically, regionally and internationally related to areas beyond national jurisdiction (ABNJ).[25] The Convention also recognizes and protects traditional knowledge (TK), or knowledge, innovations and practices of Indigenous peoples and local communities (IPLCs).[26]

Parties may advance conservation of coastal zones and marine ecosystems through establishment of monitoring measures, guidelines for sustainable management of protected areas, promotion of ecosystem restorations, mainstreaming of conservation and sustainable use of biodiversity including through incorporation into policymaking and incentivization of ecosystem conservation and good governance with a particular focus on depleted, threatened or endangered species.[27] In addition, Parties agree to cooperate on relevant capacity building and technology transfer priorities to support implementation of the Convention.[28] Parties at the 15th Conference of the Parties (COP15) in 2022 agreed on the Kunming-Montreal Global Biodiversity Framework providing both short-term (2030) and stretch goals (2050) to advance conservation and sustainable use, including of marine ecosystems, in particular Target 3, which calls for the conservation of 30% of marine and coastal areas by 2030, and the need for Parties to provide updated national biodiversity strategies and action plans illustrating alignment and pathways forward.[29]

United Nations Framework Convention on Climate Change (UNFCCC)

The United Nations Framework Convention on Climate Change (UNFCCC) (1992) in the *preamble* recognizes the 'role and importance in terrestrial and marine ecosystems of sinks and reservoirs of greenhouse gases'.[30] Article 4.1(d) and (e) empowers Parties to protect GHG sinks, cooperate on strategic planning relating to costal and riparian ecosystems and monitor and report on the status of national reservoirs.[31] Oceans and marine ecosystems play an important role in CO_2 management, having sequestered 93% of historical GHG emissions with wetlands, tidal marshes and mangroves noted as significantly more efficient sinks compared to terrestrial ecosystems.[32]

Under the Kyoto Protocol (1997), Parties reiterated the importance of conserving and restoring CO_2 sinks, noted the inclusion of human-induced land-use changes in national stocktaking exercises and implementation of annual reporting on emissions, including those removed by sinks.[33] A market mechanism was established under the Protocol through Joint Implementation (JI) encompassed in Article 6, the Clean Development Mechanism (COM) encompassed in Article 12 and modalities for trading emission amounts encompassed in Article 17, allowing Annex I Parties a modality for investment in non-Annex I jurisdictions to enable sustainable development, and for the generated Certified Emission Reductions (CER) for use in achieving compliance with their commitments under the Protocol.[34] The CDM provided an incentive for genuine and measurable emission reductions through marine ecosystem restoration,[35] was open to both public and private entities and provided a share of the proceeds of CERs reserved for administrative overhead and to assist climate-vulnerable countries with the costs of adaptation.[36]

Paris Agreement

Agreed at the 21st Conference of the Parties (COP 21), the Paris Agreement (2015) reiterated the importance of many of the UNFCCC's foundational terms and tenets, including common but differentiated responsibilities and respective capabilities, protections for climate-vulnerable states and the need to enable technology transfers to address and mitigate climate change impacts.[37] Noting the importance of maintaining the ecosystem integrity, including oceans, and with the aim of keeping the increase in global average temperatures to well below 2°C and aiming to limit global temperature rise to 1.5°C,[38] the Paris Agreement provides for parties to submit Nationally Determined Contributions (NDCs),[39] recognizes the need to conserve sinks and reservoirs, reiterated the importance of adaptation measures, particularly for vulnerable states such as small island states and coastal states, and notes approaches are to be country-driven and informed by best available science and, as appropriate, traditional knowledge.[40] Developed country Parties are to provide financial resources to support both adaptation and mitigation activities, with other parties encouraged to provide voluntary support.[41] Capacity building under the Paris Agreement is intended to be country-driven, to enhance the ability of developing countries, LDCs and SIDS to take effective action on climate change and be supported through collaboration and development of institutional arrangements.[42]

Market mechanisms are integrated through Article 6 to support voluntary cooperation in the achievement of NDCs, including through cooperative approaches that involve use of internationally transferred mitigation outcomes (ITMOs) as found in Article 6.2, and mitigation of GHG emissions through engagement with both public and private entities while promoting sustainable development as found in Article 6.4.[43] A non-market mechanism is also included via Article 6.8 to integrate a holistic approach to the implementation of NDCs and enable sustainable development in a coordinated manner, including through finance, technology transfer and capacity building.[44] Collectively, these mechanisms help incentivize investment in ocean-based projects and provide modalities for enhancing means of implementation.

Ocean issues have also increased in prominence on the agenda. At COP22, the Global Ocean Forum launched the 'Roadmap to Oceans and Climate Action' (ROCA) for broad stakeholder engagement on climate change and resilience mechanisms.[45] COP23 saw productive deliberations by Parties and non-Party stakeholders participating in the 'Talanoa Dialogue', an initiative of the Fijian Presidency to allow open sharing of experiences and raised awareness of the effects of climate change on island nations.[46] COP25 in Madrid called for a dialogue on the ocean and climate change to be held at the intersectional meetings to consider how to strengthen mitigation and adaptation action.[47]

Prior to COP26, there was limited success in raising the profile of the critical role oceans played in mitigation and adaptation to climate change.[48] Building on the momentum coming out of the informal consultations,[49] COP26 saw recognition of the need to maintain the integrity of ocean ecosystems, drawing linkages to the UN decade for action on ecosystem restoration,[50] called on Parties to conserve and protect marine ecosystems, considered intersections with ocean-based action through integration into a work program and initiated an annual dialogue on oceans and climate change during the intersessional meetings.[51] At COP27, the Parties extended the mandate of the dialogue, noting it was open to observers, and called for integration of ocean-based action into their strategies and NDCs.[52]

COP28 saw the first global stocktake under the Paris Agreement, with Parties calling for preservation and restoration of oceans and coastal ecosystems, a scale-up of ocean-based mitigation, adaptation and resilience actions, and encouraged implementation of multi-sectoral nature-based solutions, with linkages drawn to the 2030 Global Biodiversity Framework.[53] Other relevant outcomes of the UAE Consensus include the operationalization and capitalization of the loss and damage fund,[54] and reiteration of the need for Parties to double climate finance for adaptation as part of the UAE Framework for Global Climate Resilience.[55] Parallel announcements of note included formation of Ocean Resilience and Climate Alliance with an initial pledge of $US 250 million toward ocean-based solutions in vulnerable marine areas,[56] the launch of the Financial Roadmap for Mangrove Protection and Restoration[57] and the launch of the Global Fund for Coral Reefs, with a capitalization of US$ 200 million for investment in coral restoration efforts.[58]

The normative obligations as well as outcomes from multiple stakeholders demonstrate global advancement toward a robust, multi-actor approach to climate and ocean action. The commitments by Parties give rise to localized mechanisms for the fulfillment of the global agreements and ultimately draw jurisdictions closer to achieving their ocean preservation goals. With oceans included in the thematic calendar of COP along with nature and land use, 43 jurisdictions in the Commonwealth and overall 93 coastal States including ocean-based elements in their NDCs,[59] the ocean climate nexus remains an area of deep importance on the climate agenda.

Contributions to Increasing Ambition on Climate Change through Law: Thematic Strategies for National and Regional Implementation

Considering the transboundary effects of harm to the marine environment, States are encouraged to implement the climate objectives both at national and regional levels. As a result of the disproportionate impact of climate change across different territories, implementation mechanisms have taken different dimensions relative to the needs and peculiarities of a country or region.

This section provides a survey of law and governance approaches adopted at the national and regional levels and draws linkages to relevant international programs. Rooted in the Paris Agreement through use of national adaptation plans as part of adaptation planning processes,[60] examinations of climate actions focus on the adaptation process, especially with respect to normative and structural developments.[61] While the term 'national adaptation plan' (NAP) is applicable to all countries, divergence in terminology, scope and institutional structure differ across planning systems. Jurisdictions were selected to provide global representation, both national and regional implementation plans, and aimed to include a focus on approaches adopted or applicable to coastal or island nations.[62] The review highlights law and governance experiences relating to: (i) policy implementation, (ii) institutional framework, (iii) capacity-building, (iv) indigenous knowledge and climate adaptation and (v) finance.

Policy Implementation

Climate adaptation benefits from clear policies which drive the national climate objective. The Philippines established the Philippines Climate Change Act of 2009 to drive the promotion of sustainable development and the protection of future generations as key components.[63] In view of the prescient threats that climate change poses to the Philippines as a maritime state, the Act includes the recognition of

> the vulnerability of the Philippine archipelago and its local communities, particularly the poor, women, and children, to potential dangerous consequences of climate change such as rising seas, changing landscapes, increasing frequency and/or severity of droughts, fires, floods and storms, climate-related illnesses and diseases, damage to ecosystems, biodiversity loss that affect the country's environment, culture, and economy

as key influences to advance cooperation with the global community through the activities of the Philippines at both national and international levels.[64] The Act recognizes and incorporates the need to involve all levels of public and private actors in addressing climate change and associated impacts, particularly involving those that impact vulnerable communities.[65]

Australia's policy toward protecting the fragile ecosystems in its marine environment influenced the creation of marine protected areas (MPAs) through the enactment of the Australian Great Barrier Reef Marine Park and Other Legislation Amendment Act 2008, as amended in 2017. These laws, which established the Great Barrier Reef Marine Park, balance the need to protect the environment with the economic value of the ecosystem. The Great Barrier Reef Marine Park was established in 1975 in order 'to provide for the long-term protection and conservation of the environment, biodiversity and heritage values of the Great Barrier Reef Region'.[66] Beyond its economic and social yield, the Park caters to the interests of the nation, particularly the Indigenous communities who are inhabitants.[67] In evaluating and responding to the needs of the area for both short- and long-term viability, the domestic policy advances adaptation and resilience in line with Article 7 of the Paris Agreement.

Environmental Impact Assessment (EIA) has proven to be a vital tool and precondition for implementing States' climate agenda. A key example of an EIA law in this context is the Seychelles Environmental Protection Act, which codifies the nation's EIA requirements. Under the terms of the Seychelles EIA law, EIAs for proposed developments and other projects must contain essential information to identify the location, purpose and intended use of the project.[68] Beyond these background elements, the filing must identify: (a) the direct or indirect effects that the activity has on the characteristics of the ecosystem; (b) any remedial measures to be taken; (c) the adverse impacts on the environment if implemented in the proposed manner; (d) irreversible impact resulting from the activity; and (e) the proposed compensation for loss or damage to the environment.[69] Under the Act, the project proponent is required to provide an assessment of alternative measures and locations to those planned, along with a statement as to why these alternatives would not be appropriate.[70] This strengthens the provisions of the Seychelles Protected Area Policy of 2013, which gives institutional support for a multi-actor comanaged MPA project involving both the government and the local communities.

A similar approach was adopted by the island nation of Kiribati, which has acted to protect significant aspects of its marine natural resources through the Phoenix Islands Protected Area Regulations 2008 and the Phoenix Islands Protected Area Conservation Trust Act 2009. The Regulations designate the environmentally significant and sensitive Phoenix Islands area as 'a protected area for terrestrial and marine resources'.[71] At the same time, the Regulation seeks to allow limited and sustainable use of the Phoenix Islands through the granting of appropriate licenses and permits for approved activities.[72] Other nations, like South Africa and Mauritius, are utilizing their NDCs to align their climate policy, outline mitigation and adaptation priorities and advance ambition while formal climate change legal instruments are under development.[73]

Regionally, the 2008 EU Marine Strategy Framework Directive illustrates a collaborative policy approach to preserving the marine environment.[74] In the Framework Directive, the EU established a long-term policy 'to achieve or maintain good environmental status in the marine environment' with the EU and within the laws and policies of its Member States.[75] These strategies are intended to include measures to control and prevent pollution that impacts marine ecosystems, including oceans, and to 'protect and preserve the marine environment, prevent its deterioration, or, where practicable, restore marine ecosystems in areas where they have been adversely affected'.[76] As a whole, the Framework Directive is intended to create marine strategies founded on and implementing ecosystem-based approaches to activities across the spectrum of regulation.[77]

Grounded in the treaty regime of the EU, the Framework Directive is intended to function at multiple levels to provide protection for marine resources within Member States and within the EU as a whole.[78] In this vein, it ensures that marine strategies and policies throughout the EU reflect the protection of marine ecosystems from damage that is a result of transboundary pollution or other forms of degradation.[79] The Framework Directive provides a broad definition of what constitutes pollution, which allows adaption in the face of changes in scientific and other knowledge regarding marine ecosystems in the short- and long-term.[80] The approaches adopted in the Framework Directive aim to foster adaptation and resilience measures for the marine ecosystems within the EU's territory, and help advance Article 2(1)(b) of the Paris Agreement.

Institutional Framework

Through the Philippines Climate Change Act, a Climate Change Commission was created as the sole policy-making body to coordinate and oversee the implementation of the terms of the Act.[81] The multi-stakeholder Commission comprises of relevant heads of ministries, leaders of regional and municipal authorities, business and the private sector, academia and non-governmental organizations.[82] Included in the non-governmental representatives is the requirement that at least one member have a background in disaster risk reduction, indicating the importance of including resilience and associated regimes in the core governance system for the Act.[83] This Commission is also mandated with formulating a national Framework Strategy for Climate Change, developing and commenting on other laws and regulations, and 'recommending key development investments in climate-sensitive sectors such as water resources, agriculture, forestry, coastal and marine resources, health, and infrastructure to ensure the achievement of national sustainable development goals',[84] and ensuring the involvement and coordination of sub-national authorities in addressing climate vulnerabilities.[85] The Commission is one of the most active climate strategy institutions in Asia, constantly pushing for sustainability and low-carbon initiatives, as well as advancing a collaborative disaster risk reduction strategy through the Sendai Framework in Asia and the Pacific.[86]

In implementing the terms of the Great Barrier Reef Act, the Australian legislature created a designated regulatory and oversight body known as the Great Barrier Reef Marine Park Authority.[87] This body is empowered with jurisdiction over the Great Barrier Reef and is required to ensure 'ecologically sustainable use' of the marine resources in the area, including evaluation of activities and proposals using specific statutorily defined principles.[88] Under the terms of reference of the Authority, 'ecologically sustainable use' covers: (i) consideration of the precautionary principle and the principle of inter-generational equity, (ii) integration of both longterm and shortterm environmental, economic, social and equitable considerations, and (iii) inclusion of conservation of biodiversity and ecological integrity as fundamental factors in decisionmaking.[89] Recently, the Authority discovered extensive coral bleaching suffered by Australia's Great Barrier Reefs. It has moved to carry out wider surveys while also designing strategies to address climate emissions, which it considers a threat to the reef.[90] In Seychelles, an environmental authority oversees the implementation of and compliance with the terms enacted for carrying out EIAs.[91] The Authority coordinates the statutory requirements for the preparation, review and evaluation of information relating to a proposed development or other activity,[92] and is empowered to suspend approval of the EIA or cancel the project altogether.[93]

The Phoenix Islands Protected Area Conservation Trust was created by Kiribati as a separate legal entity that is empowered under national law to enter into agreements and act in ways that ensure the protection and conservation of the natural resources and biodiversity within the Phoenix Islands.[94] As part of this function, the Trust may provide funding to the Kiribati government to serve as compensation to offset the loss of potential economic exploitation of the Phoenix Islands as a way to soften the economic impacts of conservation and preservation.[95] The Regulations are geared toward not only protecting the environmental and natural resources found in the Phoenix Islands territory for citizens of Kiribati but also to the international community as a whole by encouraging the designation of the territory as a UNESCO World Heritage site.[96] An essential element of the Regulations is the creation of the Phoenix Islands Protected Area (PIPA) Management Plan and the PIPA Committee to generate and implement it.[97] As the entity charged with generating the Management Plan, the Committee is also given oversight of ensuring that the terms of the Management Plan are updated as necessary and that they are in compliance with international legal regimes.[98] The Management Plan is required to 'ensure that all activities that take place in the PIPA are designed for the benefit of present and future generations'.[99] Overall, the Management Plan places a great deal of emphasis on protection and conservation of the biodiversity in the Phoenix Islands, especially marine biodiversity, with an emphasis on ensuring the short- and long-term viability of species in the territory.[100] At the same time, there is a balance between the need to protect and conserve the territorial ecosystem, benefits of responsible research in the territory and potential economic and societal impacts to certain limited uses of the territory for recreational activities.

Capacity-Building

Acknowledging the disproportionate impact of climate change on the marine environment across countries and the differing levels of development required to conduct pre-assessment procedures and implement often financially demanding tools for marine protection, capacity building is a credible way to speed up the pace of global implementation. Capacity building needs of developing countries and SIDS as particularly climate-vulnerable have been regularly communicated through periodic submissions.[101] 74% of NDCs noted capacity building as a precondition of NDC implementation,[102] and it has been noted by the Secretariat as the most frequently requested type of support.[103]

On the multilateral level, the Marrakech Capacity Building Framework adopted in 2001, and its three reviews, have informed capacity-building efforts under the UNFCCC.[104] This Framework includes 15 areas of focus for capacity building in developing countries, as well as six priority areas for LDCs and SIDS. These priority areas include strengthening institutions, establishing research and training centers, assessment of vulnerability and implementation of adaptation measures and strengthening of meteorological and hydrological services. Resources are provided through the Capacity-building Portal, the Paris Committee on Capacity Building (PCCB) and a range of parallel initiatives and partnership-developed materials.[105] For SIDS, capacity building has been emphasized more than ever before as the paramount goal is building resilience to external shocks, and this is divided into short- and long-term measures ranging from climate education and enlightenment to supporting the process for structural transformation which will yield sustainable development.[106]

Despite the broad need, domestic legal approaches have focused on capacity building and educational needs to a lesser extent.[107] Under the Climate Change and Carbon Market Initiatives Act of the Bahamas, the Prime Minister is provided deference to develop institutional arrangements to support capacity building through domestic, regional or multilateral approaches in line with obligations under the Paris Agreement.[108] In Law No. 19355, Uruguay created in the President's Office the National Secretariat of Environment, Water and Climate Change to coordinate with public and private institutions achievement of public policies on climate change, and it empowered the National Secretariat of Science and Technology to, among other things, determine the needs and promote the development of national capabilities.[109]

Mexico, in the General Law on Climate Change, empowers the National Institute of Ecology and Climate Change to foster scientific, technical and innovation-related capacity building on climate change and sustainable development in coordination with the Secretariat of Public Education and national institutions of higher learning,[110] participate in the design of funding mechanisms to support research and provide technical assistance to domestic projects and programs.[111] The Philippines empowers their Climate Change Commission to facilitate capacity building for adaption, local planning and implementation and oversight of initiatives in climate-vulnerable communities.[112] All relevant government agencies are required to allocate funding from their annual budgets for development and implementation of training and capacity building.[113] In addition, as a component of the National Strategic Framework and program on Climate Change, the Department of the Interior and Local Government (DILG) and Local Government Academy, in conjunction with the National Economic and Development Authority, are to develop capacity building programs for local governments and vulnerable communities.[114]

Development of institutional arrangements at the domestic, regional and international level have been the primary approach to advancing capacity building for developing and emerging economies, particularly SIDS.

Indigenous Knowledge and Climate Adaptation

Indigenous peoples and local communities (IPLCs) are disproportionately affected by climate change.[115] Simultaneously, IPLCs are holders and curators of Traditional Knowledge (TK) which can be beneficial in advancing achievement of international commitments related to climate change and furthering sustainable development.

Under the UNFCCC, the Local Communities and Indigenous Peoples Platform (LCIPP) was created at COP23. Recognizing that Parties should respect, promote and consider rights of IPLCs in developing climate solutions, the LCIPP aims to strengthen innovations and practices grounded in TK to respond to climate change, to enable an exchange of experiences to share best practices relating to both adaption and mitigation and enhance engagement of IPLCs in the UNFCCC processes.[116] A Facilitative Working Group was established with joint leadership and balanced representation of seven parties from the five UN regions, SIDS and LDCs, and seven representatives of Indigenous Peoples.[117] Under the first workplan, training, outreach, recommendations on engagement and mapping of policies and good practices that provide for involvement of IPLCs in climate action were collected.[118] At COP26 a second three-year workplan was adopted, recommending a focus on ecosystem management and inviting Parties and stakeholders to enhance engagement with IPLCs in responding to climate change.[119] The LCIPP marked an important evolution incorporating a dedicated modality for discourse and integration of TK into international climate architecture.[120]

Indigenous TK has been applied in multiple contexts in marine ecosystems. In Niue, conservation practices have drawn on traditional experts' and elders' deep understanding of ecosystems and migratory patterns.[121] The Cook Islands recognize conservation practices leveraging TK, with a broad definition provided in the domestic legal framework encompassing conservation, transport, navigation and technologies, among others.[122] The Polynesian peoples apply the concept of *rahui* – a person, place or thing of importance that is set aside – to marine ecosystems in area-based management approaches deployed in areas of Rapa iti, Fakarava and New Zealand.[123] Fiji empowers their National Adaption Plan (NAP) Steering Committee to be informed by TK of all Fijians in the development, review and updating of strategic plans relating to adaptation.[124] In addition, TK is utilized in ocean planning through the National Ocean Policy Steering Committee and national climate change policy.[125]

TK is increasingly being introduced into law and governance arrangements at the international and national levels, enhancing recognition, protection and conservation while providing greater opportunities for application toward sustainable development. Importantly, both indigenous and scientific knowledge are being recognized as complementary in accelerating climate resilience, especially in small island nations.

Finance

Mobilization of finance is critical to advancing ambitious climate action both in adaptation and mitigation activities, as well as enabling responses to loss and damage.

The Bahamas established an institutional mechanism for acceptance and deployment of climate finance, including policy planning and reporting, as well as technology transfer for application in mitigation and adaptation.[126] In Peru, the Ministry of Environment and Ministry of Finance established guidelines for use of climate finance in a strategic and complementary manner to optimize the catalytic function, and to provide capacity building to public institutions and project proponents to increase access and effective management of funding.[127]

The Philippines established the People's Survival Fund to facilitate long-term finance flows to address climate change.[128] Governed by a multi-stakeholder board inclusive of government, civil society, academia and industry, the Fund supports adaption activities including: ecosystem management, early warning systems, and risk guarantees for insurance and community development.[129] Similarly, Tuvalu developed a Climate Change and Disaster Survival Fund to provide assistance in recovery and rehabilitation from impacts of climate change and natural disasters.[130] Providing for both immediate vital services as well as supporting a long-term coordinated response, citizens may apply to the Fund for natural disaster response, emergency relief, and recovery to build back, rehabilitate and embed resilience.[131] Antigua and Barbuda similarly established the Sustainable Island

Resources Framework Fund (SIRF Fund) to support regional environmental projects, build ecosystem resilience and provide support measures for adaptation, mitigation and loss and damage.[132]

In 2018, Seychelles, in partnership with the World Bank and the Global Environment Facility, issued the first blue bond, innovating conservation finance.[133] Existing powers granted to the Minister of the Development Bank of Seychelles for issuance of financial instruments were coupled with the Conservation and Climate Adaptation Trust (CCAT), an institutional framework enabling acceptance of international finance and debt swaps, to allow the nation to raise US$15 million in climate finance through international investment in a 10-year blue bond providing a 6.5% rate of return.[134] Continuing to leverage debt for nature swaps,[135] amendments were made in 2020 to further expand the role of the CCAT to develop and administer funds from a broad range of sources including bonds, grants, investments, loans, or guarantees for climate adaptation and mitigation or furtherance of sustainable development in the blue economy.[136]

Collectively, these measures provide an institutional architecture and pathways to mobilize and administer climate-related finance for advancement of climate resilience and sustainable development.

Conclusion

Current governance challenges at the ocean-climate nexus illustrate the complexity, fragmentation and limitations of international legal regimes in advancing ambition. Facilitative compliance under the Paris Agreement has enabled ongoing reporting by Parties; however, significant gaps remain, with implementation of current NDCs keeping humanity on a 2.5°C trajectory.[137] Troublingly, the World Meteorological Organization (WMO) confirmed 2023 as the hottest year on record, with ocean heat content reaching its highest levels recorded.[138] Progress on global adaption also remains slow,[139] with shortfalls in means of implementation – both human and financial resources – hindering efforts in capacity-constrained jurisdictions and further enhancing the risk to climate-vulnerable communities.

The ITLOS *Advisory Opinion* illustrates both the vulnerability experienced by SIDS as well as the critical need for clarity on the deep intersectionality of international legal obligations at the ocean-climate nexus, with the Tribunal confirming the deleterious consequences of climate change especially on SIDS, defining the stringent standard of due diligence obligations for combatting climate change impacts and ocean acidification and calling upon States to take measures against damage to the marine environment by anthropogenic greenhouse gas emissions.[140] In parallel, the request by the UN General Assembly for an Advisory Opinion from the International Court of Justice seeks clarity on the obligations of States under international law to protect the climate system and consequences of breach with particular emphasis on SIDS and future generations.[141] Collectively, efforts under international courts and tribunals seek to foster clarity and compliance with international norms and obligations while mobilizing efforts toward enhanced climate ambition and action.

Effective climate laws adopted at the national and regional level play an important function to remove barriers, create institutional frameworks and enable finance flows to be effectively deployed for adaptation and mitigation efforts and to help address loss and damage. Law and governance approaches should be inclusive of women, children and Indigenous People, grounded in the precautionary approach and respect for human rights, rooted in both science and Indigenous knowledge, provide for transparency and access to justice and support the most vulnerable to address the impacts of climate change.[142] Surveyed approaches highlight pathways for establishment of policy approaches, institutional frameworks, building of capacity, protection of indigenous peoples and local communities (IPLCs) and enabling finance flows for adaptation, mitigation and loss and damage.

Emphasis must remain on further development and operationalization of the legal architecture, both internationally and nationally, to enable equitable, inclusive and ambitious climate responses at the ocean-climate nexus.

Notes

1 Jamie Shutler and Andy Watson, 'The Oceans Are Absorbing More Carbon Than Previously Thought' World Economic Forum Report (1 October 2020) <www.weforum.org/agenda/2020/10/oceans-absorb-carbon-seas-climate-change-environment-water-co2; According to the report, evidence suggests that this figure could be higher>.

2 IOC-UNESCO, 'State of the Ocean Report', pilot edition (IOC-UNESCO 2022) <https://unesdoc.unesco.org/ark:/48223/pf0000381921>.

3 Intergovernmental Panel on Climate Change, *Special Report on the Ocean and Cryosphere in a Changing Climate* (IPCC 2019).

4 Freedom-Kai Phillips and Alexandra Harrington, 'Legal Approached towards the Achievement of SDG 14' in W Leal Filho and others (eds), *Clean Water and Sanitation. Encyclopaedia of the UN Sustainable Development Goals* (Springer International Publishing 2022) [Phillips and Harrington]; Sandra Diaz and others, *Summary for Policymakers of the Global Assessment Report on Biodiversity and Ecosystem Services of the Intergovernmental Science-policy Platform on Biodiversity and Ecosystem Services* (IPBES 2019).

5 *United Nations Convention on the Law of the Sea*, 10 December 1982, 1833 UNTS 3, 21 ILM 1261 (entered into force 16 November 1994) [UNCLOS].

6 *Convention on Biological Diversity*, 5 June 1992, 31 ILM 822 (1992) (entered into force 29 December 1993) [CBD].

7 *United Nations Framework Convention on Climate Change*, 9 May 1992, 1771 UNTS 107, 31 ILM 849 (entered into force 21 March 1994). [UNFCCC]

8 *Adoption of the Paris Agreement,* 12 December 2015, Dec 1/CP.21, FCCC/CP/2015/L.9, UNTS No 54113 (entered into force 4 November 2016). [Paris Agreement]

9 Phillips and Harrington (n 4); Freedom-Kai Phillips and Konstantia Koutouki, 'International Law and Marine Ecosystem Governance: The Climate Change Nexus' in Paul Harris (ed), *Climate Change and Ocean Governance: Politics and Policy for Threatened Seas* (CUP 2019). [Phillips and Koutouki]

10 Kojima Chie, 'Integration of General Principles of International Environmental Law into the Law of the Sea: Assessment and Challenges' (2023) 14 Marine Policy 1. [Chie]

11 UNCLOS (n 5), Article 192.

12 ibid, UNCLOS, Articles 194, 207–12; *Request for an Advisory Opinion Submitted by the Commission of Small Island States on Climate Change and International Law*, 21 May 2024, ITLOS Reports 2024, paras 173, 179, 385 [ITLOS Advisory Opinion].

13 *In the matter of the South China Sea Arbitration before an Arbitral Tribunal constituted under Annex VII to the 1982 United Nations Convention on the Law of the Sea (Republic of the Philippines v. People's Republic of China),* Award, 12 July 2016, PCA Case No. 2013–19, para 941 [South China Sea Award].

14 ibid, South China Sea, para 940.

15 UNCLOS (n 5), Article 197; ITLOS Advisory Opinion (n 12), paras 395–399: the tribunal interpreted the standard of the due diligence obligation as 'stringent obligations' given the potentially deleterious effects of climate change and ocean acidification on the marine environment.

16 ibid, UNCLOS at Article 202.

17 ibid, UNCLOS Article 194(1–2), 194(5); South China Sea (n 13) para 943; ITLOS Advisory Opinion (n 12), paras 198–203, 225–226, 243, 245–258, 401–404.

18 CBD (n 6), Article 2; South China Sea Award (n 13) para 945.

19 Chagos Marine Protected Area Arbitration (*Mauritius v. United Kingdom*), Award, 18 March 2015, PCA, Case No.2011–03, p. 128, para 320; ITLOS Advisory Opinion (n 12), paras 403–406.

20 See Chie (n 10) para 3.3; Warwick Gullett, 'The Contribution of the Precautionary Principle to Marine Environmental Protection' in *Frontiers in International Environmental Law: Oceans and Climate Challenges* (Brill Nijhoff 2021).

21 *Agreement under the United Nations Convention on the Law of the Sea on the conservation and sustainable use of marine biological diversity of areas beyond national jurisdiction*, 19 June 2023, A/

CONF.232/2023/4*, Article 17–22, 40–44 [BBNJ]; At the time of publication, the BBNJ Agreement has not yet entered into force.

22 Article 17(c), Annex I(e–h): Indicative criteria for identification of areas includes (f) 'Vulnerability, including to climate change and ocean acidification' among other relevant criteria.

23 Phillips and Koutouki (n 9).

24 CBD, CBD (n 6) Article 1.

25 ibid, CBD, Article 5–6, 8, 14.

26 ibid, CBD, Article 8(j).

27 ibid, CBD, Article 7, 8(a–f), 10–11; ITLOS Advisory Opinion (n 12), paras 404–405: 'habitat' as defined through Article 2 of the CBD, calls on Parties to focus on preservation of depleted, threatened or endangered species as identified in the Convention on International Trade in Endangered Species of Wild Fauna and Flora and linking obligations in the CBD to the ecosystem approach specified in Article 194(5) of the UNCLOS.

28 ibid, CBD, Article 8(m), 16–18.

29 CBD, Decision 15/4: Kunming-Montreal Global Biodiversity Framework (19 December 2022), CBD/COP/DEC/15/4, para 12 (Target 3), 16(a).

30 UNFCCC (n 7) at preamble.

31 ibid, UNFCCC, Article 4.1(d),(e), 4.2(a-c).

32 Christian Nellemann and others, *Blue Carbon: A Rapid Response Assessment* (UNEP GRID-Arendal 2009); C Duarte and others, 'Seagrass Community Metabolism: Assessing the Carbon Sink Capacity of Seagrass Meadows' (2010) Global Biochemical Cycles 24, GB4032.2010; Paul Lavery and others, 'Variability in the Carbon Storage of Seagrass Habitats and Its Implications for Global Estimates of Blue Carbon Ecosystem Service' (2013) 8 PLoS One e73748; Dan Laffoley and Gabriel Grimsditch (eds), *The Management of Natural Coastal Carbon Sinks* (IUCN 2009).

33 *Kyoto Protocol to the United Nations Framework Convention on Climate Change,* 10 December 1997, 2303 UNTS 148, UN Doc. FCCC/CP/1997/7/Add.1 (entered into force 16 February 2005), Article 2, 3.3, 5.1, 7.1.

34 ibid, Kyoto Protocol, Article 12(1–3).

35 ibid, Kyoto Protocol, Article 12(5); See: Project 5265: Oceanium mangrove restoration project (Senegal); restoration conducted on the Sine Saloum and Casamance deltas, on the southeast Atlantic coast of Senegal using CDM Methodology, AR-AMS0003: Afforestation and reforestation project activities implemented on wetlands, version 3.0 (2013).

36 ibid, Kyoto Protocol, Article 12(8–9).

37 Paris Agreement, *supra* note 8, preamble.

38 ibid at preamble, Article 2(a).

39 ibid at Article 3, 4(2, 4).

40 ibid at Article 5(1), 7(5).

41 ibid at Article 9(1–3).

42 ibid at Article 11.

43 ibid, Paris Agreement, Article 6(1–2, 4).

44 ibid, Paris Agreement, Article 6(8).

45 Biliana Cicin-Sain and others, *Toward a Strategic Action Roadmap on Oceans and Climate: 2016 to 2021* (Global Ocean Forum 2016) <https://globaloceanforumdotcom.files.wordpress.com/2013/03/strategic-action-roadmap-on-oceans-and-climate-november-2016.pdf>.

46 UNFCCC, 'Overview of Inputs to the Talanoa Dialogue' (23 April 2018), paras 119, 123, 126, 129 <https://unfccc.int/sites/default/files/resource/Overview%20of%20inputs%20to%20the%20Talanoa%20Dialogue.pdf>.

47 UNFCCC, Decision 1/CP.25: Chile Madrid Time for Action, FCCC/CP/2019/L.10 (2019) para 30–31.

48 Mitchell Lennan and Elisa Morgera, 'The Glasgow Climate Conference (COP 26)' (2022–02) 37(1) The international Journal of Marine and Coastal Law 137–51. [Lennan and Morgera].

49 UNFCCC, 'Joint COP26 Presidency Event – Informal Consultation on Oceans and Climate' (29 June 2021) <https://unfccc.int/sites/default/files/resource/Joint%20COP26%20Presidency%20Event%20Summary.pdf>.

50 Lennan and Morgera (n 48); UNGA Resolution 73/284 United Nations Decade on Ecosystem Restoration (2021–2030) (6 March 2019), A/RES/73/284.

51 UNFCCC, Decision 1/CP.26 Glasgow Climate Pact (8 March 2022) FCCC/CP/2021/12/Add.1, preamble, para 21, 58, 60–61.
52 UNFCCC, Decision 1/CP.27 Sharm el-Sheikh Implementation Plan (17 March 2023) FCCC/CP/2022/10/Add.1, 49–50.
53 UNFCCC, Decision 1/CMA.5 Outcomes of the First Global Stocktake (advanced version) (14 December 2023), paras 33, 35, 55–56, 63, <https://unfccc.int/sites/default/files/resource/cma5_auv_4_gst.pdf>.
54 UNFCCC, Decision -/CP.28/-/CMA.5 Operationalization of the new funding arrangements, including a fund, for responding to loss and damage referred to in paragraphs 2–3 of decisions 2/CP.27 and 2/CMA.4 (advanced version) (14 December 2023); UNFCCC, 'COP28 Agreement Signals "Beginning of the End" of the Fossil Fuel Era', Press Release (13 December 2023) <https://unfccc.int/news/cop28-agreement-signals-beginning-of-the-end-of-the-fossil-fuel-era>.
55 UNFCCC, Decision -/CMA.5 Glasgow–Sharm el-Sheikh work programme on the global goal on adaptation referred to in decision 7/CMA.3 (advanced version) (14 December 2023), para 31.
56 Blomberg, 'Coalition of Philanthropic Funders Unveil More Than $250 Million Ocean Resilience and Climate Alliance to Supercharge Ocean-Based Climate Solutions', Press Release (2 December 2023) <www.bloomberg.org/press/coalition-of-philanthropic-funders-unveil-more-than-250-million-ocean-resilience-and-climate-alliance-to-supercharge-ocean-based-climate-solutions/>.
57 Mangrove Breakthrough, 'The Mangrove Breakthrough Financial Roadmap' (2023) <https://climatechampions.unfccc.int/wp-content/uploads/2023/11/SY031_MangroveBreakthrough_2023_v7_JG.pdf>.
58 Global Fund for Coral Reefs, 'COP28 Coral Reef Breakthrough Launch Event' (4 December 2023) <https://globalfundcoralreefs.org/news/cop28/#:~:text=In%20addition%20to%20mobilising%20greater,conservation%20returns%20up%20to%20%242.5>; LMK Lobe, 'COP28: UNEP Launches Global Targets and Funding to Save Coral Reefs' (4 December 2023) <https://earthjournalism.net/stories/cop28-unep-launches-global-targets-and-funding-to-save-coral-reefs>.
59 The Commonwealth, '"Blueing" the NDCs A Review of the Nationally Determined Contributions of Commonwealth Coastal and Island Countries for Ocean-Based Actions and Commitments' (30 November 2023) <https://thecommonwealth.org/publications/blueing-ndcs-review-nationally-determined-contributions-commonwealth-coastal-island>; Ocean Conservancy, 'Ocean-based Climate Solutions in Nationally Determined Contributions' (June 2030 Update) <https://oceanconservancy.org/wp-content/uploads/2023/11/NDC-Tracker-June-2023-updated-11-21-23.pdf>.
60 UNFCCC (n 7) Article 7.9.
61 Anja Bauer, Judith Feichtinger and Reinhard Steuerer, 'The Governance of Climate Change Adaptation in 10 OECD Countries: Challenges and Approaches' (2012) 14(3) Journal of Environmental Policy & Planning 279–304. See also Mullan Michael and others, 'National Adaptation Planning. Lessons from OECD Countries' OECD Environment Working Papers, No. 54 (2013) <www.oecd-ilibrary.org/environment/national-adaptation-planning_5k483jpfpsq1-en>.
62 Phillips and Harrington (n 4): Selected jurisdictions include: the EU, Philippines, Australia, Niue, New Zealand, Fiji, Seychelles, Tuvalu Antigua and Barbuda, Cook Islands, Mexico, Kiribati, and Vanuatu.
63 Philippines Climate Change Act (2009) Section 2.
64 ibid at 2.
65 ibid.
66 Australia Great Barrier Reef Marine Park Act (1975) Article 1.
67 ibid at Article 2A.
68 Seychelles Environmental Protection Act (2012) Article 15(3).
69 ibid at Article 15 (3)(d) – (h).
70 ibid at Article 15(3)(i).
71 Phoenix Islands Protected Area Regulations 2008 (2008) Article 2.
72 ibid.
73 Sanita van Wyk, 'Climate Change Law and Policy in South Africa and Mauritius: Adaptation and Mitigation Strategies in Terms of the Paris Agreement' (2022) 30(1) African Journal of International and Comparative Law 1–24.
74 Directive 2008/56/EC of the European Parliament and of the Council of 17 June 2008 establishing a framework for community action in the field of marine environmental policy (Marine Strategy Framework Directive).
75 ibid at Article 1(1).

76 ibid at Article 1(2).
77 ibid at Article 1(3).
78 ibid at Article 2; M Gehring, FK Phillips, E Lees, 'The European Union' in J Vinuales and E Lees (eds), *The Oxford Handbook of Comparative Environmental Law* (OUP 2019) 149–70.
79 ibid at Article 2(1).
80 ibid at Article 3(8) (defining pollution as "the direct or indirect introduction into the marine environment, as a result of human activity, of substances or energy, including human-induced marine underwater noise, which results or is likely to result in deleterious effects such as harm to living resources and marine ecosystems, including loss of biodiversity, hazards to human health, the hindering of marine activities, including fishing, tourism and recreation and other legitimate uses of the sea, impairment of the quality for use of sea water and reduction of amenities or, in general, impairment of the sustainable use of marine goods and services").
81 Philippines Climate Change Act (2009) sect 4.
82 ibid at 5.
83 ibid.
84 ibid at 9(f).
85 ibid at 9 (m).
86 'Philippines, National Climate Change Action Plan (2011–2028)', Climate Change Commission <https://climate.emb.gov.ph/wp-content/uploads/2016/06/NCCAP-1.pdf>.
87 Australia Great Barrier Reef Marine Park Act (1975). Article 6–7.
88 ibid at Article 3AA.
89 ibid at Article 3AB.
90 Helen Regan, 'Australia's Great Barrier Reef Suffers Extensive Coral Bleaching as Scientists Fear Seventh Mass Bleaching Even' *CNN* (28 February 2024) <www.cnn.com/2024/02/29/australia/australia-great-barrier-reef-bleaching-intl-hnk-scn/index.html>.
91 Great Barrier Reef Act Article 15(6).
92 Seychelles Environmental Protection Act (2012) Article 15.
93 ibid at Article 15(6) – (8).
94 Kiribati, 'Phoenix Islands Protected Area Conservation Trust Act 2009' (2009) Article 4, 6.
95 Phoenix Islands Protected Area Regulations 2008 (2008) at Article 6(2).
96 ibid at Article 5.
97 ibid at Article 6.
98 ibid.
99 ibid at Article 8(2).
100 ibid at Article 8(3).
101 Africa Group. (2015). Submission by Sudan on behalf of Africa group: Third comprehensive review of the implementation of the framework for capacity building in developing countries under the convention and the Kyoto protocol; See also submission by LDC (2015). Submission by Angola on capacity building.
102 UNFCCC, 'Nationally Determined Contributions under the Paris Agreement Synthesis Report by the Secretariat' 26 October 2022, FCCC/PA/CMA/2022/4.
103 WP Pauw and others, 'Conditional Nationally Determined Contributions in the Paris Agreement: Foothold for Equity or Achilles Heel?' (2020) 20(4) Climate Policy <www.tandfonline.com/doi/full/10.1080/14693062.2019.1635874>; UNFCCC, 'First Report on the Determination of the Needs of Developing Country Parties Related to Implementing the Convention and the Paris Agreement', Executive Summary (Standing Committee on Finance, 2022), para 59, 65 <https://unfccc.int/sites/default/files/resource/54307_2%20-%20UNFCCC%20First%20NDR%20summary%20-%20V6.pdf>.
104 UNFCCC, Marrakesh Accords (2/CP,7, 3/CP,7, 4/CP.7), 21 January 2002, FCCC/CP/2001/13/Add.1; Mizan Khan and others, *Capacity building under the Paris Agreement* (Routledge 2018).
105 UNFCCC, 'Capacity-building' <https://unfccc.int/topics/capacity-building>.
106 UNCTAD, *Building Resilience in Small Island Developing States* (UNCTAD 2022) <https://unctad.org/system/files/official-document/aldcinf2022d2_en.pdf>.
107 UN, 'Report of the Special Rapporteur on the Promotion and Protection of Human Rights in the Context of Climate Change', Ian Fry, 28 July 2023, A/78/255, para 12.
108 Bahamas, 'Climate Change and Carbon Market Initiatives Act 2022', 20 May 2022, para 18(g) <https://faolex.fao.org/docs/pdf/bha211771.pdf>.

109 Uruguay, Law No. 19355 National Budget of Salary Expenses and Investments, Financial Year 2015–2019 (30 December 2015), para 33–34 <www.impo.com.uy/bases/leyes/19355-2015>. [Bahamas, CMIA]

110 Mexico, General Law on Climate Change (amended in 2023), Article 22(XIII-XIV) <https://cdn.climatepolicyradar.org/navigator/MEX/2012/general-law-on-climate-change_59bbc39608493f5839b06d68b399fc06.pdf>. [General Law]

111 ibid General Law, Article 22(XVII) (XIX-XXI).

112 Philippines, 'Administrative Order: Implementing Rules and Regulations of Republic Act 9729' ("Climate Change Act 2009") (20 January 2010), Rule VI, Sec 1(n), Rule IV, Sec 4 <https://cdn.climatepolicyradar.org/navigator/PHL/2010/administrative-order-implementing-the-climate-change-act-2009_003950cfe76892f3936ed0a7a494b01f.pdf> [Implementing Rules and Regulations Act 9729]

113 ibid, Implementing Rules and Regulations Act 9729, Rule X Sec 2.

114 Philippines, 'An Act Establishing the People's Survival Fund to Provide Long-Term Finance Streams to Enable the Government to Effectively Address the Problem of Climate Change' (Climate Change Act 2009 Amendment) (2011), Sec 11 <https://cdn.climatepolicyradar.org/navigator/PHL/2011/an-act-establishing-the-people-s-survival-fund-to-provide-long-term-finance-streams-to-enable-the-government-to-effectively-address-the-problem-of-climate-change-climate-change-act-2009-amendment_6daecc281e82c833dfa8826c13dd6578.pdf>. [Philippines, PSF 2011]

115 UN, 'Indigenous Peoples Disproportionately Impacted by Climate Change, Systematically Targeted for Defending Freedoms', Speakers Tell Permanent Forum, 17th Session HR/5389 (18 April 2018) <https://press.un.org/en/2018/hr5389.doc.htm>.

116 UNFCCC, Decision 2/CP.23 Local communities and Indigenous Peoples platform, 8 February 2018, FCCC/CP/2017/11/Add.1, preamble, para 5.

117 UNFCCC, Decision 2/CP.24 Local communities and Indigenous Peoples platform, 19 March 2019, FCCC/CP/2018/10/Add.1, para 2–3, 9.

118 UNFCCC, Report of the Facilitative Working Group of the Local Communities and Indigenous Peoples Platform, 20 August 2021, FCCC/SBSTA/2021/1, para 21–48.

119 UNFCCC, Decision 16/CP.26 Local communities and Indigenous Peoples platform, 8 March 2022, FCCC/CP/2021/12/Add.2, para 6–10.

120 CY Mulalap and others, 'Traditional Knowledge and the BBNJ Instrument' (2020) Marine Policy 122. [Mulalap]

121 Niue, 6th National Report to the Convention on Biological Diversity, Government of Niue (2020) <www.cbd.int/doc/nr/nr-06/nu-nr-06-en.pdf>

122 Cook Islands, '4th National Report to the Convention on Biological Diversity', Cook Islands Government (2011) <www.cbd.int/doc/world/ck/ck-nr-04-en.pdf>; Cook Islands, Traditional Knowledge Act (No.7 of 2013), Sec 4(1)(viii) (xii–xiii) <https://cook-islands.tradeportal.org/media//Traditional%20Knowledge%20Act%202013%207.pdf>.

123 Mulalap (n 120); T Bambridge (ed), *Legal Pluralism in Polynesian Traditional Management of Resources and Territories* (ANU Press 2016); see: T Bambridge, 'The Law of Rahui in the Society Islands',119–36; C Ghasarian, Protection of Natural Resources through a Sacred Prohibition: The rahui on Rapa iti', 139–54; L Thorax, 'From Traditional to Modern Management in Fakarava', 155–64; J Ruru and N Wheen, 'Providing for Rāhui in the Law of Aotearoa New Zealand' (2011) 120(2) The Journal of the Polynesian Society 169–182.

124 Fiji, Climate Change Act (Act no. 43 of 2021), 24 September 2021, Sec 67(3)(l), https://cdn.climatepolicyradar.org/navigator/FJI/2021/climate-change-act-2021_f6a7919aec964e5973f530d3c4dda566.pdf. [Fiji Climate Change Act]

125 ibid, Fiji Climate Change Act, Sec 27(4)(j), 83(5)(l).

126 Bahamas, CMIA (n 108) Sec 18(1)(e-f).

127 Peru, Ley Marco Sobre Cambio Climatico (Ley No 30754) (2018), Article 23.3 <https://cdn.climatepolicyradar.org/navigator/PER/2018/framework-law-no-30754-on-climate-change_7cf09911ebbf8b694c94a750cb8523b3.pdf>. [Peru, Climate Change Framework]

128 Philippines, PSF 2011 (n 114), Sec 18.

129 ibid, Philippines, PSF 2011, Sec 20–21.

130 Tuvalu, Climate Change and Disaster Survival Fund Act 2015 (No. 11 of 2016), Sec 4–5 <https://cdn.climatepolicyradar.org/navigator/TUV/2016/climate-change-and-disaster-survival-fund-act-2015-no-11-of-2016_2489d680791edb3e52eff44ed9044885.pdf>. [Tuvalu, CCDSFA]

131 ibid, Tuvalu, CCDSFA, Sec 6–7, 13–14.

132 Antigua and Barbuda, Environmental Protection and Management Act 10/2019, Sec 92 <https://cdn.climatepolicyradar.org/navigator/ATG/2019/environmental-protection-and-management-act-10-2019_c539ce172a00270381fb91d9cfa80280.pdf>

133 World Bank, 'Seychelles Launches World's First Sovereign Blue Bond', Press Release No: 2019/066/ENV (29 October 2018) <www.worldbank.org/en/news/press-release/2018/10/29/seychelles-launches-worlds-first-sovereign-blue-bond>.

134 Seychelles, 'Development Bank of Seychelles (Guarantee) (No. 16) Order 2013' <https://seylii.org/akn/sc/act/si/2014/2/eng@2014-01-13>; Seychelles, 'Conservation and Climate Adaptation Trust of Seychelles Act (Act 18 of 2015). Official Gazette' (19 November 2015) Article 4-6 <https://cdn.climatepolicyradar.org/navigator/SYC/2015/conservation-and-climate-adaptation-trust-of-seychelles-act_39fac95867f6bc121862a0f1f043e839.pdf>; Seychelles, 'Public Debt Management Act (Act 32 of 2008)', consolidated version of 2012 <http://www.finance.gov.sc/uploads/files/Act%2032%20of%202008%20Public%20Debt%20Management%20Act%20_0.pdf>; Seychelles, 'Delegation of Authority' (Public Debt Management Order, 2018) (12 January 2018) <https://seylii.org/akn/sc/act/si/2018/2/eng@2018-01-12>.

135 Seychelles, 'Delegation of Authority (Public Debt Management Order, 2020)' (31 August 2020) <https://seylii.org/akn/sc/act/si/2020/114/eng@2020-08-31>.

136 Seychelles, 'Conservation and Climate Adaptation Trust of Seychelles (Amendment) Act 2022' (Act 23 of 2022) <https://cdn.climatepolicyradar.org/navigator/SYC/2015/conservation-and-climate-adaptation-trust-of-seychelles-act_76582152c22744ad9b1b69788688f66d.pdf>.

137 UNEP, 'Emissions Gap Report 2023' (November 2023) <www.unep.org/resources/emissions-gap-report-2023>.

138 WMO, 'State of the Global Climate 2023' (March 2024) <https://wmo.int/publication-series/state-of-global-climate-2023>.

139 UNEP, 'Adaptation Gap Report 2023' (November 2023) <www.unep.org/resources/adaptation-gap-report-2023>.

140 ITLOS Advisory Opinion (n 12), para 122.

141 UNGA, Resolution 77/276: *Request for an advisory opinion of the International Court of Justice on the obligations of States in respect of climate change* (1 March 2023) <www.icj-cij.org/sites/default/files/case-related/187/187-20230630-req-03-00-en.pdf>.

142 UN, 'Report of the Special Rapporteur on the Promotion and Protection of Human Rights in the Context of Climate Change', Ian Fry (28 July 2023), A/78/255, para 68–74.

17

LEGAL AND GOVERNANCE CHALLENGES FOR THE IMPLEMENTATION OF NDCS IN MOROCCO, TUNISIA AND JORDAN

Hassan Agouzoul, Afef Hammami-Marrakchi, Abdelnaser Zeyad Hayajneh, Markus W. Gehring and Gwyneth Boone

Introduction

The Paris Agreement, as discussed in previous chapters, is a 'groundbreaking climate initiative'[1] aiming to stop global temperature increase well below 2°C.[2] One mechanism by which this global effort calls individual participating countries to action is through 'nationally determined contributions'.

Nationally Determined Contributions (NDCs) are a key component of the Paris Agreement. NDCs serve as the primary vehicle by which countries outline comprehensive national climate action plans and their commitments to reducing greenhouse gas (GHG) emissions to address climate change and are thus essential to the success of the Paris Agreement. NDCs include national goals around mitigation (reducing greenhouse gas emissions) and adaptation (addressing the impacts of climate change). The contributions are 'nationally determined', meaning that each country decides what actions it can take as a Party to the Paris Agreement, based on national circumstances, capacities, and capabilities.

NDCs typically include information on a country's emission reduction targets, policies, and the measures the country commits to take to achieve those targets, as well as information on how they plan to adapt to the impacts of climate change. The details of NDCs can vary widely from one country to another. Some countries may pledge absolute emission reductions, while others may commit to reducing the intensity of emissions or increasing the percentage of renewables in their energy output.

Because of the way that the NDCs were integrated within the Paris Agreement, they are not legally binding under international law. Thus, the failure of a participant country to implement their NDC commitments would not put that country in breach of its treaty obligations.

Despite not being substantially legally binding, the NDCs that have been included in the Agreement are procedurally binding.[3] This means that once a participant country ratifies the Paris Agreement, its NDCs become binding insofar as they cannot be revised except by revisions that advance the country's previous NDCs. Thus, each successive NDC should be drafted 'with a view to enhancing to level of [the county's] ambition (known as the "progression" principle)'.[4]

DOI: 10.4324/9781003276678-20

In this way, the Paris Agreement encourages countries to regularly update and enhance their NDCs, with the expectation that successive NDCs will reflect increased ambition over time. Another procedurally binding mechanism of the NDCs is the preparation and communication of successive NDCs every five years, as well as the regular provision of national GHG inventories and information necessary to track progress in countries' implementation and achievement of their NDCs, which encourages communication and transparency in the participating countries.

NDCs are central to the success of the Paris Agreement. 'It is countries' implementation of their NDCs, in the context of support to long-term low-carbon development pathways, that will achieve, or miss, the Paris Agreement's target of well below 2°C global warming'.[5] The first 'global stacking' of the NDCs took place in 2023, and it will follow every five years to determine whether the pledges are sufficient to meet the 1.5°–2°C warming limit set out by the Paris Agreement.[6]

Implementing NDCs can be challenging for many countries, particularly those with limited recourses or those facing economic and developmental constraints. International support and finance mechanisms are therefore crucial to support these countries in meeting their national commitments.

The cases of Morocco, Tunisia and Jordan provide lessons learned from efforts to address the legal and governance challenges of climate change at the national level. Based on recent research and legal assessments, this chapter will offer insights and potential options for structuring appropriate legal, policy, and institutional frameworks at the national level. Based on new analysis by national experts, the chapter will review current legal structures and explore the possibilities for appropriate and legal innovation to enable countries such as Morocco, Tunisia and Jordan to address the mitigation, adaptation, and financial opportunities associated with climate change.

This chapter will canvass the EBRD legal Transition Team's report on progress, potential, and obstacles in realizing NDCs in selected countries.[7] The chapter will begin by highlighting efforts made in Morocco, Tunisia, and Jordan to move their NDCs forward. The key sectors reviewed will include renewable energy, energy efficiency, transportation, agriculture and land-use, and water.[8] Next, the chapter will address the legal, regulatory, and institutional barriers the respective countries face in integrating measures which support climate change adaptation and mitigations and outline recommendations to address these barriers.

The chapter will demonstrate that responsibility for NDC implementation in Morocco, Tunisia and Jordan will require the cooperation of both the public and private sectors toward achieving climate adaptation and mitigation goals. Further, it will highlight strategies for other countries facing barriers in implementing their NDCs and present recommendations to address these barriers.

The EBRD Report focused on the NDCs of Jordan, Tunisia and Morocco. These three countries have built their Nationally Determined Outcomes from pre-existing government climate change actions and therefore already had some level of institutional and legal support in place.[9] Despite the existence of these supports, The ERBD Report found that institutional and legal gaps remain in the NDCs implementation across all three countries, creating barriers to fully realizing the countries' objectives.

The EBRD Report aims to review the laws, regulations, policies, and institutional mandates in the three countries in key sectors, namely those of renewable energy, energy efficiency, agriculture and land use, water, and transportation to understand where the countries must focus their legal reforms if they hope to achieve their NDC objectives.[10]

While certain challenges and required innovations are country-specific, the Report asserts that others can be seen across two or more of the three countries: namely, the lack of transparency in climate change mitigation and adaptation data, limited financial aid and technical capacity, and limited cross-Ministerial and public engagement in climate mitigation and adaptation measures.[11]

Morocco, Tunisia, and Jordan's NDCs have similar legal status.[12] All three countries signed and ratified the Paris Agreement, meaning that the Agreement is part of the law of the three countries in accordance with their respective constitutional frameworks.[13] Prior to signing and ratifying the Paris Agreement, the countries' commitments to the Agreement are understood as intended nationally determined outcomes, or iNDCs, which can be modified. Indeed, Morocco amended and enhanced its NDCs prior to ratification.[14] When the countries sign and ratify the Paris Agreement, their iNDCs become procedurally binding NDCs per the 'no backsliding principle' discussed in this chapter's Introduction.[15]

NDCs submitted by countries under the Paris Agreement then become 'persuasive for initiation, guidance, and interpretation of government policy and standards' and represent 'major development in climate change policy and may guide governments, private financial and other institutions investments'.[16] This is in part because while NDCs themselves are not legally binding, specific commitments under the NDC framework can be, in the form of regulations and by-laws supported by formal institutional mandates. The legality of regulations and by-laws is the case within Morocco, Tunisia, and Jordan and can encourage investment when they are applied.[17]

Morocco

The Kingdom of Morocco is located in the Maghreb region of North Africa. The Kingdom has the sixth-largest economy in Africa and is considered a 'middle income country', meaning that its income per capita lies between those countries designated low- and high-income countries by the World Bank.[18]

Morocco submitted its NDCs to the UNFCCC Secretariat in June of 2015.[19] Morocco's commitments under the Paris Agreement include strong mitigation strategies, such as emission reduction targets and a transformation of the energy sector to increase renewable energy and energy efficiency. Morocco's NDCs also include adaptation goals for 2020 and 2030, though it is unclear whether the country will be able to reach these goals without the financial support of the international community. The total cost of Morocco's NDCs is USD 50 billion, of which USD 24 billion is conditional on international financing.[20] The most expensive goals are also for the most vulnerable sectors, with Morocco projecting a minimum cost of USD 35 billion to integrate adaption programs into the sectors of water, forestry, and agriculture.

Morocco's Clean Energy Transition

After hosting the UNFCCC 22nd Conference of the Parties (COP 22) in 2016 where the Paris Agreement entered into force, the 'highest possible authorities' have been working on the development of application of Morocco's NDCs, with varying degrees of consultation with civil society stakeholders.[21] The Moroccan Competence Centre for Climate Change (4C) has been established to 'build capacity, awareness and engagement across Morocco and regionally on questions of climate change'.[22] The 'Moroccan Energy Security Plan', initiated in 2008, hopes to reduce Morocco's reliance on external energy providers through the energy sector's transition to solar, wind, and hydroelectric power.[23] Governmental authorities have developed national plants to address the effects of climate change with a focus on the energy sector, which will account for 50% of the country's pledged 42% reduction of GHG emissions by the year 2030.[24] The strategies also implicate the agriculture and waste sectors, which account for 9.7% and 13% of the targeted GHG reduction, respectively.[25]

Morocco has committed to 52% installed electricity production capacity from renewable sources by 2030 and is recognized as a regional leader in the development of renewable energy.[26] Despite this leadership, Morocco remains 'energetically vulnerable', since it relies heavily on external energy sources, with over 91% of Morocco's energy needs imported.[27]

In order to improve this energy vulnerability caused by population growth and energy dependency, many of Morocco's climate change goals have been grounded in national renewable energy investment. Researchers in Morocco are studying ways to harness solar, wind, and hydroelectric power, all of which Morocco has strong potential to harness because of its favorable environment, including 3,500 kilometers of coastal area and 9 million hectares of forest.[28] These efforts make up the larger 'Moroccan energy security plan', aimed at reducing Morocco's dependency on foreign energy sources.[29]

Morocco has made significant investments in renewable energy over the past decade. These include the Noor Solar Complex, one of the world's largest solar power facilities, launched in 2016.[30] Morocco has also invested in wind energy projects. The Tarfaya Wind Farm is one of the largest wind farms in Africa, with a capacity of over 300MW. Morocco is also investing in large-scale wind energy, solar farms, and research around hydraulic energy, per the country's NDC.

Morocco has developed a supportive legislative framework and created two new specialized governmental agencies to support its clean energy transition and to encourage private sector involvement in renewable energy development.[31] These agencies are the Morocco Agency for Sustainable Energy (MASEN), responsible for managing sustainable energy in the Kingdom, and the Moroccan Agency for Energy Efficiency (AMEE), responsible for developing and implementing national and sectoral plans to improve energy efficiency in the Kingdom. These institutional actions have attracted investments from domestic and international companies, such as EBRD, who have provided loans up to USD 4.6 million for solar panel installation.

In concert with the broad legislative framework, Morocco has also developed specific legal regimes. The first is Law No. 58–15, launched in 2016, which modified and updated the previous Renewable Energies Law in the country, establishing a legal framework for small-scale renewable energy production and including innovations like increasing the threshold of hydroelectric plants from 12 to 30MW, legally allowing the sale of excess energy production, and opening low-voltage renewable energy markets.[32] These regulations support the broader goals of creating legal infrastructure around the authorization declaration system, allowing energy developers to invest in the supply, sale, and export of electricity produced based on contracts, further encouraging investments in renewable energy.

Morocco's Reduction in Energy Consumption

In addition to its clean energy transition endeavors, Morocco has committed to reducing energy consumption in the country by 15% by the year 2030 and to completely phase out fossil fuel subsidies. The goal of reducing energy consumption by 15% involves several diverse initiatives and regulations. The country's Law No. 47–09 (known as the 'Law on energy efficiency') is the primary legal instrument being used across primary economic sectors, including construction and transportation industries.[33] The law works by laying a foundation for future thermal regulation, introducing energy and energy-wasted reduction mechanisms, and setting minimum efficiency standards that must be met by all equipment sold. It mandates energy audits for companies and institutions involved in the production, transmission, and distribution of energy in the country.

In the construction industry, the government of Morocco has focused on incentivizing energy-efficient buildings by introducing mandatory minimums for energy-efficient performance, Thermal Regulation for Buildings, and by setting minimum energy requirements for all appliances and electrical equipment sold (the 20–20 initiative).[34] In the transportation sector, the government has introduced the National Climate Change Plan, which includes measures to change the fuels used in transportation, encouraging energy-efficient transport (public transit, car-pooling, walking, etc.), the introduction of compulsory technical inspections on cars every year, and issuing a prohibition on the importation of vehicles older than five years.[35]

Morocco has committed to afforest 50,000 hectares of land per year. Motivated by the need to combat deforestation, enhance biodiversity, protect watersheds, and contribute to global climate change mitigation efforts, the High Commission for Water, Forests and Desertification Control aims to achieve 1.5 million new hectares of reforestation by 2030.[36] Morocco's commitment encompasses both reforestation (replanting trees in areas where forests have been lost) and afforestation (establishing forests in areas that were not previously forested).[37]

Morocco's investment in renewable energy has positioned it as a regional leader in clean energy development. The country has hosted international conferences and initiatives on renewable energy and has sought to share its experiences and expertise with other African nations. At the same time, Morocco's NDCs are ambitious, and their success will depend in large part on the participation of governmental bodies, including the Ministry of Agriculture and the Ministry of the Economy of Finance, discussed further in Part 2.

Legal and Institutional Barriers and Opportunities

Implementing Morocco's ambitious NDC faces several challenges despite the country's commendable environmental performance. First, there's the risk of reduced pressure for implementation over time as global attention shifts to other priorities. Second, the Kingdom's administrative culture remains compartmentalized, requiring improved inter-ministerial coordination for ambitious NDC goals. Third, a gap persists between rule-making and implementation due to ongoing issues with the rule of law, exemplified by challenges faced by the newly established Moroccan Police for the Environment. Fourth, regional disparities and incomplete stakeholder ownership hinder the advanced regionalized process that is critical for NDC implementation. Fifth, balancing economic development with environmental preservation is complicated by Morocco's expanding role in Africa, including large-scale projects with potential environmental impacts, like the gas pipeline. Finally, the State Secretariat in Charge of Sustainable Development, housed within the Ministry of Energy, Mines, and Sustainable Development, faces challenges in convening relevant stakeholders due to perceived limitations in influence. Successful NDC implementation will depend on broader ministerial ownership and collaboration beyond the Environment Ministry.

Tunisia

Tunisia, also located in North Africa, has recently adopted a new Constitution which provides 'strong foundations for the elaboration and implementation of the country's NDC'.[38] Despite this constitutional strength and generally peaceful political transitions, the country is still recovering following its 2011 revolution. The country continues to face challenges, including declining economic growth in sectors like investment, revenues, and services, rising levels of unemployment, and other economic barriers. Tunisia is considered a lower-middle income economy.[39]

Tunisia signed the Paris Agreement in April of 2016 and ratified in February 2017. Through ratification, the Paris Agreement entered into the domestic law of Tunisia and has 'a higher value than laws'.[40]

The NDC of Tunisia is not legally binding, having been set up by an Ad Hoc Government Committee at the Ministry of Environment and Sustainable Development, not formally part of the Ministry of Environment.[41] Nevertheless, some elements of Tunisia's NDC have been formalized into domestic law and are already operational.

Tunisia's Mitigation Strategies

Tunisia's NDCs include a commitment to reduce greenhouse gas emissions by 41% below business-as-usual (BAU) levels by 2030. Tunisia aims to achieve this goal through five Nationally Appropriate Mitigation Actions (NAMAs): forestry, cement, electricity, sanitation, and buildings. Tunisia estimates that it can reduce 13% of its carbon intensity through domestic efforts, while the additional 28% will have to come from international support. Tunisia will require a total of USD 17.5 billion in investment in order to support its NDCs' execution.[42]

Tunisia's mitigation measures focus on the most GHG-emitting sectors: energy, manufacturing and waste, and transport, while the country's adaptation measures will focus on the most vulnerable sections: agriculture and water.[43] The NDCs focus on renewable energy resources; energy efficiency; adaptation and mitigation through changes in Agriculture, Forestry and Other Land Use (AFOLU); and water/waste management, including reduction through reforms to water resource management.[44]

Legislative and Institutional Support in Tunisia

Tunisia's NDCs are ambitious. For example, the Tunisian energy sector accounts for 75% of the country's total emissions. Harnessing the emissions reductions promised in Tunisia's NDC mitigation strategy, the carbon intensity from this sector is projected to be reduced by 46% by 2030, compared to 2010.

If Tunisia is to successfully implement these ambitious aims, it will require considerable legislative and institutional support. Fortunately, significant support with several overarching strategies and policies is already in place, as well as sector-specific laws and regulatory frameworks.

In terms of legally binding instruments, three central Tunisian laws exist for the increased use of renewable energy: the Law on Electricity Generation from Renewable Energies of 11 May 2015; the Law on Air Quality of 4 June 2007, and the Law on Energy Management of 2 August 2004, as amended in 2009.[45] While these instruments are a good starting point, Tunisia still lacks a clear national policy framework, as well as the required legal and regulatory framework for the uptake of renewable energy projects.[46]

Tunisia's ambitious aim is to increase the use of renewable energy from 4% (2015) to 30% (2030). This goal is not only important for the execution of Tunisia's commitments under the Paris Agreement but may also help to improve the troubling energy deficit because of a declining fossil fuel reserve.[47]

Another NDC goal for Tunisia is to promote energy efficiency in all sectors, including industrial, building, transport, and agricultural in order to decrease primary energy demand by 30% by 2030.[48] Guided by the Ministry of Industry and Technology (MIT) and the National Energy Efficiency Agency (NEEA), Tunisia aims to implement government measures to facilitate the move to renewable energy and energy efficiency. Unlike the uptake of renewable energy projects, Tunisia has a somewhat comprehensive framework to address promoting energy efficiency.[49] However, the country has still not allocated sufficient funds to support the implementation of increased energy efficiency.[50]

Finally, Tunisia aims to improve the agricultural sector's contributions to mitigation and adaptation as an important priority in their NDCs. Besides Tunisia's commitments under the Paris Agreement, this priority reflects a growing concern around agricultural production and food security, as well as the sustainable development of food and water resources in the country.[51]

Once again, there are several legal and institutional enablers of this priority, namely the Law on Protection of Agricultural Land of 11 November 1983, as amended in 1995 and, more recently, in 2016; Orientation Law on Agriculture of 27 July 2004; Draft Code of Incentives to Investors, and Agricultural Biologic Law of 5 April 1999, which is supported by implementing regulations on Organic Farming and the Plant Protection Act of 3 August 1992. While these laws, as well as Tunisia's Forest Code, all provide opportunities for climate adaptation and mitigation strategies and incentivize the plantation of forests and pastoral tree species, they have not yet been implemented by private actors. Unfortunately, the laws only partially address the objectives outlined in Tunisia's NDCs.

Finally, Tunisia aims to implement water resources adaptation projects to transfer and rescue treated wastewater and to improve and secure the water supplies of large urban centers.[52] Tunisia, like many countries in North Africa and the Middle East, faces significant concerns and challenges regarding water supplies. These concerns are driven by a combination of factors, including increasing water demand, climate change, and limited water resources. Tunisia's new Constitution even includes the right to water for all citizens.[53]

Tunisia's NDCs seeks to 'consolidate and complement relevant policies, regulations and actions by addressing related challenges with regards to water resources, coastal planning and development, agricultural ecosystems, tourism and health.'[54]

Legal and Institutional Barriers and Opportunities

Tunisia faces challenges in achieving its renewable energy targets due to various legal and institutional barriers. These include a lack of transparency, low energy tariffs, complex administrative procedures, and the monopoly of the Tunisian Electricity and Gas Company (STEG).[55] To address these barriers, clear action points, legal reforms, and improved monitoring are recommended. Additionally, subsidies on electricity prices hinder the competitiveness of renewable energies, and there is a need for institutional and budgetary reforms in subsidy frameworks.[56] Administrative procedures for renewable energy are cumbersome and discourage private investment, thus simplification is essential. Furthermore, legal reforms should prioritize transparent processes for tariff setting and establish a truly independent energy authority. The law also restricts independent production of electricity for local consumption, further impeding private development. Additionally, legal ambiguities and low-capacity limits deter international investors. To encourage renewable energy investment, revisions to existing laws and regulations are necessary, along with increased transparency and streamlined procedures.

Jordan

Jordan is situated in the Middle East, and boasts a diverse geography characterized by arid deserts, fertile valleys, and the Dead Sea. Despite its limited natural resources and challenging environmental conditions, Jordan has managed to establish a relatively stable and diverse economy. Jordan is considered an upper-middle-income country.

Jordan submitted its NDC to the UNFCCC Secretariat in September of 2015 and it ratified the Paris agreement in November of 2016. Jordan's NDC was developed with the country's Ministry of Environment and in cooperation with national governmental and private stakeholders. The NDC is a high priority for Jordan, as the country is already suffering environmental degradation and other adverse effects of climate change. While the NDC is not legally binding, it is meant to guide budgetary, policy, and institutional reforms within the country.[57] Further, the Paris Agreement strongly encourages countries who have ratified it to improve and strengthen their legal frameworks to support NDC achievement.

Jordan's Emission Reduction Commitments

Jordan currently amounts to approximately 0.06% of the world's emissions. These emissions are divided across five main sectors: energy including transport, waste, industry, agriculture, and land use, land-use change, and forestry (LULUCF). Per Jordan's NDC, the country has committed to reduce its GHG emissions by 14% before 2030. The commitment is divided into a 1.5% unconditional reduction and a 12.5% reduction conditional on international financial aim and support.[58]

Energy use is the dominant sector for GHG emissions, representing 73% of the total,[59] and the country faces a growing demand for energy. As such, the Jordanian NDC has a focus on energy efficiency and renewable energy projects as its main mitigation focus. Jordan has taken some key decisions in these sectors to encourage international investment, some of which are discussed in the following section.

Jordan's Commitment to Renewable Energy

Jordan has committed to increase renewable energy from 2% overall energy in 2013 to 10% in 2020.[60] This NDC is supported by high-level policy documents including the National Climate Change Policy 2013–2020, which aims to provide 'a holistic nationwide policy with strategic objectives and policies for mitigation and adaptation' and offers frameworks for mitigation strategies. The commitment is also supported by the country's 2025 National Vision and Strategy, which sets a nationwide target of 11% renewable energy to total energy mix by 2025.

Another important legal tool for the implementation of Jordan's NDC is the National Strategy and Action Plan for Transitioning Towards the Green Economy 2016–2025 ('Green Economy Strategy'), which is still under development. The Green Economy Strategy aims to reduce dependence on petroleum and increase renewable energy usage, including solar technology for various facilities like mosques, schools, and industrial sites. Currently, small-scale entities generate 30MW of solar electricity. Additionally, the Green Economy Strategy plans to introduce nuclear power in the near future to diversify the energy mix and stabilize the economy against oil price fluctuations. However, this initiative faces significant opposition due to concerns regarding environmental and safety issues, as well as transparency regarding emergency environmental impact assessments.

Legal and Institutional Barriers and Opportunities

Jordan faces several legal, institutional, political, financial, and practical obstacles hindering the achievement of its renewable energy target. Political instability and the refugee crisis pose significant challenges, impacting the country's ability to take necessary measures for renewable energy expansion. Financial constraints, including chronic budget deficits and dependence on aid, impede the provision of sufficient incentives and infrastructure development. In legal and institutional terms, the Renewable Energy and Efficiency Law (REEL) outlines a complex process for obtaining licenses, potentially discouraging projects.[61] Gaps in investor awareness regarding incentives, complexities in customs duties exemptions, and restrictions on private-to-private transmission further hinder progress. The need for local production of renewable components, while emphasized in NDC, raises concerns about potential trade barriers.[62] Overcoming these challenges requires addressing administrative complexities, enhancing awareness, and conducting thorough assessments to reform and improve Jordanian laws on energy efficiency and renewable energy.

To enhance energy efficiency in Jordan, improved monitoring and enforcement of regulations are crucial. Additional funding mechanisms and financial incentives should be established to mitigate risks for investors and alleviate upfront costs for energy conservation projects. Clear communication with stakeholders and training initiatives, similar to those mandated in the European Union, can facilitate the uptake of financial incentives and promote energy efficiency techniques among installers and builders. Implementing energy performance certificates, alongside training for certifiers and awareness campaigns for building owners and tenants, can provide valuable information and guidance on improving energy performance. Regular inspections of energy-intensive appliances, coupled with market forces driven by higher energy prices, can further incentivize energy efficiency efforts.

Conclusion

The NDCs outlined in the Paris Agreement represent a crucial aspect of global efforts to combat climate change. These contributions serve as the cornerstone for individual countries' climate action plans, outlining their commitments to mitigate greenhouse gas emissions and adapt to the impacts of climate change. While not legally binding, NDCs carry significant weight as a procedural obligation upon a country's ratification of the Paris Agreement, setting a framework for future action and ambition.

The cases of Morocco, Tunisia, and Jordan provide valuable insights into the challenges and opportunities associated with NDC implementation at the national level. Despite their varying socioeconomic contexts and environmental challenges, these countries have demonstrated a commitment to addressing climate change through ambitious mitigation and adaptation measures outlined in their NDCs.

Morocco, for example, has embarked on a clean energy transition, investing heavily in renewable energy projects and implementing supportive legislative frameworks to attract private investment. The establishment of specialized governmental agencies and the enactment of laws promoting renewable energy and energy efficiency signify Morocco's proactive approach to NDC implementation.

Similarly, Tunisia has set ambitious targets for reducing greenhouse gas emissions and increasing renewable energy usage. The country has implemented various laws and policies to support these goals, although challenges remain in terms of administrative complexities and financial constraints.

Jordan faces unique challenges, including political instability and financial constraints, yet remains committed to its renewable energy targets outlined in its NDC. The country has developed strategies and action plans to transition toward a green economy, although legal and institutional barriers must be addressed to facilitate progress.

Across all three countries, efforts to enhance energy efficiency and promote renewable energy are central to NDC implementation. However, achieving these goals requires addressing various legal, institutional, financial, and practical obstacles. Streamlining administrative processes, enhancing stakeholder engagement, and providing financial incentives are essential steps toward overcoming these challenges.

The success of NDC implementation in Morocco, Tunisia, Jordan, and other countries will depend on collaborative efforts between governments, private sectors, and international partners. By addressing barriers and capitalizing on opportunities, these countries can make significant strides toward achieving their climate goals outlined in the Paris Agreement, ultimately contributing to global efforts to combat climate change and build a sustainable future for all.

Notes

1 Arrach Abdeljabbar and others, *'Assessment of Key Policy, Legal and Institutional Mechanisms Required for the Development and Implementation of the Nationally Determined Contributions (NDC): Selected SEMED Countries*' (European Bank for Reconstruction and Development 2017) 6.
2 ibid.
3 ibid 15.
4 ibid 7.
5 ibid.
6 UNFCCC Secretariat, 'Synthesis Report on the Aggregate Effect of the Intended Nationally Determined Contributions' Conference of the Parties 21st Session (30 October 2015) UN Doc FCCC/CP/2015/7.
7 The EBRD, in cooperation with CISDL, the Lauterpacht Centre for International Law at the University of Cambridge, and McGill University, as well as in-country legal experts, conducted a legal research project into legal measures for achievement of the nationally determined contributions in the selected jurisdictions. The outcome report is a by-product of this research project and is intended to inform policy-making moving forward.
8 Abdeljabbar and others (n 1) 8.
9 ibid.
10 ibid.
11 ibid.
12 ibid 8, 22.
13 ibid 16, 22.
14 ibid 22.
15 ibid.
16 ibid.
17 ibid.
18 ibid 72, 73; see also Accelerating Middle-Income Countries' Progress Towards Sustainable Development (Policy Brief No. 155, UN Department of Economic and Social Affairs 2023).
19 ibid 71.
20 Royaume du Maroc, 'Contribution Déterminée au Niveau National – Actualisée' [Nationally Determined Contribution – Updated] (UNFCCC 2021).
21 Abdeljabbar and others (n 1) 72.
22 ibid.
23 ibid 74.
24 ibid.
25 ibid.
26 Royaume du Maroc (n 20); see also ibid at 73.
27 Abdeljabbar and others (n 1) 73.
28 Irene García and Anna Leidreiter, 'A Roadmap for 100% Renewable Energy in Morocco' (World Future Council 2016).
29 Abdeljabbar and others (n 1) at 74.

30 'Noor Solar Power Complex, Morocco' (*Environmental Justice Alliance,* 18 July 2023) <https://ejatlas.org/print/noor-solar-power-complex-ouarzazate> accessed 10 October 2023.
31 Namely, the Morocco Agency for Sustainable Energy (MASEN) and the Moroccan Agency for Energy Efficiency (AMEE, or l'Agence Marocaine pour l'Efficacité Energétique) per Abdeljabbar and others (n 1) 74.
32 Abdeljabbar and others (n 1) at 74–75.
33 ibid 76.
34 ibid 76–77.
35 ibid 77.
36 ibid 78.
37 ibid.
38 The 2022 Constitution enshrines the principle of climate security.
39 'The Situation of Children in Tunisia – Country Factsheet: September 2022' (UNICEF 2022).
40 The 2022 Constitution enshrines the principle of the superiority of approved treaties over domestic law.
41 It's is composed of two special committees relating to adaptation and mitigation created on 7 February 2020
42 Ministry of Environment, GIZ, 2002.
43 ibid.
44 In 2023, Tunisia has adopted a new and ambitious National Ecological Transition Strategy (NETS). Its aims to reduce the heightened threats to its natural resources which are vulnerable to the impacts of climate change.
45 ibid.
46 ibid 53.
47 ibid 50.
48 ibid 56.
49 ibid.
50 ibid 59.
51 ibid 60.
52 ibid 62.
53 Constitution (2022) Article 44.
54 Abdeljabbar and others (n 1) 62.
55 ibid at 53.
56 ibid.
57 ibid at 26.
58 ibid 27.
59 ibid.
60 ibid.
61 ibid at 32.
62 ibid.

18

LEGAL CONTRIBUTIONS TO INCENTIVISING INVESTMENT FOR PARIS AGREEMENT ADAPTATION AND RESILIENCE IN UKRAINE

Oleksandr Diachuk, Mariia Stolbova, Markus W. Gehring and Gwyneth Boone[1]

Introduction

As discussed in the previous chapters, the Paris Agreement was ratified by 195 States,[2] who in so doing transformed their 'intentions' (intended Nationally Determined Contributions, or 'iNDCs') into national action plans (Nationally Determined Contributions, or 'NDCs'). The NDCs are the central mechanism by which global stocktaking can take place on whether the world will meet the Agreement's target of less than 2 °C global warming.[3]

Following the Paris Agreement, the 24th Meeting of the Conference of the Parties (COP 24) to the United Nations Framework Convention on Climate Change (UNFCCC) took place in Katowice, Poland, in December 2018. During COP 24, the States Parties a adopted 'rule book'[4] called the 'Katowice Outcomes', which provides a framework for the implementation of the Paris Agreement.[5] The Outcomes outline how to track national efforts and enhance capacity for adaptation and mitigation measures to climate change.[6]

The Katowice Outcomes represent a 'key milestone' for international sustainable development law by outlining procedure rules around the implementation of the Paris Agreement. The Outcomes also sent a 'signal to investors to take to opportunities outlined in the States' NDCs seriously',[7] allowing investment in line with the goals of the Paris Agreement.

The State Parties' NDCs are directly impacted by the Katowice Outcomes. The Outcomes establish a common set of guidelines for transparency accountability and reporting; clarify the process for the global stockade; provide guidance on how the NDCs should be prepared, communicated and updated and provide flexibility in the formulating and updating of NDCs.

The global stocktake of NDCs is a periodic assessment of the parties' collective progress towards the Paris Agreement goals. 'A Party-driven process conducted in a transparent manner',[8] the stocktake is conducted every five years to inform countries in enhancing their NDCs. The first stocktake took place in 2023. The stocktake aims to update parties on whether the world will meet the Agreement's less than 2°C global warming target.[9]

DOI: 10.4324/9781003276678-21

As States discuss the implementation of their NDCs on market and non-market actors, the Katowice Outcomes shape how decisions to revise the NDCs are made. The report on which this chapter is based, which was drafted prior to the invasion of Ukraine by Russia,[10] provides vital information for how these decisions should be made, including how reporting and transparency mechanisms can help with stakeholder reengagement and in attracting climate finance for 'climate-resilience'.[11]

This chapter focuses on the importance of investment for countries such as Ukraine to set and achieve progressively more ambitious Nationally Determined Contributions to the global response to climate change. It considers the legal and governance reforms and measures that can assist Paris Agreement implementation in aspiring European Union (EU) member states. Based on new research and analysis supported by the European Bank for Reconstruction and Development (the 'EBRD') and the Centre for International Sustainable Development Law (the 'CISDL'),[12] the chapter considers good legal practices from across the EU and analyses appropriate legal, policy and institutional measures to promote investment into climate adaptation and resilience at the national level in Ukraine. The impacts of the war on Ukraine's climate and other law and policy are beyond the scope of the report and chapter, which focus on the Country's valiant experiences prior to the conflict.

By examining the case of Ukraine, prior to the conflict, the chapter offers examples of key challenges implementing the Paris Agreement provisions on mitigation, adaptation and resilience and finance, and identifies potential legal and governance solutions at the national level. By assessing current structures and exploring the possibilities for appropriate legal innovation, the chapter provides recommendations to enable contries Ukraine to address climate change and promote more sustainable development.

The Case Study of Ukraine

The Legal and Institutional Framework to Address Climate Adaptation and Resilience in Ukraine

Ukraine ratified the Paris Agreement on 15 July 2016[13] and committed to taking actions to mitigate climate change and adapt to its impacts. Ukraine's NDCs included a reduction of GHG emissions of at least 40% from 1990, with a focus on improving forest conservation and sustainable land use practices to sequester carbon and protect biodiversity by 2030.[14] These goals are in progress.

In July of 2021, Ukraine submitted an updated NDC to the UNFCCC, updating its 40% target to a more ambitious target of 65% reduction of GHG emissions below 1990 levels. Targeted sectors for these reductions include remodeled buildings, electricity and heat, energy supply, transportation and industry.[15] Emissions from waste and agriculture are expected to stay at 1990 levels. The emission reduction targets cover all economic sectors within Ukraine's current geopolitical boundaries, including currently conflicted territories.[16]

Following the ratification of the Paris Agreement, Ukraine established three key national frameworks to govern its NDCs and climate change action: the Concept for Implementation of State Policy on Climate Change until 2030 (the 'Concept'); the Action Plan to the Concept for implementation of State Policy on Climate Change until 2030 (the 'Action Plan') and the Ukraine 2050 Low Emission Development Strategy (the 'LED Strategy').[17]

The Concept provided a general commitment framework for addressing climate change in the energy, municipal, agricultural and transportation industries.[18] The Concept included an internal system for emissions trading complete with a special authorized body established, monitoring, reporting and verification of GHG emissions and improvements to environmental taxation.[19] Overall, the Concept outlined Ukraine's approach to mitigating greenhouse gas emissions, with less of a focus on adapting to the impacts of climate change and more on transitioning to a more sustainable and low-carbon economy.[20]

The Action Plan is more detailed in terms of concrete steps that must be taken to achieve Ukraine's NDCs, including 49 measures for mitigation and adaptation.[21] Most of the measures involve the development of strategies and are not concrete actions in and of themselves. One such measure is providing for the development and adoption of a full climate change adaptation strategy for the country by 2020, aimed to take effect by 2030.

The Action Plan also contains the 'Low Carbon Development Strategy', which would bring emissions to 66–69% down from 1990.[22] The Action Plan works at the municipal, territorial and national levels to promote the development of adaptation plans, and integrates public-private partnership in climate change action.[23] The Action Plan has been criticized for having various strategies for integration of programs, rather than concrete actions.[24]

There are several notable legal documents governing environmental protection in Ukraine: 1) the Law of Ukraine "On Environmental Impact Assessment" (the 'EIA'); 2) the Law of Ukraine 'On Strategic Environmental Assessment' (the 'SEA'); 3) the Regulation 'On Criteria for Determining Planned Activity, its Expansion and Change, which are not Subject to the EIA' No. 1010; 4) the Regulation 'On Procedure for Conducting Public Discussion while Preparing the EIA' No. 989; and 5) the Regulation 'On Procedure for the Transfer of Documentation to Provide the EIA Conclusion and the EIA Funding and on Procedure for Maintaining the Unified Register on the EIA' No. 1026. Two of the legal documents outlined in the following paragraphs.

The EIA law works on integrating public and private participation in environmental protection. It works by providing a legal procedural framework for company activities that involve construction, reconstruction, re-engineering or liquidation of objects and other activities that are understood as interfering with the environment.[25] In this way, the EIA law is understood as contributing to transparency in climate mitigation decision-making in public and private spheres.

The SEA law provides another procedural framework, this time for the preparation of methods, the creation of advisory bases, the preparation of environmental and ecological assessments and approval documents.[26] Once again, the SEA law is understood as a contribution to transparency in climate mitigation in the country.

The legal status of the implementation of Ukraine's climate change commitments was reviewed in the UNDP's October 2017 Report, 'Incorporation of the recommendations regarding implementation of the UN Framework Convention on Climate Change in Ukraine'.[27]. The report analyzes the policies, programs and legal documents put in place following the ratification of the Paris Agreement and recommendations given in 2015. The report finds that out of 194 recommendations, 72 have been fully or partially implemented, while another 112 recommendations have not been effectively implemented.[28] Across sectors, less than half of the recommendations have been implemented, with the exception of the energy sector, where 13 out of 15 recommendations have been partially or fully implemented.[29]

Lengthy implementation is caused by several factors, outlined in the report. The challenge is that while most of the recommendations at the national level have been built into strategies and plans, these require time and stable leadership for implementation. The report explains that implementation can take anywhere from two to four years to develop and adopt laws, which can be challenging to execute with political turnover and international pressures.[30]

The report explains that several of the climate change initiatives in Ukraine are supported by international donors and institutions. The EBRD, for one, was financing a reform project office with the Ukrainian Ministry of Environmental Protection and Natural Resources and a one-year expert support group project on the implementation of the Paris Agreement with the Ministry of Environmental Protection and Natural Resources.[31] The projects are slowed by barriers including the current conflict after Russian invasion and ongoing national security, concerns, also 'national understanding inertia' around the prioritization of climate change mitigation efforts over adaptation and high economic instability.[32]

Beyond the EBRD, there are other international donors providing support for the development of adaptation plans for cities and villages.[33]

The analysis of Ukraine's current national frameworks and legal tools supporting its NDCs causes several priority sectors of focus to emerge. The first of these is renewable energy, aiming for a consumption to represent 12% of nationwide energy consumption by 2025 and 25% by 2035. Next are the agricultural and food sectors, where adaptation methods will be essential to accommodate the industry within the national plan. There is also a focus on municipal governance and infrastructure and capacity building for climate change adaptation mechanisms in local communities. Finally, waste management infrastructure is targeted through the introduction of recycling programs and the reduction of household and industrial waste production.[34]

Ukraine's NDC Priority Sectors for Sustainable Development Law and Policy

Climate Resilience and Adaptation for the Energy Sector

Ukraine's NDCs prioritize increasing renewable energy generation, from 2% for 2018 to 25% in 2030. This prioritization has led to the institution of key legal regimes in the country. Given Ukraine's historical dependence on fossil fuels, the need to transition to renewable energy and improve energy efficiency transcends all economic sectors in the country.[35]

Progress was made prior to the conflict: the end of 2019 saw the renewable energy market represent almost 13% of the energy sector. 25,000 residential homes in Ukraine are currently using green energy, and 30% of green energy investments in Ukraine are made by foreign direct investments (FDIs). 1433 regulatory acts and green tariffs in the country have helped with this application.[36] In 2020, the new Ukrainian law amended 'some laws in Ukraine regarding the improvement of the conditions for supporting the production of electricity from alternative energy sources', allowing the retroactive protection of foreign investments related to the application of the 'green' feed-in tariff.[37]

Despite the progress, there are issues in the legal and institutional implementation for climate change adaptable and renewable energy. The report explains that one of the most glaring issues is the lack of action plans and roadmaps for the realization of the strategies and plans at the national level, as well as the lack of coordination between ministries and other national bodies.[38] Once again, there is a lack of consistent and strong political pressure to implement these plans and strategies at the national level and across sectors.[39]

Another persistent issue with implementation is the lack of predictability and clarity of the legislation.[40] When the legislation is constantly in a state of flux, securing investors and business planning becomes challenging. For example, despite the feed-in tariff having been implemented in Ukraine in 2009, it was significantly amended in 2014 and then was substituted with tariff auctions in 2020.[41] This continual change creates an opacity around climate change regulation in the country, coupled with a significant increase in the cost of this and similar projects across the energy sector in Ukraine.[42]

The report encourages increasing transparency in the market to help with these issues.[43] Germany can be seen as an example. In 2016, Germany legislated for the transparency of the energy grid through its Incentive Regulation Ordinance (Anreizregulierungsverordnung).[44] Through establishing publication obligations for the regulator and monitoring obligations for the operator, Germany increased visibility and transparency for the energy sector. This transparency could be operationalized in the Ukrainian context through the decision to trade green energy on the Prozorro platform, reflected in the Government Decision No. 1175 in December of 2019.[45] The report suggested that the use of an online platform like Prozorro may lead to more supported and efficient markets and would help institute publication and monitoring obligations on the national energy grid.[46]

Another significant barrier on the green energy transition in Ukraine was how the legislation accommodated different scales of financing. Legislation lacked support mechanisms for small- and medium-scale projects. Further, following the change from fixed green tariffs to the tariff auction system in 2020, all new green projects passed through auctions in order to qualify for state support.[47]

Other difficulties included a rapidly developed 2019 electricity market law that caused malfunctions and debts. The law 'fails to foresee the effective participation in the market of all the participants and lends heavily on public service obligations.'[48] With private sector investment and support of climate project financing being crucial in developing a public-private partnership, 2019 fell short of its aims.

The report suggested several reasons for further cultivating these private-public partnerships. First, the report suggested that 'transparent and reliable' private-public relationships can help to stabilize and clarify the climate for green investments in Ukraine.[49] Further, a 'well-structured public fund' to support these partnerships could act as a 'public finance partner' and help to encourage further private investment. Lastly, the report emphasized the importance of investor protection in the form of bilateral or multilateral investment treaties to encourage investment.

The Ukrainian government sought to support these actions by supporting investment in national adaptation and resilience mechanisms that prioritize climate action.[50] Policies included creating export guarantee schemes and export insurers to incentivize climate action. International law already supports these private-public partnerships, with the World Trade Organization (WTO) Code on Government Procurement allowing governments to establish their own criteria for procurement.[51] The WTO Code supports the Katowice Outcomes, which mandate transparency, enhancing governmental procurement abilities and addressing adaptation and resilience measures.[52]

Recommendations for improving legal and institutional frameworks for climate resilience and adaptation in the energy sector in Ukraine included a critical focus on energy storage units to control the price fluctuation between seasons, improving grid connection and improving Ukraine's energy audits and management regulation. These regulations would needed to be legislated on the national level and be adopted by Ukraine.

For consumers, the task was more focused on diversifying energy sources, both to ensure energy independence and toward decreasing energy consumption. One strategy for these goals would be creating energy 'procumers' (both producers and consumers) by incentivizing energy management systems for households, favorable regulations for households to use green sources like solar panels and using blockchain as a platform for selling electricity and investing in other green processes.

Climate Change Adaptation and Resilience for Agriculture

Agriculture is a key economic sector in Ukraine, with over 70% of Ukrainian territory consisting of fertile lands and the rural population relying heavily on 'smallholder farming'.[53] Significant environmental impacts of climate change on this sector may include changes in soil quality and subsequent reduced harvests and would impact some of the most economically vulnerable Ukrainians.

Climate change impacts Ukraine's agriculture section in a variety of ways. For example, a climate-change induced reduction of water in the southern parts of Ukraine may lead to a loss of upwards of 70% of crops that grow in the Southern regions. Volatile weather may also cause the loss of some crops, leading to threats for small business farming. A lengthening insect activity season may also lead to the decrease of forest and some crops.[54] Suggestions for business and legislative measures in reaction to these threats included the development of water-efficient and weather-resistant technologies for the sector, both of which must be supported by legislative stimulation.

Also of concern was the monopolistic leasing of agricultural land by agri-industrial corporations who tend to over-harvest lands in the short term and do not consider the long-term impacts of their lease. There was discussion in the country to reform these practices and introduce new policies on soil treatment. The report recommends that adaptations for climate change scenarios be integrated into this agricultural reform work.[55]

Research was being done to assess opportunities to reform state policy for the adaptation of the agricultural sector. One of the major bodies doing this research is the Food and Agriculture Organization of the UN, which developed the 'Draft Strategy for Climate Change Adaptation of the Agriculture, Forest and Fish Industries by 2030'. The central concept of the Draft Strategy is the idea of 'climate smart agriculture', with institutional, regulatory, technology and science and stimulation of innovation dimensions. More research was being done by EBRD, which generated 'Support to the Government of Ukraine on updating its nationally determined contribution', with adaptation objectives for the Ukrainian Agricultural sector. Finally, the EU helped to create the 'Clima East' project, which offered a concept of state policy of the adaptation of the Ukrainian agricultural industry.[56]

Climate Adaptation and Resilience in Ukraine's Infrastructure Sector

The Nation Plan discussed earlier enumerated the need to adapt different rural and urban centers to the realities of climate change. Such a strategy would involve evolving directives to local administrative and construction bodies to begin to bring adaptation to the municipal sector. These directives might include adapting buildings to be more efficient with heating and cooling needs, building up a more resilient water supply system for municipalities and creating greener infrastructure like urban forestry, urban and peri-urban agriculture.[57] These goals highlight how essential municipal, local, regional and multi-faceted industry cooperation is for meeting Ukraine's 2030 objectives.

Ukraine's Ministry of Infrastructure aimed to have at least 15% of electric cars on the road by 2020, as well as development and financial stimulation to continue to increase usage and production of electric cars by 2033. Despite this aim, the Ministry encountered issues in implementing the relevant regulations in urban areas where public transportation is often privatized and administered by for profit-entities. Despite these challenges, Ukraine was successful in securing financing from public, private and international sources to support this goal, which promised to be the initial foundations on which to build.[58]

Ukraine had also developed a 'National Strategy on Waste Management until 2030'. Waste was one of the key sectors on which the country is focusing its efforts. In 2016, Ukraine households produced 11 million tons of waste, equivalent to approximately 9 thousand hectares of landfills. The National Strategy plans to create approximately 800 waste stations by 2030, reduce household waste by 55% and create a national registry for waste generation sources. The legal barriers with the model were highlighted. First, the environmental inspection agencies, historically used to control business rather than protect the environment, were unbalanced with their control power, and a rebalancing of legal and regulatory intervention was recommended to ensure they did not become subject to corruption. Second, the environmental tax was recommended to be refocused and refined to make sure that it was squarely directed at environmental protection. Finally, there a lack of business models available for waste management was identified.

Recommendations to Develop the Strategy for Climate Change Adaptation Resilience in Ukraine

Despite the responsibility to draft the country's climate change adaptation strategy falling on Ukraine's Ministry of Environmental Protection and Natural Resources, the strategy due to lack of resources this was not yet fully completed when the war began. Meanwhile, the Ministry was also tasked with developing Ukraine's second set of NDCs and developing effective carbon budgets and sectoral policies and measures for different economic sectors and recommendations about sustainable investment goals. Additional challenges included compliance, enforcement and implementation in Ukraine, with experts citing a lack of knowledge, urgency, consistency and expertise in the field. It was therefore recommended that the Ukrainian government seek assistance internationally for best adaptation practices.

The ERBD contributed a project, titled 'Support to the Government of Ukraine on Updating its Nationally Determined Contribution (NDC)', which was funded by the Swedish International Development Agency (SIDA) and was implemented by the Institute for Economics and Forecasting of the National Academy of Sciences of Ukraine.

Ukraine had undergone extensive legal and institutional development in the decade before the conflict, toward incentivizing adaptation and resilience. Although there were still challenges and gaps, it was possible to envision a future of scaled-up investment in climate change adaptation and resilience under Ukraine's NDCs.

Legal and Institutional Recommendations

This section analyzes some international legal innovations and good practices as inspiration to incentivize potential routes to climate adaptation and mitigation in Ukraine. It addresses the prioritization of climate adaptation and resilience; accountability and oversight mechanisms; transparency and reporting frameworks; accessing and managing climate finance and strengthening the engagement of non-governmental stakeholders.

Prioritization of Climate Adaptation and Resilience

Prioritization of climate adaptation and resilience had begun to increase across Ukraine, especially through political commitment to climate adaptation. This prioritization can be done through different mechanisms. National plans and policies could include clearer and stronger policies around adaptation and resilience. The law needed to fully implement these policies and rid themselves of detrimental gaps. This prioritization had already begun, with the Ukrainian Law 'On the Core Principles (strategy) of the State Ecological Policy of Ukraine for the Period till 2030',[59] which confirmed the country's commitment to its Paris Agreement obligations around emissions reduction and climate change adaptation. It did so by stimulating companies to reduce GHG emissions, reduce energy and resources intensity and maintaining environmental conditions of the Ukrainian climate system that do not pose risks to human health, well-being or the environment.

Despite these first steps, there was a broad scope of work on adaptation in legislation that remained to be done. The report suggested the example of the United Kingdom's (UK) regulatory reform processes and Climate Change Act 2008 as an international comprehensive tool addressing these issues.[60] Specifically, the UK's integration of a 'climate change checklist' in this legislation was considered potentially instrumental in ensuring that adaptation and resilience are taken into account when drafting laws across sectors.

Accountability and Oversight Mechanisms

Next, accountability and oversight mechanisms needed to be established to ensure a uniformly applied and responsive system of regulation and development. These mechanisms were recommended to include and be responsible to sub-national governmental actors and multi-faceted industries, so as to be effective. Laws are thus required to establish the coordination and oversight systems necessary in order to achieve national targets.

The report suggested that Ukraine could create 'coordination working groups' on climate change across sectors and within regional state administrations. France offered an example of how these working groups might look, with the 2019 French Law on Energy and Climate having created a 'High Council for Climate Chapter IIBIS'. As an independent body, the High Council is made up of 12 members appointed to five-year terms for their scientific, technical and economic expertise in the fields of climate and ecosystem management, the reduction of GHG emissions and adaptation and resilience to climate change.[61] The High Council shares similarities with the Climate Change Committee in the UK. These kinds of independent councils can facilitate transparency and inter-sector communication.

Denmark offered another example of how working groups might look, having established a national task force with specific expertise in local adaptation and resilience issues. This task force produced adaptation and resilience, as well as early warning tools, including a notable web-based mapping of weather patterns for various time horizons, allowing adaptation, flooding and erosion specialists to provide the Danish Environmental Protection Agency and Coastal Authority with support and guidance in preventative and adaptation solutions to changing weather patterns.[62]

Transparency and Reporting Networks

Progress had been made in establishing more effective communications and reporting on climate change adaptation and resilience. Still, Ukraine must establish regulations for sectorial and cross-cutting monitoring, reporting and verification (MRV) systems and improve communication between levels of government on data collection and reporting.

Germany has addressed some of these communications problems through legal and governance reform. Specifically, the German Federal Environment Ministry is obliged to produce an annual report under the Climate Action Programme entitled the 'Climate Action Report', which primarily contains mitigation information. The information is then incorporated by Germany's Federal Economic Ministry in its annual report on energy transitions. The information in these reports is consulted extensively and ultimately used to create new legal obligations. It offered an illustrative example for Ukraine to consider, should this one day be possible.

Accessing and Managing Climate Finance

Ukraine had worked toward accessing and managing climate finances through meeting the conditions of access to the Adaptation Fund and the Green Climate Fund. Specifically in the area of electric vehicles, discussed in a previous section, Ukraine had been successful in securing both public and private investment from international sources. These efforts, pervade more sectors, including the energy sector, to make sure that they would be well positioned to apply for and receive further climate financing and investment.

Once again, Denmark provides an example with their public 'Storm Council', a body appointed by the Business Minister of Denmark, that provides insurance for floods and major incidents and disasters by uniting stakeholders through innovation toward a common goal. The Council works by deciding 'whether a storm surge has taken place. The Council also handles cases involving compensation following flooding from waterways and lakes. In addition, the Council makes decisions in cases concerning subsidies for reforestation after storms'.[63] Pay-outs from the body are financed by a storm tax which constitutes a small part of fire insurance payments for homes. The Danish example highlights the importance of combining efforts from central government, local government and private insurance actors to be able to provide fair compensation for losses in the event of damage. These institutions will become increasingly important for natural disasters, especially those related to climate change.

Another example comes from the City of Toronto adopting the Climate Change, Clean Air and Sustainable Energy Action Plan in 2007. It aims to measure the increased risk to vulnerable urban populations and people working outdoors by 'Urban Heat Islands', a phenomenon that occurs when infrastructure absorbs and retains heat. The City has taken steps against this phenomenon, doubling the tree canopy and incentivizing further tree planting on private land through initiatives like the 'Eco-Roof Incentive Program', which funded over 100 green and cool roofs on buildings across the city. These examples may be worth considering, should such laws and policies be advanced again in the future.

Strengthening the Engagement of Non-Government Stakeholders

Lastly, Ukraine could harness its experience with engaging non-Party stakeholders across local, regional and national levels. Ukraine had success in this form of engagement before in the development of their sustainable transportation infrastructure, as these measures were successful among both individuals and local government systems.[64] This stakeholder engagement was a challenge for Ukraine both in climate adaptation and resilience. NGOs in the country have been actively engaging, but there was hesitation from the private sector to become involved, as many Ukrainian companies saw these measures as the government's responsibility.

Once again, Germany provides an illustrative example on how to stimulate this kind of engagement. When Germany established its Scientific Expert Council in 2019, several government ministries helped to bring together different stakeholder engagement. This stakeholder engagement is now enshrined into the Federal Climate Act 2019.[65] The Act, at Section 9, determines that the federal government seek public consultation at regular intervals from federal states, municipalities, business associations and civil society organizations as well as science platform climate protection and scientific advisory bodies of the government. In this way, business accusations are very involved as public consultees in the German climate program decision-making process. It would be to Ukraine's advantage once possible to begin a similar process of uniting public and private stakeholders and ensure that the public has the information to understand the critical nature of the issue.

Conclusion

Under the Katowice Outcomes, implementation of NDCs under the Paris Agreement involves coordinating laws, regulations and policies at the national and sub-national levels. As the report demonstrated with the case study of Ukraine, prior to the Russian invasion, this coordination could happen, and when gaps exist, they could be identified and addressed across states and systems. Innovative solutions and sharing successful measures internationally can allow these gaps to be filled and systems improved.

In the case of Ukraine, sector-specific barriers and opportunities for improvement of climate adaptation and resilience has been identified. The national analysis revealed that there are several common cross-sectoral legal and institutional barriers to achieving climate adaptation and resilience.

Notes

1 The authors would like to thank Adv. Alina Sviderska for her valued insight and support in the drafting of this chapter. The report and study shared were, as noted, completed before the war, and this chapter is provided as a record of experience should peace and re-building begin one day.
2 'Paris Agreement: Status of Ratification' (*United Nations Climate Change*) <https://unfccc.int/process/the-paris-agreement/status-of-ratification>.
3 Alina Syiderska and others, 'Legal Assessment of Paris Agreement Implementation to Mobilize Investment in Climate Adaptation and Resilience: International Law Review with Survey of Good Practices and Country Study of Ukraine' (European Bank for Reconstruction and Development 2020) 10.
4 ibid 9.
5 'The Katowice Climate Package: Making the Paris Agreement Work for All' (*United Nations Climate Change* 2018) <https://unfccc.int/process-and- meetings/the-paris-agreement/paris-agreement-work-programme/katowice-climate-package> accessed 18 October 2023.
6 Syiderska and others (n 3) 11, Table 2.
7 ibid 17.
8 'Global Stocktake' (*United Nations Climate Change*) <https://unfccc.int/topics/global-stocktake?gclid=CjwKCAjwp8OpBhAFEiwAG7NaEuQ1CViTG6_2S92-nRQ2EDU_SXzaAendnWVYew0yypT9dHGgu3HQ8hoChzgQAvD_BwE> accessed 18 October 2023.
9 Syiderska and others (n 3) 10.
10 See generally ibid.
11 ibid. 11.
12 See generally, ibid.
13 ibid 39.
14 ibid.
15 'CAT Climate Target Update Tracker: Ukraine' (*Climate Action Tracker*, 31 July 2021) <https://climateactiontracker.org/climate-target-update-tracker/ukraine/#:~:text=On%2031%20July%202021%2C%20Ukraine,%2D%2064%25%20below%201990)> accessed 20 October 2023.
16 ibid.
17 ibid 40.
18 Syiderska and others (n 3) 40.
19 ibid.
20 ibid.
21 33 of the measures are aimed at climate change mitigation, and 16 are aimed at adaptation.
22 Approved by the Ukrainian Cabinet of Ministers in 2018.
23 Syiderska and others (n 3) 40.
24 ibid.
25 ibid.
26 ibid.
27 Olga Maruschevska and Maksym Mordan, 'Incorporation for the Recommendations Regarding Implementation of the United Nations Framework Convention on Climate Change in Ukraine' (UNDP 2017).
28 Syiderska and others (n 3) 42.
29 ibid.
30 ibid 43.

31 EBRD, 'Support to the Government of Ukraine on Updating its Nationally Determined Contribution: Executive Summary for Policy Makers' (European Bank for Reconstruction and Development 2021).
32 Syiderska and others (n 3) 43.
33 Voice of Nature, 'Climate Change Adaptation Plan for Orlovka' (Climate Forum East 2015).
34 Syiderska and others (n 3) at 44.
35 ibid 45.
36 ibid.
37 Про внесення змін до деяких законів України щодо удосконалення умов підтримки виробництва електричної енергії з альтернативних джерел енергії (Відомості Верховної Ради (ВВР), 2020, № 50, ст.456) [On Amendments to Some Laws of Ukraine Regarding the Improvement of the Conditions for Supporting the Production of Electricity from Alternative Energy Sources (Information of the Verkhovna Rada (VVR), 2020, No. 50, Article 456)].
38 Syiderska and others (n 3) 46.
39 ibid.
40 ibid.
41 Galyna Trypolska, 'Support Scheme for Electricity Output from Renewables in Ukraine, Starting in 2030' (2019) 62 Economic Analysis and Policy 227.
42 Syiderska and others (n 3) 47.
43 ibid.
44 ibid.
45 ibid.
46 ibid.
47 ibid 48.
48 ibid.
49 ibid 49.
50 ibid.
51 ibid 50.
52 ibid.
53 ibid 55.
54 ibid 56.
55 ibid.
56 'Development of National Economic Policies for Rural Adaptation to Climate Change in Ukraine' CEEF2016–083-UA (CEEF2016–083-UA, Clima East 2017).
57 Syiderska and others (n 3) 60.
58 ibid.
59 Про Основні засади (стратегію) державної екологічної політики України на період до 2030 року (Відомості Верховної Ради (ВВР), 2019, № 16, ст.70) [On the Core Principles (strategy) of the state ecological policy of Ukraine for the period till 2030 (Information of the Verkhovna Rada (VVR), 2019, No. 16, Article 70)].
60 Syiderska and others (n 3) at 67.
61 ibid 69–70.
62 ibid 70.
63 ibid at 74.
64 ibid at 78.
65 Federal Climate Change Act of 12 December 2019 (Federal Law Gazette I, p. 2513), as last amended by Article 1 of the Act of 18 August 2021 (Federal Law Gazette I, p. 3905) (Germany).

19

LEGAL AND GOVERNANCE RESPONSES TO LOSS AND DAMAGE IN BANGLADESH AND ZAMBIA

M. Hafijul Islam Khan and Pamela Towela Sambo[1]

Introduction

Climate-related events, such as floods and cyclones and the slow-onset processes like sea-level rise and desertification, are resulting in loss and damage all over the world.[2] The 2018 Special Report on Global Warming of 1.5°C by the Intergovernmental Panel on Climate Change (IPCC) stated that economic and non-economic losses and damages associated with climate change are increasing gradually, especially in Small Island Developing Countries (SIDs) and Least Developed Countries (LDCs).[3] Moreover, the IPCC AR6 Working Group II (2022) report warns that existing financial, governance and institutional arrangements are insufficient to comprehensively address current and projected losses and damages, especially in the most climate-vulnerable parts of the world.[4]

In 2022, at the 27th Conference of Parties in Egypt (CoP 27), parties established funding arrangements including a Loss and Damage Fund at the global level to respond to loss and damage that goes beyond adaptation.[5] Further, a transitional committee developed some recommendations to operationalize the Fund and funding arrangements, which were adopted at CoP 28 in 2023.[6] The Loss and Damage Fund will provide financial resources in responding, to economic and non-economic loss and damage associated with the adverse effects of climate change, within the context of ongoing and ex-post approaches to address loss and damage, including rehabilitation, recovery and reconstruction.[7] A board established at CoP28/CMA5 works further to operationalize the fund, while several countries pledged over 700 million USD to contribute to the fund.[8]

Despite these international efforts, the reality is that loss and damage have imposed additional legal and governance challenges for LDCs like Bangladesh and Zambia at local, national and regional levels. The cases of Bangladesh and Zambia, as two of the countries most vulnerable to climate change, present opportunities to investigate this reality of loss and damage and to identify these at the national level. This chapter assesses the current state of governance structures and explores the potential appropriate legal innovations to enable Bangladesh and Zambia to deal with loss and damage associated with climate change impacts.

DOI: 10.4324/9781003276678-22

Climate-Related Loss and Damage

'Loss and damage' refers to the negative consequences that arise from the unavoidable risks of climate change, such as rising sea levels, prolonged heatwaves, desertification, the acidification of the sea and extreme events, such as bushfires, species extinction and crop failures. These effects cannot be mitigated and adapted. As the climate crisis unfolds, these events will happen more frequently and with increasing severity, resulting in an increase in 'irreversible losses (i.e. loss of human life, species, land to rising seas) and damages of significant economic cost (i.e. destroyed infrastructure)'.[9] Climate change-related sudden-onset events, such as floods, cyclones and sudden collapse of riverbanks, as well as more gradual slow-onset processes, such as sea level rise, salinization, coastal erosion, changing rainfall patterns and drought, cause significant losses and damages to communities. Despite implementing strategies to cope with climate change impacts, many vulnerable communities have reached their limits in adapting to climate change, incurring significant losses and damages. Loss and damage are understood as impacts induced by climate change which individuals, families and their communities can neither cope with nor adapt to.[10]

Loss and damage that cannot be avoided can be categorized as causing either economic or non-economic losses and damage. Economic loss and damage are those that can be accounted for in formal accounting processes.[11] Non-economic loss and damage (NELD) are intangible, difficult to process and put a financial value to such losses.[12] NELDs are often not accounted for in formal accounting process and often left unaddressed. In terms of nature, it is comparatively easy to understand and address economic loss and damages like damage to property and damage to infrastructure. However, it is difficult to understand, assess and address non-economic loss and damage.[13] For both economic and non-economic loss and damage assessment, there is a need for appropriate tools and methods, which the Executive Committee of the Warsaw International Mechanism for Loss and Damage is currently developing.

Climate mitigation, adaptation and loss and damage exist on a continuum. Adequate mitigation can avoid the potential risk of the future loss and damage, and effective adaptation measures can minimise the scale of loss and damage resulting from climate impacts.[14] However, inadequate mitigation and adaptation measures have already caused unavoidable loss and damage, which must be addressed with ongoing and ex-post approaches like rehabilitation, recovery and reconstruction. In situations where the impacts of climate change are particularly extreme or rapid, such as the southwest coastal belt of Bangladesh, and where populations are especially exposed to these impacts, fundamental changes to a social-ecological system may be needed.[15] Transformation therefore refers to the altering of economic, social, technological and political attributes within a system, such as the change in value systems that can happen when shifting to other locations in the form of collective resettlements, altered legislative and governance structures, financial institutions etc. For successful transformation to take place, planning for transformational approaches should include early consultation with and participation of stakeholders, including the host communities where such transformation adaptation is likely to take place, as well as the relocated population most likely to shift to the new locations.[16] All arguments, including ethical implications, must be carefully considered to avoid irreversible costs.

Overview of Loss and Damage in Bangladesh

Bangladesh is particularly vulnerable to the combined impacts of sea level rise, increased rainfall variability, frequent and extreme cyclones and changes in runoff patterns in the Ganges-Brahmaputra-Meghna delta.[17] Climate change impacts are thus a major concern for the low-lying deltaic floodplains. Future climate projections for Bangladesh indicate that annual precipitation is expected to rise by 5.6% and 9.7% by 2050 and 2100 respectively, with drier winter periods and intense summer rainfall.[18] Under a low-emission scenario, average annual temperatures in Bangladesh could rise by less than 2°C, or exceed 3°C under a high-emission scenario;[19] when combined with an increase in annual sea level rise of 27 cm and 62 cm, this could see an increase in the areas flooded by a further 10 and 20% respectively, increasing the total area exposed to higher levels of salinity and flooding.[20] These will have serious implications: Future losses and damages incurred by Bangladesh are expected to be higher, with extreme events increasing in intensity, frequency and duration.

As a result of the aforementioned climate change impacts, Bangladesh is at risk of many economic and non-economic losses and damages. Regarding economic loss and damage, agriculture, which is a key source of income in Bangladesh, is at risk.[21] Bangladesh also faces many non-economic losses and damages due to climate change impacts, including loss and damage to socio-cultural features, health and education. For example, extreme weather events such as cyclones, flooding, droughts and sea-level rise have consistently been reported to have affected health of the communities in Bangladesh. Storm surges from cyclones and sea-level rise have increased salinity in groundwater and pond water used by coastal communities for drinking, exposing coastal communities to increased levels of salinity.[22] Health professionals are increasingly seeing evidence of (pre)-eclampsia and gestational hypertension in pregnant women in the southern coastal belt, and these have been found to be associated with drinking saline water.[23]

Extreme weather events may also contaminate drinking water with sewage, increasing the transmission of infectious disease, skin diseases, kidney diseases and waterborne diseases.[24] Conversely, people in drought-prone areas increasingly suffer from dehydration and heat stroke, especially among the elderly and children.[25] According to Andrei et al. (2015) and Umma et al. (2011), deterioration of drinking water sources has increased insect pest infestation diseases in livestock, affecting food security in the region. Food consumption along with food-purchasing capacity are also reduced because of drought. Furthermore, a decline in water quality has led to a greater risk of waterborne diseases in both humans and cattle in the affected areas.[26]

Climate impacts are also impacting children's education in Bangladesh. Cyclones, floods and sea-level rise damage school infrastructure, disrupting educational activities and affecting children's education.[27] In situations where schools are used as shelters during disasters, both primary and secondary school students are left with no education for a considerable period of time. Schools which do remain open have other difficulties; access to school is further impeded for children and teachers alike due to damaged roads and bridges. Further, loss of teaching materials, school furniture and other teaching equipment also make it difficult for teachers and students to return to school. Extreme events damage school infrastructure and repair takes a long time, delaying reconstruction of the water supply and sanitation facilities, causing inconvenience for the children – girls in particular are discouraged from attending schools as a result. Moreover, damaged infrastructure leaves children exposed to physical harm from unstable buildings.[28]

Apart from injuries, emotional distress from lack of access to food, loss of shelter and loss of loved ones often bar children from participating in educational activities.[29] Many children are displaced or migrate with their families after disasters, leaving behind friends, while others become involved in income-earning activities and are thus unable to concentrate further on their education. Many children who do join school often continue to work in the mornings and attend school in the afternoon. As a consequence, children with poor school attendance or poor academic performance eventually drop out of school. In extreme situations, children end up becoming the sole income-earning members of their family, resulting in their dropping out of school and education altogether.[30] After becoming displaced, many children drop out of school because they cannot afford to pay for education-related expenses.[31] Climate change has also had an impact on underage marriage in Bangladesh.[32] The aftermath of disasters sees an increase in child marriages, especially for girls.[33] Fearing the loss of all their material wealth (homes/land/agricultural produce/cattle), families marry off their underage daughters, forcing many girls to drop out of school.

Overview of Loss and Damage in Zambia

Africa is projected as the hotspot of 'vulnerability to the adverse impacts of human-induced climate change'.[34]

Zambia is a Sub-Saharan African country with a land area of 752,614 square kilometers, though only 34 percent of the land is effectively used for agriculture. The country consists mostly of plateau with an elevation between 950 meters to 1500 meters above sea level. It has a population of about 20 million people, of which 65% live in rural areas. Climate change impacts in Zambia have permeated agriculture, human health, wildlife and essentially the entire economy. Zambia, as a party to the UNFCCC, Kyoto Protocol, Paris Agreement and other regional instruments on climate change (such as the SADC Protocol on Environmental Management for Sustainable Development), has made efforts to forestall the negative effects of climate change.

Zambia is already experiencing various severe impacts of climate change, including loss of human life and significant loss of biological diversity. As of 29 February 2024, the drought situation in the country has been declared a national disaster and emergency pursuant to the Disaster Management Act, No. 13 of 2010. The drought, precipitated by climate change, has had 'devastating consequences on many critical sectors such as agriculture, water availability, and energy supply, risking [our] national food security and livelihoods of millions of [our] people'.[35] The result is that the entire economic fibre of the country is at stake. Specific climate impacts include

> a huge decrease in agricultural productivity, a significant increase in the deaths of wild animals, a flooding of some parts of the country, a decrease in tourism, dried out rivers, the risk of Victoria Falls to dry out, and an increased spread of diseases such as malaria due to the increasing number of mosquitoes.[36]

As of 16 April 2024, approximately 900 million United States dollars is required to provide emergency 'life-saving' relief to 6.6 million Zambians who are adversely affected by the current drought disaster and emergency.[37]

Research has shown that climate change has had a serious impact on farm yields and requires land and labor adjustments to prevent losses in wealth in most of rural Zambia. As of 2021, it was projected that climate change impacts in Zambia would slow the development process and cost the country approximately USD 13.8 billion loss in GDP. The Government of Zambia has integrated climate change concerns in its policies, programmes, plans and strategies to support a low-carbon and climate-resilient development pathway and the attainment of the middle-income status envisioned in the country's Eighth National Development Plan and Vision 2030.

Legislation and Institutional Arrangements for Addressing Loss and Damage

Mechanisms for responding to climate change are varied and can include legislation, regulations, policies and decrees that refer specifically to climate change; or that relate to reducing energy demand, promoting low-carbon energy supply, tackling deforestation, promoting sustainable land use, sustainable transportation or adaptation to climate. In this vein, some relevant laws and policies in climate change mitigation and adaption in Bangladesh and Zambia are briefly discussed.

Climate Change-Related Legislation, Policies and Institutional Arrangements

Bangladesh

Bangladesh prepared a National Adaptation Plan of Action (NAPA) in 2005[38] to address the adverse impacts of climate stimuli, including climate variability and extreme events, and to promote sustainable development. The NAPA process has been advanced through the adoption of the Bangladesh Climate Change Strategy and Action Plan (BCCSAP) of 2008 (reviewed in 2009), which provides the climatic context, considers socio-economic realities and outlines policies and programmes based on broad areas of intervention.[39] The BCCSAP was formulated to streamline the activities to combat climate change.

Loss and damage are implicitly covered in the BCCSAP, under different programmes. For example, the Strategy proposes responses necessary for livelihood protection in ecologically fragile areas and the protection of livelihoods of vulnerable socio-economic groups to ensure equitable and sustainable development. In some cases, the activities are aimed at providing protection for the loss of employment, income and property from various sources to persons, households and enterprises through devising an effective insurance system by the government.

The BCCSAP 2009 proposed an institutional framework for implementation strategies and actions as an integral part of national development policies, plans and programmes, including strengthening existing institutions. The Climate Change Unit (CCU) established under the MoEF facilitates the implementation of the BCCSAP under the overall guidance of the National Environment Committee chaired by the Prime Minister and the National Steering Committee on Climate Change headed by the Minister of the MoEF. The BCCSAP also highlighted the need for cooperation across sectors by identifying the need for climate change focal points in all relevant ministries.[40]

The Bangladesh Climate Change Trust Fund (BCCTF) was established under the Trust Fund Act 2010 to support climate change-related projects in Bangladesh.[41] Bangladesh submitted its Intended Nationally Determined Contributions (INDCs) to UNFCCC in 2015 and recently reviewed it in 2021, which proposed a 5% unconditional reduction in GHG emission from Business as Usual (BAU) scenarios by 2030 and a 10% conditional reduction in GHG emission with support from the international community starting in 2011.[42] Bangladesh also adopted a National Adaptation Plan (NAP) in 2022 for the years 2023–2030, with an underlying objective of reducing risks and vulnerabilities to climate change impacts in Bangladesh.[43] The Government of Bangladesh also developed the NDC-NAP implementation framework; within this framework, Bangladesh can minimize the potential risk of loss and damage. Other policies which may address loss and damage include the Bangladesh Delta Plan, 2100, Mujib Climate Prosperity Plan, the climate-inclusive updated National Environment Policy, 2018 and the updated Standing Order on Disaster, 2019. However, there remains a need for a comprehensive national loss and damage plan of action with adequate institutional structures.

Zambia

At present, there is no climate change-specific legislation in Zambia; a draft Climate Change Bill has been under discussion for a considerable period of time. Such legislation would strengthen the coordination of the climate change response by enhancing the regulation of carbon markets, including ensuring environmental integrity and benefit sharing in the proceeds of the carbon markets with local communities. Further, the legislation would facilitate the establishment of a climate change fund which would support national climate change mitigation and adaptation programmes and projects.

Policies regarding loss and damage must precede the enactment of the climate change legislation. As a result of this procedural requirement, the National Policy on Climate Change (NPCC) of 2016 is currently undergoing review and will likely project the Ministry of Green Economy and Environment as the focal point for all climate change matters in the country.

The NPCC of 2016, developed to contribute to the achievement of the overall objective of the UNFCCC, which Zambia signed on 11 June 1992 and ratified on 28 May 1993, provides the country's integrated national response to climate change. It has made great efforts towards addressing fragmentation in handling climate change issues in sector-specific policies, strategies and plans. The NPCC 2016 seeks to promote and strengthen adaptation measures, sustainable land-use management practices, climate change mainstreaming into policies, strategies and plans and promotes investment in climate-resilient and low-carbon development pathways.

Environment-Related Legislation and Institutional Arrangements

Bangladesh

The Ministry of Environment and Forests and Climate Change (MoEFCC) is responsible for environmental management at the national level, including the formulation and monitoring of environmental policy and legislation, and controlling all executing agencies like Department of Environment (DoE), Forest Department (FD), Bangladesh Forest Research Institute, Bangladesh Forest Industries Development Corporation and Institute of Forestry and Environmental Sciences. Further, it coordinates other inter-ministerial (e.g. water, industrial, transport, mining etc.) environmental issues.

The FD works as an executing agency for the protection, control, conservation, expansion and maintenance of the national forest resources. Its administrative and managerial units are divided according to particular divisions, ranges and best-level areas in the national forest. The National Environmental Council is organized and chaired by the Prime Minister. It functions through an Executive Ministerial Committee headed by the MoEFCC and a Divisional Environment Committee headed by the Divisional Commissioner. The MoEFCC is primarily responsible for environmental protection (SACEP, 2002). Thus, legislative and institutional frameworks exist in Bangladesh to address loss and damage caused by environmental injury, which provide the opportunity to also address loss and damage associated with climate change. However, these need to be amended to incorporate specific provisions on climate change impacts and the associated vulnerabilities, including how to address loss and damage resulting from climate vulnerabilities.

Article 18A of the Constitution of Bangladesh guides Bangladesh's environment and climate change-related regulatory regime,[44] as well as three additional pieces of legislation. The Bangladesh Environment Conservation Act 1995 (ECA)[45] is Bangladesh's primary environmental legislation. The ECA contains provisions on environmental harm,[46] including the narrow possibility of taking into consideration the harm caused by climate change. The Environmental Conservation Rules, adopted in 1997 and updated in 2023, provide detailed rules for addressing environmental harm.[47] In addition, environmental courts, established by the Environmental Court Act of 2010, have heard disputes regarding legislation regulating water, forest, agriculture, fisheries, energy, industry and transport in Bangladesh. The Biodiversity Act, adopted in 2017,[48] and the Water Act of 2013 may also address loss and damage related to biodiversity and ecosystems. However, these recourses provide narrow redress and are unlikely to be accessible to many affected communities.

Zambia

Despite the absence of climate change-specific legislation, the Constitution of Zambia, Amendment Act No. 2 of 2016, Water Resources Management Act, 2010, Environmental Management Act, 2011 and the Forest Act, 2015, make some reference to climate change.

Article 257(g) of the Constitution obliges the State to establish and implement mechanisms that address climate change, providing a constitutional basis upon which appropriate measures can be implemented for purposes of addressing climate change effects in the country.

According to its preamble, the purpose of the Water Resources Management Act is to, *inter alia*, 'create an enabling environment for adaptation to climate change', whereas the forest domestication provision of the UNFCCC is the conservation, preservation and sustainable management of forests.

The Environmental Management Act 2011 ('the EMA, 2011') is the framework environmental legislation in the country and provides integrated environmental management, protection and conservation of the environment and the sustainable management and use of natural resources. Section 9(2)(g) of the EMA obliges the Zambia Environmental Management Agency (ZEMA) to 'research or sponsor research on the effects of climate change on human beings and the environment'. In addition, section 41(1)(d) of the EMA, 2011 obliges the Minister and the relevant authority to prepare guidelines for the management of environmental emergencies, including natural and climate change related to disaster such as floods, cyclones, droughts and major pest infestations or the introduction and spread of invasive alien species.

There has been a recent legislative attempt to introduce at least three climate change-specific provisions into the EMA, 2011 via the Environmental Management (Amendment) Act No. 8 of 2023 (the 'Amendment Act, 2023'). The three new provisions are important in ensuring that the country's NDCs are manageable and to increase predictability in the process of accounting for loss and damage.

First, the Amendment Act, 2023 defines 'green economy' in the context of environmental management in Zambia as:

> an economy that allows for low carbon emission, resource efficiency and social inclusiveness, resulting in improved human well-being and social equity while significantly reducing environmental risks and ecological scarcities.[49]

The inclusion of 'green economy' shows, in a practical way, that the obligations under the UNFCCC are being streamlined into all sectors of the country's economy. In specific reference to the central thesis of this chapter, low carbon emission monitoring, coupled with improved human well-being and social equity, lie at the core of loss and damage.

Secondly, Section 6 of the parent legislation provides principles governing environmental management. Curiously, none of the 12 itemized principles specifically allude to climate change management in the country. It is therefore progressive that Section 3 of the Amendment Act, 2023 introduced the need to integrate 'low carbon emissions, resource efficiency and social inclusiveness' in development programmes, creating a foundation for developing and supporting Zambia's efforts to set and achieve progressively more ambitious NDCs.

Thirdly, the Amendment Act, 2023 provides several environmental-focused roles for ZEMA, including mandating that it, in collaboration with an appropriate authority, mainstream green economy and environment in national planning.[50]

Disaster Management-Related Legislation and Institutional Arrangements

Bangladesh

The Government of Bangladesh (GoB) has achieved significant success in reducing climatic disaster-related casualties. In doing so, over time it has moved away from the earlier concept of responding post-disaster to the more cost-effective approach of pre-disaster mitigation and preparedness. The Standing Orders on Disaster Management (SODMs) was adopted in 2010 and updated in 2019, outlining the responsibilities of the government vis-à-vis rehabilitation, resettlement and disaster management in Bangladesh.[51] The latest SODMs adopted in 2019 by the Ministry of Disaster Management and Relief (MoDMR) are influenced by Sendai Framework for Disaster Risk Reduction (SFDRR), 2015–2030. MoDMR is also developing a Plan of Action to Implement Sendai Framework for Disaster Risk Reduction (SFDRR), 2015–2030, which recognizes that 'climate change has the potential to exacerbate the frequency and intensity of disasters that is adversely jeopardizing the assets and majority of livelihood segments and thus the wellbeing of the millions of people'.[52]

Within the government, the MoDMR has been assigned as the national focal point for loss and damage associated with sudden-onset events. This leaves behind slow-onset processes, and no institutional arrangement for addressing slow-onset processes. Some of the greatest loss and damage is expected to be caused by slow-onset processes.[53] The MoDMR is mandated to drive national risk reduction reform programmes to address disaster management issues. The ministry's responsibility is to reduce the risk of people, particularly the disadvantaged and vulnerable, from the effects of natural, environmental and human-induced disasters/hazards and to manage an efficient emergency response system.

The Disaster Management Act of Bangladesh (DMA),[54] adopted in 2012 (DMA, 2012), marked an important shift in recognizing climate change-induced loss and damage as within the ambit of the definition of disaster. It was passed to facilitate a more coordinated, objective-driven and stronger disaster management system.[55] The DMA aims at setting up an institutional mechanism for disaster management, reducing vulnerabilities, rehabilitation and providing humanitarian assistance to the victims of both disasters and climate change impacts.[56] The DMA also established the National Disaster Management Council to formulate policy and strategy on disaster management and to provide and implement guidelines on disaster management.[57] In addition, it envisaged the establishment of a Department of Disaster Management to implement the strategies of disaster management.[58] The Disaster Management Fund, also established under the DMA, operates at both national and district levels and is utilized to support disaster management efforts and provide humanitarian assistance to affected people.[59]

The DMA allows a person or organization negatively affected by a disaster to sue for compensation from a person or organization responsible for this disaster before a competent court in accordance with the Civil Procedure Code. The court will determine the amount of compensation to be paid and pass the order on accordingly.[60] However, this provision needs to be elaborated and further rules or guidelines adopted on the assessment of loss and damage, determination of compensation and liability for related loss and damage. Nevertheless, the DMA is considered an important legal milestone in that it recognizes loss and damage associated with climate change as a consequence of disaster and the linkage between natural and climate change-induced disaster (Ibid., s. 2). The Act has been adopted very recently and needs to be applied in practice through the suggested institutional arrangements.

Zambia

The Disaster Management Act, No. 13 of 2010 provides the legal basis for the existence of the national disaster management structure and policy. As shown earlier in this chapter, this legislation has facilitated the declaration of the 2024 drought situation as a national disaster and emergency. The Disaster Management Act empowers DMMU to mobilize resources under emergency situations and to compel all partners to provide information to DMMU for effective coordination and leadership. It is mandatory for line ministries, industries and organizations to give priority to installation of minimum standards of preparedness. In order to implement these policy measures, the Government shall review and harmonize laws and regulations at the local level and review and adopt/sign or domesticate sub-regional, regional and international conventions that facilitate effective disaster management. It is noteworthy that the provisions of the Disaster Management Act do not specifically address climate change-related disasters; however, the National Disaster Management Policy, 2015 (currently under revision), makes specific reference thereto.

The Policy document provides for the 'need to build resilient and adaptive communities in order to withstand the effects of climate change"' Some of the activities designed for achieving this include community-based awareness and education programmes on climate change issues; reduction of community vulnerability to climate variability and change; and empowering communities to manage and reduce disaster risks from climate variability and change by giving them access to necessary information and services.

The institutional arrangements for the National Disaster Management Regime are designed by the Disaster Management Act read together with the National Disaster Policy, 2015. The overall responsibility for national disaster management shall remain with the Office of the Vice-President, while the implementation of disaster management activities and programmes in the country shall be done through the Disaster Management and Mitigation Unit (DMMU). The DMMU shall exercise its responsibilities through the National Disaster Management Council, Disaster Management Technical Committee and appropriate broad-based committees at Provincial, District and Satellite levels.

The National Disaster Management Council is chaired by the Vice-President, with the Minister of Defence being the Vice-Chairperson. This is the supreme policy-making body for nationwide disaster management in the country and consists of other part-time members who are presidential appointees.

Innovative Governance Approaches

This section analyzes some of the innovative governance approaches towards addressing the effects of climate change in Bangladesh and Zambia.

Risk Management Approaches

The Warsaw International Mechanism (WIM) has compiled a compendium of Comprehensive Risk Management approaches from five geographical regions from 349 case studies and technical reports to address the economic and non-economic loss and damage associated with the extreme weather events and slow-onset events.[61] According to the UNFCCC, the Comprehensive Risk Management (CRM) framework is a combination of tools and measures that seeks to avoid and minimize loss and damage, build long-term resilience for vulnerable communities, reducing vulnerability where possible and supporting vulnerable communities where loss and damage are unavoidable. Under the CRM framework, approaches to address loss and damage include assessing the risk; reducing the risk; retaining the risk; transferring the financial risk; and transformational approaches to build back better.[62]

Innovative Approaches in Bangladesh

Addressing loss and damage incurred from slow-onset processes and extreme events would require a good understanding of the climatic events and patterns, as well as implementation of long-term policies. The existing policies and institutions developed for reducing the risk of disasters, disaster management and minimizing climate impacts though climate change adaptation. But these actions are not nearly enough to address the multitude of losses and damages expected in the future.

The government of Bangladesh has launched the Mujib Climate Prosperity Plan ('the Plan'). The Plan shifts Bangladesh's recent trajectory from one of vulnerability to one of resilience. One of the Plan's principal aims is to maximize resilience with loss and damage financing through Mujib locally led adaptation hubs, including by increasing gender responsiveness, strengthening the digital economy, enhancing financial protections and expanding Bangladesh's green economic partnerships. Additionally, the Plan is aiming to promote well-being and traditional living to take advantage of 21st-century technologies together with inherently sustainable traditional lifestyle practices and living. Such an innovative approach in the long run is expected to address slow-onset processes of climate change as well as many of the non-economic losses and damages stemming from climate change.

The newly formulated NAP released in 2022 offers a multilevel, inclusive institutional structure based on the existing institutional framework, conforming with horizontal and vertical links to carry local adaptations towards the national level and vice versa. The NAP enforces adoption of this multilevel structure for better use of existing institutional arrangements. As such, adaptation-related scopes of work, roles and responsibilities will be defined and integrated into the existing organogram and mandated under the proposed policy regime. The National Environment Council (NEC), headed by the Honourable Prime Minister of the Government of the People's Republic of Bangladesh, provides necessary oversight of the implementation of the National Environment Policy. Furthermore, the National Technical Advisory Committee (NTACCC) will play a key role in coordination, communication and engagement within the MoEFCC, MoP, MoF, ERD and other sectoral ministries addressing many of the previous siloed characteristics of the ministries and departments which prevented coordinated planning and action from taking place.

Innovative Approaches in Zambia

Some innovations include the Constituency Development Fund (CDF), cited as an example of a system that could facilitate the disbursement of international climate finance. CDF is a fund designed by the Zambian Government to address community needs for sustainable development projects, first established in the country in 1996. Each of the country's 156 constituencies submit plans for building projects, economic empowerment schemes and skills training programmes, with approved plans receiving a part of the US$1.5million allocated to each constituency as at 2024.

In research addressing the question of how the CDF can be shaped to harness external investment in climate-related sustainable development projects, it has been shown that 'the CDF offers great promise as a new development policy for Zambia'. This is possible, subject to recommendations broadly related to:

(i) optimizing the CDF's processes;
(ii) enhancing monitoring and evaluation;
(iii) strengthening governance and inclusion; and
(iv) maximizing impact and additionality.[63]

Further, the Zambian Securities and Exchange Commission (SEC) has introduced the option of issuing green bonds to finance businesses activities that have environmental benefits.[64] The emergence of green bonds as a platform for raising funds for projects with environmental advantages is part of the larger notion of green financing as a new financing mechanism to address climate change;[65] as of the end of 2023, the country's inaugural green bond had been issued to the Copperbelt Energy Corporation.[66] The Government of the Republic of Zambia has pledged to facilitate green financing by creating an enabling policy and regulatory framework to promote innovative financing for climate change interventions. For instance, in the 2022 and 2023 national budget speeches, the government explained undertakings on the promotion of green bonds, carbon trading and enactment of climate change legislation to facilitate the establishment of a National Climate Change Fund.[67]

Looking Forward: Recommendations for Further Research

In research conducted through a structured review of existing literature, series of deliberative dialogues, key informant interviews and consultations with representatives of affected communities and countries in least developed countries (LDCs) and Small Island Developing States (SIDS), the authors concluded that there is urgent need to develop national and sub- national level strategies and action plans to address loss and damage risks.[68] The research made the following key findings:

(i) Actions to address loss and damage must be implemented urgently and at scale, alongside adaptation actions.
(ii) Loss and damage risks are multidimensional and demand a comprehensive approach;
(iii) The losses and damages that disproportionately impact marginalized groups and people living in poverty must be prioritized;
(iv) Addressing loss and damage effectively requires a layering of measures;
(v) Addressing loss and damage requires a locally led, whole-of-society approach.[69]
(vi) Addressing loss and damage by accessing appropriate technical and financial resources.

In order to address these findings, the authors recommend that:

(i) Act now to address loss and damage risks using available approaches and sources of finance.
(ii) Take a pragmatic approach that is grounded in the multidimensional and intersectional risks of the marginalized groups and people living in poverty who are most at risk from climate impacts in the Global South.
(iii) Prioritize the losses and damages that affect those who are most at risk.
(iv) Recognize the multidimensional, intersectional and dynamic nature of loss and damage risks.

(v) Develop comprehensive strategies and action plans to address loss and damage risks that layer complementary measures.
(vi) Support highly vulnerable countries and communities to assess their loss and damage risks using robust approaches.

Further, methods, tools and guidelines to assess multidimensional loss and damage risks in disaggregated ways that take the evolving climate and other scenarios into account do not exist and must therefore be developed. Such approaches must ensure that they integrate robust data on the multidimensional and intersectional vulnerabilities and exposure of marginalized groups and people living in poverty. They must integrate an assessment of the likelihood that avoidable loss and damage risks will transform into unavoidable residual risks and identify the triggers or warning signs that indicate when the limits to adaptation are being reached or breached. Developing such tools must be a priority for the international community and research institutions.

Finally, it is important to note the various different ways to evaluate loss and damage when considering future research and issues. According to Van der Geest, there are a number of scientific, technical and normative ways of evaluating loss and damage which help in developing policy, including technical, legal, climate science and human rights-based approaches.[70] For example, a legal perspective places importance on establishing norms and helping to adjudicate in an orderly and transparent fashion when disputes arise. Discussions about compensation for loss and damage tend to be dominated by scholars and practitioners with a legal perspective. A financial and economic perspective focuses on the impacts of climate change on economic performance, cost-efficiency and cost-benefit analyses of different measures to avoid loss and damage and the cost of dealing with losses and damage that have not been or cannot be avoided. Conversely, non-economic perspectives underscore the lack of attention for loss and damage to entities that are not commonly traded in markets, such as identity, trust, belonging, social cohesion, traditional knowledge, cultural heritage, landscapes and ecosystems. These issues are not well-expressed in monetary terms but are of vital importance to society and may be damaged or lost as climate change unfolds. A non-economic loss and damage perspective is about values, about what matters for different types of actors.

Conclusion

A country case study of Bangladesh can be helpful in understanding the nature of loss and damage and the policy needs of vulnerable communities and national governments. This country-level needs assessment as a bottom-up approach can provide policy guidance not only for national governments but also regional and international governance structures for loss and damage. Within this bottom-up approach, this chapter attempts to understand the scientific, socio-economic, socio-ecological, and socio-legal aspects of loss and damage and sustainable development challenges in Bangladesh. It further identifies the right approaches and financial, technical, and capacity supports needed for the vulnerable communities and government of Bangladesh to deal with loss and damage and to promote sustainable development. With that understanding of the nature and required approaches for addressing loss and damage, this chapter identifies the legal and governance challenges for the government of Bangladesh through assessing the current state governance structures and further explores appropriate and innovative legal and governance structures for Bangladesh to deal with loss and damage associated with climate change by accessing required technical and capacity building supports and the financial resources.

Regarding Zambia, there is an urgent need to enact climate change-specific legislation, with a national fund for loss and damage. It is possible in this regard to utilize the Environment Fund under the EMA, as it is yet to be operationalized and would be best suited to climate-specific innovations in the country. Alternatively, the Forest Act makes provision for carbon credits, as does the Mines and Minerals Act. These funds could be coordinated under the umbrella of the Ministry of Green Economy and Environment for purposes of climate loss and damage. Addressing loss and damage incurred from slow-onset processes and extreme events would require a good understanding of the climatic events and patterns as well as implementation of long-term policies. The existing policies and institutions aim to reduce the risk of disasters, support disaster management and minimize climate impacts through climate change adaptation. But these actions are not nearly enough to address the multitude of losses and damages expected in the future. The future may not actually be too distant in this instance, because the 2024 declaration of a national disaster and emergency has already shown the extent of loss and damage that must be anticipated and therefore needs urgent and structured mechanisms. As the drafting process of the country's first-ever climate change legislation is on course, it is anticipated that these observations will be taken on board and actualized.

Considering the scale and scope of loss and damage facing both countries, robust and multi-layered laws and policies are urgently required.

Notes

1 The authors would like to thank Ms. Lydia Young (JD 2023, UVic) for her assistance in drafting and editing this chapter.

2 Laurens M Bouwer, 'Observed and Projected Impacts from Extreme Weather Events: Implications for Loss and Damage' in Reinhard Mechler and others (eds) *Loss and Damage from Climate Change: Concepts, Methods and Policy Options* (Springer 2019).

3 IPCC, *Global Warming of 1.5°C. An IPCC Special Report on the Impacts of Global Warming of 1.5°C* (Valerie Masson-Delmotte and others eds) (Intergovernmental Panel on Climate Change (IPCC) 2018).

4 IPCC, *Climate Change 2022: Impacts, Adaptation and Vulnerability. Contribution of Working Group II to the Sixth Assessment Report of the Intergovernmental Panel on Climate Change* (H-O Pörtner and others eds) (Intergovernmental Panel on Climate Change (IPCC) 2022).

5 Decision 2/CP.27; decision 2/CMA.4.

6 Decision 1/CP.28; decision 5/CMA.4.

7 ibid.

8 David W South, 'Loss and Damage Fund – Operationalized at CoP28 but Funding and Allocation Process Unresolved' (2024) 40(7) Climate and Energy 29.

9 Kees van der Geest and Koko Warner, 'Editorial: Loss and Damage from Climate Change: Emerging Perspectives' (2015) 8(2) International Journal of Global Warming 133; Cass R Sunstein, 'Irreparability as Irreversibility' (2017) Supreme Court Review 93; Reinhard Mechler and others (eds), *Loss and Damage from Climate Change: Concepts, Methods and Policy Options* (Springer Nature 2019).

10 Kees van der Geest and Koko Warner, 'Loss and Damage from Climate Change: Local-level Evidence from Nine Vulnerable Countries' (2013) 5(4) International Journal of Global Warming 367.

11 See Yohei Chiba, Rajib Shaw and Sivapuram Prabhakar, 'Climate Change-related Non-economic Loss and Damage in Bangladesh and Japan' (2017) 9(2) International Journal of Climate Change Strategies and Management 166 for examples.

12 See Chiba and others (n 11); James Morrissey and Anthony Oliver-Smtih, 'Perspectives on Non-Economic Loss and Damage: Understanding Values at Risk from Climate Change' (*Loss and Damage in Vulnerable Country Initiative*) <www.lossanddamage.net> accessed May 2014 for examples; see also Olivia Maria Serdeczny, Steffen Bauer and Saleemul Huq, 'Non-economic Losses from Climate Change: Opportunities for Policy-oriented Research' (2018) 10(2) Climate and Development 97.

13 David Frame and others, 'Climate Change Attribution and the Economic Costs of Extreme Weather Events: A Study on Damages from Extreme Rainfall and Drought' (2020) 162 Climatic Change 781.

14 Saleemul Huq, Erin Roberts and Adrian Fenton, 'Loss and damage' (2013) 3 Nature Climate Change 947.

15 UNFCCC, Executive Committee of the Warsaw International Mechanism for Loss and Damage, 'Compendium on Comprehensive Risk Management Approaches' <https://unfccc.int/documents/200759> accessed 17 April 2024.

16 Jon Barnett and others, 'A Science of Loss' (2016) 6(11) Nature Climate Change 976.

17 Masroora Haque and others, 'Towards Establishing a National Mechanism to Address Losses and Damages: A Case Study from Bangladesh' in Reinhard Mechler and others (eds), *Loss and Damage from Climate Change* (Springer 2019); Winston H Yu and others, *Climate Change Risks and Food Security in Bangladesh* (Routledge 2010).

18 IPCC, *Climate Change 2014: Synthesis Report. Contribution of Working Groups I, II and III to the Fifth Assessment Report of the Intergovernmental Panel on Climate Change* (Core Writing Team, RK Pachauri and LA Meyer eds, IPCC); Yu and others (n 17).

19 IPCC 2014 (n 18); Sjouke Philip and others, 'Attributing the 2017 Bangladesh Floods from Meteorological and Hydrological Perspectives' (2019) 23(3) Hydrology and Earth System Sciences 1409.

20 IPCC 2014 (n 18).

21 For a discussion of the impacts of economic loss and damage on agriculture in Bangladesh, see Yu and others (n 17); see also Md Arfanuzzaman and others, 'Evaluation of Adaptation Practices in the Agriculture Sector of Bangladesh: An Ecosystem Based Assessment' (2016) 4(1) Climate 11; see also Asif Anik, Ram Ranjan and Thiagu Ranganathan, 'Estimating the Impact of Salinity Stress on Livelihood Choices and Incomes in Rural Bangladesh' (2018) 30(8) Journal of International Development 1414; see also H Tuihedur Rahman and others, 'Climate Change Research in Bangladesh: Research Gaps and Implications for Adaptation-related Decision-making' (2018) 18(7) Regional Environmental Change 1535; see also Rashedul Islam and Shigeru Tabeta, 'Shrimp vs Prawn-rice Farming in Bangladesh: A Comparative Impacts Study on Local Environments and Livelihoods' (2019) 168 Ocean & Coastal Management 167.

22 Susmita Dasgupta and others, 'River Salinity and Climate Change: Evidence from Coastal Bangladesh' in *World Scientific Reference on Asia and the World Economy* (World Scientific 2015) 205; Mahin Al Nahian and others, 'Drinking Water Salinity Associated Health Crisis in Coastal Bangladesh' (2018) 6(2) Elementa: Science of the Anthropocene <https://doi.org/10.1525/elementa143> (Mahin Al); Paolo Vineis, Chan Queenie and Aneire Khan, 'Climate Change Impacts on Water Salinity and Health' (2011) 1(1) Journal of Epidemiology and Global Health <https://doi.org/10.1016/j.jegh.2011.09.001>; see Susmita Dasgupta and others, 'The Impact of Aquatic Salinization on Fish Habitats and Poor Communities in a Changing Climate: Evidence from Southwest Coastal Bangladesh' (2017) 139 Ecological Economics 128 for a discussion of the increase of salinity and its impacts; see also Nahian and others (n 22).

23 Aneire Ehmar Khan, 'Drinking Water Salinity and Maternal Health in Coastal Bangladesh: Implications of Climate Change' (2011) 119(9) Environ Health Perspect 1328; Kei Asayama and Yutaka Imai, 'The Impact of Salt Intake during and after Pregnancy' (2018) 41 Hypertension Research 1; Mahin Al (n 22).

24 MA Rakib and others, 'Severe Salinity Contamination in Drinking Water and Associated Human Health Hazards Increase Migration Risk in the Southwestern Coastal Part of Bangladesh' (2019) 240 Journal of Environmental Management 238.

25 Rahib Shaw and others, 'Overview Asian Monsoon Drought and Characteristics of Asian Monsoon Drought' (2011) Droughts in Asian Monsoon Region 1–24.

26 Nesar Ahmed, Shirley Thompson and Marion Glaser, 'Global Aquaculture Productivity, Environmental Sustainability, and Climate Change Adaptability' (2019) 63 Environmental management 159.

27 Owasim Akram, Jefarson Chakma and Amina Mahbub, 'Continuing Education in Disaster-affected Schools in Bangladesh: An Evaluation of the Education in Emergencies Project (2012) 22(2) Children Youth and Environments 249; M Shirin, HA Mita, and S Hussain, *Education in Emergency: Exploring Options for Continued Education during Disasters in Bangladesh* (Government of Bangladesh 2014) <https://reliefweb.int/report/bangladesh/education-emergency-exploring-options-continued-education-during-disasters> accessed 18 April 2024.

28 Mary-Laure Martin, 'Child Participation in Disaster Risk Reduction: The Case of flood-Affected Children in Bangladesh' (2010) 31(8) Third World Quarterly, 1357; Shirin and others (n 27).

29 Carolyn Kousky, 'Impacts of Natural Disasters on Children' 26(1) Future of Children 73; Kazi Shahidur Rahman and others, 'Education in Emergency: Exploring Options for Continued Education during Disasters in Bangladesh' (*Government of Bangladesh* 2014) <https://reliefweb.int/report/bangladesh/education-emergency-exploring-options-continued-education-during-disasters> accessed 18 April 2024.

30 Martin (n 28).

31 See Christie McLeod, Heather Barr and Katherina Rall, 'Does Climate Change Increase the Risk of Child Marriage? A Look at What We Know – And What We Don't – With Lessons from Bangladesh and Mozambique' (2019) 38(1) Columbia Journal of Gender & Law 96.

32 Heather Barr, 'Climate Change Is Forcing Bangladeshi Girls into Child Marriage' (*Human Rights Watch* 2015) <www.hrw.org/news/2015/06/09/climate-change-forcing-bangladeshi-girls-child-marriage> accessed 18 April 2024.

33 McLeod, Barr and Rall (n 31).

34 See UNECA/ACPC (2014) 'Loss and Damage in Africa' <https://archive.uneca.org/sites/default/files/PublicationFiles/acpc-loss-and-damage-report_final_en.pdf≥ accessed 20 August 2023 for a list of evidence which has led to this conclusion.

35 Republic of Zambia, 'Presidential Statement on the Declaration of Drought as a National Disaster and Emergency' (2023) <https://estatements.unmeetings.org/estatements/14.0485/20230305140000000/582jnvwNMpIH/stkqtBAAqGrd_en.pdf> accessed 18 April 2024; see also Oxfam International, 'Over Six Million People Face Hunger, Malnutrition and Water Scarcity in Zambia, Oxfam Warns' (*Oxfam* 06 March 2024) Press Release <www.oxfam.org/en/press-releases/over-six-million-people-face-hunger-malnutrition-and-water-scarcity-zambia-oxfam> accessed 18 April 2024.

36 Couroche Kalantary, 'Climate Change in Zambia: Impacts and Adaptation' (2010) 1(2) Global Majority E-Journal 85, 86.

37 Agence France-Presse, 'Zambia Requests $900 Million in Relief for Drought' (*VOA Africa* 17 April 2014) <www.voaafrica.com/a/zambia-requests-900-million-in-relief-for-drought/7573448.html> accessed 18 April 2024).

38 Ministry of Environment and Forest Government of the People's Republic of Bangladesh, 'National Adaptation Programme of Action (NAPA)' (November 2005) <https://acrobat.adobe.com/id/urn:aaid:sc:US:5331a801-b922–48bc-9e98-d9dc2cdb5762> accessed 18 April 2024; see also UNDP, 'Bangladesh National Adaptation Programme of Action (NAPA) Document – November 2005 <www.adaptation-undp.org/resources/bangladesh-national-adaptation-programme-action-napa-document-november-2005> accessed 18 April 2024.

39 Ministry of Environment and Forests Government of the People's Republic of Bangladesh, 'Bangladesh Climate Change Strategy and Action Plan 2009' (September 2009) <https://acrobat.adobe.com/id/urn:aaid:sc:US:7ade5b35-29a1-46ad-9ea9-1639fc163f8e> accessed 18 April 2024.

40 M Shamsuddoha, M Islam, M A Haque, M F Rahman, E Roberts, A Hasemann and S Roddick, 'Local Perspective on Loss and Damage in the Context of Extreme Events' in *Insights from Cyclone-Affected Communities in Coastal Bangladesh. Loss and Damage in Vulnerable Countries Initiative* (UK DFID, 2013).

41 Act No. 57 of 2010, Ministry of Environment, Forest and Climate Change, Government of the People's Republic of Bangladesh.

42 Ministry of Environment and Forest Government of the People's Republic of Bangladesh, 'Nationally Determined Contributions (NDCs)' (August 2021) <https://unfccc.int/sites/default/files/NDC/2022-06/NDC_submission_20210826revised.pdf> accessed 18 April 2024.

43 Ministry of Environment and Forest Government of the People's Republic of Bangladesh, 'National Adaptation Plan of Bangladesh (2023–2050)' (October, 2022) <file:///C:/Users/sky/Downloads/NAP-Bangladesh-2023.pdf> accessed 20 April 2024.

44 The Constitution of the People's Republic of Bangladesh' (Act No. of 1972), Article 18A: The State shall endeavour to protect and improve the environment and to preserve and safeguard the natural resources, bio-diversity, wetlands, forests and wild life for the present and future citizens [accessible at: http://bdlaws.minlaw.gov.bd/act-367/section-41505.html].

45 Act No. 1 of 1995, Ministry of Environment, Forest and Climate Change, Government of the People's Republic of Bangladesh

46 ibid, section (s.) 8 states that any person affected or likely to be affected by pollution or environmental degradation may apply to the Director General of the Department of Environment (DoE) in the manner prescribed by the rules to remedy the damage or apprehended damage; s. 7 outlines the procedures to determine and provide compensation for environmental and ecological harm, including remedial measures for harm done to ecosystems; s. 7 (3) of the ECA outlines the scope of environmental damage assessment and required corrective measures including compensation, stating that the Director General may impose duties upon any specialist and other persons to determine compensation or to adopt corrective measures.

47 SRO No. 197-law/1997 Environmental Conservation Rules, 1997; Ministry Environment, forest and Climate Change, Government of the People's Republic of Bangladesh
48 Bio-diversity Act 2017 (Act No. 2of 2017), Ministry of Environment, Forest and Climate Change, Government of the People's Republic of Bangladesh
49 Section 2, Environmental Management (Amendment) Act No. 8 of 2023
50 Section 4 (a); See Section 4 (b) for a list of ZEMA's legal responsibilities.
51 GoB, SODMs, 2019.
52 MoDMR (2018), Plan of Action to Implement Sendai Framework for Disaster Risk Reduction (SFDRR), 2015–2030. Ministry of Disaster Management and Relief, Government of the People's Republic of Bangladesh.
53 Siegele, 2012.
54 The Act defines disasters as phenomena including natural disasters, manmade disasters or climate change, giving examples such as cyclones and saline water intrusion. The DMA contains a definition of rehabilitation, which includes the rehabilitation of livelihood and repairing of infrastructure. It also includes provisions for the resettlement and planned relocation of those affected if needed after a disaster (Ibid., s. 2[15]).
55 GED, 2015.
56 DMA, 2012.
57 ibid s. 4.
58 ibid s 7(2).
59 ibid s 32.
60 ibid s 49.
61 Warsaw Compendium (n 15).
62 Erin Roberts and Mark Pelling, 'Climate Change-related Loss and Damage: Translating the Global Policy Agenda for National Policy Processes' (2018) 10(1) Climate and Development 4; UNFCCC, 'A Literature Review on the Topics in the Context of Thematic Area 2 of the Work Programme on Loss and Damage: A Range of Approaches to Address Loss and Damage Associated with the Adverse Effects of Climate Change', FCCC/SBI/2012/INF.14 (2012). UNFCCC, 'Compendium on Comprehensive Risk Management Approaches' (2019).
63 Alex Money and others, 'Mobilising Investment for Climate-compatible Growth through Zambia's Constituency Development Fund. Climate Compatible Growth Programme' (*gov.uk* 2023) Working Paper <www.gov.uk/research-for-development-outputs/mobilising-investment-for-climate-compatible-growth-through-zambias-constituency-development-fund> accessed 18 April 2024; see also <www.smithschool.ox.ac.uk/news/how-can-climate-finance-help-shape-loss-and-damage-projects-zambias-innovative-development> accessed 23 September 2023.
64 Genesis Analytics & Bourse Consult, 'Zambia Capital Markets Development Master Plan – Draft Final Market Assessment Report' (10 January 2020) <www.seczambia.org.zm/wp-content/uploads/2020/05/Market-Assessment-Report-2019–1.pdf> accessed 18 April 2024.
65 Chris Mfula, 'COP28: Zambia's First Green Bond to Be Issued by Year-end by Copperbelt Energy Corp' (*Reuters* 5 December 2023) <www.reuters.com/sustainability/cop28-zambias-first-green-bond-be-issued-by-year-end-by-copperbelt-energy-corp-2023-12-05/> accessed 18 April 2024.
66 Copperbelt Energy 'CEC Announces Registration of Zambia's First Green Bond' (5 December 2023) <https://cecinvestor.com/cec-announces-registration-of-zambias-first-green-bond/>.
67 Mumbi Mulenga, 'Green and Sustainable Finance in Zambia – Part 1' (*Moira Mukuka Legal Practioners* 26 January 2022) <www.moiramukuka.com/green-and-sustainable-finance-in-zambia/#:~:text=Green%20bonds%20have%20been%20developed,sustainable%20agriculture%20and%20forestry%20> accessed 18 April 2024; see also '2023 Budget Address by Honourable Dr. Situmbeko Musokotwane, MP, Minister of Finance and National Planning Delivered to the National Assembly' (30 September 2022) <www.parliament.gov.zm/sites/default/files/images/publication_docs/2023%20Budget%20Speech.pdf> accessed 18 April 2024.
68 Simon Addison and others, 'Addressing Loss and Damage. Practical Insights for Tackling Multidimensional Risks in LDCs and SIDS' (*International Institute for Environment and Development* 2022) Working Paper IIED <http://pubs.iied.org/21046IIED> accessed 29 August 2023.
69 ibid.
70 van der Geest and Warner (n 9).

PART 4

Compliance and Implementation of the Paris Agreement through International Legal Innovation

20

OPERATIONALIZING THE PARIS AGREEMENT IMPLEMENTATION AND COMPLIANCE COMMITTEE (PAICC)

Christina Voigt[1]

Introduction

The Parties drafting the Paris Agreement recognized the importance and necessity of creating an implementation and compliance mechanism which would contribute to the Agreement's effectiveness. At the same time, there was a strong desire amongst Parties to ensure that the Agreement, and any resulting compliance mechanism, retained respect for state sovereignty.[2] As a result, through Article 15 of the Paris Agreement, the Parties established the Paris Agreement Implementation and Compliance Committee (PAICC).[3]

The PAICC is a constituted expert body under the Paris Agreement. It comprises of 12 members and 12 alternate members reflecting broad scientific, technical, socio-economic, and legal expertise. Membership is geographically representative, with two members from each of the UN's five regional groups, as well as one member from Small Island Developing States (SIDs) and one member from the Least Developed Countries (LDCs). Members are elected by the Conference of the Parties serving as the meeting of the Parties to the Paris Agreement (CMA), and co-chairs are elected by the members of the PAICC. The CMA is responsible for ensuring that the PAICC's composition remains equitably representative and respects the goal of gender balance. By including a variety of members with differing backgrounds, the CMA can ensure that the PAICC is best equipped to address the wide range of implementation and compliance issues that may come before it.[4]

Through three distinct modes of commencement, the PAICC facilitates implementation of and compliance with the Paris Agreement, rather than punishing non-compliance.[5] This chapter outlines the ways in which the PAICC contributes to the effectiveness of the Paris Agreement.

The Paris Agreement Implementation and Compliance Committee (PAICC)

The PAICC is the compliance mechanism established under Article 15 of the Paris Agreement. Article 15 contains the following three provisions:

1. A mechanism to facilitate implementation of and promote compliance with the provisions of this Agreement is hereby established.

DOI: 10.4324/9781003276678-24

2. The mechanism referred to in paragraph 1 of this Article shall consist of a committee that shall be expert-based and facilitative in nature and function in a manner that is transparent, non-adversarial and non-punitive. The committee shall pay particular attention to the respective national capabilities and circumstances of parties.
3. The committee shall operate under the modalities and procedures adopted by the Conference of the Parties serving as the meeting of the Parties to this Agreement at its first session and report annually to the Conference of the Parties serving as the meeting of the Parties to this Agreement.[6]

The negotiators of Article 15 were inspired by Article 15 of the Minamata Convention on Mercury, which contains similar arrangements, though that Article establishes a Compliance Committee 'as a subsidiary body of the Conference of Parties'.[7] Both articles emphasize that the Compliance Committee is 'facilitative in nature' and 'shall pay particular attention to the respective national capabilities and circumstances of the Parties'.[8] While Article 15 of the Minamata Convention sets out the Compliance Committee's composition, such detail for the PAICC is contained under a Decision adopted by the Conference of the Parties at COP 21 in 2015.[9]

In 2018, the CMA adopted the modalities and procedures for 'the effective operation' of the PAICC.[10] These modalities and procedures include the 'purpose, principles, nature, functions and scope' of the PAICC, institutional arrangements including membership and frequency of meetings, initiation and process, details on measures and outputs, and consideration of systemic issues.[11] In 2022 in Sharm El-Sheikh, the CMA adopted the full set of Rules of Procedure for the PAICC.[12] These Rules are intended to be 'read together with and in furtherance of the modalities and procedures' and further facilitate implementation and compliance of the Paris Agreement.[13]

The PAICC's Facilitative Nature and Functions

The first international treaty-internal compliance procedure was established in 1992, pursuant to Article 8 of the Montreal Protocol.[14] This original compliance procedure was non-incriminating and facilitative, establishing an Implementation Committee to, among other things, 'secur[e] an amicable solution' to non-compliance matters.[15] Most subsequent compliance procedures resemble the Montreal Protocol's facilitative model,[16] including the PAICC under the Paris Agreement. Conversely, the Kyoto Protocol compliance mechanism is somewhat of an outlier in that 'went goes beyond a merely facilitative approach by referring to consequences to be applied in cases of non-compliance'.[17] This was achieved through a specific enforcement branch within the Compliance Committee.[18] Further, all compliance requirements under the Kyoto Protocol only apply to Annex I Parties. There is no analogous enforcement within the PAICC, which applies to all Parties of the Agreement.

As laid out in Article 15, the PAICC is a fundamentally facilitative in nature, rather than a punitive or adversarial body. As a result, it primarily seeks to encourage Parties' compliance with the Paris Agreement, rather than to sanction issues of non-compliance. It is not a dispute resolution body, nor does it impose penalties on States that are in violation of legal obligations under the Paris Agreement.[19] In effect, by including Article 15 within the text of the Paris Agreement, Parties agreed to accept responsibility for their actions through agreeing to an oversight committee which would help facilitate their compliance.

The PAICC, in its composition and procedural methods, has been specifically tailored to match the unique characteristics of the Paris Agreement, and as a result, its effectiveness is largely determined by the willingness of the Parties to engage with its processes.[20]

This approach is also reflected in the committee's decision-making efforts, which are based on consensus. Members must make all efforts to reach a consensus on any issue that comes before the committee. However, once efforts to reach consensus have been exhausted, and no consensus could be reached, the PAICC may come to a decision based on a majority of votes, with at least three quarters of members present and voting.[21] This alternative voting option ensures that the PAICC can engage in effective decision-making processes, even in cases where consensus cannot be reached.[22]

Modes of Initiation

The PAICC modalities and procedures identify three ways in which the PAICC may initiate considerations of issues: 1) self-referral by a Party;[23] 2) committee initiation, where a Party has not complied with a legally binding provision of the Paris Agreement;[24] and 3) discretionary initiation, in cases of significant and persistent inconsistencies of reported information.[25]

Self-Referral by a Party

One way in which an issue may be considered by the PAICC is if an individual Party makes a direct submission to the committee regarding any difficulties it is having with implementation of or compliance with its obligations under the Paris Agreement. A Party can make such a submission with regards to any provision of the Paris Agreement that relates to its own implementation or compliance efforts. This differentiates this mode from the other modes of initiation, which are restricted in scope regarding which provisions the PAICC has the mandate to initiate proceedings on its own. When a Party decides to make a submission to PAICC, it creates the opportunity for the PAICC to help that Party fulfill its obligations under the Paris Agreement by offering assistance and solutions to parties' individual implementation or compliance issues.[26] This mechanism reflects the understanding that non-compliance may arise due to lack of capacity rather than lack of willingness of a Party to fulfill its obligations. Giving Parties the option to self-refer their own implementation or compliance challenges creates the opportunity for Parties to enhance their ability to comply with the provisions of the Paris Agreement, shifting the PAICC's focus to preventing non-compliance and fostering compliance in the first place, ultimately fulfilling the objective of the Paris Agreement.[27]

The PAICC retains discretion over whether or not to initiate a case once a Party has decided to bring its submission before it. The PAICC will undergo a preliminary examination of the Party's submission in order to ensure that it is related to a proper implementation or compliance issue.[28] This ensures that the PAICC is not burdened with frivolous cases.[29]

Committee Initiation Where a Party is not in Compliance with a Legally Binding Provision

The second mode through which the PAICC may initiate proceedings with a Party occurs when a Party fails to act in accordance with a binding provision of the Paris Agreement. This applies in the following circumstances, as set out in paragraph 22(a) of Decision 20/CMA.1, Annex:

22. The Committee:

(a) Will initiate the consideration of issues in cases where a Party has not:

(i) Communicated or maintained a nationally determined contribution under Article 4 of the Paris Agreement, based on the most up-to-date status of communication in the public registry referred to in Article 4, paragraph 12, of the Paris Agreement;

(ii) Submitted a mandatory report or communication of information under Article 13, paragraphs 7 and 9, or Article 9, paragraph 7, of the Paris Agreement;
(iii) Participated in the facilitative, multilateral consideration of progress, based on information provided by the secretariat;
(iv) Submitted a mandatory communication of information under Article 9, paragraph 5, of the Paris Agreement;

Under the Paris Agreement, Parties are obligated to participate in several mandatory processes, such as communicating their Nationally Determined Contributions (NDCs) as well as submitting Biennial Transparency Reports (BTRs). These mandatory processes are set out in Article 4 paragraph 12, Article 9 paragraph 5, and Article 13 paragraphs 7 and 9:

Article 4

2. Each Party shall prepare, communicate and maintain successive nationally determined contributions that it intends to achieve. Parties shall pursue domestic mitigation measures, with the aim of achieving the objectives of such contributions.
9. Each Party shall communicate a nationally determined contribution every five years in accordance with decision 1/CP21 and any relevant decisions of the Conference of the Parties serving as the meeting of the Parties to this Agreement and be informed by the outcomes of the global stocktake referred to in Article 14.

12. Nationally determined contributions communicated by Parties shall be recorded in a public registry maintained by the secretariat.[30]

Article 9

5. Developed country Parties shall biennially communicate indicative quantitative and qualitative information related to paragraphs 1 and 3 of this Article, as applicable, including, as available, projected levels of public financial resources to be provided to developing country Parties. Other Parties providing resources are encouraged to communicate biennially such information on a voluntary basis.[31]

Article 13

7. Each Party shall regularly provide the following information:

(a) A national inventory report of anthropogenic emissions by sources and removals by sinks of greenhouse gases, prepared using good practice methodologies accepted by the Intergovernmental Panel on Climate Change and agreed upon by the Conference of the Parties serving as the meeting of the Parties to this Agreement; and
(b) Information necessary to track progress made in implementing and achieving its nationally determined contribution under Article 4.

. . .

9. Developed country Parties shall, and other Parties that provide support should, provide information on financial, technology transfer and capacity-building support provided to developing country Parties under Articles 9, 10 and 11.[32]

11. . . . In addition, each Party shall participate in a facilitative, multilateral consideration of progress with respect to efforts under Article 9, and its respective implementation and achievement of its nationally determined contribution.

Importantly, these obligations stem from Articles of the Paris Agreement that contain individual, binding obligations, through the use of the word 'shall.' As a result, these provisions give rise to legally binding duties that Parties must meet, and where the PAICC determines that when Party has failed to meet one of these mandatory provisions, it must commence proceedings against that Party.[33] This procedure is non-discretionary in the sense that the PAICC does not have discretion over whether or not to commence proceedings, as it does in the other modes of initiation.[34] However, there may still be some discretion in determining *when* it is appropriate for the committee to initiate a consideration of issues under this mode.

Importantly, the PAICC is not responsible for assessing the content or quality of a Party's NDC or mandatory reporting.[35] If, for example, a Party submits an NDC that is lacking sufficient ambition, this will not trigger review by the PAICC. Rather, the PAICC is solely responsible for addressing gaps in parties' fulfillment of their procedural obligations under the Paris Agreement; that is, whether the Party submitted their NDC or the mandatory elements of the BTR at all. Moreover, this mode of initiation will be triggered where a Party fails to submit their NDC within the deadline for doing so. Under the Paris Agreement, Parties must submit their NDCs 9–12 months prior to the relevant session of the CMA.[36] Once this margin lapses, the PAICC will initiate proceedings for non-communication.[37] The same applies to the submission of the biennial finance communication under Article 9(5) and for the mandatory elements of the BTR under Article13. BTRs are for the first time due on 31 December 2024, and biennially thereafter.

Discretionary Initiation in Cases of Significant and Persistent Inconsistencies

The third mode of initiation of PAICC is linked to the Technical Expert Review (TER) report. Under the Paris Agreement processes, TER teams are responsible for reviewing the BTRs submitted by parties.[38] Where a TER team in its report identifies in its recommendations an issue with a Party's reporting, PAICC may initiate a case where it considers that this is an issue of 'significant and persistent' inconsistencies in a Party's mandatory reporting under Article 13 paragraphs 7 and 9.[39] Notably, this third mode requires the consent of the respective Party.[40]

As outlined in Article 13, as part of the Enhanced Transparency Framework under the Paris Agreement, parties are required to submit regular national inventory reports and other mandatory information. Moreover, developed countries are required to submit information regarding their support provided to developing countries. The TER teams will then review the consistency of the information reported in Parties' BTRs (and national inventory reports if they were submitted as a self-standing report) with the Modalities, procedure and guidelines (MPGs) for reporting.[41] The TER team may issue a 'recommendation' to an 'area of improvement' of the Party's performance in relation to the *shall* provisions in the MPGs for reporting. In cases of 'significant and persistent' inconsistencies in reporting of the 'shall' requirements, the PAICC may initiate a case against a Party in this mode where a recommendation has been issued in a TER report. As a result, because the TER team is limited in scope to reviewing certain processes under Article 13, the PAICC's ability to initiate a case under the third mode is limited to this scope as well.

The PAICC retains discretion over whether to commence its own review based on a TER recommendation. The PAICC must review both the recommendation in the TER report, as well as any written comments provided by the Party, in order to determine whether a 'significant and persistent' inconsistency exists between the information sources.[42] There is no defined threshold for 'significant and persistent' in the Modalities and Procedures or the Rules of Procedure for PAICC, however the term's plain language meaning suggests that where a Party fails to respond to repeated recommendations to improve its performance and inconsistencies persist, the 'significant and persistent' inconsistency threshold might have been crossed.[43]

Further, any PAICC review under this mode of initiation requires the Party's consent. This requirement exists as a way for Parties to retain sovereignty over their actions under the Paris Agreement and again reflects the facilitative, rather than adversarial, nature of the PAICC's mandate. However, this requirement for consent is not detrimental to the PAICC's ability to fulfill its mandate, even in cases where a Party may not wish to provide its consent. If the PAICC's consideration of the case is made public, a Party may face political pressure to engage with and respond to the PAICC's initiation request in a cooperative manner.[44] As previously discussed, parties accepted the jurisdiction of the PAICC by including Article 15 of the Paris Agreement, thereby signaling their intention for an effective compliance mechanism to exist. As a result, refusing to give consent to participate in PAICC processes may reflect poorly on the Party in the international arena, and signal a lack of commitment to the goals of the Paris Agreement as a whole. Moreover, even where a Party does opt to withhold consent, the PAICC may include this in its annual report to the CMA, which could in turn lead to mounting pressure from the CMA itself.

In some cases, a Party's lack of capacity, rather than will, may lead to a finding of 'significant and persistent' inconsistencies. Where that occurs, the PAICC's decision to request consent to initiate a review may fulfill the necessary function of bringing these inconsistencies to political attention, thereby prompting a Party to address these inconsistencies itself, or to request support from the PAICC where necessary.[45]

The PAICC may also identify systemic issues that come up during the course of its work, which affect several parties' abilities to implement or comply with the provisions of the Agreement. The PAICC may then bring these systemic issues to the attention to the CMA in its annual report, who may act on them accordingly.[46] The PAICC may also provide recommendations to the CMA on how to address issues of a systemic nature.

Measures and Outputs

The modalities and procedures adopted at the CMA's first meeting also set out an open-ended list of the PAICC's various measures:

- Engaging in a dialogue with the Party to share information, identify challenges and recommend solutions (paragraph 30 (a))
- Assist the Party in engaging with the appropriate finance, technology and capacity-building bodies and arrangements under or serving the Paris Agreement in order to identify possible challenges and solution (paragraph 30 (b))
- Make recommendations to the Party with regard to those challenges and solutions and communicate them, with the consent of the Party concerned, to the relevant support bodies or arrangements (paragraph 30 (c))
- Recommend development of an action plan (paragraph 30 (d))
- Issue findings of fact in relation to matters listed in paragraph 22 a (paragraph 30 (e)).[47]

The CMA carefully composed this list of measures it can adopt with the goal of ensuring that the work conducted by the PAICC serves to complement, rather than duplicate, other processes under the Paris Agreement.[48]

Conclusion

The PAICC has an important role in enhancing parties' implementation of and compliance with the Paris Agreement. Given its primarily facilitative nature, it functions to encourage compliance, rather than to punish non-compliance, thus reflecting Parties' shared willingness to fulfill their obligations under the Paris Agreement while retaining sovereignty over their decision-making processes. Despite its short life, there is already some indication that the PAICC has been effective in fulfilling its mandate. The PAICC initiated and resolved its first two cases in 2023, and quite rapidly so. This may indicate that that the PAICC is effective, and that Parties are taking its work seriously. Moreover, while the PAICC is still relatively new, and because its role is not strictly defined but rather left to evolve, it will be crucial to study Parties' willingness to participate in its processes, and its resulting effects on their compliance with obligations under the Paris Agreement, in the coming years.

Notes

1 The author would like to thank Adv. Samantha Andison (JD 2024, University of Victoria, Research Fellow, CISDL) and Adv. Lydia Young (JD 2023, University of Victoria, Associate Fellow, CISDL) for their research, drafting and substantive insights. This chapter shares the work of Christina Voigt, 'The Compliance and Implementation Mechanism of the Paris Agreement' (2016) 25 RECIEL 161; Christina Voigt and Xiang Gao, 'Accountability in the Paris Agreement: The Interplay between Transparency and Compliance' (2020) Nordic Environmental LJ 31; Gu Zihua, Christina Voigt, and Jacob Werksman 'Facilitating Implementation and Promoting Compliance with the Paris Agreement Under Article 15: Conceptual Challenges and Pragmatic Choices' (2019) 9 CL 66.
2 Voigt (n 1) 161.
3 UNFCCC Decision 1/CP.21, Adoption of the Paris Agreement (29 January 2016) Report of the Conference of the Parties on its Twenty-First Session, Held in Paris from 30 November to 13 December 2015 (2015) UN Doc FCCC/CP/2015/10/Add.1 paras 102–3.
4 Zihua, Voigt, and Werksman (n 1) 66.
5 Voigt and Gao (n 1) 31, 56.
6 UNFCCC Decision 1/CP.21 (n 3) Article 15.
7 See Minamata Convention on Mercury (adopted 10 October 2013, entered into force 16 August 2017) 3202 UNTS 54669 (Minamata Convention) Article 15(1).
8 UNFCCC Decision 1/CP.21 (n 3) Paris Agreement Article 15(2); ibid Article 15(1).
9 ibid para 102.
10 UNFCCC Decision 20/CMA.1, Modalities and Procedures for the Effective Operation of the Committee to Facilitate Implementation and Promote Compliance Referred to in Article 15, Paragraph 2, of the Paris Agreement (19 March 2019) Report of the Conference of the Parties serving as the meeting of the Parties to the Paris Agreement on the third part of its first session, held in Katowice from 2 to 15 December 2018 (2018) UN Doc FCCC/PA/CMA/2018/3/Add.2.
11 ibid.
12 See UNFCCC Decision 24/CMA.4, Rules of Procedure of the Committee to Facilitate Implementation and Promote Compliance Referred to in Article 15, Paragraph 2, of the Paris Agreement (21 December 2022) Report of the Conference of the Parities Serving as the Meeting of the Parities to the Paris Agreement.
13 ibid rule 1.
14 UN Environment Programme Decision IV/5: Non-Compliance Procedure (25 November 1992) Fourth Meeting of the Parties to the Montreal Protocol; see Gerhard Loibl, 'Compliance Procedures and

Mechanisms' in Malgosia Fitzmaurice (ed), *Research Handbook on International Environmental Law* (2nd edn, Edward Elgar 2021) 293; the Montreal Protocol itself (Montreal Protocol on Substances that Deplete the Ozone Layer (adopted 16 September 1987, entered into force 1 January 1989) 1522 UNTS 26369 Chapter XXVII) only contained a provision indicating that Parties 'at their first meeting' would determine the procedures and institutional mechanisms needed to address non-compliance (see Article 8). See also Christina Voigt and Caroline Foster (eds) *Non-Compliance Mechanisms Versus International Courts* (CUP 2024).
15 UN Environment Programme Decision IV/5 (n 14) Appendix IV.
16 Loibl (n 14) 296.
17 ibid 295. Note that the Kyoto Protocol's compliance obligations only apply to its Parties listed in Annex I UNFCCC.
18 UNFCCC Decision 27/CMP.1, Procedures and Mechanisms Relating to Compliance under the Kyoto Protocol (30 March 2006) Report of the Conference of the Parties Serving as the Meeting of the Parties to the Kyoto Protocol on its First Session, held at Montreal from 28 November to 10 December 2005 (2005) UN Doc FCCC/KP/CMP/2005/8/Add.3.
19 Edith Brown Weiss, 'Invoking State Responsibility in the Twenty-First Century' (2002) 96 AJIL 798; Dinah Shelton, *Commitment and Compliance: The Role of Non-binding Norms in the International Legal System* (OUP 2003).
20 Voigt and Gao (n 1) 47.
21 ibid 48.
22 Zihua, Voigt, and Werksman (n 1) 10.
23 Decision 20/CMA.1 (n 10) annex para 20.
24 ibid annex para 22(a). The PAICC considered its first two cases in 2023, both of which arose under this initiation mode. See UNFCCC, Annual Report of the Paris Agreement Implementation and Compliance Committee to the Conference of the Parties serving as the meeting of the Parties to the Paris Agreement (25 September 2023) 5th Session of the Conference of the Parties Serving as the Meeting of the Parties to the Paris Agreement (2013) UN Doc FCCC/PA/CMA/2023/4 para 13.
25 ibid annex para 22(b).
26 Zihua, Voigt, and Werksman (n 1) 17–18.
27 Nils Goeteyn and Frank Maes, 'Compliance Mechanisms in Multilateral Environmental Agreements: An Effective Way to Improve Compliance?' (2011) 10 Chinese JIL 791, 800.
28 UNFCCC Decision 24/CMA.4 (n 12) annex para 2.
29 Zihua, Voigt, and Werksman (n 1) 17–18.
30 UNFCCC Decision 1/CP.21 (n 3) Paris Agreement Article 4.
31 ibid Article 9.
32 ibid Article 13.
33 ibid 19–22.
34 Voigt and Gao (n 1) 54.
35 Zihua, Voigt, and Werksman (n 1) 20.
36 Decision 1/CP.21 (n 3) para 25.
37 ibid 21.
38 UNFCCC Decision 1/CP.21 (n 3) Paris Agreement Articles 13(5) and 13(6).
39 ibid 25.
40 Zihua, Voigt, and Werksman (n 1) 24.
41 UNFCC, Decision 18/CMA.1 Modalities, Procedures and Guidelines for the Transparency Framework for Action and Support Referred to in Article 13 of the Paris Agreement (19 March 2019) Conference of the Parties Serving as the Meeting of the Parties to the Paris Agreement (2018) UN Doc FCCC/PA/CMA/2018/3/Add.2.
42 Zihua, Voigt, and Werksman (n 1) 24–25.
43 Voigt and Gao (n 1) 51.
44 Zihua, Voigt, and Werksman (n 1) 25–26.
45 ibid.
46 ibid 52.
47 Voigt and Gao (n 1) 53, citing UNFCCC Decision 20/CMA.1 (n 10) annex para 30.
48 ibid 46.

21

SUBMITTING MANDATORY REPORTS UNDER THE PARIS AGREEMENT TRANSPARENCY FRAMEWORK

Christopher Campbell-Duruflé and Raúl Salas Reyes

Introduction

A thought-provoking tension has emerged in the scholarship on the Paris Agreement's Enhanced Transparency Framework and reporting in global environmental governance more broadly. On the one hand, it is generally recognized that transparency of State Parties' climate actions can create opportunities for evidenced-based policy-making at the national level and offer new avenues to hold states accountable.[1] Ultimately, as revealed by Article 13's goal to "build mutual trust and confidence and to promote effective implementation" and "to provide a clear understanding of climate change action," treaty Parties hope that these benefits will bring about more ambitious mitigation, adaptation and support actions than they would have adopted otherwise. On the other hand, many authors have warned against transparency's possible adverse effects. These include diverting resources from substantive climate actions toward reporting challenges, lack of accountability for the goals that were set, marginalization of the issues that are not the object of reporting and, in cases where such issues include broader justice challenges, policy-making that further entrenches inequality.[2]

In this context, we identify three current challenges with the operation of the Enhanced Transparency Framework that could produce such adverse effects, rather than the benefits associated with Article 13. We focus on: 1) the risk that Parties fail to take the particular vulnerability of certain groups into consideration as they enhance their reporting on mitigation (Section 5), 2) the risk that Parties' reporting on the climate finance provided fail to allow meaningful comparisons between individual countries' levels of support, and thus ultimately to contribute to closing the outstanding finance gap (Section 6) and 3) the risk that Parties' enhanced reporting of adaptation fail to enhance their capacity to avoid conflicts between adaptation, mitigation and sustainable development objectives (Section 7).

In response to these challenges, it is recommended that Parties adopt a transformative approach to transparency, defined in Section 4 as one that improves options for State accountability, enhances capacity for substantive action at the national and subnational levels and considers social inequality in the design and implementation of climate actions. Under each challenge, we identify concrete proposals to achieve such ends while recognizing that the pursuit of transformative transparency is

DOI: 10.4324/9781003276678-25

an ongoing process. A crosscutting theme to which we return in the conclusion is the opportunity for academia to assist Parties and other stakeholders in the momentous transparency efforts ahead.

Transparency Under the UNFCCC and the *Cancun Agreements*

Article 13 of the Paris Agreement builds on and enhances Parties' reporting obligations found in the United Nations Framework Convention on Climate Change (UNFCCC). To summarize, the UNFCCC provides that each country shall publish every four years a National Communication that outlines the actions taken to implement the Convention, "taking into account their common but differentiated responsibilities and their specific national and regional development priorities, objectives and circumstances."[3] Among others, developed country Parties included in Annex I of the UNFCCC shall provide estimated impacts of mitigation policies and measures, projections of future trends in GHG emissions and removals, assessments of anticipated climate change impacts, information on domestic adaptation policies and (in the case of Annex II Parties) information on financial, technological and capacity-building support provided to non-Annex I Parties.[4] The UNFCCC also contains an obligation for Annex I Parties to submit GHG inventories, which have been presented on a yearly basis since 1996.[5]

In the case of developing country Parties not included in Annex I, by comparison, the 2002 guidelines offer greater flexibility regarding both content and frequency of National Communications. Specifically, non-Annex I Parties should provide a description of their national and regional development priorities, a national inventory of GHG emissions to the extent permitted by their capacities, a general description of the steps taken or envisaged to implement the Convention, information on steps taken to integrate climate change considerations into social, economic and environmental policies and a description of financial, technical and capacity needs.[6]

Parties also agreed to report between National Communications as part of the Monitoring, Reporting, and Verification (MRV) framework established in the non-binding Cancun Agreements.[7] Every two years since 2014, Annex I Parties have been expected to submit Biennial Reports that contain additional information on GHG emissions and trends, information on their quantified economy-wide emission reduction target and their progress to achieve it through mitigation, the use of market-based mechanisms as well as land use activities, GHG emission projections, the provision of financial, technological and capacity-building support to non-Annex I Parties and domestic self-assessment arrangements.[8]

In the case of non-Annex I Parties, Biennial Update Reports should contain updates of national circumstances and institutional arrangements, national GHG inventories "consistent with capacities, time constraints, data availabilities and the level of support provided by developed countries (sic) Parties for biennial update reporting," information in a tabular format on actions to mitigate climate change and their effects, information on constraints and gaps, related financial, technical and capacity-building needs and information on domestic MRV arrangements.[9] Least developed country parties (LDCs) and small island developing States (SIDS) may submit such reports at their discretion.

Transitioning to the Paris Agreement's Enhanced Transparency Framework

All Parties will continue to submit National Communications under the Convention. However, Biennial Reports and Biennial Update Reports will be replaced. Instead, Parties to the Paris Agreement agreed to submit BTRs and National Inventory Reports (NIRs) by the end of 2024, with NIRs due yearly for developed country Parties and biennially for other Parties, except for LDCs and SIDS, which can still submit at their discretion.

The modalities, procedures and guidelines for the Enhanced Transparency Framework (hereinafter "modalities"), adopted at COP 24 in Katowice, reveal that the changes brought about by the Paris Agreement are mainly in legal form and level of detail, rather than frequency of reporting, and generally introduce more challenges for developing countries than for developed countries. For example, the recommendation that developing country Parties present biennial updates on their emission inventories is replaced by an obligation to submit an NIR. Furthermore, the tabular information on mitigation actions and their effects presented in Biennial Update Reports should be replaced by far more detailed information on mitigation actions, policies and measures that assist in the implementation of NDCs. Another example is the new requirement to report projections of emissions and removals 15 to 20 years into the future.[10] Additionally, the *2006 IPCC Guidelines for National Greenhouse Gas Inventories for National Inventory Reports* will be applicable instead of the 1996 version, which will require developing countries to recalculate emission time series since 1990 for consistency and to enhance institutional arrangements.[11] Another consequential change for developing countries is the requirement to report information on indicators to track progress toward achieving their NDCs and to provide information on their accounting approach.

Changes in the transparency requirements that apply to developed country Parties are subtler, beyond the fact that yearly NIRs and BTRs are the object of legal obligations. Van Asselt and Kulovesi observe that

> simply following the existing transparency arrangements was not politically feasible for most developed countries, as this would have meant maintaining the largely bifurcated approach of the Convention and the Protocol, with different sets of rules for reporting and review for developed and developing country Parties.[12]

One of the most notable reporting expansions for developed countries is their obligation to present biennial communications on projected levels of climate finance under Article 9(5) of the Paris Agreement. However, such reports are not part of the Enhanced Transparency Framework strictly speaking, and will not be subject to Technical Expert Review and Facilitative Multilateral Consideration of Progress. By contrast, Mayer draws attention to the possibility of minor regressions in stringency for developed countries, for example in the case of the modalities for estimating GHG emissions that appear more permissive than those previously applicable.[13]

Between Counter-Productive and Transformative Transparency

A growing body of literature warns that transparency requirements may not always deliver on their promise of positive environmental outcomes. For example, Park and Kramarz argue that reporting frameworks that fail to engage with Parties' underlying choices may forego an important potential for learning, transformation and the resolution of disagreements regarding how to tackle global environmental challenges.[14] Commenting on urban climate governance, Hughes, Geist and Tozer warn that policy-making based on global reporting initiatives may marginalize important social justice considerations if it results in "redirect[ing] policy attention and resources away from initiatives specific to the local context and toward efforts required to conform with standards determined elsewhere."[15]

Specifically considering the Paris Agreement, Weikmans, van Asselt and Roberts identify several barriers to the considerable amount of new information to be generated being "comparable, intelligible, and complete," thereby limiting its potential to result in more ambitious climate action by states.[16] Gupta and van Asselt have even cautioned that "an ever-growing focus on developing country transparency within the UNFCCC" could "*distract from* the search for more far-reaching accountability" regarding Parties' substantive actions if it resulted in the prioritization of capacity-building.[17] To summarize, we describe as counter-productive those transparency frameworks that entrench the *status quo* or even have adverse effects on the pursuit of environmental goals and social equality.

The risk that transparency efforts could yield counter-productive effects does not entail a need to move away from the Paris Agreement's Enhanced Transparency Framework, but rather heightened caution against the pitfalls of creating new reporting obligations. We adopt the adjective "transformative" to refer to the transparency frameworks that overcome this challenge by bolstering states' readiness (both technical and political) to take action as a result of their involvement. For Weikmans and Gupta, for example, transparency is transformative when it enhances "accountability, mutual trust and ultimately, more ambitious climate actions from all."[18] Ciplet et al. go even further by defining transformative transparency as a process that may empower actors "to effectively disrupt systems and practices of inequality and to encourage more just governance."[19]

Based on this overview of the literature, we retain the following three features of transparency frameworks as telltales of their transformative potential: 1) improving options to hold State Parties accountable for their substantive actions through the Paris Agreement's mechanisms (e.g., Facilitative Multilateral Consideration of Progress, Global Stocktake) and other avenues beyond the treaty, 2) enhancing States' capacity to take substantive mitigation and adaptation actions at the national and subnational levels and 3) encouraging States to take inequalities (based on poverty, gender, age, race and other grounds of discrimination) into account in doing so. In the remainder of this chapter, we use these three criteria to identify concrete options to address current challenges with the Enhanced Transparency Framework. We recognize that not all options may fully satisfy all three criteria or completely allow avoiding counterproductive effects. In this sense, achieving transformative transparency is better understood as an ongoing process rather than as a destination.

Proposal 1: Centering Social Inequality When Enhancing Reporting on Mitigation Action

Challenge Overview

As previously indicated, transitioning from the submission of Biennial Reports and Biennial Update Reports to that of BTRs will bring about important quantitative and qualitative changes. Developing countries particularly are at very different stages in the development of national systems to monitor the effects of mitigation actions and produce national GHG inventory reports due to capacity constraints. By way of example, at the time of writing, only 66 out of 155 developing countries had submitted their first Biennial Update Reports to the Secretariat, only 24 Parties had submitted at least one NIR despite four rounds of update reports having been completed and only 40 NIRs had been submitted as standalone documents.[20]

Yet the experience accumulated under the UNFCCC shows that reporting on the effects of mitigation policies and measures also presents challenges for developed countries. According to one recent assessment, Annex I countries "are generally struggling to adhere to the reporting requirements on achievement of targets" in their Biennial Reports, for reasons other than lack of capacity.[21] Furthermore, the same study observed no pattern of improvement from one Biennial Report to the other, which suggests a lack of transformative impact of the pre-Paris MRV framework for states that have ample access to resources.

One more specific issue that both developed and developing countries will face in their BTRs is to report on the non-GHG effects of their mitigation action. Indeed, the modalities call on Parties to identify qualitative or quantitative indicators to track progress toward their NDCs.[22] For example, the modalities recommend the provision of information on the mitigation potential of economic diversification plans, adaptation actions that have mitigation co-benefits (e.g., home and buildings thermal-retrofits to increase resilience to heat waves and that integrate energy efficiency measures) or the economic and social impacts of response measures (e.g., impacts of mitigation actions in the forestry sector on gender equality).[23] Yet the lack of experience, expertise and methods under all three headings[24] may defeat the Enhanced Transparency Framework's goal "to provide a clear understanding of climate change action" and make comparisons between Parties almost impossible.

Fostering Transformative Transparency

There is no doubt that greater resources are needed to support capacity-constrained parties as they prepare to enhance their levels of reporting, such as the funding channeled through the Capacity-building Initiative for Transparency and the Global Environmental Facility. The fact that the USD 100 billion goal of yearly climate finance adopted in 2010 and restated in 2015[25] has not yet been achieved is a major concern: according to the Organisation for Economic Co-operation and Development (OECD), public climate finance was only to reach USD 67 billion in 2020.[26] Parties explicitly recognized the interconnectedness of transparency and support in Article 13(14) and (15) of the Paris Agreement and agreed to review the collective finance goal upward in 2025.

How can addressing the challenges identified here have a transformative impact and avoid possible counter-productive effects, such as diverting resources and policy attention from climate action as a result of parties' application for additional resources and efforts to better fulfill the modalities? Dagnet et al. point to the common problem presented when support for enhancing transparency is used to rely on consultants to prepare National Communications and Biennial Update Reports without a long-term engagement. If contracts are done on a report-by-report basis, much of the capacity developed through reporting cannot be used toward enhanced substantive climate policy.[27] Supporting the development of stronger institutional arrangements could allow parties to work more productively with different actors – including with consultants, civil society and academia – to build long-term relationships that enhance analytical capacity.[28]

As emphasized by the modalities' call on Parties to include population, geographical and economic profiles in the BTRs,[29] climate policies do not impact all sectors of society equally. Climate action can either address environmental injustices or further entrench the disadvantages of certain groups. For example, one hypothesis that has received heightened attention is that incentivizing electric vehicle uptake through tax credits underserves lower-income and racialized communities.[30] It is thus key that States enhance their capacity to report on social inequalities relevant to their NDC targets, for example by using disaggregate data regarding social vulnerability to climate change due to poverty, gender, age, race, minority status or disability.[31] In the words of Hughes, Geist and Tozer, "capacities are needed to allow decision-makers to engage with local data that reflects social and spatial differences."[32]

The Initiative for Climate Action Transparency has paved the way forward by developing a set of guidance for Parties to report on the extent to which actions taken to achieve their NDC also promote "transformational" change toward global decarbonization and the full implementation of the Sustainable Development Goals.[33] Another example is UNDP's Climate Promise programme, which provides technical assistance for countries to enhance their NDCs while increasing climate resilience and supporting sustainable development priorities. Requests have focused on the themes of finance, energy, gender, nature-based solutions and forests, thereby providing antecedents to center economic and social impacts in BTRs.[34]

To conclude, reinforcing the long-term capacity of both developed and developing countries to report on social inequality in their NDC implementation and to act on this data appears as key to address the technical and political challenges described in this section. The calls to include population, geographical and economic profiles in BTRs, to describe domestic arrangements for stakeholder engagement and to identify indicators to track progress on NDC implementation provide excellent opportunities to do so. Even though introduced by more hortatory language ("may also," "should," "is encouraged"), the modalities' provisions on non-GHG mitigation benefits, longer-term emissions trends and the economic and social impacts of response measures also offer significant potential for a more transformative approach to transparency.[35]

Proposal 2: Clarifying Methodological and Substantive Issues Surrounding Financial Support Provided

Challenge Overview

In large part, BTRs continue Annex II countries' levels of reporting based on the UNFCCC. In their Biennial Reports, developed countries currently use common reporting formats to account for "new and additional" climate finance and to distinguish between support to mitigation and to adaptation actions. The modalities under the Cancun Agreements call on Parties to "use any methodology to be developed under the Convention" for this purpose or, alternatively, to describe the methodology used. No such methodology has been developed to this date. Each Annex II Party is also called on to describe "how it seeks to ensure that the resources it provides effectively address the needs of non-Annex I Parties with regard to climate change adaptation and mitigation."[36]

The modalities for BTRs put even greater emphasis on developed countries' descriptions of the definitions used to account for public climate finance as well as the private finance mobilized. At the time of writing, moreover, Parties had still not adopted the "common tabular formats" necessary to report on finance as agreed to at COP 24.[37] In terms of Parties' individual contributions to the collective 100 billion goal, the modalities call on each of them to explain "[h]ow the information provided reflects a progression from previous levels in the provision and mobilization of finance," "[h]ow it seeks to ensure that support provided . . . effectively addresses the needs and priorities of developing country Parties," and "[h]ow it seeks to ensure that support provided and mobilized through public interventions is in line with the long-term goals of the Paris Agreement."[38]

One key challenge with developed countries' reporting on climate finance provided arises at the intersection of technical and political uncertainties. Under the first heading, building mutual trust and confidence will be difficult if meaningful comparisons between Parties' individual contributions cannot be made. For example, the OECD's assessment that public climate finance reached USD 64.3 billion in 2018 (including export credits) has been widely criticized by civil society observers that dispute the inclusion of bilateral funding that is not directly related to climate action and of loan figures (alongside grants).[39] Indeed, even with preferential interest rates, loans risk putting additional pressure on Parties on the long run by inflating their public debt. By contrast with the OECD, Oxfam's assessment places total net public climate finance between USD 19 and 22.5 billion for 2017–2018.[40] In the words of Roberts et al., "clear rules for what counts as climate finance need to be agreed" for developing countries' support needs to be adequately addressed.[41]

Under the second heading, building mutual trust will be equally difficult without agreement on how to determine whether individual state's contributions show sufficient "progression," "effectively" address developing countries' needs and are "in line" with the collective yearly goal. In one case, for example, civil society organizations challenged Canada's pledge of CDN 800 million yearly as not amounting to its "fair share" of global efforts, which they had set at CDN 1.8 billion yearly based on a comparison of its gross national income with that of other donor countries.[42] Yet in the absence of political agreement on including more precise guidance in the BTR modalities, Parties may take a range of approaches to describing their contributions. In the worst cases, continuous reporting on finance without clarity on how individual shares relate to the collective goal could obscure the need for more ambitious contributions to close the outstanding finance gap.

Fostering Transformative Transparency

How can reporting on climate finance have a transformative impact on donor countries and avoid counterproductive effects such as diverting attention from individual countries' levels of support or delaying the clarification of methodological and substantive issues? This question has obviously been alive since the adoption of reporting requirements in the UNFCCC. We provide three suggestions that focus on the role that academia and civil society can play to accompany Parties in presenting their BTRs starting in 2024.

One first opportunity is for researchers to engage with the outputs of the Technical Expert Review of BTRs regarding support provided by developed countries and other Parties, with a focus on methodological issues. Under Article 13(9) of the Paris Agreement, independent experts will assess Parties' BTRs every two years from the viewpoint of "consistency" with the modalities and identify possible "areas of improvement" with regard to reporting, without reviewing "the adequacy of a Party's support provided" or "mak[ing] political judgments."[43] Researchers have an important role to play in critically assessing the Technical Expert Review of BTRs, for instance with regard to the methods used by Parties to identify climate finance instruments and avoid double-counting (grants, equity, loans, etc.), to determine that support is "new and additional" (by contrast with support that was already projected), to monitor the effectiveness of the support received and to account for private climate finance mobilized through public interventions.

A second opportunity for researchers is to analyze the large amount of data that will be generated by Technical Expert Reviews in order to compare Parties' levels of reporting. Weikmans and Gupta have already proposed developing transparency indicators that could allow ranking countries based on timeliness and completeness.[44] For example, they shed light on the fact that Annex II Parties' reporting about support provided under the UNFCCC is weaker than that relating to mitigation action, although it has tended to improve over time. To maximize its transformative potential, future research building on this precedent could draw from the experience of other international ranking initiatives to encourage a race to the top in Parties' levels of support.[45]

A third and last opportunity is for researchers to propose new approaches to dividing equitable shares of finance provision, based on the approaches taken by Parties in their BTRs when addressing "progression," how "effectively" they address developing countries' needs and whether their support is "in line" with the collective goal. Parties were unable to adopt more specific guidance in the Paris Agreement or the BTR modalities regarding individual countries' finance contributions and may never be able to fully agree on this divisive issue. This makes the contribution researchers that propose new burden-sharing formula and that may foster convergence in Parties' reporting all the more important. Existing proposals have often relied on indicators of individual countries' responsibility for climate change and capacity to provide climate finance, such as their historical emissions and their national income.[46]

To conclude, academia and civil society have a considerable opportunity to encourage support-providing Parties to better consider the needs of capacity-constrained countries (which are often more vulnerable to climate change) and to improve options for their accountability during the Facilitative Multilateral Consideration of Progress and the Global Stocktake. Their engagement with unresolved methodological and substantive issues could encourage greater convergence between Parties' approaches or, at the very least, provide meaningful comparisons that would be impossible by relying solely on Parties' BTRs. Lastly, while beyond the scope of this chapter, better understanding the delivery and effectiveness of support could also increase the accountability of support-receiving Parties.

Proposal 3: Integrating Reporting on Adaptation, Mitigation and Sustainable Development

Challenge Overview

With regard to adaptation, the main normative change brought about by the Enhanced Transparency Framework is one of legal form. Article 13(8) of the Paris Agreement introduces a recommendation ("should") to report on climate adaptation goals in replacement of the invitation to develop National Adaptation Plans contained in the Cancun Agreements.[47] The modalities do not designate BTRs as the only possible vehicle; the Adaptation Communications introduced at Article 7(1) may be submitted either as part of NDCs, National Communications or National Adaptation Plans.[48] The Enhanced Transparency Framework also calls on Parties to provide greater detail in their reporting on adaptation. The modalities contain two tiers of information to be presented, including information on climate impacts, risks and adaptation policies under the first tier ("should provide") and information on loss and damage under the second tier ("may provide").[49]

Parties' reporting on adaptation may be expected to face the three types of challenges already identified in this chapter: namely, lack of resources by capacity-constrained countries for timely and complete reporting on adaptation, lack of legal certainty regarding what level of action is required from individual countries under Article 7(9) and in light of the global goal adopted at Article 7(1) and lack of technical clarity regarding how to define and measure specific adaptation actions. Under this last heading, for example, Lesnikowski et al. point out that the "fuzziness of adaptation as a policy area" makes it "difficult to define and track, especially in relation to policy issues like development or disaster risk management."[50] Ford and Berrang-Ford similarly argue that "adaptation science remains the poor cousin of mitigation science, with significant differences in understanding and scientific development between the two."[51]

Once again, building mutual trust and confidence will be difficult if there is no widely agreed methodology to determine if a given policy (e.g., promoting shrimp aquaculture in agricultural areas to adapt to saltwater intrusions) effectively reduces climate impacts on at-risk populations, and if meaningful comparisons between parties cannot be made. Moreover, Parties decided at COP 21 that their Adaptation Communications would not undergo a Technical Expert Review or be the object of the Facilitative Multilateral Consideration of Progress, two processes which could have contributed to the clarification of methodological challenges and legal uncertainties over time.

Fostering Transformative Transparency

Just as in the case of mitigation action, there is no doubt that addressing the current "adaptation finance gap" is key to enhancing transparency under the Paris Agreement. Only 18% of bilateral climate finance and 20% of multilateral climate finance were projected for adaptation in 2020,[52] contrasted with the aim of achieving a "balance" between both types of funding affirmed at Article 9(4) of the Paris Agreement and annual adaptation costs expected to reach US$140 to 300 billion in 2030 and US$280 to 500 billion in 2050.[53] Lack of capacity to take adaptation action, *a fortiori*, is likely to entail lack of capacity to report on such actions.

Beyond the challenge of increasing support to capacity-constrained Parties, how can enhanced reporting on climate impacts and adaptation policies have a transformative impact, and avoid counter-productive effects such as diverting resources and policy attention from actual adaptation efforts or even furthering adaptation actions that entrench the vulnerability of certain groups? A case study of shrimp aquaculture to adapt to saltwater intrusions in Bangladesh has shown how policies may enhance adaptation for certain groups while leaving more vulnerable groups behind. Indeed, even though shrimp aquaculture has successfully expanded into a large export commodity, increased salinity and destruction of local ecosystems have also resulted in the loss of livelihoods for landless farmers, protest and violence.[54] As Wenta, McDonald and McGee have put it, in order to achieve true resilience, adaptation "decision-making processes should explicitly consider the inequitable distribution of climate hazards and benefits."[55]

In this context, building synergies between reporting on adaptation, mitigation and sustainable development emerges as a key approach to resolving the reporting challenges identified here. On the one hand, there is mounting evidence of the benefits of enhancing capacity for reporting and policy-making on mitigation and adaptation in an integrated way. Doing so could reduce monitoring and reporting costs, prevent conflicts between both objectives and better capture the mitigation co-benefits envisioned at Article 4(17) of the Paris Agreement.[56]

On the other hand, enhancing transparency of adaptation must lead to increased capacity to address the need of particularly vulnerable groups to be transformative. In the words of the UN Special Rapporteur on human rights and the environment, a "rights-based approach should be applied in order to tackle the root causes of vulnerability, such as poverty, inequality, discrimination and marginalization, and not merely the symptoms of climate change impacts."[57] One promising innovation is to establish "mechanisms, support and incentives to gather input from vulnerable people and communities" to support integrated policy-making under the Paris Agreement, the Sustainable Development Goals' Voluntary National Reviews and the Sendai Framework's Monitor.[58] Indeed, Article 7(5) of the Paris Agreement provides a strong base for doing so by specifically identifying the importance of gender perspectives and Indigenous, traditional and local knowledge. Likewise, the modalities call on Parties to provide information on their demographics, "sectoral economic, social and/or environmental vulnerabilities," stakeholder involvement and "[h]ow adaptation increased resilience and reduced impacts."[59]

To conclude, clarifying the methodological challenges and legal uncertainties faced by Parties in their reporting on adaptation in BTRs or other communications offers a considerable opportunity for transformative transparency. Reinforcing the long-term capacity of both developed and developing countries to report on adaptation in a way that is integrated with mitigation and sustainable development, that actively takes social inequality into account and that strengthens policy-making capacities, offers particular promise.

Conclusion

Throughout this chapter, we identified technical and political challenges to the operation of the Enhanced Transparency Framework. Our goal was not to be comprehensive, and many other similar issues with reporting on mitigation, support, and adaptation may stand in the way of achieving Article 13's goals to provide a clear understanding of climate change action, to build mutual trust and confidence between treaty Parties and to promote effective implementation.

Building on emerging research in international relations and international law, we call on parties to address these transparency challenges in a transformative way. As laid out in Section 4, such an approach improves Parties' capacity to take substantive climate actions and avoids the risk that enhanced reporting will provide no safeguard against policies that further entrench inequality. We refer to research on incentivizing electric vehicle uptake through tax credits, promoting shrimp aquaculture in agricultural areas, or including loans alongside grants in accounting for climate finance to show that such policies are far from being hypothetical.

We focus on three overarching proposals for transformative transparency under Article 13 of the *Paris Agreement*, namely 1) centering social inequality when enhancing reporting on mitigation action, 2) clarifying methodological and substantive issues surrounding financial support provided and 3) integrating reporting on adaptation, mitigation and sustainable development. Under each heading, we identify existing initiatives that could pave the way forward and specific provisions of the modalities where pursuing our proposals could be nested. Interestingly, our approach calls on Parties to take the provisions introduced by hortatory language ("may also," "should," "is encouraged") as seriously as those introduced by the imperative "shall" in order to make visible issues that might otherwise be overlooked.

Also of particular interest is the need for academia to contribute to this transformative path. Specific opportunities include partnering with government agencies to enhance their long-term analytical capacity to consider social inequality, ranking countries based on timeliness and completeness of reporting in order to encourage a race to the top (in reporting and in substantive actions), proposing new approaches to dividing equitable shares of climate finance based on the terms of the Paris Agreement and of the modalities and developing new methodological tools to track adaptation in a way that is integrated with mitigation and sustainable development.

Notes

1 See for example: Yamide Dagnet and Kelly Levin, 'Transparency (Article 13)' in Daniel Klein and others (eds), *The Paris Agreement on Climate Change: Analysis and Commentary* (OUP 2017) and Daniel Bodansky, Jutta Brunnée and Lavanya Rajamani, *International Climate Change Law* (OUP 2017), Chapter 7.

2 See Section 4. These include: Susan Park and Teresa Kramarz (eds), *Global Environmental Governance and the Accountability Trap* (The MIT Press 2019), Sara Hughes, Sarah Giest and Laura Tozer, 'Accountability and Data-Driven Urban Climate Governance' (2020) 10 Nature Climate Change 1085; Aarti Gupta and Harro van Asselt, 'Transparency in Multilateral Climate Politics: Furthering (or Distracting From) Accountability?' (2019) 13 Regulation & Governance 18, and Romain Weikmans, Harro van Asselt and J Timmons Roberts, 'Transparency Requirements Under the Paris Agreement and their (Un)Likely Impact on Strengthening the Ambition of Nationally Determined Contributions (NDCs)' (2020) 20(4) Climate Policy 511.

3 UNFCCC, Article 4(1)(j) and 12.

4 Decision 6/CP.25, Revision of the UNFCCC reporting guidelines on national communications for Parties included in Annex I to the Convention, Annex Guidelines for the preparation of national communications by Parties included in Annex I to the Convention, Part II: UNFCCC reporting guidelines on national communications.

5 Decision 3/CP.1, Preparation and submission of national communications from the Parties included in Annex I to the Convention, 7 April 1995, UN Doc FCCC/CP/1995/7/Add.1 at para 2. See also: Decision 3/CP.5, Guidelines for the preparation of national communications by Parties included in Annex I to the Convention, Part I: UNFCCC reporting guidelines on annual inventories, 4 November 1999, UN Doc FCCC/CP/1999/6/Add.1.
6 Decision 17/CP.8, Guidelines for the preparation of national communications from Parties not included in Annex I to the Convention, 1 November 2002, UN Doc FCCC/CP/2002/7/Add.2.
7 Decision 1/CP.16, The Cancun Agreements: Outcome of the work of the Ad Hoc Working Group on Long-term Cooperative Action under the Convention, 15 March 2011, UN Doc FCCC/CP/2010/7/Add.1. (Cancun Agreements)
8 Decision 2/CP.17, Outcome of the work of the Ad Hoc Working Group on Long-term Cooperative Action under the Convention, 11 December 2011, UN Doc FCCC/CP/2011/9/Add.1, Annex I, UNFCCC biennial reporting guidelines for developed country Parties.
9 Decision 2/CP.17, *idem*, Annex III, UNFCCC biennial update reporting guidelines for Parties not included in Annex I to the Convention.
10 Decision 18/CMA.1, Modalities, procedures and guidelines for the transparency framework for action and support referred to in Article 13 of the Paris Agreement, 15 December 2018, UN Doc FCCC/PA/CMA/2018/3/Add.2, Annex, at paras 59 and following.
11 ibid at paras 26–28 and 57.
12 Harro van Asselt and Kati Kulovesi, 'Article 13 – Enhanced Transparency Framework for Action and Support' in Geert Van Calster and Leonie Reins (eds), *The Paris Agreement on Climate Change* (Cheltenham, UK 2021) 310.
13 Benoit Mayer, 'Transparency Under the Paris Rulebook: Is the Transparency Framework Truly Enhanced?' (2019) 9 Climate L 40 at 59.
14 Park and Kramarz (n 2) 220.
15 Hughes, Giest and Tozer (n 2) 1087.
16 Weikmans, van Asselt and Roberts (n 2) 522.
17 Gupta and van Asselt (n 2) 31. (Emphasis in original) See also: Aarti Gupta and Michael Mason, 'Disclosing or Obscuring? The Politics of Transparency in Global Climate Governance' (2016) 18 Current Opinion in Environmental Sustainability 82.
18 Romain Weikmans and Aarti Gupta, 'Assessing State Compliance with Multilateral Climate Transparency Requirements: "Transparency Adherence Indices" and their Research and Policy Implications' (2021) 21(5) Climate Policy 635. See also: Gupta and van Asselt (n 2).
19 David Ciplet and others, 'The Transformative Capability of Transparency in Global Environmental Governance' (2018) 18(3) Global Environmental Politics 130 at 137.
20 UNFCCC, 'Biennial Update Report submissions from Non-Annex I Parties' <https://unfccc.int/BURs>.
21 Weikmans and Gupta (n 18) 643.
22 Decision 18/CMA.1 (n 10) para. 65 and following.
23 See for example: Bishnu Prasad Devkota and Irmeli Mustalahti, 'Complexities in Accessing REDD+ Benefits in Community Forestry: Evidence from Nepal's Terai Region' (2018) 20(3) The International Forestry Review 332.
24 Decision 18/CMA.1 (n 10) para. 80–90.
25 Decision 1/CP.21, Adoption of the Paris Agreement, 12 December 2015, UN Doc FCCC/CP/2015/10/Add.1 at para 53. See also: *Cancun Agreements* (n 7) para 98.
26 OECD, *2020 Projections of Climate Finance towards the USD 100 Billion Goal*, Technical Note (OECD Publishing 2016). Civil society observers have challenged this figure, as discussed in Section 6.
27 Yamide Dagnet and others, 'Building Capacity for the Paris Agreement's Enhanced Transparency Framework: What Can We Learn from Countries' Experiences and UNFCCC Processes?' Project for Advancing Climate Transparency Working Paper (Washington, DC 2019). See also: Frauke Röser and others, 'Ambition in the Making: Analysing the Preparation and Implementation Process of the Nationally Determined Contributions under the Paris Agreement' (2020) 20(4) Climate Policy 415.
28 See also: Röser and others (n 27) 415 at 424.
29 Decision 18/CMA.1 (n 10) Annex at paras 59–63.
30 See for example: Shuocheng Guo and Eleftheria Kontou, 'Disparities and Equity Issues in Electric Vehicles Rebate Allocation' (2021) 154 Energy Policy 112291 and Kathryn Canepa, Scott Hardman and Gil Tal, 'An Early Look at Plug-in Electric Vehicle Adoption in Disadvantaged Communities in California' (2019) 78 Transport Policy 19.

31 See: Office of the UN High Commissioner for Human Rights, Report of the Office of the UN High Commissioner for Human Rights on the Relationship between Climate Change and Human Rights, 15 January 2009, UN Doc A/HRC/10/61 at 42.
32 Hughes, Giest and Tozer (n 2) 1088.
33 See: Initiative for Climate Action Transparency, *Transformational Change Methodology: Assessing the Transformational Impacts of Policies and Actions* (KH Olsen and N Singh eds, UNEP DTU Partnership 2020) and Initiative for Climate Action Transparency, *Sustainable Development Methodology: Assessing the Environmental, Social and Economic Impacts of Policies and Actions* (D Rich, R Song and KH Olsen eds, UNEP DTU Partnership 2020).
34 UNDP Climate Promise Progress Report, *Special Edition: NDCs and Inclusivity*, November 2020 at 9.
35 Decision 18/CMA.1 (n 10) Annex at paras 83, 89 and 90.
36 Decision 2/CP.17 (n 8) Annex I, at 13–16. See also: Decision 9/CP.21 Methodologies for the reporting of financial information by Parties included in Annex I to the Convention, 10 December 2015, UN doc FCCC/CP/2015/10/Add.2, Annex, Revised common tabular format for the "UNFCCC biennial reporting guidelines for developed country Parties."
37 Decision 18/CMA.1 (n 10) at para 12(a).
38 ibid, Annex I, para 121. See also Decision 12/CMA.1, Identification of the information to be provided by Parties in accordance with Article 9, paragraph 5, of the Paris Agreement, 15 December 2018, UN Doc FCCC/PA/CMA/2018/3/Add.1, Annex.
39 OECD, *Climate Finance Provided and Mobilised by Developed Countries in 2013–18* (OECD Publishing 2020) 6.
40 Oxfam International, *Climate Finance Shadow Report 2020* (Oxfam GB 2020) at 8. See also: CARE International, 'Climate Adaptation Finance: Fact or Fiction?' (CARE International January 2021).
41 JT Roberts and others, 'Rebooting a Failed Promise of Climate Finance' (2021) 11 Nature Climate Change 180.
42 Brian Tomlinson and AidWatch Canada, 'The Reality of Canada's International Climate Finance' (AidWatch Canada 2020) at 10. See also: Climate Action Network Canada, 'Equity and International Mitigation Finance – Submission on Canada's Mitigation Finance for the Post-2020 Climate Finance Package' (Climate Action Network Canada 2020).
43 Decision 18/CMA.1 (n 10) 146–49.
44 Weikmans and Gupta (n 18).
45 See for example: Judith G Kelley and Beth A Simmons, 'Introduction: The Power of Global Performance Indicators' (2019) 73(3) Intl Organization 491.
46 See for example: Edward A Page, 'Distributing the Burdens of Climate Change' (2008) 17(4) Environmental Politics 556, Florian Egli and Anna Stünzi, 'A Dynamic Climate Finance Allocation Mechanism Reflecting the Paris Agreement' (2019) 14(11) Environmental Research Letters 1 and Simon Caney, 'Cosmopolitan Justice, Responsibility, and Global Climate Change' (2005) 18(4) Leiden J Intl L 747.
47 *Cancun Agreements* (n 7) para. 14–15.
48 Decision 9/CMA.1, Further guidance in relation to the adaptation communication, including, inter alia, as a component of nationally determined contributions, referred to in Article 7, paragraphs 10 and 11, of the Paris Agreement, 15 December 2018, UN Doc. FCCC/PA/CMA/2018/3/Add.1 at 4.
49 Decision 18/CMA.1 (n 10) paras 106–14 and 116.
50 Alexandra Lesnikowski and others, 'What Does the Paris Agreement Mean for Adaptation?' (2016) 17(7) Climate Policy 825 at 827.
51 James D Ford and Lea Berrang-Ford, 'The 4Cs of Adaptation Tracking: Consistency, Comparability, Comprehensiveness, Coherency' (2016) 21 Mitigation and Adaptation Strategies for Global Change 839 at 856.
52 OECD (n 26) 20.
53 UNEP, *The Adaptation Gap Report 2020* (UNEP 2020) at xiv. See also: UNEP, *The Adaptation Finance Gap Report* (UNEP 2016).
54 Ross Westoby and others, 'Sharing Adaptation Failure to Improve Adaptation Outcomes' (2020) 3(4) One Earth 388 at 389.
55 Joseph Wenta, Jan McDonald and Jeffrey S McGee, 'Enhancing Resilience and Justice in Climate Adaptation Laws' (2019) 8(1) Transnational Environmental Law 89 at 110.
56 Yamide Dagnet and others (n 27) 18.

57 Report of the Special Rapporteur on the issue of human rights obligations relating to the enjoyment of a safe, clean, healthy and sustainable environment, Safe Climate Report, 15 July 2019, UN doc A/74/161 at para 85.
58 United Nations Climate Change Secretariat, *Opportunities and options for integrating climate change adaptation with the Sustainable Development Goals and the Sendai Framework for Disaster Risk Reduction 2015–2030*, 2017 at 20.
59 Decision 18/CMA.1, *supra* note 10, Annex at para 108–14.

22

OPERATIONALIZING ARTICLE 6 OF THE PARIS AGREEMENT

Michael A. Mehling[*]

Introduction

Article 6 of the Paris Agreement enables Parties to engage in voluntary cooperation as they implement their nationally determined contributions (NDCs). Specifically, Article 6 sets out three pathways for voluntary cooperation:

- cooperative approaches through the use of internationally transferred mitigation outcomes (ITMOs) in Article 6.2;
- a new crediting mechanism, sometimes referred to as the 'Sustainable Development Mechanism,' in Article 6.4; and
- a framework for non-market approaches in Article 6.8.[1]

Although Article 6 omits explicit reference to carbon markets, it 'firmly anchors market mechanisms in the Paris Agreement'[2] with the two options set out in Article 6.2 and 6.4, and thereby leverages the promise of such mechanisms to reduce the cost of achieving agreed climate policy outcomes. By enabling mitigation activities to occur in jurisdictions with lower abatement cost, such cooperation not only helps alleviate the economic burden of climate action, but also creates a price signal in line with the 'polluter pays' principle while unlocking new sources of climate finance for developing countries.[3]

Recent studies suggest that the compliance flexibility introduced by Article 6 can significantly reduce the overall costs of achieving the temperature stabilization goals of the Paris Agreement, with one estimate suggesting economic efficiency gains from cooperative implementation of existing NDCs of approximately US$ 300 billion per year in 2030.[4] Such cost reductions, in turn, could increase the latitude of countries to scale up global climate ambition by unlocking additional resources that can be diverted to mitigation activities.[5] Calculations of the additional mitigation achievable by reinvesting avoided cost are, again, staggering, and would roughly allow doubling already pledged emission reductions through 2030.[6]

Given the persistent shortfall between currently pledged NDCs and the ambition required to achieve the temperature stabilization targets of the Paris Agreement,[7] international cooperation under Article 6 has been described as a necessary 'tool to promote more mitigation action . . . and

DOI: 10.4324/9781003276678-26

pave the way for progress within the next NDC cycle.'[8] Critics have countered that Article 6 could weaken ambition under the Paris Agreement if it lacks sufficient integrity or creates a distorted incentive for future NDCs.[9] With a synthesis report of NDCs confirming that a majority of Parties intend to use Article 6 as a source of climate finance or as a means to achieve pledged emission reductions,[10] the stakes for Article 6 are high.

Importantly, however, the treaty provision that constitutes Article 6 in the Paris Agreement is sparsely worded and replete with vague concepts.[11] Such 'constructive ambiguity' – often a deliberate choice to accommodate conflicting viewpoints – can compromise implementation of Article 6 by leaving room for divergent interpretations of key operational elements and creating uncertainty.[12] Ever since the Paris Agreement was adopted, Parties have therefore been engaged in developing rules and guidance for implementation of Article 6.[13] Just as Article 6 was the last provision Parties agreed upon when the Paris Agreement was adopted, however, its operationalization continues to defy broad international consensus. In the next section, the history of negotiations on operational details of Article 6 is traced to identify key areas of disagreement that have so far stood in the way of a definitive, and legally certain, outcome.

Operationalizing Article 6: Faultlines in the Negotiations

In the decision formally adopting the Paris Agreement and several provisions of the treaty itself, Parties set out mandates to elaborate decisions with operational details on a broad set of issues ranging from mitigation and adaptation to transparency, accounting, compliance, and assessment of progress.[14] Scheduled to conclude during the Meeting of the Parties to the Paris Agreement (CMA) in December 2018 in Katowice, Poland,[15] this process – formally known as the 'Work Program under the Paris Agreement' (PAWP)[16] – resulted in a comprehensive set of decisions that is colloquially referred to as the 'Paris Rulebook.'[17] A series of agenda items in this work program eluded consensus at Katowice, however: the operational details of Article 6.

Working through the Subsidiary Body for Scientific and Technical Advice (SBSTA), Parties had been locked in negotiations on decisions that provide guidance on cooperative approaches under Article 6.2 and elaborate rules, modalities, and procedures for Article 6.4. For years, delegates had already debated a succession of formal and informal texts of varying length, detail, and maturity, with numerous options and extensive bracketed text revealing the heterogeneity of views across parties. When Parties were unable to reach agreement on operational decisions for Article 6.2 and 6.4 in Katowice, the sheer volume of unresolved technical questions was blamed for the unsatisfactory outcome. Following that meeting, the number of brackets indicating disputed text in the draft decisions on Article 6 exceeded 600 at its highest point.[18]

By the next climate summit in Madrid one year later, progress had been achieved on many of the technical issues, but negotiations ultimately derailed due to a more limited number of political rather than technical disagreements: the fault lines featured in this section. As subsequently convened informal consultations and technical dialogues showed, these divisions – reflecting not only divergent circumstances and economic interests, but also very different understandings of the nature and objectives of Article 6 and the Paris Agreement more generally – remained deeply entrenched. Despite going into overtime during both the Katowice and the Madrid negotiations, Parties failed to bridge their differences on several key issues in the operationalization of Article 6, ultimately mandating SBSTA to build on existing progress and elaborate new recommendations for adoption during the next climate summit, scheduled to convene in Glasgow in 2020.[19]

An unprecedented hiatus in the climate negotiations followed due to the global pandemic caused by the novel coronavirus, with the Glasgow summit postponed until 2021. Parties scrambled to make up for lost time, yet a successful outcome in Glasgow was far from guaranteed. Discussions resumed virtually in the second half of 2020, but remained informal, hampered by the unfamiliar format. Despite a constructive series of multilateral consultations with Heads of Delegation (HoDs) and coordinators of regional negotiating groups convened by the Presidencies of the Madrid and Glasgow summits, and informal technical expert dialogues hosted by the SBSTA Chair, progress in 2021 remained slow. Reviewing the outcomes of informal ministerial consultations in July 2021, the facilitators of those meetings warned that 'progress on Article 6 was well behind time, and any further delays on a deal in Glasgow on Article 6 might erode ambition, transparency, accountability, and support.'[20]

Parties consistently identified a limited number of issues in the Article 6 negotiations that remained unresolved ahead of the Glasgow summit, formally known as the 26th Session of the Conference of the Parties to the United Nations Framework Convention on Climate Change, or COP26.[21] Among the most contested issues were:

- accounting for Article 6.4 reductions generated outside the scope of host Party NDCs;
- generating finance from Article 6.2 to support adaptation action (share of proceeds);
- transitioning unused emission units generated before 2020 to meet NDC targets;
- ensuring overall mitigation in global emissions (OMGE) under Article 6.2; and
- baseline setting and additionality determination under the Article 6.4 mechanism.

Of these topics, the first three were singled out by Parties as highly political and thus 'most in need of ministerial level discussion.'[22] Many other issues – including mostly technical issues, such as the reporting and review cycle or metrics for cooperative approaches, and more political issues, such as other uses of emission reductions or reference to respect for human rights – likewise remained unresolved, although they were considered less likely to prompt political gridlock in Glasgow and beyond.

Given the inability to convene formal negotiations and reach even preliminary closure on any of the underlying matters, the divisions carried forward to COP26 in Glasgow were numerous, although virtually every unresolved issue had seen several compromise options emerge. 'Bridging proposals' outlined at an informal ministerial meeting in July 2021, for instance, were welcomed by several Parties, although not all felt that those proposals adequately reflected their interests or concerns. As with all prior climate negotiations, thus, the Glasgow summit once again underscored that 'nothing is agreed until everything is agreed',[23] meaning that an agreed outcome will often emerge as a result of mutual concessions and arrangements. How that process would unfold, and which Parties would be willing to relent on one or more concerns in return for accommodation of their central priorities, remained unpredictable all the way to and even during COP26.

Building on compromise options that had already been present in the draft decision texts released two years earlier by the COP25 Presidency, informal consultations convened under SBSTA resulted in four iterations of negotiated language on each agenda item related to Article 6, culminating in draft decision texts forwarded to the CMA halfway through COP26, on 6 November 2021.[24] While these texts reflected a level of progress towards consensus, persistent disagreements on matters of principle still manifested themselves both in fundamental elements as well as technical details during the negotiations, often seeing Party views resurface that had been supposedly conceded when the Paris Agreement was originally adopted.[25] Ministerial consultations during the second week of COP26 resulted in additional iterations of draft text, and after several Parties finally compromised on their starting positions and negotiating 'red lines,' the CMA adopted formal decisions on each agenda item during the closing plenary of 13 November 2021: guidance on cooperative approaches under Article 6.2;[26] rules, modalities, and procedures for the mechanism established by Article 6.4;[27] and a work programme under the framework for non-market approaches referred to in Article 6.8.[28]

Several factors contributed to a successful outcome in Glasgow where previous negotiations had failed. Discussions benefitted from a markedly improved knowledge base relative to COP25 in Madrid, for instance, with a clearer understanding of the environmental and economic implications of alternative compromise options,[29] as well as a better sense of Party positions and the 'red lines' of key delegations. Availability of this information rendered it possible to envision potential landing zones based on reciprocal concessions of different country groups and bargaining across multiple agenda items. Still, the compromise options under consideration continued to entail extensive trade-offs, with no option satisfying all Parties in equal measure.[30]

Perhaps the most important factor, therefore, was the political pressure to conclude the last unfinished item in the work program for the 'Paris Rulebook,' which reached a high point as the latest assessment report of the Intergovernmental Panel on Climate Change (IPCC) issued a forceful warning about the scale and pace of the climate crisis, public demonstrations for increased climate action continued around the world, and several parties – including the European Union and the United States – unveiled domestic decarbonization strategies that represented a progression over previous efforts. Together, these converging factors focused the attention of all relevant actors on the need for closure on Article 6, starting with the SBSTA Chair and UK COP26 Presidency, and ultimately extending to the entire international community.

A Rulebook for Article 6: Progress in Glasgow and Beyond

Taken together, the three decisions adopted in Glasgow to operationalize Article 6 of the Paris Agreement amount to 36 pages of definitions, participation requirements, reporting obligations, institutional and procedural aspects of governance, as well as a first set of details on the infrastructure of Article 6. Parties also mandated further negotiations on a number of issues of a primarily technical nature for future sessions. As mentioned in the previous section, accurate accounting of ITMO transfers under Article 6 had been a priority for Parties as they entered the Glasgow negotiations; in the final decisions, this preoccupation with the environmental integrity of cooperation through Article 6 was reflected in an obligation to carry out a 'corresponding adjustment', a double-entry bookkeeping process meant to prevent double counting of emission reductions by requiring the host Party – or seller – to add the quantity of emission reductions transferred to its emissions balance while the acquiring Party – or buyer – subtracts the respective emissions from its emissions balance, all in a manner 'that ensures transparency, accuracy, completeness, comparability and consistency.'[31]

A breakthrough in the negotiations was secured when Parties agreed that such an adjustment would take place irrespective of whether the underlying mitigation activities fall within the scope of an NDC or not. Corresponding adjustments are mandatory at the time of host Party authorization for all three uses of ITMOs envisioned under Article 6.2: a transfer to an acquiring Party for use toward its NDC; 'international mitigation purposes' such as the Carbon Offsetting and Reduction Scheme for International Aviation (CORSIA) established under the International Civil Aviation Organization (ICAO); and 'other purposes' entailing use by non-Party actors towards voluntary targets.[32] For emission reductions issued under Article 6.4 (A6.4ERs), a corresponding adjustment is required at the moment of first transfer after these are authorized for use towards the achievement of NDCs or for other international mitigation purposes, and is also required when A6.4ERs are authorized for other purposes.[33] Some concerns remained about the application of a corresponding adjustment by Parties with a single-year target in their NDC,[34] where Parties requested SBSTA to elaborate further guidance.

In Glasgow, Parties also reached an agreement on the divisive issue of whether and how to transition unused legacy credits – or Certified Emission Units (CERs) – and project activities from the Clean Development Mechanism (CDM) of the Kyoto Protocol into the Paris Agreement regime. Some Parties and country groupings had strongly opposed any use of CERs generated before 2020 to meet NDC targets, highlighting the significant overhang of such units and the risks posed by allowing their use for achievement of the temperature stabilization targets of the Paris Agreement.[35] Other Parties, including a number of major emitters, had conversely emphasized the importance of an unrestricted carryover of units to retain investor confidence. Proposals to find middle ground by specifying cut-off dates for the issuance of units or the registration of underlying activities, a deadline for the use of legacy units, and other limitations, were initially rejected as arbitrary by those Parties holding a significant number of unsold CERs. Updated analysis showing that CER volumes issued by 2020 would lie at a more conservative end of estimates[36] paved the way for agreement on a limited carryover of CERs to those issued under projects registered after 2013, with unit use only allowed toward achievement of the first NDC;[37] likewise, only CDM activities registered by the end of 2023 can be carried over, and will have to comply with the rules under Article 6.4 after 2025.[38]

Another important feature of the decisions reached in Glasgow was the establishment of a Supervisory Body to oversee the operation of Article 6.4 and perform a variety of governance functions, such as developing and approving methodologies and standardized baselines, maintaining a registry, accrediting designated operational entities for verification tasks, and registering activities and issuing A6.4ERs.[39] It is also tasked with levying a mandatory share of proceeds – set at 5% of A6.4ERs at issuance plus a monetary contribution – for adaptation and administrative expenses, and ensuring the delivery of overall mitigation in global emissions through mandatory cancelation of 2% of all issued 6.4ERs.[40] Some Parties had furthermore requested that the share of proceeds and overall mitigation in global emissions be mandatory for cooperative approaches under Article 6.2, but the final compromise only included language that 'strongly encouraged' participating Parties to contribute resources for adaptation, in particular through contributions to the Adaptation Fund, and to cancel ITMOs that will not be counted toward any Party's NDC or for other international mitigation purposes.[41]

Despite the progress achieved in Glasgow, not all matters required to enable full operationalization of Article 6 were ultimately resolved during COP26, including further technical work on how to apply corresponding adjustments, reporting formats and technical expert reviews (TER), and the development of necessary infrastructure. Similarly, the Supervisory Body was mandated with an extensive work program to elaborate its rules of procedure and provisions for the development and approval of methodologies, validation, registration, monitoring, verification and certification, issuance, renewal, first transfer from the mechanism registry, and other processes under Article 6.4. Thus, in no small measure was the successful outcome in Glasgow owed to a conscious decision to defer certain agenda items to future negotiating sessions. Parties resumed discussions on these and other issues at the next session of the CMA during COP27 in Sharm el-Sheikh in 2022, yet negotiations since Glasgow have only achieved incremental progress.

On Article 6.2, for instance, Parties have become mired in discussions about technical minutiae such as the design and interoperability of registries, the role, form, and functions of a centralized accounting and reporting platform (CARP), the scope, procedure, and reporting format for TERs, and initial reporting outlines as well as standardized tables for an agreed electronic format (AEF).[42] In Sharm el-Sheikh, disagreements between Parties on the transparency of information subject to technical expert review resulted in a compromise that was heavily criticized by environmental advocacy groups and other stakeholders because it allows Parties to designate any information as confidential without providing a justification.[43] Similarly, Party views differed on the level of centralization of the future registry infrastructure for Article 6.2, revealing divergent preferences on the degree of multilateral oversight and prompting adoption of a bridging proposal in the form of an accounting and recording registry. Similar divisions on the appropriate balance between centralized authority and flexibility of Parties to determine the implementation of cooperative activities also characterized the next session of the CMA in Dubai in 2023, which altogether failed to agree on further guidance on Article 6.2.[44]

Article 6.4 has likewise seen Parties engaged in tedious negotiations on implementation issues since Glasgow, including the rules of procedure for the Supervisory Body, the eligibility of selected mitigation activity types, questions of host Party reporting, the registry, and processes for implementing the use of CERs toward NDCs.[45] Rapid growth of activity in the voluntary carbon market prompted a discussion of whether Article 6.4ERs that have not received host country authorization for use toward NDCs or other international mitigation purposes, and are thus not subject to a corresponding adjustment, can be used to offset emissions and for claims of carbon neutrality. On this question, Parties decided to introduce a new concept, designating such units 'mitigation contribution A6.4ERs' that may only be counted toward the 'reduction of emission levels in the host Party.'[46] Parties have also been divided on the issue of mitigation activities that remove greenhouse gases from the atmosphere, with Supervisory Body recommendations on nature-based and technological removal activities unable to secure consensus on contentious issues such as permanence, reversals, and leakage. Again, no decision on Article 6.4 was adopted in Dubai in 2023.

While negotiations since Glasgow have thus been able to advance some of the more technical issues, such as reporting outlines and formats, fundamental disagreements persist on the need for and extent of multilateral governance and centralized decision making, ultimately precluding adoption of any relevant decisions during the most recent session of the CMA. Critical issues that need to be resolved to fully operationalize Article 6, such as work on methodologies, baseline setting, and additionality for Article 6.4 activities, have been held back by these divisions on matters of principle. Under Rule 16 of the draft rules of procedure governing decision making by the parties, agenda items that are not completed during one session will automatically carry over to the agenda of the next session.[47] Still, if the latest negotiating sessions are any indication, the same fault lines that already burdened negotiations when the Paris Agreement was first adopted, and only allowed finalization of the Paris Rulebook because escalating political pressure forced a temporary breakthrough in Glasgow, continue to surface in the current implementation phase. Ironically, the very concerns about ambition and integrity that have compelled some parties to resist compromise outcomes may thus be resulting in a more loosely organized and nationally driven operational architecture for cooperation under Article 6, as discussed in the next section.

Implementation of Article 6: State Practice

Given the permissive nature of international law,[48] anything Parties fail to agree on remains, by default, within their sovereign discretion. Consequently, when Parties have argued during past negotiations that an absence of rules to operationalize Article 6 would not necessarily prevent parties from engaging in voluntary cooperation through carbon markets,[49] they correctly described the legal situation at least for the ability to transfer ITMOs through cooperative activities under

Article 6.2. Indeed, the wording of Article 6.2 intentionally calls for cooperative approaches to be implemented 'consistent with guidance,' rather than 'subject to guidance,' which would have implied conditionality on the adoption of such guidance. Rather, because Article 6.2 relies on parties for its implementation and does not necessarily depend on centralized governance processes or institutions, cooperative approaches remain viable even if Parties fail to finalize all operational details by way of implementing decisions, as has been the case with the latest round of negotiations in Dubai during COP28.

Indeed, a number of parties and international organizations are already piloting cooperative approaches under Article 6 to explore the opportunities offered by this policy mechanism and to inform the further development of operational rules. Most piloting activities focus on capacity building, establishing the necessary infrastructure, and creating an enabling environment for engagement in Article 6 transfers. Multilateral initiatives, such as the Transformative Carbon Asset Facility (TCAF) established by the World Bank, the Supporting Preparedness for Article 6 Cooperation (SPAR6C) programme hosted by the Global Green Growth Institute (GGGI), or the Article 6 Support Facility operated by the Asian Development Bank (ADB), aim to provide developing countries with capacity building and technical support to help them develop and test mitigation projects under Article 6. At the bilateral level, only a few pilot initiatives have progressed to the implementation phase, with Switzerland signing the first bilateral agreement – a mitigation outcome purchase agreement (MOPA) – with Peru in late 2020, and Japan entering into bilateral and commercial agreements on ITMO transfers with partner countries and project developers through its already existing Joint Crediting Mechanism (JCM).[50] Despite their early stages of development, piloting activities have already yielded a number of valuable insights for the practical operation of Article 6.

As of March 2024, the Article 6 Pilot Pipeline Database maintained by the UNEP Copenhagen Climate Centre (UNEP-CCC) listed 140 pilot projects in several dozen host countries, with funding for these activities originating from Australia, Japan, Monaco, Norway, Singapore, South Korea, Sweden, and Switzerland.[51] Only four of these pilot projects had already seen release of Authorization Statements and submission of the mandatory Initial Reports, but the fact that these steps had already been taken allowed for the first issuance ever of ITMOs on 15 December 2023 under a cooperative approach involving Switzerland and Thailand. Most activities follow a baseline-and-credit approach, aiming at emission reductions through interventions in energy supply, energy demand, waste, land use, and blue carbon. Through these various activities, over US$ 1.8 billion have been mobilized for Article 6 piloting activities, with ITMO prices – where disclosed – ranging from US$ 23.50 to 36 per ton of CO_2e.[52]

A periodic mapping exercise conducted under the Climate Finance Innovators project has identified a number of common patterns and tentative lessons from these piloting activities for the further operationalization and future implementation of Article 6. First, piloting activities can be distinguished by whether they explicitly aim at generating ITMOs or adaptation benefits (ABs) under Article 6, or are covered by its rules and procedures, such as linked emissions trading systems (ETS) enabling international transfers of emission allowances between Parties.[53] Second, many of the foregoing activities have already progressed to implementation, although these mostly have the character of capacity building activities, and it remains unclear whether sustained demand for ITMOs will emerge over the longer term.[54] Third, contractual structures have become diversified, but share a focus on environmental integrity, for instance by including provisions on the avoidance of double counting of mitigation outcomes, enhancement of NDC ambition in the host country, sharing of benefits and prevention of overselling, and applying robust methodologies for baseline and additionality.[55] Fourth, piloting activities have reflected the changed incentive structure under the Paris Agreement, with host countries showing greater reluctance to commit to a transfer of mitigation outcomes they may eventually need to meet their own NDCs. Accordingly, the initiative to cooperate has typically originated with the prospective buyer countries. Fifth, and finally, while uncertainty about the operational details of Article 6 may have slowed down the pace of piloting activities, further decisions are clearly not seen as a necessary condition for cooperative approaches under Article 6.2.

While voluntary cooperation under Article 6.2 will thus most likely proceed no matter what, failure to finalize the rules, modalities and procedures for Article 6.4 may mean that the latter never sees a similar level of participation. With its more centralized architecture, Article 6.4 relies on the Supervisory Body for its operation, which in turn is subject to the authority and guidance of the CMA. The stakes for an agreed outcome at upcoming climate summits are thus disproportionately higher for Article 6.4. Interactions between the Supervisory Body and Parties in the CMA do not promise an easy process going forward, however: while the existence of a constituted body should accelerate progress by virtue of allowing more frequent meetings and ideally a less politicized setting, matters of principle – including the recurring disagreements on the appropriate levels of flexibility and multilateral oversight – keep entering the discussions and preventing adoption of Supervisory Body recommendations. Still, Parties have already made ample use of the provision allowing a transition of legacy activities and units under the CDM, with transition requests submitted for 1,274 Project Activities, 113 Programmes of Activities, and 933 Component Project Activities as of 29 February 2024, potentially carrying over almost 900 million tons of CO_2e.[56]

Outlook

Although operational details on Article 6 eluded agreement for the first five years after the Paris Agreement was adopted, interest in market approaches to climate change mitigation has continued to grow apace. From the steady expansion of domestic emissions trading systems to record levels of activity in the voluntary carbon market and, more recently, a growing number of Article 6 pilot initiatives, this momentum may translate into the political pressure needed for full operationalization of Article 6 at future climate negotiations. Key elements of the implementation framework remain unresolved, including further rules on accounting, reporting, and host Party authorization, which in turn risks delaying the establishment of national institutional frameworks. If the aspiration of Article 6 – according to its wording – is to 'allow for higher ambition in [Parties'] mitigation and adaptation actions' by reducing the cost of implementation and fostering investment flows, then lacking uptake could impede adoption of more ambitious pledges in the next NDC cycle in 2025.

For that aspiration to be realized, however, Article 6 has to secure a high standard of environmental integrity. Experience with earlier carbon markets – including, in particular, the market for credits issued under the CDM – leaves little doubt that robust governance, both at the multilateral level and in the bilateral arrangements between parties, will be critical for the enduring viability of Article 6. If its operationalization is unable to ensure alignment with the temperature stabilization goals of the Paris Agreement, it will only be a matter of time before flawed or fraudulent activities are revealed to the public and confidence in the market dwindles, as it already did once under the Kyoto Protocol. That does not, however, mean that negotiators should always err on the side of the most ambitious option for each issue currently under discussion. While the 'San José Principles for High Ambition and Integrity in International Carbon Markets'[57] may have commendable intentions, for instance, some of the principles, if interpreted and applied literally, could effectively prevent Article 6 from fulfilling its potential to enable ambition by lowering the cost of achieving mitigation targets.[58]

A balance between stringency and flexibility, that is, between nationally determined implementation and centralized oversight authority, is therefore essential. Whether Parties at future negotiations can overcome their past divisions to achieve such a balanced outcome is everything but certain. With the 'Paris Rulebook' now finalized, concerns and preferences that Parties have been willing to set aside in the interest of full operationalization, including deeply held views about the nature and objectives of the Paris Agreement, risk being drawn to the surface during continued negotiations on Article 6. Already, as the analysis in this chapter has shown, Parties are alternatingly invoking specific provisions of the Paris Agreement and general principles and objectives to justify their position, echoing the recursive argumentation patterns of international relations more generally.[59] Yet full operationalization of Article 6 is not altogether out of reach. Parties have not remained idle since COP26. As they reconvene in Baku, Azerbaijan, later in 2024, they will be equipped with both a better understanding of the implications of alternative policy choices, and a better sense of the viewpoints and positions of their fellow Parties. Improved knowledge may, in the end, be the key to unlocking the transformative potential of Article 6.

Notes

* I gratefully acknowledge valuable comments on an earlier version received from Aglaja Espelage, Andrei Marcu, Axel Michaelowa, Giuseppe Montesano, Nicolò Sartori, and Robert Stowe, as well as support from the Enel Foundation and the Harvard Project on Climate Agreements. Opinions and remaining errors are my own.

1 Article 6.8 on non-market approaches is not further considered in this chapter; for further details, however, see Karsten Karschunke, Thomas Forth and Axel Michaelowa, 'Operationalizing Article 6.8 & 6.9 of the Paris Agreement' (Deutsche Emissionshandelsstelle (DEHSt) 2021) <https://www.carbon-mechanisms.de/fileadmin/media/dokumente/Publikationen/Bericht/A_6.8_6.9_Virtual_seminar_Key_messages.pdf>.

2 Benito Müller, 'Article 6: Market Approaches under the Paris Agreement' (European Capacity Building Initiative (ECBI) 2018) Policy Brief 7 <https://ecbi.org/news/article-6-market-approaches-under-paris-agreement>.

3 Michael A Mehling, 'Market Mechanisms' in Lavanya Rajamani and Jacqueline Peel (eds), *The Oxford Handbook of International Environmental Law* (2nd edn, OUP 2021).

4 James E Edmonds and others, 'How Much Could Article 6 Enhance Nationally Determined Contribution Ambition toward Paris Agreement Goals through Economic Efficiency?' (2021) 12 Climate Change Economics 2150007.

5 Michael A Mehling, Gilbert E Metcalf and Robert N Stavins, 'Linking Heterogeneous Climate Policies (Consistent with the Paris Agreement)' (2018) 48 Environmental Law 647.

6 Pedro Piris-Cabezas, Ruben N Lubowski and Gabriela Leslie, 'Estimating the Potential of International Carbon Markets to Increase Global Climate Ambition' (2023) 167 World Development 106257; Edmonds and others (n 5).

7 Taryn Fransen and others, 'Taking Stock of the Implementation Gap in Climate Policy' (2023) 13 Nature Climate Change 752; UNEP, *Emissions Gap Report 2023: Broken Record* (United Nations Environment Programme 2023) <https://wedocs.unep.org/bitstream/handle/20.500.11822/43922/EGR2023.pdf>.

8 Malin Ahlberg, 'Enhancing Ambition: Carbon Pricing as a Tool to Step up Mitigation Efforts' (2018) 6 Carbon Mechanisms Review 22, 23–24.

9 Lambert Schneider and Stephanie La Hoz Theuer, 'Environmental Integrity of International Carbon Market Mechanisms Under the Paris Agreement' (2019) 19 Climate Policy 386.

10 Nicolas Kreibich, 'Analysis of the role of Article 6 in Parties' NDCs' (Umweltbundesamt 2024) Fact Sheet 03/2024 <https://www.umweltbundesamt.de/publikationen/analysis-of-the-role-of-article-6-in-parties-ndcs>; UNFCCC, 'Nationally Determined Contributions under the Paris Agreement: Synthesis Report by the Secretariat. UN Doc. FCCC/PA/CMA/2023/12' <https://unfccc.int/sites/default/files/resource/cma2023_12.pdf>, para. 7.

11 On the negotiating history of Article 6, see Andrew Howard, 'Voluntary Cooperation (Article 6)' in Daniel Klein and others (eds), *The Paris Agreement on Climate Change: Analysis and Commentary* (OUP 2017) 178–95.

12 Harro van Asselt, Kati Kulovesi and Michael A Mehling, 'Negotiating the Paris Rulebook: Introduction to the Special Issue' (2018) 12 Carbon & Climate Law Review 173, 173.
13 UNFCCC, Decision 1/CP.21, Adoption of the Paris Agreement, Report of the Conference of the Parties on its Twenty-First Session, Addendum, Part 2, UN Doc. FCCC/CP/2015/10/Add.1 (29 January 2016), para. 36.
14 Section III of Decision 1/CP.21 (n 13).
15 Formally the Third Part of the First Session of the CMA, see UNFCCC, Decision 1/COP.23, Fiji Momentum for Implementation, Report of the Conference of the Parties on its Twenty-third Session, UN Doc. FCCC/CP/2017/11/Add.1 (8 February 2018), para. 2.
16 UNFCCC, Decision 1/CMA.1, Matters Relating to the Implementation of the Paris Agreement, Report of the Conference of the Parties Serving as the Meeting of the Parties to the Paris Agreement on the First Part of its First Session, Addendum, Part Two, UN Doc. FCCC/PA/CMA/2016/3/Add.1 (31 January 2017), paras. 5–7.
17 For commentary, see Lavanya Rajamani and Daniel Bodansky, 'The Paris Rulebook: Balancing International Prescriptiveness with National Discretion' (2019) 68 International and Comparative Law Quarterly 1023.
18 Simon Evans and others, 'COP26: Key Outcomes Agreed at the UN Climate Talks in Glasgow', CarbonBrief (15 November 2021) <https://www.carbonbrief.org/cop26-key-outcomes-agreed-at-the-un-climate-talks-in-glasgow>.
19 UNFCCC, Decision 9/CMA.2, Matters relating to Article 6 of the Paris Agreement, Report of the Conference of the Parties serving as the Meeting of the Parties to the Paris Agreement on its Second Session, Addendum, Part Two, FCCC/PA/CMA/2019/6/Add.1 (16 March 2020), para. 2.
20 UNFCCC, Report by Minister Grace Fu (Singapore) and Minister Sveinung Rotevatn (Norway) on the Informal Ministerial Consultations on Article 6 of the Paris Agreement on 7 and 12 July (26 July 2021) 2 <https://unfccc.int/sites/default/files/resource/Article%206%20Ministerial%20Consultations%20Report%20Back.pdf>.
21 UNFCCC, Co-Chairs' Summary of the Presidencies' Consultations on Article 6 of the Paris Agreement (Cooperative Approaches, the Mechanism, the Framework for Non-market Approaches) (29–30 March 2021) 1 <https://unfccc.int/sites/default/files/resource/Co-chairs_Summary_Article_6.pdf>.
22 UNFCCC, Heads of Delegation Briefing on Informal Ministerial Consultations on Article 6 of the Paris Agreement, Summary by the Chair (23 June 2021) 2 <https://unfccc.int/sites/default/files/resource/20210623_Chairs_Summary_Art6.pdf>.
23 Andrei C Marcu and Virender K Duggal, 'Negotiations on Article 6 of the Paris Agreement: Road to Madrid' (Asian Development Bank (ADB) November 2019) 4 <https://www.adb.org/sites/default/files/publication/541016/sdwp-063-negotiations-article-6-paris-agreement.pdf>.
24 IISD Reporting Services, 'Glasgow Climate Change Conference: 31 October-13 November 2021' (16 November 2021) 12(793) Earth Negotiations Bulletin 23 <https://enb.iisd.org/sites/default/files/2021-11/enb12793e_1.pdf>.
25 Evans and others (n 18).
26 UNFCCC, Decision 2/CMA.3, Guidance on Cooperative Approaches referred to in Article 6, paragraph 2, of the Paris Agreement, Report of the Conference of the Parties serving as the Meeting of the Parties to the Paris Agreement on its Third Session, Addendum, Part Two, FCCC/PA/CMA/2021/10/Add.1 (8 March 2022) <https://unfccc.int/sites/default/files/resource/cma2021_10_add1_adv.pdf>.
27 UNFCCC, Decision 3/CMA.3, Rules, Modalities and Procedures for the Mechanism established by Article 6, paragraph 4, of the Paris Agreement, ibid.
28 UNFCCC, Decision 4/CMA.3, Work Programme under the Framework for Non-market Approaches referred to in Article 6, paragraph 8, of the Paris Agreement, ibid.
29 Uncertainty about matters such as potential volumes of CERs and other units issued under the Kyoto Protocol by the end of 2020 were cited by several Parties as a reason for their inability to agree to suggested compromise options during previous negotiations, and some even conceded that they would 'potentially be open to changing their positions' based on more robust data. Calls for further analysis were met from research and environmental advocacy groups as well as the UNFCCC Secretariat, see IISD Reporting Services, 'Summary of the May-June 2021 Climate Change Conference: 31 May-17 June 2021' (21 June 2021) 12(780) Earth Negotiations Bulletin 12 <https://enb.iisd.org/sites/default/files/2021-06/enb12780e.pdf>.
30 With regard to different scenarios for the transition of legacy CERs, for instance, see the tradeoffs identified by Sandra Greiner and others, 'CDM Transition to Article 6 of the Paris Agreement: Options Report'

(Koru Climate and Climate Focus, March 2017) 43–44 <https://www.climatefocus.com/sites/default/files/CDM%20Transition%20Options%20Report%20v2.0.pdf>.

31 Wolfgang Obergassel and others, 'Turning Point Glasgow? An Assessment of the Climate Conference COP26' (2021) 15 Carbon & Climate Law Review 271, 275.

32 Decision 2/CMA.3 (n 26) para. 1.

33 Decision 3/CMA.3 (n 27) para. 43–44.

34 In such cases, the guidance on Article 6.2 allows countries to choose between two methods: application to an indicative multi-year emissions trajectory or budget consistent with achievement of the NDC, or 'averaging' over the number of elapsed years in the NDC implementation period, see Decision 2/CMA.3 (n 26), para. 7.

35 Some early third-party analyses suggested that unrestricted carryover of CERs could weaken pledged ambition under the Paris Agreement by almost 40%; see Climate Analytics, 'Article 6 Needs Ambition, not Time Wasting: The Carryover of Pre-2020 Credits Could Fatally Undermine the Paris Agreement' (Climate Analytics 2019) 3 <https://climateanalytics.org/media/carry_over_ca_briefing_11dec2019.pdf>.

36 UNFCCC, 'Article 6 of the Paris Agreement: Informal Technical Expert Dialogues. CDM Transition' <https://unfccc.int/sites/default/files/resource/Art.%206%20_presentation%20ITEDs%20CDM%20transition.pdf>; see also Axel Michaelowa and others, 'Volumes and Types of Unused Certified Emission Reductions (CERs)' (Perspectives and Zurich University of Applied Sciences (ZHAW) 2021) <https://www.zhaw.ch/storage/sml/institute-zentren/cee/PCG-ZHAW_unused_CERs_final_clean_PAC.pdf>.

37 Decision 3/CMA.3 (n 27) para. 75.

38 ibid para. 73.

39 ibid paras. 3–24.

40 ibid paras. 66–70.

41 Decision 2/CMA.3 (n 26), paras. 37–39.

42 UNFCCC, Decision 6/CMA.4, Matters relating to cooperative approaches referred to in Article 6, paragraph 2, of the Paris Agreement, Report of the Conference of the Parties serving as the Meeting of the Parties to the Paris Agreement on its Fourth Session, Addendum, Part Two, FCCC/PA/CMA/2022/10/Add.2 (17 March 2023) <https://unfccc.int/documents/626570>.

43 ibid, Annex II: Guidelines for the Article 6 Technical Expert Review Referred to in Decision 2/CMA.3, Annex, Chapter V (Review) para. 22; see also Aruna Chandrasekhar and others, 'COP27: Key Outcomes Agreed at the UN Climate Talks in Sharm el-Sheikh', CarbonBrief (21 November 2022) <https://www.carbonbrief.org/cop27-key-outcomes-agreed-at-the-un-climate-talks-in-sharm-el-sheikh>.

44 Wolfgang Obergassel and others, 'Through the Desert towards Fresh Water – or Just a Fata Morgana? An Assessment of COP28 in Dubai' (Wuppertal Institute for Climate, Environment and Energy 2023) 10 <https://wupperinst.org/fa/redaktion/downloads/publications/COP28-Report_en.pdf>.

45 Wolfgang Obergassel and others, 'Last Call for 1.5 Degrees: COP27 in Sharm El Sheikh Schedules Fund for Loss and Damage for Departure While Mitigation Stays Grounded' (2022) 16 Carbon & Climate Law Review 225.

46 UNFCCC, Decision 7/CMA.4, Guidance on the Mechanism Established by Article 6, paragraph 4, of the Paris Agreement, Report of the Conference of the Parties serving as the Meeting of the Parties to the Paris Agreement on its Fourth Session, Addendum, Part Two, FCCC/PA/CMA/2022/10/Add.2 (17 March 2023) <https://unfccc.int/documents/626570>, Annex I, para. 29b.

47 UNFCCC, Organizational Matters: Adoption of the Rules of Procedure. Note by the Secretariat, Conference of the Parties, Second Session, FCCC/CP/1996/2 (22 May 1996) <https://unfccc.int/sites/default/files/resource/02_0.pdf>, Rule 16.

48 Case of the S.S. Lotus (*France v. Turkey*), Judgment, 1927 P.C.I.J. (ser. A) No. 10, at 45–47 (7 September 1927).

49 See, e.g., the EU position expressed during COP25: IISD Reporting Services, 'Summary of the Chile/Madrid Climate Change Conference: 2–15 December 2019' (18 December 2019) 12(775) Earth Negotiations Bulletin 15 <https://enb.iisd.org/events/chilemadrid-climate-change-conference-december-2019/summary-report-2-15-december-2019>.

50 Sandra Greiner and others, 'Article 6 Piloting: State of Play and Stakeholder Experiences' (Climate Focus and others 2020) <https://www.climatefocus.com/sites/default/files/Climate-Finance-Innovators_Article-6-piloting_State-of-play-and-stakeholder-experiences_December-2020.pdf>.

51 Copenhagen Climate Centre, 'Article 6 Pipeline' (Copenhagen: UN Environment Programme 2024) <https://article6pipeline.org>.

52 Stephan Hoch and others, 'The Landscape of Article 6 Implementation' (Climate Finance Innovators 2023) 20 <https://www.carbon-mechanisms.de/fileadmin/media/dokumente/Publikationen/Bericht/CFI-Guidebook-the-landscape-of-article-6-implementation-Nov_2023.pdf>.

53 ibid 11–15.

54 ibid 22.

55 Sandra Greiner and others, 'Moving Towards Next Generation Carbon Markets: Observations from Article 6 Pilots' (Climate Focus and others 2019) <https://www.carbon-mechanisms.de/fileadmin/media/dokumente/Publikationen/Studie/Studie_2019_CFI_Article_6_Pilots.pdf>.

56 Copenhagen Climate Centre (n 51).

57 Costa Rica and others, 'San Jose Principles for High Ambition and Integrity in International Carbon Markets' (30 October 2019) <https://cambioclimatico.go.cr/sanjoseprinciples/about-the-san-jose-principles>.

58 Michael A Mehling, 'Governing Cooperative Approaches under the Paris Agreement' (2020) 46 Ecology Law Quarterly 765–828.

59 Martti Koskenniemi, *From Apology to Utopia: The Structure of International Legal Argument* (CUP 2006).

23
INCENTIVIZING INTERNATIONAL FINANCE FOR NET ZERO PARIS AGREEMENT IMPLEMENTATION

Wendy Miles KC and Douglas Leys KC

Introduction

The **Paris Agreement** by virtue of Article 2.1(c) states as follows:

> This Agreement in enhancing the implementation of the Convention, including its objective, aims to strengthen the global response to the threat of climate change, in the context of sustainable development and efforts to eradicate poverty, including by:
>
> (c). . .**making finance flows consistent with a pathway towards low greenhouse gas emissions and climate-resilient development.**[1] (emphasis supplied)

The primary aim of the Paris Agreement is to induce a substantial shift in the global economy by redirecting financial resources away from unsustainable practices and infrastructure towards sustainable alternatives.[2]

These alternatives should meet societal needs, emit lower levels of greenhouse gases (GHGs), and demonstrate greater resilience to climate impacts.[3] Article 2.1(c) explicitly highlights the importance of aligning financial flows to support the transition towards low GHG emissions and climate-resilient development.[4] To achieve this goal, significant changes are necessary in incentives, disincentives, cooperative climate action, and individual behaviours. The traditional international financial institutions are not readily geared to implement these requirements. The predominant reason why is that their capital structure was not geared for this kind of activity.

Article 9 of the Paris Agreement specifically addresses the mobilization of climate finance as a key tool for driving this transformation.[5] Scaling up climate finance and its effective deployment will be integral to advancing both mitigation and adaptation strategies, as well as attracting larger private finance contributions.

The foundation for Articles 2.1(c) and 9 of the Paris Agreement are to be found in the United Nations Framework Convention on Climate Change (UNFCCC). Article 11 establishes and defines a financial mechanism.[6] The operation of that financial mechanism was initially vested in the Global Environmental Facility (GEF), which is an independent body that performs similar

DOI: 10.4324/9781003276678-27

functions under other environmental treaties. In 2010 the Green Climate Fund (GCF) was established by the Conference of the Parties (COP), the highest decision-making body under the UNFCCC, pursuant to the 2010 Cancun Agreements, to serve as the other operating mechanism.[7] This chapter is primarily concerned with the efforts of the GCF to operationalize Articles 2 and 9 of the Paris Agreement by mobilizing financial flows as well as the financial instruments used to do so. It demonstrates the wide array of financial instruments in the GCF and how the GCF is able to deploy its capital in a manner different from the traditional international financial institutions, thus creating a financial window for financial flows to help realize the net zero ambitions envisaged in its efforts to mitigate and adapt to the rigours of climate change.

The Green Climate Fund

The GCF serves as a vital platform for mobilizing and distributing climate finance to support developing countries in their endeavours to mitigate and adapt to climate change.[8] Its primary goal is to facilitate low-emission and climate-resilient development, with a particular focus on assisting vulnerable nations and those with limited resources.[9] The GCF provides funding for various projects and programmes in areas such as renewable energy, energy efficiency, climate resilience, and sustainable land use. It plays a significant role in facilitating financial transfers to developing countries, enabling them to take climate action. The GCF's governance involves a board composed of an equal number of representatives from both developed and developing countries.[10]

Pursuant to paragraph 29 of its Governing Instrument, the GCF requires funding to be provided by developed country parties to the UNFCCC, although it may also receive financial inputs from a variety of other sources, both public and private. These provisions empower the GCF with the authority to raise finance and define the parameters in which the process may occur. As previously mentioned, there is another operating entity under the UNFCCC, i.e. the GEF. It uses a similar contribution-based financing system, although it splits its funds among five conventions. The GCF occupies a unique space in climate finance and, unlike other international finance development institutions whose fundraising activities cover a range of sources from capital market transactions to leveraging their share capital and other assets, the GCF now relies exclusively on voluntary contributions for a single purpose. This may change in the future. The GCF therefore has a unique advantage among international financial institutions. It is not constrained in devising its financial instruments to be primarily concerned with a return to shareholders and investors. At the same time it has a raft of policies to ensure that the use of its resources is prudently and efficiently managed.[11]

Financial Instruments

In order to discharge its mandate under the Paris Agreement, the GCF deploys a raft of financial instruments tailor made to specific circumstances to ensure that they are used in a sustainable and paradigm-shifting manner.[12] These instruments are as follows: grants, concessional loans, equity investments, subordinated debt, results-based payments, guarantees, and blended finance.[13] These instruments will be discussed *seriatim.*

Grants (Non-reimbursable and Reimbursable)

The (GCF) utilizes both non-reimbursable and reimbursable grants as part of its arsenal to finance climate activities. These grant types support different purposes and activities within the realm of climate change mitigation and adaptation.[14] Non-reimbursable grants are typically distributions of financial resources with no repayment obligations on the part of the recipients. The grants are disbursed on conditions and are frequently attached to milestones in terms of activities and eligibility for further disbursements. Reimbursable grants are typically distributions of financial resources which contain a repayment obligation on part of the recipients. They are often used where a project or activity has the prospect of a return on investment, especially where private sector actors are involved. Once the project has been successfully implemented and there is a positive return on investment, the recipient is required to repay the grant, often with an interest component attached to it. In other cases it may just be the return of capital deployed by the GCF. It is possible to offer examples of how the GCF employs these grant types:

(a) Non-reimbursable grants can be used for:

  (i) Capacity-building: The GCF provides non-reimbursable grants to support capacity-building activities, including training programs, workshops, and technical assistance, aimed at enhancing the capacity of developing countries to address climate change effectively.
  (ii) Project Preparation: These are non-reimbursable grants to help cover the costs associated with project preparation activities, such as feasibility studies, environmental assessments, and financial structuring. These grants enable countries to develop robust and bankable climate projects.
  (iii) Technology Transfer: Non-reimbursable grants can be used to facilitate technology transfer from developed to developing countries. This support includes activities like technology assessments, pilot projects, and the deployment of climate-friendly technologies.

(b) Reimbursable grants can be used for:

  (i) Project Implementation: The GCF provides reimbursable grants to support the actual implementation of climate projects on the ground. This funding can cover a range of activities, including the construction of renewable energy infrastructure, climate resilience measures, ecosystem restoration, and sustainable agriculture initiatives.
  (ii) The GCF can also approve reimbursable grants in the form of loans that are given to eligible recipients, typically with a repayment obligation over time. These loans support climate-related projects and activities, helping countries finance their climate action plans.

It is important to note that the GCF considers a combination of non-reimbursable and reimbursable grants to cater to the diverse needs of recipient countries. The specific mix of grant types utilized by the GCF depends on project requirements, country priorities, and the nature of the climate initiatives being supported.

Concessional Loans

The GCF offers concessionary loans as a financial instrument to support climate-related projects and activities in developing countries. Concessionary loans provided by the GCF have certain characteristics that differentiate them from traditional commercial loans. The following is an overview of the regime for the GCF's concessionary loans.

Below-Market Interest Rates: The GCF provides loans at interest rates that are typically lower than those offered by commercial lenders. These below-market interest rates make the loans more affordable for recipient countries and help address financial barriers associated with climate change projects.

Longer Repayment Periods: The repayment periods for GCF concessionary loans are generally longer compared to commercial loans. This flexibility allows recipient countries to repay the loans over an extended timeframe, considering the long-term nature of climate change projects that necessitate significant investments and potential revenue generation.

Flexible Terms and Conditions: The terms and conditions of GCF concessionary loans can be customized to suit the specific requirements of the recipient country and the project being financed. This flexibility enables countries to structure the loans in a manner that aligns with their capacity and priorities.

Preference for High-Impact Projects: The GCF prioritizes financing projects that have a high potential for climate mitigation and adaptation impact, particularly in vulnerable and less developed countries. Concessionary loans are often directed towards initiatives that contribute significantly to greenhouse gas reduction, foster climate resilience, and promote sustainable development.

Enhanced Access for Developing Countries: The GCF aims to enhance access to climate finance for developing countries that may have limited access to traditional sources of financing. Concessionary loans are an important instrument for providing financial resources to support climate-related projects in these countries, helping bridge the funding gap.

While the specifics of concessionary loan arrangements may vary depending on project requirements and country circumstances, the overall regime for GCF concessionary loans is designed to offer flexible and affordable financing options to promote climate action in developing nations. The GCF can do so because it does not access its resources from the capital markets; accordingly, there is no benchmark return for creditors and investors. Because it relies exclusively on voluntary contributions from developed country members, it is not constrained by this factor.

Equity Investments

The GCF has the capacity to use equity investments as part of its arsenal of financial instruments in its efforts to mobilize and deploy climate finance. Equity investments involve the purchase of shares or ownership stakes in companies or projects with the aim of earning a financial return while promoting climate action. The purpose of equity investments made by the GCF serve multiple objectives. They not only provide financial returns to support the Fund's sustainability, but also promote climate-related initiatives by investing in companies or projects that contribute to mitigation, adaptation, and sustainable development. The following are the main types of equity investments undertaken by the GCF:

Direct Equity Investments: The GCF can directly acquire equity stakes in specific companies or projects that align with its objectives. These investments provide the GCF with ownership rights and influence over decision-making processes.

Indirect Equity Investments: The GCF may also invest in equity funds or venture capital funds that specialize in climate-related sectors. Through these indirect investments, the GCF indirectly supports a portfolio of companies or projects working on climate solutions.

Illustrative examples of equity investments by the GCF include:

Renewable Energy Projects: The GCF may make equity investments in renewable energy projects, such as solar or wind farms. These investments can provide the GCF with financial returns while supporting the expansion of clean energy generation.

Climate-Resilient Infrastructure: The GCF may invest in companies involved in building resilient transportation systems or sustainable urban development projects.

Sustainable Agriculture Initiatives: The GCF may also support equity investments in companies or projects focused on sustainable agriculture practices, such as agroforestry, organic farming, or climate-smart technologies. These investments can help promote resilient food production systems.

Climate Technology Start-ups: Equity investments by the GCF can enable support for climate technology start-ups and innovative ventures working on cutting-edge solutions for climate mitigation and adaptation. These investments help nurture a pipeline of innovative companies addressing climate challenges.

Equity investments made by the GCF are guided by its investment guidelines and assessment criteria that consider both financial viability and climate impact. Such investments provide the GCF with the potential for financial returns while fostering transformative climate action through targeted investments in companies and projects.

Subordinated Debt

The GCF can utilize subordinated debt instruments as part of its climate finance activities. Subordinated debt involves providing loans or financial instruments that have a lower priority of repayment compared to other debt obligations. The purpose of the GCF's subordinated debt instrument is to provide concessional financing to support climate-related projects and activities in developing countries. It allows the GCF to address specific financial needs and leverage additional investment by taking on a lower repayment priority.

The GCF may offer various types of subordinated debt instruments, such as:

Subordinated Loans: The GCF can provide loans to recipient countries or projects that are considered subordinated or junior to other debt obligations. These loans have a lower priority in the order of repayment in the event of default or liquidation.

Subordinated Bonds: The GCF may issue subordinated bonds as a form of debt instrument. Subordinated bonds have a lower claim on assets or cash flows compared to other senior or unsecured debt obligations.

A few instances of how these subordinated debt instruments may be used by the GCF include:

Climate-Resilient Infrastructure: The GCF's subordinated debt instrument can support infrastructure projects with a focus on climate resilience. For example, the GCF may provide subordinated loans to finance the construction of climate-resilient transportation systems, water infrastructure, or resilient urban development projects.

Renewable Energy Ventures: Subordinated debt instruments from the GCF can facilitate investments in renewable energy projects, such as solar or wind farms. By providing subordinated loans or bonds, the GCF helps attract additional private investment in these ventures.

Adaptation and Mitigation Initiatives: The GCF's subordinated debt instrument can be used to support adaptation and mitigation projects. For instance, the GCF may offer subordinated loans to finance initiatives aimed at coastal protection, climate-smart agriculture, or ecosystem restoration.

Small and Medium-Sized Enterprises (SMEs): The GCF's subordinated debt instrument can target SMEs that play a critical role in climate action. Subordinated loans can provide financing options to SMEs engaged in climate-related sectors like energy efficiency, sustainable manufacturing, or green technologies.

These examples illustrate how the GCF's subordinated debt instrument can be employed to provide flexible and concessional financing for a range of climate-related projects and initiatives. By taking on a lower repayment priority, the GCF can incentivize private investment and support transformative climate action in developing countries.

Results-Based Payments

Results-based payments refer to funding provided by the GCF to recipient countries based on the achievement of specific climate-related targets or results. These payments are typically made as a reward or incentive for successful implementation of projects or programmes that yield positive outcomes in terms of reducing GHG emissions, enhancing climate resilience, or advancing sustainable development. The following are some examples of different areas in which the GCF provide results-based payments. Some, like sustainable forest management, are already in train in those programmes in the Congo and Peru:

Renewable Energy Projects: If a recipient country successfully implements a renewable energy project, such as a wind farm or solar power plant, and meets predefined criteria for clean energy generation and emission reductions, they may receive results payments from the GCF.

Climate Resilience Programs: If a country implements initiatives to strengthen its resilience to climate change impacts, such as implementing flood control measures or building climate-resilient infrastructure, and achieves specific resilience outcomes, results payments may be provided by the GCF.

Sustainable Forest Management: The GCF may offer results payments to countries that effectively implement sustainable forest management practices, leading to carbon sequestration, reduced deforestation rates, and biodiversity conservation.

Energy Efficiency Initiatives: If a country implements energy efficiency measures in buildings, industries, or transportation sectors, resulting in reduced energy consumption and lower greenhouse gas emissions, they may receive results payments from the GCF based on the achieved energy savings.

Low-Carbon Transportation Projects: The GCF may provide results payments to countries that successfully implement projects or programmes promoting low-carbon transportation options, such as the development of electric vehicle infrastructure or efficient public transportation systems.

It is important to note that the specific criteria for results payments and the types of projects eligible for funding can vary depending on the GCF's guidelines and priorities. Countries seeking results payments from the GCF must demonstrate measurable results and meet specified evaluation criteria to qualify for funding based on their achievements in addressing climate change and sustainable development goals.

Guarantees

The GCF utilizes guarantees as a financial instrument to support climate finance projects and activities. Guarantees are risk-mitigation mechanisms that help attract private sector investment by providing assurance against potential financial losses. The GCF employs guarantees to mobilize and leverage additional private sector investment for climate-related projects. By offering guarantees, the GCF can enhance the creditworthiness of projects and reduce perceived risks for private investors, stimulating their involvement in climate finance initiatives. Guarantees essentially act as a form of insurance, providing financial protection and promoting confidence in a project's viability. The following provide some examples of how the GCF utilizes guarantees:

Renewable Energy Projects: The GCF may offer investment guarantees to encourage private sector participation in renewable energy projects. These guarantees can minimize the risk of financial losses associated with technology performance, reimbursement of project debt, or revenue streams from energy sales. By providing this assurance, the GCF attracts private investors to finance renewable energy initiatives, such as solar or wind power projects.

Energy Efficiency Initiatives: Guarantees can also be used to support energy efficiency projects. For instance, the GCF may provide guarantees that cover potential default risks associated with financing energy-efficient building retrofits or industrial energy management projects. This helps incentivize private investment and accelerates the adoption of energy-saving technologies.

Climate Resilience Measures: The GCF may employ guarantees to encourage private sector engagement in building climate resilience. For example, guarantees can support projects focused on creating climate-resilient infrastructure, such as flood protection systems or resilient urban planning. By ensuring a level of financial security, these guarantees attract private investment in climate adaptation initiatives.

Sustainable Agriculture and Forestry: Guarantees can be used to foster private sector involvement in sustainable agriculture and forestry projects. For instance, the GCF may provide guarantees to minimize financial risks related to sustainable farming practices or reforestation efforts, encouraging private investors to engage in climate-smart agricultural projects or sustainable land management initiatives.

Worthy of note is that while guarantees can be an effective tool in leveraging private investment, their specific application and deployment may vary depending on the GCF's guidelines and priorities. Each guarantee arrangement is tailored to the specific project or sector, considering the risks involved, the targeted outcomes, and the needs of private investors.

Blended Finance

The GCF utilizes blended finance as a financial instrument to mobilize and leverage both public and private sector resources for climate finance projects. Blended finance involves combining different sources of capital, including grants, concessional loans, and market-rate investments, to support sustainable development initiatives. The GCF employs blended finance to catalyze private sector investment and maximize the impact of its climate finance activities. By combining public funds with private sector resources, the GCF aims to bridge the financing gap for climate projects and encourage sustainable investments at scale. Blended finance mechanisms allow for the allocation of public funds strategically to mobilize additional private investment, thereby creating a multiplier effect and promoting sustainable development outcomes. The following examples demonstrate how the GCF uses blended finance in its efforts to discharge its mandate:

Renewable Energy Projects: The GCF may utilize blended finance to support renewable energy projects, such as large-scale solar or wind power installations. By providing concessional loans or grants, the GCF can reduce project costs and lower the level of risk for private investors. This blended finance approach helps attract private sector investments and accelerates the deployment of renewable energy infrastructure.

Climate-Resilient Infrastructure: Blended finance can be employed to fund climate-resilient infrastructure projects, such as resilient urban planning or flood mitigation measures. The GCF may offer a mix of grants and concessional loans to partially finance these projects, making them more attractive for private investors seeking sustainable and climate-resilient investment opportunities.

Sustainable Agriculture and Land Use: Blended finance can be utilized to promote sustainable agriculture and land use practices. The GCF provides grants or concessional loans to support activities like agroforestry or sustainable farming initiatives. By blending public and private resources, the GCF encourages investment in sustainable agriculture, which can enhance food security, reduce emissions, and promote climate resilience.

Energy Efficiency Improvements: Blended finance mechanisms can be employed to finance energy efficiency projects in buildings, industries, and transportation. The GCF may offer concessional loans or grants to support the implementation of energy-saving technologies and practices. This approach helps stimulate private sector investments in energy efficiency and contributes to reducing GHG emissions.

It is important to note that the exact structure and mix of financial instruments in blended finance mechanisms utilized by the GCF can vary depending on project-specific factors, priorities, and risk considerations. The GCF aims to leverage its available resources to attract additional private sector funding and promote sustainable and climate-resilient development.[15]

Conclusion

A Report published by the United Nations in 2022 entitled 'Accessing Climate Finance: Challenges and Opportunities for Small Island Developing States' emphasizes the vulnerability of SIDS to climate change and their limited financial capacity to address it.[16] The article identifies barriers to accessing climate finance, including the lack of financial instruments, technical expertise, complex application processes, and inadequate institutional frameworks. Insofar as the lack of financial instruments are concerned, the GCF is lowering the threshold for the hitherto-difficult barriers.

The Paris Agreement emphasizes the need for financial flows to be consistent with low GHG emissions and climate-resilient development. The GCF plays a crucial role in mobilizing and distributing climate finance to support developing countries in their climate actions. As demonstrated here, the GCF utilizes various financial instruments to achieve its objectives.

Grants, both non-reimbursable and reimbursable, are utilized by the GCF to support capacity building, project preparation, and technology transfer. Concessional loans provide affordable financing options with below-market interest rates and longer repayment periods. Equity investments involve acquiring ownership stakes in climate-related companies or projects to earn financial returns while promoting climate action.

The GCF also uses subordinated debt instruments, which have a lower repayment priority, to provide concessional financing for climate-related projects. Results-based payments are provided based on the achievement of climate-related targets or outcomes. Guarantees mitigate risks and attract private sector investment, while blended finance combines public and private resources to bridge the financing gap and maximize sustainable development outcomes.

These financial instruments cater to the diverse needs of recipient countries and help incentivize climate action by providing flexible and affordable financing options. By leveraging financial resources and catalyzing private sector involvement, the GCF contributes to the implementation of the Paris Agreement and supports the transition to a low-carbon and climate-resilient future. It is hoped that developing countries, including SIDS, will utilize these instruments and in their efforts to access finance will catalyze the GCF to open up the full array of instruments available, some of which remain rarely used up to the time of writing.

Notes

1 Paris Agreement to the United Nations Framework Convention on Climate Change, adopted 12 December 2015; entered into force 4 November 2016.
2 See further Daniel Bodansky 'Paris Agreement' (2021) United Nations Audiovisual Library of International Law <https://legal.un.org/avl/pdf/ha/pa/pa_e.pdf> accessed 21 April 2024.
3 For an analysis on the sustainable developments dimensions in this context see Marie-Claire Cordonier Segger, 'Advancing the Paris Agreement on Climate Change for Sustainable Development' (2016) 5 Cambridge Journal of International and Comparative Law 202.

4 Paris Agreement (n 1)
5 ibid.
6 For further reading see UNFCCC, 'Summary and Recommendations by the Standing Committee on Finance' (2022) <J0156_UNFCCC BA5 2022 Summary_Web_AW.pdf> accessed 21 April 2024.
7 Green Climate Fund <https://www.greenclimate.fund/> accessed 21 April 2014.
8 To review the interconnectedness between climate change, decarbonization, and green finance see Chengbo Fu, Lei Lu, and Mansoor Pirabi, 'Advancing Green Finance: A Review of Climate Change and Decarbonization' (2024) 2(1) Digital Economy and Sustainable Development -Springer Nature 1–23.
9 UNFCCC, 'Governing Instrument: Green Climate Fund' (15 March 2012) FCCC/CP/2011/9/Add.1, Dec 3/CP.17, Article 1.2.
10 UNFCCC, 'Governing Instrument: Green Climate Fund' (15 March 2012) FCCC/CP/2011/9/Add.1, Dec 3/CP.17, Article 2.9.
11 Green Climate Fund (n 7). See further Green Climate Fund Strategic Plan 2024–2027 <Strategic Plan | Green Climate Fund> accessed 21 April 2024.
12 For further reading see Mohammad Al-Saidi 'Green Climate Fund (GCF): Role, Capacity Building, and Directions as a Catalyst for Climate Finance' in Leal Filho and others (eds), *Climate Action Encyclopaedia of the UN Sustainable Development Goals* (Springer 2020).
13 For guidelines on GCF's investment frameworks see Green Climate Fund <Investment framework | Green Climate Fund> accessed 21 April 2024.
14 For further reading on climate mitigation finance within the ambit of the Paris Agreement and green finance see Muhammad Asif Khan and others, 'Does Green Finance Really Deliver What Is Expected? An Empirical Perspective' (2021) 22(3) Borsa Istanbul Review 586.
15 To further engage new themes in green finance refer to HMNK Mudalige, 'Emerging New Themes in Green Finance: A Systematic Literature Review' (2023) 9(108) Future Business Journal 1–20.
16 Laetitia De Marez and others, Climate Finance Access Network, 'Accessing Climate Finance: Challenges and Opportunities for Small Island Development States' (UN-OHRLLS, 2022) <www.un.org/ohrlls/sids%20climate%20financing%20report%202022> accessed February 2024.

24

ADVANCING PARIS AGREEMENT ALIGNMENT IN MULTILATERAL DEVELOPMENT BANKS

Hyfa Azeez, Thomas M. Clark, Vesselina Haralampieva, Christina Pak and Michael Strauss[1,2]

Introduction – The Role of Multilateral Development Banks in Climate Finance

The Paris Agreement establishes binding commitments of climate mitigation and adaptation within the broader framework of climate action.[3] Climate finance plays a key role in mitigation efforts, as it mobilises large-scale capital to build the sustainable infrastructure required to reduce emissions. Climate finance is equally important for adaptation, given the significant scale of investments needed to build adaptive, resilient, and sustainable economies envisioned by the Paris Agreement.[4] Whilst public finance plays an essential role in tackling the climate crisis, it is insufficient to deliver the climate change objectives.[5] Strong private sector participation is critical in bridging the gaps in climate finance to achieve meaningful progress.[6]

In this context, Multilateral Development Banks (MDBs) are uniquely placed to leverage capital and steer financial flows towards low-carbon and climate-resilient activities, due to their regional and global reach and the significant pool of capital made available through their shareholders.[7] In terms of capital, each MDB has individually committed to support increased climate finance levels and in 2022, MDB climate finance reached a new record high of approximately $100 billion.[8] MDBs often provide concessional climate finance, supported by contributions from donors and member countries, to help finance projects in developing countries. This lower cost of financing enables MDBs to offer more favourable terms to borrowers, therefore reducing the overall cost of investment.

MDBs' efforts range from supporting governments on legal and regulatory reforms and capacity building, to designing innovative financial products with co-investors, to offering technical assistance to private sector clients and helping them unlock green finance.

The Landscape of Climate Finance: Challenges and Opportunities

Whilst in the past decade climate finance has reached record numbers and key institutions have demonstrated concerted efforts to combat climate change, unprecedented levels of funding and resource allocation are required to further advance mitigation and adaptation measures. It is understood that approximately EUR 185 trillion is required to achieve Net Zero by 2050, and hence the current financial flows must increase by at least 300% in order to achieve the Paris Agreement targets.[9] MDBs play a pivotal role in closing this gap, given the manner in which they coordinate

DOI: 10.4324/9781003276678-28

their work to achieve stakeholder alignment, international collaboration, knowledge dissemination, legal and regulatory reform, and stakeholder accountability.[10]

The implications of climate change present a dual challenge for developing countries, affecting both their climate objectives and developmental goals.[11] Given that these challenges are closely connected, MDBs play an instrumental role in leveraging the institutional and financial support required for a just transition. The strong reliance of many developing countries on carbon-intensive energy sources can sometimes lead to deficient legal and regulatory frameworks and a reduced political incentive to commit to the green transition.[12] Even in the face of great urgency, the absence of strong legal and regulatory framework and political will may contribute to gaps in the enabling environment and insufficient financial innovation to encourage the flow of capital towards green investments.[13]

MDBs have identified two key areas to address the challenges faced by developing countries in accessing climate finance:

(i) Mobilisation of private capital: MDBs actively engage with investors to identify deterrents to sustainable investment and use their expertise, knowledge, and capital to incentivise allocation and alignment with the Paris Agreement goals; and
(ii) Systemic reform of the economic systems: MDBs foster an enabling environment that extends beyond financial support by providing expertise, knowledge, and technical assistance to address the challenges of sustainable development.

Insights from the Experience of the EBRD

The primary objective of the EBRD in its climate initiatives is to facilitate the emerging markets' and developing economies' transitions not only to low-carbon economies but also inclusive, resilient, equitable, and competitive economies. Consequently, EBRD views the low-carbon transition as an economic and social opportunity rather than a mere cost.[14] EBRD defines transition through six fundamental qualities: competitive, well-governed, inclusive, green, integrated, and resilient.[15]

Key Milestones and Achievements in Climate Finance and Paris Agreement Alignment

EBRD is the first MDB to be fully aligned with the Paris Agreement as of 1 January 2023. This implies that every investment project undergoes rigorous screening for alignment with the goals of the Paris Agreement ('Paris Alignment'), reflecting an equal commitment to both mitigation and adaptation goals. EBRD's Paris Alignment is facilitated by an operational framework developed jointly with other MDBs. This joint approach comprises six building blocks: (i) alignment with mitigation goals; (ii) adaptation and climate-resilient operations; (iii) accelerated contribution to the transition through climate finance; (iv) strategy, engagement, and policy development; (v) reporting; and (vi) alignment of internal activities.[16]

Using the first two building blocks set out here, EBRD has developed a methodology to determine Paris Alignment of its projects. The methodology is divided into three parts:

1) Directly financed projects – These projects must demonstrate alignment with the Paris Agreement by ensuring they support both climate mitigation and adaptation goals. This involves assessing the project's contribution to reducing greenhouse gas emissions and enhancing climate resilience.

2) Intermediated finance with partner financial institutions (PFIs) – The primary requirement for such projects is that PFIs have robust environmental and social management systems and commit to aligning their financial flows with the goals of the Paris Agreement, including excluding high-emission activities. PFIs may also be encouraged to climate-proof their portfolio and business practices and develop climate transition plans.
3) Other financial instruments not otherwise covered by (1) and (2) – This category includes equity instruments, bonds, and other financial products. The EBRD evaluates these instruments for alignment with climate goals, focusing on supporting green finance markets, and climate-friendly investments. In particular, when the use of proceeds is not clear and there is a risk of misalignment, the EBRD looks 'beyond the project' and engages with the client to support its systemic transition towards low-carbon, climate resilient, and sustainable business model (i.e., the 'counterparty' approach).[17]

EBRD also addresses the other building block of the MDBs' joint approach by steering towards Paris Alignment in its internal activities.[18] EBRD is the first MDB to sign up to the Task Force for Climate-related Financial Disclosures and published its fourth report in 2023.[19]

Impact Assessment: EBRD's Contributions on the Ground

EBRD's 2022 climate finance for low- and middle-income economies rose to $4.3 billion from $3.9 billion in 2019, and for high-income economies reached $2.5 billion from $ 1.1 billion in 2019. In total, the EBRD's climate finance for 2022 increased by 35% from 2019 to reach $6.8 billion in 2022. In addition to its own climate finance contributions, EBRD focuses on mobilising from the private sector. EBRD's total climate private mobilisation stood at $10 billion in 2022.[20]

EBRD has an impressive track record in financing renewable energy projects, having financed more than 18 GW of renewable energy capacity since 2006. In 2022, EBRD deployed capital for its largest renewables project to date by arranging two syndicated loans worth a combined $520 million to help construct two wind power plants in Uzbekistan, with a total installed capacity of 1 GW.[21]

In addition, EBRD is increasing its focus on projects that play a critical role in the circular economy. For example, EBRD committed a total financing package equivalent to around EUR 120 million in 2023 to support the construction of a greenfield recycling facility in southern Poland. This facility will extract and recycle rare metals from e-waste for use in the manufacture of new products, which will decrease the associated greenhouse-gas emissions by up to 98%.[22]

The EBRD is working with several countries on their plans to transition from fossil fuels, invest in clean energy, and attract climate finance.[23] At COP28, for instance, North Macedonia launched its Just Energy Transition Investment Platform with the aim of mobilising up to EUR 3 billion in investment by 2030 to speed up the country's energy transition. The platform, supported by EBRD, represents a milestone for the historically coal-dependent country and highlights its ambition to transform its economy to a low-carbon, low-cost, and secure paradigm.[24]

The EBRD's Legal Transition Programme (LTP) supports governments and regulators to develop policies and legal frameworks that align with the climate goals and provide the legal certainty needed to unlock green finance. In addition, LTP engages with private and public sector clients to enhance their corporate climate governance, supports them to formulate their climate strategy and transition plans, and disclose in line with international best practices, creating strong demonstration effect in the respective sector and beyond.

Closely linked to the climate change challenge is the broader issue of environmental, nature, and biodiversity degradation – an excessive price paid for the world's economic prosperity over the past few decades. The EBRD has announced its Approach to Nature, which highlights the Bank's plans for intervention and engagement through the mix of investment, blended finance, technical assistance, and capacity building.

Insights from the Experience of the ADB

The Asia and the Pacific region is at the center of the climate crisis in terms of both the impact and potential to combat climate change. Consequently, ADB has placed tackling climate change at the top of its development agenda and aims to play a leading role in helping the region pursue a path of low-carbon and climate-resilient development.

Initiatives and Commitments Towards Climate Finance and the Sustainable Development Goals

ADB has been at the forefront of climate action and has made substantial commitments towards climate finance and the Sustainable Development Goals. Notably, it was the first MDB to establish a climate risk screening and management framework for its operations, disclose project-level data for all its climate projects, be accredited by the Green Climate Fund, and implement a comprehensive long-term climate change operational framework, as evidenced by its recently published climate change action plan for 2023–2030.[25]

To become Asia and the Pacific's Climate Bank, ADB recently adopted a comprehensive road map, featuring a new operating model to enable climate and private sectors shifts as well as new ways of working.[26] Furthermore, it has made commitments to align its operations with the goals of the Paris Agreement, with 100% alignment of sovereign operations since July 2023 and 100% alignment of private sector operations by July 2025.[27] Moreover, ADB has elevated its climate finance ambition to $100 billion from its own resources by 2030. It will also leverage its own funds to mobilise climate finance from private sector, philanthropies, capital markets, donors and other sources and enable climate investments. Additionally, ADB's capital management reforms will unlock $100 billion in new funding over the next 10 years to support the region's overlapping, simultaneous crises, including the climate crisis.[28]

In terms of financial commitments, ADB allocated $7.11 billion in climate finance in 2022, with $4.28 billion (60.2%) expected to contribute to mitigation and $2.83 billion (39.8%) to adaptation. Climate mitigation efforts focused primarily on transport and energy sectors, while adaptation projects focused on agriculture, natural resources, rural development, and transport sectors. Geographically, significant climate finance was allocated to Southeast Asia and South Asia, followed by Central and West Asia, East Asia, and the Pacific regions.[29]

Enabling a low-carbon transformation requires substantial investment, as well as innovation. ADB has been driving innovation in climate finance through initiatives such as the Energy Transition Mechanism (ETM), Innovative Finance Facility for Climate in Asia and the Pacific (IF-CAP) and the Climate Action Catalyst Fund (CAF), as well as innovative private sector projects. For example, at COP26 in Glasgow, ADB launched the ETM which will support the early retirement of coal-fired plants, while boosting the share of clean energy in electricity systems of participating countries.[30] Under ADB's ETM, an agreement has been signed with the Government of Indonesia to early retire the 660-megawatt coal-fired power plant Cirebon-1.[31] In May 2023, ADB launched the IF-CAP which is the first leveraged guarantee mechanism for climate finance to be adopted by an MDB. IF-CAP donor partners will provide guarantees for parts of ADB's sovereign loan portfolios to enable ADB to free up capital to increase lending for climate investments.[32] More recently, at COP28 in Dubai, ADB launched the Climate Action Catalyst Fund, a first-of-its-kind carbon fund under the Paris Agreement, which will mobilise innovative carbon finance through the purchase of carbon credits to catalyse investments in transformative mitigation actions in ADB developing member countries (DMCs).[33]

Furthermore, ADB has been able to increase the number of renewable energy projects in its DMCs through innovative project financing solutions, such combining its sovereign loan and transaction advisory services for the development of the largest utility-scale photovoltaic project in Cambodia, enabling the lowest-ever solar PV tariff in Southeast Asia.[34] ADB has also utilised blended financing structure to help build a 600 MW wind power plant in Laos PDR to export and sell power to neighboring Vietnam, which will be the largest wind power plant in Southeast Asia. This landmark 600 MW Monsoon Wind Power Project in Lao PDR involved a blended financing structure, deploying several debt tranches offering a combination of concessional tenors and pricing, alongside market priced MDB and commercial debt to address bankability gaps.[35]

Enabling Whole-of-Economy Shifts through Systematic and Integrated Approach

ADB recognises that the low-carbon transition requires a holistic approach, including policy, legal and regulatory and institutional reforms, and capacity building fundamental to enhancing climate action and attracting climate finance. Through its policy-based, results-based lending and sector development programs, ADB has been supporting reforms to enable whole-of-economy shifts. For example, ADB approved its first climate policy-based loan to the Philippines which will support a systematic approach to addressing climate change.[36]

Moreover, ADB recognises the instrumental role of law and the rule of law in tackling climate change, ultimately to help achieve inclusive and sustainable development.[37] Through ADB Office of the General Counsel's Law and Policy Reform (LPR) Program, ADB has been supporting reforms to strengthen legal and regulatory frameworks and build the capacity of implementing parties towards low-carbon and green transition.[38] For example, through its Legal Readiness for Climate Finance and Climate Investment Program,[39] the LPR Program has been addressing legal barriers to attracting private climate finance including reforms to improve the business climate, assisting to establish carbon market laws and regulations and drafting transformative framework climate change laws to enable whole-of-economy shifts. At the same time, ADB's LPR Program has been investing in green courts and benches and judicial education programs on commercial, environmental and climate change laws and access to justice issues, training lawyers on climate and environment laws and sustainable finance, and strengthening climate and environmental legal education to build the next generation of climate and green leaders.

Conclusions and Future Directions

Climate change is a human crisis at its core, and MDBs and legal experts play an important role in navigating the intersectionality of its challenges.[40] The MDBs' joint statement at COP28 was cognisant of the magnitude of the climate crisis, thus extending the focus of their activities to nature and biodiversity, long-term strategies (LTS), and country-led platform, amongst others.[41] As global climate action gears up to achieve the goals set by the Paris Agreement, climate finance and innovative knowledge solutions are key tools in navigating the transition towards a just, sustainable, and resilient future.

Given the operational and other challenges faced by the MDBs, it is imperative to explore innovative financing mechanisms such as ADB's IF-CAP. Drawing on the scale and scope the IF-CAP is designed to deliver in addressing the climate crisis, ADB President Masatsugu Asakawa identifies its impact as twofold: first in the way ADB's business is conducted and second in the way it addresses climate change.[42] This dual innovation meets the unique challenges encountered by MDBs in climate finance, and paves the way for peer institutions.

Leveraging private sector engagement through blended finance is becoming increasingly essential to meet climate finance goals. Blended finance poses challenges where there is a lack of legal readiness or a uniform framework for its deployment and implementation.[43] MDBs such as the ADB and EBRD play a key role in steering legal reforms and governance initiatives that establish industry standards for predictability, transparency, and accountability.

From a brief review of the current trends and practices in climate finance and legal innovations, it is clear that MDBs such as the EBRD and ADB are not merely following the climate action trend; they are leading the way. The financial, legal, and knowledge initiatives and innovations driven by the MDBs will be crucial in enabling the global efforts to achieve the goals of the Paris Agreement.

Notes

1 The views expressed in this publication are those of the authors and do not necessarily reflect the views and policies of the respective institutions or the governments they represent. The institutions do not guarantee the accuracy of the data included in this publication and accepts no responsibility for any consequence of their use. The mention of specific companies or products of manufacturers does not imply that they are endorsed or recommended by the respective institution in preference to others of a similar nature that are not mentioned. By making any designation of or reference to a particular territory or geographic area in this document, the institutions do not intend to make any judgements as to the legal or other status of any territory or area.

2 This chapter reprises aspects of the remarks of EBRD General Counsel Michael Strauss and ADB General Counsel Thomas M. Clark at the Climate Law and Governance Day, Engaging in Global Stocktake Through Legal Lenses, 5 December 2023, Dubai COP28. It also builds upon previous works by ADB Principal Counsel Christina Pak and EBRD Senior Counsel Vesselina Haralampieva, with thanks for their insights and contributions.

3 Paris Agreement (adopted 12 December 2015, entered into force on 4 November 2016) 3156 UNTS 79 (Paris Agreement) Articles 4, 7.

4 United Nations, 'Why Finance Climate Action' (UN) <https://www.un.org/en/climatechange/why-finance-climate-action> accessed 19 April 2024.

5 UN Climate Change News, 'From Billions to Trillions: Setting a New Goal on Climate Finance' (UN, 29 April 2024) <https://unfccc.int/news/from-billions-to-trillions-setting-a-new-goal-on-climate finance#:~:text=The%20first%20Needs%20Determination%20Report,not%20fully%20cost%20for%20 adaptation.> accessed 8 July 2024.

6 United Nations Environment Programme, *Adaptation Gap Report 2023: Underfinanced. Underprepared. Inadequate Investment and Planning on Climate Adaptation Leaves World Exposed* (UNEP 2023) Ch. 4, p. 55 <https://doi.org/10.59117/20.500.11822/43796>.

7 See for further reading on the unique organisational nature of MDBs, see: Chris Humphrey, *Financing the Future: Multilateral Development Banks in the Changing World Order of the 21st Century* (online edn, OUP 2022) <https://doi.org/10.1093/oso/9780192871503.001.0001> accessed 17 April 2024.

8 European Investment Bank (EIB), 'Multilateral Development Banks Provide Record Climate Finance of Close to USD61 Billion for Low- and Middle-Income Economies in 2022' (EIB, 12 October 2023) <https://www.eib.org/en/press/all/2023-376-multilateral-development-banks-provide-record-climate-finance-of-close-to-usd61-billion-for-low-and-middle-income-economies-in-2022> accessed 20 April 2024.

9 European Climate, Infrastructure and Environment Executive Agency, 'Bridging the Climate Financing Gap: Seizing the Opportunity' (European Commission Sustainable Energy Week, 22 February 2024) <https://sustainable-energy-week.ec.europa.eu/news/bridging-climate-financing-gap-seizing-opportunity-2024-02-22_en> accessed 20 April 2024.

10 Rockefeller Foundation, *Reimagining the Role of Multilateral Development Banks: Full Report* (The Rockefeller Foundation 2021) <https://www.rockefellerfoundation.org/wp-content/uploads/2021/07/Reimagining-the-Role-of-Multilateral-Development-Banks-Full-Report-July-2021.pdf> accessed 23 April 2024.

11 See for further research: Alexander Thompson, 'The Global Regime for Climate Finance: Political and Legal Challenges' in Kevin R Gray, Richard Tarasofsky, and Cinnamon P Carlarne (eds), *The Oxford Handbook of International Climate Change Law* (online edn, OUP 2016) <https://doi.org/10.1093/law/9780199684601.003.0007> accessed 20 April 2024.

12 See for further reading on legal and regulatory aspects of mobilising climate finance: Megan Bowman, 'Turning Promises into Action: "Legal Readiness for Climate Finance" and Implementing the Paris Agreement' (2022) 16(1) Carbon & Climate Law Review 41 <https://ssrn.com/abstract=4083998> accessed 20 April 2024.

13 Commonwealth Secretariat, *Accessing Development and Climate Finance: Issues and Challenges in the Commonwealth Countries* (Commonwealth Secretariat 2023) <https://production-new-commonwealth-files.s3.eu-west-2.amazonaws.com/s3fs-public/2023-05/Accessing_Development_and_Climate_Finance_UPDF.pdf> accessed 21 April 2024.

14 European Bank for Reconstruction and Development (EBRD), *The EBRD Just Transition Initiative: Sharing the Benefits of a Green Economy Transition and Protecting Vulnerable Countries, Regions and People from Falling Behind* (EBRD 2020) <https://www.ebrd.com/what-we-do/just-transition-initiative> accessed 30 April 2024.

15 European Bank for Reconstruction and Development (EBRD), *Annual Report 2018: Our Transition Qualities* (EBRD 2018) <https://2018.ar-ebrd.com/our-transition-qualities/> accessed 30 April 2024.

16 The joint MDB approach to alignment with the objectives of the Paris Agreement was presented at the United Nations Climate Change Conference (COP24) in 2018 (EBRD, 2018). The MDBs involved in the development of the joint approach are the African Development Bank, the ADB, the Asian Infrastructure Investment Bank, the EBRD, the European Investment Bank, the Inter-American Development Bank Group, the Islamic Development Bank, the New Development Bank, and the World Bank Group. See presentation by the MDBS involved: *Presentation on MDB Paris Alignment Approach: Linkages with Climate Finance* <https://unfccc.int/sites/default/files/resource/MDB%20CF%20and%20PA%20finance%20UNFCCC%20Oct%202023_NES_EIB.pdf?> accessed 30 April 2024.

17 EBRD, *Methodology to Determine the Paris Agreement Alignment of EBRD Investments* (EBRD 2024).

18 EBRD, *Approach to the Paris Agreement Alignment of the EBRD's Internal Activities* (EBRD 2022).

19 Nigina Mirbabaeva, 'EBRD's Fourth TCFD Report Shows Progress on Mainstreaming Climate Considerations' (EBRD, 17 October 2023) <https://www.ebrd.com/news/2023/ebrds-fourth-tcfd-report-shows-progress-on-mainstreaming-climate-considerations.html> accessed 8 July 2024.

20 EIB, *2022 Joint Report on Multilateral Development Banks 'Climate Finance* (EIB 2023) <https://www.ebrd.com/documents/climate-finance/2022-joint-report-on-multilateral-development-banks-climate-finance.pdf> accessed 21 April 2024.

21 Anton Usov, 'EBRD Invests Record US$ 900 Million in Uzbekistan' (EBRD, 26 January 2023) <https://www.ebrd.com/news/2023/ebrd-invests-record-us-900-million-in-uzbekistan.html> accessed 21 April 2024.

22 Svitlana Pyrkalo, '€120 Million to Elemental for E-waste Recycling in Poland' (EBRD, 12 January 2023) https://www.ebrd.com/news/2023/120-million-to-elemental-for-ewaste-recycling-in-poland.html> accessed 21 April 2024.

23 Vanora Benett 'EBRD Launches Approach to Nature' (EBRD, 9 December 2023) <https://www.ebrd.com/news/2023/ebrd-launches-approach-to-nature.html> accessed 2 May 2024.

24 Vanora Benett 'North Macedonia Launches Just Energy Transition Investment Platform at COP28' <https://www.ebrd.com/news/2023/north-macedonia-launches-just-energy-transition-investment-platform-at-cop28.html> accessed 2 May 2024.

25 Asian Development Bank (ADB), *Climate Change Action Plan, 2023–2030* (ADB 2023) <https://www.adb.org/documents/climate-change-action-plan-2023-2030> accessed 30 April 2024.

26 ADB, *Organizational Review: A New Operating Model to Accelerate ADB's Transformation Toward Strategy 2030 and Beyond* (ADB 2022) <https://www.adb.org/documents/organizational-review-adb-transformation-toward-strategy-2030> accessed 30 April 2024.
27 ADB, 'ADB Commits to Full Alignment with Paris Agreement' (ADB, 8 July 2021) <https://www.adb.org/news/adb-commits-full-alignment-paris-agreement> accessed 20 April 2024.
28 ADB, 'Capital Adequacy Framework' (ADB) <https://www.adb.org/capital-adequacy-framework> accessed 30 April 2024.
29 ADB, *Climate Finance in 2022* (ADB 2022) <https://www.adb.org/sites/default/files/related/543511/climate-finance-2022.pdf> accessed 20 April 2024.
30 ADB, 'Energy Transition Mechanism' (ADB) <https://www.adb.org/what-we-do/energy-transition-mechanism-etm> accessed 30 April 2024.
31 ADB, 'New Agreement Aims to Retire Indonesia 660-MW Coal Plant Almost 7 Years Early' (ADB, 3 December 2023) <https://www.adb.org/news/new-agreement-aims-retire-indonesia-660-mw-coal-plant-almost-7-years-early> accessed 30 April 2024.
32 ADB, 'Q&A: Innovative Finance Facility for Climate in Asia and the Pacific (IF-CAP)' (ADB, 2 May 2023) <https://www.adb.org/news/features/qa-innovative-finance-facility-climate-asia-pacific-if-cap> accessed 30 April 2024.
33 ADB, 'ADB Announces Start of Climate Action Catalyst Fund' (ADB, 8 December 2023) <https://www.adb.org/news/adb-announces-start-climate-action-catalyst-fund> accessed 30 April 2024.
34 ADB, 'ADB-Supported Solar Project in Cambodia Achieves Lowest-Ever Tariff in ASEAN' (5 September2019)<https://www.adb.org/news/adb-supported-solar-project-cambodia-achieves-lowest-ever-tariff-asean> accessed 30 April 2024.
35 ADB, 'ADB Signs Loan for First Cross-Border Wind Power Project in Asia for First Plant in Lao PDR and Largest in Southeast Asia' (ADB, 1 March 2023) <https://www.adb.org/news/adb-signs-loan-first-cross-border-wind-power-project-asia-first-plant-lao-pdr-and-largest> accessed 21 April 2024.
36 ADB, 'Philippines: Climate Change Action Program, Subprogram 1' (ADB, 2022) <https://www.adb.org/projects/55268-001/main> accessed 8 July 2024.
37 ADB's corporate Strategy 2030 provides 'the rule of law is needed to sustain development momentum and to ensure that the benefits of growth are equitably and widely shared'. ADB, *Strategy 2030: Achieving a Prosperous, Inclusive, Resilient, and Sustainable Asia and the Pacific* (ADB 2018) 8 <https://www.adb.org/sites/default/files/institutional-document/435391/strategy-2030-main-document.pdf> accessed 20 April 2024.
38 ADB, 'ADB's Law and Policy Reform Program' (ADB) <https://lpr.adb.org/> accessed 30 April 2024.
39 See for further reading on the legal barriers to climate finance in Asia-Pacific: Takako Morita and Christina Pak, 'Legal Readiness to Attract Climate Finance: Towards a Low-Carbon Asia and the Pacific' (2018) 12(1) Carbon & Climate Law Review 6 <https://www.jstor.org/stable/26478081> accessed 21 April 2024.
40 Michael Strauss and Harry Boyd-Carpenter, 'The EBRD'S Climate and Sustainability Agenda: The Role of Law And Lawyers in Delivering on the Paris Agenda' (2022) EBRD Law in Transition Journal <https://2022.lit-ebrd.com/green-transition/> accessed 2 May 2024.
41 See joint statement of the MDBs at COP28: 'COP28 Multilateral Development Banks (MDB) Joint Statement' (IFC, 3 December 2023) <https://www.ifc.org/en/statements/2023/cop28-mdb-joint-statement> accessed 2 May 2024.
42 Opening statement by Masatsugu Asakawa, President, Asian Development Bank, at the President's press conference at the 56th Annual Meeting, 2 May 2023, Incheon, Republic of Korea.
43 See for further reading: Naomi Sander and Selin Bakare, 'Legal Critiques and Barriers in Blended Finance' in *Unlocking Legal Pathways for Blended Finance* (Global Alliance of Impact Lawyers 2024).

25

EXPLORING LOW-CARBON AND ENERGY-EFFICIENT PROCUREMENT AS A TOOL FOR PARIS AGREEMENT IMPLEMENTATION[1]

Jellie Molino

Emerging International Instruments and Initiatives on SPP

Sustainable Public Procurement[2] (SPP) is now widely recognized as a strategic lever to drive innovation and improve the sustainability performance of public and private sector organizations worldwide,[3] although it remains voluntary among procurement entities. The challenge, therefore, in mainstreaming SPP rests on a solid international policy foundation,[4] which includes international procurement instruments such as the United Nations Commission on International Trade Law (UNCITRAL) Model Law on Government Procurement and the World Trade Organization (WTO) Government Procurement Agreement (GPA), among others. Multilateral environmental treaties (METs) can also provide strong political leadership among global multi-stakeholder partnerships in working together for a systematic implementation of SPP to promote the 2030 Sustainable Development Goals (Agenda 2030). Preferential trade agreements, such as the Comprehensive and Progressive Agreement for Trans-Pacific Partnership (CPTPP), with strong climate change chapters (e.g. provisions on the transition to a low-emission and resilient economy), could also be a way to mitigate GHG emissions through economic partnership agreements with trade policy instruments, e.g. government procurement.[5]

The first of these instruments was the UNCITRAL Model Law on Government Procurement ('Model Law'), recommended by the United Nations General Assembly (UNGA) in a resolution of 9 December 2011 (General Assembly Resolution 66/95). The UNGA called for cooperation and coordination among international organizations for the modernization and harmonization of public procurement laws.[6] States Parties are required to enact or amend (if already existing) their procurement regulations[7] to implement, among other things, socio-economic procurement policies.[8] Accordingly:

> any socio-economic policies[9] may or must be taken into account in qualification requirements (e.g., environmental, ethical and other standards), in the description of the subject matter of the contract, and in the design of the evaluation criteria (e.g., to give credit for compliance with socio-economic policies beyond any minimum required).[10]

DOI: 10.4324/9781003276678-29

Articles 9[11] and 11[12] of the Model Law stipulate that the state must specify ethical standards[13] and establish exceptional criteria, such as environmental consideration[14] and standards.[15]

In 2012, the United Nations General Assembly adopted the outcome document of the United Nations Conference on Sustainable Development (Rio+20) entitled 'The Future We Want'. Paragraphs 224–226 of the document set out the sustainable consumption and production commitments of the heads of state and government and high-level representatives who met in Rio de Janeiro, Brazil, from 20 to 22 June 2012. As a result, they adopted the '10-Year Framework of Programmes (10YFP) on Sustainable Consumption and Production Patterns', which includes, inter alia, areas on SPP.

Subsequently, the United Nations Environment Protection Programme (UNEP) published the 'Guidelines for the Implementation of Sustainable Public Procurement' to give governments direction for the design and implementation of sustainable public procurement policies and action plans.[16] The guidelines set out steps that countries can follow to create a policy framework that legitimizes SPP actions. These include institution building, reviewing legal policies, formulating a policy and action plan for SPP, and capacity building training.

As the central procurement unit of the United Nations, the United Nations Office for Project Services (UNOPS) incorporated 'best practices for sustainable procurement' into the 2014 revision of the 'UNOPS Procurement Manual: Revision 5'.[17] Some of the sustainability provisions incorporated in the UNOPS Procurement Manual include the ineligibility of suppliers suspected of social and/or environmental malpractices;[18] conducting a sustainable procurement risk assessment;[19] the use of transparent social and environmental requirements;[20] a transparent list of sustainable requirements in the request for proposal (RFP)[21] purchasing more sustainable products;[22] inclusion of mandatory and well-defined sustainability requirements in the criteria;[23] cumulative analysis methodology for the RFP to promote sustainability;[24] use of landed cost and transport cost in tender evaluation;[25] use of more sustainable packaging and shipping instructions;[26] and use of progressive indicators during contract management[27]

The revised WTO GPA, which entered into force on 6 April 2014,[28] also instructs the Committee[29] to

> undertake further work to facilitate the implementation of this Agreement and the negotiations foreseen in paragraphs 7 and 8 (a) (iii) of Article XXII on the Final Provisions of the GPA,[30] through the adoption of work programmes for . . . sustainable procurement by 6 April 2017 or three years from the date of its entry into force (6 April 2014).[31]

On 15 March 2015, the 10YFP partners recommended the application of the six principles on SPP, namely: 1) good public procurement is SPP; 2) SPP implementation requires leadership; 3) SPP contributes to broad policy objectives; 3) SPP involves all stakeholders; 4) SPP implementation is based on sound organizational management principles; and 5) SPP monitors its outcomes and results. They recommended including these principles in their procurement policies and frameworks and applying them in their procurement practices.[32]

In the same year, the Organization for Economic Co-operation and Development (OECD) expanded on the core principles of the 2008 OECD Recommendations on Enhancing Integrity in Public Procurement, recommending the pursuit of a balance between the secondary policy objectives[33] and the primary objective of procurement in any public procurement system. The 2015 OECD Fifth (5th) Recommendation on Public Procurement[34] calls not only for the use of public procurement in the pursuit of secondary policy objectives but also for the development of an appropriate strategy to integrate secondary policy objectives into public procurement systems.

In doing so, the OECD encourages the use of an appropriate impact assessment methodology to measure the effectiveness of procurement in achieving secondary policy objectives.

The year 2015 also marked the 'new global agenda for a sustainable future', when the 193 members of the United Nations unanimously adopted the 2030 Agenda.[35] The 17 Sustainable Development Goals (SDGs) have become the world's best plan to build a better world for people and our planet by 2030. The SDGs are a call to action by all countries – poor, rich and middle-income – to promote prosperity while protecting the environment.[36] Of the 17 Goals, it is SDG 12 on sustainable consumption and production that directly promotes sustainable procurement among public procurers. Target 12.7 specifically promotes SPP practices in accordance with national policies and priorities.

In the same year, the Paris Agreement, under the United Nations Framework Convention on Climate Change (UNFCCC), set the ambition for global action to reduce greenhouse gases, requiring all sectors to commit to a low-carbon transition to bring net emissions to zero in the second half of this century, especially the government,[37] through SPP.

International organizations like UNOPS are also at the forefront of green infrastructure, as evidenced by its involvement in the construction of a zero-emission UN regional hub in Panama City and its pioneering role in the procurement of fuel-efficient (hybrid) ambulances in Peru.[38] Indeed, UNEP has already pointed out that the reduction of greenhouse gas emissions is the most frequently cited and quantified benefit of sustainable public procurement, e.g. it promotes innovation, regional economic development, generates job opportunities, improves occupational health and safety and reduces waste generation.[39]

The benefits associated with SPP are not limited to environmental impacts, but can include everything from social and health benefits to economic and political ones.[40] The public sector can also benefit from potential cost savings.[41] SPP could save both money and resources through the use of life-cycle costing. For example, all product life-cycle costs, such as operation and maintenance costs, can reduce the total cost (compared to the purchase price) in cases like the purchase of energy-efficient equipment, where savings will be achieved due to lower energy use, or even the application of end-of-life recycling.

An increasing number of countries around the world consider the environmental and social impact of their public spending and have implemented SPP or GPP policies.[42] Governments can take the lead in demanding more sustainable products at scale, thus stimulating markets to produce these goods and demonstrating the feasibility of innovative solutions that companies often follow, as well as creating private markets for sustainable products.[43] Manufacturers who are hesitant to develop better products due to demand uncertainty can participate in public procurement that guarantees a certain amount of new products will be purchased by the government; for example, the United States and Sweden have successfully used public procurement to induce the launch of more energy-efficient appliances such as refrigerators and freezers.[44]

Despite the valuable impact of SPP, its implementation remains a major challenge for the following reasons: a) habit and difficulty in changing purchasing behaviour; b) lack of suppliers of sustainable goods, vendors or services; c) complexity of comparing cost/value assessments; d) difficulty of including factors broader than environmental considerations; e) perception that the process and results are more costly or time-consuming.[45]

Although there is no single global strategy to address the challenges of implementing sustainable public procurement, there are numerous international (e.g. Marrakech Task Force, International Green Purchasing Network – IGPN, Local Governments for Sustainability – ICLEI, North American Green Purchasing Initiative – NAGPI and EUROPE 2020), national (e.g. SPP programmes in the OECD, SPP programmes in Africa, SPP programmes in Asia, SPP programmes in South America) and even local initiatives that have been undertaken to promote and implement SPP.[46]

One such initiative was GPP 2020, the most recent project funded by the EU's Intelligent Energy programme to integrate low-carbon procurement across Europe[47] through central purchasing bodies (CPBs).[48] Energy and CO2 reductions were measured over the entire life cycle of products, services and works.[49] GPP 2020 compared the CO2 savings between emissions from previous or 'standard' tenders and the GPP tenders used by GPP 2020 procurement partners.[50] To ensure the sustainability of the project, GPP 2020 organized a capacity-building programme, including training courses and exchanges, with participating CPBs.

The other initiative is the evaluation of the integration of the three pillars of sustainable development (i.e. economic, social and environmental) into the procurement system using the OECD Methodology for the Evaluation of Procurement Systems for Sustainable Public Procurement (MAPS SPP). Like the OECD MAPS module, the OECD MAPS SPP module provides a harmonized tool for the evaluation of SPPs, addressing the following aspects from the perspective of sustainability (1) legal, regulatory and policy framework; (2) institutional arrangements and inter-ministerial cooperation; (3) strategic plans for SPP implementation and capacity building; (4) sustainable procurement cycle; (5) sustainable procurement operations; (6) private sector and other stakeholder involvement; (7) monitoring, evaluation and reporting; (8) ethics; (9) awareness raising, communication and outreach and (10) networking.[51]

Recently, MAPS SPP was tested to evaluate SPP in Norway based on the four pillars of the OECD Methodology for the Evaluation of Procurement Systems (MAPS) – Pillar 1 on Legal, Regulatory and Policy Framework, Pillar 2 on Institutional Framework and Management Capacity, Pillar 3 on Public Procurement Operations and Market Practices and Pillar 4 on Accountability, Integrity and Transparency of the Public Procurement System. Interestingly, the evaluation showed that while Norway has a solid foundation for SPP in the area of legal and regulatory framework, it has weaknesses in the implementation and adoption of SPP throughout its public procurement system, including its accountability framework, which led to a recommendation on the need to consider a multidimensional approach in its strategic policy framework for SPP.[52]

Although measurement in terms of uniform definitions of SPP remains a challenge,[53] an advanced definition of Low Carbon Procurement (LCP) has been presented as a 'process whereby organizations seek to purchase goods, services, works and utilities with a reduced carbon footprint over their life cycle and/or that lead to the reduction of the organization's overall carbon footprint, considering its direct and indirect emissions".[54] Accordingly, Carbon Management (CM) must be considered for the purchase of: a) goods and services that will be owned and controlled by the organization and that lead to the reduction of its direct emissions through the purchase of lower-carbon alternatives for internal energy production and consumption; b) energy from third-party sources not owned by the organization that lead to the reduction of its indirect energy emissions (e.g. through the purchase of energy directly from non-carbon or lower-carbon sources) and/or energy-efficient goods and services that can also lead to a reduction in indirect energy emissions; and c) upstream and downstream goods and services not owned by the organization that lead to a reduction in other indirect emissions (e.g. through the purchase of products or services with an overall reduced life-cycle footprint compared to alternatives, including considerations from extraction to disposal).[55]

Although it may seem that, like other SPP initiatives, LCP is too technical to be understood and implemented, examples of LCP best practices prove otherwise. Through GPP 2020, more than 100 low-carbon tenders have been implemented by over 40 public authorities in eight countries,[56] resulting in calculated savings of over 900,000 tonnes of CO2 and 140,000 toe (tonnes of oil equivalent) over three years.[57] The highest CO2 reduction was recorded in the infrastructure project 'A6 Almere Motorway Reconstruction' in the Netherlands, with a savings of 52800 t CO2 eq and 15048 toe of energy savings.[58]

While SPP has not been included among the main topics of the climate negotiations (e.g. some of the negotiating priorities for achieving the long-term goals of the Paris Agreement include ambitious mitigation actions, adaptation and reporting targets, loss and damage, scaled climate finance, technology development and transfer, capacity building and transparency of actions and support),[59] its impact on the overall goal of combating climate change through GHG/CO2 reduction cannot be underestimated. Best practices have shown that SPP or LCP (to be more precise) have contributed to the reduction of CO2 and could be one of the best possible tools for implementing the Paris Agreement.[60]

Drivers for Low-Carbon and Energy-Efficient Procurement

Public procurement is responsible for the release of 7.5 billion tonnes of CO2 into the atmosphere or close to 15% of annual GHG emissions,[61] equivalent to those from the United States (also 15%, which makes the United States the second-highest carbon dioxide emitter by country), and half of that of China with 30% annual GHG emissions (the top carbon emitters by country).[62] The vast majority of these emissions – up to 70% of the total – stem from the activities of just six industries: defense and security (1.3 billion tonnes), transport (0.9), waste management services (0.9), construction (0.9), industrial products (0.6), utilities (0.6) and others (2.3).[63] With this impact, governments have the responsibility of decarbonizing their purchases.

As an emerging aspect of green public procurement (GPP), decarbonizing public procurement requires the valuation of carbon dioxide – financially, socially and environmentally – to environmental savings in a particular procurement on the idea that GHG emissions associated with a product, service and supply chain can be calculated and measured to reveal the true cost of the publicly procured goods or services.[64]

In fact, government organizations worldwide have already identified the need to start tracking and managing their GHG emissions, both to demonstrate environmental leadership and to prepare for future reporting policies and regulations. In the US, for example, Executive Order 13514, which former President Obama signed on October 5, 2009, required federal agencies to report and reduce their GHG emissions over time.[65] In this calculation, GHG emissions are divided into three categories: Scope 1, 2 and 3. Scope 1 emissions are defined as those caused directly by an organization's activities, while scope 2 emissions count indirect emissions resulting from an organization's energy consumption. Scope 3 emissions include all other indirect emissions caused along an organization's value chain.[66] In green public procurement, for example, procuring entities can use GHG emission as a source selection factor by requiring, the use of offeror self-certifications to report GHG emissions.[67]

There are at least three strategies by which low-carbon emissions can be promoted in public procurement – by adopting a low-carbon public procurement policy, or by integrating low-carbon emissions standards or criteria in the procurement cycle, or through the use of eco-labelling.

Low-Carbon Procurement Policies

Greenhouse gas reduction is not a new concept in terms of SPP. As early in 2011, the Marrakech Task Force on Sustainable Public Procurement, led by Switzerland, reported how New Zealand's 'Sustainable Public Procurement Initiative', implemented since 2006, had reduced waste and carbon emissions, paving the way for New Zealand as a 'world-leading sustainable economy'.[68]

The EU, for example, has implemented EU eco-design that has already decreased the EU's carbon emissions by 19% while increasing GDP by more than 44%, making the EU one of the most energy-efficient economies in the world, producing fewer greenhouse gases per unit of GDP than most other major economies.[69] In addition, the EU also has started to regulate carbon dioxide emissions (CO2) from cars and vans,[70] and has strengthened energy performance targets for buildings, including near-zero emission standards for all new buildings from 2020, resulting in a quarter reduction in GHG emissions per capita. In 2012, average emissions per capita in EU Member States and Iceland fell to 9 tonnes CO2 equivalent.[71]

Even the world's largest purchaser, the US federal government,[72] has a policy that 'requires federal agencies to ensure that 95 per cent of new contract actions for products and services are energy efficient or otherwise environmentally preferable'.[73] President Barack Obama's 2009 Executive Order 13514 specifically states that

> [federal agencies must] ensure that 95% of new contracts . . . for products and services . . . are energy-efficient (Energy Star or Federal Energy Management (FEMP)), water-efficient, bio-based, environmentally preferable, e.g., Electronic Product Environmental Assessment Tool (EPEAT) certified, ozone-friendly, contain recycled content, or are non-toxic or less toxic alternatives, where such products and services meet agency performance requirements.[74]

The same executive order encourages agencies to consider carbon intensity in product purchasing decisions by requiring each agency to report and reduce its direct and indirect greenhouse gas emissions.[75]

President Biden expanded the federal agencies' requirements by issuing Executive Order No. 14057 on December 8, 2021, otherwise known as 'Catalyzing Clean Energy Industries and Jobs through Federal Sustainability', which set out several goals to both address climate change and catalyze clean energy industries and jobs: (1) Achieve 100% carbon pollution-free electricity by 2030, including 50% on a 24/7 basis; (2) Reach 100% zero-emission vehicle acquisition by 2035, including 100% light-duty acquisitions by 2027; (3) Achieve net-zero building emissions by 2045, including a 50% reduction by 2032; (4) Reduce Scope 1 and 2 greenhouse gas emissions by 65 percent from 2008 levels by 2030; (5) Establish targets to reduce energy and potable water use intensity by 2030; (6) Reduce procurement emissions to net zero by 2050; (7) Have climate-resilient infrastructure and operations; (8) Develop a climate- and sustainability-focused workforce; (9) Advance environmental justice and equity-focused operations and (10) Accelerate progress through domestic and international partnerships.

Even the US Congress recognizes strategic public procurement in the fight against climate change by incorporating a provision on direct spending for green products or vendors in the recently enacted 2022 Inflation Reduction Act (IRA). Though not a procurement law, IRA includes significant provisions related to federal spending, for example, regarding federal purchases of environmentally-sound building products. Section 60502 and 60503 of the IRA provides the General Services Authority with $2.15 billion for low-embodied carbon materials in building projects, along with $250 million to be invested in green materials for federal properties.[76]

An increasing number of countries around the world consider the environmental and socio-economic impact of their public spending and have implemented SPP or GPP policies.[77] Governments can take the lead in demanding more sustainable products at scale, thus stimulating markets to produce these goods and demonstrating the feasibility of innovative solutions that companies often follow, also creating private markets for sustainable products.[78] Manufacturers who are hesitant to develop better products due to demand uncertainty can participate in public procurement that guarantees a certain amount of new products will be purchased by the government; for example, the United States and Sweden have successfully used public procurement to induce the launch of more energy-efficient appliances such as refrigerators and freezers.[79]

States have also taken some action, with California adopting a Buy Clean law in 2017, which provides a threshold for emissions intensity above which companies cannot bid for government contracts, and other states providing preferential procurement treatment for low-carbon materials, such as the Low Embodied Carbon Climate Leadership Act (LECCLA) introduced in New York and New Jersey, with provisions for a 5% discount to bids with the lowest emissions and another 3% discount for producers that use any carbon capture, utilization, or storage technology, or other breakthrough technology. A discount of this size would make bids more competitive, incentivizing immediate adoption (and pairing) of existing off-the-shelf solutions (e.g., energy efficiency; cement mixes that use less clinker; concrete mixes that replace some cement with alternative materials) and longer-term investments to tackle harder-to-abate segments of the supply chain (e.g., process emissions from making a key input to cement).[80]

Low-Carbon Tenders

Low-carbon tenders are rarely a standard tender document but usually incorporate provisions for either an increase of consumption and production of electricity from renewable sources or decrease of energy consumption or the use of criteria for environmentally friendly products or services including CO2 reporting. They can be categorized into five types of tenders: 1) product-centered tenders, 2) tenders for services related to public buildings, 3) tenders for services that produce transport emissions, 4) tenders that produce emission on the service providers' facilities and 5) tenders for design, architectural and engineering services.[81]

In some instances, low-carbon tenders are used to introduce low-carbon criteria even on the procurement of conventional fossil-fueled products, such as vehicles that are still powered by gasoline or diesel[82] (see Table 25.1. for technical specifications for low-carbon fossil fueled van).

In a low-carbon tender, the performance clauses are just as important as the clauses defining the requirements of the products to be purchased. Performance conditions must be clearly defined to ensure that suppliers are aware of these obligations and are able to consider them when calculating their offer price. Public procurers, in turn, need to have a clear picture of the lifespan of a product within their organizations and take particular care in transposing their expectations into contractual clauses, as changes to contracts during their lifespan are only permitted in specific cases.[84]

Eco-label Use

There has been growing interest in sector-specific market-based performance standards as pathways to decarbonization. In the US, for example, performance standards already play a significant role in the transportation and buildings sectors at both the federal and state level. These include federal Corporate Average Fuel Economy (CAFE)[85] and carbon dioxide emissions standards and state-level zero-emission vehicle standards for light-duty vehicles, as well as efficiency standards for appliances. A growing number of states have adopted clean energy standards (CES) for the electric power sector, and a number of CES bills have been introduced in Congress.

In fact, Ecolabel Index has listed at least 50 ecolabels that include assessment of carbon footprints and/or carbon emissions reduction or greenhouse gas emissions from the 456 ecolabels

Table 25.1. Tender for low-carbon fossil-fueled van[83]

Tender for low-carbon fossil fueled van:

Description: Supply of a conventional fossil fueled large panel van demonstrating a CO2 improvement of at least 10% of the New European Drive Cycle (NEDC) against comparable conventional models. Proposals which deliver a greater than 10% improvement on NEDC, as well as the potential for substantial greater improvements in urban and suburban drive cycles, are strongly encouraged:

Vehicle attributes	*Specifications*	*Demonstration*
CO2 NEDC	Minimum 10% improvement over an equivalent conventional vehicle, larger improvements preferred	The proposal should include independently validated test results for the CO2 emissions of the proposed low-carbon van on the NEDC. Should this data not be immediately available, the proposal should detail a methodology to attain these results
CO2 non-NEDC	Demonstration of greater improvements in CO2 emissions over duty cycles appropriate for the target market	Should the contractor have such information available, the tender bid can be augmented by including independent test results for the proposed low-carbon van on appropriate non-legislative drive cycles
Regulated emissions (Euro standard)	The proposed low-carbon van must comply with the appropriate emissions legislation in force at the time of the procurement of new vehicles	Contractors are encouraged to provide vehicles with regulated emissions performance exceeding the minimum requirements and showing early attainment of future Euro standards (Euro 5)
On-board technology	Vehicles may provide on-board technologies that achieve reductions in the CO2 emissions of the vehicle under targeted usage conditions, such as methods that encourage and/or create more efficient driving style	Should the contractor have such devices available, e.g., passive (driver informative) systems that encourage efficient driver behavior, and with the increased use of on-board GPS tracking in some fleets, active (drive independent system that adapt the vehicle performance or behavior for greater efficiency for the location); the proposals can be augmented by including details of these devices and their operation. However, any savings must be over and above the base CO2 savings requirements
Life cycle CO2	A life cycle CO2 analysis should show significant life cycle CO2 savings over a conventional vehicle	The proposal should include validated full life cycle analysis of CO2 emissions generated by the proposed low vehicle in production, operation and disposal

that it currently tracks in 199 countries;[86] the first of which was recorded in 1981 – the R-2000, a voluntary performance-based standard that focuses on energy performance and is managed by the Natural Resources of Canada using second-party certification (i.e., verification is done by the organization issuing the certification, e.g., an association creating its own quality market) for buildings (i.e., R-2000 homes are those that use 30% less energy to operate compared to conventional new homes).

This was followed in 1992 by Energy Star: US Certification, a voluntary government-backed programme, which marks the national symbol for energy efficiency. Products that earn Energy Star marks prevent greenhouse gas emissions by meeting the strict energy efficiency guidelines set by the U.S Environmental Protection Agency. Unlike R-2000, Energy Star uses third-party certification or an independent assessment declaring that specified requirements pertaining to the products have been met.

Since then, third party-certification (often managed by non-profit organizations) has become the preferred conformity assessment for purposes of verification due to the assurance of independent third parties that the objective requirements for various product categories (see Figure 25.1) have been met.

GIZ (2020) has recorded some of the best practices highlighting possible strategies on the use of eco-labels to promote sustainable public procurement in Southeast Asia. These include setting a directory of eligible labels based on minimum environment criteria, which serves as government-endorsed directory that is linked legally to public procurement regulations, i.e., making it mandatory for public procurers to procure from the directory, e.g., MyHIJAU Mark & Directory in Malaysia, or requiring state agencies to give preference to products awarded with eco-labels, e.g., South Korea. In Thailand, the government introduced a grace period of two years for green products and services to enter the 'Green Cart', which serves as Thailand's green catalogue for SPP.[87]

While decarbonization requirements in eco-labels vary from classification of products and/or products categories across different sectors, carbon emission limit targets and energy-efficiency remain the topmost requirements for labelling climate-friendly products.

International Best Practices on Low-Carbon and Energy-Efficient Procurement

Some of the international best practices on low-carbon and energy-efficient procurement focus on (1) energy-efficient building, green building, and net zero building, (2) target setting for GPP and (3) international organizations initiatives for low carbon and energy efficient procurement.

Energy Efficient Building, Green Building, and Net Zero Carbon Building

Unlike energy efficient buildings, green buildings include many other environmental aspects apart from energy efficiency, such as water efficiency, waste management and the use of green materials in construction. Green buildings should not be confused with net-zero carbon buildings, which have achieved net-zero carbon emission by reducing energy consumption and are powered from on-site and/or off-site renewable energy sources. Unlike green buildings, net-zero carbon buildings need to generate renewable energy and are usually low-rise buildings to produce a sufficient amount of renewable energy to satisfy building demand. Net-zero carbon buildings are less common than green and energy-efficient buildings.[88]

To date, very few infrastructure projects have focused on reducing carbon emissions (more particularly on embodied carbon emissions) or becoming net-zero. To encourage more net-zero embodied carbon buildings, some agencies have started to provide incentives or requirements for net-zero buildings. For instance, the Buy Clean California Act has required Environmental Product Declarations (EPDs) for certain materials being specified for state-building projects, starting on January 1st, 2020. Additionally, in 2016, the City of Vancouver published its Zero Emissions Building Plan establishing specific targets and actions for achieving zero emissions in all new buildings by 2030.

Target Settings for GPP Programs

The introduction of low-carbon criteria in GPP, to be successful, requires clear quantitative targets that can be applied to all overall programmes and to specific goals. They can be categorized into four: 1) adoption of targets (i.e., the adoption of LCPP), 2) industry-level targets (i.e., adoption of industry certifications e.g., Energy Star programme in the US or the Concrete Sustainability Council eco-label in Belgium), 3) project-level targets (i.e., project-level life-cycle assessment such as LCA indicators and GWP, decreased CO2 emissions such as the CO2 Performance Ladder in The Netherlands or project-level environmental impact assessment such as DuboCalc environmental cost indicator) and 4) product-level targets, such as greenhouse gas emissions reduction (GWP of the product).[89]

The 2021 white paper by the World Economic Forum in collaboration with the Boston Consulting Group on catalyzing the net zero economy through GPP highlights the importance of creating a transparent baseline (i.e., current status of emissions for which the procurement function is both directly and indirectly responsible) including the decarbonization value proposition (i.e., reduction in total emissions needed to, for example, implement a net zero procurement programme) before setting a realistic emission targets reflecting the Paris Agreement goals whilst leveraging on science-based targets.

For example, in the case of public procurement for works, it is important to identify the total emissions that construction materials are generating, i.e., that cement represents 25% of the construction sector's total emissions can be used as a baseline for setting the target for reduction of emissions in public procurement of works through the use of low-carbon emissions materials,[90] such as clinker substation with fly ash and blast furnace slag in cement production.[91]

Conclusion

Governments can have an impact on CO2 emission reductions through green public procurement (GPP) by leading the way in greening the market through public sector purchases by, for example, (a) displaying a willingness to procure green products through subsidies or grants to suppliers who are willing to go green or accept a higher purchase price in favor or choosing a green product (which in many cases will still have a lower cost over its life cycle than a non-green product) or (b) by holding companies accountable not only for how they spend their money, but also for their emissions (CO2 budgeting) (PEFA, 2021).

Despite this potential, very few countries have yet to leverage their purchasing power in accelerating their National Determined Contributions (NDC) ambitions. Even developed countries that are known for championing the use of public procurement in reducing their CO2 emissions, such as South Korea and Singapore, have not reported about public procurement in their most recent NDCs submission, i.e., Singapore has included in its long-term climate strategy the role of public procurers in taking the lead towards decarbonization, yet inadvertently failed to report about it in their updated NDCs.

While several international best practices have been recorded on the use of LCPP to combat climate change, particularly on the integration of low-carbon considerations in every stage of the public procurement cycle, the challenge of finding "Climate Champions" among public procurers remains: not because of lack of motivation to do so, but due to systemic protocols in ensuring that reporting countries will even think of the potential of their purchasing power in carbon emission reductions.

Notes

1 Gratitude to Prof. Gabriella Racca of the University of Turin and to Mr. Farid Yaker and Ms. Agnes Wierzbicki of UNEP for their invaluable comments in developing this chapter.

2 Sustainable procurement ensures that the products and services purchased by an organization provide good value for money on a life-cycle cost basis and generate benefits not only for the organization, but also for the environment, society and the economy. See Simon Clement, John Watt and Abby Semple, *The Procura Manual, A Guide to Implementing Sustainable Procurement* (3rd edn, ICLEI European Secretariat 2016) <www.procuraplus.org/fileadmin/user_upload/ManualProcura_online_version_new_logo.pdf> accessed 14 April 2024. Sustainable procurement becomes sustainable public procurement when the procuring entities are public organizations.

3 UNEP, Global Review of Sustainable Public Procurement (2017) <www.unep.org/resources/report/2017-global-review-sustainable-public-procurement> accessed 14 April 2024

4 See also Ron Watermeyer, 'Facilitating Sustainable Development through Public and Donor Procurement Regimes: Tools and Techniques' (2004) PPLR, 1, 30–55.

5 Comprehensive and Progressive Agreement for Trans-Pacific Partnership (CPTPP, also known as TPP11 or TPP-11) (trade agreement between Australia, Brunei, Canada, Chile, Japan, Malaysia, Mexico, New Zealand, Peru, Singapore and Vietnam as original parties and with the accession of United Kingdom on 16 July 2023) (signed on 8 March 2018 and entered into effect 60 days after the ratification by at least half of the signatories or on 30 December 2018). See Chapters 15 on Government Procurement and 20 on Environment of CPTTP <www.mfat.govt.nz/assets/Trade-agreements/CPTTP/Comprehensive-and-Progressive-Agreement-for-Trans-Pacific-Partnership-CPTTP-English.pdf> accessed 14 April 2024. See also Rafael Leal-Arcas, 'Climate Change Mitigation from the Bottom up: Preferential Trade Agreements to Promote Climate Change Mitigation' (2013) Carbon & Climate L. Rev. 34

6 UNCITRAL, Part I – A (1)(5) of the Guide to Enactment of the UNCITRAL Model Law on Procurement Regulation (2014) <https://uncitral.un.org/sites/uncitral.un.org/files/media-documents/uncitral/en/guide-enactment-model-law-public-procurement-e.pdf> accessed 14 April 2024.

7 UNCITRAL, UNCITRAL Model on Public Procurement (2014) <https:uncitral.un.org/sites/uncitral.un.org/files/media-documents/uncitral/en/2011-model-law-on-public-procurement-e.pdf> accessed 14 April 204/Article 4. Article 4 of the Procurement Regulations states that 'The (name of the body or authority responsible for promulgating the Procurement Regulations) is authorized to promulgate regulations to realize the objectives and implement the provisions of this Act'.

8 Supra (n 5). See also Caroline Nicholas, 'The 2011 UNCITRAL Model Law on Public Procurement' (2012) PPLR, 3, NA111–123. ('The second [amendment to the 2011 Model Law] is to allow for the inclusion of "socio-economic" evaluation criteria, i.e. as an exemption from the materiality rule, provided that such criteria are stated objectives of government policy (i.e. recorded in procurement regulations or other laws) and are subject to the full transparency regime applicable to evaluation criteria').

9 Supra (n 6). Article 2 (o) of the UNCITRAL Model Law on Government Procurement defines 'socio-economic policies' as 'environmental, social, economic and other policies of this State authorized or required by the procurement regulations or other legal provisions of this State to be taken into account by the procuring entity in procurement procedures. (The issuing State may expand this subparagraph by providing an illustrative list of such policies)'.

10 Articles 9 and 10 of the Model Law. ibid.

11 Section 9 (2)(a) of the Model Law stipulates that 'Suppliers or contractors shall meet the following criteria that the procuring entity deems appropriate and relevant to the circumstances of the particular contract: (a) that they have the necessary professional, technical and environmental qualifications, professional and technical competence, financial resources, equipment and other physical facilities, managerial capacity, reliability, experience and personnel to perform the contract'. ibid.

12 Article 11(2)(b) stipulates that 'The evaluation criteria relating to the subject matter of the contract may include: (b) the cost of operation, maintenance and repair of the goods or of the construction; the time of delivery of the goods, of completion of the construction or of provision of the services; the characteristics of the subject matter of the contract, such as the functional characteristics of the goods or of the construction and the environmental characteristics of the subject matter; and the terms of payment and guarantee relating to the subject matter of the contract'. Ibid.

13 Article 9(1) of the Guide, supra at note 15.
14 Article 11(4), ibid.
15 Article 11(5), ibid.
16 UNEP, 'Sustainable Public Procurement Implementation Guidelines: Introducing UNEP's Approach' (2012) <https://wedocs.unep.org/handle/20/500/11822/32157> accessed 14 April 2024.
17 UNOPS Procurement Manual (2014, updated in 2021) <https://www.unops.org/SiteCollectionDocuments/Procurement/UNOPS%20procurement%20manual%20EN.pdf> accessed 14 April 2024.
18 These include repeated instances of violations of waste disposal regulations, paragraph 3.3 on the ineligibility of suppliers, ibid 33.
19 Section 4.1 on procurement strategy, ibid 36.
20 Section 4 on the types of requirements specifications for works, ibid., p. 40); carrying out the assessment of sustainability impacts during the project level procurement planning (para. 4.3.3 on project level procurement planning, ibid., p. 43); including the availability of sustainable products, their cost, their practical implications and the supplier's sustainability practices in the market research. (Section 5.2. on market research, ibid., 46).
21 These include the technical capacity to deliver the sustainability components of the contract, the corporate responsibility of the supplier, approaches to reduce emissions, increasing national capacity Para. 6.3.1.4 on Request for Proposal, Ibid. at page 58; optional Request for Proposal procedure to promote sustainability Para.3.2 on Selecting the solicitation method for works, Ibid. at page 59; encouraging SME participation through lot design in tenders Para 6.5.1 (q) on Fractional Orders, Ibid. at page 75; use of recycled packaging materials Para 6.5.3 on Contractual Information, Ibid. at page 76; open, inclusive and transparent communications Para. 6.5.1 (q) on Fractional Orders, Ibid. at page 75; use of recyclable packaging materials Para. 6.5.3 on Contractual Information, Ibid. on page 76; open, inclusive and transparent communication with suppliers on the UNOPS sustainability approach Para. 6.7 on Communication with Suppliers, Ibid. on page 79; inclusion of technical expertise in the technical evaluation team for complex requirements Para. 8.2 on Evaluation Committee, Ibid. on page 103.
22 These include 100 per cent recycled paper compared to traditional paper and the lowest price within the given product category. Paragraph 8.4.1. Most advantageous and technically acceptable offer, ibid 104.
23 Section 8.4.2. on the lowest and substantially compliant price offer, ibid 105.
24 Section 8.4.3. on cumulative analysis methodology, ibid 106.
25 Section 8.6 on commercial evaluation, ibid 108.
26 Section 12.2.1 on packaging, ibid 150.
27 Section 1.2. on the evaluation of supplier performance, Ibid. at page 158.
28 Robert D. Anderson, "The coming into force of the revised WTO Agreement on Government Procurement, and related developments" (2014) PPLR, S. NA160-NA163
29 WTO, Revised Agreement on Government Procurement (amended on 30 March 2012) <https://www.wto.org/english/docs_e/legal_e/rev-gpr-94_01_e.htm> accessed 14 April 2024. Committee means the Committee on Government Procurement established by Article XXI:1. Article XXI:1 provides that 'There shall be a Committee on Government Procurement composed of representatives of each Party. The Committee shall elect its own Chairman and shall meet as required, but not less than once a year, for the purpose of giving the Parties the opportunity to consult with each other on any matter relating to the operation of this Agreement or the pursuit of its objectives and to carry out such other responsibilities as may be assigned to it by the Parties'.
30 ibid. Article XXII:7 states that 'Within three years of the date of entry into force of the Protocol Amending the Government Procurement Agreement, adopted on 30 March 2012, and periodically thereafter, the Parties shall enter into further negotiations with a view to improving this Agreement, reducing and progressively eliminating discriminatory measures and achieving the widest possible scope of its coverage among all Parties on the basis of reciprocity, taking into account the needs of developing countries'.
31 See generally Robert Anderson, 'The Revised WTO Government Procurement Agreement: The Evolution of the Global Footprint, Economic Impact and Political Significance' (2019) PPLR 3, 71–91.
32 The 10YFP SPP Programme, Principles of Sustainable Procurement (March 2015) <https://www.oneplanetnetwork.org/sites/default/files/10yfp_spp_programme_principles_of_sustainable_public_procurement.pdf> accessed 14 April 2024.
33 Secondary policy objectives refer to a range of goals such as sustainable green growth, small and medium-sized enterprise development, innovation, standards for responsible business conduct or

broader industrial policy goals, which governments increasingly pursue through the use of procurement as a policy lever, in addition to the primary objective of procurement. OECD, 'Recommendation of the Council on Public Procurement' (2015) <https://www.oecd.org/gov/public-procurement/OECD-Recommendation-on-Public-Procurement.pdf> accessed 14 April 2024

34 ibid.

35 United Nations, 'Historic New Sustainable Development Agenda Unanimously Adopted by 193 UN Members' (Press Release, 25 September 2015) <https://sustainabledevelopment.un.org/content/documents/8371Sustainable%20Development%20Summit_final.pdf> accessed 14 April 2024

36 Transforming Our World: the 2030 Agenda for Sustainable Development, also known as 'The 2030 agenda for Sustainable Development' (adopted by all United Nations Member States in 2015) <https://sdgs.un.org/2030agenda> accessed 14 April 2024.

37 See in general Jellie Molino, 'Sustainable Public Procurement in the Green Climate Fund: A "Walk-the-talk" Strategy on Climate Change' (2019) PPLR 4, 154–69.

38 ibid.

39 UNEP, 'Measuring and Communicating the Benefits of Sustainable Public Procurement (SPP): Baseline Review and Development of a Guidance Framework' (2016) <http://www.upphandlingsmyndigheten.se/globalassets/publikationer/rapporter/measuring-and-communicating-the-benefits-of-sustainable-public-procurement-spp-baseline-review-and-development-of-a-guidance-framework.pdf> accessed 1 March 2023.

40 See generally, UNEP, 'Measuring and Communicating the Benefits of Sustainable Public Procurement (SPP): Baseline Review and Development of a Guidance Framework' (2016) <http://www.upphandlingsmyndigheten.se/globalassets/publikationer/rapporter/measuring-and-communicating-the-benefits-of-sustainable-public-procurement-spp-baseline-review-and-development-of-a-guidance-framework.pdf> accessed 1 March 2023. (UNEP has classified the benefits of SPP into three: (1) environmental benefits (i.e. reduction of greenhouse gas emissions; reduction of energy, water and fuel consumption; reduction of waste generation; improvement of air quality; efficient use of materials; reduction of the use of hazardous substances; maintenance of biodiversity); (2) social benefits (i.e. creation of employment opportunities; improvement of occupational health and safety; improvement of social inclusion; promotion of economic opportunities for Indigenous Peoples; promotion of equal employment opportunities; promotion of fair and ethical trade; support for small and medium-sized enterprises); and 3) economic benefits (i.e. cost reduction; promotion of innovation; promotion of regional economic development; development of markets for sustainable products and services; enhanced reputation; reduced risk).

41 ibid. (Citing the report 'Baseline Review: Measuring and Communicating the Benefits of Sustainable Public Procurement and BuySmart Network's Guide to the Business Case & Benefits of Sustainability Purchasing', March 2007).

42 UNEP, 'Sustainable Consumption and Production Indicators for Future SDGS' (March 2015) <https://www.iisd.org/sites/default/files/publications/sustainable-consumption-production-indicators-future-sdgs_0.pdf> accessed 1 March 2023.

43 ibid.

44 See in general Carl Dalhammar, Jessica Luth Richter and Erika Machacek, 'Energy Efficiency Regulations, Market and Behavioural Failures and Standardisation' in Eleonore Maitre-Ekern, Carl Dalhammar and Hans Christian Bugge (eds), *Preventing Environmental Damage from Products* (CUP 2018).

45 United Nations, *UN Procurement Practitioner's Handbook* (2022) <www.ungm.org/Shared/Knowledge-Center> accessed 14 April 2024.

46 See in general Oshani Perera, Nupur Chowdhury and Anandajit Goswami, 'State of Play in Sustainable Public Procurement' (2007) <https://www.iisd.org/pdf/2007/state_procurement.pdf> accessed 14 April 2024.

47 See in general Nancy Clinton, 'The Path to a Low-Carbon Economy is Paved By Central Purchasing Bodies' (2015), Public Spend Forum Europe <http://publicspendforumeurope.com/2015/02/17/the-path-to-a-low-carbon-economy-is-paved-by-central-purchasing-bodies/> accessed 1 March 2023.

48 ibid.

49 ibid.

50 ibid.

51 OECD, 'Methodology for Evaluating Procurement Systems for Sustainable Public Procurement' (2018) <https://www.oecd.org/gov/public-procurement/methodology-assessing-procurement/> accessed 14 April 2024.

52 OECD, 'Sustainable Public Procurement in Norway: Testing the MAPS Module on Sustainable Public Procurement' (2020) <http://www.mapsinitiative.org/assessments/MAPS%20Norway%20SPP.pdf> accessed 1 March 2023.

53 See in general Fernandeo Correia and others, 'Low Carbon Procurement: An Emerging Agenda' (2013) 19 Journal of Purchasing and Supply Management 58–64.

54 ibid.

55 ibid.

56 The Netherlands, Germany, Austria, Slovenia, Croatia, Spain, Italy and Portugal.

57 ICLEI, GPP Final Report (2020) <http://www.gpp2020.eu/low-carbon-tenders/measuring-savings/> accessed 1 March 2023.

58 Reconstruction Highway A6 Almere, Rijkswaterstaat, The Netherlands (2020) <http://www.gpp2020.eu/fileadmin/files/Tender_Models/GPP_2020_Tender_Model_Reconstruction_A6_Almere_RWS_April_2016.pdf> accessed 1 March 2023. See also Inga Geach, 'Investigating the Role of Sustainability in Contractor Selection and Evaluation' (2016) Sustainability Scholarship <http://www.ciob.org/sites/default/files/View%20Inga%27s%20full%20report%20here.pdf> accessed 1 March 2023. ('In the construction sector, zero-carbon buildings, BREEAM requirements, preference for local and responsible sourcing of labour and materials, and the Considerate Constructors Scheme have become increasingly important to maintain a positive image of the sector').

59 See in general Neier Henrik, Neyer Judith and Radunsky Klaus, 'International Climate Negotiations – Issues at Stake in View of the COP 24 UN Climate Change Conference in Katowice and beyond' (2018) <https://www.europa.eu/Reg.Data/etudes/STUD/2018/626092/IPOL-STU(2018)626092_EN.pdf> accessed 14 April 2024

60 See also Jorge Nunez Ferrer, 'The EU's Public Procurement Framework: How the EU's Public Procurement Framework Contributing to the Achievement of the Objectives of the Paris Agreement and the Circular Economy Strategy?' (2020), Briefing Requested by the IMCO Committee, European Parliament <https://www.europarl.europa.eu/RegData/etudes/BRIE/2020/648770/IPOL_BRI(2020)648770_EN.pdf> accessed 14 April 2024.

61 World Economic Forum, 'Green Public Procurement: Catalyzing the Net-Zero Economy' (2022) <https://www.weforum.org/publications/green-public-procurement-catalysing-the-net-zero-economy/> accessed 14 April 2024.

62 EPA, Emissions by Country (2020, citing data from Climate Watch) <https://www.epa.gov/ghgemissions/global-greenhouse-gas-emissions-data> accessed 14 April 2024.

63 Supra (n 61).

64 L Olmsted, 'A Common Taxonomy for Carbon: How States and Cities Public Procurement to Combat Climate Change' (2020) 49 Pub. Cont. L.J. 691.

65 World Resources Institute and LMI, The Greenhouse Gas Protocol for the U.S. Public Sector (2010) <https://ghgprotocol.org/sites/default/files/2022–12/us-public-sector-protocol_final_oct13.pdf> accessed 14 April 2024.

66 European Commission, Eco-Management and Audit Scheme (EMAS) Implementation tools (2017) <https://green-business-ec.europa.eu/publications/emas-toolkit-instruction-manual_en> accessed 14 April 2024.

67 Supra (n 65).

68 Alex Kopp, Marrakech Task Force on Sustainable Public Procurement led by Switzerland, Activity Report (2011) <http://www.sustainableprocurement.eu.com/documents/MTFonSPPReportCSD19FINAL.pdf> accessed 14 April 2024.

69 Yannis Maniatis, 'Setting the International Climate Negotiations Pace for COP-21 in Paris' (2014–2015) 16 Whitehead J. Dipl. & Int'l Rel. 33, cited in Molino (n 47).

70 See generally The Clean Directive (EU Directive 2019/1161), which aims to increase the share and zero emission vehicles in contracts tendered by public authorities in the 27 EU countries by setting the national targets for procuring vehicles. <https://eur-lex.europa.eu/eli/dir/2019/1161/oj> accessed 14 April 2024.

71 ibid.

72 Shawna D Ganley, 'Federal "Green" Product Procurement Policy in the United States' (2013) Center for Climate Change Law, Columbia Law School.

73 ibid.

74 ibid.

75 'President Obama's 2009 executive order also encourages agencies to factor carbon intensity into product purchasing decisions by requiring each agency to report and reduce its direct and indirect GHG emissions. These reporting requirements are generally modeled on the Public Sector Protocol, prepared by the World Resources Institute's (WRI) GHG Protocol Initiative,53 as well as EPA's Private Sector GHG Reporting Program (GHGRP). The order requires agencies to report and reduce these emissions, although it does not specify a minimum percentage reduction that agencies must achieve' (ibid.).

76 Christopher Yukins and Nathaniel Green, 'Feature Comment: The Inflation. Reduction Act: A New Role for Green Procurement?' (2022) 64(33) The Government Contractor.

77 UNEP, Sustainable Public Procurement Global Review (2022) <https://www.oneplanetnetwork.org/knowledge-center/sustainable-public-procurement-2022-global-review-parts-i-and-ii> accessed 14 April 2024.

78 ibid.

79 Dalhammar (n 54).

80 Chris Neidl and Caleb Woodal, A Design Guide to State and Local Low-Carbon Concrete Procurement (2022) <https://www.nrdc.org/sites/default/files/low-carbon-concrete-procurement-guide.pdf> accessed 14 April 2024.

81 ICLEI, GPP 2020 – Procurement for a low-carbon economy (2020) <https://iclei-europa.org/publications-tools/?c=search&uid=Nri0LyGg> accessed 14 April 2024.

82 See also EPA, Questions and Answers: Greenhouse Gas Emissions from a Typical Passenger Vehicle (March 2018) for guidance on the other sources of GHG emission from a vehicle, which can be used as basis for designing technical specifications in the procurement of conventional vehicles with less GHG emissions, e.g., less tailpipe emissions. <https://nepis.epa.gov/Exe/ZyPDF.cgi?Dockey=P100U8YT.pdf> accessed 14 April 2024.

83 Department for Transport, Low Carbon Vehicle Procurement Programme: Supply of Lower Carbon and All-electric Vans (Framework Agreement dated 11 June 2009) <https://assets.publishing.service.gov.uk/government/uploads/systems/uploads/attachment_data/file/167911/low-carbon-vehicle-framework.pdf> accessed 14 April 2024.

84 See for example Article 72 of Directive 2014/24/EU, which provides for conditions for amending contracts and framework agreements without a new procurement procedure. In addition, contracts may be amended without a new procurement procedure if the value of the amendment is below both (i) the threshold values and (ii) 10% of the initial contract value for service and supply contracts and 15% of the initial contract value for works contracts. For further details on performance clauses, especially those related to environmental performance, see Directorate-General for Environment (European Commission), ICLEI – Local Governments for Sustainability, *Buying Green! A Handbook on Green Public Procurement* (3rd edn, *European Commission* 2016).

85 Corporate Average Fuel Economy (CAFÉ) refers to standards in the United States, which was first enacted by Congress in 1975 to improve fuel economy of cars and light trucks that are produced for sale in the United States, which was later expanded to include GHG emissions standards and covered medium- and heavy-duty vehicles. For more information, please see the U.S. Department of Transportation, 'Corporate Average Fuel (CAFÉ) Standards' <https://www.transportation.gov/mission/sustainability/corporate-average-fuel-economy-cafe-standards> accessed 14 April 2024.

86 Using key terms such as 'carbon, climate and greenhouse gas', author searched for ecolabels from the 456 listed labels in Ecolabel Index and was able to list 51 ecolabels <https://www.ecolabelindex.com> accessed 1 March 2023.

87 Siddharth Prakash, Tobias Schleicher and Mirja Michalscheck, 'Barrier Analysis and Strategies for Ecolabels and Sustainable Public Procurement Implementation' (2021) <https://www.oeko.de/fileadmin/oekodoc/Barrier-Analysis-report.pdf> accessed 14 April 2024.

88 Dina Azhgaliyeva and Dil Rahut, 'Promoting Green Buildings: Barriers, Solutions, and Policies' (2022), Asian Development Bank Institute Working Papers Series <https://www.adb.org/sites/default/files/publication/812801/abdi-wp1331.pdf> accessed 14 April 2024. ('The green building concept has evolved over time. Initially, a green building was defined only in terms of environmental performance (citing Kua and Lee 2002, Yoshida and Sugiura 2010 but has evolved to include sustainable and environmentally-friendly construction methods and products (citing Hoffman and Henn 2008, Allwood and others 2011, Hertwich and others 2020). In recent years, the efficient use of resources, the improvement of air quality and reducing pollution have been added to the characteristics of a green or sustainable building (citing Haapio and Viitaniemi 2008, Kibert 2016, Li and others 2016'.)

89 Ali Hasanbeigi and Dinah Shi, 'Target Setting for Green Public Procurement Programmes' (October 2021) <https://industrialenergyaccelerator.org/wp-content/uploads/IDDI-Report-Target-Setting-for-Green-Public-Procurement-Programs_20211004_b-4.pdf> accessed 14 April 2024.

90 Supra (n 71).

91 Johanna Lehne and Felix Preston, 'Making Concrete Change: Innovation in Low-carbon Cement and Concrete' (2018), Chatham House Report, The Royal Institute of International Affairs <https://www.chatamhouse.org/2018/06/making-concrete-change-innovation-low-carbon-cement-and-concrete> accessed 14 April 2024.

26

REGULATING THE DISCLOSURE OF CLIMATE-RELATED FINANCIAL RISKS

Professor Marie-Claire Cordonier Segger, Lara Douvartzidis and David Gayle[1]

Introduction

The average annual climate finance flows for the year 2021/2022 reached almost USD 1.3 trillion, almost double the recorded flow of the year before.[2] The majority of these funds went to mitigation finance. Developed economies continue to mobilise the most climate finance, primarily from private sources, and private actors provided 49% of the total climate finance in this period (USD 625 billion).[3] Yet in the average scenario, the annual finance needed per year is around $8.1 trillion to $9 trillion, jumping to $10 trillion each year for the years 2031 to 2050 – inaction costs trillions more than doing the work to facilitate climate financial flows, and investment decisions increasingly need to reflect this.[4]

Under Article 2(1)(c) of the Paris Agreement, finance flows are to be made consistent with a pathway towards low greenhouse gas emissions and climate-resilient development, and this provision is to be read in the context of sustainable development and efforts to eradicate poverty. The financial sector, including insurance, banking, and capital markets, are key vehicles to allocate capital needed for the just transition and are essential contributors in assessing and managing risk and distributing information in financial markets – in other words, Article 2(1)(c) cannot be met, and the finance cannot flow, without them.[5] Recognising the barriers to finance flows and the role in which the financial sector plays in dismantling those barriers, the Financial Stability Board set up the Task Force on Climate-Related Financial Disclosures (TCFD) to confront this.[6] Eight years, eleven key recommendations and numerous status reports later, in late 2023 the TCFD disbanded, having fulfilled its mandate. Acknowledging that sustainable development and Nationally Determined Contribution (NDC) realisation requires significant financial investment and recognising the intense financial pressures of the financial sector in accounting for losses and opportunities related to climate change,[7] this chapter seeks to assess the progress of the TCFD and regulatory trends at a domestic level on its effective implementation, and with an illustrated example from one of the co-authors of how economic liability may be assessed in the insurance company context.

This chapter shares initial findings from one co-author's examination of the potential for Directors' and Officers' liability insurance (D&O) coverage to limit the responsibility of carbon majors for climate litigation damages, by either absorbing the costs arising from lawsuits, or by providing insurance against personal liability, affecting incentives to reduce or manage climate-related risks. Consideration is given as to whether carbon majors are being 'enabled' by D&O insurance

DOI: 10.4324/9781003276678-30

coverage, but does not extend to examining insurance firms and their potential exposures to litigation-related claims via their corporate insureds, in a manner comparable in scope to the Bank of England's Climate Biennial Exploratory Scenario (CBES).[8] Rather, the chapter focuses on whether D&O insurance may be preventing shareholder litigation cases[9] from having significant financial impact on the directors and officers of corporations and how this can inform the ongoing prudential regulation of general insurers in the context of the net zero transition. This analysis is based on a recent study undertaken by one co-author, which illuminates interconnections between climate litigation risk and insurance cover, with the aim of both informing and bolstering the prudent management of climate-related financial risks in the future.

Climate-Related Risk Disclosure in Policy and Law

The Paris Agreement is a bottom-up structure that relies on commitments from parties to build and elaborate on the transparency and compliance framework within.[10] It does not create a carbon market in and of itself, but it provides foundations and possibility – including for a global carbon market. To be consistent with Article 2(1)(c) of the Paris Agreement and to meaningfully advance the Sustainable Development Goals (SDGs) and its 169 time-bound targets by 2030, governments and financial markets must prioritise a range of trade-related and financial measures to make the finance flow.[11] Financial flows are one of four enabling conditions to facilitate the deployment of response options to climate change and sustainable development.[12] Advancing and aligning economic priorities with climate change considerations such as disclosure of climate-related financial risk is key to fostering sustainable development,[13] and many countries have indicated their support in this endeavour.[14]

Over the last decade disclosure recommendations and guidance have been issued to assist the financial sector, which has resulted in some steps being taken by national financial regulators to align financial flows within their jurisdiction to be consistent with a pathway towards low greenhouse gas emissions and climate-resilient development. This section will assess the relevant international recommendations issued over the last eight years and then examine domestic responses to this.

The Task Force on Climate-related Financial Disclosures (TCFD)

In April 2015, the G20 Finance Ministers and Central Bank Governors requested that the Financial Stability Board (FSB) review how the financial sector should consider and incorporate climate-related issues. Following this, in December 2015 the FSB formed the TCFD for the purpose of identifying and providing information needed by the financial sector "to appropriately assess and price climate-related risks and opportunities".[15] With this, the TCFD was born.

In 2017, the TCFD issued its flagship report containing 11 recommendations for companies in the financial sector centred around four core elements, as follows:[16]

Governance: Disclose the organisation's governance around climate-related risks and opportunities.

Recommended Disclosures:

- Describe the board's oversight of climate-related risks and opportunities.
- Describe management's role in assessing and managing climate-related risks and opportunities.

Strategy: Disclose the actual and potential impacts of climate-related risks and opportunities on the organisation's businesses, strategy and financial planning where such information is material.

Recommended Disclosures:

- Describe the climate-related risks and opportunities the organisation has identified over the short-, medium- and long-term.
- Describe the impact of climate-related risks and opportunities on the organisation's businesses, strategy and financial planning.
- Describe the resilience of the organisation's strategy, taking into consideration different climate-related scenarios, including a 2°C or lower scenario.

Risk management: Disclose how the organisation identifies, assesses and manages climate-related risks.

Recommended Disclosures:

- Describe the organisation's processes for identifying and assessing climate-related risks.
- Describe the organisation's processes for managing climate-related risks.
- Describe how processes for identifying, assessing and managing climate-related risks are integrated into the organisation's overall risk management.

Metrics and Targets: Disclose the metrics and targets used to assess and manage relevant climate-related risks and opportunities where such information is material.

Recommended Disclosures:

- Disclose the metrics used by the organisation to assess climate-related risks and opportunities in line with its strategy and risk management process.
- Disclose Scope 1, Scope 2 and, if appropriate, Scope 3 greenhouse gas (GHG) emissions, and the related risks.
- Describe the targets used by the organisation to manage climate-related risks and opportunities and performance against targets.

The target audience of this report were investors, lenders and insurance underwriters (the 'primary users'); however, at the date of the report the FSB noted that the TCFD *should*:

> determine whether the target audience of users of climate-related financial disclosures should extend beyond these primary users.[17] This foundational report provided the financial sector an opportunity to understand, appropriately assess and price climate-related risk and opportunities, and "to help increase consistency and comparability around the world?[18]

The aim of the TCFD was to provide a singular, accessible framework[19] in which to operate and to contribute to sustainable finance regulation more broadly, which has arguably become a global phenomenon.[20]

Following strong demand from markets, on 3 November 2021 the Trustees of the IFRS Foundation announced the formation of the International Sustainability Standards Board (ISSB).[21] This announcement took place at COP26 in Glasgow, the same forum that saw the formation of the Glasgow Financial Alliance for Net Zero (GFANZ) – with both initiatives citing the objective of the Paris Agreement to limit global temperature increases to 1.5 degrees Celsius from pre-industrial levels.[22] These newly formed organisations can be seen as a visual and decisive link between the Paris Agreement, obligations towards financial flows and action to support this.

On 25 July 2023 the International Organization of Securities Commissions called on its 130 member jurisdictions "to consider ways in which they might adopt, apply or otherwise be informed by the ISSB standards within the context of their jurisdictional arrangements, in a way that promotes consistent and comparable climate-related and other sustainability-related disclosures for investors." From there, these recommendations have permeated national financial sectors in the form of legislative amendment to existing disclosure rules, including in the US, Canada, the UK and European Commission.

In June 2023, the ISSB issued two standards – IFRS S1 and IFRS S2 – as the next step in actioning TCFD's recommendations.[23] IFRS S1 contains disclosure requirements for companies to communicate with investors about sustainability-related risks and opportunities in the short-, medium- and long term. IFRS S2 contains specific climate-related disclosures to be used in tandem with IFRS S1. Both sets of standards fully incorporate the recommendations of the TCFD. and the disclosures themselves are designed to be included in the same 'reporting package' as financial statements.[24] Positively, the Brazilian Ministry of Finance and the Comissão de Valores Mobiliários (CVM) announced that it will incorporate IFRS S1 and S2 within the mandatory framework commencing on 1 January 2026.[25]

In September 2023, the TCFD issued its fourth and final Status Report (the 2023 Status Report), which provided information on action by governments, regulators and standard setters and made key findings in relation to the upwards trend of companies disclosing TCFD-aligned information. The 2023 Status Report found a 40% increase in companies disclosing with at least five of the 11 recommended disclosures since 2020, yet only 4% of companies issued disclosures in line with all of them.[26] The report also observed that further work was needed by the ISSB or other appropriate bodies, including in relation to operationalising the ISSB Standards within domestic legal frameworks to ensure consistent disclosures across jurisdictions, and ensuring focus remains on 'decision-useful disclosures' on other sustainability topics including sustainable development, and to see the linkages between climate-related and sustainability issues especially in company transition plans.[27] Shortly after this report was issued, and at the request of FSB, the TCFD was disbanded – it had fulfilled its mandate and passed the baton to ISSB to continue ratcheting up its recommendations.[28]

State Parties are reacting to these international standards by moving to implement the TCFD recommendations and ISSB standards at a domestic level in line with the Paris Agreement. With these developments, the money could flow with greater ease and speed.

United Kingdom

In 2022, the United Kingdom introduced mandatory disclosure rules regarding climate change by way of amendment to the Companies Act 2006, with numerous complementary legal opinions also being issued regarding the scope of directors' duties in the context of climate- and nature-related disclosures.[29] On 17 January 2022, the Department for Business, Energy and Industrial Strategy issued two regulations amending sections 414C, 414CA and 414CB of the Companies Act 2006 mandating climate-related financial disclosure requirements for companies (the 2022 FD Regulations) in line with TCFD recommendations.[30] This amendment inserts the term 'sustainability' alongside 'non-financial' and mandates that non-financial and sustainability information must contain the climate-related financial disclosures of the company. Section 414CB (2A) was inserted in the Act to provide a definition of *climate-related financial disclosures*. This definition includes:

(a) a description of the company's governance arrangements in relation to assessing and managing climate-related risks and opportunities;
(b) a description of how the company identifies, assesses, and manages climate-related risks and opportunities;
(c) a description of how processes for identifying, assessing, and managing climate-related risks are integrated into the company's overall risk management process;
(d) a description of –

    (i) the principal climate-related risks and opportunities arising in connection with the company's operations, and
    (ii) the time periods by reference to which those risks and opportunities are assessed;

(e) a description of the actual and potential impacts of the principal climate-related risks and opportunities on the company's business model and strategy;
(f) an analysis of the resilience of the company's business model and strategy, taking into consideration different climate-related scenarios;
(g) a description of the targets used by the company to manage climate-related risks and to realise climate-related opportunities and of performance against those targets; and
(h) a description of the key performance indicators used to assess progress against targets used to manage climate-related risks and realise climate-related opportunities and of the calculations on which those key performance indicators are based.

These amendments apply to relevant companies reporting for the financial years starting on or after 6 April 2022 and are accompanied by a non-binding guidance for the benefit of publicly quoted companies, large private companies and LLPs (the 2022 FD Guidance).[31] This guidance makes clear that physical and transition risks can have a material impact on the value of companies and their assets, and that disclosure of material climate-related financial information can help support investment decisions.

Reflecting on the importance for national frameworks such as the 2022 FD Regulations to consider the SDGs, although the 2022 FD Guidance does not reference the SDGs itself, it does reference a report issued on 18 October 2021 titled "Greening Finance: A Roadmap to Sustainable Investing", which contained an outline of strategy for disclosures on climate change and sustainability. This 2021 report does not explicitly discuss the SDGs, either; however, there is reference to a further, earlier report issued in September 2019 by HM Government which sought to understand the UK public's demand for opportunities to invest in the SDGs (based on a survey to members of the public).[32] Using various findings from this survey, this report acknowledged that because individuals within the UK are not able to invest directly into green bonds, it is therefore "feasible" for institutional investors such as insurance companies to do so, as these green bonds were seen as an "effective tool" for sustainability and impact.[33] As a result, we see implicit, not explicit, acknowledgement that climate-related financial disclosure is an effective tool to further the SDGs.

In sum, while climate-related financial disclosures are now mandatory in the UK for larger companies, clarification as to the direct relationship of these disclosures with sustainable development and the Paris Agreement could improve, as could the cross-referencing of the SDGs within sustainability-related reporting publications.

Canada

In May 2021, the Government of Canada announced the formation of the Sustainable Finance Action Council (SFAC) for the purpose of integrating sustainable finance into Canadian industry practice.[34] On 13 March 2024, the newly formed Canadian Sustainability Standards Board (CSSB) released proposed Canadian Sustainability Disclosure Standards (CSDS 1 and CSDS 2).[35] These standards align with IFRS S1 and S2 with modifications for the Canadian landscape, including a suggested voluntary adoption date of 1 January 2025 and mandatory disclosure date beginning on or after 1 January 2027 (including reporting on Scope 3 greenhouse gas emissions).[36] Comments on the draft standards were due on 10 June 2024, with the CSSB welcoming feedback from all interested parties.

The EU

Within the European context, and contrary to the US position, climate- and sustainability-related issues are a core focus of financial policymaking and align with wider policy acceptance of the Paris Agreement and adoption of the SDGs.[37] Sustainability-related disclosures were first imposed in the EU via the Sustainable Finance Disclosures Regulation (SFDR), which was far-reaching in its approach.[38] The SFDR requires transparency on how sustainability is considered in investment and renumeration policies, as well as pre-contractual disclosures and marketing in relation to financial instruments. Although this approach was criticised due to a lack of definition and broad application, the EU's stance on climate and sustainability related disclosures is arguably innovative as compared to the US Securities and Exchange Commission (SEC's) approach.[39]

Additionally, the EU Corporate Sustainability Reporting Directive (CSRD) introduces mandatory sustainable disclosure rules by way of amendment to the Non-Financial Reporting Directive. Commencing on 1 January 2024, the CSRD applies to large companies with more than 500 employees and requires these companies to report not only on risks and opportunities of sustainability, but also the sustainability impacts of their businesses in their value chain.[40] This is commonly referred to as a double materiality approach.[41] At the time of writing, the Corporate Sustainable Due Diligence Directive (CSDDD) has just been approved by the EU Parliament – should the Directive enter into force, this would provide yet another layer of regulation by requiring companies caught by the directive to provide climate transition plans and report on environmental and human rights due diligence periodically – noting that the financial sector is excluded in the current text.

United States

The US Securities and Exchange Commission (SEC) established a Climate Taskforce in 2021 to consider implementing the TCFD US SEC recommendations into its markets.[42] It introduced proposed rules in 2022 and established an enforcement mechanism in April 2023. On 6 March 2024, the SEC formally adopted new rules for companies to disclose climate-related risks, and for larger companies to disclose carbon dioxide emissions.[43] That same day, the SEC were sued by 10 US states[44] on the grounds that "the final rule exceeds the agency's statutory authority and otherwise is arbitrary, capricious, an abuse of direction, and not in accordance with law".[45] The plaintiffs seek a declaration that the rule is unlawful and for the court to vacate the SEC's final action.

The SEC is also defending its position in the US Federal Court, having been sued by fracking company Liberty Energy, who oppose the new SEC listing rule.[46] On 14 March 2024, the Chamber of Commerce, Texas Association of Business and Longview Chamber of Commerce also filed a petition against the SEC for review of this order.[47] On Friday 15 March 2024, Judges Jones, Higginson and Wilson of the Fifth Circuit Court of Appeals ordered that the SEC rule be halted pending the outcome of litigation.[48] Whether this string of litigation will have a long-term effect on climate-related financial disclosures remains to be seen, but given the strong stance of the EU, the extraterritorial effect of the CSRD and the introduction of CSSB standards by Canada (where companies like Liberty Energy also operate), climate-related financial disclosure is arguably becoming a market standard, regardless of whether the SEC or equivalent mandates it to be so. For example, in defending its position in the Fifth Circuit Court of Appeals, counsel for the SEC made the salient point that the sole petitioner suing the SEC (Liberty Energy) is a publicly traded company that already publicly disclosed climate-related information.[49]

TCFD Implementation: A Rapidly Advancing Development

While divergent approaches exist to climate- and sustainability-related disclosure at a national or supranational level[50] (such as jurisdictions where states are or are not supportive of federal/EU disclosure initiatives), broad motivators and commonalities can be identified, including investor protection and motivation for clarify and consistency in the market, as well as the wish to reduce instances and risks of greenwashing.[51] Nevertheless, in the cover letter of the 2023 Status Report, Michael R. Bloomberg wrote, "[a]lthough companies continue to make progress in their disclosures, significant gaps in data remain. In particular, reporting the impact of climate change on companies' businesses, strategies, and financial planning is still lagging behind".[52]

Common governance frameworks like the ones cited here are an attempt to harmonise and concretise TCFD to internalise financial externalities at risk due to climate change, and while progress is being made, additional issues such as data availability, quality and accessibility remain unresolved.[53] Senior leadership across the Board is needed to assist with this integration to internalise these externalities and meaningfully drive the transition forward, including by way of recognition of the interdependence of climate- and biodiversity-related risks and management of these issues within broader governance structures.[54] Setting the tone at the top facilitates change throughout an organisation to drive the transition and imparts genuine signals to financial markets, consumers and the broader community that alignment with the Paris Agreement is a priority for the organisation.

Additionally, questions arise as to whether mandatory disclosure will actually lead to investor capital transfer from the private sector and whether the finance will flow as needed.[55]

If the transition is not occurring fast enough, governments and companies alike risk being Party to litigation, as climate litigation becomes more likely as a means to secure climate justice.[56] This may also include litigation in the insurance sector for damage related to natural disasters.[57] For context, in 2022 roughly 45% of global economic losses due to natural disasters were covered by insurance.[58] That equates to only $125 billion of the total $284 billion being 'insured losses', and these insured losses have more than doubled over the previous five-year period.[59] Investment trends and the current transition are being influenced in part by financial markets which are in turn shaped by insurance trends.

Directors' and Officers' Liability for Climate Litigation

Directors' and Officers' Liability Cover

While historically, UK companies were prohibited from providing indemnity to their directors for negligence, default, breach of duty and breach of trust,[60] the Companies Act 1989 validated the corporate purchase of directors & officers (D&O) insurance to provide defence for 'any proceedings (whether civil or criminal) in which judgment is given in [the director's] favour or [the director] is acquitted'.[61] D&O is thus specifically designed to provide coverage for the types of legal liability incurred by board members as a result of their oversight or day-to-day management of company affairs, protecting directors' personal wealth from exposure in the event of a 'good faith' error,[62] but also allowing some protection to shareholders (albeit indirectly) against legal damages which could threaten the financial integrity of the company itself, assuming exoneration.[63] Despite the clear utility of such an insurance cover, D&O remains somewhat esoteric, and has few parallels among the class of professional liability lines available to corporations.[64]

Indeed, as to the particular *types* of D&O coverage, there exist three distinct 'sides' of product intended to cover liability for different aspects of litigation risk. The first 'side' of coverage allows the protection of directors' and officers' personal financial assets when the corporations they manage are not able to indemnify them (whether for legal or financial reasons), so that these individuals are not bankrupted by legal proceedings or by damages claims brought by plaintiffs. By comparison, the second cover allows corporations to recover the damages from legal proceedings when they defend their own directors and officers, and the third cover provides protection to corporations *themselves* when these are the named defendants in cases.[65] All three 'sides' of D&O insurance are often purchased by companies simultaneously, with the first side of cover regularly forming part of the benefits or compensation package for board members (whether executive or non-executive officers) when undertaking senior management functions.

Private Climate Litigation Risk for Prudential Regulators and the Public Sector

The risks arising from private climate litigation have begun to be considered by some prudential regulators. For example, the Bank of England Prudential Regulation Authority (PRA) took a relatively innovative approach as early as 2015 when considering the impact of so-called climate-related liability risks on the insurance sector,[66] conceptualising private climate litigation as part of a package of risks insurers may face more routinely as the physical and transition-related impacts of climate change continue to unfold. More recently, the PRA included a dedicated climate litigation scenario as part of its 2021 Climate Biennial Exploratory Scenario, in which general insurance participants were required to detail their potential exposures to hypothetical litigation cases brought against their corporate insureds.[67] Further, in its 2020 *Good Practice* report, De Nederlandsche Bank recognised that a failure to integrate climate-related risks into business-as-usual risk management processes could result in 'reputational and legal risks'.[68] Indeed, the Network for Greening the Financial System, a global coalition of central banks and supervisors dedicated to sharing best practices in the management of climate-related financial risks,[69] recognised in 2020 that transition-related risks may "lead to higher legal liabilities or D&O insurance claims".[70] Each of these examples suggests central banks and supervisors are beginning to show awareness of private climate litigation risk, highlighting the utility of further academic studies which deepen understanding of these issues and complement prudent management of the surrounding risks.

In addition, several public sector organisations, think tanks, NGOs and research bodies have published reviews and assessments of climate litigation risk, intended either as a guide for firms or to further general risk management strategies. Of particular note is a 2019 comparative paper published by the Commonwealth Climate Law Initiative, which specifically explores the implications of shareholder-derivative claims, and the role D&O products may play in absorbing some of the losses arising from private climate litigation cases.[71] The Geneva Association,[72] the UN Environment Programme Finance Initiative (via their Principles for Sustainable Insurance)[73] and the International Association of Insurance Supervisors[74] have all also published guidance on the nature of climate litigation risk (specifically for insurers), often garnering information from the industry via public consultations. The prevalence of publications from these non-private actors highlights the growing importance of climate litigation risk, as well as the diversity of voices and interested parties joining the conversation beyond what was originally only lawyers or academics. Finally, an annual report on climate change litigation published by the LSE Grantham Research Institute (LSE GRI)[75] provides expansive detail on trends appearing in the case data (both public and private cases) and offers comprehensive summaries of the current issues and global coverage of cases.[76]

Climate-Related Risk Disclosure, Climate Litigation and Protection Gaps

A study of several firms conducted by a co-author of this chapter[77] on insurance exposures to climate litigation-related losses suggests that D&O underwriters[78] only provide coverage to *some* corporations involved in carbon-intensive sectors (but few overall), and that this is currently provided as coverage to corporations within jurisdictions particularly sensitive to litigation.[79] In this light, the co-author's study suggests policies were broad enough to hypothetically cover a shareholder-derivative claim scenario.[80] Although firms appear to write policies in highly litigious jurisdictions and confirmed that their policies could hypothetically respond to a shareholder-brought suit, the co-author's initial survey results may suggest the possibility of an insurance protection gap, given the low availability of cover for carbon major corporations in litigious jurisdictions.[81] The co-author's investigations challenged initial expectations that corporations are likely to view D&O cover as an opportunity to avoid the full financial responsibility arising from lawsuits, as underwriters signalled a tendency not to provide abundant cover to carbon major corporations, preferring instead to write business for only a few of these companies overall.[82] In addition, he found that certain insurers do not write cover for any carbon-intensive companies or sectors, suggesting that the appetite for these risks is diverse across the market.[83]

Emerging Insurance Protection Gap

Further, and perhaps most interesting as an outcome of the co-author's research, it can be argued that insurers are becoming concerned about the potential for a *protection gap* emerging within the D&O market, within which underwriters actively avoid writing business for carbon major firms with the intention of limiting their own exposures. Such a protection gap may mean corporations self-insure, or encounter difficulties obtaining the cover to assist in withstanding the financial damages that may arise from shareholder-derivative climate litigation. The idea that these companies rely on D&O insurance contracts to avoid the financial impact of lawsuits becomes less realistic in this context.

Conclusions

Significant developments have occurred in the last decade regarding climate financial flows. The formation of the TCFD, the establishment of GFANZ, NZLA and the formalisation of ISSB standards are all grounded by the Paris Agreement and were willed into existence within the COP arena, especially at COP21 (Paris) and COP26 (Glasgow). Imbuing global financial disclosure practices with the spirit of both Article 2(1)(c) of the Paris Agreement and the SDGs can be better achieved by an understanding of the evolving nature of fiduciary duties in the context of climate change and by the TCFD recommendations, now enshrined in ISSB S1 and S2. Individual steps by countries to adopt ISSB regulations and to encourage alignment of disclosure laws with TCFD where possible (and despite pushback) is evidence of progress in this regard.

Regarding insurance and litigation, one co-author notes the potential of a protection gap emerging amongst D&O insurance underwriters in the UK market (that may have parallels in other jurisdictions), with material implications for firms in obtaining coverage for litigation losses. The underexplored interaction between corporate D&O coverage and climate litigation is just one aspect of the broader narrative of climate litigation risk. Future research could build on these themes by sizing insurance exposures quantitatively (as has been pursued within the Bank of England's CBES for general insurers), or by examining another of the various financial actors involved in this story in further detail (e.g., banks). Increasing collective understanding of climate-related transition risks will further equip the financial sector – and society – towards a just transition.

Notes

1 The authors wish to thank colleagues from the Glasgow Financial Alliance for Net Zero, the Net Zero Lawyers Alliance and the Climate Law and Governance Initiative for their insights and collaboration.

2 Barbara Buchner, Baysa Naran, Rajashree Padmanabhi, Sean Stout, Costanza Strinati, Dharshan Wignarajah, Gaoyi Miao, Jake Connolly and Nikita Marini, Climate Policy Initiative 'Global Landscape of Climate Finance' (2 November 2023) Figure ES4 <https://www.climatepolicyinitiative.org/publication/global-landscape-of-climate-finance-2023/> accessed 22 March 2024. Note: Climate finance flows tracked in this report represent targeted climate mitigation and adaptation-specific project-level allocation of capital.

3 ibid 6.

4 ibid; Megan Bowman, 'Turning Promises into Action: 'Legal Readiness for Climate Finance' and Implementing the Paris Agreement' (2022) 16(1) Carbon & Climate Law Review 41–55; Commonwealth Climate and Law Initiative and Climate Governance Initiative, 'Developments in Climate-related Litigation, Disclosures and Due Diligence Requirements: What Board Directors Need to Know' (17 November 2023) <https://hub.climate-governance.org/article/developments_litigation_dsclosures_due_diligence_Nov_23> accessed 22 March 2024.

5 Bowman (n 4) 41–55; Trude Myklebust, 'Climate-related Financial Risks: Considering an Emerging Framework for Assessment and Disclosure in a Regulatory Perspective', European Business Law Review (2022) 450; Justin Macinante, 'Climate Impact Measurement in Climate Finance and Carbon Markets' (2020) 14(3) Carbon & Climate Law Review 203 <https://www.jstor.org/stable/27076689>.

6 Mark Carney, 'Breaking the Tragedy of the Horizon – Climate Change and Financial Stability', Speech given at Lloyd's of London (London, 29 September 2015); Bowman (n 4) 41–55.

7 Marie-Claire Cordonier Segger, 'Crafting Trade and Investment Accords for Sustainable Development: Athena's Treaties' (Oxford 2021; online edn, Oxford Academic 19 August 2021); Marie-Claire Cordonier Segger, 'Advancing the Paris Agreement on Climate Change for Sustainable Development' (2016) 5 Cambridge Journal of International and Comparative Law 202–37; Ick Jin and Yunhee Kim, 'Analysis of the Impact of Achieving NDC on Public Climate Finance' (2017) 7(4) Journal of Sustainable Finance & Investment 309–34; Megan Bowman and Stephen Minas, 'Resilience through Interlinkage: The Green Climate Fund and Climate Finance Governance' (2019) 19(3) Climate Policy 342–53.

8 See for instance: Bank of England, 'Key Elements of the 2021 Biennial Exploratory Scenario: Financial Risks from Climate Change' <https://www.bankofengland.co.uk/stress-testing/2021/key-elements-2021-biennial-exploratory-scenario-financial-risks-climate-change>.

9 Caroline Flammer, Michael Toffel and Kala Viswanathan, 'Shareholder Activism and Firms' Voluntary Disclosure of Climate Change Risks' (2021) 42(10) Strategic Management Journal, 1850–79.

10 Nicolas Kreibich and Hanna Wang-Helmreich, Chapter 6 'Linking Carbon Tax Systems under the Paris Agreement: Potentials and Risks' in Stefan E Weishaar and others (eds) *The Green Market Transition The Green Market Transition: Carbon Taxes, Energy Subsidies and Smart Instrument Mixes Critical Issues in Environmental Taxation series* (Edward Elgar Publishing 2017) vol 19 at paragraph 6.4.2 at 87.

11 Marie-Claire Cordonier Segger, *Crafting Trade and Investment Accords for Sustainable Development: Athena's Treaties* (Oxford, 2021; online edn, Oxford Academic, 19 August 2021) <https://doi-org.eux.idm.oclc.org/10.1093/oso/9780198831341.001.0001> accessed 15 March 2024; Marie-Claire Cordonier Segger, 'Advancing the Paris Agreement on Climate Change for Sustainable Development' (2016) 5 Cambridge Journal of International and Comparative Law 202–37; Marie-Claire Cordonier Segger, Marios Tokas, and Markus W Gehring, 'Trade and Sustainability in EU-Americas Trade Relations' (2023) 50 LIEI 3, 227–38 <https://kluwerlawonline-com.eux.idm.oclc.org/journalarticle/Legal+Issues+of+Economic+Integration/50.3/LEIE2023011> accessed 19 March 2024: *see also:* Harro van Asselt, Michael A Mehling, and Kati Kulovesi, 'The Evolving Architecture of Global Climate Law' *Research Handbook on Climate Change Mitigation Law* (Edward Elgar Publishing 2022) 17–42; *see further* United Nations Environment Programme (UNEP) 'The Financial System We Need: Aligning the Financial System with Sustainable Development' (2015) <https://www.unep.org/resources/report/financial-system-we-need-aligning-financial-system-sustainable-development> accessed 18 March 2024,

World Resources Institute and World Business Council for Sustainable Development, 'The Greenhouse Gas Protocol: A Corporate Accounting and Reporting Standard' (March 2004) <https://ghgprotocol.org/corporate-standard> accessed 18 March 2024.

12 Energy and Climate Intelligence Unit, John Lang, IPCC Explainer: Climate Change Synthesis Report (March 2024) <https://eciu.net/analysis/infographics/ipcc-explainer-infographic-synthesis-report-climate-2023> accessed 20 March 2024.

13 Marie-Claire Cordonier Segger, *Crafting Trade and Investment Accords for Sustainable Development: Athena's Treaties* (OUP, 2021) 3–6.

14 European Commission, Guidelines on Non-Financial Reporting: Supplement on Reporting Climate-Related Information, OJ C 209 (20 June 2019) section 1.1; Within the EU context, support was voiced for proposed disclosures regarding natural, social and human capital alongside an expression of concern regarding the difficulty of disclosure on human and social capital: European Commission Summary of the written comments provided by stakeholders (20 February – 20 March 2019) paragraph 3.2 page 6 <https://finance.ec.europa.eu/publications/commission-guidelines-non-financial-reporting_en#:~:text=summary%20of%20the%20written%20comments%20provided%20by%20stakeholders> accessed 20 March 2024.

15 Task Force on Climate-Related Financial Disclosures, 'About' (2024) <https://www.fsb-tcfd.org/about/> accessed 19 March 2024.

16 Task Force on Climate-Related Financial Disclosures, *Final Report: Recommendations of the Task Force on Climate-related Financial Disclosures* (2017) 14.

17 ibid, page 2.

18 Task Force on Climate-Related Financial Disclosures, *2023 Status Report* (2023).

19 ibid page ii; see also footnote 8: Principles for Responsible Investment, 'Meeting the TCFD Recommendations in the 2018 PRI Reporting Framework' (18 December 2017); Climate Disclosure Standards Board (now part of the IFRS Foundation), Framework for Reporting Environmental and Social Information (January 2022); Sustainability Accounting Standards Board (now part of the IFRS Foundation), TCFD Implementation Guide (1 May 2019).

20 Nathan de Arriba-Sellier, 'The International Regulation and Coordination of Sustainable Finance' in D Dam-de Jong and F Amtenbrink (eds), *Netherlands Yearbook of International Law* (vol. 52, t.m.c. asser press 2021) 192.

21 International Sustainability Standards Board <https://www.ifrs.org/groups/international-sustainability-standards-board/> accessed 22 March 2024.

22 GFANZ <https://www.gfanzero.com/> accessed 22 March 2024.

23 IFRS Foundation, 'ISSB issues inaugural global sustainability disclosure standards' (26 June 2023) <https://www.ifrs.org/news-and-events/news/2023/06/issb-issues-ifrs-s1-ifrs-s2/> accessed 20 March 2024.

24 ibid.

25 IFRS, 'Brazil Adopts ISSB Global Baseline, as IFRS Foundation Trustees Meet in Latin America' (20 October 2023) <https://www.ifrs.org/news-and-events/news/2023/10/brazil-adopts-issb-global-baseline/> accessed 20 March 2024.

26 FSB, '2023 TCFD Status Report: Task Force on Climate-related Financial Disclosures' (12 October 2023) <https://www.fsb.org/2023/10/2023-tcfd-status-report-task-force-on-climate-related-financial-disclosures/> accessed 18 March 2024; see also Task Force on Climate-Related Financial Disclosures, *2023 Status Report* (2023).

27 ibid.

28 In September 2023 the Taskforce on Nature-Related Financial Disclosures issued recommendations for companies, see: Taskforce on Nature-related Financial Disclosures (TNFD) Recommendations (September 2023) <https://tnfd.global/publication/recommendations-of-the-taskforce-on-nature-related-financial-disclosures/> accessed 18 March 2024.

29 *See* Commonwealth Climate and Law Initiative reports at: https://commonwealthclimatelaw.org/resources/.

30 Companies (Strategic Report) (Climate-related Financial Disclosure) Regulations 2022 <https://www.legislation.gov.uk/uksi/2022/31/made> and the Limited Liability Partnerships (Climate-related Financial Disclosure) Regulations 2022 <https://www.legislation.gov.uk/uksi/2022/46/contents/made>; for further information regarding the timeline leading up to the issuance of these regulations, see the useful background provided by the Financial Conduct Authority here: https://commonwealthclimatelaw.org/resources/.

31 Mandatory climate-related financial disclosures by publicly quoted companies, large private companies and LLPs (21 February 2022) <https://www.gov.uk/government/publications/climate-related-financial-disclosures-for-companies-and-limited-liability-partnerships-llps> accessed 20 March 2024.

32 Department for International Development, 'Investing in a Better World: Results of UK Survey on Financing the SDGs' (25 September 2019) 31 <https://www.gov.uk/government/publications/investing-in-a-better-world-results-of-uk-survey-on-financing-the-sdgs> accessed 20 March 2024.

33 ibid.

34 Government of Canada Department of Finance, 'Canada launches Sustainable Finance Action Council' (12 May 2021) <https://www.canada.ca/en/department-finance/news/2021/05/canada-launches-sustainable-finance-action-council.html> accessed 20 March 2024.

35 Financial and Reporting Assurance Standards Canada, 'Media Release – Canadian Sustainability Standards Board Announces First Canadian Sustainability Disclosure Standards for Public Consultation' (13 March 2024) <https://www.frascanada.ca/en/sustainability/projects/adoption-csds1-csds2/media-release-cssb-public-consultation> accessed 20 March 2024.

36 ibid. See also Sarah Marsh, Scott Morrison and Jennifer Lawson, PwC 'Canada's Draft Sustainability Disclosure Standards' (14 March 2024) <https://www.pwc.com/ca/en/today-s-issues/environmental-social-and-governance/insights/need-to-know-about-csds.html> accessed 20 March 2024.

37 Myklebust (n 5) 450; *see also* European Commission, The European Green Deal, COM (2019) 640 final (11 December 2019).

38 European Union Regulation 2019/2088 of the European Parliament and Council on sustainability-related disclosures in the financial services sector (27 November 2019) (2019) OJ L317/1.

39 Arriba-Sellier (n 20) 52, 201.

40 Directive (EU) 2022/2464 of 14 December 2022 amending Regulation (EU) No 537/2014, Directive 2004/109/EC, Directive 2006/43/EC and Directive 2013/34/EU, as regards corporate sustainability reporting (2022) OJ L322/15.

41 On the discussion of double materiality and market-based governance approaches to meet public interest goals in sustainable finance, see Iris H Chiu, 'The EU Sustainable Finance Agenda: Developing Governance for Double Materiality in Sustainability Metrics' (2022) 23(1) European Business Organization Law Review 87–123.

42 US Securities and Exchange Commission 'SEC Announces Enforcement Task Force Focused on Climate and ESG Issues' (4 March 2021) <https://www.sec.gov/news/press-release/2021-42> accessed 18 March 2024; see also Colin Myers, 'Financing Our Future's Health: Why the United States Must Establish

Mandatory Climate-Related Financial Disclosure Requirements Aligned with the TCFD Recommendations' (2020) 37(2) Pace Environmental Law Review 415.

43 U.S. Securities and Exchange Commission, 'Press Release: SEC Proposes Rules to Enhance and Standardize Climate-Related Disclosures for Investors' 21 March 2022; U.S. SEC, 'Enforcement Task Force Focused on Climate and ESG Issues' 11 April 2023.

44 West Virginia, Georgia, Alabama, Alaska, Indiana, New Hampshire, Oklahoma, South Carolina, Wyoming, Commonwealth of Virginia.

45 Petition to the Court (6 March 2024): https://ago.wv.gov/Documents/SEC%20Climate%20Disclosure%20Petition%20for%20Review.pdf.

46 Rachel Frazin, 'Court Halts SEC Climate Disclosure Rule' (*The Hill*, 15 March 2024) accessed 19 March2024<https://thehill-com.cdn.ampproject.org/c/s/thehill.com/policy/energy-environment/4535659-court-halts-sec-climate-disclosure-rule/amp/>.

47 Petition to the Court (14 March 2024): <https://www.bloomberglaw.com/public/desktop/document/LibertyEnergyvSECDocketNo24601095thCirMar062024CourtDocket/2?doc_id=X6KO2DQUQJ58Q6O2SPBT850PDUJ> accessed 20 March 2024.

48 ibid.

49 ibid: see Liberty Energy Annual Report Form 10-K (2024) page 5–6, 8, 16–17 related to climate change and ESG disclosures: https://otp.tools.investis.com/clients/us/liberty_oilfield_services/SEC/sec-show.aspx?Type=html&FilingId=17249425&Cik=0001694028.

50 See, for example updates in Korea: Financial Services Commission 'FSC Chairman meets with banking sector to discuss measures to boost climate finance (19 March 2024) <https://www.fsc.go.kr/eng/pr010101/81909> accessed 22 March 2024 and 'Authorities meet to discuss ESG disclosure standards' (14 February 2024) noting that the Korea Sustainability Standards Board (KSSB) to formulate draft proposal for ESG disclosure standards expected to be introduced in April 2024 <https://www.fsc.go.kr/eng/pr010101/81707> accessed 22 March 2024; updates in China via UNPRI <https://www.unpri.org/sustainability-issues/climate-change/TCFD-Capacity-Building-Series-for-China>; updates in Kenya via Wambui, Reuben Muhindi. 'Climate-Related Financial Risks for Kenyan Banks: An Analysis of Loan Portfolios and GHG Emissions' Geneva: Graduate Institute Publications (2021) <https://directory.doabooks.org/handle/20.500.12854/85481> accessed 18 March 2024; Central Bank of Kenya, 'TCFD a Desirable Benchmark for Proposed Disclosure Framework: 2021 Guidance on Climate-Related Risk Management for the Banking Sector' (October 2021) <https://www.centralbank.go.ke/2021/10/15/guidance-on-climate-related-risk-management/> accessed 18 March 2024.

51 Arriba-Sellier (n 20) 52, 203.

52 Task Force on Climate-Related Financial Disclosures, *2023 Status Report* (2023).

53 Thanh Ngo and others, 'Climate Risk Disclosures and Global Sustainability Initiatives: A Conceptual Analysis and Agenda for Future Research' (2023) 32(6) Business Strategy and the Environment 3705–20; see also Paul Griffin and Amy Myers Jaffe, 'Challenges for a Climate Risk Disclosure Mandate' (2021) 7 Nature Energy 2–4.

54 Commonwealth Climate and Law Initiative and Climate Governance Initiative, 'Developments in Climate-related Litigation, Disclosures and Due Diligence Requirements: What Board Directors Need to Know' (17 November 2023) <https://hub.climate-governance.org/article/developments_litigation_dsclosures_due_diligence_Nov_23> accessed 22 March 2024; *see also* Centre for Policy Development 'Hutley Opinions' on directors' duties and climate risk <https://cpd.org.au/work/2021-hutley-opinion-greenwashing-repor/> (2021; 2019; 2016).

55 Brandon D Stewart, 'Shining Some Sunlight on Mandatory Corporate Climate-Related Disclosure/Faire La Lumiere Sur La Divulgation Corporative Obligatoire Reliee Au Climat' (2021) 17(1) McGill Journal of Sustainable Development Law 34.

56 Michael Burger and Maria Antonia Tigre, Columbia Law School, 'Global Climate Litigation Report: 2023 Status Review' (July 2023) 62–63 <https://scholarship.law.columbia.edu/sabin_climate_change/202/> accessed 20 March 2024; Robert Dixon and others, 'The Role of Environmental Initiatives in Encouraging Companies to Engage in Environmental Reporting' (2005) 23(6) European Management Journal 702–16.

57 See information on the Asian Development Bank and its financing practices in the context of the 'Disaster Risk Index 2022'; see also its policies regarding disaster and emergency assistance <https://www.adb.org/what-we-do/topics/climate-change> and <https://www.adb.org/what-we-do/topics/climate-change/disaster-risk-management>; see also Regional Workshop on Climate Finance: Role of Insurance in

Financing Climate Risk <https://www.adb.org/news/events/regional-workshop-climate-finance-role-insurance-financing-climate-risk>

58 Swiss Re Institute, 'In 5 Charts: Continued High Losses from Natural Catastrophes in 2022' (Swiss Re, 29 March 2023) <https://www.swissre.com/institute/research/sigma-research/sigma-2023-01/5-charts-losses-natural-catastrophes.html> accessed 19 March 2024.

59 ibid.

60 Noel O'Sullivan, 'Insuring the Agents: The Role of Directors' and Officers' Insurance in Corporate Governance' (1997) Journal of Risk and Insurance 545–56.

61 Companies Act, 1989, 137 1,3(b)ii available at <https://www.legislation.gov.uk/ukpga/1989/40/section/137#commentary-c18769671>

62 Martin Boyer, 'Directors' and Officers' Insurance and Shareholder Protection' (20114) Journal of Financial Perspectives 2.

63 ibid.

64 John E Core, 'On the Corporate Demand for Directors' and Officers' Insurance' (1997) Journal of Risk and Insurance 63–87.

65 Sides B & C therefore offer some level of balance sheet protection to corporations.

66 Bank of England, *The Impact of Climate Change on the UK Insurance Sector* (Prudential Regulation Authority 2015) <https://www.bankofengland.co.uk/prudential-regulation/publication/2015/the-impact-of-climate-change-on-the-uk-insurance-sector>.

67 See the results from this exercise at <https://www.bankofengland.co.uk/stress-testing/2022/results-of-the-2021-climate-biennial-exploratory-scenario>.

68 De Nederlandsche Bank, *Good Practice, Integration of Climate-Related Risk Considerations into Banks' Risk Management* (De Nederlandsche Bank 2020) <https://www.dnb.nl/media/jwtjyvfn/definitieve-versie-gp-en-qa-klimaatrisico-s-banken.pdfactice Risico Management Banken (dnb.nl)>.

69 See <https://www.ngfs.net/en>.

70 Network for Greening the Financial System, *Guide to Climate Scenario Analysis for Central Banks and Supervisors* (2020) <ngfs.net/sites/default/files/medias/documents/ngfs_guide_scenario_analysis_final.pdf>.

71 Janis P. Sarra and Cynthia Williams. Commonwealth Climate and Law Initiative (2018). See also Commonwealth Climate and Law Initiative, Primer on Climate Change: Directors' Duties and Disclosure Obligations Second Edition (July 2022) 49 <https://commonwealthclimatelaw.org/wp-content/uploads/2022/07/CCLI-CGI-Primer-2022.pdf> accessed 20 March 2024.

72 The Geneva Association, *Climate Change Litigation – Insights into the Evolving Global Landscape* (The Geneva Association 2021) <genevaassociation.org/sites/default/files/climate_litigation_04-07-2021.pdf>.

73 UN Environment Programme Finance Initiative, *Liability Risk and Adaptation Finance* (Minter Ellison, UNEP FI 2021) <https://www.unepfi.org/themes/climate-change/liability-risk-and-adaptation-finance/s Environment – Finance Initiative (unepfi.org) >.

74 *Application Paper on the Supervision of Climate-related Risks in the Insurance Sector* (IAIS, October 2020).

75 Joana Setzer and Catherine Hingham, *Global Trends in Climate Change Litigation: 2023 Snapshot Report* (London School of Economics Grantham Research Institute on Climate Change and the Environment June 2023).

76 Both the LSE GRI and Columbia University maintain online databases of climate litigation cases, upon which the study in this chapter depends for up-to-date and reliable case law data. Available at <https://climate-laws.org/> (LSE GRI), and <http://climatecasechart.com/climate-change-litigation/> (Columbia).

77 David Gayle, 'Feeling the Heat: The Role of Liability Insurance in Preventing Corporate Responsibility for Climate-Related Losses' (July 2021) <https://papers.ssrn.com/sol3/papers.cfm?abstract_id=4769447>. According to the co-author's study, some firms were unable to complete the pre-interview questionnaire or declined to do so. These eight firms consisted of four D&O underwriters, one broker, two insurance trade bodies and one law firm specialising in climate litigation and insurance-related lawsuits.

78 ibid 16.

79 The United States, Australia, United Kingdom and European Union are considered most sensitive to litigation, according to data available from the LSE Grantham Research Institute. Available at <https://www.

lse.ac.uk/granthaminstitute/wp-content/uploads/2022/06/Global-trends-in-climate-change-litigation-2022-snapshot-1.pdf>.

80 Gayle (n 78) 16; Cynthia Clark and Elise Crawford, 'Influencing Climate Change Policy: The Effect of Shareholder Pressure and Firm Environmental Performance' (2012) 51(1) Business & Society 148–75.

81 ibid.

82 ibid.

83 ibid.

27

EXAMINING LITIGATION ASPECTS OF NATIONALLY DETERMINED CONTRIBUTIONS

Amelia Burnette, Kate McKenzie and Francesco Sindico

An Overview: The Paris Agreement and the Rise of Domestic Climate Change Litigation

The Paris Agreement sets out to strengthen the global response to the threat of climate change and avert the worst of climate impacts by keeping a global temperature rise to below 2°C above pre-industrial levels, and to pursue efforts to further limit this to 1.5°C. The stakes for meeting these limits are high, as extreme heatwaves, heavy precipitation, droughts and tropical cyclones, attributed to human influence on the climate system, are intensifying, alongside reductions in polar sea ice, snow cover and permafrost.[1] While staying below 2°C may avert the worst of dangerous global impacts, multiple climate tipping points are likely to be crossed at even 1.5°C, and every fraction of a degree matters.[2] This pulls into sharp focus the critical importance of countries making material strides towards doing their 'fair share' to mitigate greenhouse gas emissions. Keeping 1.5°C in sight will mean 'phasing down coal power, halting and reversing deforestation, speeding up the switch to electric vehicles and reducing methane emissions'.[3]

The structure of the Paris Agreement puts in motion a framework designed to push parties towards achieving these global temperature limits by requiring individual countries to develop nationally determined contributions (NDCs), committing to future greenhouse gas reductions and adaptation measures. The process of developing, revising and strengthening the NDCs aims to ratchet up and aggregate ambition towards meeting the Paris Agreement goals over time,[4] and each Party's NDC is to reflect its highest possible ambition towards meeting the long-term temperature goals.[5] Despite the presence of an enhanced transparency framework,[6] a global stocktake[7] and a compliance system,[8] the Agreement does not have a specific mechanism to ensure that the NDCs in fact do reflect the highest possible ambition towards mitigating greenhouse gases. Neither is there a specific enforcement mechanism within the Paris Agreement to ensure domestic climate policies rise to the level of highest possible ambition and are appropriately implemented and enforced nationally, as envisioned by the Agreement.[9] Therefore, efforts towards assuring countries' NDC commitments result in effective, durable and enforceable climate policies are playing out in multiple spheres external to the Paris Agreement – political, legislative and judicial. In this context, litigation has emerged as a tool with potential to push countries towards meeting the Agreement's overarching goals.[10]

DOI: 10.4324/9781003276678-31

Since the adoption of the Paris Agreement in 2015, there has been a rise in litigation being deployed globally, with increasing frequency and by a range of actors, to compel more ambitious action on climate change.[11] Notably, climate change litigation itself involves a vast array of cases, spanning varied jurisdictions, legal systems, types of claims and objectives.[12] Within climate change litigation, for example, are cases where individuals and groups impacted by climate change, like youth, Indigenous Peoples, women and seniors, as well as communities and environmental NGOs, have challenged the adequacy of climate laws and policies that countries have enacted.[13] Although these cases may bear similarity in factual background and argumentation, the underlying legal theories use a wide variety of grounds, such as tort, human rights and international or administrative law, amongst others.[14]

As part of this growing trend, national courts are being tasked with evaluating the strength of domestic climate mitigation measures in a range of contexts, from scrutinizing climate policies to reviewing decisions on greenhouse-gas-emitting projects. As parties increasingly resort to the courts to adjudicate controversies over the pace and substance of measures to mitigate climate change, litigation in domestic courts has emerged as one forum with potential to compliment the ratcheting framework of the Paris Agreement. Recognizing this, the IPCC includes climate litigation as a potentially 'powerful force in climate governance' with the capacity to drive more ambitious climate action on the part of states.[15]

The analysis that follows considers a specific type of climate case arising in multiple jurisdictions, where climate litigation in national courts intersects commitments made through NDCs. The objective of focusing on these early cases is to highlight the potential direction of travel of NDC-related litigation and what it might or might not accomplish.

Domestic Litigation Meets NDCs

The mitigation measures that individual countries commit to through their NDCs are central to achieving the goals of the Paris Agreement. Every country that is party to the Paris Agreement is under a legally binding obligation to prepare and submit an NDC.[16] The Agreement does not itself impose specific greenhouse gas reductions on particular countries, regions or industries. Instead, individual countries are responsible for developing their own NDCs that reflect their highest level of ambition, taking into account their 'common but differentiated responsibilities and respective capabilities'.[17] The Paris Agreement further requires parties to 'pursue' domestic mitigation measures with the aim of achieving the objectives of their NDCs.[18]

The NDCs must be submitted to the UNFCCC secretariat, and the Agreement builds in transparency[19] by making the NDCs available in a public registry.[20] However, the Paris Agreement does not address the enforcement of the strength or ambition of measures reflected in the NDCs.[21] Furthermore, domestic climate policies implementing mitigation measures fall outside of the scope of the Agreement. To be sure, the Paris Agreement uses unequivocal language in imposing a requirement to pursue domestic mitigation measures to achieve NDC objectives,[22] but the review of the sufficiency of those domestic measures is not within the scope of the Paris Agreement compliance mechanism and is, therefore, deferred to individual countries. As a consequence, *how* countries meet their NDC commitments, for example, the specific climate legislation and policy changes that are needed to achieve the commitments reflected in their NDCs, is deferred to national governance and politics. The practical effect is that the real potential for scrutinizing domestic commitments to address climate change and meet the goals of the Paris Agreement lies at the national level and increasingly involves the courts.

As courts are tasked with adjudicating disputes concerning domestic climate policies, the NDCs are also increasingly the subject of adjudication in domestic fora, either because they are directly challenged or are relevant to adjacent domestic policies or decisions that are challenged. Here, we track the progression of NDCs alongside the emergence of domestic litigation, before turning to key trends in litigation relating to NDCs.

Climate change cases relating to NDCs demonstrate potential to shape the substance and pace of countries' responses to climate change. We group these emerging cases into three types. First, we consider the potential of cases that challenge the sufficiency of countries' NDCs or climate policies to close ambition or enforcement gaps between domestic commitments and the Paris Agreement goals. Next, we turn to cases that resort to domestic courts to challenge NDCs as a means of preventing regressive NDCs or backsliding in ambition. Lastly, we examine the potential of NDCs to shape climate impact assessment for projects or authorizations with significant consequences to countries' attainment of mitigation or adaptation commitments. We conclude by reflecting on the potential for this type of domestic climate litigation to compliment the ratcheting framework of the Paris Agreement.

Closing Ambition Gaps Between Domestic Climate Policies and the Paris Agreement

The parties' first NDCs were requested when they ratified the Paris Agreement, although many parties developed and submitted versions of their intended NDCs years earlier, in conjunction with the Conferences of the Parties leading up to the Paris Agreement.[23] The parties must submit successive NDCs every five years.[24] Each successive NDC must be stronger than the prior, representing a progression and party's 'highest possible ambition', taking into account 'common but differentiated responsibilities and respective capabilities, in the light of different national circumstances'.[25]

Several years on from the adoption of the Paris Agreement, most parties have submitted NDCs through which they have committed to specific greenhouse gas reductions and mitigation measures.[26] Although the ambition reflected in each country's NDC is not reviewed under the Paris Agreement's compliance regime, the 'collective progress' towards meeting the Paris Agreement's goals is assessed through the global stocktake that happens every five years, the first of which occured in 2023.[27] The outcomes of the stocktake are to inform the direction of revised NDCs.[28]

With the first stocktake cycle came confirmation that major gaps exist between the NDCs and achieving the Paris Agreement's temperature limits.[29] Even with full implementation of the commitments made in the NDCs, including their conditional elements, the 'mitigation ambition' was determined to be not yet consistent with modelled mitigation pathways keeping global warming to either 2°C or 1.5°C.[30] In line with UNFCCC assessments, UNEP's Emissions Gap Report found that new and updated NDCs, including their conditional elements, would lead to a temperature increase of approximately 2.4°C, and were therefore 'woefully insufficient' to meet Paris Agreement temperature limits.[31]

Based on the identifiable gaps between projected greenhouse gas emissions and the reductions needed to keep global warming well below 2°C or limiting it to 1.5°C, the reports convey an urgent need for more ambitious reductions in countries' NDC targets between now and 2030.[32] The assessment of longer-term mitigation goals in NDCs, by comparison, gave reason for measured optimism, as an increasing number of parties have embraced some version of the Paris Agreement's aim[33] to reach climate neutrality or net zero emissions between 2030 and mid-century.[34] This trend towards net-zero emissions by mid-century, while encouraging, also underscores the need for policies in the interim period to assure attainment of long-term goals,[35] with one report asserting that ambitious targets 'matter little unless they go hand in hand with ambitious policies and accelerated implementation'.[36]

Punting these reductions to the future will come at a cost. Failure to attain adequate reductions by 2030 will necessitate substantial reductions thereafter, essentially requiring deeper and faster reductions in global emissions[37] and implicating concerns about the achievability of a just transition to net zero emissions by mid-century.

Crucially, these projections are based on the optimistic assumption that the commitments within the NDCs will be fully implemented. That underlying assumption cannot be assured by the Paris Agreement alone. Therefore, in light of the urgent need for more ambitious NDCs, and the necessity for commitments within the NDCs to be actually implemented through enforceable domestic policies,[38] attention has turned to other strategies for increasing ambition, including domestic climate litigation.[39]

A look at several cases confirms both the possibilities and limitations of domestic climate litigation to promote accountability in domestic climate policies, assure their alignment with NDCs and to push for greater ambition within NDCs.

National Policies Lagging Behind Nationally Determined Contributions

With the submission of NDCs forecasting national mitigation measures and commitments, multiple cases have challenged domestic climate policies as out of step with the NDCs. Among these, two cases in European countries animate the potential use of commitments within NDCs as a basis to challenge the sufficiency domestic climate policies.[40]

Belgian courts considered the relevance of mitigation targets within the NDC of the EU and its member states in evaluating whether the government's response to climate change was in breach of its duty of care. In response to a case brought by an organization and thousands of citizens, the Brussels Court of First Instance found domestic climate policies insufficient to comply with the civil code and fundamental rights, but citing separation of powers grounds, declined injunctive relief setting specific targets.[41] On review, the Court of Appeals considered that mitigation targets reflected in the European Green Deal, which had been transmitted to the UNFCCC and adopted into European climate law, were relevant to defining the government's standard of care.[42] The court determined that a 55% reduction in greenhouse gases by 2030 compared to 1990, consistent with these commitments, was a minimum threshold, below which Belgian authorities cannot go without violating fundamental rights and the general duty of care.[43] As this minimum had been validated at European level, the court also found granting injunctive relief did not infringe separation of powers.[44]

Courts in the Czech Republic have similarly considered the applicability of commitments within the EU's NDC as a basis to evaluate domestic climate policies. The Municipal Court of Prague determined that the failure of multiple government ministries to develop sufficient mitigation measures contravened Article 4(2) of the Paris Agreement and unlawfully interfered with the applicants' right to a healthy environment under the Czech Charter of Fundamental Rights and Freedoms.[45] The court reasoned that the Czech Republic's independent obligation to comply with the Paris Agreement included a requirement to implement domestic mitigation measures.[46] Although the Czech Republic has not provided its own NDC, the court found the NDC for the EU and its member states, committing to reduce greenhouse gas emissions by 55% by 2030 compared to 1990,[47] applicable to assessing whether interference with a right has occurred.[48] On appeal, the Supreme Administrative Court disagreed, determining that the collective commitment within the EU NDC does not oblige the Czech Republic to individually reduce greenhouse gas emissions by a commensurate amount, as member state obligations are part of ongoing political and legislative processes.[49]

Although the architecture of the specific claims considered by the courts differed somewhat, these cases illustrate the ways that targets within NDCs may be used to frame the shortcomings of national policies. If an NDC can be found to have specific binding effect at the national level, the forecasted reduction targets can aid in identifying the gap in domestic climate policies, potentially defining the remedy. Even when NDCs are not viewed as legally binding within the context of a national court's review, they may nonetheless assist in supplying the factual framework or standard of care to evaluate the sufficiency of domestic policies. NDCs developed for purposes of complying with state obligations under the Paris Agreement will be difficult for governments to assail from an evidentiary standpoint. For these reasons, NDCs can be expected to play an ongoing role in evaluating the strength of domestic policies in the context of judicial review.

Inadequate Nationally Determined Contributions

In addition to improving alignment between domestic policies and the commitments made under the Paris Agreement, claimants have also sought judicial review of the NDCs themselves as a means to boost the ambition and commitments of governments. In light of the urgent need for more ambitious mitigation and adaptation measures in States' NDCs, but the absence of a clear pathway to compel such measures at the international level, domestic courts have been called upon to directly assess NDCs developed by national governments under theories that government decisions relating to NDCs are subject to judicial review.

A question playing out in the context of these types of cases is whether government decisions related to NDCs are reviewable or are solely within the discretion of the political branches of government. These cases have reached differing conclusions. For example, a New Zealand court considered challenges to two decisions made by a government minister setting New Zealand's 2050 emissions reduction target pursuant to a legislative process and setting a 2030 target in its NDC under the Paris Agreement.[50] The plaintiff sought review on common-law grounds of the 2030 target within the NDC, arguing that the target, which was set in the exercise of the Crown's prerogative powers, was 'irrational and unreasonable' as 'the global scientific consensus shows the NDC falls short of the extent and speed of reductions needed to stabilize greenhouse gas concentrations' to prevent dangerous climate impacts.[51] In considering its power to review claims related to setting the NDC target, the court emphasized that 'it may be appropriate for domestic courts to play a role in Government decision-making about climate change policy'.[52] However, the court found the NDC target was within the discretion of the Minister and that the appropriate decision-making processes had been followed.[53] With regard to the 2050 target set by legislation, the court found error with the Minister's failure to reconsider the target after the release of the IPCC AR5 report, but the court stopped short of ordering relief, as an incoming administration committed to revisiting the mid-century target.[54] Legislative amendments[55] that followed introduced the goal of carbon neutrality by 2050 and established the Climate Change Commission to advise the government.[56] Although New Zealand also updated its NDC,[57] it was again in the crosshairs of domestic litigation, this time based on alleged errors in the Commission's advice relating to the NDC that plaintiff, a non-profit group of lawyers, asserted would allow emissions to continue to increase over the next decade instead of keeping New Zealand on course to meet revised targets.[58] While agreeing that the Commission could have been more transparent in its advice, the court did not find the kind of serious error or improper decision warranting intervention had occurred.[59]

While these cases demonstrate the possibility of challenging the decisions of national governments that result in inadequate NDCs, notably, courts continue to grapple with the kind of policy decisions (or omissions) that are both within the purview of the judiciary and merit court intervention. In *Misdzi Yikh v. Canada*, for example, two houses of the Wet'suwet'en Indigenous group asserted that the Canadian government's climate change policies are inadequate to ensure that Canada meets its international commitments and does not violate constitutional and human rights. The suit alleged both that Canada's NDC is insufficient and that, even so, Canada is not on track to meet those commitments.[60] The claims were initially dismissed on justiciability grounds in a ruling that characterized climate change as 'inherently political'.[61] However, on appeal the court disagreed that claims should be considered non-justiciable just because 'climate change is complex' and the legislation 'reflects a political choice' on how to address it, finding once those choices are made, the law is not immune from judicial scrutiny.[62]

Generally, concerns about the complex policy and scientific questions involved in responding to climate change permeate judicial review of government decisions on national climate change policy, and the case outcomes vary, from finding specific interventions and relief warranted,[63] to declining to exercise review or to grant specific relief.[64] To the extent that a legal grounding for judicial review can be found in particular domestic legal systems, claims testing the sufficiency of NDCs likely will continue to arise as the public sector works to ensure the NDC commitments lead to sufficiently ambitious and concrete reductions. Furthermore, challenging NDCs – even where reviewability falls in a grey area – may be viewed as a strategy to assure that inadequate NDCs are not cemented into, or used to justify, similarly lacklustre domestic policies.

Preventing the Backward Slide of NDCs

Core to the Paris Agreement's ratcheting framework is a requirement for NDCs to strengthen, not weaken, over time. As countries amend their NDCs at five-year intervals, each successive NDC must represent a 'progression' beyond the previous NDC and reflect that Party's 'highest possible ambition'.[65] Although countries can take into account different national responsibilities, capabilities and circumstances, their NDCs must progress in ambition.[66] Domestic litigation may compliment this part of the Paris Agreement's ambition mechanism, to the extent it can provide a forum to challenge an NDC that backslides in its ambition and commitments.

Already courts have considered challenges to NDCs on the grounds that they are impermissibly regressive, rather than progressive. As countries continue to balance the requirement to show 'progress' in their international commitments on the one hand, and possible pressure to reduce or cushion the burden of these commitments domestically on the other, courts are likely to be called upon to decide whether changes in methodologies, baseline assumptions and targets in NDC updates are effectively a regression from commitments made in earlier NDCs.

Courts in Mexico and Brazil have considered successive NDCs that were challenged through legal actions against government ministries. An environmental organization challenged Mexico's revised 2020 NDC in a legal action premised on constitutional grounds, arguing Mexico's mitigation commitments were regressive.[67] Following an appeal of an initial dismissal, and entry of a separate preliminary order suspending the 2020 NDC, a court assessing the merits on appeal determined the environmental group had not offered sufficient proof, in light of the technical and scientifically complex nature of the matter, to establish a violation of the right to a healthy environment.[68]

Courts in Brazil have likewise encountered challenges related to updates to its NDC. In two cases in federal courts in Brazil, plaintiffs argue that changes underlying the accounting for emissions effectively make the updated NDC less ambitious. In the earlier case, youth activists sought an injunction of the 2020 NDC because of an accounting manoeuvre[69] which they argued effectively allows an increase in greenhouse gas emissions compared to the earlier NDC.[70] The case was deemed within the jurisdiction of the court, as the Paris Agreement has been enacted into federal law in Brazil.[71] However, the court rejected the requested injunction, noting that the NDC included a goal of climate neutrality by 2060, maintained earlier interim emissions reduction targets, and its alleged regressive effect was a matter warranting expert technical review.[72] Meanwhile, in another case in Brazil, dozens of civil society organizations filed a suit against the Environmental Ministry and Brazilian government challenging the 2020 NDC based on changes in baseline calculations and the elimination of a commitment to reduce deforestation by 2030. While that case remained under consideration,[73] Brazil again updated its NDC in 2022.[74]

As Brazil is one of the largest GHG emitters in the world,[75] and parties to the Paris Agreement remain far from reaching their emissions reduction goals, the stakes of seemingly technical questions related to baselines and methodologies are not insignificant. What may appear as incremental shifts can amount to large changes in allowable emissions. Cases that challenge backsliding NDCs have the potential to play a role as a backstop either directly, through judicial intervention, or indirectly, by increasing the visibility of what litigation highlights as impermissible shifts in emission baselines or future projection, thereby increasing the chance of accountability through other channels (political, diplomatic, public).[76]

NDCs, Authorizations of Specific Projects, and Environmental Reviews

Through their NDCs, countries have committed to targets for GHG emissions reductions, and many have projected specific mitigation strategies (e.g., power generation shifts, reforestation) and identified greenhouse gas budgets as well as trajectories for peak and decline of greenhouse gases.[77] Cases have demonstrated that these commitments, made at the international level, can have relevance to national, project-level assessment of climate impacts. While the Paris Agreement directly contemplates a relationship between NDCs and the pursuit of 'domestic measures' implementing those policies, decisions about specific projects, from new coal-burning power plants to logging authorizations, lie at the national level. As countries are faced with requests to authorize greenhouse gas-intensive projects, the NDCs can become a basis to bring enhanced accountability to environmental impact reviews.

In South Africa, the environmental review for a coal-fired power plant was invalidated following a challenge in court because it omitted a climate change impact assessment. In doing so, the High Court relied on the commitments in South Africa's NDC.[78] Although the NDC did not directly address the new power plant, a climate impact assessment was 'necessary and relevant to ensuring that the proposed coal-fired power station fits South Africa's peak, plateau and decline trajectory as outlined in its NDC' as well as 'its commitment to build cleaner and more efficient than existing power stations'.[79] Similarly invoking an NDC in the context of a state project or practice, in litigation brought on behalf of girls living near gas flares in the Ecuadorian Amazon, a court not only found that authorized flaring violated multiple rights under Ecuador's Constitution, but also that the authorization of gas flaring activities disregards international commitments made by Ecuador, including to reduce emissions from the energy sector as reflected in its NDC.[80]

The relationship between NDCs and project authorizations is not limited to greenhouse gas-emitting industries, as countries also rely on mitigation strategies like carbon sinks to achieve their long-term mitigation goals. A court in India, for example, considered its NDC's reliance on reforestation as a primary mitigation strategy in considering whether the State of

West Bengal may cut hundreds of trees in order to construct and widen roads.[81] Noting India's stated goal of increasing tree cover as a means to enhancing its carbon sink and meeting its Paris Agreement obligations, the court constituted an expert committee to develop 'scientific and policy guidelines' to govern decisions relating to the 'cutting of trees for developmental projects'.[82]

In both of these cases, the NDC did not itself compel a specific outcome, but provided a basis for a court to consider whether the state had evaluated the consequences of an activity alongside its own climate mitigation objectives reflected in its NDC. Where attainment gaps exist between domestic policies and commitments made in NDCs, parties and courts may leverage NDC commitments as a basis to require climate impact reviews in specific projects.

In addition to highlighting gaps between NDCs and actions taken by countries on the ground as a basis for requiring climate impact assessments, it is possible that cases challenging a specific project could also highlight the shortcomings within an NDC as it relates to a specific project approval. Aspects of NDCs may be viewed as shielding GHG-intensive projects, for example, because they contain inflated carbon budgets[83] or anticipate near-term reliance on fossil fuels before making a later shift to renewables.

Conclusion

Early forerunner cases in NDC-related litigation point to key themes arising in domestic fora. While it is too early to analyze the long-term import of these types of cases or anticipate all of the indirect results or follow-on effects, it is possible to glean some insights and gauge where NDC litigation trajectories might follow broader climate change litigation trends.

First, it is clear that the litigation horizon is extending beyond the emission reduction targets, such as concretizing climate neutrality. Governments are under pressure to justify climate accounting methods, choices made between sectors, and the pace and speed of emission reductions leading up to 2030 and beyond. Second, these cases can become complex and draw heavily from the findings and approaches of IPCC reports, as well as other country- and region- specific scientific reports and GHG accounting. Despite the complexity of these cases and the policy questions they overlap, judges are not categorically shying away from the NDCs. Third, however, their reviewability is likely to be an ongoing sticking point in domestic litigation. Moreover, the cases reflect some inclination of courts to consider how similar complexities have been navigated in other jurisdictions,[84] which is consistent with adjudication trends in climate litigation more broadly. Lastly, a domestic mechanism implementing the Paris Agreement can assist in closing the gap between international Paris Agreement obligations and domestic policy and could improve the footing for judicial review, but this is not dispositive.

Although the outcome and role of individual domestic cases within their respective jurisdictions is going to vary widely, initial indications are that this type of domestic climate litigation has potential to compliment the attainment of the Paris Agreement temperature goals, particularly by providing a mechanism to highlight or close the gap between domestic policies and NDCs, and by serving as a forum to enforce principles of non-regression in NDCs.

Notes

1 Valérie Masson-Delmotte and others (eds), 'Summary for Policymakers' in *Climate Change 2021: The Physical Science Basis. Contribution of Working Group I to the Sixth Assessment Report of the Intergovernmental Panel on Climate Change* (CUP in press, 2021) (IPCC 2021 Summary for Policymakers) SPM-10, SPM-19, SPM-28.

2 David I Armstrong McKay and others, 'Exceeding 1.5°C Global Warming Could Trigger Multiple Climate Tipping Points' (2022) 377 Science eabn7950.
3 United Nations Climate Change Conference 'Presidency Outcomes, The Glasgow Climate Pact' (2021) 7 <https://ukcop26.org/wp-content/uploads/2021/11/COP26-Presidency-Outcomes-The-Climate-Pact.pdf> accessed 4 November 2022.
4 United Nations Climate Change, 'Key aspects of the Paris Agreement' <https://unfccc.int/process-and-meetings/the-paris-agreement/the-paris-agreement/key-aspects-of-the-paris-agreement> last accessed 4 November 2022.
5 Paris Agreement to the United Nations Framework Convention on Climate Change (adopted 12 December 2015, entered into force 4 November 2016) UNTS I-54113 (Paris Agreement) Article 4(3).
6 ibid Article 13.
7 ibid Article 14.
8 See, e.g., ibid Article 15.
9 ibid Article 4(2).
10 See Lennart Wegener, 'Can the Paris Agreement Help Climate Change Litigation and Vice Versa?' (2020) 9 Transnational Environmental Law 17, 36.
11 This trend is widely recognized. See, e.g., Anna Berti Suman and Amelia Burnette, 'A Place for People's Knowledge in Climate Evidence: Exploring Civic Evidence in Climate Litigation' (2024) Review of European, Comparative & International Environmental Law < https://doi.org/10.1111/reel.12552>; Joana Setzer and Catherine Higham, 'Global Trends in Climate Change Litigation: 2023 snapshot' (GRI 2023) www.lse.ac.uk/granthaminstitute/wp-content/uploads/2023/06/Global_trends_in_climate_change_litigation_2023_snapshot.pdf (accessed 18 October 2023); Katerina Mitkidis and Theodora N Valkanou, 'Climate Change Litigation: Trends, Policy Implications and the Way Forward' (2020) Transnational Environmental Law 6.
12 Maryam Golnaraghi and others, 'Climate Change Litigation – Insights into the Evolving Global Landscape' (April 2021) The Geneva Association 1, 32; Joana Setzer and Lisa Benjamin, 'Climate Litigation in the Global South: Constraints and Innovations' (2020) 9 Transnational Env L 77; Jacqueline Peel and Jolene Lin, 'Transnational Climate Litigation: The Contribution of the Global South' (2019) 113 AJIL 679.
13 Cases challenging 'whole-of-government policies and decisions', which can include a state's NDC, may be referred to as 'government framework litigation' cases. See, e.g., Joana Setzer and Catherine Higham, 'Challenging Government Responses to Climate Change through Framework Litigation' (GRI 2022) 2 <https://www.lse.ac.uk/granthaminstitute/wp-content/uploads/2022/09/Challenging-government-responses-to-climate-change-through-framework-litigation-final.pdf> accessed 25 October 2023.
14 See F Sindico, MM Mbengue and K McKenzie, 'Climate Change Litigation and the Individual: An Overview' in F Sindico and MM Mbengue (eds), *Comparative Climate Change Litigation: Beyond the Usual Suspects* (Springer 2021) 9–17.
15 NK Dubash and others, 'National and Sub-national Policies and Institutions' in PR Shukla and others (eds) *IPCC, 2022: Climate Change 2022: Mitigation of Climate Change. Contribution of Working Group III to the Sixth Assessment Report of the Intergovernmental Panel on Climate Change* (CUP 2022) Ch. 13–29 to 13–20 with regard to increasing academic agreement of climate litigation's role in climate governance.
16 See Paris Agreement (n 5) Article 4(2).
17 ibid 4(3).
18 ibid 4(2).
19 ibid 4 (12).
20 See NDC Registry (UNFCCC) <https://unfccc.int/NDCREG> accessed 4 November 2022.
21 Paris Agreement (n 5) Article 15 with regard to the Paris Agreement Implementation and Compliance Committee, which reviews the NDCs and may exert influence to ensure compliance with requirements regarding communication, content and transparency, although it does not evaluate the strength or sufficiency of the NDCs.
22 'Parties *shall* pursue domestic mitigation measures, with the aim of achieving the objectives of such contributions,' Paris Agreement (n 5) Article 4(2) (emphasis added).
23 See, e.g., 'Warsaw Outcomes' (UNFCCC) <https://unfccc.int/process/conferences/the-big-picture/milestones/outcomes-of-the-warsaw-conference> accessed 13 September 2022. Furthermore, at COP 21 Parties were invited 'to communicate their first nationally determined contribution no later than when the Party submits its respective instrument of ratification, acceptance, approval or accession of the Paris Agreement;

if a Party has communicated an intended FCCC/CP/2015/10/Add.1 5 nationally determined contribution prior to joining the Agreement, that Party shall be considered to have satisfied this provision unless that Party decides otherwise.' Adoption of the Paris Agreement, Decision 1/CP.21 (12 December 2015) paragraph para 22 <https://unfccc.int/resource/docs/2015/cop21/eng/10a01.pdf#page=2>.

24 Paris Agreement (n 5) Article 4(9).

25 ibid 4(3).

26 The October 2021 update of the key findings of the NDC report synthesizes 'the 165 latest available NDCs, representing all 192 Parties to the Paris Agreement, including the 116 new or updated NDCs communicated by 143 Parties, recorded in the interim NDC registry on 12 October 2021, covering 94.1 percent of the total global emissions in 2019, which are estimated at 52.4 Gt CO2eq without LULUCF'; UNFCCC, 'Nationally determined contributions under the Paris Agreement: Revised synthesis report by the secretariat' (25 October 2021) 2021FCCC/PA/CMA/2021/8/Rev.1 (2021 Synthesis Report: NDCs) 1 <https://unfccc.int/sites/default/files/resource/cma2021_08r01_E.pdf> accessed 4 November 2022.

27 Paris Agreement (n 5) Article 14. 'Global Stocktake' (UNFCCC) <https://unfccc.int/topics/global-stocktake> accessed 4 November 2022 (Global Stocktake).

28 ibid.

29 UNFCCC, 'Technical dialogue of the first global stocktake: Synthesis report by the co-facilitators on the technical dialogue' (8 September 2023) FCCC/SB/2023/9 (2023 Synthesis Report: Technical Dialogue) para 94 <https://unfccc.int/documents/631600> accessed 30 October 2023.

30 2023 Synthesis Report: Technical Dialogue (n 29) para 94, 99. If the mitigation actions in the latest NDCs are not fully implemented and supported, those identified gaps will be larger. ibid para 100.

31 UNEP, 'Emissions Gap Report 2022: The Closing Window: Climate crisis calls for rapid transformation of societies' (2022) (2022 Emissions Gap Report) XVI; 26 <https://wedocs.unep.org/bitstream/handle/20.500.11822/40874/EGR2022.pdf?sequence=1&isAllowed=y accessed O24 October 2023> accessed 24 October 2023.

32 ibid 36; see 2021 Synthesis Report: NDCs (n 26) para 15.

33 Paris Agreement (n 5) Article 4.1.

34 2021 Synthesis Report: NDCs (n 26) para 74; 2023 Synthesis Report: Technical Dialogue (n 29) para 107.

35 See UNEP, 'The Emissions Gap Report 2021: The Heat is On' (2021) (2021 Emissions Gap Report) para 26 <https://wedocs.unep.org/bitstream/handle/20.500.11822/36990/EGR21.pdf> accessed 4 November 2022, noting an urgent need for 'net-zero targets to be backed up by near-term actions' to assure their achievability. UNEP's 2020 Emissions Gap Report likewise described the growing trend in 'committing to net-zero emissions goals by around mid-century' as 'the most significant and encouraging climate policy development of 2020', but cautioned that to 'remain feasible and credible' the commitments must be 'urgently translated into strong near-term policies and action' and reflected in NDCs. UNEP, Emissions Gap Report 2020 (UNEP, 2020) (2020 Emissions Gap Report) VII <www.unep.org/emissions-gap-report-2020> accessed 4 November 2022.

36 2022 Emissions Gap Report (n 31) 15.

37 2021 Synthesis Report: NDCs (n 26) para 15.

38 The UN's 2020 emissions gap report noted 'two steps are urgently required' to make progress towards achieving the temperature goal of the Paris Agreement by 2030: 'First, more countries need to develop long-term strategies that are consistent with the Paris Agreement, and second, new and updated NDCs need to become consistent with the net-zero emissions goals', 2020 Emissions Gap Report (n 35) VII.

39 See Violetta Ritz, 'Towards a Methodology for Specifying States' Mitigation Obligations in Line with the Equity Principle and Best Available Science' (2022) Transnational Env L 1, 2 with regard to arguments being advanced with increasing 'vehemence' that states' actions and omissions that contribute to climate change can amount to a violation of states' legal obligations; Goran Dominioni, 'Pricing carbon effectively: a pathway for higher climate change ambition' (2022) 22 Climate Policy 7, 897–905 with regard to carbon pricing mechanisms to enable higher ambition.

40 See, e.g., Climate Action Tracker's assessment of EU policies and action, finding a notable difference between the European Commissions' proposed emissions reductions and those actually implemented at the national level, Climate Action Tracker, 'EU' <https://climateactiontracker.org/countries/eu/policies-action/> accessed 2 October 2023.

41 *VZW Klimaatzaak v Kingdom of Belgium and Others,* Brussels Court of First Instance, No.167 (17 June 2021) [Unofficial English Translation] s 2.3.2.

42 *VZW Klimaatzaak v Kingdom of Belgium and Others*, Brussels Court of Appeal, Nos. 2021/AR/1589, 2022/AR/737 and 2022/AR/891 (30 November 2023) [Unofficial English Translation] para 63, 198–202, 244 (*Klimaatzaak*).
43 ibid para 284, discussing violations under Articles 2 and 8 of the European Convention of Human Rights.
44 ibid para 286. The court excepted from its injunction the Walloon Region, which was found not to be in breach of its obligations. After the ruling, the Flemish Region announced its intent to appeal.
45 See *Klimatická žaloba ČR v Czech Republic*, Prague Municipal Court, Judgment No. 14A 101/2021 (15 June 2022) [Unofficial English Translation], para 328 with regard to finding an unlawful interference with Article 35(1) of the Charter, which is part of the Czech Republic's constitutional code.
46 The court determined that the textual requirement to *pursue* mitigation measure, includes an obligation to *implement* mitigation measures aimed at achieving the objective of NDCs, when read in conjunction with the more prescriptive language of the underlying UNFCCC. According to the court's reasoning, Article 4(1)(b) of the UNFCCC requires Parties to implement mitigation measures set out in national programmes, and that obligation is further specified in the Paris Agreement's Article 4(2)(a): 'Each of these Parties shall take corresponding measures on the mitigation of climate change', ibid para 248.
47 ibid para 251.
48 ibid.
49 *Klimatická žaloba ČR v Czech Republic*, Supreme Administrative court, Judgment No. 9 As 116/2022–166 (20 February 2023) [Unofficial English Translation], para 2, 119 (*Klimatická žaloba*). In further proceedings, the Municipal Court issued a new judgement dismissing the lawsuit in October 2023, and plaintiffs filed a cassation complaint. 'News' (Klimazaloba) <https://www.klimazaloba.cz/aktuality/> accessed 25 June 2024.
50 *Thomson v Minister for Climate Change Issues* (2018) 2 NZLR 160, para 73, 99.
51 ibid para 161.
52 ibid para 133.
53 ibid para 179.
54 ibid para 178.
55 See Climate Change Response (Zero Carbon) Amendment Act 2019 (2019/61).
56 See 'New Zealand: Cases Against the State Challenging National Climate Policy', C2LI <www.c2li.org/case/cases-challenging-the-state-for-ineffective-climate-action-12/> accessed 4 November 2022.
57 See 'Nationally Determined Contribution', New Zealand Ministry of the Environment <https://environment.govt.nz/what-government-is-doing/areas-of-work/climate-change/nationally-determined-contribution/> accessed 4 November 2022, with regard to New Zealand's first Nationally Determined Contribution which was updated on 31 October 2021, setting a target of a 50 percent reduction of net emissions below 2005 level by 2030.
58 In *Lawyers for Climate Action NZ v. The Climate Change Commission,* a group New Zealand lawyers alleged that errors by the country's Climate Change Commission invalidate its advice on the NDC and its recommendations on budgets. 'LCANZI Challenge to Climate Change Commission Advice Starts Today' (LCANZI, 18 February 2022) <https://www.lawyersforclimateaction.nz/news-events/ccc-jr-hearing-starts-today> accessed 4 November 2022.
59 Following dismissal of the proceeding in *Lawyers for Climate Action NZ Incorporated ('LCANZI') v The Climate Change Commission* (2022) NZHC [3064], plaintiff appealed on grounds stated in *LCANZI v The Climate Change Commission*, Court of Appeal of New Zealand, Docket: CA714/2022, Appellant's Submissions (26 September 2023).
60 *Misdzi Yikh v. Canada,* Federal Court, Docket: T-211–20, Statement of Claim (10 February 2020), para 49, 52.
61 *Misdzi Yikh*, 2020 FC 1059, para 77.
62 *La Rose v. Canada*, 2023 FCA 241, para 32, 33. The court considered lower court rulings in two climate cases together, including *Misdzi Yikh*, reversing in part and allowing leave to amend in both cases claims alleging violations of section 7 of the Canadian Charter of Rights and Freedoms.
63 See *Commune de Grande-Synthe v France*, Conseil D'Etat, N° 427301 (1 July 2021); *Klimaatzaak* (n 42) reversing lower court's ruling that declined to grant injunctive relief.
64 See *Klimatická žaloba* (n 49).
65 Paris Agreement (n 5) Article 4(3).
66 ibid Article 4(3).
67 Plaintiffs argued Mexico's 2020 revision had raised the baseline for GHG emission reduction and eliminated a peaking commitment, effectively allowing for additional emissions. *Greenpeace Mexico v Instituto*

Nacional de Ecología y Cambio Climático and Others, Eleventh Collegiate Court in Administrative Matters of the First Circuit, R.A.(I) 81/2021 (21 September 2021).

68 *Greenpeace Mexico v Instituto Nacional de Ecología y Cambio Climático and Others*, Eleventh Collegiate Court in Administrative Matters of the First Circuit, Amparo in Revision 159/2022 (15 December 2022).

69 Press Release, 'Young Activists Sue Brazilian Government for "Carbon Trick Maneuver"' *Observatório do Clima* (14 April 2021) <www.oc.eco.br/en/jovens-processam-governo-por-pedalada-climatica/> accessed 4 November 2022.

70 *Six Youths v Minister of Environment and Others*, Federal Civil Court of São Paulo, Ação Popular nº 5008035–37.2021.4.03.6100 (*Six Youths*), Petition (13 April 2021).

71 See Federal Decree No.9.073/2017 (enacting the Paris Agreement).

72 *Six Youths*, Decision (28 May 2021). The government agencies contested the jurisdictional determination, *Six Youths*, Contestation (1 July 2021). A final decision on the merits is pending at the time of writing. See further discussion in Maria Antonia Tigre, 'The 'Fair Share' of Climate Mitigation: Can Litigation Increase National Ambition for Brazil?' (2023) 16 Journal of Human Rights Practice 25.

73 *Laboratório do Observatório do Clima v Minister of Environment and Brazil*, 7th Federal Environmental and Agrarian Court of the Judiciary Section of Amazonas, No. 1027282–96.2021.4.01.3200, Petition (26 October 2021).

74 Climate Action Tracker assessed the 2022 update as stronger than the 2020 NDC but weaker than the 2016 NDC, as it still allows higher emissions than Brazil's first submission. 'Brazil' (Climate Action Tracker, 5 September 2022) <https://climateactiontracker.org/countries/brazil/> accessed 4 November 2022.

75 The Carbon Brief Profile: Brazil (Carbon Brief, 7 March 2018) <https://www.carbonbrief.org/the-carbon-brief-profile-brazil/> accessed 2 October 2023. Brazil is also the largest greenhouse gas emitter in Latin America. Brazil: Climate Change Fact Sheet (13 November 2022) <https://www.usaid.gov/sites/default/files/2023-03/2022-USAID-Brazil-Climate-Change-Country-Profile.pdf> accessed 2 October 2023.

76 For example, litigation can 'create ratcheting effects by raising public awareness and mobilizing NGOs to challenge climate policy, and by providing impetus for government review of the adequacy of targets or measures'; Wegener (n 10) 34; Jacqueline Peel and Jolene Lin (n 12) ('[m]any advocates and practitioners see their climate litigation work as contributing to the global effort to address climate change, and their cases are often accompanied by campaigns that seek to appeal to a wider national, or international, audience' at 696).

77 See 2021 Synthesis Report: NDCs (n 26) paras 27–30, 63.

78 *Earthlife Africa Johannesburg v The Minister of Environmental Affairs and Others*, High Court of South Africa Gauteng Division, Pretoria, Case No. 65662/16, Judgment (6 March 2017), para 90.

79 *Earthlife Africa Johannesburg v The Minister of Environmental Affairs and Others*, High Court of South Africa Gauteng Division, Pretoria, Case No. 65662/16, Judgment (6 March 2017), para 90, following additional environmental review, the government re-authorized the project, and NGOs challenged in court the adequacy of the climate impact assessment. After the applicants and defendants reached an agreement, the court issued an order in November 2020 setting aside all governmental authorizations for the coal-fired power plant; see *Earthlife Africa NPC and Others v The Minister of Environmental Affairs and Others*, High Court of South Africa Gauteng Division, Pretoria, Case No. 21559/2018, Order (19 November 2020).

80 *Herrera Carrion et al. v. Ministry of the Environment et al.*, Provincial Court of Justice of Sucumbío, Judgment No. 21201202000170 (July 29, 2021).

81 *Association for Protection of Democratic Rights v The State of West Bengal and Others*, Supreme Court, Special Leave Petition no. 25047 of 2018, Order (25 March 2021) ('[u]nder the Paris Agreement, India has committed itself to Nationally Determined Contributions in 2015, wherein one of the stated objectives is to create an additional carbon sink of 2.5 to 3 billion tonnes of CO2 equivalent through additional forest and tree cover by 2030,' at 3).

82 ibid.

83 See, e.g., *Fundación Greenpeace Argentina y Ots. v Estado Nacional y Ots.* Federal Court of Mar del Plata N° 2, No. 58/2022, Petition (13 January 2021) with regard to highlighting deficiencies in Argentina's NDC regarding carbon budget projections in connection with challenging offshore fossil fuel exploration activities.

84 See *Klimaatzaak* (n 42) para 169 (referencing reasoning by the Dutch Supreme Court in *Urgenda*); *Klimatická žaloba ČR* (n 51) (referring, among others, to the Constitutional Court of Germany in *Neubauer et al.*, the United States Supreme Court, in *Massachusetts v EPA*, and Supreme Court of the Netherlands, *Urgenda*).

PART 5

Future Directions for Law and Governance on Climate Change

28

ACHIEVING INCREASED AMBITION THROUGH INTERNATIONAL TRIBUNALS

Rosa M. Fernández Egea and Pau de Vilchez Moragues[*]

The Role of Climate Litigation

There has been an exponential increase in climate-related cases at the national level, representing diverse claims, plaintiffs and defendants.[1] Cases at the domestic level are brought against States or governments, and increasing attention is paid to regional and international courts or semi-judicial bodies, deriving largely from the intersection between climate change and human rights.[2]

Climate litigation is brought as a response to regulatory failures and the inadequacy of executive and legislative responses to global warming.[3] Courts increasingly appear as suitable institutions to respond to allegedly unlawful actions or omissions regarding climate change.

Following the adoption of the Paris Agreement in 2015, States are obliged to regularly submit their commitments in terms of GHG emissions reductions (known as Nationally Determined Contributions (NDCs)).[4] Since then, the number of laws, regulations and policies regarding climate change has significantly increased,[5] offering an additional cause of action at the domestic level. Indeed, there are already cases in which national plans to reduce GHG emissions have been brought before domestic courts alleging their inconsistency with the temperature target set in Article 2 of the Paris Agreement,[6] and in some instances courts have considered targets as insufficient and therefore unlawful.

Despite judicial decisions at the domestic level since 2015,[7] there is still a considerable diversity in the outcomes of domestic climate litigation regarding the obligations of States to tackle global warming and the legal grounds underpinning such obligations.[8]

The dire situation in terms of GHG emissions and warming of the atmosphere, as well as the short amount of time available to reduce GHG emissions at a level compatible with the targets set in the Paris Agreement,[9] highlight the potential impact that a decision by an international court could have compared to the painstaking process of exhausting all possible remedies in every single national jurisdiction. Moreover, some countries have greatly contributed to GHG emissions since the Industrial Revolution, while others have contributed to a very limited extent to those emissions. Considering that these latter countries will usually suffer the gravest consequences of global warming and they often lack the resources to properly respond to the climate crisis, it is understandable that some of them are seriously considering going before an international court to obtain an appropriate remedy.[10]

DOI: 10.4324/9781003276678-33

This chapter assesses the potential of the most relevant international and regional courts and quasi-judicial bodies in terms of climate litigation.

The Role of Climate Litigation through International Tribunals with General Jurisdiction: The International Court of Justice

In the absence of an international judicial forum on environmental matters, the International Court of Justice (ICJ) could be an appropriate forum to solve this type of dispute, given that it has universal jurisdiction and, under Article 36 of the ICJ's Statute, no dispute can be excluded *rationae materiae* (because of the matter) from its jurisdiction.

Obstacles such as acceptance of its jurisdiction, the existence of a dispute between the states involved, or the limitation of states' standing can explain the scarcity of environmental cases before the ICJ so far.

In its advisory role, the Court will not face the aforementioned obstacles, fulfilling its fundamental role as the guardian of international law.[11] One of the main challenges the Court will face on environmental matters concerns how to address State responsibility for climate change.

Many aspects and norms of international law potentially relevant regarding climate change would benefit from a clarification by the ICJ. Climate litigation is based on basic general principles that have not been created by the climate change regime, but which can be read and developed on its light, such as no harm, due diligence, good faith, cooperation, prevention, precaution and inter- and intra-generational equity, among others. An advisory opinion on this matter, although not binding, would bring much-needed coherence in a fragmented corpus of law such as environmental law – as well as human rights law and public international law in general – by bringing norms, obligations and principles together and analysing their interaction in the framework of climate change.[12]

There are additional advantages for a possible advisory pronouncement of the Court, like endorsing the existing scientific consensus on the anthropogenic origin of many environmental problems, as well as their seriousness and dangerousness.[13] Moreover, the Court could help define the responsibilities of countries regarding climate change, providing solid arguments to vulnerable countries that are asking for deeper and bolder mitigation and adaption action by richer countries, as well as demanding much-needed finance to develop their own mitigation and adaptation policies, especially to address the increasing loss and damage derived from global warming.[14]

Therefore, despite the existence of procedural obstacles, some States have considered the possibility of requesting an advisory opinion to the ICJ on climate change as a relevant means to respond to current pressing environmental problems that require a response from international law.

Small Island Developing States (SIDS) have been particularly active on the matter. In 2002, following their decision not to ratify the Kyoto Protocol, Tuvalu threatened both the United States and Australia with bringing them before the ICJ for their contribution to global warming.[15] Some years later, in 2011, Palau announced that it was considering submitting to the UN General Assembly a proposal to request an advisory opinion from the ICJ on the matter.[16]

In 2016, the IUCN World Conservation Congress adopted a resolution directed at generating support at the UN General Assembly for a request of and advisory opinion to the ICJ regarding the principle of sustainable development in view of the needs of future generations.[17]

More recently, students from all over the Pacific islands at the University of the South Pacific, in Vanuatu, launched a campaign in 2019 asking island states from the region to request an advisory opinion from the ICJ.[18] Shortly after, the government of Vanuatu joined in their efforts,[19] with the support of an experienced team of lawyers,[20] and took up diplomatic efforts to bring such a proposal to the UNGA. Thus, in September 2021 it publicly announced its intention to build up a coalition of states in the UNGA to seek an advisory opinion of the ICJ, gathering the support of Caribbean states,[21] the Pacific Island states,[22] and around 1,500 civil society organisations from around the world.[23]

Finally, after several previous drafts, the UN General Assembly adopted Resolution 77/276 on 29 March 2023, requesting "an advisory opinion of the International Court of Justice on the obligations of States in respect of climate change", which was filed before the Court on 12 April of the same year.

The role of Climate Litigation through Regional Human Rights Courts and United Nations Human Rights Committees

Human rights are mentioned in the Preamble of the Paris Agreement (the first MEA to explicitly refer to human rights), which calls for a systemic interpretation of the obligations in the Agreement in the sense that when parties take action to address climate change, they should respect, promote and consider their obligations concerning human rights.[24]

This perspective has recently been strengthened by the decision of the Supreme Court of Brazil in the case of *PSB et al. v. Brazil* (on Climate Fund), in which the high court affirmed that the Paris Agreement is a human rights treaty, thus having precedence over ordinary laws in the Brazilian legal system.[25]

This link between human rights and climate change has been highlighted, analysed and described in detail by the UN Special Rapporteurs on human rights and the environment, first Professor John Knox and, since 2018, Professor David R. Boyd.[26] It has culminated with the appointment in 2022 of a new Special Rapporteur on the promotion and protection of human rights in the context of climate change, a position currently held by Elisa Morgera.[27]

There are many advantages in bringing climate litigation before regional human rights courts that should not be underestimated and that might help to overcome some of the shortcomings of international environmental litigation, such as mandatory jurisdiction, locus standi, and strong human rights conventions.[28]

The European Court of Human Rights

The absence of an explicit recognition of a right to enjoy a healthy environment in the European Convention for the Protection of Human Rights and Fundamental Freedoms (the European Convention on Human Rights, ECHR) of 1950, and its annexes, has not prevented the European Court of Human Rights (ECtHR) from ruling on a considerable number of cases with environmental content.[29]

The most notable examples regard cases where severe environmental damage may affect the right to life (Article 2) and the right to the enjoyment of a person's home or to their family and private life (Article 8).

Attacks on the right to private and family life are not only those of a material or bodily nature but can include immaterial or incorporeal interferences, such as noise, polluting emissions, odours or other disturbances. If these damages or environmental risks are of a serious nature, they may affect the well-being of people and deprive them of the enjoyment of their home, impairing their private or family life.[30]

On 9 April 2024, the Court delivered its first judgment on a climate change case (*KlimaSeniorinnen v Switzerland*), building upon the aforementioned case law on environmental issues. The

ECtHR considered that the Swiss State had violated both Articles 8 (right to private and family life) and 6 (right to a fair trial) of the Convention for failing to adopt timely and appropriate measures to tackle global warming, as well as for failing to properly examine the merits of the plaintiffs' case without convincing reasons. This judgment will have important repercussions on forthcoming cases before the Court – and the domestic courts of State parties to the Convention – since it has established jurisprudence both regarding the content of State obligations regarding climate change, as well as regarding locus standi (the individuals' claims were dismissed for failing to prove specific victim status, but an NGO was considered to have standing). On the same day, the Court also dismissed two other applications on procedural grounds.[31]

The Inter-American Court of Human Rights

Article 11 of the 1988 Additional Protocol on Economic, Social and Cultural Rights (San Salvador Protocol) to the 1969 American Convention on Human Rights (San José Convention) provides that everyone has the right to live in a healthy environment and to have basic public services and that States' parties must promote the protection, preservation and improvement of the environment. The Inter-American Court of Human Rights (IACtHR) includes within the scope of this right the fundamental right to receive appropriate information on the environmental risks of a given activity.[32]

As the Court affirmed in 2017, the right to a healthy environment "is included among the economic, social and cultural rights protected by Article 26 of the American Convention",[33] thus making it also opposable to State Parties to the San José Convention, which have not ratified the Protocol of San Salvador.

These are relevant and *à propos*, in case of a future complaint regarding state obligations in relation to climate change, and the Court itself has recalled that "environmental degradation and the adverse effects of climate change affect the effective enjoyment of human rights".[34]

Environmental protection is particularly relevant in relation to the human rights of Indigenous Peoples,[35] especially through the safeguarding of their ancestral lands, which also means the safeguarding of the natural resources contained therein. This has been confirmed both by the Inter-American Commission[36] as well as the Inter-American Court of Human Rights itself.[37]

The Court has already stated that the right to a healthy environment of a group of Indigenous People had been violated by illegal logging, livestock exploitation and barbed wire on their ancestral lands that were being carried out without their consent.[38] The Court considered that these activities affected the environment to such an extent that they altered the traditional way of alimentation and accessing water of these communities, also damaging their cultural identity.

The Inter-American Court of Human Rights has shown a special interest and openness towards environmental issues related to the protection of human rights, especially concerning the most vulnerable populations. In this sense, it is expected that it will be able to play an important role in the definition of climate obligations and their enforceability, both in its contentious and consultative jurisdiction.

On 9 January 2023, Colombia and Chile filed a joint request for an advisory opinion from the IACtHR regarding State obligations on the matter of climate change and human rights.[39]

United Nations Human Rights Treaty Bodies

Human rights tribunals are not the only international forums to bring a "claim" on climate and human rights. There are also several human rights bodies that are delivering decisions on the matter.[40]

These committees and commissions are not international tribunals *stricto sensu*,[41] and their decisions are not binding.[42] They are nevertheless quasi-judicial in nature, and their decisions are becoming increasingly relevant for identifying human rights obligations in relation to climate change. For environmental activists, these Treaty Bodies have become an additional instance at the international level to denounce the inactivity of their States in the fight against climate change and other serious environmental problems. That has been the case so far with the Committee on the Rights of the Child and the UN Human Rights Committee.

In 2019, 16 children filed a petition before the Committee on the Rights of the Child against Argentina, Brazil, France, Germany and Turkey for allegedly violating their rights under the UN Convention on the Rights of the Child for not sufficiently mitigating climate change in a manner consistent with the temperature target set in the Paris Agreement.[43] The Committee, through a strict reading of its procedural rules, did not rule on the merits of the petition, because domestic remedies had not been exhausted, but nevertheless, the decision on the admissibility of the petition includes several findings that are particularly relevant on the matter.[44] The Committee affirmed that:

> the authors have sufficiently justified, for the purposes of establishing jurisdiction, that the impairment of their Convention rights as a result of the State party's acts or omissions regarding the carbon emissions originating within its territory was reasonably foreseeable.[45]

In September 2022, the United Nations Human Rights Committee rendered a decision in *Daniel Billy et al. v. Australia*,[46] the first instance of climate litigation linked to human rights and in favor of Indigenous People in Australia.[47] The Committee affirmed its competence to verify whether the human rights referred to had been violated because of breaches of international climate agreements. It stated that Australia's failure to take adequate climate change timely and effective adaptation measures constitutes a violation of Articles 17 and 27 pf the ICCPR, by unwarranted interference with their rights to home, private and family life and to enjoy their culture, respectively. Therefore, in its decision, the Committee called on Australia to compensate the islanders for the damage suffered, to consult with indigenous communities to assess needs and to take the necessary and sustained measures to ensure their survival on the islands.

This decision also represents a significant step forward from its previous decision on the first communication regarding climate change, *Teitiota v. New Zealand*, delivered in 2019.[48] In *Teitiota*, the Committee rejected the petitioner, a Kiribati national, claim that New Zealand's refusal to grant him refugee status on climate grounds had violated his right to life, as recognised in Article 6 of the ICCPR. The petitioner affirmed that

> sea-level rise in Kiribati has led to a shortage of living space, which in turn has led to violent conflicts over land that endanger the author's life, and environmental degradation that has also led to the contamination of the freshwater supply with salt water.[49]

The Committee, however, considered that the risk of flooding and disappearance of the island where the petitioner lived was not expected to happen before at least 10 to 15 years' time, leaving enough time to domestic authorities and the international community to take adequate measures and, therefore, there was no imminent risk to his life.

The Role of Climate Litigation through International Tribunals with Special Jurisdiction *Rationae Materiae*

The International Tribunal for the Law of the Sea

The International Tribunal for the Law of the Sea (ITLOS) was established by the 1982 Convention on the Law of the Sea (UNCLOS) as one of the means to settle disputes concerning the application and interpretation of the Convention that may arise between the Parties. Its statute also allows the Tribunal to hear matters that are submitted in relation to other international agreements when the dispute is related to the material scope of UNCLOS, and those international agreements confer jurisdiction to the ITLOS.[50]

There are relevant environmental issues that have been dealt with by the Tribunal since it started operating. In its contentious competence, the ITLOS has dealt with matters relating to overfishing (the 1999 *Bluefin tuna agreement, New Zealand and Australia v. Japan*;[51] and the 2009 *Swordfish Conservation and Sustainable Exploitation of Swordfish Stocks in the Southern Eastern Pacific Ocean, Chile v. European Union*)[52], maritime contamination by radioactive materials (the 2001 *MOX plant, Ireland v. United Kingdom*)[53], or by oil extractions (the *delimitation of the maritime border between Ghana and Côte d'Ivoire in the Atlantic Ocean of 2017, Ghana v. Ivory Coast*).[54]

Tuvalu and Antigua and Barbuda signed an agreement in October 2021 for the establishment of the Commission of Small Island States on Climate Change and International Law. The Agreement establishes that the Commission "shall be authorized to request advisory opinions" from ITLOS.[55] On 12 December 2022, the International Tribunal for the Law of the Sea received a request from the Commission of Small Island States on Climate Change and International Law to render an advisory opinion on the following legal questions:

> What are the specific obligations of State Parties to the United Nations Convention on the Law of the Sea (the "UNCLOS"), including under Part XJI:
>
> (a) to prevent, reduce and control pollution of the marine environment in relation to the deleterious effects that result or are likely to result from climate change, including through ocean warming and sea level rise, and ocean acidification, which are caused by anthropogenic greenhouse gas emissions into the atmosphere?
> (b) to protect and preserve the marine environment in relation to climate change impacts, including ocean warming and sea level rise, and ocean acidification?[56]

On the 21st of May 2024, the Court delivered its unanimous advisory opinion, crucially finding that GHG emissions constitute pollution to the marine environment as per UNCLOS, and therefore States are under a stringent obligation of due diligence to, *inter alia*,"take all necessary measures to prevent, reduce and control marine pollution from anthropogenic GHG emissions and to endeavour to harmonize their policies in this connection", as well as to "take measures necessary to conserve the living marine resources threatened by climate change impacts and ocean acidification", taking into account the best available science.[57]

WTO Dispute Settlement System

International trade and the environment are closely connected. Not only does international trade have a considerable environmental impact, but measures directed at the protection of the environment may impose restrictions on imports and exports that might be considered inconsistent with WTO rules.[58] 'Environmental' disputes have developed under the General Agreement on Tariffs and Trade (GATT). Although this agreement does not refer at any time to the protection of the environment, it includes a series of exceptions to the violation of its rules when decisions and regulations are adopted for certain legitimate objectives included in the Agreement.

Trade 'jurisprudence' has undergone an evolution from 'environmental blindness' to a gradual opening to non-commercial interests, coming to recognise the right of GATT States Parties to define their environmental and health policies, even if they entail a certain restriction on trade.[59]

Thus far, no case before WTO dispute settlement bodies has had a direct link with climate change, although several have concerned renewable energies, like *US-Certain Measures Relating to the Renewable Energy Sector (DS 510)*,[60] brought by India in response to the dispute previously initiated by the United States, *India – Certain Measures Concerning Solar Cells and Solar Modules (DS456)*.[61]

For some decades now, the EU has been pursuing an active policy of restricting the use of fossil fuels due to their contribution to climate change. That is why the use of biofuels based on agri-food products has been promoted, to facilitate compliance with the EU self-imposed goals on renewable energy in different sectors, such as transport. However, the production of palm oil causes the deforestation of some tropical forests, which not only has implications in terms of habitat loss for certain species, but also destroys important natural carbon sinks which are fundamental to mitigate global warming. Consequently, the EU adopted a gradual reduction in the use of palm oil-derived biofuels, with a total ban by 2030.[62] However, Malaysia and Indonesia consider these measures disproportionate and arbitrary, arguing that they are based on criteria of dubious scientific basis and do not take into account the specific circumstances of each State or the land management policy they carry out.[63]

The outcome of these cases will have important consequences regarding the margin of discretion of States when it comes to configuring domestic policies on renewable energy and climate change mitigation (as well as biodiversity).

It might also be expected that the EU carbon border adjustment mechanism[64] will be challenged before the dispute settlement system for not complying with WTO Law.[65] The WTO Dispute settlement bodies may also have a relevant role in stopping measures that are both environmentally harmful and trade-restrictive, such as fossil fuel subsidies.[66]

International Criminal Court

Serious interference and disruption of the natural environment is increasingly being persecuted by domestic criminal systems, and there is even a proposal to add the crime of ecocide to the list of international crimes persecuted by the International Criminal Court (ICC).[67]

Although such a crime has not yet been established at the international level, some argue that actions or omissions that have a serious and deleterious impact on the environment that could have grave consequences on human beings could be included under the notion of crimes against humanity. On 12 October 2021, AllRise, an Austrian NGO, filed a complaint before the ICC prosecutor against Jair Bolsonaro, President of Brazil at the time. The NGO argued that Bolsonaro's policies facilitated the deforestation of the Amazon Rainforest, seriously endangered the Indigenous Peoples that inhabit it and indirectly threatened the rest of the planet's population through climate change, given the important role of the Amazon as a carbon sink.[68]

There is still much work to be done in this field: for example, defining the crime of ecocide and its elements, as well as finding the consensus among States to include it in international treaties. Nevertheless, it is clear that climate change can have a direct impact on other well recognised international crimes, such as genocide, war crimes, crimes against humanity or crimes of aggression.[69]

Conclusion

Climate litigation is well established at the domestic level in many jurisdictions with several cases already decided by the highest courts in some countries. However, at the international level, climate litigation is only slowly emerging, with only a handful of contentious cases and advisory opinions.

The aim of this chapter has been to delineate the prospects of a climate claim filed in some of the most relevant international and regional jurisdictions, throwing light on the possible obstacles and outcomes of this type of case through an examination of the previous case law of these courts and quasi-judicial bodies.

International tribunals that deal with disputes between States, such as the ICJ and the International Tribunal of the Law of the Seas, can have a relevant role within their advisory jurisdiction, where they can take a broader look at the interaction of different international regimes.

There are also some hurdles that need to be taken into account when considering climate litigation before an international court. First, broader consent is needed, since international litigation needs jurisdiction, which in turn requires States' consent. Second, causality is essential within a contentious case, but is less of an issue in advisory opinions. And third, enforcement of international courts' decisions remains highly unsatisfactory, often depending on the will of the affected State.

Nevertheless, international climate litigation brings more advantages than disadvantages. First, States will not only be accountable for their actions and inactions before their own citizens, but also before the international society. Even if it is only through 'naming and shaming', countries will feel the pressure of not doing enough to contain climate change, and the need to enact more ambitious legislation and policies that are better aligned with their international obligations.

International climate change litigation has also the potential to raise awareness on climate change and its effects,[70] as well as providing enhanced visibility of affected communities and vulnerable groups, such as children and future generations. Confronted with a high probability of disaster at a global scale, courts – and international courts – appear as a bastion of last resort for these vulnerable groups and communities.[71] In addition, a positive decision by an international tribunal will have an inspiring effect for other courts, both at the international and the domestic level,[72] thus ensuring a broader impact. Given the already ongoing transnational dialogue among jurisdictions dealing with climate claims,[73] it is to be expected that judges and tribunals will more easily incorporate the reasoning and grounds adopted by an international court than those endorsed by domestic courts from a different country and legal tradition.

Moreover, international courts also help to clarify international norms and principles: they can identify environmental customary rules, clarify their content and binding nature or even contribute to the creation of emerging environmental norms.

It is to be expected that the clear stance taken this year by both the ECtHR and ITLOS, unmistakably recognising the obligation of States to take all adequate measures to counter climate change in the face of the extraordinary and longstanding risks that it poses, will be taken into account by the rest of international and regional courts and para-judicial bodies dealing with global warming, particularly the ICJ, as well as national jurisdictions. A global problem needs a global assessment and response. Even if emissions occur at the national level, their effects have a global dimension. International courts integrate laws and regulations from different levels and jurisdictions; they deal with transnational legal experiences. International courts should thus play a fundamental part in the multilevel dialogue that should take place in order to give an adequate response to the global climate emergency.

Notes

* This chapter has been written within the research project: 'El papel de la ciudadanía y de los jueces en la litigación climática', Call IDP-UB 2021 B, funded by the Observatori de Dret Públic IDP Barcelona. This contribution is updated to March 2024. All links were accessed March 2024.

1 UNEP, 'The Status Of Climate Change Litigation: A Global Review' (2017) <https://wedocs.unep.org/handle/20.500.11822/20767>; UNEP, 'Global Climate Litigation Report: 2020 Status Review' <https://wedocs.unep.org/bitstream/handle/20.500.11822/34818/GCLR.pdf?sequence=1&isAllowed=y>; Joana Setzer and Catherine Higham, 'Global Trends in Climate Change Litigation: 2022 Snapshot' (LSE, 2022) <www.lse.ac.uk/granthaminstitute/publication/global-trends-in-climate-change-litigation-2022/> accessed 27 March 2024.

2 OHCHR, 'Human Rights and Climate Change: Overview' <www.ohchr.org/EN/Issues/HRAndClimateChange/Pages/HRClimateChangeIndex.aspx>.

3 Sam Varvastian, 'The Human Right to a Clean and Healthy Environment in Climate Change Litigation' (2019) Max Planck Institute for Comparative Public Law & International Law (MPIL) Research Paper No 2019–09, 3 <http://dx.doi.org/10.2139/ssrn.3369481>.

4 Paris Agreement to the United Nations Framework Convention on Climate Change (Paris Agreement, adopted 22 April 2016, entered into force 4 November 2016) TIAS No. 16–1104, arts 3–4.

5 Joana Setzer and Lisa C Vanhala, 'Climate Change Litigation: A Review of Research on Courts and Litigants in Climate Governance' (2019) 10 Wiley Interdisciplinary Reviews: Climate Change 3, 1–19.

6 As Gastón Medici-Colombo affirms, climate litigation may serve as a complement to the Paris Agreement (see Gastón Medici-Colombo, 'You cannot be serious!: Crisis climática, autorización de proyectos carbono-intensivos y su control judicial' (Doctoral Thesis, Universitat Rovira i Virgili, 2021) 156 <http://hdl.handle.net/10803/672813>).

7 See, for example, *Urgenda Foundation v. the Netherlands*, ECLI:NL:HR:2019:2006 (Supreme Court of the Netherlands, 2019).

8 Pau de Vilchez Moragues, *Climate in Court: Defining State Obligations on Global Warming Through Domestic Climate Litigation* (Edward Elgar 2022).

9 To have a very likely chance to limit the increase in global mean temperature to 1.5ºC by the end of the century, GHG emissions should be halved by 2030 (UNEP, 'Emissions Gap Report 2022: The Closing Window – Climate crisis calls for rapid transformation of societies: Executive Summary' (2022) 8 <https://wedocs.unep.org/20.500.11822/40874>).

10 Annalisa Savaresi, 'Chapter 16: Inter-State Climate Change Litigation: "Neither a Chimera nor a Panacea"' in Ivano Alogna, Christine Bakker, and Jean-Pierre Gauci (eds), *Climate Change Litigation: Global Perspectives* (Brill | Nijhoff 2021) 366–92.

11 According to Jorge Viñuales: 'the main role of the ICJ with regard to the development of international law is arguably not that of a ground-breaking body but rather that of a stock-taking institution or, to put it in somewhat more colourful terms, that of being the gate-keeper and guardian of general international law' (Jorge Viñuales, 'The Contribution of the International Court of Justice to the Development of International Environmental Law: A Contemporary Assessment' (2008) 32 Fordham Int'l L J 232, 258).

12 Rosa M. Fernández Egea, 'La Función Consultiva de la CIJ al Servicio de la Lucha Contra el Cambio Climático' in Soledad Torrecuadrada García-Lozano and Eva M. Rubio Fernández (eds), *La Contribución de la Corte Internacional de Justicia al Imperio del Derecho Internacional en Tiempos Convulsos: Aproximaciones Críticas* (Aranzadi 2023) 209-237.

13 Phillippe Sands, 'Climate Change and the Rule of Law?: Adjudicating the Future in International Law' (Lecture at the UK Supreme Court, 17 September 2015) 14–15 <www.supremecourt.uk/docs/professor-sands-lecture-on-climate-change-and-the-rule-of-law.pdf>.

14 Margaretha Wewerinke-Singh, Julian Aguon, and Julie Hunter, 'Chapter 17: Bringing Climate Change before the International Court of Justice: Prospects for Contentious Cases and Advisory Opinions' in Ivano Alogna, Christine Bakker, and Jean-Pierre Gauci (eds), *Climate Change Litigation: Global Perspectives* (Brill | Nijhoff 2021) 403.

15 Holley Ralston, Britta Horstmann, and Carina Holl, 'Climate Change: Challenges Tuvalu' (Greenwatch 2004) 16; Rebecca Elizabeth Jacobs, 'Treading Deep Waters: Substantive Law Issues in Tuvalu's Threat to Sue the United States in the International Court of Justice' (2005) 14 Pac Rim L & Pol'y J 103, 105.

16 Douglas A Kysar, 'Climate Change and the International Court of Justice: Seeking an Advisory Opinion on Transboundary Harm from the Court' (2013), Yale Law School Public Law Research Paper nº 315, 2013, 93 <https://ssrn.com/abstract=2309943>.

17 IUCN, 'WCC-2016-Res-079-EN Request for an Advisory Opinion of the International Court of Justice on the Principle of Sustainable Development in View of the Needs of Future Generations' <https://portals.iucn.org/library/node/46496>.

18 'Pacific Climate Resistance' <www.pacificclimateresistance.org>.

19 'Vanuatu ICJ Initiative' <www.vanuatuicj.com/> accessed 27 March 2024; A brief summary of the initiative can be found at <https://drive.google.com/file/d/19Rud1vucOQhsaayzh81lgf9jCP2GinWl/view>.

20 BlueOceanLaw, 'Pacific Firm to Lead Global Legal Team Supporting Vanuatu's Pursuit of Advisory Opinion on Climate Change from International Court of Justice' (23 October 2021) <www.blueoceanlaw.com/blog/pacific-firm-to-lead-global-legal-team-supporting-vanuatus-pursuit-of-advisory-opinion-on-climate-change-from-international-court-of-justice>.

21 The Conference of Heads of Government of the Caribbean Community (CARICOM) gave "their support for Vanuatu in its pursuit of an Advisory Opinion from the International Court of Justice on the rights of present and future generations to be protected from Climate Change" in March 2022 (See: Caricom, 'Communique – Thirty-Third Inter-Sessional Meeting of CARICOM Heads of Government' <https://caricom.org/communique-thirty-third-inter-sessional-meeting-of-caricom-heads-of-government/>.

22 The Pacific Island States, at the twenty-first meeting of the Pacific Islands Forum in July 2022, called on "the UN General Assembly for a resolution requesting the International Court of Justice to provide an advisory opinion on the obligations of states under international law to protect the rights of present and future generations against the adverse impacts of climate change, and looked forward to close collaboration in the development of the specific question to ensure maximum impact in terms of limiting emissions to 1.5 degrees, including obligations of all major emitters past, present and future." <https://forumsec.org/publications/report-communique-51st-pacific-islands-forum-leaders-meeting>.

23 Lagapoiva Cherelle Jackson, "Vanuatu's Push for Legal Protection from Climate Change Wins Crucial Support' *The Guardian* (London, 10 May 2022) <www.theguardian.com/world/2022/may/11/vanuatus-push-for-legal-protection-from-climate-change-wins-crucial-support>.
One organisation is the World's Youth for Climate Justice Platform <www.wy4cj.org/>.

24 Sébastien Duyck and others, 'Human Rights and the Paris Agreement's Implementation Guidelines: Opportunities to Develop a Rights-based Approach' (2018) 12 Carbon and Climate L Rev 3, 191.

25 Climate Case Chart, 'PSB et al v Brazil (on Climate Fund)' <http://climatecasechart.com/non-us-case/psb-et-al-v-federal-union/>.

26 The reports of the former and current Special Rapporteurs on human rights and the environment, John H Knox and David Boyd, respectively, are available at <www.ohchr.org/EN/Issues/Environment/SREnvironment/Pages/AnnualReports.aspx>.

27 ONCHR, 'Special Rapporteur on Climate Change' <www.ohchr.org/en/specialprocedures/sr-climate-change>.

28 See also Riccardo Luporini and Annalisa Savaresi, 'International Human Rights Bodies and Climate Litigation: Don't Look Up?' (2022) The Review of European, Comp & Int'l Envt L (RECIEL) 2022.

29 See ECtHR, 'Factsheet – Environment and the ECHR (July 2022) <www.echr.coe.int/documents/fs_environment_eng.pdf> accessed 27 March 2024; ECHR, 'Guide to the Case-law of the European Court of Human Rights: Environment' (30 April 2022) <https://echr.coe.int/Documents/Guide_Environment_ENG.pdf>.

30 Some paradigmatic examples are the cases *López Ostra v. Spain* (1994), *Guerra et al. v. Italy* (1998), *Moreno Gómez v. Spain* (2002), and *Martínez Martínez v. Spain* (2012); The ECHR jurisprudence is accessible at <https://www.echr.coe.int/hudoc-database>.

31 For a general idea and summary of the cases, see ECtHR Factsheet on Climate Change (24 April) <https://prd-echr.coe.int/documents/d/echr/fs_climate_change_eng>.

32 *Claude Reyes y otros c. Chile* (2006) <www.corteidh.or.cr/docs/casos/articulos/seriec_151_esp.pdf>.

33 Advisory Opinion OC 23–17 (n 56), para 57.

34 ibid para 47.

35 The 1997 Draft American Declaration on the Rights of Indigenous Peoples establishes that Indigenous Peoples have the right to a safe and healthy environment, a necessary condition for the enjoyment of the right to life and collective well-being (Article 13) <www.cidh.org/Indigenas/Cap.2g.htm>.

36 Interamerican Commission of Human Rights, 1985, as. *Yanomami c. Brasil* <www.cidh.oas.org/annualrep/84.85sp/Brasil7615.htm>.

37 IACtHR, 'case of the Mayagna Community (Sumo) Awas Tingni v. Nicaragua' <www.corteidh.or.cr/docs/casos/articulos/Seriec_79_esp.pdf> accessed 25 January 2024, and of 2014, 'case of the Kuna indigenous peoples of Madungandí and Emberá de Bayano and their members v Panama' <www.corteidh.or.cr/docs/casos/articulos/seriec_284_esp.pdf>.

38 IACtHR, 'Case of the Indigenous Communities Members of the Association Lhaka Honhat (Our Land) v. Argentina' <www.corteidh.or.cr/docs/casos/articulos/seriec_400_ing.pdf>.

39 The request as well as the written submissions and numerous *amicus curiae* are accessible at: <https://www.corteidh.or.cr/observaciones_oc_new.cfm?lang=en&lang_oc=en&nId_oc=2634>.

40 Monica Feria-Tinta, 'Chapter 14 Climate Change as a Human Rights Issue: Litigating Climate Change in the Inter-American System of Human Rights and the United Nations Human Rights Committee' in Ivano Alogna, Christine Bakker, and Jean-Pierre Gauci (eds), *Climate Change Litigation: Global Perspectives* (Brill | Nijhoff 2021) 310–42.

41 They are composed of independent experts, chosen by the States' parties, to monitor and control the implementation of various international human rights agreements. The acceptance of their jurisdiction is not presumed but must be expressly accepted by States parties to those conventions.

42 They merely record violations, remind States of compliance with their international commitments and make recommendations, but without binding legal effect. Despite this, there are some interesting domestic decisions on the matter: See Casla, K., 'Supreme Court of Spain: UN Treaty Body individual decisions are legally binding', *Ekil:Talk!* (1 August 2018) <www.ejiltalk.org/supreme-court-of-spain-un-treaty-body-individual-decisions-are-legally-binding>.

43 ClimateCaseChart, '*Sacchi et al v. Argentina et al*' <https://climatecasechart.com/non-us-case/sacchi-et-al-v-argentina-et-al/>.

44 Decision adopted by the Committee on the Rights of the Child under the Optional Protocol to the Convention on the Rights of the Child on a communications procedure in respect of Communication No. 104/2019, CRC/C/88/D/104/2019.

45 ibid 12.

46 Views adopted by the Committee under article 5(4) of the Optional Protocol, concerning communication No. 3624/2019, CCPR/C/135/D/3624/2019 <https://tbinternet.ohchr.org/_layouts/15/treatybodyexternal/Download.aspx?symbolno=CCPR%2fC%2f135%2fD%2f3624%2f2019&Lang=en>.

47 Maria Antonia Tigre, 'U.N. Human Rights Committee finds that Australia is Violating Human Rights Obligations towards Torres Strait Islanders for Climate Inaction" (Climate Law Blog at the Sabin Center for Climate Change Law, 27 September 2022) <https://blogs.law.columbia.edu/climatechange/2022/09/27/u-n-human-rights-committee-finds-that-australia-is-violating-human-rights-obligations-towards-torres-strait-islanders-for-climate-inaction/)>; Iraida Giménez and Eulalia Petit de Gabriel, 'Cambio Climático y Derechos Humanos: El Caso de los Isleños del Estrecho de Torres" (Aquiescencia: International Law Blog, 24 October 2022) <https://aquiescencia.net/author/eulaliawladimir/>.

48 Views adopted by the Committee under article 5(4) of the Optional Protocol, concerning communication No. 2728/2016, CPR/C/127/D/2728/2016 <https://tbinternet.ohchr.org/_layouts/15/treatybodyexternal/Download.aspx?symbolno=CCPR/C/127/D/2728/2016&Lang=en>.

49 ibid para 3.

50 *Statute of the International Tribunal for the Law of the* Sea, arts 20–22 <https://www.itlos.org/fileadmin/itlos/documents/basic_texts/statute_en.pdf>.

51 ITLOS, 'Southern Bluefin Tuna Cases (New Zealand v Japan; Australia v Japan), Provisional Measures' <www.itlos.org/index.php?id=62>.

52 ITLOS, 'Case Concerning the Conservation and Sustainable Exploitation of Swordfish Stocks in the South-Eastern Pacific Ocean (Chile/European Union)' <www.itlos.org/index.php?id=99>.

53 ITLOS, 'The MOX Plant Case (Ireland v United Kingdom), Provisional Measures' <www.itlos.org/index.php?id=102>.

54 ITLOS, 'Dispute Concerning Delimitation of the Maritime Boundary Between Ghana and Côte d'Ivoire in the Atlantic Ocean (Ghana/Côte d'Ivoire)' <www.itlos.org/en/main/cases/list-of-cases/case-no-23/>.

55 Agreement for the Establishment of the Commission of Small Island States on Climate Change and International Law, 3447 UNTS 1 (entered into force 31 October 2021) Article 2(2).

56 See ITLOS, *Request for an Advisory Opinion Submitted by the Commission of Small Island States on Climate Change and International Law* (Request for Advisory Opinion Submitted to Tribunal) <www.itlos.org/en/main/cases/list-of-cases/request-for-an-advisory-opinion-submitted-by-the-commission-of-small-island-states-on-climate-change-and-international-law-request-for-advisory-opinion-submitted-to-the-tribunal/>.

57 *Request for an Advisory Opinion Submitted by the Commission of Small Island States on Climate Change and International Law (No. 31)* (Advisory Opinion of 21 May 2024) <https://www.itlos.org/fileadmin/itlos/documents/cases/31/Advisory_Opinion/C31_Adv_Op_21.05.2024_orig.pdf>.

58 On the one hand, commercial activity contributes to environmental degradation, since the goods to be exchanged must be produced, transported, consumed and disposed of; all these actions produce different impacts on the natural environment. On the other hand, in the interest of safeguarding the environment, barriers to trade are introduced, consisting of restrictions or conditions on the import or export of certain products, sometimes in application of an international agreement.

59 The Appellate Body report in the 1998 *US-. Import Ban on Certain Shrimp and Shrimp Products* (WT/DS58/AB/R) is a particularly relevant decision in that regard. However, it is only on rare occasions that it has been possible to derogate from a national regulation under that provision as in the case *European Community-Measures affecting asbestos and asbestos-containing products* of 2001 (WT/DS135) and the case *US – Import Ban on Certain Shrimp and Shrimp Products – Malaysia's Recourse to Article 21.5 (DS58/RW)*.

60 WTO, 'DS510: United States – Certain Measures Relating to the Renewable Energy Sector' <www.wto.org/english/tratop_e/dispu_e/cases_e/ds510_e.htm>.

61 WTO, 'DS456: India – Certain Measures Relating to Solar Cells and Solar Modules' <www.wto.org/english/tratop_e/dispu_e/cases_e/ds456_e.htm>.

62 The 2018 EU Renewable Energy Directive (known as the RED II Directive) states that by 2030 the EU must reach at least 32% renewable energy use. In addition, it establishes the objective of limiting the use of biofuels, bio-liquids or unsustainable biomass fuels, with their elimination foreseen by 2030.

63 Commission Delegated Regulation (EU) 2019/807 complements the RED II Directive by establishing the criteria for determining which raw materials are unsustainable due to the high risk of sink disposal. The criteria basically consist of checking whether these are extensive crops and whether they affect a percentage of land with high carbon stocks.

64 Regulation (EU) 2023/956 of the European Parliament and of the Council of 10 May 2023 Establishing a Carbon Border Adjustment Mechanism, PE/7/2023/REV/1 <https://eur-lex.europa.eu/legal-content/EN/TXT/?uri=CELEX%3A32023R0956>.

65 On this matter and the tense relationship between WTO and climate change regimes, see Harro van Asselt, 'Chapter 19 Trade and Climate Disputes before the WTO: Blocking or Driving Climate Action?', in Ivano Alogna, Christine Bakker and Jean-Pierre Gauci (eds), *Climate Change Litigation: Global Perspectives* (Brill | Nijhoff 2021) 433–61.

66 Within the WTO, the Fossil Fuel Subsidy Reform (FFSR) has been launched in order to rationalise and phase out inefficient fossil fuel subsidies.

67 Through the Stop Ecocide Foundation, the Independent Expert Panel proposed a consensus definition of ecocide in June 2021, available at <www.stopecocide.earth/legal-definition>.

68 AllRise, 'Letter of Support for the Communication to the International Criminal Court of Crimes Committed by the Brazilian Government' (12 October 2021) <https://static.poder360.com.br/2021/10/Bolsonaro-Haia-crimes-ambientais-out-2021.pdf>; see also <https://www.theplanetvs.org/>.

69 Nema Milaninia and Jelena Aparac, 'Chapter 21 Climate Change Litigation before the International Criminal Court: Prospects in Theory and Practice' in Ivano Alogna, Christine Bakker and Jean-Pierre Gauci (eds), *Climate Change Litigation: Global Perspectives* (Brill | Nijhoff 2021) 482.

70 Medici-Colombo, 'You Cannot Be Serious!' (n 6) 149.

71 ibid 376–77.

72 ibid 148.

73 Pau de Vilchez Moragues (n 8).

29

PRIORITIZING GENDER LAW AND POLICY ASPECTS OF CLIMATE ACTION

Anusheh Fawad

Introduction: Understanding Gender and Climate Change Impacts

The impacts of climate change affect the lives of all individuals, regardless of their socioeconomic status.[1] However, those living in poverty or low-income households will face a disproportionate burden due to climate-related disasters.[2] Those living in poverty often lack the resources and infrastructure to cope with the intensified challenges caused by climate change.[3] Consequently, they are more susceptible to loss of livelihood, displacement, and reduced access to essential services, exacerbating the existing inequalities. Gender plays a pivotal role in determining how individuals experience and adapt to climate change.[4] Historical gender inequalities deeply entrenched in customs, social practices, and economic institutions perpetuate disparities between men and women.[5] These factors influence the range of work responsibilities, access to resources, and vulnerability to climate-related risks.[6]

Gender, as a socially constructed concept, is not a fixed trait but rather a fluid and contextual notion.[7] It is deeply intertwined with power structures that pervade all levels of society. The unequal distribution of resources, power, and privileges along gender lines has far-reaching consequences, extending to the realm of environmental resources and opportunities. Resurrección (2013) and Kronsell (2018) have pointed out the critical link between gender, power, and environmental access.[8] The relationship between gender and power dynamics plays a significant role in determining the distribution of resources and opportunities necessary for climate resilience. Socially constructed gender roles and stereotypes further compound these challenges, often limiting women's mobility and economic agency, thus inhibiting their ability to adapt effectively to changing environmental and economic conditions.[9]

Projections by UN Women reveal that a significant number of women and girls live in extreme poverty worldwide.[10] Gender inequalities persist in areas such as poverty rates, bodily autonomy, access to resources, and violence against women, making them more vulnerable to climate change impacts.[11] The alarming rate of environmental degradation caused by human activity exacerbates climate change effects, leading to environmental devastation and human suffering.[12] Extreme weather events, restricted human mobility, increased pandemic risks, and threats to livelihoods pose serious challenges to human dignity and basic rights, including access to clean water, food,

DOI: 10.4324/9781003276678-34

education, and self-determination.[13] Extensive research underlines that women and girls are particularly susceptible to these challenges due to inherent gender disparities, which increase their vulnerability to the adverse effects of climate change.[14]

Legal barriers and discriminatory practices hinder women's economic opportunities and their access to resources.[15] The World Bank Group's research reveals that despite efforts towards gender equality, women across 178 economies, totaling 2.4 billion women of working age, still lack legal rights equal to men's.[16] Numerous countries have legal barriers hindering women's economic opportunities, with some prohibiting them from certain jobs and lacking laws against workplace sexual harassment.[17] Additionally, a significant number of economies impose restrictions on women's property rights, freedom of movement, and agency.[18] In certain countries, husbands have the authority to prevent their wives from working, inheritance rights are unequal between widows and widowers, and women's testimonies are accorded lower evidentiary value compared to men's.[19] Furthermore, women's limited rights to own land and property hinder poverty reduction, access to markets, food security, and development.[20] Notably, women in the Global South represent around 43% of the agricultural labour force but own only about 15% of the land.[21] These disparities perpetuate gender inequalities, affecting women's economic and social empowerment worldwide.

Gender discrimination is not specific to a region or a country's economic status; gender inequalities happen to be among the most pervasive inequalities throughout the world. Gender inequalities persist in the Global North, evident in gender wage gaps, gender-based violence, and limited bodily autonomy.[22] For instance, the overturning of Roe v. Wade in the United States denies women, girls, and pregnant individuals access to safe reproductive health services, leading to economic hardships, especially for marginalized communities.[23] Women in low-income households could face financial struggles due to restricted access to safe abortions, leading to additional costs and exacerbating existing financial burdens, and disproportionately impacting women of color and those in poverty.[24] Moreover, this perpetuates gender inequality by limiting women's decision-making autonomy over their bodies and reproductive health, undermining women's agency and perpetuating social injustices.[25] Additionally, the lack of access to safe and legal abortion services may force women into unsafe procedures, endangering their health and lives, with far-reaching social and economic consequences, including increased healthcare costs and decreased workforce participation.[26] Furthermore, climate change exacerbates gender-based violence in the aftermath of natural disasters, making it more challenging for women and girls to cope with and respond to the impacts of climate change which impede their basic human rights.[27] Climate change also directly impacts human health through worsening air quality, contaminated drinking water, and increased risks of pandemics from zoonotic diseases like COVID-19.[28] Loss of habitat due to deforestation, a significant cause of climate change, forces animals to migrate and potentially contact other animals or people, increasing the risk of spillover infections.[29] The novel coronavirus, a zoonotic disease, resulted in millions of deaths and revealed a hidden rise in domestic violence globally, underscoring the interconnectedness of these issues.[30] According to UN Women, France saw a 30% increase in domestic violence after its lockdown in March; domestic violence reports in Argentina increased by 25% and in Hubei, China, the epicenter of the COVID-19 outbreak, police reported that domestic violence tripled in February 2020 compared to the previous year.[31]

As we continue to grapple with the impacts of climate change, it is important to consider and incorporate the perspectives and experiences of those most vulnerable. Most literature recognizes that to limit or reduce gender inequalities, policies addressing climate change should be representative of the diverse needs and concerns of all people.[32] The basic tenet of gender equality is that all people are equal beings in that they are deserving of equal rights, including equal access to decision-making and equal representation in policies. Despite this acknowledgment, women's involvement in political and economic spaces, especially at executive levels of decision-making in climate-related institutions, remains imbalanced.[33] Climate calamities and this existing power imbalance have led scholars and gender advocates to call upon governing bodies to create policies and programs that respond to the needs and interests of men and women. Feminist movements have played a vital role in advocating for "women's inclusion as crucial to achieving justice, promoting women's interests and making use of women's resources for the good of society."[34] As a result of feminist advocacy over the past few decades, there has been a noticeable rise in incorporating gender considerations into environmental policy.[35]

A Brief Timeline: Gender and Environmental Governance in the International Arena

The intersection of gender and environmental issues in the international arena has evolved significantly over the years. While discussions concerning women's roles in the environment and development emerged as early as the 1970s, it was not until 1984 that concrete action was taken by the United Nations Environment Programme (UNEP), with the establishment of the Senior Women's Advisory Group on Sustainable Development.[36] The advisory group initiated research into the linkages between women's exclusion, their roles, and the impacts of development on both women and environmental degradation. One significant outcome of the advisory group's efforts was the Nairobi Forward-looking Strategies for the Advancement of Women, adopted in 1985 at the World Conference to Review and Appraise the Achievements of the UN Decade for Women. This landmark report officially integrated environmental concerns into the discourse on women, highlighting the interconnectedness of environment, gender, and development. The Nairobi Forward-looking Strategies for the Advancement of Women report emphasized that women, particularly those living in poverty, often face livelihood disruptions due to natural and man-made disasters, forcing them into marginal environments and depriving them of their means of sustenance.[37] To address these challenges, the Nairobi Forward-looking Strategies for the Advancement of Women emphasized the importance of assessing the environmental impacts of policies, programs, and projects on women's health, activities, and sources of employment and income to mitigate negative effects and promote gender-responsive approaches.[38]

Another critical milestone occurred during the UN Fourth World Conference on Women in Beijing in 1995, with the adoption of the Beijing Platform for Action (BPfA). The BPfA recognized the environment as one of the 12 critical areas for women and underscored the vital role of women in fostering sustainable consumption and production patterns and natural resource management.[39] Yet it also acknowledged the persistent absence of women in decision-making related to environmental and natural resource management, leaving their valuable expertise and advocacy skills marginalized.[40] The BPfA marked a monumental victory for women's empowerment, emphasizing the principle of shared power and responsibility to enable women's active involvement in all spheres of life (UN, 2010). It identified gender equality as a fundamental prerequisite for sustainable development and called for gender mainstreaming, which entails considering gender-specific and diverse interests in policy design, implementation, and evaluation.[41]

The 2030 Sustainable Development Agenda, introduced in 2015, has emerged as a significant global framework, placing considerable emphasis on gender equality (SDG 5) and climate change (SDG 13) as fundamental objectives.[42] This Agenda recognized the intricate interplay between gender inequalities and climate change, underscoring the need to address these issues to advance sustainable development. Notably, the United Nations Development Program's report, "Gender and Climate Change," played a pivotal role as a critical link between gender and climate issues, shedding light on how both elements acted as obstacles to sustainable development.[43] By advocating for gender-responsive approaches, the report highlighted the potential to empower women while fostering zero-carbon and climate-resilient futures. The inclusion of gender perspectives within climate governance proved crucial as it helped shape policies and measures that consider the specific challenges women face in relation to climate change.[44] The prioritization of gender equality in combating climate change is of utmost importance in creating more inclusive and effective solutions that benefit all, and the 2030 Sustainable Development Agenda stands as a cornerstone in the journey toward a more equitable and sustainable future.[45]

As a result of these significant milestones, gender equality and women's empowerment are seen as key components of environmental sustainability and governance. These developments have laid the foundation for the creation of monumental global frameworks explicitly addressing the intersection of gender and environmental issues.[46] They have become instrumental in guiding international efforts to ensure gender-responsive approaches and policies in climate action and environmental management.[47]

Gender and Climate Change Governance

Gender integration into the international climate arena has undergone a gradual and evolving process. Extensive research and empirical evidence have unveiled the differential impacts of climate change on women and men, elucidating how existing gender inequalities exacerbate the vulnerability of women to climate-induced disasters.[48] Over the years, key legal instruments have emerged, addressing the inclusion of gender perspectives in climate governance and actions.

The United Nation Framework Convention on Climate Change (UNFCCC) has incorporated over 50 decisions that address gender equality, contributing to shaping implementation mechanisms under the Convention.[49] Efforts by women's rights organizations and allies played a crucial role in gaining momentum for gender equality and women's rights in the climate regime.[50] During the Conference of Parties (COP) meetings, held annually to discuss climate change and coordinate international climate actions, gender equality and women's empowerment increasingly became integral components of the agenda. Women's rights organizations and advocates actively engaged with delegates and policymakers, advocating for the integration of gender considerations in climate policies and actions.[51] As COP meetings progressed, the commitment to gender equality within the UNFCCC framework strengthened. The UNFCCC Secretariat organized technical workshops for parties to support the implementation of decisions aimed at promoting gender balance and increasing women's participation in climate negotiations and representation in related bodies.[52] These workshops facilitated the transformation of perspectives on topics such as mitigation and technology development, shifting from gender-neutral to gender-responsive approaches.[53] The recognition of gender issues within the climate discourse led to the creation of climate instruments that further solidified the commitment to gender-responsive climate action.

Lima Work Programme on Gender

The Lima Work Programme on Gender (LWPG), established in 2014, plays a crucial role in advancing gender equality in the context of climate change within the framework of the United Nations Framework Convention on Climate Change (UNFCCC). It was developed to support the implementation of key UNFCCC decisions, specifically Decisions 36/CP.7, 1/CP.16, and 23/CP.18, which aimed at promoting gender balance and enhancing the participation of women in

UNFCCC negotiations and representation.[54] The LWPG, under the mandate of the UNFCCC Secretariat, was tasked with organizing technical workshops for parties to facilitate the implementation of the aforementioned decisions. These workshops were instrumental in assisting parties in identifying tools and best practices to design gender-responsive climate change policies.[55] By providing guidance and capacity-building opportunities, the LWPG has fostered a shift in perspectives, helping transform discussions on topics such as mitigation and technology development from being gender-neutral to gender-responsive.[56]

Through the workshops conducted under the LWGP, parties were able to recognize and address the differentiated impacts of climate change on women and men. This transformation towards gender-responsive approaches in climate policymaking and action was crucial in promoting gender equality and women's empowerment in the climate change discourse. As a result of the LWGP's efforts and the increased focus on gender considerations, gender equality commitments gained momentum during the Conference of Parties at its twenty-first session (COP 21) in Paris.[57] This momentum led to significant progress in integrating gender perspectives into climate change negotiations and decisions, ultimately enhancing the inclusivity and effectiveness of climate policies and actions.[58]

Paris Agreement

The Paris Agreement, adopted in 2015, marked a significant milestone in recognizing the importance of gender equality and women's empowerment in the context of climate change. This landmark international climate agreement became the first to explicitly mention gender equality in its preamble, acknowledging the pivotal role that gender considerations play in achieving fair and sustainable outcomes.[59] Central to the Paris Agreement are the Nationally Determined Contributions (NDCs), which serve as individual countries' commitments to combat climate change. NDCs are critical components of the agreement, as they outline each country's specific climate actions and measures. Recognizing the transformative potential of NDCs, the Paris Agreement encouraged parties to incorporate gender considerations into their NDC planning processes.[60] The mandate for gender-responsive adaptation actions and capacity-building activities within the Paris Agreement also played a vital role in highlighting the importance of including gender considerations. This provision emphasizes the need to ensure that women have the means and opportunities to influence climate change decisions and participate fully in climate-related processes.[61]

In addition to the explicit recognition of gender equality in the agreement's preamble, the UNFCCC and the Parties also committed to two important goals under the dedicated gender and climate change agenda. Firstly, there is a focus on improving gender balance and increasing the participation of women in all UNFCCC processes, including participation in delegations and bodies established under the Convention.[62] Secondly, there is an emphasis on increasing awareness and support for the development and effective implementation of gender-responsive climate policies at regional, national, and local levels.[63]

The Paris Agreement's integration of gender considerations and its commitment to gender-responsive actions represented a significant step forward in recognizing the role of gender equality in climate change mitigation and adaptation efforts. It reinforced the importance of empowering women in shaping climate-related decisions and actions at all levels. As countries continue to implement and update their NDCs, the Paris Agreement's focus on gender equality and gender-responsive approaches serves as a critical framework for advancing climate actions that are equitable, sustainable, and resilient for all.

The Paris Rulebook

In December 2018, global leaders and climate advocates convened at the 24th Conference of the Parties (COP) in Katowice, Poland, where they finalized the Paris Rulebook. This comprehensive set of guidelines was established by the Conference of the Parties serving as the meeting of the Parties to the Paris Agreement (CMA) to facilitate the implementation of various aspects of the Paris Agreement by 2020. The Paris Rulebook demonstrated a significant commitment to gender considerations within climate change governance. Notably, it showcased increased gender coverage in matters related to Nationally Determined Contributions (NDCs), adaptation communications, technology and transparency frameworks, and finance.[64] By requesting information on and consideration of gender responsiveness in the planning process of parties' NDCs, the Rulebook represented a major achievement, as efforts to address gender-responsive mitigation had been ongoing since the Copenhagen COP 15.[65]

The Paris Rulebook also recognized the importance of addressing gender responsiveness in adaptation actions. The section 'Elements for reporting adaptation communications' specifically requested information on gender-responsive adaptation actions and traditional knowledge, knowledge of Indigenous Peoples, and local knowledge systems related to adaptation.[66] Additionally, the technology framework decision placed significant emphasis on gender by urging parties to design and implement the Technology Mechanism in a manner that considers gender,[67] fosters gender-responsiveness through innovation,[68] facilitates enabling environments for promoting endogenous and gender-responsive technologies for mitigation and adaptation,[69] and provides support under the framework through gender-responsive collaboration and stakeholder engagement.[70] It actively encouraged gender-responsive approaches to guide the implementation of the Paris Agreement. It rectified the gender blindness that was prevalent in the Paris Agreement, as evidenced by the inclusion of more gendered language across various sectors, including mitigation and technology.

The Paris Rulebook holds immense importance for gender and climate change in the international arena. Acknowledging and incorporating gender considerations across key areas of climate governance reinforced the commitment to gender equality and women's empowerment in the fight against climate change. The Rulebook provides parties with a roadmap to integrate gender perspectives for the implementation of the Paris Agreement, enabling more inclusive and effective climate policies and actions. As parties continue to implement the Paris Agreement, the gender-responsive provisions in the Rulebook serve as a foundation for advancing gender equality and resilience in the face of climate challenges.

Integrating Gender-Responsive Perspectives in Climate Policies

There are various definitions for the term "gender-responsive," but the core concept remains the same – to address and bridge gender gaps in policies and programs. The report 'Pocket Guide to Gender Equality Under the UNFCCC' refers to "gender-responsive" as:

> Policies and approaches that entail identifying needed interventions to address gender gaps in sector and government policies, plans and budgets; considering gender norms, roles and relations for women and men and how they affect access to and control over resources; and considering women's and men's specific needs, although these nuances are not always clear cut. Changes are planned or made that respond to the inequities in the lives of men or women within a given social setting and aim to remedy these inequities.[71]

Based on this definition, gender-responsive measures aim to address the specific needs of women and men within a given social context and seek to rectify existing inequities. By incorporating gender-responsive perspectives into climate policies and programs, societies can work towards fostering inclusivity and fairness, promoting gender equality, and enabling meaningful participation and influence for all individuals in the pursuit of sustainable development.[72]

Mainstreaming Gender in Climate Adaptation

Mainstreaming gender in climate adaptation has been a critical endeavor to ensure that climate policies and actions address the distinct vulnerabilities and needs of both women and men. The concept of mainstreaming gender involves integrating gender considerations into all stages of climate adaptation planning, implementation, and evaluation.[73] This approach aims to go beyond simply targeting women as a specific group and instead recognizes the importance of understanding and addressing gender norms, roles, and relations that shape individuals' experiences and capacities in the face of climate change.

Case Study: 'Improving Resilience of Vulnerable Coastal Communities to Climate Change in Viet Nam (2017–2022)'

The 'Improving Resilience of Vulnerable Coastal Communities to Climate Change in Viet Nam (2017–2022)' project was a climate adaptation initiative jointly implemented by the United Nations Development Programme (UNDP) and the Green Climate Fund (GCF) in partnership with the Government of Vietnam. The project aimed to enhance the resilience of coastal communities in Vietnam to the impacts of climate change, specifically focusing on rising sea levels, extreme weather events, and other climate-related challenges.[74] To ensure a gender-responsive approach in its implementation, the project incorporated a Gender Action Plan (GAP) proposed by the GCF. The GAP included various objectives and actions to promote gender equality and the active participation of women throughout the project, including:

- ensuring women's role in reviewing beneficiary selection and monitoring;
- gender-balanced employment;
- ensuring users' outreach, information campaign, and development of communication and dissemination strategy included women;
- Women's active participation in planning and decision-making regarding the relocation of livelihoods and activities outside of protected mangrove areas as required;
- Increasing gender sensitivity among Government staff and community members involved in project implementation, and
- Increasing consistent application of gender-disaggregated data and gender-smart indicators.[75]

In 2021, the Gender Action Plan was effectively executed in all 10 Project Management Units (PMUs)/Provincial Project Management Units (PPMUs), leading to significant outcomes.[76] Notably, 68.57% of houses were handed over to woman-headed households, and women accounted for 45.6% of participants in mangrove planting and regeneration activities.

Additionally, 37.4% of women actively participated in livelihood training and implementation. The project also witnessed the involvement of women in community-based disaster risk management and adaptation training, with 44% of commune staff and 13% of the Community-Based

Disaster Risk Management group discussion leaders being women. The collaboration with the Viet Nam Women's Union at national and provincial levels played a vital role in effectively monitoring and ensuring gender inclusion throughout the project's execution. The project succeeded in integrating gender considerations and benefits, resulting in women actively participating in community risk reduction practices. Women represented 50.7% of participants in planning sessions, underscoring their significant involvement and contributions in shaping climate resilience strategies at the community level. Moreover, the project demonstrated a commitment to environmental and social safeguards, implementing safeguard systems at national, provincial, and local levels in compliance with applicable laws and regulations in Vietnam.

In 2022, the plan for the project was to continue implementing the updated Gender Action Plan, focusing on specific gender targets.[77] These included ensuring that at least 50% of beneficiaries from the housing program were women, promoting the engagement of around 30% of women in the mangrove program, and providing approximately 40% of women farmers with access to climate information. The project persisted in its efforts to conduct training and monitoring activities to effectively undertake gender actions and integrate gender-differentiated considerations into the Livelihoods Plan. The project's gender-responsive approach played a significant role in empowering women, enhancing their involvement in decision-making processes, and addressing gender-specific vulnerabilities in the face of climate change impacts.

Prioritizing gender in climate planning, as demonstrated by the 'Improving Resilience of Vulnerable Coastal Communities to Climate Change in Viet Nam (2017–2022)' project, holds immense significance in addressing climate change challenges effectively and promoting sustainable development. By recognizing and addressing the specific needs, roles, and vulnerabilities of women and men, gender-responsive climate planning ensures more inclusive and equitable outcomes.[78] Women, especially in vulnerable communities, often play crucial roles in climate adaptation, disaster risk reduction, and natural resource management. Integrating gender considerations helps empower women by providing them with opportunities for meaningful participation in decision-making processes and leadership roles.[79]

Moreover, gender-inclusive approaches enhance the effectiveness and efficiency of climate interventions by leveraging diverse perspectives and knowledge. Through the active involvement of women and men, climate projects can create more resilient and adaptive solutions that better serve the needs of communities, foster social cohesion, and promote long-term sustainability.[80]

Gender and Climate Mitigation Efforts

Research and exploration of women's capacity to contribute to climate change mitigation strategies have been relatively limited compared to studies on gender and climate adaptation. According to the Clean Development Mechanism (CDM) 2012 assessment, out of a total of 3,864 CDM projects, only five of the projects included gender-related elements in their design and implementation.[81] Climate change mitigation efforts are often centered around technological solutions aimed at reducing greenhouse gas (GHG) emissions. However, the participation of women in the science and technology field remains inadequate, leading to their exclusion from these processes.[82] Nevertheless, women can play crucial roles as key actors and stakeholders in climate change initiatives, especially when actively involved in planning and decision-making processes.[83] In response to critiques of a gender-neutral or absent approach, there has been a upsurge in recognizing gender equality within climate change initiatives. This growing awareness highlights the importance of adopting gender-responsive approaches in climate policies and projects to promote inclusivity, effectiveness, and sustainability in addressing climate challenges.[84]

Case Study: 'Promoting Risk Mitigation Instruments and Finance for Renewable Energy and Energy Efficiency Investments' – Argentina

The 'Promoting Risk Mitigation Instruments and Finance for Renewable Energy and Energy Efficiency Investment' is an initiative implemented by the Inter-American Development Bank (IDB) in Argentina in partnership with the Green Climate Fund. The primary objective of this project is to mobilize investments in renewable energy and energy efficiency, thereby supporting Argentina's transition toward a sustainable, low-carbon energy system.[85] By reducing greenhouse gas emissions and promoting cleaner and more efficient energy practices, the project aligns with Argentina's climate and environmental goals, contributing to enhanced energy security and environmental sustainability.[86]

The project's commitment to integrating gender considerations is reflected in its implementation of a comprehensive gender assessment and the formulation of a Gender Action Plan (GAP). The gender assessment has facilitated a deeper understanding of how men and women utilize energy in Small and Medium-sized Enterprises (SMEs), leading to targeted interventions aimed at promoting gender equity and empowering women within the energy sector.[87] As women's active participation in decision-making processes and technical roles is recognized, their valuable perspectives can contribute to more inclusive and effective climate mitigation strategies. Furthermore, the project's gender-sensitive capacity-building and training initiatives hold the potential to increase women's participation in the energy sector and enhance their access to financing and credit facilities. This empowerment of women entrepreneurs enables them to play a more significant role in renewable energy and energy efficiency investments, thereby fostering sustainable development and bolstering climate mitigation efforts.

The GAP outlines a set of important activities and sets targets to promote gender equality within the energy sector, including:

- Conducting a gender baseline study on financing women-led SMEs and participation of women in relevant engineering and construction activities of eligible projects in Argentina;
- 100% of all companies considered for GCF financing will receive information about proposed gender activities (internship, capacity building, working environment);
- 30% of SMEs and TSPs receiving GCF financial support contractually agree and plan for the implementation of at least one gender activity;
- 40% of SMEs and TSPs initiate implementation of agreed gender activities;
- At least 20% of women participate in capacity-building activities in the program; and
- Creation of one knowledge platform module to share experiences with financing women-led projects, SMEs, and technology providers to encourage female participation in the sector.[88]

As the project progresses, it will continue to engage with SMEs and technology providers, fostering gender-sensitive practices, and encouraging women's active involvement. By integrating gender-responsive approaches, the project aims to ensure that both men and women have equal access to resources, opportunities, and decision-making processes. This alignment with relevant gender equality policies underscores the project's dedication to mainstreaming gender considerations in climate mitigation initiatives.[89] The project's outlook holds promise for promoting a more inclusive and sustainable energy sector in Argentina. By empowering women and enhancing their participation in the energy industry, the project aims to address gender disparities and promote gender equality in climate change mitigation. The project's prioritization of integrating gender and climate mitigation represents a crucial step toward building a more resilient, equitable, and sustainable future for Argentina.

Integrating gender considerations into climate mitigation efforts holds paramount significance for both gender equality and international climate law. Recognizing that gender equality is a core development objective, incorporating gender perspectives in climate strategies ensures that climate actions address the diverse needs and experiences of men and women.[90] By promoting women's active participation in decision-making processes, technical roles, and entrepreneurial opportunities within the energy and climate sectors, gender integration fosters women's empowerment and contributes to sustainable development.[91] Furthermore, aligning climate initiatives with international climate law frameworks, such as the Paris Agreement, underscores the global commitment to mainstreaming gender in climate actions. Prioritizing gender equality in climate mitigation strategies not only ensures inclusivity and social justice but also enhances the effectiveness and resilience of climate responses.

Conclusion: Areas for Further Advancements

Despite the progress to integrate gender considerations into climate policies, several significant challenges persist in effectively addressing gender disparities in climate action.[92] One of the key obstacles is the limited representation of women in decision-making processes related to climate policies and projects.[93] Women's voices and perspectives often remain underrepresented, leading to a lack of gender-responsive approaches in climate initiatives. Another challenge is the inadequate financing and investment in gender-responsive climate projects. Insufficient funding for gender-responsive initiatives limits the scope and impact of such projects, impeding progress toward gender equality in climate action.[94]

Furthermore, there is a need for greater awareness and capacity-building among policymakers, stakeholders, and communities regarding the importance of gender-responsive approaches in climate action. Many decision-makers may not fully understand the significance of considering gender dimensions in climate policies and may lack the knowledge and tools to implement gender-inclusive measures effectively.[95] Additionally, data collection and research on gender-specific climate impacts remain insufficient in many regions. Robust gender-disaggregated data is essential for informed decision-making and evidence-based policy development.[96] Without comprehensive data, it becomes challenging to develop targeted interventions and policies that address the unique challenges faced by women and men in the context of climate change.[97] Addressing these global challenges requires a collective effort from governments, international organizations, civil society, and the private sector. It is essential to prioritize gender-responsive approaches in climate action, allocate adequate funding for gender-specific projects, promote women's meaningful participation in decision-making, and strengthen capacity-building initiatives.[98]

In conclusion, continued efforts are necessary to prioritize gender in climate action and ensure its prominent integration into climate policy rather than being marginalized as a peripheral aspect. Addressing these challenges demands a deliberate and steadfast commitment to incorporate gender-responsive approaches throughout climate policies and initiatives. By recognizing the central importance of gender equality in all facets of climate planning and implementation, substantial progress can be achieved toward fostering a more sustainable and equitable future for all.

Notes

1 Intergovernmental Panel on Climate Change Press Release, 'Climate Change: A Threat to Human Wellbeing and the Health of the Planet. Taking Action Now Can Secure our Future' (28 February 2022).

2 Stephane Hallegatte, Marianne Fay and Edward B Barbier, 'Poverty and Climate Change: Introduction' (2018) 23(3) Environment and Development Economics 217.

3 ibid.
4 UN Development Programme (Global Gender and Climate Alliance), 'Gender and Climate Change: Overview of Linkages Between Gender and Climate Change' (2013); Seema Arora-Jonsson, 'Virtue and Vulnerability: Discourses on Women, Gender and Climate Change' (2011) 21(2) Global Environmental Change 744; Seema Arora-Jonsson, 'Forty Years of Gender Research and Environmental Policy: Where do We Stand?' (2014) 47 Women's Studies Intl Forum 295.
5 Justina Demetriades and Emily Esplen, 'The Gender Dimensions of Poverty and Climate Change Adaptation' (2009) 39(4) IDS Bulletin 24.
6 Arora-Jonsson, 'Forty Years' (n 4).
7 Susan A Farrell and Judith Lorber, *The Social Construction of Gender* (Mayfield Publishing Company 1991).
8 Bernadette P Resurrección, 'Persistent Women and Environment Linkages in Climate Change and Sustainable Development Agendas' (2013) 40 Women's Studies Intl Forum 33; Anicca Kronsell, 'The Contribution of Feminist Perspectives to Climate Governance' in Susan Buckingham and Virginie Le Masson (eds), *Understanding Climate Change through Gender Relations* (1st edn, Taylor & Francis Group 2017).
9 Sherilyn MacGregor, '"Gender and Climate Change": From Impacts to Discourses' (2010) 6(2) J of the Indian Ocean Region 223.
10 Ginette Azcona and Antra Bhatt, 'Poverty Deepens for Women and Girls, According to Latest Projections' (*UN Women*, 1 February 2022).
11 Bina Agarwal, 'Environmental Action, Gender Equity and Women's Participation' (1997) 28 Development and Change 1, 1; Anna Kaijser and Annica Kronsell, 'Climate Change Through the Lens of Intersectionality' (2013) 23 Environmental Politics 3, 417; MacGregor (n 10).
12 Irene Dankelman, *Gender and Climate Change: An Introduction* (Taylor & Francis Group 2012).
13 The Lancet, 'Climate and COVID-19: Converging Crises' (2021) 397(10269) The Lancet 71; CJ Carlson and others, 'Climate change Increases Cross-Species Viral Transmission Risk' (2022) 607 Nature 555; Saloni Gupta, Barry T Rouse and Pranita P Sarangi, 'Did Climate Change Influence the Emergence, Transmission, and Expression of the COVID-19 Pandemic?' (2021) 8 Frontiers in Medicine.
14 Minu Hemmati M and Ulrike Röhr, 'A Huge Challenge and a Narrow Discourse: Ain't No Space for Gender in Climate Change Policy?' (2007) 74(9) Women and Environment Intl [page]; Agarwal (n 12).
15 World Bank, 'Nearly 2.4 Billion Women Globally Don't Have Same Economic Rights as Men' (1 March 2022) <www.worldbank.org/en/news/press-release/2022/03/01/nearly-2–4-billion-women-globally-don-t-have-sa me-economic-rights-as-men>.
16 World Bank, *Women, Business and the Law 2022* (World Bank Publications 2022).
17 ibid.
18 ibid.
19 ibid.
20 'Insecure Land Rights for Women: A Threat to Progress on Gender Equality and Sustainable Development' (*OHCHR* 2017) <https://www.ohchr.org/en/special-procedures/wg-women-and-girls/insecure-land-rights-women-threat-progress-gender-equality-and-sustainable-development>.
21 'These Numbers Prove that Rural Women are Crucial for a Better Future. But They're not Getting what they Need to Succeed.' (*IFAD* 7 March 2022) <https://www.ifad.org/en/web/latest/-/these-numbers-prove-that-rural-women-are-crucial-for-a-better-future>; The Food and Agriculture Organization of the United Nations, 'The Gender Gap in Land Rights' (FAO 2018).
22 UN Department of Economic and Social Affairs, 'Achieving Gender Equality, Women's Empowerment and Strengthening Development Cooperation: Dialogues at the Economic and Social Council' (United Nations 2010); Geraldine Terry, 'No Climate Justice without Gender Justice: An Overview of the Issues' (2009) 17(1) Gender & Development 5.
23 Liza Fuentes, 'Inequity in US Abortion Rights and Access: The End of Roe Is Deepening Existing Divides' (Guttmacher Institute 2023) <www.guttmacher.org/2023/01/inequity-us-abortion-rights-and-access-end-roe-deepening-existing-divides>; Samantha Artiga and others, 'What Are the Implications of the Overturning of Roe v. Wade for Racial Disparities?' (KFF 2022) <www.kff.org/racial-equity-and-health-policy/issue-brief/what-are-the-implications-of-the-overturning-of-ro e-v-wade-for-racial-disparities/.>.
24 Karine Coen-Sanchez and others, 'Repercussions of Overturning Roe v. Wade for Women Across Systems and Beyond Borders' (2022) 19 Reproductive Health.
25 Zara Abrams, 'Abortion Bans cause Outsized Harm for People of Color' (2023) 54(4) Monitor on Psychology 24.

26 Artiga and others (n 25).
27 Bharat H Desai and Moumita Mandal, 'Role of Climate Change in Exacerbating Sexual and Gender-Based Violence against Women: A New Challenge for International Law' (2021) 51(3) E.P.& L 137; MacGregor (n 10).
28 Jitendra Mishra, Priya Mishra and Naveen Kumar Arora, 'Linkages Between Environmental Issues and Zoonotic Diseases: With Reference to COVID-19 Pandemic' (2021) 4(3) Environmental Sustainability 455.
29 Michelle Marie Esposito and others, 'The Impact of Human Activities on Zoonotic Infection Transmissions' (2023) 13(10) Animals.
30 Pâmela Rocha Vieira, Leila Posenato Garcia and Ethel Leonor Noia Maciel, 'Isolamento Social e o Aumento da Violência Doméstica O que isso nos Revela?' [The Increase in Domestic Violence during the Social Isolation: What Does It Reveal?] (2020) 23 Revista Brasileira de Epidemiologia; Laura C Hudson, Eve J Lowenstein and Leonard J Hoenig, 'Domestic Violence in the Coronavirus Disease 2019 Era: Insights from a Survivor' (2020) 38(6) Clinics in Dermatology 737.
31 Brad Boserup, Mark McKenney and Adel Elkbuli, 'Alarming Trends in US Domestic Violence during the COVID-19 Pandemic' (2020) 38(12) The American Journal of Emergency Medicine 2753.
32 Senay Habtezion, 'Gender and Climate Change: Overview of Linkages Between Gender and Climate Change' (United Nations Development Programme 2016); Bridget Burns and Camille Andre, 'Ensuring Women's Access and Influence on Climate Change Policy (WEDO 2015).
33 Hemmati and Rohr (n 15); Macgregor (n 10).
34 Mona Lena Krook and Pippa Norris, 'Beyond Quotas: Strategies to Promote Gender Equality in Elected Office' (2014) 62(1) Political Studies 2.
35 Chantal de Jonge Oudraat and Michael E Brown, 'Gender, Climate Change, and Security: Making the Connections' (Wilson Center, 25 January 2022) <https://www.wilsoncenter.org/article/gender-climate-change-and-security-making-connections>.
36 Maria Nieves Rico, 'Gender, the Environment and the Sustainability of Development' (Economic Commission for Latin America and the Caribbean 1998).
37 World Conference to Review and Appraise the Achievements of the United Nations Decade for Women, 'Report of the World Conference to Review and Appraise the Achievements of the United Nations Decade for Women: Equality, Development and Peace' (15–26 July 1985) UN Doc A/CONF.116/28/Rev.1 para 244.
38 ibid para 227.
39 Ioana Borza, 'Review of the Implementation in the EU of Area K of the Beijing Platform for Action: Women and Environment' (European Institute for Gender Equality 2012).
40 The Fourth World Conference on Women Resolution I: Beijing Declaration and Platform for Action (Beijing 15 September 1995) para 249.
41 Jacqui True, 'Mainstreaming Gender in Global Public Policy' (2003) 5(3) I Feminist J of Politics 368.
42 United Nations, 'Transforming Our World: The 2030 Agenda for Sustainable Development' (2015) UN Doc A/RES/70/1.
43 United Nations Framework Convention on Climate Change Secretariat, 'Guidelines or Other Tools for Integrating Gender Considerations into Climate Change Related Activities under the Convention' (2016).
44 UN Women, *Turning Promises into Action: Gender Equality in the 2030 Agenda for Sustainable Development* (UN Women Headquarters 2018).
45 Organisation for Economic Co-operation and Development, *Gender and the Environment: Building Evidence and Policies to Achieve the SDGs* (OECD Publishing 2021).
46 Organisation for Economic Co-operation and Development, *Gender Equality and the Empowerment of Women and Girls: Guidance for Development Partners* (OECD Publishing 2022).
47 'Five Big Wins Ushered in by the Landmark Beijing Platform for Action' *UN Women* (20 March2020)<https://www.unwomen.org/en/news/stories/2020/3/compilation-five-wins-ushered-in-by-beijing-platform-for-action>.
48 Otzelberger (n 16).
49 Maria Prebble and Ana Rojas, 'Gender in Mitigation Actions' (ICUN and USAID 2016).
50 Benoit Mayer, 'Human Rights in the Paris Agreement' (2016) 6 Climate L 109.
51 Bridget Burns and Ronit Anspach, 'Report on Women's Participation in UN Climate Negotiations' (WEDO 2012).

52 Mary Robinson Foundation – Climate Justice, 'Women's Participation: An Enabler of Climate Justice' (2015).
53 ibid.
54 UNFCCC Draft decision -/CP.20. Lima Work Programme on Gender (2014).
55 UNFCCC Secretariat (n 45).
56 UNFCCC, 'Implementation of the Lima Work Programme on Gender and its Gender Action Plan' UNFCCC 51st Session (9 December 2019) UN Doc FCCC/SBI/2019/15.
57 ibid.
58 ibid.
59 Sébastien Duyck and others, 'Delivering on the Paris Promises: Combating Climate Change while Protecting Rights: Recommendations for the Negotiations of the Paris Rule Book' (CIEL, IWGIA, RFN, CARE, WEDO, AIPP and ITUC 2017)
60 UNFCCC Secretariat (n 45).
61 UNFCCC, 'Adoption of the Paris Agreement' Conference of the Parties 21st Session (15 December 2015) FCCC/CP/2015/L.9/Rev.1.
62 UNFCCC, 'Report on Gender Composition' Conference of the Parties 21st Session (21 September 2015) UN Doc FCCC/CP/2015/6.
63 'Adoption of the Paris Agreement' (n 63).
64 Sophia Huyer, *Gender Equality in National Climate Action: Planning for Gender-Responsive Nationally Determined Contributions* (UNDP 2016).
65 Ana Rojas, 'Advancing Gender Equality, Women's Empowerment and Indigenous Rights from COP24 to COP25 through the Paris Rulebook' (*IUCN* 21 December 2018) <https://iucn.org/news/gender/201812/advancing-gender-equality-womens-empowerment-and-indigenous-rights-cop24-cop25-through-paris-rulebook>.
66 UNFCCC, 'Proposal by the President, Informal Compilation of L-documents' (15 December 2018) 17.
67 ibid 58.
68 ibid 59.
69 ibid 61.
70 ibid 62.
71 Bridget Burns, 'Pocket Guide to Gender Equality' (ECBI 2017) 53.
72 NB Chauhan and Vinaya Kumar, 'Gender Responsive Climate Change Strategies for Sustainable Development'. (2016) 57(2) Productivity 182; Gayle Nelson, *Gender Responsive National Communications Toolkit* (UNDP 2015).
73 Margaret Alston, 'Gender Mainstreaming and Climate Change' (2014) 47 Women's Studies International Forum 287; Office of the Special Adviser on Gender Issues and Advancement of Women, *Gender Mainstreaming: An Overview* (United Nations 2002).
74 United Nations Development Programme, 'Factsheet for the project 'Improving resilience of vulnerable coastal communities to climate change in Viet Nam.'
75 United Nations Development Programme, *Gender Action Plan for FP013: Improving the Resilience of Vulnerable Coastal Communities to Climate Change Related Impacts in Viet Nam* (Green Climate Fund 2021).
76 United Nations Development Programme, *2020 Annual Performance Report for FP013: Improving the Resilience of Vulnerable Coastal Communities to Climate Change Related Impacts in Viet Nam* (Green Climate Fund 2021).
77 ibid.
78 Alston (n 75).
79 UN Women, 'Implementation of Gender-Responsive Climate Action in the Context of Sustainable Development' (2016).
80 Green Climate Fund, 'Mainstreaming Gender in Green Climate Fund Projects' (2017).
81 Prebble and Rojas (n 51).
82 Commission on the Status of Women, 'Key Policy Initiatives and Capacity Building on Gender Mainstreaming: Focus on Science and Technology' Commission on the Status of Women 55th Session (2 February – 4 March 2011) UN Doc E/CN.6/2011/CRP.5.
83 Susan Markham, *Women as Agents of Change: Having Voice in Society and Influencing Policy* (World Bank 2013).

84 Nora Götzmann and Nicholas Bainton, 'Embedding Gender-Responsive Approaches in Impact Assessment and Management, Impact Assessment and Project Appraisal' (2021) 39(3) Impact Assessment and Project Appraisal 171.
85 Inter-American Development Bank, *Promoting Risk Mitigation Instruments and Finance for Renewable Energy and Energy Efficiency Investments* (Green Climate Fund 2018).
86 ibid.
87 Inter-American Development Bank, *Gender Assessment for FP064: Promoting Risk Mitigation Instruments and Finance for Renewable Energy and Energy Efficiency Investments* (Green Climate Fund 2018).
88 ibid.
89 Green Climate Fund, 'Mainstreaming Gender' (n 82).
90 Agnes Otzelberger, *Gender-Responsive Strategies on Climate Change: Recent Progress and Ways Forward for Donors* (BRIDGE/IDS 2011).
91 WEDO, *Gender at COP24: A Quick Overview on the Integration of Language Related to Gender Equality at COP24* (Women's Environment and Development Organization 2018).
92 Arora-Jonsson 'Forty Years' (n 4).
93 Nina Jeffs, *Why Women's Leadership is Key to Climate Action* (Climate Champions 8 March 2022).
94 OECD Organization for Economic Cooperation & Development, *Development Finance for Gender-Responsive Climate Action* (OECD Development Co-operation Directorate 2022); Karen Judd and others, *Gender Budget Initiatives: Strategies, Concepts and Experiences* (The United Nations Development Fund for Women 2001).
95 Ulrike Röhr and others, *Gender into Climate Policy Toolkit for Climate Experts and Decision-Makers* (GenderCC – Women for Climate Justice 2009).
96 UNFCCC, 'Differentiated Impacts of Climate Change on Women and Men: the Integration of Gender Considerations in Climate Policies, Plans and Actions; and Progress in Enhancing Gender Balance in National Climate Delegations' UNFCCC 50th Session (12 June 2019) UN Doc FCCC/SBI/2019/INF.8.
97 ibid.
98 UNFCCC Secretariat (n 45).

30

EXPLORING THE POTENTIAL OF THE PARIS AGREEMENT TO DECOLONIZE INTERNATIONAL LAW

Mrinalini Shinde

Introduction

The Preamble to the United Nations Framework Convention on Climate Change (UNFCCC)[1] emphatically states that

> the largest share of historical and current global emissions of greenhouse gases has originated in developed countries, that per capita emissions in developing countries are still relatively low and that the share of global emissions originating in developing countries will grow to meet their social and development needs.

It acknowledges that "the global nature of climate change calls for the widest possible cooperation by all countries . . . in accordance with their common but differentiated responsibilities and respective capabilities and their social and economic conditions" (CBDRRC). The UNFCCC was adopted in 1992 and currently has 197 parties. These parties are divided into Annex I and Non-Annex I Parties, in effect distinguishing developed and developing country parties, respectively. The entire UNFCCC legal regime is based on the principle of CBDDRRC, which in turn is based on the acknowledgment that historic responsibility for global carbon emissions must be accounted for when parties bind themselves to emissions reductions. Subsequent instruments under the UNFCCC, the Kyoto Protocol[2] and the Paris Agreement,[3] codified the CBDRRC in a more evolved manner with more specific obligations.

The Industrial Revolution, which resulted in the most significant increase in global anthropogenic climate emissions, is connected with the colonial project, the extraction and consumption of natural resources, particularly minerals and oils by colonisers. Within international law, the *Declaration on the Granting of Independence to Colonial Countries and Peoples* affirmed the right to self-determination of all people, calling for an end to colonialism. According to Pahuja, international law (IL), when studied through a decolonial lens, is based on two fundamental understandings: one view that IL uses law to continue the "subjugation of colonized peoples by the imperial powers in a distortion of international law's true spirit" and therefore examines how these vestiges can be removed to broaden the scope of IL, and another view that presupposes IL as "always been

DOI: 10.4324/9781003276678-35

encompassed by and in the service to empire . . . the very doctrines and institutions of international law are understood to have been moulded by the powerful in order to serve their interests."[4]

Based on this nexus between industrialisation, resource extraction and historic responsibility for climate change inherent to international climate change law, I wish to examine the following questions in this chapter: first, what are the primary critiques of international law from a decolonial perspective, particularly with respect to the origins of international law, the functioning of the United Nations and the relationships between nations? And second, to what extent did the UNFCCC in its text, debates and declarations leading up to its formation address the concerns of colonialism that exist within international law? I will refer to both secondary sources and literature, as well as primary legal instruments and decisions to answer these questions.

Decolonising International Law

This section provides insights into the theoretical and historical literature that addresses how international law has extended the colonial project, especially as it relates to the focus on the UNFCCC. Antony Anghie, one of the foremost scholars of the Third World Approaches to International Law (TWAIL) school critiques and analyses international law from the perspective of the Global South. Anghie explains that international law is composed essentially of doctrines and principles that originated in Europe, emerging from European history, and were dispersed outside of Europe through international law, such as the legal concept of sovereignty. Anghie explains how the concept that sovereign states exercised absolute control over their territory emerged from the Treaty of Westphalia in 1648 and was extended to non-European states through the use of international law. This was particularly achieved through decolonisation when former colonised territories gained independence and became new sovereign nations, particularly as members of the United Nations. Anghie argues that this process, using institutional mechanisms of international law, has effectively made colonialism only a thing of the past by extending the Westphalian model in a display of retrospective equality using the concept of sovereignty.[5] Anghie states that one reason international law addressed questions such as democracy and human rights was to justify itself as a project, which also resulted in decolonisation and the inclusion of newly independent countries as members. However, he says that this "generated a new set of issues, namely the reconciliation between the concepts of universality, equality, and participation, newly espoused by international law and the previous history of exclusion and disempowerment experienced by the colonized." Europe was then faced with the quandary of preventing "the disruption of international order that would ensue if the developing world were allowed to articulate its history of exploitation" using its new access to international law, and the reason to exclude the developing world from international law as the new nations demanded reparations.[6]

As Mitchell points out, since the basis of international law is a kind of new natural law which needs no one central legislator to understand its core principles but is accepted as a set of norms about justice that all civilized nations agree to, international law can further enforce the European origins of what is understood as universally just, especially when interpreting custom, where "courts must always decide whose custom is to be treated as dispositive, and whose disregarded."[7]

Oumar Ba makes a strong claim that from the TWAIL perspective, international law as a legal regime is not legitimate, as it continues the exploitation and subservience of the Third World and legitimises it. TWAIL seeks to understand how international law is used to maintain racial hierarchies of norms and institutions. International criminal law, for example, practically operates as a space for political transactions, where prosecution can be pursued arbitrarily, and results in a legal regime that characterises crimes such as genocide, war crimes and crimes against humanity as being the crimes committed by only those kinds of people who must be controlled or tamed by international law. Ba observes:

> Alternatively, the West is exonerated from the capacity of committing such crimes. For instance, the portrayal of the planners and executioners of the Holocaust as being distant, an aberration in the European march toward enlightened civilization, exonerates European culture, which is an attempt to reestablish Europe as the producer of universal values and legitimate the West as the purveyor and arbiter of values, norms, and institutions.[8]

In addition, there is also resistance to international human rights protection which "privilege the individual over his or her group" for being "grounded in norms and values that are derived from European and Western culture," a topic that continues to be a question of debate amongst scholars.[9]

Sandhya Pahuja, another leading scholar on the decolonisation of international law, explains that it was by design that as more nations were decolonised, the concepts of development and underdevelopment in international law and its institutions were born. She argues:

> According to this deeply historicist account, the non-universality of the newly formed nations was understood in contradistinction to the universal (Western) nations and was maintained once again through the idea that non-modern forms of social organization existed in the historical past and that the present Western nations were exemplars of the future for those nonmodern nations.[10]

Pahuja further explains that this project was furthered by the emphasis on the idea of modernity, that resistance to the modern or Western set of ideals becomes backward or archaic by definition and this characterisation required and justified intervention by international institutions to modernise the Third World, such as interventions by the World Bank or International Monetary Fund, which sought to liberalise economies, aiding the neoliberalisation and modernisation project in tandem. These interventions were aided by the creation of the concept of universal values.[11]

In explaining the extent of Eurocentrism in international law, Martti Koskenniemi says that it enables:

> lawyers from all over the world to communicate with each other by invoking widely shared historical associations and a normative teleology in which an idealized Europe, coded as nationhood, capitalism, modernity or rule of law marks the horizon of its imagination.[12]

After the events of the Second World War, international law transcended from being a project of civilisation to that of modernisation, focusing on technological development, conservation of resources, ensuring global security and protecting human rights.[13]

However, economic policies promulgated by international institutions have rendered complete self-government difficult given how developing nations' governments were "made subservient to unequal economic development." Promotion and expansion of commerce came "at the expense of the social and political integrity of that society," and the characterisation of poverty and underdevelopment as being an endemic problem of developing societies resulted in a focus on good governance or democratic reforms of seemingly backward nations, without an effort to reform the international economy as a whole which endorses exploitative commercial practices. These institutions are largely controlled by the developed states, whose own policies often lie beyond the scrutiny and focus of these institutions.[14] For example, as Anghie and Chimni point out, during the Yugoslavia and Rwanda conflicts, which resulted in the creation of the International Tribunals for Rwanda and for Yugoslavia, which tried individuals responsible for the conflicts, it was evident that:

> policies authored by international financial institutions (IFIs) the World Bank and the International Monetary Fund, in which powerful actors of the international system play a dominant role, were in part responsible for creating the wider environment in which these human rights violations took place.[15]

However, this liability was not examined, let alone prosecuted, for failure of existing institutions to prevent those situations for whose prevention they were created.

By the 1980s and 1990s, while there was increasing disillusionment with international law, we also saw its expansion: new branches emerging, such as international refugee law, environmental law, trade law and space law.[16] At the beginning of the 1990s, there was a renewed interest in international environmental law, also marked by the United Nations Conference on Environment and Development in 1992 (Rio Earth Summit). This also led to an increase in scholarship on understanding how international environmental law was ignoring the interests of the Third World, and the importance of respecting the principle of common but differentiated responsibility.[17]

Traditional Knowledge and Indigenous Communities within IL

While international law remains the arena of nations, rather than member states, environmental legal scholarship has focused heavily on the role of local communities, Indigenous People and those whose rights to resources and a healthy environment have been usurped not only by international commerce and exploitation and the international economic order, but also by the nation states to whom they belong, owing to the allegiance of nation states to this economic order. The UNFCCC houses The Local Communities and Indigenous Peoples Platform (LCIPP)[18] and one of the nine constituencies within the non-governmental organisations; non-Party stakeholders admitted to the UNFCCC process are the Indigenous peoples organisations (IPO) constituency.[19] It then becomes crucial to examine the role of indigenous communities and traditional knowledge in decolonising international law.

The concept of traditional knowledge entered international law starting in the 1990s. The UN Convention on Biological Diversity (CBD), arising out of the Rio Earth Summit, formalised it for the first time, and in 2000, the World Intellectual Property Organization (WIPO) established the "Intergovernmental Committee on Intellectual Property and Genetic Resources, Traditional Knowledge and Folklore" (IGC). In 2001, the World Trade Organization (WTO), in Article 19 of the Doha Declaration,[20] included the consideration of traditional knowledge within its Trade-Related Aspects of Intellectual Property Rights (TRIPS) Agreement. Subsequently, the Food and Agriculture Organization of the United Nations (FAO) and the World Health Organization (WHO) examined traditional knowledge with respect to food and medicine.[21] In 2015, the Paris Agreement, under the UNFCCC, in Article 7 discussing adaptation stated that:

> Parties acknowledge that adaptation action should follow a country-driven, gender-responsive, participatory and fully transparent approach, taking into consideration vulnerable groups, communities and ecosystems, and should be based on and guided by the best available science and, as appropriate, traditional knowledge, knowledge of indigenous peoples and local

knowledge systems, with a view to integrating adaptation into relevant socioeconomic and environmental policies and actions, where appropriate.[22]

Indigenous legal perspectives, along with traditional knowledge of nature, and natural systems play an important role in the protection of the environment, management of land and ecological sustainability,[23] such as land tenure regimes based on community rights instead of private rights, which is especially necessary when communities combat scarcity of resources, soil degradation and loss of vegetation arising from climate change. However, owing to the paradox within international law that upholding the right to self-determination of peoples also upholds state sovereignty, which can lead to a conflict of laws of sorts for the interests of Indigenous Peoples, decolonising international law becomes vital because through the "development of an inclusive legal system, Indigenous peoples and other minority groups will have a voice where they have previously struggled to be heard."[24] The recognition and enforcement of community-based land tenure regimes of Indigenous Peoples is an important strategy to combat climate change and environmental destruction, and indigenous communities struggle to protect their community-based tenure from States as well as corporation, an illustration of how indigenous communities within international law have historically operated within the self-determination and sovereignty paradox of international law.[25]

Indigenous communities are also excluded from processes that can alleviate their immediate conditions through migration. Over a period of roughly 150 years during European colonisation, over 62 million Europeans migrated to nations to politically and economically dominate the people that are now excluded today from the international law project, ensuring "the flow of human and natural resources overwhelmingly for the benefit of Europe and its settler colonial satellites." This was only possible in the absence of the immigration control that exists today, preventing disenfranchised communities from travelling similarly to seek better environmental conditions.[26]

Tuck and Yang discuss "white harm reduction models," which treat white supremacy as a public health issue, and the models seek to reduce inter alia "the deep harm it has caused non-white people over generations." With the escalation of the climate crisis and consequent increase in violence and poverty, a similar model to the "settler harm reduction model" can help in providing pathways that lead to both an acknowledgement of the inherent harm perpetrated by settlers, instead of settlers moving towards innocence through history,[27] but also to inform how state institutions in justice, education utilities and administration are designed to actively reduce that harm, instead of indigenous identities existing at the margins of state functions.

In the project of colonisation, growth of wealth was measured as it was distributed amongst the ruling or capital-owning class, and the deprivation of local communities and the destruction of their local ecosystems was externalised. As Howitt states, "under the conditions created by settler colonialism, environmental capital in general – and land, water, timber, minerals, and fossil fuels in particular – were free and effectively unlimited. They became the property of the sovereign settler-colonial states."[28] In the process, climate risks to local populations arising out of this degraded landscape are disproportionate and an impact of being a network externality during colonisation, and climate injustice is part of the many injustices suffered by indigenous communities in postcolonial times.[29]

With this theoretical background regarding the inherent challenges in decolonising international law and the impact of colonisation not just on developing States, but on local communities, especially in the context of environment and climate change law, the following section focuses particularly on the UNFCCC, its Kyoto Protocol and the Paris Agreement in order to understand the role of the UNFCCC in decolonising international law.

Examining the Paris Agreement for Spaces of Decoloniality

In examining the decoloniality within the Paris Agreement, it is important to note that Parties to the UNFCCC and the Paris Agreement have historically aligned themselves on the North-South axis, reflecting their colonial identities to a large extent. As Fridahl points out,

> though some countries might be more or less dependent, the global South has formed coalitions that underline their position in the world system, a position that to a large degree form arguments and possibilities in the negotiations. The same holds for the global North.[30]

Political groupings have also shaped the narrative of the negotiations under the UNFCCC process, with the groups playing certain roles based on their helping or inhibiting progress in negotiations on different topics of mutual interest.[31] An example of a strong negotiating block within the non-Annex I Parties is the "Alliance of Small Island States" (AOSIS), which represents the interests of its island state members, which are uniquely vulnerable to the impacts of climate change.[32] The AOSIS managed to make significant inroads in the UNFCCC process, including achieving prominent seats on constituted and governing bodies within a process which was otherwise limited to the five major regional groups of the United Nations, such as the COP Bureau, the Executive Board of the Clean Development Mechanism (CDM) and the boards of the Adaptation Fund and the Green Climate Fund.[33]

The UNFCCC divided its parties into Annex I (industrialised countries that were members of the Organisation for Economic Co-operation and Development), Annex II (Annex I Parties not including those economies in transition) and non-Annex I Parties (mostly developing countries). Within non-Annex I Parties, least developed countries (LDCs) as classified by the United Nations are given special status in participation.[34] This categorisation was also reflected in the Kyoto Protocol. However, the Paris Agreement created a distinction between developed and developing country parties, mentioning the special status of the LDCs and small island developing States (SIDS). As discussed previously, the preamble of the UNFCCC considers the historic responsibility of developed countries for emissions; the Paris Agreement did not include the language, although it continued to recognise common but differentiated responsibilities and respective capabilities and their social and economic conditions (CBDRRC).[35] The following section discusses six avenues within the UNFCCC and Paris Agreement that exhibit the potential for decoloniality.

Historical Emissions

> There are various existing approaches to measuring national responsibility for climate change. Negotiations and agreements under the UNFCCC are focused on current territorial emissions. Based on this approach, China's responsibility is more than double that of the USA, and India comes just behind the European Union. When it comes to climate change, however, what matters is stocks of CO2 in the atmosphere, not annual flows; so responsibility must be measured in terms of each country's contribution to cumulative historical emissions.[36]

In examining the Paris Agreement from a decolonial lens, the very term "historical and current global emissions" as mentioned in the preamble is loaded in its implications, as they ask developed country parties to account for the emissions from which they have already benefitted and which resulted in their developed status. An innovative method of understanding historic emissions could involve switching from a production-based metric (which countries produce the most emissions) to that of a consumption-based metric, which takes into consideration the carbon footprint of goods and services consumed by States. This is because exports from China and other high-emitting developing country parties are consumed in low-emitting States. Fossil fuels when burnt can also be geographically far from the origin of extraction. Therefore, as proposed by Davisa, Peters and Caldeira, "understanding the distribution of interests along this supply chain may facilitate international efforts to limit CO2 emissions from the burning of fossil fuels."[37] Such an approach then would aid in the phasing out of consumption behaviours which are high in emissions (characteristic of the Global North) without penalising Global South countries for the production of emissions in their pathways towards industrialisation in the process of emission reduction for mitigation of climate change.

Common but Differentiated Responsibilities

At the heart of the Paris Agreement's decoloniality is the principle of common but differentiated responsibilities and respective capabilities and their social and economic conditions (CBDRRC). The idea of differentiation in responsibility is not unique to the UNFCCC. The International Labour Organisation (ILO) has recognised how conditions of labour cannot be uniformly enforced and are affected by factors such as climate and economic opportunity, and parties to the General Agreement on Tariffs and Trade (GATT) created "nonreciprocal trade concessions" and differentially favourable tariffs to benefit developing countries. The idea that the five permanent members of the Security Council have veto power is an effective differentiation of responsibility in the UN Charter itself.[38]

CBDRRC as included in the Paris Agreement confers a shared obligation with differentiated responsibilities, not only through emission reductions, but also by expecting developed country parties to contribute climate finance in accordance with their responsibility and capacity, along with differentiated procedural requirements in monitoring and reporting for parties.[39] During the negotiations before the Paris Agreement was adopted, the Global North countries were dissatisfied with the manner in which the principle put undue burden on them within the realm of the Kyoto Protocol, which had put emission reduction targets on the Annex I countries while non-Annex I countries were involved in reduction on a voluntary basis.[40] There is a shared understanding that CBDRRC is recognising that climate change is a common responsibility of all parties and based on their responsibilities for historical emissions, and their current national capacity will inform their ability to reduce emissions. Predictably, this has led to developing countries drawing a line in the sand regarding historic responsibility of developed country parties, which have in turn resisted the idea and focused on aspects such as capacity-building and technological transfer.[41]

In 1997, the Brazilian government submitted what is referred to colloquially as the Brazilian Proposal, which emphasised that the UNFCCC process should be based in equity, and the burdens on the Annex I Parties should reflect past emissions and their effects as they have impacted the current climate. While the Brazilian proposal was not adopted, it did give rise to a coherent interpretation of what historical responsibility could be defined as and how it could be quantified.[42] Developing countries have participated in the treaty based on the perception of equity that CBDRRC provides, operating in a manner similar to affirmative action. While it is logical that costs be allocated on the basis of responsibility, which was reflected in the Brazilian proposal, developed country parties have the defence of ignorance, of being unaware of the consumption of the carbon budget that occurred during their industrialisation process, which coincided with colonisation to an extent. So, the developing legal regime under the Paris Agreement must create a basis for liability for the allocation of costs of emissions, irrespective of knowledge or moral basis of responsibility, for the CBDRRC to be effectively operationalised.[43]

Loss and Damage

Article 8 of the Paris Agreement contains the provisions addressing loss and damage within the context of climate change, which is a remarkable space of decoloniality given its basis in accounting for loss suffered by countries from the impacts of climate change through damages which must be paid by those responsible: in effect an avenue for climate reparations. As discussed, the pursuit of reparations by the Global South has been a long-held apprehension of the Global North within the international law project. Article 8 states that

> Parties recognize the importance of averting, minimizing and addressing loss and damage associated with the adverse effects of climate change, including extreme weather events and slow onset events, and the role of sustainable development in reducing the risk of loss and damage.[44]

It established that Parties "Parties should enhance understanding, action and support, including through the Warsaw International Mechanism, as appropriate, on a cooperative and facilitative basis with respect to loss and damage associated with the adverse effects of climate change." One of the areas of cooperation and facilitation envisioned is the resilience of communities, livelihoods and ecosystems.[45] The Warsaw Mechanism works through its various thematic groups "to minimize and address loss and damage associated with climate change impacts, including extreme weather events and slow onset events."[46] However, loss and damage as characterised within the Paris Agreement run the risk of being framed as an issue of neoliberal economic intervention based on risk transfer and insurance, rather than reparations. In 2015, the COP requested the

> Executive Committee of the Warsaw International Mechanism to establish a clearing house for risk transfer that serves as a repository for information on insurance and risk transfer, in order to facilitate the efforts of Parties to develop and implement comprehensive risk management strategies[47]

This framing "rhetorically minimizes questions of culpability and ignores certain types of events and consequences that fall outside of the 'insurable risk' category," as noted by Vanhala and Hestbaek.[48]

While practising decoloniality, the use of scientific evidence is crucial in determining the outcomes of loss and damage payments. Scientists such as Otto and others have established that even though international law may not require loss and damage to be quantitatively assessed, it is possible using certain predictive modelling to quantify both loss and damages reliably, and "the fact that it is possible to provide such quantifications will greatly advance the possibility of an informed discussion on whether such information is useful, necessary, and should be included in multinational agreements."[49]

As a result of decades of action by developing countries, and civil society, COP27 in Egypt established a Loss and Damage Fund. This included the demands by 134 developing countries at COP25 in Madrid regarding the establishment of such a fund.[50] While the fund was not established in Madrid, or in Glasgow at the following COP meeting, continued efforts by developing countries led to financing for loss and damage being included in the COP27 agenda, and the establishment of the fund.[51] The next years will be crucial in determining how the fund will operate, its modalities and most importantly how effectively developed countries pay into the fund, and how effectively vulnerable parties are able to access those funds. Serdeczny and Lissner propose in their agenda for research regarding such a loss and damage fund that there is still considerable normative research necessary on who contributes to the fund.[52] There is significant debate regarding the nature of the donors, especially whether emerging economies should contribute to the Fund given the current emissions, or whether historical emissions and responsibility should play a greater role.[53] Serdeczny and Lissner suggest that "estimating how many people or communities benefit from different eligibility scenarios, and clarifying underlying normative principles, could increase the transparency of various options."[54]

Local Communities and Indigenous Peoples

In 2015, in its 21st session while adopting the Paris Agreement, the COP recognised:

> the need to strengthen knowledge, technologies, practices and efforts of local communities and indigenous peoples related to addressing and responding to climate change, and establishes a platform for the exchange of experiences and sharing of best practices on mitigation and adaptation in a holistic and integrated manner.[55]

In 2017, the COP established the 'Local communities and Indigenous Peoples platform'[56] and clarified the working modalities of the platform in 2018.[57] Institutionally, the Paris Agreement has emphasised the need for increased participation of local communities within the process through the organisation of knowledge-sharing, facilitative sharing of views and stakeholder workshops. However, the UNFCCC process has been accused of tokenising indigenous communities for the optics of an inclusive process, especially during the COP25 in Madrid in 2019, during which women and indigenous activists, part of observer organisations, were escorted out of the venue by police and their entry badges rescinded for a day when they staged a demonstration, owing to security concerns.[58] At the same meeting, civil society leaders from the Māori community in New Zealand were manhandled and denied opportunities to participate in the talks.[59] While international law through the Paris Agreement continues to recognise and expand the participation of indigenous communities in climate negotiations, instances such as these illustrate the potential power relations that exist between the international law project and communities, and the potential for use of force, even optically, reinforces the need for decolonising the practice of international environmental law.

Shortcomings in Procedure: Consensus versus Voting

Over 25 years of negotiations at the Conference of Parties to the UNFCCC (COP) have resulted in a legal regime based on reciprocity, wherein high-emitting States, including some previously colonised States, bargain over their reduction of emissions to the extent that their economically competing States also reduce obligations, characterised particularly by the historic conflict over emission reductions between the two largest emitters: the United States and China. The UNFCCC regime as a sub-species of international law places sovereignty at the highest level, and States then justify limited reductions in line with economic interests in accordance with their sovereignty. Reciprocity-based international rule-making has been criticised by scholars, as it has been shown that the negotiated outcomes from consensus-based decision-making are determined by the lowest common denominator of the least ambitious negotiating Party. The least ambitious Party will determine the collective ceiling for progress which, combined with a regime of reciprocity, creates outcomes that are disconnected from scientific advice on emission reduction in accordance with the goals of the Paris Agreement. This unfortunate and widening gap between negotiated ambition and recommended scientific thresholds creates a practically failing legal instrument, a failure which will then disproportionately impact citizens of previously colonised nations, local communities and Indigenous Peoples who are vulnerable to climate change and its impacts.[60] The question of voting versus consensus has prevented the UNFCCC COP from formally adopting its rules of procedure because of differences over rules regarding voting. As clarified by the UNFCCC secretariat, the draft rules except the rule on voting are followed by the COP, and consensus is then followed as the default method of decision-making,[61] except the decision to amend the Convention itself, which can be done through three-fourths majority if it is impossible to reach consensus.[62]

This method of assuming "default consensus" was first created when Saudi Arabia along with other oil-producing states did not agree to the voting rule, creating a precedent for future COP Presidents to use it as the ad-hoc method. For example, in 2013, Russia, Ukraine and Belarus during an intersessional meeting ended the negotiation track regarding an amendment to the provisional agenda about holding "a formal discussion of meeting procedures," which dealt with "matters most important to vulnerable nations relating to climate adaptation, forest protection, and the framework for a legal instrument to deal with climate-related catastrophic loss and damage." This procedural problem within the UNFCCC, which has the power to prevent significant progress, must be taken seriously by those advocating for greater ambition and efficiency of the process.[63] In Warsaw in 2018, and in Madrid in 2020, in the pursuit of an elusive consensus the COP negotiations far exceeded the planned time slot for the meetings, causing undue stress to those delegations of small or developing country parties who do not have the resources or manpower to man all negotiation rooms or share the burden of overtime work for unplanned delays and extensions which are becoming normalised.[64]

There have been instances, such as in the Cancun COP16 in 2010, where COP President Patricia Espinosa gavelled through a decision despite an objection by Bolivia, creating a new understanding of consensus that has been perceived as being a procedurally problematic decision: that the interpretation of consensus should not rest on the personal decision of the COP President. Therefore, beyond the substantive elements of international climate change law becoming conceptually decolonised, the procedural aspects of the UNFCCC must also address the failures of its consensus-based decision-making process, as it comes at the cost of the interests of those most vulnerable. It would not be unique or revolutionary, given that other international environmental law conventions such as the Convention on International Trade in Endangered Species, International Whaling Convention, Montreal Protocol and Convention on Biological Diversity all provide for voting-based decision-making.[65]

Conclusion

This chapter in essence sought to examine first how international law as a project can be decolonised and how to analyse its working from a decolonial lens, and second, to examine how the Paris Agreement can be decolonised, using theoretical concepts within the decolonial historicist theory of international law. The Paris Agreement, in addressing climate change with its demarcation of developed and developing country parties within the core of its construction and guided by the CBDRRC, is also dealing with one of the biggest consequences of colonialism: industrialism that gave rise to increased carbon emissions, leading to climate change. As we can observe through the various spaces discussed in this chapter: from accountability to historic emissions, the avoidance of quantified accounting of differentiated responsibilities, the use of market mechanisms to skirt around the issue of liability for loss and damage, the limited involvement of most vulnerable local communities and Indigenous Peoples in decision-making and the flaws of the consensus-based decision-making procedures, the Global North, including previous colonial powers, continues to exert their influence over the fortunes and welfare of developing nations. Not all nations come to the negotiation table with clean hands, and there is little attempt in earnest to recognise this inequity. The structures and institutions of international law support and legitimise these inherent power imbalances, since *prima facie*, all nations are equal sovereign States. Along with the skewed discussion on emission reductions, an increased focus on adaptation or resilience to climate change also reinforces the idea that the Global South, developing countries or local communities have to take responsibility for the impacts of climate change and climate disasters, when in reality, the "neo-liberal economic system that values unlimited growth and unsustainable extraction of natural resources, is contributing to climate volatility, while rapid urbanisation, other forms of environmental degradation and wealth disparity are increasing disaster risk."[66] A truly decolonised UNFCCC and Paris Agreement would codify and recognise this reality.

Notes

1 United Nations Framework Convention on Climate Change (entered into force 21 March 1994) 1771 UNTS 107, 165.
2 Kyoto Protocol to the United Nations Framework Convention on Climate Change (entered into force 16 February 2005) 2303 UNTS 162.
3 Paris Agreement, parties to the 1992 United Nations Framework Convention on Climate change (adopted 12 December 2015, entered into force 4 November 2016) 3156 UNTS 79.
4 Sundhya Pahuja, 'The Postcoloniality of International Law' (2005) 46 Harv Int'l LJ 459.
5 Antony Anghie, 'The Evolution of International Law: Colonial and Postcolonial Realities' (2006) 27 Third World Q. 739, 740.
6 Antony Anghie, 'The Heart of My Home: Colonialism, Environmental Damage, and the Nauru Case' (1993) 34 Harv Int'l L J 445, 496.
7 Ryan Martinez Mitchell, 'International Law as Project or System?' (2020) 51 Geo J Int'l L 623, 688.
8 Oumar Ba, 'International Justice and the Postcolonial Condition' (2017) 63 Africa Today 45, 52.
9 Darren C Zook, 'Decolonizing Law: Identity Politics, Human Rights, and the United Nations' (2006) 19 Harv Hum Rts J 95, 99.
10 Pahuja (n 4) 464.
11 ibid 465.
12 Martti Koskenniemi, 'Histories of International Law: Dealing with Eurocentrism' (2011) 19 Rechtsgeschichte 152, 154.
13 Pahuja (n 4) 159.
14 Antony Anghie, 'Colonialism and the Birth of International Institutions: Sovereignty, Economy, and the Mandate System of the League of Nations' (2002) 34 NYU J Int'l L & Pol 513, 624.
15 Antony Anghie and BS Chimni, 'Third World Approaches to International Law and Individual Responsibility in Internal Conflicts' (2003) 2 Chinese J Int'l L 77, 89–90.
16 BS Chimni, 'International Law Scholarship in Post-colonial India: Coping with Dualism' (2010) 23 LJIL 23, 44.
17 ibid 45.
18 UNFCCC secretariat, 'Local Communities and Indigenous Peoples Platform' <https://unfccc.int/LCIPP#:~:text=The%20Local%20Communities%20and%20Indigenous,a%20common%20concern%20of%20humankind> accessed 21 February 2021.
19 UNFCCC secretariat, 'Admitted NGOs' <https://unfccc.int/process-and-meetings/parties-non-party-stakeholders/non-party-stakeholders/information-by-category-of-observer/admitted-ngos#eq-2> accessed 21 February 2021.

20 Article 19, Declaration on the Trips Agreement and Public Health WT/MIN(01)/DEC/W/2, dated 14 September 2001.
21 Karen Tucker, 'Unraveling Coloniality in International Relations: Knowledge, Relationality, and Strategies for Engagement' (2018) 12 Int. Political Sociol. 215, 217.
22 Paris Agreement (n 3) Article 7(5).
23 Amy Maguire, 'Contemporary Anti-Colonial Self Determination Claims and the Decolonisation of International Law' (2013) 22 Griffith L Rev 238, 262.
24 ibid.
25 Lara Domínguez and Colin Luoma, 'Decolonising Conservation Policy: How Colonial Land and Conservation Ideologies Persist and Perpetuate Indigenous Injustices at the Expense of the Environment' (2020) 9 Land 1, 4.
26 E Tendayi Achiume, 'The Postcolonial Case for Rethinking Borders' (2019) 66 Dissent 27, 29.
27 Eve Tuck and K Wayne Yang, 'Decolonization is not a metaphor' (2012) 1 Decolonization: Indigeneity, Ed. Soc. 1, 21–22.
28 Richard Howitt, 'Decolonizing People, Place and Country: Nurturing Resilience across Time and Space' (2020) 12 Sustainability 1, 5.
29 ibid 6.
30 Mathias Fridahl, 'Historical Responsibility in the UNFCCC' Centre for Climate Science and Policy Research Report 07:01, 56 <www.researchgate.net/publication/228855588_Historical_Responsibility_in_the_UNFCCC> accessed 21 February 2021.
31 Lau Øfjord Blaxekjær and Tobias Dan Nielsen, 'Mapping the Narrative Positions of New Political Groups under the UNFCCC' (2015) 15 Climate Policy 751, 762.
32 Carola Betzold, Paula Castro and Florian Weiler, 'AOSIS in the UNFCCC Negotiations: From Unity to Fragmentation?' (2012) 12 Climate Policy 591.
33 ibid 594.
34 UNFCCC Secretariat, 'What Are Parties & Non-Party Stakeholders?' <https://unfccc.int/process/parties-non-party-stakeholders/the-big-picture/what-are-parties-non-party-stakeholders> accessed 21 February 2021.
35 Kevin Anderson, John F Broderick and Isak Stoddard, 'A Factor of Two: How the Mitigation Plans of "Climate Progressive" Nations Fall Far Short of Paris-compliant Pathways' (2020) 20 Climate Policy 1290, 1294.
36 Jason Hickel, 'Quantifying National Responsibility for Climate Breakdown: An Equality-Based Attribution Approach for Carbon Dioxide Emissions in Excess of the Planetary Boundary' (2020) 4 Lancet e399.
37 Steven J Davisa, Glen P Peters, and Ken Caldeira, 'The Supply Chain of CO2 Emissions' (2011) 108 Proc. Natl. Acad. Sci. 18554.
38 Rowena Maguire, 'The Role of Common but Differentiated Responsibility in the 2020 Climate Regime: Evolving a New Understanding of Differential Commitments (2013) 7 Carbon & Climate L Rev 260, 261.
39 Miriam Prys-Hansen, 'Differentiation as Affirmative Action: Transforming or Reinforcing Structural Inequality at the UNFCCC?' (2020) 34 Global Society 353, 356–57.
40 Raoni Rajão and Tiago Duarte, 'Performing Postcolonial Identities at the United Nations' Climate Negotiations' (2018) Postcolonial Studies 1, 5.
41 Jutta Brunnée and Charlotte Streck, 'The UNFCCC as a Negotiation Forum: Towards Common but More Differentiated Responsibilities' (2013) 13 Climate Policy 589, 590.
42 Mathias Fridahl and Björn-ola Linnér, 'Technology Obscuring Equity: Historical Responsibility in UNFCCC Negotiations' (2008) 8 Climate Policy 339, 341.
43 Derek Bell, 'Global Climate Justice, Historic Emissions, and Excusable Ignorance' (2011) 94 Monist 391, 393.
44 Paris Agreement (n 3) Article 8.
45 ibid Article 8(4)(h).
46 UNFCCC Secretariat, 'Introduction to Loss and Damage' <https://unfccc.int/topics/adaptation-and-resilience/the-big-picture/introduction-to-loss-and-damage> accessed 21 February 2021.
47 Decision 1/CP.21, FCCC/CP/2015/10/Add.1 para 48.
48 Lisa Vanhala and Cecilie Hestbaek, 'Framing Climate Change Loss and Damage in UNFCCC Negotiations' (2016) 16 Global Environmental Politics 111, 127.
49 Friederike EL Otto and others, 'Assigning Historic Responsibility for Extreme Weather Events' (2017) 7 Nature 757, 759.

50 Arthur Wyns, 'COP27 Establishes Loss and Damage Fund to Respond to Human Cost of Climate Change' 7 Lancet Planetary Health Newsdesk <https://doi.org/10.1016/S2542-5196(22)00331-X> accessed 21 April 2023.
51 ibid.
52 Olivia Serdeczny and Tabea Lissner, 'Research Agenda for the Loss and Damage Fund' 13 Nat Clim Chang 412 (2023) <https://doi.org/10.1038/s41558-023-01648-x> accessed 21 April 2023.
53 ibid.
54 ibid.
55 Decision 1/CP.21, FCCC/CP/2015/10/Add.1 para 135.
56 Decision 2/CP.23, FCCC/CP/2017/11/Add.1.
57 Decision 2/CP.24, FCCC/CP/2018/10/Add.1.
58 Fiona Harvey, 'Activists Protest at "Sidelining of Social Justice" at UN Climate Talks' *The Guardian* (12 December 2019) <www.theguardian.com/environment/2019/dec/12/activists-protest-un-climate-talks> accessed 21 February 2021.
59 Michael Neilson, 'COP 25: Māori Leader Calls Out Global Climate Change Summit for Treating Indigenous Peoples Like "Tokens"' *New Zealand Herald* (17 December 2019) <www.nzherald.co.nz/nz/cop-25-maori-leader-calls-out-global-climate-change-summit-for-treating-indigenous-peoples-like-tokens/5FMQTMF3OMC73U4IRZRUYJXC4Y/> accessed 21 February 2021.
60 Amy Maguire and Jeffrey McGee, 'A Universal Human Right to Shape Responses to a Global Problem? The Role of Self-Determination in Guiding the International Legal Response to Climate Change' (2017) 26 Rev. Eur. Community Intl. Envt'l L. 54, 55.
61 UNFCCC Secretariat, 'A Guide to the Climate Change Convention Process' (2002) <https://unfccc.int/resource/process/guideprocess-p.pdf> accessed 21 February 2021.
62 UNFCCC (n 1) Article 15.
63 Jesse Vogel, 'The Problem with Consensus in the U.N. Framework Convention on Climate Change' (2014) 32 Philo. Public Policy Q. 14.
64 ibid 19.
65 ibid 15.
66 Loretta Pyles, 'Decolonising Disaster Social Work: Environmental Justice and Community Participation' (2017) 47 Br. J. Soc. Work 630, 631.

31

ADDRESSING HUMAN MOBILITY IN INTERNATIONAL LAW ON CLIMATE CHANGE AND BEYOND

Cosmin Corendea and Chhaya Bhardwaj

Human Mobility and Migration: Definition and Scope

The last few decades have seen a rise in studies on human mobility as a study of global human migration[1] and climate change.[2] One of the earliest works by Berry is considered one of the first attempts to trace the phenomenon of human mobility by studying population on the move.[3] The forms of human mobility are becoming increasingly diverse today.[4] While the terms "mobility" and "migration" are used interchangeably and as synonyms to each other, the term "mobility" (and "mobility studies") is more holistic.[5] The studies on mobility are conducted to promote social equity and to ease out daily mobilities in human lives.[6] The term "migration" is broadly defined as "the act of moving from one place to another";[7] mobility is an important social response to difficult situations, like climate change.[8] In 2010, the United Nations Human Development Programme (UNDP) prepared a report on mobility and migration, recognizing the complexity of the use of these two terms.[9] The report states that:

> In different country contexts, however, and in different languages, the phrase "migration" can have different meanings . . . The use of other terms such as "mobility" and "movement," or more specific phrases such as "temporary" or "seasonal labour migration" may more clearly describe the form of movement under discussion.[10]

The report distinguishes various forms of movement and migration, stating that "mobility entails freedom to seek opportunities to improve living standards, while migration is a broader term".[11] In the 21st century, the line between migration and mobility has been blurred, and differ globally from a social and cultural perspective.[12] This means the categories are not definitive and will almost always overlap. The "relation between migration, return migration, tourism, transnationalism and diaspora is crucial to mobilities research".[13] Human mobility is deemed as efficient in enhancing a human income, education, health and overall human development.[14] In its sociological sense, human mobility is a tool for human development and to strengthen the foundations of living standards. The World Bank also recognizes that human mobility is a "broader trend".[15]

DOI: 10.4324/9781003276678-36

The advisory opinion by the Tribunal for the Law of the Sea, also acknowledges the IPCC sixth assessment report findings that climate change and associated hazards are "growing driver(s) of involuntary migration and displacement".[16]

People migrate internally and across borders both voluntarily and involuntarily (forcibly). People choose to migrate voluntarily and willingly based on their goals.[17] Forced or involuntary migration, on the other hand, are linked to migration due to "force, compulsion or coercion".[18]

The UNHCR reported that by the end of 2022, 108.4 million people were forcibly displaced due to conflict, violence, human rights violations and events seriously disturbing public order,[19] both across and within the borders.[20] In addition to this, the Internal Displacement Monitoring Centre reports that by the end of 2022, 71.1 million people were internally displaced people, due to conflict and disasters as major reasons, amongst others.[21]

Relationship between Climate Change and Human Mobility

Scientists are also studying forms of human mobility in the context of climate change.[22] These forms of human mobility include migration, displacement and planned relocation.[23] One of the recent studies by Boas on climate change and human mobility challenges the narrative of "climate-induced migration" and recommends pursuing it from an inquisitorial perspective rather than a submissive perspective that accepts the assumption that climate change causes mass migration.[24] The interlinkages between mobility and both slow- and sudden-onset disasters is well established.[25] Managing mobility can reduce risks arising out of disasters.[26] Climate change, sea-level rise and other disasters are predicted to displace millions of people, causing humanitarian and national security crises.[27] There are many natural and manmade environmental activities that can influence mobility of people, both directly and indirectly.[28]

Although linkages between climate change and human movement are established,[29] the absolute connection between the two is not fully materialized.[30] One reason for this disjunction is the relationship between climate change and disasters.[31] Some disasters like floods and sea-level rise[32] are "adverse effects of climate change" which drive migration, rather than climate change itself. This reasoning justifies Boas's understanding of climate mobilities.[33] McAdam recognizes human movement due to disasters and climate change and discusses displacement-related issues generally in the context of climate change and disasters together.[34] She also agrees conflict may stem from climate change and disasters causing pressure on natural resources.[35]

Factor that influence migration today, other than that of climate change, are intertwined with climate change and complexify mobility issues. Migration "may speed up when a critical climate threshold is reached", but the projections remain "highly uncertain".[36]

The Human Rights Committee (HRC), in *Teitiota v. New Zealand*,[37] concluded that climate-induced displaced peoples can be protected if their life is at imminent risk.[38] Such cases may increase as migration related to slow-onset disasters increases.[39] Other drivers of migration, like violence, may be interlaced in such cases, but will require more scientific studies to unravel the complexities.

Displacement or human mobility is also an adverse impact of climate change.[40] IPCC states that "climate change over the 21st century is projected to increase displacement of people".[41] Climate change could produce eight million refugees in the Pacific Islands, and 75 million in the Asia-Pacific region.[42] For "Small Island Developing Nations" (SIDS), climate change is already occurring,[43] such as frequent flooding and storm surges, increased food and water shortage, and individuals are experiencing loss of land and being forced from their homes.[44]

Migration may be beneficial, but it also causes tension.[45] Lambert defines climate migrants as individuals whose "movement is triggered" in a vast part "by the effects of climate change".[46] The aforementioned complexities may make this definition non-inclusive or non-comprehensive.

Under the international climate change frameworks, "human mobility" covers displacement of populations, migrations and planned relocation at local, regional and international level.[47] The United Nations Framework Convention on Climate Change (UNFCCC) explicitly specifies the "need to avert, minimize and address climate displacement",[48] while the United Nations Security Council warns of mass climate migration with the risk of aggravating conflicts.[49] The Cancun Agreement is one of the first international instruments that contemplated human mobility in the context of climate change, inviting all Parties to undertake adaptation action, including "measures to enhance understanding, coordination and cooperation related to national, regional and international climate change induced displacement, migration and planned relocation".[50] Boas's recent research challenges the usage of "climate change induced" in the legal document.[51]

UNFCCC primarily aims at protecting ecosystems and humans from the "adverse effects of climate change".[52] Article 1 states that adverse effects are "changes . . . resulting from climate change which has significant deleterious effects on . . . . human health and welfare". The climate policy is developed around this human-centric approach and is supported by states.[53] UNFCCC recognizes climate change as a key driver of migration.[54] The Paris Agreement includes elements of human movement under the umbrella of adaptation,[55] including strategies to support population, enhance resilience of communities and pan for internal or cross-border migration and consented adaptation as an adaptation strategy.[56] Additionally the Warsaw International Mechanism (WIM Excom) for Loss and Damage creates a task force to address climate change migration through its Task Force on Displacement (TFD).[57] In COP24, Parties were invited to develop laws and policies to address displacement caused by the adverse impacts of climate change, taking into consideration respective human rights of the displaced populations.[58] The Paris Agreement reflects the need to ensure protection of people's rights regarding climate migration,[59] acknowledging that Parties should respect, promote and consider their respective obligations to human rights when addressing climate change.[60] Migration associated with climate change may have negative effects on human security in destination countries.[61]

WIM Excom established the TFD to understand human mobility in the context of climate change under the Paris Agreement.[62] Its objective is "to enhance research, data collection, risk analysis and sharing of information to better map, understand and manage human mobility related to the adverse impacts of climate change" and to promote integration of human mobility into national planning.[63] The TFD asserts that human mobility in the context of climate change includes migration, displacement and planned relocation, both internal and cross-border.[64]

Several other international environmental treaties contain disaster-induced cross-border displacement or have developed ancillary frameworks to address this.[65]

A final and more nuanced complexity of human mobility in the context of climate change concerns the forms of human mobility. Human mobility encompasses forms of movement other than internal mobility and cross-border mobility,[66] including migration, displacement and planned relocation.[67] The TFD report does not take into consideration re-settlement as a form of human mobility in the context of disaster or climate change, likely because the term "resettlement" is used in the context of development-related displacement.[68] A United Nations University publication recommends considering "resettlement" as a form of migration in the context of climate change.[69]

Nationally Determined Contributions (NDCs): Meaning, Scope and Current Status

The pledges, i.e. NDCs, are voluntary pledges submitted to the UNFCCC Secretariat.[70] These binding state party commitments are distinct from non-party stakeholders and actors.[71] Under the Paris Agreement, parties are obligated to communicate their NDCs every five years.[72] The first NDCs or INDCs were submitted in 2015. Updated NDCs were due in 2020; however, due to COVID-19, many countries missed this deadline. The United States's re-entering of the Paris Agreement may positively impact climate change.[73] The US has submitted an updated and enhanced NDC, backed by domestic actions and executive orders to ensure climate justice in the wake of climate change.

NDCs were central to the global stocktaking that took place in 2023.[74] While there are guidelines like the IPCC Guidelines to report GHG inventories at the state level,[75] there is a lack of guidance on other sectors concerning climate change,[76] including migration and human rights.

In 2015–16, over 180 countries had submitted the NDCs.[77] The NDCs are reflective of the parties' geography, demographic, vulnerability to climate change and resources. Thus, it is difficult to predict the contents of an NDC.[78] Additionally, NDC contents can be changed; the rules of international treaty amendments[79] do not apply. Some NDCs include topics which may not be within the scope of the Paris Agreement or the UNFCCC. The Paris Agreement is in alignment with international human rights law,[80] but the protection of human rights is not a defined obligation. Human rights should be considered during global stocktaking.[81]

NDCs originate from the principle that the states parties "should protect the climate system for the benefit of present and future generations of human kind on the basis of equity and in accordance with their common but differentiated responsibilities [CBDR] and respective capabilities".[82] All countries have different responsibilities, due to differing contributions to emissions, and different resources to take action;[83] developed and developing countries would never agree to a common internationally binding treaty to combat climate change due to these differences.[84]

The NDCs represent self-assessment of party responsibilities, resources and capabilities, and set pathways to achieve ambitions. There are no penal actions if a state fails to achieve its goals. The NDCs are modifiable and can change with parties' circumstances.[85]

Elements of Human Mobility in NDCs

Due to the uniqueness of each NDC, it can't be ascertained, unless researched, which elements of climate action dominate the NDCs and which elements of climate actions are missing from specific NDCs. The missing elements may not even be needed by the country who submits the NDC. However, the NDCs can be analyzed not only for good stocktaking, but also to understand the sectors in which the countries are taking climate action and the sectors which remain rather excluded from the NDCs.

NDCs shed light on domestic frameworks, including legislative, executive and judicial actions concerning climate change and human mobility. In August 2018, the WIM ExCom released two reports that mapped "how climate and displacement is included in . . . National Determined Contributions (NDCs) and national communications".[86] Out of the 193 countries that submitted the (I) NDCs, 20 percent refer to human mobility.[87] Out of 18 countries who submitted new NDCs, only one – Uruguay – contains human mobility. Sri Lanka and Venezuela removed mobility from their original (I)NDCs. These reports were released in 2018 and do not encompass all the newly updated NDCs, including that of the United States.

In 2022, 36 countries updated their NDCs.[88] All 193 countries submitted at least a first NDC, and 151 parties communicated a new or updated NDC as of November 2, 2021.[89] Until August 9, 2021, only 81 countries had submitted new NDCs to the Secretariat, and six other countries have proposed new NDC Targets.[90] A large number of Asian and African countries have not updated their NDC targets or commitments under the Paris Agreement. Considering the victim status of many Asian-African countries, higher-emitting countries should lead climate action[91] to protect people from adverse impacts of climate change. A 2008 IOM report reveals state practices regarding consideration of environment and climate in their national migration legislations, policies or strategies.[92] Their survey of 66 countries revealed that 35 of the 66 surveyed countries refer to climate and environmental consideration in their national migration legislations.[93]

In relation to NDCs, the Chilean NDC is one of the few NDC that pledges to developing "guidelines on the effect of climate change in the phenomenon of human mobility in Chile . . . in line with related international instruments",[94] while also mentioning mobility along with transportation.[95] Similarly, the NDC of Grenada commits that it "will continue to build coherence with the NDC and Nap to comprehensively address loss and damage. This will include strengthening resilience to respond to impacts beyond the limits of adaptation and addressing human mobility and settlements".[96] Most other NDCs include mobility vis-à-vis transportation.[97] The NDC by Sierra Leone also states the need to develop alternatives for urban mobility by developing greener transportation systems and infrastructures.[98] The NDC by Cambodia speaks of an increase in positive mobility amongst its population due to enhanced transportation systems.[99] Cabo Verde also understands mobility within the country in the context of greener and electric transportation.[100]

The following part of this chapter assesses the inclusion of various elements of human mobility into the NDCs submitted by the state parties.

Migration in the NDCs

The Republic of Sierra Leone highlights that in its demographics, "rural migration to Freetown, during and since the civil conflict has increased pressure on urban water resources".[101] There is a "paradigm shift of increase in rural urban migration". This has disproportionately affected the resources and has increased the problems concerning waste, sanitation and drain flows.[102] Cabo Verde discusses at length the issues related to migration and emigration in the wake of climate change. Its NDC states that "sea-level rise and increased extreme climatic events will also result in loss of culturally and spiritually important landscapes and ultimately migration and displacement of coastal communities".[103] Georgia discusses eco-migrants as people who move from one place to another due to climate change.[104]

Demographic information is also highlighted in the NDC submitted by Tonga.[105] The Census data of the country shows that people residing in the outer islands have migrated to the main islands for education and other purposes.[106] It also states that the population is migrating due to sea-level rise.[107] In Saint Lucia[108] and Sri Lanka, there is a potential threat of migration of communities away from coastal areas due to sea-level rise and climate change.[109] Sri Lanka supports more research on the intersection of migration and climate change by stating that:

> Migration, permanent or seasonal, has clear interlinkages with the enhanced vulnerability of rural populations exposed to continued climate disasters. It is critical to study the phenomenon of migration to determine the extent of the problem, challenges of enhanced vulnerability for both rural and urban poor and the rights of those displaced from their homes

> and uprooted from livelihoods due to exacerbated climate changes . . . . Migration related analysis should be included in adaptation sectors.[110]

Papua New Guinea uses the term "climate-induced migration" in its NDC;[111] however, it does not define it. Rather, it states that "climate change affects patterns and rates of internal migration".[112] Indonesia has integrated human-rights in its NDC, similar to Sri Lanka, and recognizes its human rights obligation towards migrants.[113]

Displacement in the NDCs

The NDC of Fiji recognizes that it has developed "best practices and experience related to the preparation of the nationally determined contribution", which can be true if the integration of human mobility is read within the Fijian NDC.[114] Fijian Displacement Guidelines are an institutional and national development to address and govern the displacement of population due to climate change.[115] The updated NDC by Barbados states that it had taken socio-economic development programs "for displaced workers to mitigate the effects of the pandemics".[116] The Republic of Sierra Leone's population displacement is one of the adverse impacts of climate change.[117] The Cabo Verde's NDC also recognizes that due to climate risk and sea level rise, there will be loss of territory and biodiversity, which can lead to displacement of communities.[118] It explicitly states that by 2030, it pledges to implement the National Strategy for Disaster Risk Reduction, which will aim to:

> Expand livelihood protection policies that assist vulnerable, low-income individuals to recover from damages associated with extreme weather events; provide support and protection for internally displaced persons, persons displaced across borders and host communities.[119]

As a lower-middle-income country, Cabo Verde has voluntarily pledged to undertake protection framework for both internally and cross-border displaced persons in the wake of extreme weather events. This is a good practice that should be integrated by other countries submitting their voluntary pledges. Somalia also recognizes its specific demographic-related displacement:

> Climate change-related droughts, intermittent floods and desert locust infestation results in loss of livestock and agricultural production which account for more than 70% of GDP while employing millions directly and indirectly. The destruction of local communities' main livelihood bases continues to increase the number of internally displaced persons and resultant humanitarian crises. Furthermore, climate change and variability impacts and conflicts are interlinked in Somalia and affects the affect the most vulnerable (particularly women and children) and resource-dependent communities.[120]

The Somalian NDC's impact of displacement of communities is also founded in the widely accepted fact that low-income countries like Somalia make low contributions to greenhouse gas emissions and anthropocentric climate change; however, the impacts on these countries are disproportionately high. Liberia has committed to an adaptation action and policy measure to "develop climate health hazards risk mapping and area-based scenarios planning to responding to climate health hazards . . . e.g . . . forced migration".[121] Malawi reports in its NDC that due to extreme weather events like flooding and cyclones, hundreds of thousands of people have been displaced.[122]

Similarly, Georgia recognizes the impacts of extreme weather events on its population and uses the term "eco-migrants" for those who are displaced as a result of disaster cause by climate change or those "who are threatened to be eco-migrated due to the climate change".[123] It is committed "to identify the most vulnerable populated areas in the country with a threat of displacement due to climate change".[124] Sri Lanka also accepts that it is important to understand the rights of the persons displaced due to climate change.[125] A similar echo is resounded by the NDC of Saint Lucia.[126]

Relocation or Planned Relocation of the NDCs

The inclusion of relocation measures is not popular as NDC content. It may also be because not all countries are equally witnessing the impacts of climate change, and those countries at the forefront of vulnerability due to climate change are proactive in including relocation as a commitment under the NDCs. Due to this, the Fijian NDC recognizes its own NDC as one of the best practices. The Fijian NDC, through its planned relocation example, puts a practice before the world under which "partial and complete relocation of six climate vulnerable communities" has been successfully completed.[127] This means that six communities or indigenous groups that were facing existential crisis due to sea-level rise and climate change are moved to safer locations and their vulnerabilities have been reduced. Due to rising sea-levels, the population that lived in outer islands in Tonga "may have to relocate close[d] to the centre of the islands".[128]

Other countries that have attempted to commit to relocation through their NDC include Cuba. It "states the need to prioritize vulnerable zones . . . stating measures for the coastal protection of cities, the relocation of human settlements . . . Amongst others".[129] Georgia is another country that has expressed its interest and invited "international partners to work together on the development of protection programmes for children and their families, who are forced to relocate as a result of natural disasters or crisis induced by climate change".[130]

Papua New Guinea discusses rehabilitation and relocation projects for people in case of coastal flooding and sea-level rise and climate-induced migration.[131] The Solomon Islands mention "relocation of communities in low-lying and artificial islands";[132] however, it also says that relocation should be used as a last resort.[133] It is committed to "develop a community/human relocation guidelines and assessment tools, build capacity and implement relocation of communities as an adaptation action where and when necessary".[134]

Vietnam is another country that recognizes that its population is at a high risk and therefore mentions "formulating plans to relocate and resettle residents in areas frequently hit by floods and typhoons and areas prone to flash floods and landslides".[135] It discusses "relocating and resettling residential areas in places frequently affected by natural disaster; developing and constructing typhoon and flood resistant housing".[136] It also highlights that "for areas that cannot yet be relocated, the completion of 100% of the installation of monitoring and warning systems for floods, flash floods and landslides; ensuring that 100% critical high-risk areas have the systems for monitoring and controlling natural disaster risks".[137] Such a relocation planning is necessary for a flood-risk country like Vietnam, which loses life and property due to ongoing floods and other extreme weather events.

Other Intersections of Human Mobility in the NDCs

The NDC of Papua New Guinea uses the term "resettlement" of the "climate-induced migrants".[138] While this not a commonly used term in the context of climate change-related migration or displacement, it can be used synonymously with relocation when reading the NDC.[139] Additionally, many countries may not have specifically included the elements of human mobility – migration, relocation and displacement in their NDCs; some have mentioned disaster risk reduction national frameworks. For example, Korea has updated its new NDC by mentioning that it has integrated Disaster Risk Reduction Strategy 2019–2030.[140] Cambodia also contains a domestic law called the National Action Plan for Disaster Risk Reduction 2019–2023.[141] The Cuban government has pledged that it will maintain territorial and urban restructuring through its projects on coastal zones and hazard and vulnerability risk assessment under its disaster plans.[142] Other countries include Bhutan,[143] Bangladesh,[144] and Vanuatu[145].

Future Prospects for Human Mobility under the Paris Agreement

In 2010, Jane McAdam argued that climate change-related movement may present unique considerations and challenges.[146] Amongst the challenges, including conceptual challenges and definitional challenges,[147] were the challenges for protection frameworks for these displaced persons.[148] Today, 12% of Pacific countries, 15% of Asian countries, 35% of Central and South American countries and 23% of African countries address human mobility in their 2020/21 NDCs by region.[149] The development in both regional and national frameworks that govern climate change-related migration or displacement or relocation has increased significantly.

The WIM ExCom report identifies good practices by countries who have included the elements of human mobility in their NDCs; however, it also underscores that such cases are still limited.[150] It first highlights Togo and Colombia, who have elements of human elements in their NDC, National Adaptation Plans and National Communications.[151] The consistent inclusion of human mobility matters throughout their submissions to the UNFCCC Secretariat shows a good example of policy coherence at the national and international level. Secondly, the reports commend countries who have included climate change as a separate and distinctly identifiable section in their national domestic policies.[152] These nationally included laws or actions do not form part of the NDCs of all the countries. For example, Vanuatu has a strong national policy to protect people displaced due to climate change.[153] This policy, however, is not reflected in the updated NDC of Vanuatu.

It is important to include human mobility in the NDCs as a necessary step to reduce any potential negative impacts on people displaced or forced to migrate due to climate change.[154] Although countries are not legally under an obligation to fulfil all their voluntary pledges under the NDCs, an inclusion of variety of elements can be of co-benefit to the countries. Currently, "the implementation hinges on a variety of factors: degree of economic, social and human development within a country, reliance on internal and external funding, geographical location, stability and reliability of the governance, and natural resources endowment".[155] Moreover, inclusion of human mobility in the NDCs will be the adoption of a people-centred approach to adaptation and migration, which is considered crucial for successful climate action.[156]

The recognition through the NDC that people are at threat of migration or displacement due to climate change and extreme weather events may also likely push action, funding and support. There may be different terminologies used at the domestic or NDC levels for post-disaster relief and may include terms like rehabilitation, reconstruction, relocation, resettlement; a disaster response to protect people requires human, technical and financial capacity.[157] Currently, relocation is taking place in the absence of resources, public transportation and resources.[158] A Planned Relocation is seen as positive when people move spontaneously from rural to urban areas.[159] It is considered a good adaptive strategy, particularly in the context of rising sea levels.[160] In Fiji, the planned relocation of communities living in areas at risk of climate change and extreme weather events is currently applied by some states as a measure to avoid displacement. In Vanuatu, relocation processes are included as post-disaster measures.[161]

The Pacific region's historical experience with planned relocation processes also highlighted specific challenges and protection concerns linked to complex customary land tenure systems and cultural ties. The participants concluded that the relocation of communities requires an extensive and inclusive planning process to ensure adequate levels of consultation and participation take place with both the relocated and receiving communities. These can serve as good practices and allow other countries to develop policy models that can work in their countries.

Further, Vietnam's approach to include human mobility in its NDC reminds us that it is not possible to relocate all the people vulnerable to climate-induced displacement and migration; therefore, warning systems should be installed for their protection. Uganda recognizes that the country faces crisis-induced mass migration, in which large numbers of people are forced to leave their homes to seek alternative means of survival.[162] Uganda has included early warning for disasters and hazard trend analysis in its national adaptation policy[163] and a vulnerability assessment to protect people. Early Warning Systems prepare governments for relief of forced migrants or preventing forced migrations by reducing impelling causes.[164]

In conclusion, it is fair to state that NDCs do not carry a legally binding obligation for human mobility; however, the voluntary pledges may be discussed at the international level to track the progress of climate action within each country, take stock, and perhaps rank countries on the basis of their performance. These performances can then be used to ratchet up each country's action and commitment to climate action and protection of people on the move due to climate change.

Notes

1 Spyridon Spyratos and others, 'Quantifying International Human Mobility Patterns Using Facebook Network Data' (2019) 14(10) PLoS ONE e0224134 <https://doi.org/10.1371/journal.pone.0224134>; Valeria Bello, 'The Spiralling of the Securitisation of Migration in the EU: From the Management of a 'Crisis' to a Governance of Human Mobility?' (2022) 48(6) Journal of Ethnic and Migration Studies 1327–44; Stephen Castles, 'Social Transformation and Human Mobility: Reflections on the Past, Present and Future of Migration' (2018) 39(2) Journal of Intercultural Studies 238–51.

2 Caroline Zickgraf, 'Climate Change, Slow Onset Events and Human Mobility: Reviewing the Evidence' (2021) 50 Current Opinion in Environmental Sustainability 21–30; Lisa Thalheimer, 'Compound Impacts of Extreme Weather Events and COVID-19 on Climate Mobilities' (2023) 55(1) Area 134.

3 Josefina Dominguez-Mujica, *Global Change and Human Mobility* (Springer 2016) 3.

4 Armando Montanari, 'Human Mobility, Global Change and Local Development, Contribution to the Italian PRIN 2002, Research Programme on "Tourism and Development: Local Peculiarity and Territorial Competitivity"' (2005) Human Mobility in a Globalising World 1–2 <https://doi.org/10.4000/belgeo.12391>

5 Sandra Ponzanesi, 'Migration and Mobility in a Digital Age: (Re)Mapping Connectivity and Belonging' 2019 (20) Television and New Media 547–57. <https://journals.sagepub.com/doi/full/10.1177/1527476419857687>

6 ibid.

7 Karen Fog Olwig and Kirsten Hastrup, *Climate Change and Human Mobility: Challenges to the Social Sciences* (CUP 2012) 8.

8 ibid 15

9 Human Development Report Office, A Guidance Note for Human Development Report Teams, 'Mobility and Migration', UNDP, 2010 <http://hdr.undp.org/sites/default/files/nhdr_migration_gn.pdf>

10 ibid.

11 ibid.

12 Sasha Brown, 'Migration and Mobilities' (2020) 21 Social & Cultural Geography 1168–73 <https://doi.org/10.1080/14649365.2019.1667019>

13 Kevin Hannam, Mimi Sheller and John Urry, 'Editorial: Mobilities, Immobilities and Moorings' (2006) 2 Mobilities 1–22. https://www.tandfonline.com/doi/full/10.1080/17450100500489189?src=recsys
14 Human Development Report 2009, 'Overcoming Barriers: Human Mobility and Development', UNDP (2009) <http://hdr.undp.org/sites/default/files/reports/269/hdr_2009_en_complete.pdf> page 1.
15 See Forcibly Displaced: Toward a development approach supporting refugees, the internally displaced, and their hosts, World Bank, 2017 page.
16 *Request for an Advisory Opinion submitted by the Commission of Small Island States on Climate Change and International Law (No 31)* (Advisory Opinion of 21 May 2024) ITLOS Reports 2024, para 66.
17 Valeria Ottonelli and Tiziana Torresi, 'When Is Migration Voluntary' (2013) 47 INT'l MIGRATION REV. 783.
18 IOM, 'International Migration Law, Glossary on Migration' (2019) <https://publications.iom.int/system/files/pdf/iml_34_glossary.pdf>
19 UNHCR, 'Global Trends Report 2022' <https://www.unhcr.org/sites/default/files/2023-06/global-trends-report-2022.pdf>
20 ibid.
21 Internal Displacement Monitoring Center Report, GRID 2023 <https://www.internal-displacement.org/global-report/grid2023/>
22 Koko Warner and others, *Changing Climate, Moving People: Framing Migration, Displacement and Planned Relocation* (UNU-EHS 2013).
23 ibid.
24 See Ingrid Boas and others, 'Climate Migration Myths' (2019) 9 Nature Climate Change 901–3 <https://doi.org/10.1038/s41558-019-0633-3> for her discussion on migration/mobility terminologies.
25 'Human Mobility: Shaping Vulnerability and Resilience to Disasters', Background paper to the HFA2 Dialogue, IOM <https://www.iom.int/sites/default/files/migrated_files/What-We-Do/docs/background-paper-for-HFA2-light.pdf>
26 ibid.
27 Patrick Barnard and others, 'Dynamic Flood Modelling Essential to Assess the Coastal Impacts of Climate Change' (2019) 9(1) Scientific Reports <https://doi.org/10.1038/s41598-019-40742-z>
28 Etienne Piguet, Antoine Percoud and Paul de Gouchteneire (eds), *Migration and Climate Change* (CUP 2011).
29 Camila Bustos and others, 'Shelter from the Storm: Policy Options to Address Climate Induced Migration from the Northern Triangle', Harvard Immigration and Refugee Clinical Program, HLS Immigration Project, the University Network for Human Rights, Yale Immigrant Justice Project, and Yale Environmental Law Association, April 2021; E Piguet, 'Climate Change and Forced Migration. New Issues in Refugee Research', Research Paper No. 153 (UNHCR 2008); O Brown, *Migration and Climate Change* (International Organization for Migration 2008); C Raleigh, L Jordan and I Salehyan, *Assessing the Impact of Climate Change on Migration and Conflict* (The World Bank, The Social Development Department n.d.); K Rigaud and others, *Groundswell: Preparing for Internal Climate Migration* (The World Bank 2018) <https://openknowledge.worldbank.org/handle/10986/29461>; Bradshaw (2014) in, K Rigaud and others, *Groundswell: Preparing for Internal Climate Migration* (The World Bank 2018) <https://openknowledge.worldbank.org/handle/10986/29461>;
30 In Daniel Billy et. al. v. Australia, 2022, the Human Rights Committee acknowledged linkages between climate change and migration, but left gaps in the jurisprudence concerning right to life.
Chhaya Bhardwaj, 'Adaptation and Human Rights: A Decision by the Human Rights Committee Daniel Billy et al. v. Australia CCPR/C/135/D/3624/2019' (2023) 25(2) Environmental Law Review 154–61.
31 Elizabeth Ferris, 'Displacements, Natural Disasters and Human Rights' (*Brookings* 2008) <https://www.brookings.edu/on-the-record/displacement-natural-disasters-and-human-rights/> accessed 5 July 2021.
32 Bhardwaj (n 29) 154–61; Chhaya Bhardwaj, 'Ioane Teitiota v New Zealand (advance unedited version), CCPR/C/127/D/2728/2016, UN Human Rights Committee (HRC), 7 January 2020' (2021) 23(3) Environmental Law Review 263–71.
33 ibid.
34 Jane McAdam, 'From the Nansen Initiative to the Platform on Disaster Displacement: Shaping International Approaches to Climate Change, Disasters and Displacement' (2016) 39(4) The University of New South Wales Law Journal 1518–46; Guy S Goodwin-Gill and Jane McAdam, *UNHCR and Climate Change, Disasters and Displacement* (The United Nations Refugee Agency (UNHCR) 2017); Jane McAdam, 'Displacement in the Context of Climate Change and Disasters' (IFRC, 2021).

35 Jane McAdam, 'From the Nansen Initiative to the Platform on Disaster Displacement: Shaping International Approaches to Climate Change' (2016) 39 U.N.S.W.L.J. 1518.

36 Chi Xu and others, 'Future of the Human Climate Niche' (2020) 117 Proceedings of the National Academy of Sciences of the United States of America 11350–55 <https://www.pnas.org/content/117/21/11350>

37 Ioane Teitiota v. New Zealand (advance unedited version), CCPR/C/127/D/2728/2016, UN Human Rights Committee (HRC) (7 January 2020) <https://www.refworld.org/cases,HRC,5e26f7134.html>

38 See Teitiota's decision, esp para 2.9, 9.2, 4.6 for a discussion of the case.

39 Barbara K Bodine, Foreword, *New Challenges to Human Security: Environmental Change and Human Mobility* (Institute for the Study of Diplomacy 2017).

40 https://www.ipcc.ch/report/ar6/wg1/downloads/report/IPCC_AR6_WGI_Chapter_12.pdf

41 Page 778, WN Adger and others, '2014: Human Security' in CB Field and others (eds), *Climate Change 2014: Impacts, Adaptation, and Vulnerability. Part A: Global and Sectoral Aspects. Contribution of Working Group II to the Fifth Assessment Report of the Intergovernmental Panel on Climate Change* (CUP 2014) 755–91 <https://www.ipcc.ch/site/assets/uploads/2018/02/WGIIAR5-Chap12_FINAL.pdf>; Page 20, IPCC, '2014: Summary for Policymakers' in CB Field and others (eds), *Climate Change 2014: Impacts, Adaptation, and Vulnerability. Part A: Global and Sectoral Aspects. Contribution of Working Group II to the Fifth Assessment Report of the Intergovernmental Panel on Climate Change* (CUP 2014) 1–32 <https://www.ipcc.ch/site/assets/uploads/2018/02/ar5_wgII_spm_en.pdf>

42 Climate Change: 75 Million Environmental Refugees to Plague Asia-Pacific (August 2005) <http://www.ipsnews.net/2009/08/climate-change-75-million-environmental-refugees-to-plague-asia-pacific/>

43 United Nations Development Programme (UNDP), 'Small Island Nations at the Frontline of Climate Action' (18 September 2017) <https://www.undp.org/content/undp/en/home/presscenter/pressreleases/2017/09/18/small-island-nations-at-the-frontline-of-climate-action-.html>

44 World Health Organization, Regional Office for Europe, 'Floods in the WHO European Region: Health Effects and Their Prevention' (2013) <http://www.euro.who.int/__data/assets/pdf_file/0020/189020/e96853.pdf>

45 Xu and others (n 35)11350–55

46 Kristen Lambert, 'The Paris Agreement: Spotlight on Climate Migrants', YALE: FORESTRY ENVTL. BLOG (29 December 2015) <https://environment.yale.edulblog/2015/12/the-paris-agreement-spotlighton-climate-migrants/> at 2110

47 Paragraph 14(f) of the Cancun Decision 1/CP.16 and Doha decision 3/CP.18 paragraph 7 (a) (vi) https://environmentalmigration.iom.int/sites/environmentalmigration/files/Research%20Database/Paris_COP21-Human_Mobility-AdvisoryGroup.pdf

48 Nash, S.L. Global Policy 9, 53–63 (2018)

49 Boas, I. Climate Migration and Security. Securitisation as a Strategy in Climate Change Politics (Routledge 2015).

50 UNFCCC, Report of the Conference of the Parties on its sixteenth session, held in Cancun from 19 November to 10 December 2010, FCCC/CP/2010/7/Add.1. <https://unfccc.int/resource/docs/2010/cop16/eng/07a01.pdf>

51 ibid.

52 UNFCCC, Preamble.

53 Andrea Schapper, 'Climate Justice and Human Rights' (2018) 32(3) International Relations 275–95.

54 UNFCCC, Climate Change is a Key Driver of Migration and Food Security, 16 October 2017 <https://unfccc.int/news/climate-change-is-a-key-driver-of-migration-and-food-insecurity>; Human Rights, 'Climate Change and Cross-border Displacement: The Role of the International Human Rights Community in Contributing to Effective and Just Solutions', Policy Report (Universal Rights Group 2015) <https://unfccc.int/files/adaptation/groups_committees/loss_and_damage_executive_committee/application/pdf/cc_hr_displacement_urg.pdf>

55 Sharaban Tahura Zaman, 'Legal Protection for the Cross-Border Climate-Induced Population Movement in South Asia: Exploring a Durable Solution' (2021) 36 J. ENVTL. L. & LITIG. 187.

56 Paris Agreement Article 8; Koko Warner, Human Mobility and the Paris Agreement: Contribution of climate policy to the global compact for safe, orderly and regular migration. Input to the UN Secretary-General's report on the global compact for safe, orderly and regular migration, in response to Note Verbale of 21 July 2017, requesting inputs to the Secretary-General's report on the global compact for safe, orderly and regular migration. 19 September 2019. Bonn.

57 Paris Agreement, Conf. of the Parties on Its Twenty-First Session, at Preamble, U.N. Doc. FCCC/CP/2015/10/Add.1 (2016); WARSAW INTERNATIONAL MECHANISM (W1M) TASK FORCE

ON DISPLACEMENT (TFD), Moving FORWARD TOGETHER: AVERTING, MINIMIZING AND ADDRESSING DISPLACEMENT: THE SECOND PHASE OF THE TASK FORCE ON DISPLACEMENT 2 (3 December 2019) <https://unfccc.int/sites/default/files/resource/28112019%20 Concept%2ONote%20 and%20Programme%20TFD%20Side%2OEvent%20%28FINAL%20 DRAFT%29%20upd ated.pdf>

58 Framework Convention on Climate Change, Report of the Conference of the Parties on Its Twenty-Fourth Session, U.N. Doc. FCCC/CP/2018/10/Add.1, at 43 (Mar. 19, 2019).

59 Cosmin Corendea, Migration and Human Rights in the Wake of Climate Change: A policy perspective over the Pacific, UNU-EHS Publication Series Policy Report 2017 No. 2 <https://collections.unu.edu/eserv/UNU:6305/PolicyReport_No2_171113_online_revised_meta.pdf>

60 Paris COP Decision & Paris Agreement, U.N. Doc. FCCC/CP/2015/L.9/REV.1 (12 Dec. 2015). Preamble

61 National security implications of climate-related risks and a changing climate. RefID: 8–6475571 DoD. United States Department of Defense (2015) <https://archive.defense.gov/pubs/150724-congressional-report-on-national-implications-of-climate-change.pdf>

62 UNFCCC, 'Report of the Executive Committee of the Warsaw International Mechanism for Loss and Damage associated with Climate Change Impacts', Decision-/CP.24

63 ibid 5.

64 ibid 4.

65 See e.g. United Nations Convention to Combat Desertification, Migration, and desertification, UNCCD thematic fact sheet series No. 3 http://catalogue.unccd.int/22_loose_leaf_Desertification_migration.pdf; see also United Nations Disaster Risk Reduction, 'Sendai Framework for Disaster Risk Reduction 2015–2030', 2015 <https://www.preventionweb.net/files/43291_sendaiframeworkfordrren.pdf> (Sendai Framework) para 33.

66 The WARSAW International Mechanism for Loss and Damage Associate with Climate Change Impacts, 'Summary Report of Outputs of Activity I.1: Mapping Human Mobility and Climate Change in Relevant National Policies and Institutional Frameworks, Task Force on Displacement, First Phase of Implementation' (June 2017–April 2019) <https://unfccc.int/sites/default/files/resource/TFD%20Output%20 acitivity%20I.1.pdf>

67 ibid.

68 Migration, Displacement and Planned Relocation, United Nations High Commissioner for Refugees, 31 December 2012. This articles originally appeared in Spanish in Migracion Humana u cambio Climatico, published by Fundacion BBVA Bancomer, Mexico, 2012.

69 Koko Warner and others, 'Changing Climate, Moving People: Framing Migration, Displacement and Planned Relocation, Policy Brief', UNU-EHS Publication Series, No. 8 June 2013.

70 Anders Corr, 'Expect Climate Catastrophe: Paris Agreement Lacks Enforcement' FORBES: OPINION (1 December 2016, 10:34 PM), https://www.forbes.com/sites/anderscorr/20 16/12/0 1/expect-climate-catastrophe-paris-agreement-lacksenforcement/#24a540233130.

71 Daniel Klein and others, *The Paris Agreement on Climate Change: Analysis and Commentary* (OUP 2017) 48.

72 Paris Agreement Article 4.9

73 Dan Bodansky, 'Climate Change: Reversing the Past and Advancing the Future' (2020) 115 AJIL Unbound 80–85 <https://doi.org/10.1017/aju.2020.89>; Mark Elder, *Optimistic for US Climate Policy in the Biden Administration* (Institute for Global Environmental Strategies 2021).

74 H van Asselt and others, 'Leveraging the Global Stocktake for Effective Sectoral Climate Governance' (2023) 2(6) PLOS Clim e0000229 <https://doi.org/10.1371/journal.pclm.0000229>

75 The *2019 Refinement to the 2006 IPCC Guidelines for National Greenhouse Gas Inventories* was adopted and accepted during the 49th Session of the IPCC in May 2019. Available at: https://www.ipcc.ch/report/2019-refinement-to-the-2006-ipcc-guidelines-for-national-greenhouse-gas-inventories/

76 van Asselt and others (n 74).

77 Klein and others (n 70) 93.

78 ibid.

79 Vienna Convention on the Law of the Treaties, Article 39–41.

80 John Knox, 'The Paris Agreement as a Human Rights Treaty' in Dapo Akande and others (eds), *Human Rights and 21st Century Challenges: Poverty, Conflict, and the Environment* (online edn, Oxford Academic, 23 April 2020) <https://doi.org/10.1093/oso/9780198824770.003.0016> accessed 11 July 2023.

81 Summary report following the second meeting of the technical dialogue of the first global stocktake under the Paris Agreement, Report by the co-facilitators of the technical dialogue, UNFCCC, GST.TD.2023. SummaryReport2, 31 March, 2023; Summary report on the first meeting of the technical dialogue of the first global stocktake under the Paris Agreement, Report by the Co-facilitators of the technical dialogue, UNFCCC, GST.TD.2022.SummaryReport.1, 10 October 2022;
82 UNFCCC Article 3.1; see also Benoit Mayer, 'International Law Obligations Arising in Relation to Nationally Determined Contributions' (2018) 7 TEL 253; Stellina Jolly and Abhishek Trivedi, 'Principle of CBDRRC: Its Interpretation and Implementation Through NDCS in the Context of Sustainable Development' (2020) 11 Wash. J. Env't L. & Pol'y 309; Christina Voigt and Felipe Ferreira, '"Dynamic Differentiation": The Principles of CBDRRC, Progression and Highest Possible Ambition in the Paris Agreement' (2016) 5(2) Transnational Environmental Law 285–303.
83 Lavanya Rajamani, 'The Principle of Common but Differentiated Responsibility and the Balance of Commitments under the Climate Regime' (2000) 9 Rev Eur Comp & Int'l Envtl L 120
84 ibid.
85 For an example of how COVID affected NDCs, see Arthur Wyns, 'From Pandemic to Paris: The Inclusion of COVID-19 Response in National Climate Commitments' (2021) 5 The Lancet Planetary Health.
86 Implementation of the Workplan of the Task Force on Displacement under the Warsaw International Mechanism for Loss and Damage (WIM), United Nations Framework on Climate Change (UNFCCC), Pillar II: Policy- International/Regional Activity II.2. 'Mapping Human Mobility (Migration, Displacement and Planned Relocation) and Climate Change in International Processes, Policies and Legal Frameworks,' International Organization for Migration (IOM), Analysis Report, August 2018; Implementation of the Workplan of the Task Force on Displacement under the Warsaw International Mechanism for Loss and Damage, United Nations Framework Convention on Climate Change (UNFCCC), Pillar I: Policy/Practice – National/Subnational Activity I.1: Mapping Human Mobility and Climate Change in Relevant National Policies and Institutional Frameworks, IOM, Analysis Report, August 2018, 3 <https://unfccc.int/sites/default/files/resource/20180917%20WIM%20TFD%20I.1%20Output%20final.pdf>
87 Pillar I report, ibid.
88 Climate Action Tracker, 'Climate Targets, NDC Updates since 2022' <https://climateactiontracker.org/climate-target-update-tracker-2022/>
89 Climate Actions, 'All About the NDCs, the UN' <https://www.un.org/en/climatechange/all-about-ndcs#:~:text=So%20far%2C%20all%20193%20Parties,some%20cases%2C%20insufficient%20political%20commitment>
90 Pillar I Report, ibid.
91 Bayes Ahmed, 'Who Takes Responsibility for the Climate Refugees?' (2018) International Journal of Climate Change Strategies and Management 10.
92 Implementation of the Workplan of the Task Force on Displacement under the Warsaw International Mechanism for Loss and Damage, UNFCCC, Mapping Human Mobility and Climate Change in Relevant National Policies and Institutional Frameworks, IOM-Analysis Report, August 2008 <https://unfccc.int/sites/default/files/resource/WIM%20TFD%20I.1%20Output.pdf> (IOM Analysis Report).
93 IOM Analysis Report, Page 3.
94 NDC by Chile, UNFCCC, 2020, page 44.
95 ibid, page 92.
96 NDC by Grenada, UNFCCC, 30 November 2020, page 9.
97 NDC by the Barbados, UNFCCC, 2021.
98 NDC by the Republic of Sierra Leone, July 2021, page xi.
99 NDC by the Kingdom of Cambodia, UNFCCC, 2020, page 124.
100 NDC by Cabo Verde, UNFCCC, February 2021, page 6.
101 NDC by the Republic of Sierra Leone, July 2021.
102 ibid.
103 NDC by Cabo Verde, UNFCCC, February 2021, page 32.
104 NDC by Georgia, UNFCCC, page 11.
105 NDC by the Kingdom of Tonga, UNFCCC, 2020, page 3.
106 ibid.
107 ibid, page 27.
108 NDC by Saint Lucia, UNFCC, page 6.

109 NDC by Sri Lanka, UNFCCC, July 2021, page 41.
110 NDC by Sri Lanka, UNFCCC, July 2021, page 28.
111 NDC by Papua New Guinea, UNFCCC, 2021, page 22.
112 ibid.
113 NDC by Republic of Indonesia, UNFCCC, 2021, page 2.
114 NDC by Republic of Fiji, UNFCCC, 2020, page 9.
115 ibid.
116 NDC by the Barbados, UNFCCC, 2021.
117 NDC by the Republic of Sierra Leone, July 2021
118 NDC by Cabo Verde, UNFCCC, February 2021, page 42.
119 ibid, page 43.
120 NDC by the Federal Republic of Somalia, UNFCCC, July 2021, page 1.
121 NDC by the Republic of Liberia, UNFCCC, July 2021, page 36.
122 NDC by the Republic of Malawi, UNFCCC, July 2021, page VII.
123 NDC by Georgia, UNFCCC, page 11.
124 ibid, page 19.
125 NDC by Sri Lanka, UNFCC, 2020, page 28.
126 NDC by Saint Lucia, UNFCC, page 6.
127 NDC by the Republic of Fiji, UNFCCC, 2020, page 16.
128 NDC by the Kingdom of Tonga, UNFCCC, 2020, page 31
129 NDC by the Republic of Cuba, UNFCCC, page 5.
130 NDC by Georgia, UNFCCC, page 19.
131 NDC by Papua New Guinea, UNFCCC, 2021, page 24–25.
132 NDC by Solomon Islands, UNFCCC, 2021, Foreword.
133 ibid, page 17.
134 ibid, page 19.
135 NDC by Vietnam, UNFCCC, 2020, page 18.
136 ibid, page 21.
137 ibid, page 38.
138 NDC by Papua New Guinea, UNFCCC, 2021, page 49.
139 ibid, page 24.
140 NDC by the Democratic People's Republic of Korea, UNFCCC, New York, 19 September 2019.
141 NDC by the Kingdom of Cambodia, UNFCCC, 2020, page 133.
142 NDC by the Republic of Cuba, UNFCCC, page 11.
143 NDC by Kingdom of Bhutan, UNFCCC, 2020.
144 NDC by Republic of Bangladesh, UNFCCC, 2020.
145 NDC by Republic of Vanuatu, UNFCCC, 2020.
146 Jane McAdam, *Climate Change and Displacement: Multidisciplinary Perspectives* (Bloomsbury Publishing 2010).
147 ibid 6.
148 ibid 90.
149 Human Mobility in the Context of Climate Change, *Briefing Note Human Mobility in Nationally Determined Contributions* (SLYCAN Trust June 2021).
150 Pillar I: Report, page 3.
151 ibid, page 13.
152 ibid, page 8.
153 Government of Vanuatu, 'Draft National Policy on Climate Change and Disaster-Induced Displacement: Towards a Durable Solution for People Displaced by Climate Change and Disasters in Vanuatu 2017' (2018) <www.environmentalmigration.iom.int/vanuatu-draftnational-policy-climate-change-and-disaster-induced-displacement-2017>.
154 Liain Yamamoyo and others, 'Human Mobility in the Context of Climate Change and Disasters: A South American Approach' (2019) 10 International Journal of Climate Change Strategies and Management 66–85.
155 Farrukh Khan, 'NDC Score Card: Measuring the Nationally Determined Contributions (NDCs) under the Paris Agreement', M-RCBG Associate Working Paper Series No. 123 (May 2019).

156 Koko Warner and others, 'Integrating Human Mobility Issues within National Adaptation Plans', UNU-EHS Publication Series, Policy Brief No. 9 (June 2014).
157 Environmental Performance Review, Third Review, Georgia, 2016.
158 Alice R Thomas, 'Post-disaster Resettlement in the Philippines: A Risky Strategy' (May 2015) 49 FMR <https://www.fmreview.org/climatechange-disasters/thomas>
159 Warner and others (n 159).
160 Koko Warner and others, 'National Adaptation Plans and Human Mobility' (May 2015) 49 FMR <https://www.fmreview.org/climatechange-disasters/warner-kaelin-martin-nassef>
161 Government of Vanuatu (n 156).
162 The Republic of Uganda, *The National Policy for Disaster Preparedness and Management, Directorate of Relief* (Disaster Preparedness and Refugee Office of the Prime Minister October 2010) <https://www.ifrc.org/docs/IDRL/Disaster%20Policy%20for%20Uganda.pdf>
163 ibid.
164 Leon Gordenker, 'Early Warning of Forced Migration' (1984) 7 In Defense of the Alien 68–77 <http://www.jstor.org/stable/23141142> accessed 29 July 2021.

32

ADVANCING THE LEGAL RESEARCH, CAPACITY AND AWARENESS FOR CLIMATE LAW AND GOVERNANCE

Marie-Claire Cordonier Segger, Christina Voigt and Tejas Rao

Introduction

As preceding chapters have shown, climate change presents a multifaceted crisis with significant economic, environmental, and social challenges. The costs are staggering, with one estimate alone suggesting that the world faces over $300 billion in damages from weather and climate disasters per annum.[1] These costs reflect not only immediate damages but also long-term economic disruptions across various sectors. The World Health Organization (WHO) underscores that climate change exacerbates health inequalities, with vulnerable populations in low-income countries facing the greatest health risks from climate-related events.[2] Moreover, climate change is expected to displace millions, with the Internal Displacement Monitoring Centre (IDMC) reporting over 30 million displacements due to climate-related disasters in 2020 alone, highlighting the urgent need for climate resilience and adaptation strategies.[3] This is the imperative for comprehensive and urgent action to mitigate climate change and adapt to its unavoidable impacts, and it is against this background that contributors to this Handbook have undertaken their work.

This concluding chapter seeks to encapsulate the insights, legal innovations, and forward-thinking analyses presented across its diverse chapters, while presenting an invitation to climate law and governance considering significant capacity chasms. The Handbook not only identifies the multifaceted challenges posed by climate change, some of which have been discussed, but also highlights the pivotal role of legal and governance frameworks in addressing this global crisis. Through a detailed exploration of the intersections between climate law, international agreements, and sustainable development goals, the Handbook has provided a comprehensive roadmap for enhancing global climate ambition and ensuring a resilient future. It has examined the full spectrum of Nationally Determined Contributions (NDCs), presenting a systematic account of recent legal and institutional innovations. These innovations are pivotal for the implementation of the Paris Agreement and the achievement of the global Sustainable Development Goals (SDGs), focusing on raising ambition through law and policy, reforming national legal frameworks, and fostering effective international law and governance mechanisms.

The thematic structure of the Handbook – Challenges, Courage, Contributions, and Compliance – has aimed to provide a coherent framework for understanding the complexities of climate

DOI: 10.4324/9781003276678-37

law and governance. It has addressed the foundational context of international law and policy, courageous developments in law and governance, significant legal and institutional reforms at the domestic level, and the crucial next steps in developing the compliance regime of the Paris Agreement. Through chapters that span from the urgency of global response and the significance of climate change courage, contributions, and compliance, to operationalizing the Paris Agreement and exploring innovative financial mechanisms for climate action, the Handbook has offered a holistic view of the current legal landscape. It has showcased exemplary innovations in financial law, the potential of nature-based solutions, the intersection of human rights and climate change, the importance of public participation and access to information, and the intricate relationship between climate change and international marine biodiversity conservation. The analytical chapters by leading experts and practitioners close to ongoing climate negotiations provide readers with a front-row seat to the latest legal and institutional innovations. These innovations not only advance the implementation of the Paris Agreement but also foster a deeper understanding of how law and governance can contribute to achieving the SDGs. Moreover, the Handbook has delved into the legal aspects of diverse issues such as climate-induced migration, private financing for climate action, and the just transition, offering insights into the multifaceted nature of climate law and governance.

The Research and Capacity Chasm in Climate Law and Governance

Despite progress both internationally in advancing climate ambition and nationally developing climate responses which respond to domestic pressures that previous chapters have highlighted, there remain critical capacity limitations to the effective implementation of the Paris Agreement in a manner that secures the world's SDGs. Addressing the climate crisis requires robust legal frameworks and effective governance systems capable of catalyzing substantial change. The urgency of addressing climate change is unquestionable, yet the capacity to tackle this existential challenge through law and governance remains underdeveloped in many regions. The disparity between what is needed and what currently exists is stark, with the United Nations Environment Programme (UNEP) warning that the current commitments fall far short of those needed to prevent global warming beyond the 1.5°C threshold.[4] Legal frameworks and governance structures in many countries, particularly in the Global South, lack the complexity and enforcement mechanisms necessary to drive effective action. There is a significant capacity gap in designing, implementing, and enforcing regulations that can underpin ambitious climate action.

Global commitments to bolster climate law and governance have been enshrined in various international agreements, exemplifying a collective aspiration to address these shortcomings. The Paris Agreement includes several articles dedicated to capacity building. Article 11, for example, emphasizes the need for capacity-building support to developing countries, aligning it with national priorities and fostering country ownership of climate change actions.[5] Furthermore, Article 13 establishes an enhanced transparency framework, which provides a basis for understanding global progress and requires robust governance and legal systems to report accurately, consistently and transparently.[6] The Glasgow Climate Pact, adopted at COP26, calls for support to be scaled up and reiterates the importance of building capacities for developing countries, especially those that are particularly vulnerable to the adverse effects of climate change.[7] The Global Stocktake decision, adopted at CMA5 in Dubai (2023), recognizes the persistent gaps in capabilities that hinder effective implementation, particularly regarding technical skills, regulations, institutional governance, and strategic policy development.[8] It emphasizes that addressing these gaps is essential to achieving the ambitious goals outlined in the Agreement, such as rapid emissions reductions and net-zero targets. The decision calls for collaborative efforts to strengthen capacity-building support, including knowledge sharing platforms and the exchange of best practices among developing countries.[9] These commitments reflect a global recognition of the need for strengthened legal and governance systems to effectively enact and enforce climate action.

Recent policy, legal, and institutional innovations may illustrate the relevance of the law and governance approaches available, and ongoing climate litigation may underline the importance of access to justice and fair, reliable dispute resolution, but further efforts are necessary to actualize implementation of climate change commitments on all levels. Effective, accountable national and international law on sustainable development, especially to support Paris Agreement implementation, has never been more important. The enormity of the challenge for the law, and indeed for all disciplines and professions, is clear. With 195 Parties requiring urgent legal and institutional reform to implement their Paris Agreement commitments,[10] and only a few qualified lawyers available to assist in each country, a 'capacity chasm' is gaping in our path ahead. Indeed, in each country and region of the world, hundreds, perhaps thousands of capable, informed jurists specialized in climate change are desperately needed to bridge the gaping chasm.

Enhancing Research and Capacity: Global Initiatives and Their Impact

The best and brightest of our law students from all countries, and the world's leading centres of legal education and research face a critical opportunity to make a decisive contribution to the highest possible ambition in our global response to climate change. There are several global initiatives that are active in this space, with opportunities for legal researchers and professionals to become involved.

The Paris Committee on Capacity Building (PCCB) embodies a cornerstone of the international framework established by the Paris Agreement to fortify the response to climate change, specifically within the context of developing countries.[11] Instituted to strategically address the pronounced gaps in capacity-building, the PCCB endeavours to engender and facilitate the execution of measures necessary for effective climate action. The Committee's objectives are ambitious and multifaceted, targeting an elevation in climate change education, a boost in training quality, and an expansion in public awareness, all of which are essential for cultivating an informed and proactive approach to climate governance. Underpinning the objectives of the PCCB is a mandate of considerable breadth, cantering on the enhancement of knowledge and skills critical to climate change mitigation and adaptation. A prime aspect of this mandate is to augment global climate change education, training, and public awareness – initiatives viewed as foundational to forging widespread societal support for robust climate action. The Committee's role is to support developing nations in constructing and refining their climate governance frameworks, ensuring these structures can effectively meet the imperatives of the Paris Agreement. This includes fostering international cooperation and learning exchanges, which are vital for sharing best practices and catalyzing global progress.

The PCCB has launched various flagship projects and initiatives that have marked significant milestones in capacity-building. Among these, tailored educational programs aimed at enhancing the competencies of climate policymakers have been particularly noteworthy. Furthermore, the establishment of international platforms for knowledge exchange has facilitated the cross-pollination of ideas and experiences among climate experts and practitioners worldwide. By supporting research into the distinct capacity needs of diverse regions, the PCCB has tailored its initiatives to the unique socio-political landscapes of various countries, thereby improving the efficacy of these projects in promoting sustainable climate action.

Complementing the work of the PCCB, other global initiatives also make substantive contributions to capacity-building. The Climate Law and Governance Initiative (CLGI) operates as one component in the global effort to bridge the capacity chasm in climate law and governance.[12] This coalition brings together legal experts, scholars, and practitioners from across the globe with a shared objective: to advance climate law and governance mechanisms in both depth and reach. Through its extensive network, the CLGI fosters the development of innovative legal instruments and supportive policies that are crucial for the implementation of the Paris Agreement and the broader United Nations Framework Convention on Climate Change (UNFCCC). In its commitment to capacity building, the initiative emphasizes the importance of specialized education and training in climate legislation, policy design, and implementation strategies. This focus is crucial, considering the intricate web of legal and regulatory frameworks that intersect with climate action. Through workshops, seminars, and collaborative research, the CLGI has worked diligently to disseminate knowledge and best practices that can empower effective and informed decision-making at all levels of governance.

Furthermore, the CLGI has played a role in facilitating dialogue and knowledge-sharing among the global legal community. It serves as a platform for discussion on emerging issues in climate law, encourages the harmonization of legal frameworks across jurisdictions, and advocates for the integration of climate justice into legislative practices. Special emphasis is placed on inclusion of current and future law and policy leaders from the growing number of highly climate vulnerable countries, including by the University of Cambridge Democratising Education for Global Sustainability and Justice Programme.

This collaborative approach not only amplifies the impact of national and international climate laws but also supports the creation of a cohesive and comprehensive legal response to the climate crisis. By continuously seeking to address the capacity needs within climate law and governance, these global efforts contribute significantly to the collective effort of ensuring that legal frameworks keep pace with the evolving demands of climate change mitigation and adaptation.

Equally, the IUCN World Commission on Environmental Law (WCEL) provides a forum for capacity-building and networking among environmental law scholars, practitioners, and judges to advance legal climate literacy. IUCN WCEL operates on a global scale with individual members engaging in activities aiming at capacity-building as well as developing legal solutions to the climate crisis, both in many national contexts, as well as on the international level. As the core environmental law entity within the International Union for the Conservation of Nature, WCEL also serves to provide support and legal expertise, including on climate law, to both the IUCN Secretariat as well as to the IUCNs many member states and member organisations.

Bridging the Climate Law and Governance Research and Training Gap

Climate law and governance is a field characterized by rapid evolution and complexity, where key areas beckon for deeper legal research. Prominent among these is climate finance – a critical aspect of international agreements that warrants meticulous analysis to ensure the fair distribution and effective utilization of financial resources. Understanding the legal frameworks governing the mobilization, accounting, and transparency of climate finance is vital to ensure that funds not only reach their intended destinations but also yield maximum impact.

Another area ripe for exploration is the nascent field of climate refugee rights. As the effects of climate change intensify, so too does the potential for massive human displacement, which presents unprecedented challenges to existing legal frameworks. Legal scholars are called upon to chart the unexplored territories of international refugee law, developing new jurisprudence that can address the status, rights, and protections for those displaced by environmental factors. The complexities of this task are manifold, involving cross-jurisdictional issues and a need for international consensus that extends beyond the current scope of refugee law.

Furthermore, the role of implementation and compliance committees in climate law is another critical area demanding scrutiny. These committees are tasked with the oversight of international agreements' adherence, a role that could be enhanced through a more nuanced understanding of legal obligations, mechanisms for dispute resolution, and the integration of compliance strategies. The efficacy of these committees is paramount to the integrity of international environmental agreements, and thus a comprehensive legal inquiry into their operations and powers is indispensable.

Comprehensive training programs are essential for policymakers, legal professionals, and civil society organizations engaged in the field of climate law. Such programs must not only cover the legal aspects but also integrate a profound understanding of the scientific underpinnings of climate change. Policymakers and enforcers must be versed in the scientific consensus around climate change to ensure that legal frameworks and policies are grounded and effectively address the challenges at hand. Legal professionals, in their turn, must be equipped to interpret and apply laws in a way that reflects the complexities of environmental science, enabling them to craft robust arguments and provide sound counsel on matters of climate governance. The urgency for interdisciplinary training programs is underscored when considering the plight of highly climate-vulnerable countries, such as small island developing states (SIDS) and least developed countries (LDCs). These nations face unique challenges that demand tailored legal and policy solutions. Capacity building in these contexts requires a sensitive approach that acknowledges the vulnerabilities and harnesses the local knowledge of affected communities. Legal support must be flexible, adaptive, and culturally cognizant, fostering legal environments that can withstand the exacerbated impacts of climate change experienced by these countries.

The role of international support mechanisms in aiding these vulnerable nations is crucial. Institutions like the Green Climate Fund and Global Environment Facility are tasked with providing financial and technical assistance to countries grappling with the impacts of climate change. However, the effectiveness of these mechanisms can be enhanced by ensuring that they operate with greater responsiveness to the nuanced needs of SIDS and LDCs. This means not only providing funds but also facilitating the exchange of legal expertise, technology transfer, and institutional capacity building, thus fostering a holistic approach to climate resilience. Optimization of international support mechanisms involves a concerted effort to align resources with the specific legal and governance needs of climate-vulnerable countries. This alignment is paramount for enabling these nations to weave climate governance into the fabric of their national development plans. Doing so ensures that climate action is not seen as a separate agenda but is integral to the broader objective of sustainable development. International support should thus prioritize the building of local capacities, the enhancement of national institutions, and the support of legal frameworks that can effectively navigate the international climate policy landscape.

Looking Ahead: An Invitation to Climate Law and Governance

We stand at the vanguard of a defining era, envisaging a future where robust climate governance frameworks are not aspirational but foundational to our global society. It is a future fortified by exhaustive legal research, unwavering capacity building, and a heightened collective consciousness about the fragility and resilience of our shared home. As former US President Barack Obama has inspiringly noted, "We are the first generation to fully understand climate change and the last generation to be able to do something about it."[13] This understanding propels us towards a future where our actions are anchored in wisdom, and our policies are crafted with the precision that the severity of climate change demands.

We envision a world where robust climate governance frameworks are the bedrock upon which societies build their resilience against the relentless tide of climate change. In this envisioned future, our collective actions are underpinned by comprehensive legal research and capacity building, supported by an unwavering global awareness of the environmental and humanitarian imperatives at stake. The fabric of this future is woven with the threads of in-depth legal scholarship, enriched by an interdisciplinary melding of science and policy, and fortified by the shared dedication of the international community to safeguard our planet. This vision serves as an earnest call to action for stakeholders at all levels of society. From the deliberative chambers of international bodies to the grassroots mobilizations in local communities, each participant in this global enterprise has a crucial role to play. The path forward is not one of isolation but of collective endeavour and innovation, where the efforts of individuals and organizations are synergized towards the common goal of addressing climate challenges. It is a path that embraces the transformative power of shared knowledge, mutual support, and creative solutions, fostering a global response that is both equitable and effective.

Our final reflection rests upon the moral imperative that anchors our quest to combat climate change. It is a duty that transcends boundaries and generations – a duty to protect the most vulnerable, to preserve the richness of biodiversity, and to bequeath a habitable world to future generations. The transformative potential of enhanced climate law and governance is not merely a theoretical proposition but a tangible beacon of hope. It promises a sustainable future where justice, resilience, and a deep respect for the interconnectedness of all life are the guiding principles of our collective journey. It is an open invitation to every reader, every scholar, every policymaker, and every citizen to partake in the task of shaping a sustainable future. The insights and knowledge shared within these pages are but seeds planted in the fertile grounds of intellectual discourse, awaiting the nurturing hands of action and implementation. Let this Handbook serve as a clarion call to all who cherish our world: the time for decisive action is now. The responsibility we bear is profound, but so too is our capacity for ingenuity and perseverance. Together, we can forge a future that honours our role as custodians of the Earth, a future where the legacy of our time is not defined by the challenges we faced but by the resolve and vision with which we met them. This is our collective endeavour, a journey of transformation that begins with the recognition of our shared humanity and our united destiny on this, our only home.

Notes

1 United Nations Office for Disaster and Risk Reduction, 'Global Assessment Report on Disaster Risk Reduction 2022' <https://www.undrr.org/media/79595/download?startDownload=true> accessed 10 April 2024
2 World Health Organization, 'Fact Sheet on Climate Change' <https://www.who.int/news-room/fact-sheets/detail/climate-change-and-health> accessed 10 April 2024.
3 Internal Displacement Monitoring Centre, 'Global Report on Internal Displacement' <https://www.internal-displacement.org/global-report/grid2020/> accessed 10 April 2024
4 United Nations Environment Programme, 'Emissions Gap Report 2023' <https://www.unep.org/resources/emissions-gap-report-2023> accessed 10 April 2024.
5 Article 11, Paris Agreement.
6 Article 13, Paris Agreement.
7 Glasgow Climate Pact, UN Doc. FCCC/PA/CMA/2021/10/Add.1 (2021).

8 First Global Stocktake, UN Doc. FCCC/PA/CMA/2023/L.17 (2023).
9 First Global Stocktake, UN Doc. FCCC/PA/CMA/2023/L.17 (2023).
10 Maeve McDermott and Valeria Zambianchi, *Report on the Importance of Legal and Institutional Reforms in the Nationally Determined Contributions (NDCs) of the Paris Agreement* (CISDL 2021).
11 Paris Committee on Capacity Building <https://unfccc.int/pccb_activities> accessed 10 April 2024.
12 Climate Law and Governance Initiative <www.climatelawgovernance.org> accessed 10 April 2024.
13 Remarks by President Obama during the First Session of COP21 <https://obamawhitehouse.archives.gov/the-press-office/2015/11/30/remarks-president-obama-first-session-cop21> accessed 10 April 2024.

INDEX

[Note: Numbers in **bold** indicate a table]